BOOKS BY ANNE EDWARDS

BIOGRAPHY

Sonya: The Life of Countess Tolstoy
Vivien Leigh
Judy Garland

NOVELS

The Survivors
Miklos Alexandrovich Is Missing
Shadow of a Lion
Haunted Summer
The Hesitant Heart
Child of Night

AUTOBIOGRAPHY

The Inn and Us (with Stephen Citron)

SONYA

The Life of Countess Tolstoy

ANNE EDWARDS

Hodder and Stoughton
London   Sydney   Auckland   Toronto

ISBN 0 340 25002 X

Originally published in the United States of America in 1981
by Simon and Schuster, New York, New York.

ACKNOWLEDGMENTS

I cannot thank enough the Tolstoy Foundation and the surviving members of the Tolstoy family for their support, assistance, and cooperation, which enabled me to draw upon new material and afforded me certain rare privileges of research. My deepest debt of gratitude is to Miss Alexandra Lvovna Tolstoy (Sasha); her closest friend of forty-five years, Miss Tatiana Schaufauss; and her secretary and literary assistant, Professor Catherine Wolkonsky, who gave me access to some of Miss Tolstoy's unpublished manuscripts and memoirs and to her entire collection of photographs, and who spent many hours not just recounting the past but discounting that which was untrue or that which had been distorted. They also made me welcome in the home at the Tolstoy Foundation in Valley Cottage, New York. All the members of this "Tolstoyan Colony" were open, kind, and cooperative. I was allowed free and full access to their Russian library, shared their table, and was allowed to observe the workings of their hospital, church, and home and to talk to all those who had lived in Russia under the last Tsar and during the Revolution.

I am especially grateful to Mr. Vladimir M. Tolstoy (Sonya's grandson and Misha's son) and Mrs. Olga Tolstoy (V. M. Tolstoy's wife), who is a chief administrator of Valley Cottage and of the Tolstoy Foundation. The Vladimir M. Tolstoys received me graciously in their home, discussed their family with me, and gave me permission to reprint several of their photographs of Yasnaya Polyana.

Other members of Sonya's family who were kind enough to share their reminiscences, photographs, letters, books, and manuscripts with me were: Ms. Vera Ilyovna Tolstoy (Sonya's granddaughter; Ilyusha's daughter); Dr. Sergey M. Tolstoy (Sonya's grandson; Misha's youngest son); his charming wife, Mrs. Collette Tolstoy; and Ms. Antonina Behrs (Sonya's niece). To Dr. and Mrs. Sergey Tolstoy in Paris I owe an added debt of gratitude not only for their friendship and help but also for allowing me to take home and study Sonya's children's stories and Dr. Tolstoy's own unpublished recollections and impressions of his ancestors.

5

My appreciation as well to BBC producer Jonathan Stedall; Nigel Pope, also of the BBC; publisher Henry S. Evans; Deborah Lott, trade permissions editor of Little, Brown, publishers; Sadie Ayand of *Novosti* and the *Soviet Weekly;* and Angela Johnson of the Society for Cultural Relations with the USSR. My thanks to Catherine Sadler, who assisted me with my interviews and research in the United States; Marcelle Garfield, who proved extremely helpful in the United Kingdom; Pamela Davidson, who helped in the translations from Russian; Debbie Campbell of A. P. Watt; my invaluable New York assistant, James Robbins, who worked untiringly on transcriptions, research, and on typing the many drafts of this voluminous book; Linda Olsen, who typed the final manuscript; Kathleen Howard, who had the difficult task of copyediting it; Rebecca Head, who was always available to my queries; Sophie Sorkin; Vincent Virga; Joan Sanger and Michael Korda, my enthusiastic editors; and Hilary Rubinstein and Monica McCall, my friends and agents who both believed so long in this project.

I am also grateful to the staffs of all the libraries in which I did my research, most especially the British Museum and the Slavonic Division of the New York Public Library; and to the staffs of the Russian agencies and archives who helped me cut through the difficulties I encountered on Sonya's behalf.

And to Steve, the one person who lived with Sonya and me on a daily basis with grace, encouragement, and a great deal of tender, loving care, my everlasting devotion.

A. E.

For Monica McCall

Whose enthusiasm always gives me
an expectation of success
and whose belief has
more times than not
brought this to pass

CONTENTS

AUTHOR'S NOTE

Many of the Christian names in this book have more than one English translation. Therefore, Countess Tolstoy has been referred to in other works as Sofia, Sofya, Sofiya, Sofie, Sophie, Sonia, and Sonya. I have chosen the last spelling because it is the one her daughter Alexandra and the surviving members of the Tolstoy family prefer. For the same reason, I have used the name Lev Nikolaevich Tolstoy for the man the English-speaking world knows as Leo Tolstoy.

Russian men have a first or Christian name, their father's first name with "vich" (sometimes spelled "vitch" and called their patronymic) added, and a last or family name. Russian women use their first name, their father's first name with "evna" or "ovna" added, and their last or family name. Thus Sonya was Sonya Andreyevna Behrs before her marriage to Tolstoy. I have chosen the form Sonya Tolstoy, since the Russian feminine form (Sonya Tolstaya) is generally not used in English. This style has been applied throughout the book to all the surnames of Russian women.

It is also the custom for Russian families to employ diminutives of the names of all members. To avoid confusion I have taken the liberty of referring to members of the Tolstoy family and their inner circle by these diminutives. In Russia no outsider would ever refer to Alexandra Lvovna as "Sasha." I apologize for this and various other similar transgressions of etiquette committed for the sake of clarity.

Tolstoy was born with a title. During the reign of Peter the Great (1682–1725), Tolstoy's great-great-great-grandfather was granted the title of Count. Sonya became Countess Tolstoy upon her marriage to Tolstoy. Tolstoy later renounced his title and the Revolution disallowed it. Sonya, however, referred to herself as Countess Tolstoy until her death, and certain members of the Tolstoy family living on the continent have retained the title.

I have left the dates as entered in the Tolstoys' diaries, journals, and letters. However, before 1900 Russia followed the Julian calendar, which was twelve days behind the Gregorian calendar. From 1900 to 1918 there was a thirteen-day discrepancy between Russia and the West. In 1918 they went onto the Gregorian calendar, and dates given from that time are the same as in the West.

Sonya, Tolstoy, Tatyana Behrs Kuzminsky (Sonya's sister), and Ilya, Lev, Sergey, Tatyana, and Alexandra Tolstoy (five of Sonya's children) kept voluminous diaries, notebooks, and journals containing not only a record of events but also fragments of conversations. In all cases the conversations I have reported are a faithful reconstruction of the original as heard by one or more of the participants, or as told by Sonya or Tolstoy to one or more of the participants. Their sources are listed in the chapter notes on page 466.

A. E.

THE FAMILIES

THE BEHRS FAMILY

LYUBOV ALEXANDROVNA ISLAVINA (1826-86). Countess Tolstoy's mother.

ANDREY YEVSTAFYEVICH BEHRS (1808–68), Lyubov's husband, was a physician to the court.

Their children:

ELIZAVETA ANDREYEVNA BEHRS (Lisa) (1843–1919). Married Gavril Yemelyanovich Paulenko. After divorce, married Alexander Alexandrovich Behrs, a cousin.

SONYA ANDREYEVNA BEHRS (1844–1919). Married Count Lev Nikolaevich Tolstoy.

ALEXANDER ANDREYEVICH BEHRS (Sasha) (1845–1918). Vice governor of Orel province.

TATYANA ANDREYEVNA BEHRS (Tanya) (1846–1925). Married Alexander Mikhailovich Kuzminsky, a cousin.

PYOTR ANDREYEVICH BEHRS (Petya) (1849–1910).

VLADIMIR ANDREYEVICH BEHRS (Vlodny) (1853–74).

STEPAN ANDREYEVICH BEHRS (Styopa) (1855–1909).

VYACHESLAV ANDREYEVICH BEHRS (Slavatchka) (1861–1907).

THE TOLSTOY FAMILY

SONYA ANDREYEVNA (1844–1919) and LEV NIKOLAEVICH TOLSTOY (1828–1910) were married in 1862.

Their children:

SERGEY LVOVICH (Seryozha) (1863–1947).

TATYANA LVOVNA (Tanya) (1864–1950).

ILYA LVOVICH (Ilyusha) (1866–1933).

LEV LVOVICH (Lyova) (1869–1945).

MARYA LVOVNA (Masha) (1871–1906).

PYOTR LVOVICH (Petya) (1872–73).
NIKOLAI LVOVICH (Nikolenka) (1874–75).
VARVARA LVOVNA (1875–75).
ANDREY LVOVICH (Andreyusha) (1877–1916).
MIKHAIL LVOVICH (Misha) (1879–1944).
ALEXEI LVOVICH (Alyosha) (1881–86).
ALEXANDRA LVOVNA (Sasha) (1884–1979).
IVAN LVOVICH (Vanichka) (1888–95).

ALSO:

ALEXANDRA ANDREYEVNA TOLSTOY (1817–1918), Tolstoy's third cousin.
TATYANA ALEXANDROVNA ERGOLSKAYA (Aunt Toinette) (1795–1874), Tolstoy's third cousin.
PELAGYA ILYENISHNA YUSHKOV (Aunt Pelagya) (1798–1875), Tolstoy's paternal aunt.

PROLOGUE
1910

A Death at Astapovo

In 1910 there were many who said Russia had two tsars—Nicholas II and Lev Nikolaevich Tolstoy. But by early November it appeared that there would soon be only one emperor. The eighty-two-year-old Tolstoy lay dying at the railroad station in the remote village of Astapovo. Sonya, the wife of forty-eight years whom he had abandoned only days before, arrived in a private railroad car, and through her window she saw hundreds of torches ablaze in the midnight gloom.

Crowds thronged the little-used wayside platform waiting for some word on the great Tolstoy's condition, and she could barely make out the weatherbeaten hut in which her husband lay dying. As she stepped down from her car into the chilling night winds, Sonya looked out across the thousands of ragged peasants who wailed and chanted prayers as they stood their vigil. In the distance caravans of gypsies huddled about small fires. She recognized the city magistrate of Tula, some of Tolstoy's former students, and many landowners. The crowd seemed like a great family come together to await the death of its patriarch. The Tsar and his family, upon hearing Tolstoy was critically ill, had cut short a visit to Germany and returned to the Winter Palace. Throughout the world, newspapers reported on the last days of the man whom many, both in Russia and abroad, revered as a saint and a prophet.

Sonya resented them all—from the Tsar to the lowliest peasant. Tolstoy was her husband; she had married him when she was eighteen, and he was her entire world. Theirs had been a grand passion. Together they had had thirteen children, six of whom they had buried. These crowds knew nothing of their love, of her devotion to his literary genius. She knew they condemned her for having driven Tolstoy to the brink of his grave and thought of her as a cruel, half-mad warder whom Tolstoy had finally cast off in a

17

last heroic act. How were these strangers to understand that she was a great part of the man they so revered when he had never confessed the fact. She had lived in the shadow of Tolstoy, she realized with rancor, because her husband, fanatical in his belief that all men were equal, never extended his humanity to include women.

When Sonya, supported by her daughter Tanya and her youngest sons, Andreyusha and Misha, was recognized, she was set upon by newspapermen, while newsreel cameras (being used for the first time to cover an international "event") cranked nearby. She was dressed carelessly. Her large deep-set dark eyes were anguished; her smooth-skinned aristocratic face appeared distorted, ravaged. "Why did you try to drown yourself, Countess Tolstoy?" "Why did he run away from you and your home, Countess?" members of the press shouted at her. The crowd's babble confused and frightened her, and she sent a piercing cry to the streaked, smoky heavens. Police fought to hold back the crowd. The doctor and nurse whom she had brought with her from her home, Yasnaya Polyana, pushed their way to her side and tried to turn her back to the train. But she broke loose and marched toward the hut, at last reaching its wooden steps. A nurse and the stationmaster came out on the small veranda to prevent her from entering. All the strength Sonya had gathered to reach the hut vanished. Suddenly older than her sixty-six years, she was a shrunken, trembling, broken woman. She had come although she had been rejected by her dying husband, discouraged by all of her children and betrayed by most of them, and vilified by the world. Her violent love and determination had carried her from a sickbed to the door of this shack; she had come so far only to be turned away. Tanya held her about the waist to keep her from falling, and the doctor took her arm. She swayed and looked about wildly, but she would not be led away. Finally, afraid that she would create a disturbance that might be heard inside, they allowed Sonya to look through the windows of the hut. Not much over five feet tall, she had to stand on tiptoe.

The stationmaster's house had two small rooms. In one Sonya's three older sons and her youngest daughter, Sasha, sat around a large circular table. A number of people whom Sonya did not know stood behind them, visible through an open door. In the other room Tolstoy lay semiconscious on a narrow bed. The room was lit by a single kerosene lamp which stood on the bedside table among the litter of medicine bottles. Sonya knew that his temperature was over 104, but his pulse was strong. Everyone knew these things. Bulletins were released every hour. Still she was not prepared for the look of death that had insinuated itself on his face. She began to cry, and Tanya tried to pull her away. Understanding that if she were to be allowed to stay there any longer she must control herself, she breathed in deeply, fighting for composure. Dr. Dushan Makovitsky, Tolstoy's physician, stood over the bed checking the half-conscious man's pulse; and on the other side of the room, just emerging from the shadows, was Chertkov! *Chertkov*, the man who she believed had driven her husband from her.

Sonya gasped and faltered as she turned away. The doctor and nurse supported her while Tanya, Misha, and Andreyusha formed a tight band around her as she was helped back to the train that would be her home until Tolstoy left Astapovo alive or dead. She moved through the crowd like a small wounded animal. Finally the magistrate from Tula broke through and angrily dispersed those who pressed about her. She reached out and grasped his hand before being helped onto the train. Behind the closed curtains of her compartment she was at last concealed from the curious, but she was also separated from Tolstoy. How had she and her husband found their way to this desolate village? How could he be dying and not want her by his side? Through the sealed windows of her car Sonya could hear the crowd—the worshipful and the merely curious—and all of them closer to her husband than she in his last moments. She wept, and Tanya held her in her arms. Perhaps to understand one had to go back to the beginning.

The year was 1856, and Count Lev Nikolaevich Tolstoy, slim and handsome, stood horrified in the sordid furnished room where his older brother Dmitry lay dying of consumption. The once-happy boy who had shared his childhood was now a gaunt, livid man who smelled of sour sweat and bitter medicines. His dark eyes, immense in his drawn face, were filled with profound puzzlement. Masha, the pockmarked prostitute who had become his mistress, watched over him with sad tenderness. Tolstoy, however, felt only horror as he sat by his brother. He knew that they were alike. They had the same propensity for extreme behavior; they both swung easily from virtue to lechery, from good to evil; but in this dirty, foul-smelling room Tolstoy felt neither pity nor love for Dmitry. Dmitry cried for God's help in a hoarse, weak voice; Masha brought him a small icon, and as his fleshless hand closed around it, he muttered a fevered prayer.

Driven by a terrified revulsion, Tolstoy quickly departed and returned to the bright world of St. Petersburg, where his days and nights were filled with the glittering voices and laughter of that city's most exciting, most beautiful citizens. St. Petersburg was brilliantly alive in the winter, when the imperial family was in residence; its wide avenues were crowded with gaily decorated troikas, the sound of sleigh bells filling the air. Along the left bank of the sparkling River Neva marched regiments of grenadiers—the Preobrazhensky in their vivid red and white uniforms, the Izmailovsky in green and white, and the Semionovsky in their crisp blue and white. Tolstoy had just had his first great literary success, and every night he was invited to dinners, parties, and balls. Still he had never felt so alone. Three weeks after his visit to Dmitry he was told that his brother was dead. Thoughts of Dmitry on his deathbed haunted him. He was seized by a feeling "of horror at the inscrutability, nearness, and inevitability of death," and in panic and despair he saw the great necessity and urgency of finding a good wife and living a stronger and purer life.

He was restless, bored, irritable. He was rude, impatient, and argumentative. Invitations dwindled as few found him good company. He thought about going abroad, but with the first signs of spring in the parks and gardens of St. Petersburg his mood changed, and he decided to go to his estate, Yasnaya Polyana, which was 120 miles south of Moscow. There life would be rising from the earth and he would be close to the memories of his childhood.

After saying goodbye to his dearest friend in St. Petersburg, his charming, beautiful cousin, the Countess Alexandra Andreyevna Tolstoy, he boarded the train for Moscow, a journey that took thirty hours. The railway station smelled of acrid smoke. Porters bustled with the luggage, fur-hatted gentlemen gave orders to their servants, passengers said their goodbyes to the people who had come to see them off. There were tears, laughter, and excitement.

Sitting alone in his compartment, Tolstoy read, wrote in his diary, and ate the meals his manservant brought to him. There was plush crimson carpet beneath his feet, and his seat was deeply cushioned. In all he lacked few comforts, yet he was short-tempered and rather rudely rebuffed the overtures of the other passengers. After learning of his brother's death, he had sworn that he would never again gamble or set foot in a cabaret or a brothel. He was determined to lead a pure, good life, and he was in search of a woman to share that life with him.

In Moscow he walked in the gardens of the little Hermitage, watched the young skaters on Ice Hill, and called on friends. Just as he was about to leave for Yasnaya Polyana, he met Princess Alexandra Obolensky, with whom he had once been in love, and he extended his visit. Although she was now married to Prince Andrey Obolensky, she and Tolstoy became quickly engaged in a rather intense flirtation. Six years older than he, the Princess was an elegant, sophisticated woman with golden hair and lilac eyes; and Tolstoy commented in his diary that she was "the most charming woman I have ever met. The most highly refined artistic nature and at the same time the most moral." Fortunately, he did not have to test either the Princess's moral nature or his own; she soon left to join her husband in St. Petersburg. He was curiously elated, as though he had been saved in spite of his weakness. In this mood he encountered an old friend, Kostya Islavin, and agreed to go with him and another friend, Baron Vladimir Mengden, to visit Islavin's sister, who had a small country house at Pokrovskoye, less than an hour's drive from Moscow. The beautiful dark-haired, jet-eyed Lyubov Islavin, who had also been a childhood friend of Tolstoy's, had married an older, austere German doctor named Behrs and had a house full of exuberant children. Tolstoy often visited them when he was in Moscow; he always enjoyed the company of children and was especially fond of the gay, delightful Behrs youngsters.

As the small trap jogged over the deeply rutted road, Tolstoy and Kostya talked happily about old times. The countryside had begun to show the green mistiness of springtime. The comforting smell of damp earth being warmed by the sun came from the fields, and birds soared in the bright sky.

PART ONE
1856-1862

An Expectation of Happiness

At that time in the Rostovs' house there prevailed an amorous atmosphere characteristic of homes where there are very young and very charming girls. Every young man who came to the house—seeing those impressionable, smiling young faces (smiling probably at their own happiness), feeling the eager bustle around him, and hearing the fitful bursts of song and music and the inconsequent but friendly prattle of young girls ready for anything and full of hope—experienced the same feeling; sharing with the young folk of the Rostovs' household a readiness to fall in love and an expectation of happiness.

TOLSTOY
War and Peace

1

In the late spring of 1856 the Behrses left Moscow, as they did every year, for their country home at Pokrovskoye eight miles outside the city. The large family—there were seven high-spirited children—and their servants had barely settled when guests began to arrive. Lyubov Alexandrovna Behrs, a woman of elegant style and exceptional charm, delighted in witty friends, stimulating conversation, and amusing gossip, but this May she was at odds with herself and discerned an unfamiliar restlessness in her family. Dr. Behrs too sensed that his household had changed. His three daughters were growing up, and they had become much too aware of themselves as female. It was his middle daughter, Sonya Andreyevna, who made the German Dr. Behrs the most uneasy. She was startlingly mature and too aware of her sex for a girl three months short of her twelfth birthday; and she was at times a dreamer, and at other times so full of life that her unladylike laughter rang through the house.

Possessing wide black eyes, and a full sensuous mouth, Sonya was too striking in appearance to be called merely pretty. She loved the country house where she had been born in the summer of 1844. It was bright and spacious with a large garden and secret nooks where she could go to be alone. The house had two stories. Her parents and two of her brothers and their tutor had rooms on the ground floor, which also contained a charming guest room, a large sunny parlor, and a huge dining room, which opened onto a wide terrace. Upstairs there was a nursery for the two younger boys and their nurse, rooms for the servants and the governess, and a big light-filled bedroom, which Mrs. Behrs called "the room of the three maidens," as it was occupied by her daughters. Lisa, the older sister, was tall and good-looking, with even features, hair the color of ripe wheat, and expressive dark brown eyes. Though she smiled often, her smile did not enhance her beauty; "on the contrary, it gave her face an unnatural and therefore unpleasant expression." Less than two years separated them, but Sonya had little in common with her aloof and self-absorbed sister. Poetry bored Lisa. Small children exasperated her. Nine-year-old Tanya, who was the stormy petrel in the family and Sonya's favorite sibling, aroused her to near fury. Yet Lisa never gave way to her temper as Sonya often did.

In spite of the bucolic joys of Pokrovskoye, Sonya yearned to be back in Moscow, where plans were being made for Tsar Alexander II's coronation in the early fall. At Pokrovskoye her parents and their guests were absorbed by "the question of questions, the evil of evils, the first of all of Russia's misfortunes—serfdom and its future," and almost everyone agreed with the Tsar's recent statement that sooner or later serfdom would have to be abolished. Sonya well understood how this could affect her father's social and financial standing. He was a physician for the imperial court, with a comfortable salary, a good income from his private practice, a government apartment in the Kremlin, a house in the country; and at present he owned ten serfs. But a world upended by the abolition of serfdom would greatly change his status. Silence often ensued in these adult discussions when one of the girls entered the room. Sonya was the most intuitive of the Behrs sisters and the closest to her mother. She knew that Lyubov Alexandrovna desperately hoped each of her daughters would make a good match, marrying into the St. Petersburg nobility, to which she had a small claim (being of noble but illegitimate birth), rather than the Moscow bourgeoisie, which was her husband's world.*

St. Petersburg was the home of the Tsar and the center of Russia's aristocracy. Moscow was little more than an overgrown village. Water was still brought in in casks, and the streets were

---

* Lyubov Alexandrovna was one of three illegitimate daughters and three illegitimate sons born to Princess Kozlovsky (who had run away from her husband) and her lover, the dashing Alexander Islenyev. Prince Kozlovsky refused to give his errant wife a divorce, and so the six children of the lovers were never legitimized. The lovers were secretly married, but the union was declared invalid, and the children were never allowed to carry Islenyev's name. Instead, they were each christened Islavin. Therefore, Sonya's mother's maiden name was Islavin, which was also her brother Kostya's surname.

dirty and poorly lit. Many families kept cows, horses, mules, dogs, chickens, and ducks in their yards, and these animals often strayed into the roads. People lived simply, in a relaxed and easy way. Everyone knew everyone else. The middle and upper classes and the nobility mingled freely. The rigid stratification so characteristic of St. Petersburg society did not exist in Moscow.

The Behrses' Kremlin apartment was always full of family and friends and young people, and it was not unusual for guests to stay for months at a time. In their summer quarters at Pokrovskoye this whirl of activity seemed even more intense. Of all her parents' friends it was Count Tolstoy whose visits Sonya most enjoyed. To the young girl, he was a figure of romance, and she was fascinated by the titillating rumors about him which were whispered around the samovar. He led a tumultous, at times scandalous life, and there was much shushing in the front parlor if the children came in while his escapades were being recounted. Still, Sonya knew that he had gambled away much of his land and the large main house at Yasnaya Polyana—his mother's legacy to him. But despite the tales of roguish and even reprehensible behavior, he was always a welcome guest at the Behrses'. His good nature and flamboyant personality buoyed the whole household.

Accordingly, there was a great feeling of excited anticipation in late May at Pokrovskoye when Lyubov Alexandrovna received word from her brother Kostya that he was coming for a short visit with Count Tolstoy. As the latter jumped out of the trap, three of the young Behrs brothers ran up to him and tugged at his arms, pleading with him to join in their games. The carriage had been crowded and uncomfortable, and Tolstoy promised that if they allowed him a little rest he would play leapfrog later in the afternoon. Contented with this compromise, they scampered away, and Tolstoy went in to greet their parents.

Since the servants were at church, Lyubov Alexandrovna asked the girls to set the table and serve dinner. As they went about their tasks, Tolstoy observed how Sonya had blossomed since his last visit. Conversation at the table was gay and frivolous, but once the party moved to the parlor the talk inevitably turned to the siege and fall of Sevastopol. Tolstoy had been only twenty-six when he joined the besieged garrison of Sevastopol in November 1854 in a mood of patriotic exaltation, believing that the Russian drive through the Crimea toward the Balkans and the Bosporus was to be "another chapter in the heroic struggle of civilization against barbarism." He told the Behrs family that when he arrived the soldiers were fiery in their dedication. "Admiral Kornilov, making the rounds of his troops, instead of hailing them with 'Good health to you, lads!' called out, 'If you must die, lads, will you die?' and the soldiers shouted back, 'We will die, Your Excellency, hurrah!' "

When Tolstoy left Sevastopol a year later, nearly 100,000 men had kept that promise. Long before then his patriotic enthusiasm had died—killed by the bloody reality of war and by the realization that thousands of starving soldiers had been abandoned by a government unwilling or unable to send them relief. His first sketch of the city under siege, "Sevastopol in December 1854," was suffused with love of country and admiration of the soldiers' bravery, but in a later essay, "Sevastopol in May 1855," he wrote with a new hero in mind—Truth. The *Contemporary*, Russia's leading progressive magazine, had published these Sevastopol sketches. The first was widely acclaimed, but the second, which appeared only after extensive changes by the censor, was attacked and Tolstoy himself was charged with ridiculing Russia's brave officers. "And now it seems that I am under the strict observation of the police on account of my writings. So much for truth in war, eh!" he exclaimed.

Sonya, who sat holding her youngest brother, small Styopa, grasped the baby so close that he cried out. The idea that the dynamic and exceptional Count—a man who wrote books, was a brave officer and loved people and life so—was under police surveillance horrified her. Tears flooded her eyes, and Tanya put her arm around her sister's trembling shoulders.

Lyubov Alexandrovna, trying to bring gaiety back to the group, asked about the song "The Eighth of September," which it was rumored Tolstoy had written.

"A great part of the song was composed and sung by soldiers. I am not the only author of it," Tolstoy said.

"Sing it please," the children begged.

Their Uncle Kostya, his blond beard meticulously parted in the middle and his lapis lazuli eyes gleaming, sat down theatrically at the piano and, after playing several thunderous chords, gestured

with his long slender hand for his friend to begin. But Tolstoy
refused.

"Tanya will sing if you teach her the words," Sonya
prompted, pushing her younger sister forward.

Tanya was taught the first verse and then, her remarkable
musical talent evident, sang a duet with Tolstoy. The words were
sharp and witty and everyone laughed and called for a reprise, but
Tolstoy insisted Kostya play some Chopin waltzes and mazurkas.
He listened and smiled wistfully. "Remember, Lyubov Alexandrovna, how we danced to those tunes when we were young?"

"Of course," she answered softly.

Sonya was amazed by this exchange. She knew, of course,
that her mother was eighteen years younger than her father, but it
had never occurred to her that the fascinating, volatile Count Lev
Nikolaevich Tolstoy was a contemporary and a childhood friend of
her mother's.* Was it possible that her handsome, stately, imper-
turbable mother had once lightheartedly danced with the exuberant
Count, her hand on his shoulder, his on her waist? This disconcerting image grew less startling the more Sonya considered it.
Although her mother seldom caressed the children, Sonya had
always known that Lyubov Alexandrovna's cool demeanor hid a
tender and understanding heart. She was convinced her mother
possessed a poetic, sensitive nature much like her own. Lyubov
meant "love," and to Sonya it seemed that her mother was well
named. She could rarely discipline the children; she managed to
find money for all their needs and many of their whims; and she
encouraged each of them to develop his or her own personality and
talents.

Tolstoy had been a frequent guest in her home during her
childhood, but this visit was the first Sonya recorded at length in
her diary. She was at a most impressionable age and knew no one
whose fame could compare with this literary nobleman's. Romantic
yearnings were just beginning to stir in Sonya, but the mature and
volatile Count was nothing like the lean, pale, brooding young men
she dreamed about. With his piercing glance and extraordinary
energy, he seemed to have stepped out of a daring French novel,

* Tolstoy was only eighteen months younger than Lyubov Alexandrovna.

like the one by the notorious George Sand which she had just begun to read secretly.

Yes, like the Rostovs in Tolstoy's future masterpiece, *War and Peace*, the young people in the Behrs household had begun to show "a readiness to fall in love and an expectation of happiness." And between a worldly Count and a high-strung eleven-year-old girl a historic meeting had taken place.

2

Although she was an enthusiastic and energetic girl, quick at learning and by far the cleverest of the Behrs children, Sonya was also rather moody and inclined to spells of fancifulness. "Poor Sonya," she once overheard her father remark to her mother, "she will never be completely happy."

Sonya was not sure what constituted happiness, but she did feel great joy when a poem or novel moved her to tears. She had a passionate nature, and adolescence had brought erotic feelings which she could not understand and which frightened and depressed her. These emotions she confided to no one, although she did make note of them in her diary.

Yet that summer of 1856 brought Sonya almost unclouded happiness. She and Tanyachka and their brother Sasha, who was between them in age, formed an irrepressible triumvirate, bursting with youthful excitement and filling each day with pranks and games. And the joy of those summer days, which enveloped her like a glowing mist, intensified when the memory of Tolstoy's visit echoed gently in her thoughts.

She read his *Boyhood* and reread *Childhood*, her large dark, slightly myopic eyes brimming with tears of delight. *Le Comte* understood. He alone of all adults understood. Was he, she wondered, recalling his own young days when he wrote, "If you only go by what's real there won't be any games. And if there are no games, what is left?"

The last days of this idyllic summer were marred by her parents' arguments about Sasha. Was he to be sent to the Cadet Corps or was he to remain at home a short while longer? Sasha was only ten, too young, Dr. Behrs adamantly insisted, to leave home. But Lyubov Alexandrovna had decided that the eldest Behrs son should enjoy the social and educational advantages of the corps, and she prevailed.

Sonya's great happiness turned to fear and depression, profoundly troubled by rumors. It was whispered that boys were treated severely in the Cadet Corps, that they were wakened by a drum roll, that they were flogged if disobedient. She cried herself to sleep, but she would never have dared to speak to her parents on her brother's behalf. And so on the morning of August 11, when Sonya came down for breakfast, she found Sasha dressed in a new jacket with a white collar, his golden brown curly hair slickly combed and pomaded. Alexander Andreyevich Behrs, her precious, loving Sasha, would be leaving for the Cadet Corps directly after prayers were said to bless him in his new life, and there was nothing she could do to avert his going. What surprised her most was her brother's excitement. He even took his mother's edict "Don't climb trees, don't roll on the grass, you will spoil your suit" with shocking equanimity.

By midmorning Uncle Kostya and the priest and deacon from Pokrov had arrived, and the whole family, even the squalling Styopa, gathered in the parlor for the service. The prayers over, Sonya and Tanyachka joined Sasha as he went to say his farewells to the servants, delaying as long as possible their return to the waiting carriage that would take him away. Finally there was nothing left to be done. Sasha, determined to be brave and manly, kissed his mother's hand in a gay and gallant manner. Lyubov Alexandrovna embraced him and made the sign of the cross over his head. Then he turned slowly and approached his sisters. The Behrs family regarded most kissing as a distasteful expression of sentimentality and reserved this gesture for solemn occasions. As Sasha and the girls had never been separated, they had never kissed. With some embarrassment, therefore, Sasha kissed each of his sisters, and then, turning swiftly on the heels of his polished, squeaking boots, he jumped into the open carriage and sat stiffly, eyes straight ahead, beside his uncle.

As the carriage pulled away, raising plumes of dust, Tanya burst out crying.

"Don't be a baby," her mother scolded. "Your father is waiting for him in Moscow. And Sasha will be home again. Go, get busy with something." Lyubov Alexandrovna turned quickly into the house, fighting back her own tears. Of her three daughters only Sonya understood what her mother was suffering. Between them there had always been a rather special unspoken communication. Her mother dreaded any exposure of her vulnerability, of her secret emotions, and Sonya shared this fear.

To Sonya, the best of all the family stories was that of her parents' first meeting. When her mother was fifteen, she had fallen ill and lay close to death from what was diagnosed as "brain fever." Every doctor in Tula had been called to her sickbed, but she did not improve. Then Lyubov's father, Alexander Islenyev, heard that a Dr. Behrs, a Moscow court doctor who treated the Tsar and his family, had stopped in Tula while on his way to visit his good friend the young writer Ivan Turgenev, in the Orel district. Islenyev asked him to see his daughter; and after Andrey Yevstafyevich Behrs had examined the beautiful young patient, he gave no more thought to his journey. For nearly a month he kept an almost constant vigil at Lyubov's bedside, and as she grew well she and the gray-haired, impeccably trim physician fell in love. But marriage to a doctor of German ancestry who was rumored to have some Jewish blood was considered a misalliance for a young woman of the provincial nobility, even if her birth was illegitimate; and there was also the problem of their ages. Dr. Behrs was thirty-three, eighteen years Lyubov's senior. Although Lyubov's whole family strongly opposed the marriage, her grandmother was the most indignant. "Next you will give your daughters to musicians!" she shouted at her son. But Lyubov Alexandrovna had made her choice and would not be moved.

She had been wed when she was sixteen, and she was barely thirty when Sonya celebrated her twelfth birthday on August 22, 1856, amid a large gathering of friends and neighbors at Pokrovskoye. The Behrs family left for Moscow the next day. The Tsar's coronation was drawing near, and once home in their Kremlin apartment there was much activity as dresses and shawls were fitted and sewn. During the week, Sonya studied long hours with her German and French tutors, worked diligently at the piano, and helped her mother with the younger children. On Saturdays there were dancing lessons with Lisa, Varya, and Nikolai, the children of Count Tolstoy's sister, Marya Nikolaevna. Afternoon tea was served in the brightly lit parlor, with her mother pouring as the samovar hummed beside her. Everyone conversed in French, since Lyubov Alexandrovna was careful to maintain all the forms of polite society.

Sasha soon arrived home for his first visit, bringing with him a fellow cadet, Mitrofan Andreyevich Polivanov. Three years older than Sasha, the tall, blond, intelligent Polivanov was the son of a wealthy Kostroma landowner. The two young cadets joked and laughed at the tea table, and as Sonya smiled at their sallies she felt young Polivanov studying her. She raised her eyes and spiritedly returned his forthright gaze. Polivanov's golden hair shimmered beneath the large silver candelabra; and then, as he turned to answer a question put to him by Lisa, his sensitive aristocratic profile glowed in the candlelight. There was something appealing about Polivanov; he was much like the ideal beau Sonya yearned for— and totally unlike Count Lev Nikolaevich Tolstoy.

The morning of the Tsar's coronation was clear and frosty, and sunlight made all the gateposts glisten. The flagstone courtyard of the Behrs apartment was covered with yellow and orange oak leaves. A brisk clean breeze came through the girls' open window. Sonya woke up first. It was five o'clock, and by eight the Behrses and their daughters (the boys were too young to be invited) had to be at the Red Stairway of the Winter Palace for the ceremonies. The old housemaid Praskovya had all the girls' clothes in readiness. Never had they worn anything lovelier than these fine pastel silk dresses, although to the sister's disappointment, the skirts were short, showing that they had not yet left childhood behind. Sonya, however, was far too excited about seeing the coronation gown of Maria Alexandrovna to give the length of her skirt more than a moment's thought.

Under her thick dark brown braids plaited with flowers, Sonya's head was filled with the imagined splendors of the coronation, but the adults in the house were elated by the Coronation Manifesto of Tsar Alexander II. Taxes had been lowered for the Tsar's poorest subjects, and tax arrears amounting to forty million rubles had been canceled. A juster distribution of the poll tax was promised. Conscription was suspended for three years. Literary censorship was relaxed. Students were once more admitted to the universities without limitation. Special taxes paid by Jews were abolished. Polish nobles in the western provinces were to be able to travel freely within Russia. There was to be wide amnesty for political prisoners, and the heavy passport fee imposed under Nicholas I was to be abolished, allowing more Russians to travel abroad. It appeared that Russia was well on the road toward liberalization and domestic prosperity. (However, if the Behrses had heard the comments of Lord Granville, Queen Victoria's special envoy to the coronation, they might have been less optimistic. Granville reported that although the new Tsar looked "intelligent and amiable," he did not have much strength "either of intellect or character." In sum, he was "well-intentioned but weak as water.")

Kremlin Square was already crowded when the Behrses presented their tickets to one of the guards in splendid red, white, and gold uniforms who lined the crimson carpets which had been laid for the ceremonies. Newly erected stands filled every space between the Red Staircase and Kremlin Square's five lovely old whitestone churches with their glistening onion domes. The girls were enchanted by their fellow celebrants—Persians in black fezzes, Turks in red ones, Hussars swathed in gold and rich furs, Bokharans in curious bright-colored turbans, Siberians with huge wide-brimmed hats, and Caucasians in scarlet coats that swept the ground.

A canopy of gold cloth topped by yellow, white, and black ostrich feathers was carried to the foot of the Red Stairway. A wild roar of joy arose when the royal couple, coming from the palace, appeared at the top. The young Tsar was handsome in a blue uniform with a broad red ribbon across his chest, and the Tsarina wore a magnificent gown of white satin and gold. The cheers swelled as they descended the steps and then, sheltered by the canopy, walked slowly toward the Uspensky Cathedral. After pausing at the door to be anointed with holy oils, they entered the cathedral, followed by a procession of foreign dignitaries and court officials, among whom were the elder Behrses. Later Sonya made her mother repeat every detail of the ceremony until it was fixed firmly in her head. But even as she stood outside with her sisters, she knew in her mind what was happening in the cathedral. She could see the Tsar's jewel-encrusted robe being placed on his shoulders; she could see him place the gold and diamond crown on his head after it had been blessed by the priests. She knew that then,

a scepter and globe in his hands, he would sit upon his throne for
a moment before rising to crown the Tsarina, resting his crown
briefly upon her head and then replacing it with her own smaller
one. But now, as she stood outside with her sisters, she was content
to hear church bells and cannon blasts ring throughout the Kremlin
as the Tsar and Tsarina came out of the cathedral, their crowns
glittering in the morning sun. Leading the procession to the other
cathedrals in the square, they were blessed by priests in each of
them. Finally they left their canopy and followers and ascended
the Red Staircase alone. At the top they turned and saluted their
cheering subjects before disappearing into the palace.

The images of what she had seen and imagined would warm
Sonya during the hard, cold winter. Her fanciful musings were not
confined, however, to the glories of the coronation; the memory of
Polivanov's handsome, glowing profile gave her an unfamiliar, dis-
turbingly sensual delight. But there was one element in her day-
dreams about Polivanov that she found increasingly puzzling.
Whenever she envisaged the young cadet, she felt Count Tolstoy's
shadowy presence in her thoughts.

3

Tolstoy came to see the Behrses whenever he was in Moscow, often an unexpected but most welcome visitor. He sometimes arrived in the afternoon, sometimes in the evening, and he spent as much time with the children as he did with their parents. The Behrs children, with the exception of Lisa, were full of what he called "sparkle"—energy that filled their home with love and gaiety. They all seemed to be a "little in love," and their evident affection for him brought out Tolstoy's tenderness and high spirits.

He now treated Sonya not as a child but as an intelligent young woman. He talked to her about her mother and remarked on how much like Sonya she had been as a girl. He asked her about the books she was reading and about her hopes and ambitions, and he proffered advice. One evening he asked her to play the Adagio from Beethoven's "Moonlight Sonata" for him. Then, after assuring her that she could be a competent pianist, he carefully evaluated her performance, dwelling on both her weaknesses and strengths. He was easy to talk to, but his comings and goings filled her with anxiety. The man who used to play children's games with her had vanished. In his stead she now had an interested, affectionate friend, and she could not understand why she found this transformation disquieting or why his glances sometimes made her feel an oddly pleasant awkwardness.

She was growing prettier each day, and many of the young men whom Sasha brought home from the corps were charmed by her, as was the university student Vasily Ivanovich Bagdanov who spent the summer of 1857 with the Behrses in Pokrovskoye helping the girls with their Russian lessons. He quickly became a member of the family, but it was Sonya with whom he spent most of his time, giving her volumes of poetry by Büchner and Vogt and reciting passages from Turgenev to her. Once he impulsively grasped her hand and kissed it.

Sonya, shocked, sharply pulled away. "How dare you!" she cried and ran to tell her mother about the incident.

"It's your own fault," her mother said drily. "Take a lesson from Lisa. Things like that don't happen to her."

"Lisa is like a stone; she never pities anyone!" Sonya answered. "But I felt sorry for him the other day when he was telling me about how his little brother was operated on. That is why he dared kiss me!"

It was Polivanov to whom Sonya, a year after their first meeting, was still drawn. Young people seemed to flock to the Behrs house—Sasha's friends; Marya Nikolaevna Tolstoy's family; the Behrses' young cousin from St. Petersburg, Sasha Kuzminsky; and of course girl friends of the three sisters. But of all the youthful guests, Polivanov was the most frequent visitor, and it was apparent he returned Sonya's affection.

While Sonya was having her first flirtation, Tolstoy confessed to a friend that he was "ready to marry," adding, "If Sonya were sixteen and not fourteen, I would propose at once." At this time, however, no one in the Behrs household suspected that Tolstoy might be forming a romantic attachment to any of the girls. He was simply a good family friend who was able to communicate with young people better than most men his age.

Although his sister, Marya Nikolaevna, still despaired over his penchant for Gypsy women, his gambling, and his lamentable extravagances, and feared he was a confirmed bachelor, Tolstoy had in fact put his earlier excesses behind him and was now more anxious than ever to find a suitable wife. There had been several recent socially acceptable attachments, but none had endured.

Women were not his only concern. Following Alexander II's historic statement in early 1856 about the absolute need for changes in the serf system, Tolstoy became obsessed by the injustice of serfdom. After he left the Behrses' in the summer of 1856, he returned to his estate, Yasnaya Polyana. He called his 309 male serfs together to tell them of his plan to free them. The estate, he explained, was heavily mortgaged. He could not grant them their freedom immediately; and even if he could, liberty without land would be calamitous for them. Instead he offered each household twelve acres of land, one and a quarter acres of which would be presented outright. Each household would then buy the remainder of its acreage by paying twenty rubles a year for the next thirty years. In this way the mortgage would be paid on the land. It would then be theirs, and they would be free.

To Tolstoy's amazement his offer was spurned by the serfs in the wild belief that at his coronation the Tsar would free the serfs and give them all the land they farmed. Therefore, Tolstoy's serfs thought, he was trying to cheat them of their coming windfall.

Bitterly disappointed by the rejection of his plan, Tolstoy set out to earn the trust of his serfs. He remained at Yasnaya Polyana for five months, although he did make several brief visits to his sister, Marya, in Moscow—each time stopping to see the Behrs family as well—and to Turgenev's estate at Spasskoye Lutovinovo, which was about fifty miles from Yasnaya Polyana. But most of his days were spent in his cattle and farm yards and in his fields. By the next spring his serfs had become accustomed to seeing their master ride through the mud and melting ice wearing a plain cloth coat like their own. Many days found Tolstoy taking over the direction of the farm work from his bailiff. He sweated in the wheat fields, scything the grain with the serfs and often sharing his bailiff's lunch. But these efforts did little to shake the peasants' distrust of him.

During these months Tolstoy did not abandon his literary interests. He finished *Youth* and began several stories and plays; he read works by Dickens and Goethe, among others; and he recorded his thoughts and activities in his diary. As he wrote and worked, he was tenderly looked after by his housekeeper Agatha Mikhailovna, who had come to Yasnaya Polyana as his grandmother's maid, and by his aging and beloved Aunt Toinette, as he called his distant cousin Tatyana Alexandrovna Ergolskaya. She had come to Yasnaya Polyana to raise her cousin Nikolai Tolstoy's five small children after their mother died. An extraordinarily kind and good woman, Aunt Toinette was the only mother Tolstoy had ever known, and he remained deeply attached to her until her death.

In spite of his constant industry at this time, Tolstoy was buffeted by emotional storms. The flagrant immorality in the nearby villages appalled yet fascinated him. He noted in his diary the depraved relations of a "proprietress with her footman, a brother with his sister, a father to his son's wife, etc." His own sexual adventures with village girls, neighbors' wives, and peasant women left him filled with self-loathing; and he became convinced that only marriage would save him from a life of immorality and lechery. The women he met of marriageable age in Moscow and St. Petersburg all seemed too worldly. He decided to look closer to home and began a proper courtship of the pretty twenty-year-old Valerya Vladimirovna Arsenev, who lived only five miles away at Sudakova. But Valerya was not the ideal wife he was searching for, and their romance ended within a few months.

Tolstoy then traded the blue wool peasant tunic that he wore at Yasnaya Polyana for the elegant suits made for him by the French tailor Charmeur, one of the finest in Moscow, and returned to that city. He visited the Behrses frequently and had a brief affair with a thrice-married baroness, noting afterward in his diary, "Perhaps the whole delight consists in standing on the threshold of love."

In this cynical mood, Tolstoy took leave of Moscow in January 1857 and went off on a tour through Western Europe. The aristocratic Russian community in Paris entertained him royally, and for two months his life there was frivolous, exhausting, and gay. Then early one morning in late March he witnessed—in the spirit of a tourist seeing the sights—the execution of a criminal, François Richeux, who had robbed and killed two people. The spectacle was hideous. None of the horrors of war he had seen in the Caucasus and the Crimea had affected him so profoundly. There was "nothing at all majestic" about the "dextrous and elegant machine," as he described the guillotine. He wrote to the critic Vasily Petrovich Botkin, "I will never again look at such a thing, and I will never anywhere serve any government."

Paris had become unbearable, and the next day he left for Geneva, where his favorite cousin, Countess Alexandra Andreyevna Tolstoy, was staying. (Alexandra Andreyevna was traveling with the Tsar's sister, the Grand Duchess Marie, as the companion of her children.) He went by rail, but the French trains had none of the luxury of those in Russia, and he wrote Turgenev that the French train "is to a journey what a brothel is to love; just as convenient, but also just as humanly mechanical and deadly monotonous." Tolstoy had a delightful though short visit with his cousin and was so taken with Switzerland that he stayed there for more than two months. His plans were for an extensive stay abroad; and he wanted to visit Holland, London, Rome, Naples, Constantinople, and Odessa. A disastrous stop at the roulette wheels in Baden-Baden in early July, however, forced him to book passage home. But had his usual ill-fortune at the gaming tables not cut short his trip, some distressing news he received at this time would have. As he was packing, a letter arrived from his brother Sergey telling him that their sister, Marya, had broken with her husband (Valerian Petrovich Tolstoy—a cousin) because of his infidelities, declaring she "would not be the chief sultana in his harem."

Sonya, in Moscow, was much disturbed, first by the rumors and whispers and then by the tears of her dear friends, Marya Nikolaevna Tolstoy's children. Divorce was a word rarely heard in the Behrs household. But even more immediately disconcerting to Sonya was her mother's often-voiced plaint that her sister Lisa should be meeting "more eligible young men." Dr. Behrs went into one of his rages whenever possible suitors were mentioned, while Lisa burst into spasms of tears, in acute distress over her parents' arguments, rather than in irritation at her mother's efforts on her behalf. In fact, she confided to Sonya that she agreed with Lyubov Alexandrovna, at least to the extent that she didn't object to meeting "eligible young men."

On Sonya's part, she hoped it would take a long time for her family to find a suitable husband for Lisa, because, as was the custom, the oldest daughter must be married first. Once Lisa was wed, her mother might begin searching for suitors for her. She found that idea unspeakably depressing. Marriage was a serious matter—the end of romantic musings and youthful frivolities. And to entertain ardent thoughts for Polivanov or to dream about an older man like Tolstoy did not indicate that she was prepared to wed.

By 1858 Sonya was a young woman, a "dreamer," the most striking of the three sisters. Tanya was growing up fearless and gay, "a scamp of a girl . . . a Cossack," while Lisa had a cool, diffident beauty. The nestlings were quickly becoming swans. Tolstoy called on the Behrses often during that year. When he was visiting, everyone in the household seemed to cheer up, and the girls entered into a lively competition for his attention. He talked about literature to Lisa, played piano duets and chess with Sonya, and—still treating Tanya as a child—carried her around on his back and gave her riddles to solve. Unlike most guests, he did not have to be entertained in the drawing room. He liked to roam about the house as though he were a member of the family.

He was becoming increasingly aware of Sonya's charm. She was, of course, still naive. But therein lay her great appeal; and her air of childlike innocence "combined with the slim beauty of her figure" kept her vividly in his mind. He was attracted by "the expression of her eyes—mild, calm, and truthful—and above all her smile, which carried him into a fairyland where he felt softened and filled with tenderness, as he remembered feeling on rare occasions in his early childhood." But there was a toad in Tolstoy's enchanted garden. The young, handsome Polivanov had become part of the family group. He was openly attentive to Sonya, and she had innocently confided her feelings to Tolstoy, telling him how attractive she found Polivanov. Although Tolstoy knew that neither of them was old enough to make serious promises, he was seized by an irrational agitation whenever he was in the young man's presence, and he took to organizing outings that would not include Polivanov.

He escorted Sonya, Tanya, and Sasha on long walks to historic places in Moscow, tiring them so much that their legs would be numb on their return home. Sasha was far more reserved than either Sonya or Tanya, but what he lacked in fire he made up for in steady warmth and ready understanding. Tolstoy liked the young man enormously.

The gaiety of the Behrs family warmed Tolstoy's soul, and he was drawn frequently to their house that winter. The charm of the three sisters fascinated him. Women were on his mind constantly; and when he returned to the isolation of Yasnaya Polyana, self-restraint became insufferably difficult. Convincing himself that he needed a woman—"not for the sake of debauchery but for health's sake"—he began an affair with Axinia Bazykina, a peasant girl from his own farm whose husband was serving in the army.

Axinia was "simple, without pretense, clean, and not bad-looking, with bright black eyes, a deep voice, a scent of something fresh and strong and a full breast that lifted the bib of her apron." Everything about her seemed attractive, and though he believed it was shameful to corrupt one of his own peasants, he was not strong enough to resist temptation. They often made love in the hazel and maple thicket, concealed from the peasants at work in the fields, yet bathed in bright sunlight.

"Today, in the big old wood. I'm a fool, a brute. Her bronze flesh and her eyes. I'm in love as never before in my life. Have no other thought," he wrote in his diary in May 1858.

Guilt began to plague Tolstoy because, since Axinia was a serf and he was her master, she was not free to refuse him. Each time he met her, he vowed it would be the last. But whenever he caught a glimpse of her, he was overwhelmed with desire. He felt completely in her power, and this weakness, coupled with his monstrous sense of culpability and shame, caused him the greatest anguish he had ever suffered. He began to faithfully record his basest emotions in his diary, perhaps to try to discover the source of his obsession or perhaps to assuage his conscience by listing his every transgression. In July Axinia gave birth to their son, Timofei.

Tolstoy remained away from Yasnaya Polyana as often and as long as he could. In September he attended an election of the Tula nobility. Later that fall he took part in a bear hunt at Volochok, near St. Petersburg; he was thrown to the ground and mauled by a huge bear but miraculously escaped without serious injury. By Christmas he was in Moscow, and on New Year's Day 1859 he wrote in his diary, "I must get married this year or never."

He knew that he was using most of his energy to resist his passion for Axinia. More than ever he was convinced that a proper marriage to a respectable woman would save him from his baser instincts. But after his disappointment in Valerya, he was wary of almost all women. During the last weeks of his romance with Valerya, he had unfairly accused her of having been too encouraging to another man and had attacked her for being unwilling to change in the ways he deemed necessary if she was to become the Countess Tolstoy. Valerya, he concluded, was "intellectually lazy." In his last letter to her he admitted he was an egotist and stated flatly that the woman he married would have to "work to keep up with him," but in the two years since he had broken with Valerya, he had not found a woman who either could or would take on this challenge. There was one, Sonya, whom he could educate to his ways; but this would take time, and in the winter of 1859 he felt that he could not afford such luxury and that, though he was only thirty, he would soon be an old man.

He decided that rather than returning to Yasnaya Polyana that winter, he would visit his devoted cousin Alexandra in St. Petersburg. Eleven years his senior, she was one of the handsomest, most captivating women Tolstoy had ever known. For years they had exchanged the most intimate confidences, and there were times when he suspected he was somewhat in love with her. He was always dazzled by her silvery gray eyes, serene, intelligent smile, and sensual contralto voice. But he so enjoyed the idea that a man and woman could have a friendship not based on sex that he bested his own nature and kept his relationship with Alexandra untouched by physical passion. Alexandra respected this tacit pact between them, though she did not attempt to conceal her great admiration for him. A few months of theater parties and social rounds in St. Petersburg made him anxious to get home, and he set out for Moscow.

A new idea had taken hold of him in late spring. What was the point of writing books and articles that nine-tenths of the Russians could not read? He would start a village school at Yasnaya Polyana and do battle against illiteracy. He equipped a large upstairs room with benches and blackboards, and by the end of the summer his school had twenty students.

Suddenly he felt a new energy, a rebirth. The children took up almost all his time, and he was no longer obsessed with Axinia. Even his work on a new novel, *The Cossacks*, was given short shrift, as were the affairs of his estate. His thoughts of marriage were pushed aside by his new enthusiasm.

Then in June 1860 his brother Nikolai became critically ill with a tubercular condition and was sent to Soden, a Prussian health spa, in a desperate search for a cure. Tolstoy was distraught. The harrowing image of Dmitry on his deathbed still haunted him. Dmitry had been the black sheep of the family, and Sergey was too frivolous. But Nikolai, the oldest of the four Tolstoy brothers, had always been the one Lev Nikolaevich loved most. So, putting his school in the hands of a young university student who had become his assistant when attendance had grown, Lev Nikolaevich, his sister, Marya Nikolaevna, and her three children sailed from St. Petersburg on July 2 to be with their dying brother.

4

The golden domes of St. Petersburg's great cathedrals blazed under the wintry sky on March 17, 1861, the Sunday on which Alexander II, in the sixth year of his reign, had the Emancipation Proclamation read from the pulpits of the capital's churches. The Tsar, resplendent in full uniform and mounted on his huge black horse, reviewed a grand military parade after church services, and then in a clear voice he addressed the assembled throng: ". . . an end has been put to centuries of injustice. I expect sacrifices from the nobility . . . the loyal nobility will gather around the throne." Wild hurrahs rose from the peasants who filled the streets. The manifesto was a complex document, and the peasants who had heard it read did not fully understand it. However, two points were quite clear to them. While their total liberty would not come for two years, their slavery was at an end.

All through the day masses of cheering peasants stood in front of the palace. Wherever the Tsar went he was followed by crowds shouting their joy and his greatness. But this jubilation was short-lived; in the coming weeks and months the peasants came to understand that the Emancipation Proclamation had given them freedom but not the means to enjoy a free life.

Sixty percent of them were not given enough land to support themselves and their families. And all peasants lost their customary rights to timber and firewood from the lands of their former owners, and were denied the use of pastures and meadows. But the domestic serfs suffered the most. They were now free to leave their former masters and seek employment elsewhere. Some were able to do so, but the majority faced an impoverished and miserable future. Domestics had been closer to slaves than serfs, and their numbers were out of all proportion to the work to be performed.

For the most part they were orphans, widows, and dull-witted unfortunates and their legitimate and illegitimate issue. To this class belonged the lackeys, servant girls, cooks, coachmen, stable boys, and gardeners, as well as the many old men and women who could do no real work. They had received a monthly allowance of food and a yearly allowance of clothes, but with emancipation they were left destitute.

Tolstoy was still abroad when the Tsar's proclamation was published. He had traveled with the dying Nikolai from Soden to Frankfurt, and then to Hyeres on the southern coast of France. Like their brother Dmitry, Nikolai had suffered a slow, painful decline, finally dying in Tolstoy's arms on September 20, 1860. "Nothing in my life has ever made such an impression on me," he wrote his old friend Afanasy Afanasyevich Fet.

Tolstoy spent the next months traveling in Europe, and on his return to Russia in April 1861 he threw himself into his peasant school and his literary work. He had always condemned serfdom; but curiously, though acting fairly, he did not—now that they were emancipated—treat his peasants with exceptional generosity. He gave them no more land than the new law required, and no more rights to firewood in his forests, fish in his streams, or hunting privileges on his property. Tolstoy's former serfs, over three hundred in number, received about one-sixth of his land among them, most of which was not well irrigated and contained little wood and almost no wild game. Tolstoy now had to pay them a small wage. But with less land his taxes were lower and he no longer had the responsibility of seeing that the peasants were fed and clothed. Yet, because of his school and his writings, he was regarded as a dangerous radical by his fellow landowners in Tula.

The peasants of Yasnaya Polyana never expected more than what they received. But their emancipation did not bring them closer to Tolstoy. It was only with the children that he had mutual fond regard. With those attending his school he slid down the steepest hills of the estate, romped in the snow, played ball, walked in the woods and meadows telling them all about nature, and sat on the terrace weaving fantastic tales.

There was much work to be done in the fields of Yasnaya Polyana. An old proverb often repeated by the peasants promised, "Sow in mud and you will be a prince." So when the spring thaw made mud of the fields, the peasants prepared the land and sowed the summer grain, a task that lasted through May. This done, they worked in the fallow fields, sowing the winter grain, until St. Peter's Day in late June, when they began the haymaking. After that came the harvest, by far the busiest time of the year. Since the peasants now had more land of their own to work, they had fewer days to give to the Count's acreage, and he had to take a greater interest in the cultivation of his fields. He saw that it was unlikely that he would be able to leave Yasnaya Polyana before the harvest was in.

Aunt Toinette was good company, and that spring he did not need much other companionship. In the evenings, dressed in his blue wool tunic, he sat in a comfortable armchair in the parlor, and they discussed her favorite subject, philosophy, as well as physics and agriculture. A devout churchwoman, she never discussed religion with him, because his unorthodox beliefs upset her. She loved Lev Nikolaevich like a son. Hers was an unobtrusive love, and had she known about his affair with Axinia she would have been saddened, but she would not have censured him. Tolstoy had brought Axinia into the house as a domestic; and although he treated her in a peremptory manner, he allowed small Timofei, who was nearly three, to play at his mother's heels as she scrubbed the floors. Axinia accepted her lot without complaint, and the child's resemblance to Tolstoy was as yet unremarked.

At the end of May the governor of the province of Tula named Tolstoy arbiter of the peace to help resolve disputes between the emancipated peasants and their former masters. There was a resounding protest to this appointment from the landowners; and though Tolstoy had vowed he would never work for any government again, he took this post most seriously. His quick temper flared often during that spring and summer, and in early July he wrote in his diary, "The arbitership has involved me in quarrels with all the landowners and has injured my health."

His school continued to take up most of his free time. The children gathered around him eagerly and always greeted him with affection. Nikolai's death had left Tolstoy with morbid thoughts about his own mortality. Although his body was bronzed and strong, the scent of decay was always in his nostrils. Only his hours with the youngsters lightened his dark mood.

Fearing interference from the government, he obtained a formal authorization from the Tula authorities for his free school. While a three-room schoolhouse was being built, he held classes on the grass under an apple tree. Before the summer ended, the school was completed, and Tolstoy and the two young men who worked as his assistants moved their classes indoors. The school was non-compulsory and open to all without charge; over the door was a sign that read, "Enter and Leave Freely." Girls were excluded but the boys were from seven to thirteen years old; classes were held from eight to noon and from three to six.

Proudly Tolstoy wrote his cousin Alexandra, "Lessons often continue an hour or more beyond closing time because it is impossible to send the children away from school—they beg for more. Many even linger on till late in the evening and pass the night in a hut in the garden."

After the harvest, when there was a short respite from the work of the farm, he decided to publish a pedagogical journal and plunged into writing articles as well as teaching. It was in this new and vital frame of mind that he once again began to visit Moscow and to spend even more time at the Behrses', where his school and publishing activities were of great interest to everyone.

Lisa, who was showing some literary talent, wrote articles for his magazine; and a chance remark by Tolstoy to his sister—"I like the Behrs family particularly well, and if I ever marry, I will only marry in that family"—seemed to give substance to the gossip linking his name with that of the oldest Behrs daughter. The ladies in Lyubov Alexandrovna's circle were certain that *le Comte* was hoping to marry Lisa. After all, the other girls were still children. *Le Comte* must be in love with Lisa! Why else would he come so often to the Behrses'? Even Marya Nikolaevna gave her blessing to the match, saying, "She will make an excellent wife."

At first Lisa, who was now nineteen and thus eminently marriageable, seemed untouched by this speculation. Then, as Tolstoy visited more and more often that winter, her sisters saw a great change in her. She took to studying herself in the mirror, became more interested in clothes, and fussed with her hair; she was kinder, and even pleasant to them.

Sonya laughed at her and wrote teasing poems about her love-sick air. Lisa was undisturbed by this banter. She had begun to fall in love for the first time. She listened serenely when Sonya reminded her that she had until recently regarded Tolstoy as a rather unattractive middle-aged man and suggested that perhaps she was in love with love and not with *le Comte*. These pointed observations did not ruffle Lisa, who had begun to imagine her life as the Countess Tolstoy. But as the winter drifted into spring of 1862, Tolstoy came less often to Moscow; rumors to the contrary, he was proving to be a laggard suitor.

It was a beautiful May day and the Behrs household was in chaos. The family was leaving the next morning for Pokrovskoye, and packing was in progress in every part of the house. In the courtyard, Grigory the butler was storing china in crates; hay and straw were everywhere.

Suddenly, in the midst of this uproar, there was Tolstoy with his butler Alexei Stepanovich and two of his favorite students, Vasya Morozov and Ignat Chernox, eleven-year-old peasant boys. They adored their teacher, shared his jolly mood, and immediately joined the Behrs boys in their games. Delighted as always to see their friend, the Behrses postponed their departure for three days.

Exhausted by his work as arbiter and distraught over increasing opposition to his school, Tolstoy was in poor health. For several months a cough had plagued him, and he feared that he had contracted tuberculosis. Dr. Behrs assured him that he had not, but suggested rest and a kumiss cure (fermented mare's milk); and so Tolstoy decided to travel to the Caucasus, where he could follow this regimen. But for three days he enjoyed the Behrses' exuberant hospitality. At dinner Lisa sat beside him smiling coquettishly and speaking in an unnaturally soft voice while Sonya and Tanyachka exchanged knowing glances.

Dinner conversation centered on their visitor's problems. The landowners in Tula complained constantly that Tolstoy's decisions as arbiter were far too favorable to the peasants; for his part, he felt that this pressure had made him too solicitous about the nobility's interests. Other worries distressed him. The educational establishment had denounced him as a "pedagogical nihilist," and his school had been described as a "Jewish synagogue or a Gypsy encampment." He was said to represent a danger not only to the foundation of educational practice but also to the authority of the state, because the freedom he allowed in his classroom was close to anarchy. Tolstoy's philosophy, his detractors claimed, placed the well-being of the individual above that of the state. And his magazine had been flailed by his former colleagues on the *Contemporary*, who accused him of being "an ignoramus" in the field of education.

As Tolstoy spoke gloomily of these troubles, Sonya was unusually quiet, and whenever he glanced her way she avoided his eyes. This did not escape Tanya's attention, nor did she miss the quiver of Sonya's lips when Lisa was most cloying, or the flush that rose in Sonya's cheeks when an inconsequential question was directed at her and all eyes, including Tolstoy's, were turned on her as she answered.

Later that evening Tolstoy accompanied the Behrses and their daughters to the theater. Lyubov Alexandrovna made certain that Lisa was seated next to him, and it was clear to the younger sisters that she was trying to arrange a match. Lisa was pleased by her mother's efforts, but Tolstoy seemed cooler than usual, a circumstance all present attributed to his ill-health. After the theater, refreshments, and a sharp debate about the pros and cons of the performance, Tolstoy took his leave, coughing badly and looking, in the dim evening light, pale and painfully thin.

Lyubov Alexandrovna's matchmaking never failed to anger Dr. Behrs. Throughout the evening he had pulled at his beard, a gesture his family knew signaled extreme irritation; and on their return home he took her to task rather harshly. The doctor loved his three daughters, and though Tanya was thought to be his favorite he showed each equal concern and tenderness. He told his wife bluntly that, while he respected Tolstoy and considered him an honorable man, he was not at all sure that the Count's attentions to Lisa were those of a serious suitor. It was this new freedom that allowed Lisa to believe she could fall in love with whomever she wanted to marry. When Lyubov Alexandrovna reminded her husband that they had been "allowed" to fall in love and marry, he asked, "What if our Lisa has fallen in love with a man who has no intention of marrying her?"

"Why would he come to the house so often?" his wife countered.

"He has always been a frequent guest in our home. Must our daughter's new status as a young woman eager to marry change that? And anyway he is much too old."

"Not any older than you were when we fell in love."

"I had not led the wild life that *le Comte* has led," the doctor said in a hard voice that ended the discussion. (In fact, the doctor's judgment was astute. Back in September 22, 1861, Tolstoy had written in his diary, "L[isa] B[ehrs] tempts me; but she will not be the one. She is all reason, and has no feelings.")

Sonya had overheard her parents' disagreement, her heart beating violently, and she remained a long while at her prayers that night. Tears rose in her eyes. Without speaking to Tanya, she climbed into bed. Finally she reached over and snuffed the bedside candle. There was no light from beneath the screen that divided Lisa's area in the room from theirs. Their sister was asleep. The two girls lay in silence until the irrepressible Tanya whispered, "Sonya, do you love *le Comte?*"

"I don't know." Sonya sighed deeply. "Oh, Tanya, two of his brothers died from consumption!"

"What if they did?" Tanya replied. "He has quite a different constitution. You may be sure that Papa knows better than we do."

Sonya sobbed quietly; her heart was heavy, her mind confused. What about Polivanov? she wondered. And what about Lisa?

After Tolstoy left for the Caucasus, the Behrses set out for Pokrovskoye. Sonya rode with her mother, Petya, Lisa, and her mother's maid. Tanya, the smaller boys, the baby, and the nurse followed in a second carriage. Sasha was to join them later with Dr. Behrs. The wheels of the carriage rumbled over the cobbles, passed Petrovsky Park and the outskirts of Moscow. Sonya stared out the window while her mother and Lisa discussed plans for the autumn social season—and for a visit with the children's grandfather, Alexander Islenyev, at his estate, Ivitsy, which was only a short drive from Yasnaya Polyana.

Soon they would see *le Comte* in his own home, and that prospect cheered Sonya.

• •

July was hot and filled with summer storms. The house was, as always, alive with vivacious young people. Through the open window of "the room of the three maidens" Sonya heard the shrieks of the younger children playing in the soft warm rain. She spent almost every morning writing in her diary or working on a story. And when the words didn't come easily, she stared out the wide bowed window at the pond with its small emerald island, at the green cupolas of the village church and the winding road to Moscow.

Sonya would soon be eighteen, and if Lisa's expectations were fulfilled her mother would then turn to making "arrangements" for her. The thought terrified her. The only man she wanted to marry was Lev Nikolaevich. If she could not have him, what would become of her? She was not religious enough to become a nun, and in any case she could never give up the comfort and elegance she loved for the austerity of convent life. Nor was a dedication to writing possible, for neither her family nor Tolstoy would approve of a woman making a career of literature.

These musings did not prevent Sonya from joining in the gay summer life at Pokrovskoye. Every Sunday the house was filled with guests, and often more than twenty sat down to dinner. One visitor—Nil Alexandrovich Popov, a professor of Russian history at the University of Moscow and a young friend of Dr. Behrs's— began coming with great frequency. A bachelor of twenty-nine, he had serious gray eyes and a sallow complexion. He was then staying at a summer cottage just a mile from Pokrovskoye and was obviously quite taken by Sonya. She found him interesting, enjoyed his stories about Russia's past, and—though it could not be said that she encouraged his attentions—was amused and flattered by his grave courtship. He was, after all, a distinguished "older man," and he did fill a curious void she sensed in her life.

Invigorated by his rest cure, Tolstoy had extended his stay in the Caucasus. His sister, Marya Nikolaevna (whom he called "Mashenka"), was at Yasnaya Polyana for the summer with Aunt Toinette, and he felt confident that things were being well looked after. He was not, however, aware that the secret police suspected that an illegal press at Yasnaya Polyana was being used to print anti-government leaflets. The police decided to move against Tolstoy, and on July 13 three troikas of officers swept down on his estate. All the occupants were forbidden to leave the house, and the premises were searched. The family was not told what the police were looking for, but one man, a colonel, after reading all of Tolstoy's letters and diaries, including his private correspondence, announced that nothing suspicious had been found and ordered the officers to leave.

When he received his sister's letter telling of the police visit, Tolstoy hurried back to Yasnaya Polyana. After making sure that his family was well and no damage had been done to the house, he went to Moscow to deliver a letter of protest to the Tsar. He then came to Pokrovskoye, ostensibly to see Dr. Behrs and be assured that his health was restored. He was heavier, his color good, and his cough gone; but Sonya had never seen him so agitated. He stormed up and down the bright parlor "very much like a dark, thunderous cloud moving fast through a summer sky." The Behrs family, including the small children, perched on the edges of sofas, chairs, and stools listening to his impassioned account of the incident.

"The police officials burst upon the house about midnight!" he exclaimed. "My aunt and Mashenka were preparing for bed. They demanded the keys of all the cupboards and chests, and asked for wine and food. They rummaged through everything they could, and naturally did not discover anything with which they could in any way find fault. And as if that were not enough, one of the officials opened my writing desk, and since I take the key to this desk with me wherever I go, he broke the lock! They read aloud my private diaries and my most personal letters in Mashenka's presence. . . . My name has been dishonored by what they have done! . . . I cannot live in Russia! I must leave everything and go abroad!"

"No!" Dr. Behrs remonstrated, standing and facing Tolstoy. "This will all blow over, and you must stay here to see it through!"

"Yes, you must!" Sonya echoed.

"I'm sure everything will soon be smoothed over and forgotten," Lisa added complacently.

A few days later he returned to tell them that the Tsar, through an adjutant, had sent him an apology, expressing his regret "over this unfortunate incident." Although the sky was overcast and a heavy rain had already left the roads muddy, Tolstoy, needing to work off his frustration and anger, suggested a walk. Sonya, Lisa, Tanya, Petya, Popov, a young man named Pascault, who was Popov's student, and Tolstoy set out; and before long, dark clouds gathered over their heads and the rain burst down torrentially on them. The group ran screaming and laughing toward a nearby peasant's cottage. An old man with long shaggy yellow hair stood in the open doorway, and as they drew closer three dogs rushed out of the hut barking and then jumping on them playfully. Bowing low as he stepped aside, the peasant welcomed them to his home. The hut consisted of one large room, perhaps fifteen by thirteen feet, and had two small windows and a dirt floor. A narrow bench lined two sides of it. In one corner was a table, and in another a large brick stove which rose almost to the ceiling. The base of this stove was a platform six feet wide which was used as a bed. The hut appeared to be shared by a large family, most of whom were out working the communal field which bordered it.

With the exception of Tolstoy, the intruders were uncomfortable; he, however, began to talk with the old man about crops. A young peasant woman came in with a squalling baby in her arms. She approached the visitors shyly; then pulling up the infant's shirt and revealing an angry rash, she begged to know what she should do for her child. Popov was repelled and walked away.

"My father's a doctor," Sonya said with warm, quick sympathy. "He will give you some medicine." And then she told the woman how to get to Pokrovskoye.

Black bread and tea were offered and refused, and then the rain stopped and the hikers took their leave. As Tolstoy and Sonya walked ahead of the others, he asked if she kept a diary. She replied she had done so since she was eleven. "And what else have you been doing this summer?" he inquired.

"I have been writing a story, but I haven't finished it yet."

"A story? How did you get the notion to do such a thing? What are you writing about?"

"Oh, it's about our family," she admitted hesitantly.

"Who has read it?"

"I am reading it aloud to Tanyachka."

"And will you give it to me?"

"Oh, I couldn't do that!" she said breathlessly. Just then Lisa caught up with them, and the conversation turned to less intimate subjects.

When they reached home, Mrs. Behrs was waiting for them on the terrace, silhouetted against the glowing orange sunset. Tolstoy rushed up to her, announcing, "Lyubov Alexandrovna, I have come to tell you that your daughters are very well bred young ladies." He told her about the peasant baby and praised the girls' concern about the child.

When Tolstoy had begun speaking, Sonya was terrified that he might mention the time they spent alone on their walk home. The warm wind breathing gently from the south made her tremble, and she went inside for a shawl. Tolstoy's glance followed her. He was pacing in the sitting room when she came down to tea, long impatient steps, as if this were his home and she his *what—daughter? wife?* He stopped the moment he saw her, sat down, and took a steaming cup of tea from Lyubov Alexandrovna's hand. "How pleasant and comfortable it is here," he remarked. Popov had stayed for tea; and as the clotted cream and pastries were passed, Tolstoy gave him reproving looks.

That evening Sonya gave him her story to read. The plot involved three sisters, two of whom were in love with the same man, a character named Dublitski. Sonya, Lisa, Tanya, and their mother were thinly disguised. The story ended with the middle sister entering a convent so that the older girl could marry the man they both loved. As simplistic as the tale was, it was extremely well written, the characters quite real. Tolstoy was later to use much of Sonya's re-creation of Tanya (as well as the fictional name Natasha) in *War and Peace*. But the next morning he mentioned only that he had glanced through it. Sonya's story had, however, disturbed him so much that he had spent a sleepless night. As he had hoped, Sonya was attracted to him. And, as he had feared, her family thought it was Lisa who had caught his eye. But what disturbed him most was Sonya's description of Dublitski, obviously patterned on himself. Although energetic and intelligent, Dublitski was middle-aged and unattractive—a portrait that pained and irritated Tolstoy.

The night had been equally troubled for Sonya. It seemed inconceivable to her that her sister was not aware that something curious, unspoken, had happened between Count Tolstoy and herself that afternoon. In her diary she recalled the events of the day, dwelling on his every expression and every word. Her question to herself was whether she was right in suspecting he might be attracted to her. But as he prepared to leave he extracted a promise from Lyubov Alexandrovna to visit him with the girls at Yasnaya Polyana on their journey to the Islenyev estate in Tula. Sonya's fears were appeased. She would see him again soon.

5

Once Tolstoy had left, Sonya was in a continual state of unrest. Although she still wrote about her hopes and desires in her diary, for the first time she was reluctant to talk about them with Tanya. She sat at her bedroom window after her sisters were asleep and stared out at the moon. She read Lev Nikolaevich's *Family Happiness*, which he had published three years before, and—like Marya Alexandrovna, its seventeen-year-old heroine—she wandered alone in the garden. She found it uncanny that *le Comte* had set this story at Pokrovskoye, and she was amazed at how sensitive he was to a young woman's dreams and fantasies.

No one in the house, not even Tanya, suspected the depth of Sonya's feelings; but all concerned were elated when Lyubov Alexandrovna announced in early August that the three girls and nine-year-old Vlodny would accompany her to Ivitsy. On their way they would stop at Yasnaya Polyana to visit the Count and his sister, Marya, who was also a childhood friend of Mrs. Behrs's. For three days the house at Pokrovskoye bustled with activity. There were errands to run and purchases to be made—ribbons and pins for the girls' hair (there were bound to be festivities), music and books, food and presents. Then they drove into Moscow where the six-seated Annenskaya coach waited to take them as far as Tula.

The long ride was broken by stops at various stations where —with the provisions they had brought—tea was prepared. As dusk fell, they arrived at an inn at Serpukhov, where they stayed the night. Vlodny and Tanya explored everything—the stables, the kitchen, the harness room; but Lisa and Sonya, bound by the restrictions of being young women, remained in their room—a chilly silence separating them though they shared the same bed.

At sunrise, as the cocks crowed, the Behrs family departed for

Tula, where they spent most of the day with Lyubov Alexandrovna's older sister, Nadezhda Alexandrovna, who was married to Vladimir Xenofontovich Karnovich, the former district marshal of the Tula nobility. She was a woman more noted for gay good humor than handsomeness; and her daughters, who were close in age to the Behrs sisters, had inherited their mother's happy nature.

Tula was a dull provincial town; however, such a good time was had that the Behrses did not leave for Yasnaya Polyana until evening approached. They drove through the Zaeska forest in a glorious summer twilight. The road was lined with old lime trees purple in the dark violet light, their creamy buds shimmering from an early dew. As they emerged from the forest, they could see the fields and hillocks of Yasnaya Polyana. It was the first time Sonya had been to visit Tolstoy, the first time she had set her eyes on his beloved land. How unlike the overworked land at Pokrovskoye. Tall grass caught in the wheel spokes as the carriage drew close to the house. There were immense waist-high gray-green willows, and all around was the delightful scent of the freshly mowed meadows.

"There's the house. There it is!" Vlodny shouted.

"Where? Where?" Sonya asked. The growing dark obscured the birch trees that stretched their branches across the road ahead.

"Beyond that arch," Vlodny said.

At last Sonya made out a large frame house in the dim light. "Why, there aren't any lampposts!" she exclaimed. Vlodny laughed at her, but her sisters shared her amazement. Pokrovskoye was regarded by Muscovites as a rustic retreat, but in truth it was more like the city than the country. Though there were farms aplenty, all the main roads had lampposts, and the smaller roads leading to the gates of summer houses were also well lighted at night.

There was a great commotion as Tolstoy, his sister, and his aunt came out to greet the guests. Lyubov Alexandrovna immediately fell into the arms of Marya Nikolaevna, and the two women began to exchange laughing reminiscences.

"Do you remember our old house, Lyubochka?" asked Marya Nikolaevna.

"How could I forget it!" Lyubov Alexandrovna exclaimed. "When we were approaching Yasnaya Polyana, I looked at the spot where the house had stood, and my heart ached to see an empty space."

A pained expression came into Tolstoy's eyes, but only Sonya seemed to notice it as the others were caught up in the good-humored recollections of the two friends. There had been another house, larger and grander, on the estate; the one, in fact, in which all the Tolstoys had been born. Tolstoy had sold this house many years before to pay his gambling debts, and it had been moved by its new owner.

They went inside in a swirl of activity and chatter. As the servants brought in the visitors' bags, and Aunt Toinette's old friend and companion, Natalya Petrovna Okhotnitsky greeted them, Aunt Toinette kept up a continuous commentary in excellent French.

"Sonya is much like you, Lyubov Alexandrovna, and Tanya reminds me very much of her grandmother, the Princess Kozlov-sky, whom I knew well." Out of the corner of her eye she seemed to be studying Lisa, but she made no comment about the oldest of the three sisters.

Natalya Petrovna was a poor elderly gentlewoman whose gratitude for this home that she now shared was evident in her humble and solicitous gestures. When Aunt Toinette had entered, she had hurried to her and placed a shawl around her, and then backing away deferentially, she had stood next to Sonya and silently patted her on the shoulder.

There was something both touching and ridiculous about Tolstoy as he rushed about ordering supper for his guests and arranging beds for them, for though he had hoped the Behrses would accept his invitation, he had not expected them for another week or two.

The house was a great disappointment to Sonya. It was old-fashioned, modestly—and even in some rooms poorly—furnished. There was neither a proper salon nor guest suites. Tolstoy had decided that the sisters would share a large vaulted room on the ground floor. It had once been a storeroom, and the thick iron rings which had been used for holding saddles and hanging fresh meat were still attached to the ceiling. Against the walls stood two settees and a small chaise longue, all painted white and upholstered with blue-and-white striped canvas. The rough birchwood table had been made by a local cabinetmaker. Lev Nikolaevich was wearing a tunic belted with leather which made him look much less *le Comte*. He stood awkwardly, watching Sonya and his Aunt Toinette's maid, Dunyasha, make up the settees. When they were done, Dunyasha asked, "And what shall we do about a third bed?"

"Why not the armchair?" he suggested, and as Dunyasha pushed a chair close to the chaise longue so that a bed was formed, he clumsily unfolded a sheet. Sonya felt somewhat embarrassed. At the same time she enjoyed the sense of intimacy that had sprung up in the room.

The small squint-eyed butler, Alexei Stepanovich, was laying the table for supper as Sonya walked through the dining room into a small drawing room. A French window opened from this room onto a little balcony. Sonya went out, and within moments her host followed. The domestic sounds of the house were muffled in the evening air, and she sensed his presence even before she knew for certain that it was he. She felt "something rapturous and hitherto inexperienced."

"What are you doing here all by yourself?" he asked.

"I am admiring the view," she replied, glancing at the darkening fields.

"How serene and simple you are," he said. They spoke for some minutes, but Sonya was never quite sure what had been said. It was as if they had both appeared suddenly in the same dream.

Three of the teachers from the Yasnaya Polyana school joined the party for evening tea. Sonya was quieter than usual, while Lisa laughed and joined in the general merriment. Lisa remained in the parlor quite late, but Sonya went to their makeshift bedroom soon after tea was served. She settled into the armchair bed, and thinking about the radiance of Tolstoy's face when he saw her step down from the carriage, his self-consciousness as he prepared her bed, and the gentle studying way he had looked at her through the evening, she fell warmly and dreamily asleep.

She awoke the next morning feeling happier than she could ever remember being. Lev Nikolaevich was impatiently waiting on the terrace for the three sisters, and when they joined him he showed them about the house and the school. Then he ordered a large two-horse carriage to take them on a picnic with two neighboring families in the Zaeska forest.

"Would you like to ride with me?" Tolstoy asked Sonya as a well-bred white horse was being saddled for him.

She was wearing a billowy yellow dress trimmed in black velvet. "Yes, but I haven't got a riding habit," she replied.

A handsome gray mare named Belogubka, fitted with a side-saddle, was led out from the stable.

"There are no villas here; only the trees of the wood will see you," Lev Nikolaevich said as he helped her mount.

The two of them rode ahead of the long, narrow *katky* which carried the other picnickers. Marya Nikolaevna, who was terrified of any moving vehicle, cried out whenever the carriage lumbered over a rut. Lisa sat stiffly, furious that Sonya and not she was riding with the Count. Of course, she would never have ridden in her fine dress, and Sonya's impropriety was most irritating.

But Sonya had no thought for the dictates of decorum. That "day was different than any [she] had ever previously experienced. It was like no other day in ordinary life but was filled with flashes of magic." The road wound through a stand of century-old oaks into a wide meadow at the edge of the forest. The party stopped there and the picnic was laid out next to a haystack. Lev Nikolaevich glowed with extraordinary vitality; he insisted that everyone including Lyubov Alexandrovna and Marya Nikolaevna climb to the top of the haystack and slide down, and with great animation he led them all in singing rounds.

The next morning Lyubov Alexandrovna and her family left Yasnaya Polyana to visit her father at Ivitsy, but not before promising Lev Nikolaevich that they would stop again on their way back to Moscow.

Sonya's grandfather, Alexander Islenyev, was still exactly as Tolstoy had described him in *Childhood*. A tall imposing figure with "a habit of jerking one shoulder," he was "a strange tripping giant." His eyes were small and "perpetually twinkling, his nose large and aquiline, his head almost entirely bald, and he possessed a kind of lisp. Yet he was an elegant man, regal in bearing and educated to charm—which he instantly did."

Although Sonya knew that her grandfather, born in the last century, was about the same age as Lev Nikolaevich's Aunt Toinette, she found it difficult to regard him as the old woman's contemporary. He had remained formidable at the card table, and he still carried himself like an *homme à bonnes fortunes*.

Dressed in light loose-fitting clothes, beautiful linens with large cuffs and collars, and soft boots, he glided elegantly across his well-polished floors. He greeted his family warmly and called the girls "the young Moscow ladies" as he cheerfully winked and pinched their cheeks. Sofya Alexandrovna, his second wife, smiled and laughed as she embraced them. A noted beauty in her youth, she had become a handsome woman with dark expressive eyes. The three daughters of this marriage—Olga, Adele, and Natalya, who were half-sisters of Lyubov Alexandrovna—hurried to greet "the young Moscow ladies."

The comfortable two-story house was large and old-fashioned; and, unlike Tolstoy, the Islenyevs were ready to receive guests. Sonya and her sisters were led upstairs to a large room with three canopied beds and a window which looked out on an apple orchard. That night the house was filled with neighbors from near and far, and Grandfather Islenyev sang Gypsy songs, accompanying himself on the guitar. He was an emotional man, and whenever he sang a poignant verse his voice faltered. Gypsy music was life, he explained, while Beethoven's sonatas put him to sleep.

The next morning Sonya and Lisa were still sleeping when Tanya, already dressed, burst into their room. "*Le Comte* is coming," she cried.

"No! Really?" asked Lisa, blushing as she wakened.

"Is he alone or with Marya Nikolaevna?" Sonya asked.

"He's alone. He's come on his white horse!"

The girls quickly dressed and ran down to greet him.

"It's really been a long time since I've been in Ivitsy," he was saying to their grandfather. "The last time I stayed with you we went wolf hunting. Remember?"

"But we let the wolf get away!" Islenyev laughed. "How long did it take you to get here?"

"Three hours or more. It was so hot I let the horse walk."

His eyes then turned to Sonya, and even as he greeted the others he kept glancing at her. Sonya instantly became gay and vivacious, and there was a deepened color in her cheeks. Islenyev and his three granddaughters accompanied Tolstoy as he walked about reacquainting himself with the grounds of the old estate.

Later that morning Olga Alexandrovna drew her young niece Tanya aside. "Tanya," she asked, "why has Lisa told me that Lev Nikolaevich intends to marry her when my eyes tell me differently?"

Tanya could not answer, but the question disturbed her all through the festivities of the day and dimmed her excitement about the gala party planned for that evening.

Sonya took special care with her toilette that night. She was wearing a white dress, and was especially pleased by her mauve *suivez-moi* (a rosette worn on the shoulder with long ribbons falling down the back). The last to be ready, she descended the wide wooden staircase alone, feeling all eyes upon her. Her grandfather joined her at the foot of the stairs and, placing her hand on his arm, took her to meet his guests.

Most of the neighboring families were there—the elderly squires who played whist with Alexander Mikhailovich, their wholesome wives, and the pretty young daughters who were the belles of the countryside. The majority of the young men were soldiers from a regiment quartered not far from Ivitsy. Several guests took turns at playing lively dances on the piano. Some of the elderly men and women played cards at two tables in the music and game room while the young people danced in the much larger salon. Even before her grandfather had introduced her to everyone, Sonya had been asked to waltz and was whirling on the dance floor. Her eyes shone as she caught sight of Lev Nikolaevich standing behind a group of ladies as he watched the dancers, his glance straying quite frequently her way. After the dance she went up to him.

"How stylish you look!" he said.

"Aren't you dancing?" she asked.

"Oh, no. I'm too old for that."

While she danced, Lisa kept looking in despair toward where Sonya stood with Tolstoy.

They became involved in a conversation about women's rights and occupations. It took Lyubov Alexandrovna's pointed interference to separate them. Reluctantly Sonya danced the last dance in the cotillion with a young officer. After supper was served, Tanya was asked to sing. She shyly refused and, laughing, ran out of the room to hide in the game room. Moments later she heard footsteps and, thinking someone had been sent to bring her back to perform, ducked under the floor-length cover of the grand piano.

The footsteps were those of Sonya and *le Comte*. They sat down at a game table on which candles were still burning.

"I must go," Sonya said agitatedly, beginning to rise. "Mother will be furious at me. She was quite firm in saying I should go to my room and get some rest."

"Don't go. Sit down, Sonya Andreyevna," he said in a rather strained tone.

"So you are leaving us tomorrow," Sonya remarked, trying to break the tense mood. "What a pity you're going so soon. Why do you?"

"Mashenka is alone. And then she will be going abroad soon."

"Are you going with her?"

"No. I did want to go, but now I can't," he replied.

"We should be going back into the drawing room." She rose again and started to leave.

"Wait a minute, Sonya Andreyevna!"

He picked up a piece of chalk and, after impatiently wiping off the score written on the game table cover, began to scribble something in its place. "Try to read what I write. But I shall only write the initials."

Sonya sat down again. They were both very solemn and excited. Sonya watched, all her thoughts and feelings were concentrated on the chalk and on the large red hand that held it. The chalk squeaked to an abrupt stop. Both were silent as Sonya studied the letters.

"Y.y. & y.d.f.h.r.m.t.v.o.m.i.f.h."

Prompted by him, she began to puzzle out the sentence. "Your youth and your . . . desire . . . for happiness . . ."

"Go on, go on," he prodded.

". . . remind me . . . too vividly . . . of my . . . incapacity for happiness," she read out. She seemed (as she later wrote) "to lose all sense of time and reality; [she felt] as though at that moment she could grasp everything, conceive the inconceivable."

"Let's try again," he said, his voice trembling, and he wrote: "Y.f.h.f.i.a.m. & y.s.L. W.y. & y.s.T.p.m.?"

With less help she read rapidly, "Your family have false ideas about me and your sister Lisa. Won't you and your sister Tanya protect me?"

Tolstoy did not seem startled that she had so easily intuited his thoughts. Their state of mind "was so tense and exalted that nothing seemed to surprise [them]!"

Lyubov Alexandrovna suddenly appeared in the doorway.

"There you are! Go to bed!" she scolded. Sonya said a hasty good night, followed her mother into the hall, and ran upstairs.

Alone in the bedroom, Sonya opened her diary and wrote down the sentences she had just deciphered. She knew something serious and important had taken place between her and the Count, and she "was locking up for a while what had happened during [the] evening."

Later Tanya slipped quietly into the room; and in the morning she confessed to Sonya that she had been in the game room and had overheard her conversation with Tolstoy. She thought Sonya would be angry, but instead there was only joy and radiance in Sonya's eyes as she clasped her sister's hand.

Later that day Tanya found Lisa crying as she sat at the window of their room. "Tanya," Lisa said solemnly, "Sonya is taking *le Comte* away from me. The finery she has decked herself out in, those glances she gives him, the pains she takes to be alone with him—all these things are as clear as day to everyone."

There was little that Tanya could say to console her distraught sister. But that night when both Sonya and Lisa were asleep, Tanya slipped down to her mother's room. "I want to have a talk with you, Mama," she began. "You, Papa, and Lisa don't see things the way they really are."

"What things? What are you talking about?"

"About *le Comte* naturally. You think he intends to marry Lisa, but he's going to marry Sonya," she burst out.

Lyubov Alexandrovna was silent for a moment, and then—though this was not a subject she wanted to discuss with her sixteen-year-old daughter—she questioned Tanya further and became convinced that she had spoken the truth. This revelation kept Lyubov up late into the night. As the oldest daughter, Lisa should, according to tradition, marry first; and, more importantly, she was in love with Tolstoy. Dr. Behrs would never sacrifice one daughter's happiness for another's. And there was the added complication of the doctor's jealousy of his younger, still beautiful wife. He had made it clear that he thought Tolstoy had been overly attentive to Lyubov. He would certainly be angered to learn that Tolstoy had captured the heart of still another woman in the Behrs household.

The Behrses' return to Yasnaya Polyana several days later was quite different from their first gay arrival. Lisa was nervous, tense, and irritable; Vlodny restless; and Lyubov Alexandrovna rather stiff and distant. Sonya alone was in good spirits, but this time she looked at Yasnaya Polyana with a more calculating eye.

The house was badly in need of paint. The surrounding grounds, other than the avenue to the veranda, had not been cleared. And there were no flower beds and well-tended paths like those that gave Ivitsy so much of its charm. Weeds and burdock grew everywhere. Only in the old park was there any evidence of a gardener's skills; its paths were partly cleared and its alleys lined with linden trees. A large pond bordered the entrance to the estate, and at the far end of it was a shabby peasant village.

Although Tolstoy had obviously tried to make his home bright and cheerful for his guests, Sonya was again struck by the crudeness of its furnishings. The unpainted floors were bare; here there were no fine rugs like those that graced Ivitsy and her parents' Kremlin apartment.

Sonya did not think of herself as a snob. She knew that being a member of the nobility did not necessarily mean that one was rich. Yet in her secret heart she did desire beautiful things—rich draperies, fine porcelain and paintings, and delicately carved furniture. Of course, Lev Nikolaevich had been a bachelor for a long time and the house had never been as important to him as his land, his writing, and his school. How could he be expected to concern himself with planting flower gardens when he had to supervise the planting of the crops? And with so many demands on his time, how could he attend to woman's work in the house?

Despite its drawbacks, Sonya was pleased by the house. Unlike Ivitsy, it had sweeping views from almost every window. What was needed was a large salon and perhaps a new wide stairway and several pieces of elegant French or Italian furniture.

It rained the day the Behrs family returned to Yasnaya Polyana, and a steady downpour continued throughout the night.

The next morning the large Annenskaya coach was brought from Tula to take them back to Moscow. Marya Nikolaevna had decided to travel with them, and so goodbyes were said to Aunt Toinette and Natalya Petrovna. Sonya went by herself to look for Lev Nikolaevich. She found him standing on the small balcony where they had met on her first visit.

"I am going with you," he said simply. "How can I stay in Yasnaya Polyana now? It will be so dull and lonely."

The coach had six seats—four inside and two outside. Young Vlodny sat on his mother's lap. Tolstoy took an outside seat, and because Tanya had a cold it was decided that Lisa and Sonya would take turns sitting next to him. It was a curious journey. Sonya, wrapped in her cloak, was the first to join Tolstoy. He told her long stories of the Caucasus, of his life there during his younger days, of the beauty of its mountains. He spoke in a calm, slightly hoarse, tender voice. When night fell, they stopped at the inn at Serpukhov for supper. Lisa took Sonya aside and angrily demanded the outside seat. Lyubov Alexandrovna hurriedly quieted them and decreed Sonya *must* sit inside. But as they boarded the coach, Lev Nikolaevich guided Sonya to the rear and lifted her into the place her sister had been determined to have. Furious, Lisa could do nothing.

While everyone in the crowded carriage slept, Tolstoy talked through the night. Sonya dozed from time to time, always waking to his soft voice, his gentle smile.

It was early morning when the carriage stopped at an inn on the outskirts of Moscow. Lisa loudly complained, "It's so stuffy inside the coach," and rode the rest of the way next to a taciturn Tolstoy.

After a day in Moscow, Lyubov Alexandrovna and her children continued on to Pokrovskoye. Tolstoy took a room in Moscow in the house of a German shoemaker, but within a few days he appeared at the Behrs summer home. He invited the girls to return to Moscow with him to view the military maneuvers at which the Tsar would be in attendance.

Lyubov Alexandrovna refused permission, saying that it would be most improper for her daughters to go out alone with Tolstoy. Undaunted by her chilliness, Tolstoy walked from Moscow to Pokrovskoye almost every day. Although Lyubov made sure that Sonya and Tolstoy were given no opportunity to be alone together, they did share many joyous moments in the company of others.

For Sonya her whole life seemed to have changed. Lisa no longer disturbed her. "A powerful sense of infinite freedom" possessed her. She later wrote that "I [seemed to be] living those last days of my girlhood with a particularly strange inner light, as though my soul had suddenly awakened."

With the Tsar and Tsarina in residence in Moscow, Sonya had taken to merrily pretending she was the Empress. She would laugh and imperiously say, "When I become Empress, I'll do this or that," or "When I become Empress, I'll order this or that." One day after the horse had been unharnessed from Dr. Behrs's cabriolet, she jumped into the carriage and cried, "When I become Empress, I'll drive about in this kind of cabriolet!"

With that, Tolstoy, who had been playing with her brothers, seized the shafts of the small carriage and shouted, "I'm going to give my Empress a drive!" Pulling hard, he started up the road from the house at a trot.

"Don't, don't! It's too heavy for you!" Sonya shrieked. And finally he stopped and the two of them roared with laughter.

That night they sat with other members of the family on the veranda. "What a mad night!" Tolstoy exclaimed as he looked out at the small pond with a full moon reflected in it, seeming to transpose sky and earth.

It did not seem to matter to them that they were allowed no time alone together. They had reached the point when a glance or a touch was as meaningful as words spoken in private. Lisa, though, was still deceiving herself; and Lyubov Alexandrovna, no matter what she saw to the contrary, could not admit that her old friend was interested in Sonya and not Lisa.

But Sasha and Tanya saw and understood what was happening. "Tanya," Sasha asked when they were alone, "What are we going to do with Lisa? *Le Comte* is obviously avoiding her."

"You've noticed it too? He pulls such a long face when he's with her, and she, poor thing, doesn't see it!"

"I would like to have a little talk with her and tell her the truth."

"Better not! Leave it alone!" warned Tanya.

"Well, then, what about our little Sonya? Polivanov will be coming here one of these days."

And they fell silent, puzzled by this world of love, returned and unrequited, that they were observing for the first time.

And late at night, after returning to his Moscow room from an evening at Pokrovskoye, Tolstoy wrote in his diary.

August 23, 1862

Spent the night at the Behrses'. What a child! Or like one! What a great tangle! Oh, if only I could find my way to a clear and decent place to rest! I fear for myself; what if this desire to love is not love itself? I try to look only at her weak points and yet it is still there. What a child! How absurd!

September 8

My God! How perfectly unhappy [Lisa] would be if she were my wife! I begin to hate her at the same time as I pity her!

September 9

I started to work but I can't go on. Instead of working I wrote her [Sonya] a letter which I shall not send. Leave Moscow—I cannot, I cannot do it. . . . Did not go to sleep until three o'clock. I rhapsodized and agonized like a sixteen-year-old boy.

September 12

Lord help me! Oh God, show me what to do! Again a night of sleeplessness and torment for me who laughed at the agonies of those in love. The thing you mock becomes your master. How many the plans I intended to tell her . . . and all to no purpose . . . Lord, help me, show me what to do. Mother of God, help me. I am in love, as I never believed one could love. I am insane, I shall shoot myself if things go on any longer this way. I spent the evening at their home. She is charming in every way. And I . . . am a repulsive Dublitski . . . but I am magnificent in my love. Yes! Tomorrow I'll go to them in the morning . . . I want to go back and tell everything to all of them [the Behrses] Lord help me.

September 13

Tomorrow I'll go as soon as I get up and I'll say everything or else I'll shoot myself. It is past three at night. I have written her a letter and I'll give it to her tomorrow, that is to say today, the 14th. My God, how I dread to die. But happiness and such happiness, seems impossible. O God! Help me!

September 17, the feast day of the Blessed Martyrs, was both Sonya's and her mother's name day, and a large celebration had been planned. The Behrses were back in the Kremlin, and on the evening before the festivities a distraught Count Tolstoy appeared at their door. Since Sasha had returned home from the Cadet Corps with three friends, the house was filled with activity and Sonya was preoccupied with household chores. Tolstoy paced back and forth in the front parlor, and finally, when Sonya came into the room, he insisted she play a piano duet with him while Tanya sang to the small gathering of young people.

Sonya sat down next to him, and as they accompanied Tanya, he whispered that he felt he must tell her of his feelings for her. She played awkwardly, missing several notes. "Go on! Go on!" he ordered. And as she did, he said softly, "I love you."

"My hands," she later wrote, "trembled on the keys as I played for the tenth time the same tune from the 'Il Baccio' waltz. I had learned it by heart in order to accompany Tanya's singing."

After this musical interlude ended, he followed her to her mother's room, where she had gone to fetch a shawl.

"I wanted to speak to you," he said, "but I couldn't do it. Here is a letter which I have now been carrying in my pocket for several days. Read it. I shall wait here for your answer."

He thrust an envelope into her hand, and she turned and rushed downstairs into the bedroom she shared with her sisters. Relieved to find the room empty, she closed the door and tore open his letter.

Sonya Andreyevna, it is becoming unbearable. For three weeks I've been saying to myself, "I shall tell her now!" And yet I continue to go away with the same feeling of sadness, regret, terror, and happiness in my heart. Every night I go over the past and curse myself for not having spoken to you and wonder what I would have said if I *had* spoken. I am taking this letter with me in order to hand it to you should my courage fail me again. Your family have the false notion, I believe, that I am in love with Lisa. This is quite wrong. . . .

At Ivitsy I wrote, "Your youth and your desire for happiness remind me too vividly of my . . . incapacity for happiness." But then, and later on, I lied to myself. At that time I could have cut everything short and could have again entered my own cloister of solitary work and my absorbing labors.

Now I can do nothing. I feel I have created a disturbance in your home, and that your friendship for me, as a good honorable man, has also been spoiled. I dare not leave, and I dare not stay. You are a candid, honest girl; with your hand on your heart, and without hurrying (for God's sake, don't hurry!) tell me what to do.

Will you be my wife? If you say *yes, boldly* with all your heart, then say it, but if you have the faintest shadow of doubt, say *no.* For heaven's sake, think it over carefully. I am terrified to think of a *no,* but I am prepared for it and will be strong enough to hear it. But it will be terrible if I am not loved by my wife as much as I love you!

Just as Sonya finished reading, Lisa entered the room. Sonya clasped the loose pages to her heart.

"What is it?" asked Lisa, turning pale with a premonition of disaster.

"*Le Comte m'a fait la proposition,*" Sonya replied, her dark eyes shining.

Before Lisa could comment, the door opened again, and Lyubov Alexandrovna came in. She wanted to remind her daughters of some chores still to be done, but seeing their agitation, she immediately asked, "My dears, what has happened?"

This was the most difficult moment Sonya had ever faced. But her heart made her bold, and in a firm voice she told her mother and her sister that *le Comte* had asked her to marry him and that she loved him with every fiber of her being. Lisa stood motionless, shocked beyond reaction.

At first, deep red glowed in Lyubov Alexandrovna's cheeks. Then her expression softened.

"Do you want to marry *le Comte?*" she asked.

"Yes," Sonya answered, handing her the letter.

As Lyubov Alexandrovna read it, her hand trembled. She put it down and stood silently for a moment. "Go then and give him your answer," she said in a steady voice.

Sonya flew out of the room and up the stairs; she ran breathlessly into her mother's bedroom. Tolstoy stood in a corner, leaning against the wall, waiting. Sonya took his hands in hers.

"Well?" he asked.

"Of course—*yes,*" she cried.

Hand in hand, they left the room and went into the parlor, where her mother, Tanya, the younger boys, and Sasha and his friends congratulated them. Lisa was conspicuously absent and Dr. Behrs had not yet come home from his court duties.

Sonya's name day dawned bright and clear, and she awoke with a sense of abiding contentment. But a storm raged through the rest of the household. Dr. Behrs was absolutely opposed to the marriage and was unmoved by his wife's emotional appeal. Lyubov Alexandrovna finally went to Lisa and told her that only she could soften his resistance. However difficult it may have been for her, Lisa went to her father and "with remarkable nobility and tact" told him that "no one could stand in the way of Fate." She assured him that she wished Sonya happiness and that now that *le Comte* had chosen, she would be able to put him out of her heart. Reluctantly, and only after Sonya's tears had touched him, did Dr. Behrs give his consent.

Later that morning Tolstoy again came to the Behrs apartment, and after asking to see Dr. Behrs, he was ushered into the front parlor. As he paced agitatedly, he heard the "sound of very, very rapid light steps on the parquet floor," and to his joy, Sonya rushed into the room. All thoughts of Dr. Behrs flew from his mind; he was dazzled by her closeness and the delirious joy of seeing her dark eyes shining with the same overwhelming love as "filled his own heart. She stopped so close that she touched him. Her arms rose and her hands dropped on his shoulders." She blushed as he put his arms around her and kissed her. Her face glowing, her eyes sparkling with excitement, she told him that her parents had given their consent and were happy in her happiness. She added shyly that she had listened for his arrival so that she would be the first to tell him.

The door to Dr. Behrs's study opened, and a servant asked the lovers to go in. Lyubov Alexandrovna stood by her husband's side. Sonya ran to her and put her arms about her; the doctor in a reserved but kindly manner congratulated his daughter's prospective husband.

"When is it to be?" Lyubov Alexandrovna asked.

"When?" said Tolstoy, blushing. "Tomorrow!"

"Oh, don't, *mon cher!* What nonsense! There is the betrothal, and cards [wedding announcements] must be sent out," Lyubov Alexandrovna exclaimed.

"Well then, next week."

"He seems quite mad." Dr. Behrs laughed dryly.

"Why not next week?" asked Tolstoy, grasping Sonya's hand tightly.

"What an idea!" said Lyubov, amused by his impatience. "And the trousseau?"

Tolstoy was horror-struck by the prospect of elaborate preparations, but seeing that Sonya was quite delighted by the idea of a trousseau, he said nothing.

Finally September 23, one week thence, was set as the day of the wedding, although Lyubov declared it would take a miracle to allow her to send the announcements, have the trousseau made, and arrange the ceremony in the next seven days. Only a man as persuasive as Tolstoy could have cajoled the parents of a bride to agree to so short an engagement.

That afternoon guests began to arrive at two o'clock for the name-day celebration of Lyubov Alexandrovna and Sonya. As they often were, Lisa and Sonya were dressed alike. For this party they were wearing mauve and white *barège* gowns, bare at the neck, with mauve bows on the bodice and at the shoulders, and both wore their hair piled high on their heads. Tanya, at sixteen still considered a young girl, wore, to her indignation, a short white dress with a high collar, and her hair down.

As each guest wished her a happy name day, Lyubov Alexandrovna announced, "You may also congratulate us on the occasion of our daughter's betrothal!" Many, before she had time to explain *which* daughter, rushed over to Lisa to offer their good wishes.

Then unexpectedly Polivanov, looking quite the young dandy in his uniform of the Guards, strode into the drawing room. Tolstoy nervously studied him from across the room as Sonya's former suitor paused at a mirror and with his slender white fingers smoothed his golden hair. Sasha went quickly to his side, and

Tolstoy closely watched the young man's startled expression as Sasha spoke to him, and then his confusion as Sonya joined them and led him out of the room. Shortly after, Polivanov left abruptly without saying any goodbyes.

That evening Tolstoy's older brother, Sergey Nikolaevich, joined the Behrses and about ten other guests for dinner. The brothers were so alike that when the maid let Sergey into the house she announced excitedly that "Count Tolstoy has arrived but with darker hair!" Sergey Nikolaevich had a sharp sense of humor, a subtle mind, and great charm. He also had a reputation for behaving even more scandalously than his younger brother. Therefore, it was with some shock that Sonya noticed his flirtatious interest in the innocent Tanya. She thought that his overtures, no matter how discreet, were distasteful—not only because of Tanya's youth and his maturity, but also because of his longtime illicit relationship with a Gypsy woman with whom he had had several children. Sergey Nikolaevich made no secret of his attraction to the youngest Behrs daughter. After dinner he smilingly told his brother and Sonya that if they put off their wedding for a while, perhaps the two Behrs sisters could be married together. Still, so absorbed in her own happiness was Sonya that she dismissed this remark as frivolous chatter and later laughed about it with a blushing Tanya.

Before Tolstoy left that night, the newly engaged couple had a few minutes alone. Since the Behrses had given their consent, Tolstoy had been torn between ecstasy and anguish. Sonya's glowing youth and clear true eyes made him painfully conscious of his own jaded past. She seemed so innocent, so pure; and there was so much about himself that he had not told her. Should he marry her without telling her that he was an agnostic, that he had slept with dozens of women, that he had gambled away most of his inheritance? And if he were to tell her, how would she respond? Would she find him repulsive; would she refuse to marry him? The love in Sonya's gaze filled him with a tremendous sense of responsibility, and he decided that she *must* know all. To make sure he withheld nothing, he would give her his diary to read. And the next morning, after asking Dr. Behrs's permission, he handed Sonya the volumes that told the story of his life. Neither father nor fiancé seemed to have considered the effect Tolstoy's candid chronicle would have upon a romantic young woman who had just celebrated her eighteenth birthday. She had, of course, heard whispered innuendos about Tolstoy's adventures, and she accepted the diary with some reluctance.

"You will have me, whatever I may be?" he beseeched.

"Yes, yes!" she assured him.

Relieved, he asked her where she would like to go after the wedding. Did she want to stay for a time with the Behrses in Moscow, or go abroad, or go straight to Yasnaya Polyana. She answered, "Yasnaya Polyana," certain that this would please him. And she was quite right. He was delighted that they would start their married life *at home*.

That evening Sonya went to her room directly after dinner and began to read the diary. At first she was timid, then fascinated, then shocked, and finally appalled. She knew that he had gambled away fortunes, but she had been almost completely ignorant of his erotic life. And now, less than a week before their wedding, she discovered that the man she loved had been to bed with every sort of woman—Gypsies and whores, women who were her mother's friends, even his own serfs—and had recorded each encounter! And there was a bastard child as well.

When Tolstoy returned the next morning, Sonya greeted him alone in the front parlor. Only when he saw her tear-stained face and the shocking new maturity in her eyes did he realize the devastating effect the knowledge of his dissolute past must have had on her, and he was horrified at what he had done.

"Take those dreadful books back!" she cried, pushing away the notebooks that lay on the table before her. "Why did you give them to me?"

He explained that he had wanted her to know the worst about him, that he had felt there must never be secrecy or deception between them. As he pleaded with her to understand, he stared at her with despair, certain that he had lost her.

Seeing his agony, she was overcome by tender compassion. "It was best after all! But it is dreadful, dreadful!" she cried.

His head dropped and he whispered, "You will not forgive me?"

"Yes, I have forgiven you, but it is dreadful!" she said. But she spoke too quickly. She could not forgive him for bedding the wife of one of his own peasants, for being consumed with lust for her, and for fathering her child. And she was appalled at the possibility of seeing this former mistress and illegitimate child in the home that she would share with him for the rest of her life. And Tolstoy was too caught up in his own relief that Sonya would still have him to consider the full impact his lurid diaries must have had on such a sheltered young woman.

His best man was to be an old friend, Fyodor Ivanovich Timiryzaev, who was then the examining magistrate in the Kremlin. Timiryzaev informed him that before he could marry he must have a certificate stating that he had received communion. Being an agnostic, Tolstoy was offended by this stricture, but he did see a Kremlin priest and did receive a certificate after the priest blessed him and pronounced absolution for the sin of Tolstoy's doubts.

The few days before the wedding were filled with excitement. Guests filled the house. As more and more wedding gifts arrived, the hallway became almost impassable. The bridegroom had bought a splendid *dormeuse* (sleeping carriage), ordered a photograph of Sonya, had a photograph taken of himself, and had given Sonya a diamond brooch. Dr. Behrs gave her a gold bracelet with a locket to hold Lev Nikolaevich's photograph. Dressmakers came at dawn and stayed until midnight. And Sonya and her mother swept through all the fashionable stores, racing to complete her trousseau.

On September 23, the day of the wedding, Tolstoy unexpectedly arrived in the early morning. He was in a highly excited state and demanded to see Sonya. When told by the startled servants that it was against all custom for the bridegroom to see his bride on the day of the wedding, he brushed past them and hurried to Sonya's room. Tanya was with her, but seeing Tolstoy's distress immediately left. The betrothed couple stood facing each other amidst a confusion of trunks, travelling cases, and scattered possessions. Remembering the pain on Sonya's face as she had cast aside his diaries, and comparing himself to the handsome youthful Polivanov, Tolstoy had fallen prey to devastating doubts about whether it was right to marry this perfect, chaste, beautiful young creature whom he had known since she was a child. In a despairing tone, he muttered, "I have come to say that there is still time . . . all this business can still be put a stop to!"

Sonya swayed and Tolstoy grasped her arm to keep her from falling. She stared up at him in confusion. "What is it? What is the matter?" she asked.

He was not worthy of her, he cried. His conscience had forced him to beg her to reconsider the step she was about to take. She could not love him, not when she knew the evil he had done; she could not love an ugly old man with decaying teeth. Raging on, he grasped her shoulders and stared intently into her eyes; then, his energy suddenly spent, he turned aside as though stricken.

"I shall be unhappy, of course," he said numbly. "Let them all say what they like. Anything is better than the misfortune. . . . Anyhow, it would be better now while there is still time!"

Sonya was thoroughly frightened. "Do you mean you would cancel all the marriage plans?" she asked.

"Yes, if you don't love me."

"Are you mad? . . . What are you thinking about? Tell me everything."

"I think you cannot love me. What could you love me for?"

"Oh God, what can I do?" She wept.

"Oh, what have I done!" he gasped; and kneeling before her, he kissed her hands.

Lyubov Alexandrovna, learning that the bridegroom had violated convention and was with his bride, hurried to Sonya's room to ask him to leave. She found her daughter crying bitterly.

"You've chosen a fine time for upsetting her!" Lyubov exclaimed. "Today is her wedding day, and it's all very tiring, especially with the long journey in front of her, and there she is crying!"

Tolstoy left after Sonya reassured him that she loved him and indeed wanted to marry him and that she was not troubled by any regrets about Polivanov.

The wedding was to be at eight o'clock in the evening in the Church of the Nativity of the Blessed Virgin. At six Tanya and the bridesmaids began to help Sonya into her wedding gown. Lisa went into her mother's room to dress, and this caused some whisperings among the girls, who could easily discern a chilliness between the two sisters. Sonya's gown was filmy tulle, as fashion demanded, and the neckline was low in front but with a raised collar in back, and the long sleeves were etched with frills. Tanya helped her arrange her thick black hair and secured the long, airy tulle veil with a chaplet of fresh flowers.

By seven, looking ravishingly beautiful, Sonya was dressed and waiting, as was the custom, for the best man to come to tell her that the bridegroom was at the church. An hour later Timiryzaev had still not arrived, and Sonya was distraught. Because of his strange behavior that morning, she was sure that Lev Nikolaevich had run away. She experienced a fear that would stay with her throughout her married life. What if I lose his love? she thought. I shall die.

The great clock in the hallway chimed the half-hour. She was already thirty minutes late for her wedding. The assembled guests must be growing restless and murmuring about the impending scandal. Suddenly Tolstoy's manservant, the nearsighted little Alexei Stepanovich, burst in. Nervously he rushed to explain that when they were packing the bridegroom's luggage they had forgotten to leave a shirt out for the wedding. To make matters worse, Count Sergey Nikolaevich had taken his brother's cases with him to Yasnaya Polyana, where he was preparing the house for the bridal couple's arrival. Most terrible of all, since it was Sunday, the shops were all closed. Finally, at nine o'clock, Timiryzaev arrived to say that a shirt had been found and Tolstoy was waiting at the church. But yet another pall was cast on the occasion. Dr. Behrs was suddenly taken ill; though he was in no danger, he was too weak to be left alone, and Lyubov Alexandrovna had to stay with him.

Sonya drove to the church with Lev Nikolaevich's aunt, Pelagya Ilyenishva Yushkov, and her young brother Vlodny, who held the icon of St. Sofya with which her mother and her mother's youngest brother—her uncle Mikhail Alexandrovich Islavin—had blessed her before she left. As they rode the short distance to the church in an elegant carriage, Sonya cried, but her tears eased when she caught sight of the brilliantly lit church. The groom was waiting calmly for her in the garden, all his fears allayed. Taking her by the hand, he led her to the altar just as the choir burst forth with "Come, O Dove."

Candles burned before all the icons in the church, and these hundreds of flickering flames were reflected in the gilt frames of the

icons, the silver of the chandeliers and candlesticks, and the flag-
stones of the floor. Blazing with crimson and gold, the cavernous
church seemed to be "inundated with light." An elegant assemblage
of over three hundred guests awaited the bridal couple. The
women glowed in richly embroidered brocades, brilliant velvets
and fine satins; shoulders and arms were bare and flowers nestled
in elaborate coiffures; gloved hands held jeweled fans. The men
wore elegant swallowtail coats and white ties or their gold and
crimson regimental uniforms.

Once they had joined hands at the altar, Tolstoy never took
his eyes off Sonya. Her hair was dressed high beneath the flowing
veil and white flowers. Her long neck was framed beautifully by
the neckline of her gown, and her waist looked strikingly slender.
But what enhanced her beauty most was not the flowers, the veil,
or the "Paris" gown Lyubov Alexandrovna had managed to have
copied inside a week, but the truthfulness and trust that shone in
her eyes.

"Take the bride's hand and lead her," whispered the best man.

Sonya pressed her lips together, glancing at no one. After
much pleading by Lyubov Alexandrovna, she had agreed that Polivanov and Lisa should be members of the wedding party. Now,
as Sasha and Polivanov took turns holding the crowns over their
heads, she feared that she had made a grave error. Polivanov's
patrician face revealed no emotion, but his presence, those delicate
gentleman's hands raised above Tolstoy's head, greatly disturbed
her bridegroom, and Sonya sensed his irritation. Lyubov Alexandrovna had wanted the young man to take part in the ceremony in
order to put to rest any gossip that there was something amiss in so
rushed a wedding. No man, she reasoned, would expect to be a
part of a wedding in which his honor had been challenged, and
most of the gathering knew Polivanov had been Sonya's suitor. But
while Mrs. Behrs's regard for outward appearances might be com-
mendable, her lack of sensitivity was startling. Polivanov was fourteen years younger than the groom; taller, slimmer, and with fine
white teeth; he was a handsome fellow who caught the eyes of all
the young women. And he had loved Sonya with all the pure
passion of first love, something Tolstoy could never give her.

After Sonya and the Count had exchanged their vows, the
priest read the final prayer. The crowns were removed from their

heads and the priest congratulated the married couple. "Kiss your wife; and you, kiss your husband!" he said and took the candles they had been holding from their hands. Tolstoy kissed Sonya gently on the lips. Her face was flushed, and her eyes brimmed with tears. Tolstoy took her hand, held it, and then led her down the aisle of the church amid enthusiastic congratulations.

After the service the Count and his new Countess returned to the Behrs apartment for a small wedding reception and supper. About an hour later Sonya went to her room and changed into her new dark blue traveling suit. The *dormeuse*, drawn by six horses, stood waiting, Sonya's shiny black trunks filled with her new wardrobe strapped to its roof. Lyubov Alexandrovna fussed about and insisted they all say a prayer for the journey. Dr. Behrs, pleading illness, remained closeted in his study; it was clear that although he had given his consent he still withheld his approval. The servants crushed around to say goodbye; while Lisa cried uncontrollably, Tanya clung to Sonya a long while, unable to break away.

Just before getting into the carriage, Sonya threw her arms about her mother and sobbed. Mrs. Behrs remained composed; but as Sonya finally took her seat beside her new husband, Lyubov Alexandrovna let out a piercing cry which rang out over the grinding of the carriage wheels and the clopping of the horses' hoofs. An autumn rain beat down on the roof of the carriage, and puddles in the road reflected the dim lights of street lanterns. Sonya sat huddled in a corner weeping, exhausted, and brokenhearted at leaving her family.

Tolstoy did not know how to console her, and when her weeping showed no sign of abating, he grew angry. Having been orphaned as a young child, he was completely baffled by her distress over parting from her parents. "If leaving your family means such great sorrow to you then you cannot love me very much," he observed acerbically.

They had left Moscow and were riding through an impenetrable darkness. The night was starless and moonless; there were no lanterns. Sonya, finally dry-eyed but disconsolate, listened to the rain driving against the carriage windows. In the opposite corner her husband sat stiffly erect; she felt overwhelmed and oppressed by his presence. Suddenly he drew close to her, and his hands began to move over her body. She recoiled, and when he persisted,

she struggled forcefully to repel his caresses. He moved sharply
and quickly away.

They stopped for the night at Birulevo. A titled couple arriving in a splendid carriage drawn by six horses created quite a stir,
and they were given a large well-appointed suite. As the servants
brought in a steaming samovar, Sonya was crouched in a corner of
a sofa.

"Well, show that you are the mistress here," said Tolstoy.
"Come on, pour the tea."

She obeyed, but her hand trembled as she held a teacup out to
him. They were seated in half-darkness with only a few candles for
light. He grasped her hands, and at that moment she saw that the
fear she had felt in the *dormeuse* was actually a new sort of love—
stronger than the old and imbued with a passion she had never felt
before. Yet, for a second time that night she rejected Tolstoy's bold
and ungentle sexual overtures.

Of that night, Sonya's new husband wrote cryptically in his
"loathsome diary": "She is weepy. In the carriage. She knows
everything and it is simple . . . But she is afraid."

PART TWO
1862-1865

Something Beautiful...

She suffered, complained, triumphed in her sufferings, rejoiced in them and loved them. He saw that something beautiful was taking place in her soul, but what it was he could not understand. It was above his comprehension.

TOLSTOY
Anna Karenina

6

The journey from Birulevo to Yasnaya Polyana was a long one, taking nearly twenty hours. The rain had stopped, but the day was bleak and gray, so that the *dormeuse* was enveloped in near darkness for most of the trip. The lashing sound of the horses' hoofs as they slapped on the damp earth became almost painful in its monotony. As they rode, Lev Nikolaevich told her about the servants she would have to manage, the peasants in the village, and the neighbors, for most of whom he had little affection. He talked about his plans for the farm, the problems in his school, the opposition to his magazine, and the difficulty of finding more time to write. Sonya was quietly reflective, too embarrassed to speak freely or to use the personal form of address.

It was evening as they neared Yasnaya Polyana. Sonya pressed her face to the window, trying desperately to see the house behind the trees that lined the overgrown roadway. When the elegant *dormeuse* jolted to a stop, Lev Nikolaevich helped her down and rushed up the steps to the front door. Aunt Toinette stood beneath a flickering lantern, holding up an icon of the Holy Virgin. Standing beside her was Sergey Nikolaevich carrying a loaf of bread and a container of salt, the traditional welcoming gifts for a newly married couple. Old Auntie, Lev Nikolaevich, and his brother all smiled as Sonya walked up to join them. As she did, Aunt Toinette held the icon out toward her, and Sonya bowed down to the loose-planked wooden floor. Rising slowly, she kissed first the icon and then the members of her new family. Touched by this simple time-worn ceremony, the small group turned and entered the house.

The domestic staff greeted Sonya in the front hallway: Dunyasha, the tall, large-boned maid; diminutive Alexei Stepanovich, the manservant; Nikolai Mikhailovich, the elderly cook who played the flute and drank too much (even at this important moment he seemed unsteady on his feet); and poor feeble-minded Alyosha Gorshok, the cook's helper. Aunt Toinette's devoted personal maid, the meek, somewhat backward Axinia Maximovna, who was always just a few steps away from her mistress, managed an awkward curtsy. Agatha Mikhailovna, Tolstoy's eccentric housekeeper, had supervised the household since he had been a child. She assured Sonya that the rest of the staff—which included Indyushkin the coachman, his assistants, the charwomen, the seamstresses, laundry women, and errand boys—would pay the Countess their respects on the following day. Agatha Mikhailovna was a woman so devoted to animals that she would not eat meat or kill the smallest insect; she left milk out in saucers for mice and flies and spiders, and she nursed a seemingly endless series of puppies and kittens in her stuffy crowded room. A homely woman approaching sixty, Agatha Mikhailovna had once been quite tall but was now stoop-shouldered. She had large expressive black eyes, and in her youth it had been whispered that she was an illegitimate child of one of the Tolstoys.

From the past, Sonya knew Yasnaya Polyana was not a palatial home, but she had not been as conscious then of the total lack of luxury. The furniture was hard and plain, the rooms lighted with palm-oil candles. Warm slippers had to be worn, as none of the bedrooms had rugs (and because Aunt Toinette could not stand the sound of servants clumping on the hard floors in their heavy shoes). Of the splendor of the original white-columned house, with its thirty-six rooms and grand stairway, all that remained were the two small wings separated by a yard where the main house had once connected them. One was now occupied by the school; the other, a somewhat larger building, was to be Sonya's home.

After a short visit with the small, pudgy Natalya Petrovna, who was ill and confined to her room, a light supper was served in the dining salon on unpretentious tableware. There was no fine porcelain, no elegant plate, and the house seemed unnaturally quiet without Sonya's own gay family filling it. Yet, she felt quite comforted as she glanced nervously at her husband. A warmth instantly flushed her body; her cheeks burned crimson.

After supper they went into the front parlor. The walls were crowded with ancestral portraits. Lev Nikolaevich pointed out his

maternal grandfather, Prince Nikolai Sergeyevich Volkonsky, with
his thick, bushy black eyebrows, stiff gray wig, and elegant crimson robe. It was Volkonsky, he explained, who had built Yasnaya
Polyana. On the opposite wall was a portrait of Lev Nikolaevich's
paternal grandfather, Ilya Andreyevich Tolstoy, a plump, arrogant
man who had sent his linen to Holland twice a year to be laundered
and insisted that only French wines and Bohemian crystal grace his
table.

Although her gloomy new parlor was utterly unlike the bright
salon in the Behrs apartment, the conversation was as lively as it
had been in Moscow. Aunt Toinette, her delicate face flushed with
excitement, chattered away happily in perfect French. Lev Nikolaevich was at his most amusing, telling stories about the wedding.
After an hour or so Aunt Toinette made her excuses, blessed them,
and retired. Tolstoy rose from his chair and took Sonya's hand.
They snuffed the candles and then went to their room.

Bowls of wild autumn flowers had been placed in the room to
welcome her. Sonya glanced around and then, turning down the
wick of the oil lamp (brought out for the special occasion of her
arrival), undressed awkwardly behind a screen, shivering as she
stood on the cold bare floor. To her surprise, as she climbed into
the waiting bed, she saw that in place of a pillow Lev Nikolaevich
used a hard leather cushion which looked as if it had done service
in a carriage. He explained that he did not like either the softness
of most pillows or the texture of linen cases.

Their first night together was to strongly affect their marital
relationship for many years. The unfortunate incident in the *dormeuse* and the difficulties of their wedding night were forgotten.
Warmed by the knowledge that Yasnaya Polyana was her home,
and perhaps by a gentler, more sensitive approach on Tolstoy's
part, Sonya turned to him with newly awakened passion. She was
a warm, demonstrative woman, more erotic than she had imagined
or her husband expected.

A sensual man, Tolstoy responded fully to her. Upon rising
the next morning he wrote in his diary, "Incredible happiness! I
can't believe that this can last as long as life!" Three days later he
wrote to his cousin Alexandra in St. Petersburg, "I am writing
from the country and as I write I hear a voice upstairs, talking to
[my] brother, of my wife whom I love more than anything on

earth. I lived to be thirty-four without ever knowing that one could love so much or be so happy."

But this incredible happiness was not completely unclouded. Within a day or two of their arrival at Yasnaya Polyana, Tolstoy realized that he did not know Sonya as well as he thought he had. She took to the role of mistress of the house extremely well, Lyubov Alexandrovna's training serving her admirably. Yet it disturbed him to see her occupied and content with such mundane tasks as rearranging furniture and checking the linen supply, ordering weeds pulled out and a flower garden planted, issuing an edict that the servants must not throw the refuse into the fields near the house. And when he had taken her to the barn to watch the milking, she had become faint from the smell of the cows. Although he was disappointed that his city-bred wife was repelled by his beloved livestock, he reacted with loving indulgence. She was after all "a beautiful bird who had flown into his rather austere home and enlivened everything by her presence." At times he glimpsed the play of dark emotions in her expression which frightened him. She was nervous; often seized by an uncontrollable burst of energy, she ran wildly through the fields close to the house calling out to —*whom?* He was not sure. And while her passion in bed dazzled him, he was haunted and disturbed by her abandon and by the lust she aroused in him.

The same day that Tolstoy wrote his cousin Alexandra, Sonya wrote to her sister Tanya:

> How are you, my sweet Tanyanka? I am often sad that you are not here with me. In spite of the fact that life is simply wonderful, things would be still better if I could hear your sweet nightingale voice, if I could sit and gossip with you as we used to do. . . . I haven't yet got quite used to things. It still seems strange to me that when I am at Yasnaya I am at home.
>
> Yesterday we had our first tea upstairs around the samovar, as it should be, a happy family. Auntie is so pleased, Seryozha [Sergey Nikolaevich] is so nice, and as for Lyovochka [Tolstoy], I have no words. I am frightened and abashed that he loves me so much. Tatyana, why should he, tell me?
>
> What do you think? Could he stop loving me?
>
> I am afraid to think of the future. This is no mere idle dream as in my maiden days—I know well what life has in store for me and

am only afraid something might go wrong. Oh well, what's the use, little one, you don't understand this; when you get married you will understand. . . . I'm not yet completely settled, there are still a few trifles to take care of. It is very pleasant to unpack little by little. See here, Tanya my love, send me my low warm boots without fail. I am lost without them. It is impossible to go walking in high boots, and frosts are already at hand. Oh yes, and I forgot my powder. There is no place to get it here and it isn't worthwhile to buy it in Tula. Send all this with the dowry. Don't forget, little one, please—I need these things.

And now, farewell, my sweet. We didn't kiss each other often when we were together, but I am really going to do it this time. I send you a big kiss. Lyovochka wants to write to you and I must leave room for him.

I sign importantly, for the first time,

your sister,
Countess Sonya Tolstaya

September 28, 1862

Tolstoy's postscript followed:

If you ever lose this letter, our charming Tanechka, I shan't forgive you for a lifetime. Do me a favor. Read this letter and send it back to me. Do you feel how wonderful and touching it all is—the thoughts about the future and the powder? It makes me sad that even this little bit of her has gone away from me. . . .

Today she is wearing a cap with crimson ribbons—and it's not bad. This morning she played at being grown-up and mistress of the house—and she did it brilliantly, very much like the real thing. Farewell. This letter makes me feel that it is easy for me, and a pleasure, to write to you. I will write you often. I love you very much—very much. I know that you, like Sonya, love to be loved. That is why I write.

L. Tolstoy

To Sonya's disappointment, her husband took no interest in household affairs but spent most of the day attending to the farm and the laborers. Rising early, he dressed in a coarse tunic, loose pants, and work boots; and when she woke he was invariably gone. For the first few days he returned for early tea; they sat alone while he recounted all that was happening in the fields, telling hilariously exaggerated tales about the workers, and they laughed together. The sight and sound of him filled her with enormous pleasure, tempered slightly by the realization that the ecstasy with which he talked about his land was an emotion she did not share. With each passing day her jealousy of his life without her grew. He gave her a new diary, insisting that they must each read what the other wrote; as husband and wife they must have no secrets. She agreed and did not so much mind his reading her journal as she did having to take his diary, that loathsome object, the record and reminder of his "evil past," in her hands. Although she tried to hide her fits of depression when she was with him, she carefully noted her most somber, troubled thoughts in her diary. It was left to him to record their more lyrically ecstatic moments.

> I love her at night, or in the morning [he wrote after two weeks of marriage]. When I awake and see: she looks at me and loves. And no one, especially not I, prevents her from loving me in her manner, as she understands it. I love her when she sits close to me and we know that we love each other, as only we are able to, and she says: "Lyovochka," and then adds: "Why are chimneys built so straight?" Or: "Why do horses live so long?" . . . I love when we are alone, and I say: "What are we to do? Sonya, what are we to do?" She laughs. I love when she gets angry with me, and in a twinkling of an eye, her thoughts and words sometimes sharp, she says: "Let me be, you bore me." In a moment she smiles timidly at me. I love when she does not see me and does not know that I love her in my fashion. I love her when she is a little girl in a yellow dress and sticks out her lower jaw and tongue at me. I love when I see her head tilted backwards, her serious, frightened, childish, and passionate face.

Exuberant in his love, he rushed home from the fields hungry for her presence. Made ecstatic by the sight of her, he could not turn his eyes from her when she was in the room with him. Nevertheless he treated her in a way that, had his love not been so apparent, might have been called condescending. She was, of course, sixteen years younger than he, but his almost paternal, protective attitude had more to do with Sonya's demeanor and appearance than with the difference in their ages.

Seeing Sonya in a country setting made him more aware of

her fragility and extreme femininity, and her quickly assembled trousseau strongly emphasized these qualities. Lyubov Alexandrovna had made sure that her daughter began married life in a style befitting a countess. From her lace morning cap with its crimson satin ribbons to the hand-embroidered pointed tips of her silk slippers, she was dressed in the finest and latest of French fashions. The collars on her frocks seemed designed to enhance the delicacy of her heart-shaped face, her hairstyle to emphasize the dimple in her cheek, the colors she wore to point up her fair skin, dark eyes, and jet hair. There were times he felt she must consider him old and awkward and Yasnaya Polyana too crude. Then, though he never doubted his love for her, he found himself questioning her love for him. The image of the young Polivanov kept flashing before his eyes. She must now regret her foolish impetuosity in marrying a man old enough to have lost most of his teeth; a farmer whose aristocratic background and noble birth may have given her false hopes of an exciting and elegant life. Tortured by the fear that she was disappointed both in him and in Yasnaya Polyana, he began to accuse her of not loving him, of wishing she had not married him.

Sonya was baffled by his wild vacillations. One moment he was filled with adoration, the next he accused her of insincerity.

I have been feeling frightened ever since yesterday when he told me he did not believe in my love [she wrote in her diary on October 8]. I know why he doesn't believe in it, only I don't think I'll be able to put it into words. Ever since my early girlhood I have dreamed of a man *as a whole*, a new and *pure* man whom I would love. Those were childish dreams, but I still find it hard to give up the idea of loving a man who would always be with me, whose slightest thought and feeling I would know, who would love no one but me, and who, like myself, and unlike all other people, would not need *to sow his wild oats* before becoming good and sound. These dreams were always dear to me. As a result, I almost fell in love with P. [Polivanov]; in other words, loving my dreams, I connected P. with them. . . . When I got married, I had to admit that my old dreams were foolish, and yet I feel unable to give them up altogether. The *whole* of my husband's past is so dreadful that I don't think I will ever be able to accept it. . . . He doesn't understand that his past is a whole world of a thousand different emotions—good and bad—which will never belong to me, just as his youth, spent heaven knows on what and whom, will never be my property. Nor does he understand that I am giving him everything, that no part of myself has been spent elsewhere, and that only my childhood alone did not belong to him. . . .

Yesterday, at Grandfather's house [they had spent the day at Ivitsy], I came downstairs specially to see him, and when I saw him I was seized with an unusual feeling of love and strength. I loved him so much at that moment; I wanted to go up to him, and yet I felt that if I touched him I would not feel so happy, that it would be almost sacrilege. But I never can and never will let him see what is going on in my mind. I have so much foolish pride that everything will be lost if I ever see that he can in the least doubt me. I am irritated. What is he doing to me? Gradually I shall retreat into myself and shall poison his life. And yet I feel so sorry for him at those times when he doesn't believe in me; his eyes fill with tears and he has such a meek, wistful look. At such moments I could strangle him with love, and yet the thought pursues me: "He doesn't believe in me, he doesn't believe in me."

Their honeymoon, the first month of marriage from which each had anticipated so much pleasure, was instead a most trying time. Their quarrels were almost always initiated by him. He would seek to rouse her passion and then, when she willingly, fully responded, he was tortured, reproachful, senselessly jealous.

Today [she wrote in her diary] I suddenly felt that we would gradually drift apart and each live our own lives, that I would create my own sad world for myself, he a world full of work and doubt. And this relationship struck me as vulgar. I have stopped believing in his love. When he kisses me, I think to myself: "Well, I'm not the first woman." And it begins to hurt me that this love of mine, my first and last, should not be enough for him. I, too, have been interested in men, but only in my imagination; but he—he has known women, young and lively and pretty, with individual faces, souls, and characters, and he has loved and admired them, just as he now loves and admires me. It is vulgar; but it isn't my fault; it is the fault of his past. I cannot help it if I can't forgive God for having made people in such a fashion that they must sow their wild oats before becoming decent. I can't help it if it makes me feel sad and miserable that my husband, too, should come within that category.

The extraordinary sensual pleasure Tolstoy found with her led him almost immediately into agonies of self-reproach. His alternation between exalted sexuality and black guilt made Sonya defensive and withdrawn. She tried to conceal her feelings. Yet at times as she sat with Tolstoy, her dark eyes brimmed with unhappy tears. When he asked, "What are you crying about?" she would answer, "I'm lonely for my mother." Unable to accept this as the truth, he would refuse to let the matter drop. Once when he accused her of trying to play on his emotions, her tears stopped and she lashed out furiously at him, bitterly denouncing him as a cruel egotist. It was the first time he had seen such hostility in Sonya, and it frightened him. Condemning himself, he was now convinced that their infatuation had been exhausted by their sexual gratification. Perhaps they were both egotists, bent only on deriving as much pleasure from each other as possible. Sonya's passion, he was certain, had filled her with melancholy shame. Was marriage, he wondered, nothing but a license to commit debauchery? Tolstoy had always been concerned with the morality of sexual conduct, and in the years ahead this subject would come to obsess him.

Their quarrels continued, but after each heated exchange they soon were in each other's arms, not able to remember why they had quarreled. Later he rightly attributed all these early quarrels to their sexual behavior. Sonya knew that he thought her enjoyment of sex made her, like him, a "participant" in a crime. But she could not understand why she should feel guilty for acting as a wife to her husband.

During one quarrel, he mentioned Polivanov, with whom, he suggested, she might have been happier; she countered that his cousin Alexandra seemed a better match for him than herself. When she complained that he spent too much time in the fields with the peasants, he replied that she should take an active interest in their land and at times come with him.

"No! No!" she cried. "Suppose I should see *her?*"

The woman she was referring to was his former peasant mistress, Axinia, and he had no answer; but as his deep guilt turned into compassion, he stroked her black silken hair and kissed her delicate blue-white hands. She responded warmly, and he pulled away. That next morning Sonya wrote in her diary:

. . . it seems to me that I shall soon die.

    This is strange, now that I have a husband. I listen to him sleeping, and I am frightened to be left alone. He won't let me go near him, which is sad; physical things disgust him.

And two days later:

He grows colder and colder every day, while I go on loving him more and more. His coldness will soon become unbearable. . . . I sometimes try to console myself with the thought that it will pass and that everything will yet be right, but now I feel that it will not pass and that things will only go from bad to worse. Father writes me: "Your husband loves you passionately." Yes, he did love me *passionately*, but passion dies.

    Confused emotions in her new role as a wife occupied her for over a month. "If I am no good to him, if I am merely a doll, a *wife*, and not a *human being*—then it is all useless and I don't want to carry on this existence. Of course I am idle, but I am not idle by nature; I simply haven't yet discovered what I can do here," she wrote after several weeks had passed.

    Tolstoy, blindly believing her major problem was that she was lonely during the day, invited Lyubov Alexandrovna's pretty dark-haired half-sister Olga Alexandrovna, to visit. Sonya was happy to see her young aunt, but when Olga, who was a far more accomplished musician, played piano duets with Tolstoy, she became wildly jealous. The situation finally abated and Yasnaya Polyana became quite lively during these months. Besides Olga Alexandrovna, the Tolstoys' guests included Sergey Nikolaevich and his young son, Grisha. The youngster's presence further saddened Sonya, however, because Grisha's Gypsy mother, Masha, and Sergey Nikolaevich, though they had lived together many years, were not legally married. "Today Grisha began to talk of his papa, and I felt so sorry that he wasn't a *real* son that I nearly wept," she wrote in her diary.

    Sonya loved the children in Yasnaya Polyana school. She took them on picnics and helped them with their studies. Agatha Mikhailovna gave her a bright-eyed orphaned red setter puppy, the runt of the litter, too small for a proper hunting dog but perfect for a pet. Sonya named the dog "Dora," after a character in Dickens's

David Copperfield, one of her favorite novels, and it followed her wherever she went. Tolstoy had given her the gray mare Belogubka, and she rode whenever he had time to ride with her. Though it was only early autumn, the weather was quite cold and grew still colder toward evening. But in spite of the chill and her fear of seeing "the peasant woman," Sonya loved riding over the vast and varied land of Yasnaya Polyana, she with a hood over her head and Lev Nikolaevich in his leather coat and high boots. He was always in an affectionate and cheerful mood on these excursions, and he looked at her with delight as she rode side-saddle next to him or laughed breathlessly after besting him in a short race. During these rides she was her young, gay, spontaneous self, and both of them experienced again the joy they had shared when they had visited the peasants' hut near Pokrovskoye.

Although she loved Yasnaya Polyana, Sonya took little part in the day-to-day life of the estate. Except for the schoolchildren, she showed no interest in the peasants, their lives, or their village; she was pleasant to the house servants, gardeners, and stable boys, but seemed to avoid any contact with most of the workers on the estate. Among themselves they referred to her compromisingly as the Little Countess and drew back, casting their eyes down if they were working nearby when she and Tolstoy passed on horseback. Sonya, still terrified of encountering Axinia, did nothing to encourage a friendly rapport between herself and the peasants.

The household, including Tolstoy, generally met at four in the afternoon for tea. Sonya dressed for dinner at nine, a custom she tried to have Tolstoy adopt. His plain tunic, however, continued to appear at the dinner table. Then after a simple meal they went into the parlor, and Aunt Toinette sat in an armchair cutting the leaves of new books while Tolstoy read aloud. After Olga Alexandrovna left—and if a request was made—Sonya played the piano. Natalya Petrovna was now well; and though she mumbled, took snuff, and liked a glass of vodka before dinner, Sonya had grown quite fond of her. The two old women made a curious pair —Natalya Petrovna as round and red-faced as a plump tomato and Aunt Toinette as delicate as a small clipped bird.

A chatterbox, Natalya Petrovna told fantastic stories about the lives of landowners, army officers, and monks, which Sonya found rather boring. She amused Tolstoy, however, and with his encouragement she would rattle on until Aunt Toinette got up, kissed Sonya and Lev Nikolaevich, and signed them with a cross. Then all three ladies—Aunt Toinette, her friend, and her maid—would go off to bed.

Life at Yasnaya Polyana was quiet, perhaps too quiet for a high-spirited, romantic young girl. There was no place to wear all the beautiful clothes Sonya had bought for her trousseau, no young friends with whom to share frivolous chatter. There were no teas, parties, dancing classes, or ice skating lessons, as there had been in Moscow. Sonya spent her days discussing household affairs with Agatha Mikhailovna, listening to Aunt Toinette's stories about her husband's family, and humoring the slightly senile Natalya Petrovna.

The house did not have the gaiety of the Behrs home. Thoughts of her family were always with Sonya, making her somberly reflective but at times giving her a giddy happiness that was welcomed by Tolstoy. Together they wrote Tanya a gay letter after her tonsils had been removed.

(Lev Nikolaevich) Tatyana, dear friend, pity me, for I have a silly "sil" wife. I pronounce it just as you do.

(Sonya) He's the silly one, Tanya.

(L.N.) This news that we are both foolish must grieve you sorely. But after you have grieved, you may be comforted; we are both very satisfied in our stupidity and don't wish to be different.

(Sonya) But I want him to be intelligent.

(L.N.) Now she's embarrassed me. Can you feel how we rock with laughter all this while? I am sorry that you have had to have your tonsils cut out—will you send me a piece? Or have they already been taken to Vagankov cemetery and laid to rest under a cross with the inscription:

> *Here lie the tonsils of Tanya,*
> *Passerby, please have a look.*
> *Unbutton your vest for a comfortable breath,*
> *But don't think to rest in this nook.*

Sonya says that it is shocking to write you in such a vein. She's right. Well then, listen to me and I shall speak seriously.

[In your letters I see] your wonderful sweet nature with its laughter and its basic poetic seriousness. There is no other Tanya, but it's true that she is hard to please and that there is no better admirer than—

L. Tolstoy

I kiss Mama's hand and embrace Papa, the children and Sasha.

It seemed to Tolstoy that he and his melancholy young bride would recapture the delirious happiness of their courtship by a visit to the Behrses for the Christmas holidays. Sonya was delighted and wrote her parents immediately, adding that to avoid upsetting Lisa they would stay at a hotel.

As the cold winter began to set in and the late November days grew shorter, Sonya realized she was pregnant. Nothing could have pleased Tolstoy more, and he became ambitious as he had never before been. Interest in his school waned, his magazine was neglected. What mattered was money, and he doubled his efforts on the farm and added several enterprises—beehives, herds of sheep, even a distillery (to which Sonya objected strenuously). Sonya wanted children terribly and believed when she bore Tolstoy's child she would be able "to see things in a pure light, without his past, without all the filth which I still see in him and which makes me so unhappy."

But two weeks after discovering she was pregnant, Sonya saw Axinia for the first time.

7

Sonya and Tolstoy were both jealous by nature, often without reason, but with a fiery vehemence fueled by their passionate temperaments. Jealousy blinded their reason, made them unjust to each other, and caused both to be vindictive. On October 1, barely a week after their marriage, Tolstoy wrote in his diary, "She would rather not write to my cousin at court [Alexandra], she suspects everything." And four days later when Sonya finally agreed to write to Alexandra, she composed a frigidly polite letter in French, signing it "Your respectful niece, Countess Sonya Tolstoy."

Irritated, Tolstoy added a postscript to her note:

> I find this letter of Sonya's to you rather annoying, my dear Alexandra; I sense that direct relations between you will be quite different, but probably, however, it has to be like this. You understand that I can't speak the truth about her at present—I'm afraid of myself and afraid of the disbelief in others. . . . I'm aware of all my vileness every second when I compare myself with her—with Sonya, but "I cannot wash away the sorrowful lines." . . . She's reading this letter and doesn't understand a thing and doesn't want to understand, and there's no need for her to understand.

At which point Sonya took the pen from his hand and wrote, "I cannot leave it at that, dear Auntie. He's mistaken! I understand everything, absolutely everything that concerns him."

"Today there was a scene," he commented in his diary after this incident. "I was sad at the thought that we behave just like others. I told her that she had offended me in my feeling for [Alexandra]. She wept. She's charming. I love her even more."

Each day brought them greater disillusionment and unanticipated joys. He had fully expected her to make herself over in his image, but Sonya was far too independent to merge her individuality into his. And yet a good measure of their suffering could have been avoided if he had not demanded truth and confession from her at every turn, insisting on the exchange of the diaries, thus tormenting her with the ghosts of past loves and living images of women still important to him. Sonya then used this "truth"—these private revelations—as a weapon. During this period every entry in her diary was colored by her knowledge that it would be read by her husband. Through this unusual form of communication she could convey to him her deepest feelings, her worst fears, and she could strike out at him for the suffering she believed she had endured on his behalf. And yet the source of her greatest anguish—her jealous fear of Axinia—was never spelled out in the early pages of her diary. In fact, she did not even know the name of the peasant woman who had been her husband's mistress and had borne him a son; nor did she know if the woman and her child were still living at Yasnaya Polyana. Therefore, whenever Tolstoy left the house, she was terrified that he might be going to meet that woman.

Tolstoy had assured her that he had severed all relations with "the peasant woman" long before they married. But if that were true, Sonya wondered, why did he turn away from her in bed whenever she was overcome by waves of tenderness and passion? It seemed unlikely to her that her ardent emotions would repel him or leave him unmoved unless he was indeed having relations with another woman; and if not with "the peasant woman," with whom?

She became determined to find out the peasant woman's name and to discover whether she was still at Yasnaya Polyana. She began to talk of starting a class for the younger children on the estate, and then she asked Aunt Toinette, Natalya Petrovna, Agatha Mikhailovna, and Tolstoy's manservant, Alexei Stepanovich, for the names of any peasant children who were about five years old. But their answers were so vague and inaccurate as to be absolutely useless.

Sonya's obsession with her husband's former mistress would probably not have taken hold had she been able to generate an enthusiasm for such activities as breeding hens or pickling cucumbers. She was suffering from boredom so extreme that it could not be dispelled either by the thought of her future motherhood or by the anticipation of a visit to Moscow. She still thought Tolstoy "was brilliant, poetic, and full of *power*"; she continued to be immensely attracted to him while at the same time feeling shabbily treated, regarded as "a doll, a *wife* and not a *human being*." Her anger became a constant companion, warming her empty hours.

One cold gray morning in late November as she came down to breakfast, the chill damp house was permeated with the unpleasant smell of strong lye soap and dirty water. A broad, dark-skinned peasant woman with muscular shoulders and large breasts was on her hands and knees, scrubbing the floor of the entryway. A child of four or five played in the open doorway. Sonya snapped irritably at him, telling him to close the door. The boy stood still for a moment, staring up at her. He had fair skin, thick lips, and narrow smoky gray eyes that made her catch her breath. The youngster ran to his mother's side. Slowly the peasant woman sat back on her sturdy haunches and, as she drew her son close to her, glanced toward the mistress of the house. No words were exchanged, but the woman must have sensed her unwanted presence, for after a few moments she rose rather majestically to her feet and, grasping her child strongly by his shoulders, forced him to stand on his own.

This was a terrifying encounter for Sonya. Not only did she suspect the woman's identity, but also for the first time in her life she had looked at a peasant—a former serf—and seen her as an equal, having the same sense of pride and dignity that she had.

Sonya ran from the house, Dora barking at her heels, into the near-freezing day without cloak or bonnet. She raced across the fields, dumb with horror. This peasant woman and her child *were* —*must surely be* . . . She could not confess her suspicions—that the woman was Tolstoy's former mistress, the child his bastard son— aloud even to the tall grass about her. She took refuge in the woodshed, where she huddled under some old burlap, Dora in her arms; though Aunt Toinette, Dunyasha, and Alexei Stepanovich searched and called for her she did not return to the house until teatime.

When Tolstoy joined Sonya for tea, they sat across from each other, the steaming samovar between them, strangers suddenly. Although she was incapable of telling him what had happened, she was certain he knew that the woman had been brought in to clean the floors and that she, Sonya, had run off and hidden for most of the day.

For nearly two weeks after this "meeting" with Axinia and her son, Timofei, names she finally learned from Dunyasha, Sonya was in a state of near hysteria. She knew that an order had been given that Axinia never be used as a domestic again, but this did not calm her. Most wounding to her was her husband's insensitivity. She was appalled that he had so little regard for herself, the woman, and the child that he had allowed Axinia to continue working in the house he now shared with his holy and legitimate wife. And Axinia still remained, and would perhaps forever remain, within a short distance from the house, because Sonya was too intimidated by the situation to discuss it with him. The passages in Tolstoy's diary which she had read before their marriage flashed before her eyes. "Never so much in love!" he had written during his passionate affair with Axinia.

On December 6, 1862, she wrote in her diary, "Someday I shall kill myself with jealousy. . . . And nothing but a big fat lump of a woman. Terrible! I kept looking at his daggers and rifles with the greatest joy. One jerk—it's so easy. So long as there is no child [her own unborn child]. And there she [Axinia] is, a few yards from here. It drives me mad! I shall go out for a drive. I may meet her at any moment. So that's how he loved her! If only I could burn his diary and his whole past!"

But as always Sonya was torn between her intense loathing of Tolstoy's "terrible long past" and her great love for him. She still was awed by his brilliance and as sexually drawn to him as ever, but his rejection of her overtures filled her with shame and a sense of unworthiness. She took to going through his books and manuscripts, ferreting out and studying all his references to love and women. Growing more disgusted and depressed, she wanted to burn all he had written, for it reminded her again and again of his past. "If I could kill him and then make another man exactly like him, I should do it joyfully," she wrote in her diary.

The Russian winter had come in earnest, and high banks of snow blocked the roadways. No longer could Sonya run in the fields. The house became her world, and it was a world of fixed duties and customs that she found stultifying. She tried to be cheerful, polite, and affectionate; but she mourned her lost freedom and felt that she was "becoming enslaved to the steady passionless course of time."

The arrival of her dowry from Moscow was a welcome respite from her melancholy. It pleased her to set out her elegant green and gold porcelain tea and coffee service on the simple sideboard in the dining room and to have her carpet with its lovely rose and trellis design by her bed. Tanya had, as she had asked, sent her warm boots. But the snowfall had been exceptionally heavy and the estate was covered with deep drifts. Her boots, though snug and warm enough for winter in Moscow, were entirely inadequate in the country. Wearing fur boots that reached above his knees, Lev Nikolaevich went about muffled to the eyes in his sheepskin coat. He loved his land in winter with as great a passion as in the other seasons and was busy from early morning until late in the day making sure the animals, the bridges, the farm buildings, and the stored harvest were safe from the cold and snow.

The loneliness, the sense of isolation, the constant sound of wind in the chimneys and through the rafters, and the new sensations in her body caused by her pregnancy made Sonya increasingly nervous. Tolstoy watched her fuss with linens and china, rearrange furniture, add feminine touches here and there—new curtains in some rooms, beaded doilies on tables—with fond amusement, and yet with some disappointment, for in his opinion these were trivial occupations at best. Her jealousy offended him while at the same time the pain it caused him brought her closer to him. During the few daytime hours they spent together he was tender, loving, gentle. At night he was distant. Their quarrels were ugly and frequent. He abhorred these violent arguments as much as she did. Still he insisted that both of them reveal their true feelings, and he felt that her anger was roused by inconsequential provocation. Both felt "as if the chains that bound them were being pulled first one way, and then the other."

Yet with all the unhappiness of this period, Sonya's heart would suddenly soar when Tolstoy entered a room, his face radiant, looking as though he had a great new discovery he must tell the world about. She loved to listen to his stories, his fantastic plans for the future, his memories of his childhood. And at these times she felt he understood her as no other person could. Their differences, she would reason at such moments, were all her fault. And then, having accepted the blame, though not acknowledging it to him, she would become more tender, more forgiving.

There were, of course, many pleasant and good things about life at Yasnaya Polyana. She had grown extremely fond of Aunt Toinette and Natalya Petrovna. Some evenings Lev Nikolaevich taught her English; on others they read together. Victor Hugo's *Les Miserables* was a favorite at this time. When he was writing at night, she occupied herself with making a fair copy of the work. But as the short novel he was then writing, *Polikushka*, was a tale loosely based on his relationship with Axinia, this was a rather distressing project. Nonetheless, she did enjoy the feeling of sharing his work and did nothing to show her distaste for this story.

One night as a blizzard raged outside, they sat before the fire and he told her about a time when he was a small boy and believed he could fly. He had thought that if he held his knees together tightly with his arms and threw himself down from a great height, he would be able to soar like a bird. Alone in the nursery one evening, he decided to put his plan into execution. Crawling out a window and balancing himself on the ledge, he grasped his knees close to his body and sprang forward into the night; he landed, miraculously without one broken bone, but with a slight concussion, in the courtyard below.

"I understand!" she exclaimed, for in her "flights" across fields, away from the restraints of the house, she often felt she could simply lift off and fly if only she knew how. Tears filled his eyes and he clasped her hand tightly.

To spend the Christmas holidays in Moscow they left Yasnaya Polyana in a small one-horse sleigh, because the road to Tula was so banked with snow that nothing wider could get through. Their bags followed in another sleigh pulled along by a shaggy old jade. They made a curious caravan, but in Tula they changed to a larger vehicle. Sonya was breathless with excitement and happiness as they rode into Moscow just two days before Christmas. She looked at the city with greater interest than she ever had before. How could she have thought of it as provincial? After Tula and Yasnaya Polyana, Moscow was like a glistening Christmas tree to a child on its first Christmas morning. A winter sun made the hundreds of blue and gilt onion domes on the city's "forty times forty" churches glitter. Deep snow covered the wide avenues with their columned palaces, the maze of back streets with their rows of two-story wooden buildings. Sonya thrilled to the sound of whooping Cossacks as they thundered through Moscow's streets, the *whoosh* of carriages as they swept by, the shouts as pedestrians jumped out of the way as a troika dashed by.

Before they went to their suite at Chevrier's Inn (the most elegant small hotel in Moscow) on Gazetny Lane outside the Kremlin, they stopped to see the Behrses. Lyubov Alexandrovna, watching for them from the salon window, saw the carriage pull up and rushed out onto the veranda. There were tears and shouted greetings, much excitement, and then suddenly the younger Behrses gathered around, pulling them inside. Even Lisa welcomed them affectionately. Most of the Tolstoys' time was spent happily at the Behrses'. There was some strain, however, during the first three days, because Polivanov was Sasha's guest. Tolstoy's jealousy flared, and Sonya was relieved when her former suitor left the day after Christmas.

The Behrs house remained filled with guests through New Year's Day. Their cousin, Alexander Mikhailovich Kuzminsky, also called Sasha, who had come from St. Petersburg, was captivated by Tanya, and she was quite the coquette with her first beau. Acquaintances of the Tolstoys continually called on them at the Behrses'. Sonya was quickly caught up in the sophisticated life of the city. While her husband met with his literary friends, she and Tanya and Lyubov Alexandrovna visited places she had known so well—the Tea Palace for afternoon refreshments, the Ice Hill to watch the skaters, and most exciting for Sonya, the shops where she could see all the new Paris fashions.

Despite her pregnancy, Sonya was still slim, but she resisted the extravagantly lovely gowns. She adored bonnets and hats, however, and the milliner's shop on Mokhovaia Street had one in its window that she knew she must have. The very latest style, it was covered with thick layers of white feathers. The brim was high and pointed in the front and then swept down closely over the ears. Tied under the chin with a Persian blue bow, the bonnet set off Sonya's thick dark hair and fair complexion. Glowing with excitement, she tried it on that evening for her husband; Lyubov Alexandrovna and Tanya stood by, all three women eager to see Tolstoy's delighted appreciation, for Sonya looked quite dazzling.

"What," he exclaimed, looking at it with distaste, "is Sonya going to make calls in that Tower of Babel?"

"They wear them like that now," Lyubov Alexandrovna answered calmly.

"It is a monstrosity!" he replied. "Why can't she wear her fur cap?"

Lyubov Alexandrovna indignantly drew in her breath. "What is the matter with you, Lyovochka, for heaven's sake! If a woman paid a call wearing a cap everyone would criticize her."

"She won't be able to climb into a carriage without getting it knocked off," he countered.

"*Everyone* wears hats like this," Sonya insisted.

She did not, however, put on the controversial hat when she went calling with her husband on his friends. Nor did she wear a fur cap. Instead she chose a hat from her trousseau which he had always admired, and saved her new acquisition for excursions with Tanya or calls on her own friends. She felt slightly ill during the holidays, perhaps because of the rich food and pastries which were served wherever she went. Still she refused to cancel any of her plans for concerts or the theater; she spent hours in her favorite museums, and shopped daily for things she wanted for Yasnaya Polyana. And, though feeling intimidated by Lev Nikolaevich's literary friends—who she feared would view her with intellectual contempt—she did consent to call on them with him. The trip would have been a delight in every way, except that once again, as in the country, Sonya's jealousy erupted.

Lev Nikolaevich had accepted an invitation for dinner at the home of the writer Nikolai Mikhailovich Sushkov and his wife, Darya Ivanovna, who had been a maid of honor to the former Tsarina (the wife of Nicholas I). Literary figures, diplomats from St. Petersburg and abroad, and noted musicians and singers were always among the Sushkovs' guests, and Tolstoy dearly enjoyed the stimulating conversation at their parties. Sonya claimed she was feeling "indisposed" and stayed with her family. Actually, she was aware that the Princess Obolensky was also invited, and she knew from her husband's diary that he had once carried on an ardent flirtation with her. She did not want to meet the Princess, and she had hoped that Lev Nikolaevich would not attend the dinner party without her. But go he did, and Sonya, Lyubov Alexandrovna, and Tanya sat up waiting for his return. The clock struck twelve, then one, then *two*. Sonya was beside herself. "Mama, I'm going home. I can't wait for him any longer," she burst out.

"How can you think of it!" her mother countered. "He'll be here any minute!" As if in response to her words, the bell sounded and moments later Tolstoy strode ebulliently into the room. Sonya took one look at his joyous expression and began to sob uncontrollably. Thinking she had been worried he had met with an accident, he kissed her hands and begged for forgiveness.

"My darling, my dear one, don't be so upset. After the Sushkovs' I went to Aksakov's, and there I met Zavalishin, one of the Decembrists. I became so interested in him that I didn't notice how the time was passing!"

"And did the Princess Obolensky go with you?" Sonya asked sharply. An angry scene followed and Tolstoy turned to leave without her, but then, out of respect for Lyubov Alexandrovna (who had instantly intervened), the two left silently—but together.

Any thought of her husband enjoying the company of another woman brought back her deep hurt over Axinia. On January 14, 1863, she wrote in her diary:

I had such an unpleasant dream last night. I dreamed of an immense garden into which all our Yasnaya village girls came, and all of them were dressed up like ladies. They all went off somewhere, one by one, and the last one to leave was A., wearing a black silk dress. I talked to her, but grew so angry that, taking her child from somewhere, I began to tear it to pieces. In a terrible rage I tore off its arms and its head. Lyova came in and said that they would exile me to Siberia, and then picked up the hands and legs and all the parts, and said that, after all, it didn't matter, for it was only a doll. I looked, and, indeed, it was all cloth and cotton-wool. This annoyed me greatly.

And she ended that day's entry: "I sometimes have a silly, unconscious desire to test my power over him; it is simply a desire to see him obey me. But he will always be stronger than me, and my desire for self-assertion will pass." But it seemed unlikely that this desire would fade away as easily as she thought.

On January 29 she wrote, "I find this life in the Kremlin depressing, for it reminds me of my lazy and aimless life before my marriage. I have no longer any illusions about the aims and duties of married life since Lyova let me see that it alone isn't sufficient, but that one needs other interests as well." (Tolstoy added a comment to this entry: "I don't want anything except you. Lyova talks a lot of nonsense!")

They left Moscow the next day in a large sleigh drawn by hired post horses, and all the Behrses, as they had done after their wedding, came out on the veranda to see them off. Sonya wept inconsolably as she had before, and after Lev Nikolaevich settled her gently into a corner of the sleigh he shouted back at Tanya, "You shall come to see us with the swallows!"

He believed, perhaps naively, that Tanya's gaiety would be an antidote for Sonya's melancholia. He did not seem to realize that a young woman's fantasies can give rise to the most desperate and violent emotions. Ever since she was a girl of twelve, Sonya had idolized Tolstoy. She had imagined an ideal life with him, had dreamed fevered romantic dreams. And despite the difficulties of their "honeymoon months," she still clung to her fantasies. Even her approaching motherhood, and a moralistic husband who thought relations with a woman three months pregnant were unclean, did not dispel them. Sonya was trapped in the spider web of her own confusion. She longed for the romantic Tolstoy of her youthful fantasies while she lusted for the worldly adoring man she had married, a man who was now a censorial Tolstoy, critical and sententious. Because she refused to accept these irrevocable changes in her husband, there was now a seemingly unbridgeable dichotomy. Sonya was in love with a man who in actual fact no longer existed.

The winter blizzards gave way to sudden thaws. The Voronka, a deep stream which flowed through Yasnaya Polyana, flooded its banks; the wooden bridge was swept away by the raging waters, and for several weeks the main house was completely isolated. The school was closed, and the few people from Tula and

Ivitsy who occasionally came to visit could not reach the house. But from her bedroom window Sonya could see a hint of misty green in the Zaeska forest. The sun was warm in the deep blue early spring sky, and Lev Nikolaevich's high fur boots had been exchanged for heavily oiled waterproof ones, his bulky sheepskin coat stored until the next winter.

It was not long before the snow disappeared and the road from Yasnaya Polyana to Tula had dried. Reddish-brown shoots of nettles and chicory popped up along the fences and by the sheds, and in the distance Sonya heard the mooing of cows and the bleating of sheep released from their long winter confinement.

Since their return from Moscow, the Tolstoys had entertained few guests. The wretched condition of the country roads discouraged travel, and in any case Tolstoy disliked most of his neighbors and had few intimate associates in the district. Once in a great while the Auerbach family or the novelist Eugene Markov came down from Tula. Afanasy Fet was perhaps Tolstoy's closest friend, but he was absorbed by his own work that winter and spring. Tolstoy enjoyed their solitary life and spent long hours in his study writing while Sonya, her body now growing heavier, sat with her embroidery on that same old leather-covered sofa which had stood in the study through his father's and grandfather's time and on which he had been born. It pleased him to work with her in the room, conscious of her presence, demanding her silence.

But such intense closeness began to irritate both of them. Sonya would pull her needle through her tapestry with increasing violence as she smoldered over the slights she felt she suffered at night. Tolstoy now believed that sexual intercourse during her pregnancy was "swinish," "a crime," and "simple, coarse, direct violation of the laws of Nature." She would snap her scissors sharply to cut off a thread, and when he turned to the sound, she would stare at him and smile coolly. Provoked, he would ask her what was she thinking. Soon an argument would begin and she would run crying from the room while he sat furious, unable to go on with his work. He attributed her emotional storms to her pregnancy and to her passionate nature, which she had such difficulty subduing. Still he felt that to protect "the great work going on in [her]" she must try to curb her emotional excesses. But the more he urged calm, the more restive she became.

A week after Easter spring returned at last. The grass grew green once again. The plowing began, and Sonya, five months pregnant, felt the first movement of her unborn child. A new acceptance, a sort of armistice with her own nature, took place as her sexual yearnings began to dissolve. The quarrels became infrequent, while her admiration for her husband turned to a form of worship. Their physical relationship had become that of a devoted brother and sister.

"I love everything about him," she wrote in her diary on March 26, "his cheerful moods, as well as his bad moods, his kind, kind face, his meekness, and his impatience—everything! His face expresses everything so beautifully, that he *hardly* ever hurts my feelings."

When Sonya grew bored by the inactivity of the last months of her pregnancy, Tolstoy took her for short carriage rides around the estate, telling about his childhood at Yasnaya Polyana.

His brother Nikolai, nearly six years his senior, had been his idol. The natural leader among the four Tolstoy brothers, Nikolai was unusually gifted intellectually, spiritually, and artistically. He was an avid reader of books about freemasons and religious sects, and one day he announced to his brothers that he alone had discovered the secret of happiness for all men. He said he had written this secret on a green stick which he had buried by the edge of the ravine in the Zahak forest. Whoever found the stick and carried out the secret message would be able to destroy all evil in the world. When Tolstoy told Sonya this story, they were standing on the spot where the stick was said to have been buried, and his eyes filled with tears.

The last months of her pregnancy were mostly happy, but there were also signs of conflict to come. Sonya and Tolstoy together wrote Tanya an eight-page letter the day after Tolstoy had a curious dream about a "porcelain doll." Sonya began the letter, but after a few lines Tolstoy took over and in a serio-comic tone told how he dreamed that Sonya had come into their bedroom while he was asleep.

> I heard her opening the door, breathing and getting undressed all in my sleep. I heard her coming out from behind the screen and walking toward the bed. I opened my eyes and I saw Sonya, not the Sonya whom we know, but a Sonya made of china! . . . Do you know those

little china dolls with cold, bare shoulders and neck, and arms folded
in front but made of the same piece of china as the body, with hair
painted black and big artificial waves, with the black paint faded on
top, and with protruding china eyes also painted black at the edges
and set too widely apart, and a bodice with firm pleats, also of china
and made out of one piece? Sonya was just like that—I touched her
hand—it was smooth, pleasant to touch, cold and made of china.
. . . I said, "Are you made of china?" She replied without opening
her mouth (her mouth remained folded at the corners and daubed
with bright crimson): "Yes, I am." A chill ran down my spine, and I
looked at her legs: They too were china, and (you can imagine my
horror) they stood on a china base made from the same piece as she
was, representing the ground and painted green like the grass. Near
her left leg a little above the back of the knee was a china support
painted brown and probably representing a tree stump. It too was
made from the same piece of china as she was. I realized that without
this support she wouldn't have been able to stand up, and I became
so sad, as you can imagine—you who loved her. I still couldn't
believe my eyes and began to call her; she couldn't move without the
support and the base beneath her, and she could only rock a little bit
on her base so as to fall toward me. I heard the china bottom bumping
against the floor. I began to touch her—she was all smooth china,
pleasant to touch and cold. I tried to raise her arm—I couldn't. I
tried to put my finger, or at least my nail, between her elbow and
her side— I couldn't either. . . . I began to examine her bodice—all
of one piece with her body, top and bottom . . . one piece of pleat of
her bodice had been broken off at the bottom, and you could see
something brown. The paint on the top of her head had peeled off a
bit, and the white was showing. The paint had come off her lips in
one place, and a piece of her shoulder had broken away. But everything was so true to life that you could tell it was the same Sonya of
ours. The bodice I knew, embroidered with lace, and the black bun
of hair at the back—only made of china—and the lovely delicate
hands and the big eyes and the lips—they were all exactly alike, only
they were china—even the dimple on the chin and the shoulder
bones in front. I was in a terrible state; I didn't know what to say or
do or think; she would have been glad to help me, but what could a
china creature do? The half-closed eyes, and the eyelashes and the
eyebrows—from a distance they all looked real. She didn't look at
me, but through me, at her bed. She obviously wanted to go to bed,
and she kept rocking back and forth. I was at my wit's end, and took
hold of her and tried to carry her over to the bed. My fingers made

no impression on her cold china body and, what surprised me even more, she had become as light as a glass phial. And suddenly she seemed to shrink away, and she grew tiny, tinier than the palm of my hand, although she still looked exactly the same. I took hold of a pillow, stood her up in one corner, pummeled another corner with my fist, and laid her down there; then I took her nightcap, folded it into four, and covered her with it up to the chin. She lay there, looking exactly the same. I put out the candle and laid her down to sleep under my beard. Suddenly I heard her voice from the corner of the pillow: "Lyova, why have I become china?" I didn't know what to reply. Again she said: "Does it matter that I'm china?" I didn't want to upset her, and said that it didn't. I felt her again in the darkness—she was still cold, still china. Yet her belly was the same as when she was alive, protruding upward like a cone, and rather unnatural for a china doll. I had a strange feeling. I suddenly felt glad that she was like that, and I ceased to be surprised—it all seemed natural to me. I took her out, transferred her from one hand to the other, and put her down again by my head. She was quite happy. We went to sleep. In the morning I got up and went out without looking at her. I was so afraid of all that happened the previous night. When I came back for lunch she was just the same again as she had always been. I didn't remind her of the previous night, being afraid to upset her and Auntie. I haven't told anyone about it except you. I thought it was all over, but during these past days, whenever we are alone, the same thing has happened again. She suddenly becomes a little china doll. When she is with others, everything is normal. She isn't dismayed by this, nor am I. To be frank, however strange it is, I'm glad about it, and despite the fact that she is made of china, we're very happy.

I'm only writing to you about all this, Tanya dear, so that you can . . . find out from the doctors via Papa what it all means and whether it is bad for the future child. We're alone just now, and she is sitting by my necktie, and I can feel her sharp little nose digging into my neck. Yesterday she was left alone. I went into the room and saw Dora dragging her into a corner and playing with her, and almost breaking her. I gave Dora a thrashing and put Sonya into my waistcoat pocket and took her off to the study. However, I've now ordered a wooden box with a clasp (it was delivered today from Tula), covered on the outside with Morocco and the inside with crimson velvet, with a place made for her so that her elbows, head, and back can fit exactly into it, and she can't get broken. I'm covering it on top with suede as well.

In this story Tolstoy obviously intimates that Sonya's pregnancy has transformed her into an untouchable—a porcelain doll that by its nature can have no responsiveness or desires. Once again the Tolstoys, unable to speak of their deepest emotions, were using the written word to communicate.

Although Tanya thought the story rather odd and unsettling, she gave it to her father as Tolstoy had asked. Dr. Behrs apparently did not perceive the complex sexual revelations in the little tale, and he wrote to Sonya, "Your Lyova wrote such a fantastic piece for Tanya that even a German would never have thought of it. Amazing how fertile his imagination is. Sometimes it manifests itself in very strange forms—he managed to write eight pages about the metamorphosis of a woman into a china doll!"

Dr. Behrs arrived for a visit in mid-April, and after extracting every bit of family news she could from him, Sonya proudly took him all over the estate. She showed him Lev Nikolaevich's beehives, the pure-blood sheep they were breeding, and the newly acquired Japanese hogs with their exotic flaring snouts. They rode in a three-horse carriage through sharp winds and spring cloudbursts to see the budding orchards, the sapling pines, the experimental plantings of coffee and chicory, and even the distillery. Tolstoy had closed the school early in Sonya's confinement, but some of the former pupils were helping him and Sonya in the management of the estate. Tolstoy had decided to take charge of the day-to-day operations of Yasnaya Polyana after making "an important discovery," which he noted in his diary: "Managers, foremen, and overseers are only a burden on the farm. You can verify this by firing all the overseers, and by sleeping until ten o'clock. You will see that there will be no change for the worse. I have made this experiment and am absolutely convinced."

Thus Sonya now looked after the house, kept the accounts, and paid the laborers; and Tolstoy and his young students ran everything else. Dr. Behrs did not have to be an agricultural expert to see that the Tolstoys were dismal failures at farm management. The Japanese hogs were dying one after the other, Tolstoy was suffering from severe bee stings, green mold rimmed the wooden butter caskets, and except for the young orchard and sapling pines the fields were in a sorry state.

Before Dr. Behrs's visit, Tolstoy had confided in a letter to him that more and more he wanted to have an apartment in Moscow where they could spend three or four months each year. They could then enjoy the company of family and friends; Sonya would be delighted by the theatrical and musical performances, and he would have a library close at hand. But it seemed unlikely that, even with the most stringent economies, the Tolstoys could support two residences. As it was, Tolstoy was ashamed of the general shabbiness of Yasnaya Polyana. Unless they substantially increased their income, an annual sojourn in Moscow would remain a dream.

Dr. Behrs saw that the couple's financial state would never improve without a competent estate manager and overseer, and he was determined to find such a man for Tolstoy. He also felt that his son-in-law should be spending more time writing and was pleased when Sonya confided that Lev Nikolaevich was thinking about a new novel. Dr. Behrs did not, however, regard Tolstoy's literary work with unqualified approval. *The Cossacks* had been published in Moscow in February to quite good reviews, but the doctor believed that the novel, although well written, was seriously flawed by the inclusion of scandalous autobiographical episodes. He felt that these "indecent incidents" were the reason for the book's poor sales. "For certainly," he declared, "young girls should not be allowed to read the book!" He also found its length—two hundred pages—"discouraging." Yet he believed that if Tolstoy decided to devote himself to his writing, he would achieve the same great commercial success enjoyed by the poet and publisher Nikolai Nekrasov. "A good overseer will help," he insisted.

The late spring days with their cool breezes and bright sun were glorious. Every field and slope sparkled with bright flowers. The peasant girls blossomed into springtime finery, tying colorfully embroidered scarves over their heavy plaited hair (a single braid was worn by unmarried girls, two by married ones). Yet in spite of the delights of the season, Sonya was saddened by her father's departure, and she was eagerly awaiting Tanya's promised visit in June. Her thoughts often turned to the times they had always had together, the carefree springs and summers they had shared, and the long wonderful talks in which nothing was held back. Sonya was—for reasons she did not understand—feeling ill at ease with her husband, "shy and ashamed" about everything.

"What can the reason be?" she asked in her diary. "My conscience is clear, and I have done nothing wrong. Even when I am writing down these thoughts I feel embarrassed. . . . I am afraid to love him, and afraid that he will see this."

She sewed, played the piano, settled the accounts, transcribed his writing, and spent the better part of her days alone. Feeling bored and put-upon, she began to resent her unborn child for causing Tolstoy to grow away from her. "He has stopped loving me in the old way," she wrote on May 8. "If only he knew how much he has changed; if he could step into my shoes, he would soon realize what kind of life I am leading. But there is no help for it. He will wake up again after the baby is born."

But as Sonya's time approached, the early problems between husband and wife faded even further away. He now read medical books, and Sonya noted that he "continually examines my abdomen." He loved to place his ear to her belly and feel his child kicking. One day he burst into the bedroom carrying a book on obstetrics. "He already has toenails!" he announced. "Who?" Sonya asked, and then understanding, she joined in his happy laughter. And with the earliest days of summer the house, so long empty, began to fill with good friends—her husband's Aunt Pelagya, her aunts, her grandfather from Ivitsy, the Auerbach and the Marcus families from Tula. Seldom were there fewer than twelve at dinner, and when Sonya looked around the table, her face glowed with "the smile that could brighten a room."

8

In early June Lyubov Alexandrovna came from Moscow to help her daughter during her confinement and her first days as a new mother. Accompanying her were Tanya and her two suitors—Alexander Kuzminsky and Anatoly Shostak. Young, carefree liveliness reigned at Yasnaya Polyana, but Sonya had begun to feel like a rather neglected outsider. While she was forced to sit quietly, Lev Nikolaevich devoted much time to the visitors, taking them on outings, picnics, and rides. And he seemed fascinated by his vivacious sister-in-law, following Tanya about with a small notebook in which he jotted down all her comments and reactions.

Sonya, who so loved parties, found herself packing lunches and watching forlornly as her guests piled into the *lineika*, with its flat-cushioned side seats, which jolted up Kabatsky hill with Tanya and Lev Nikolaevich leading the way on saddle horses. And late in the afternoon she had tea waiting when they returned home full of chatter about their adventures. She confided her unhappiness to her diary, hoping that Lev Nikolaevich would take heed and pay more attention to her, but she said nothing to Tanya and put on a brave front whenever the young people were around. (Sonya was, after all, less than two years older than Tanya and the same age as Tanya's two suitors.) Tolstoy did try to soothe her, telling her that it was ridiculous of her to be jealous of Tanya, that he loved her and no other woman, and that of course he hadn't fallen under her sister's spell. The truth was that Tanya was a flirt and, without thinking of the havoc she might cause, did try to make every man she met or knew fall a little in love with her. And it seems certain that her magnetic brother-in-law, whom she had always adored and admired, would not have escaped her naive seductions.

As Sonya's confinement (June 20) drew closer—a date deter-

mined by the most careful calculations by the taciturn Dr. Shmigaro, a Pole who lived nearby—a change in Sonya became more
evident. She had become a mature woman. Suddenly it was Tanya
who felt left out as her mother and sister exchanged whispered
confidences. For that matter, Tolstoy felt like an outsider as well,
with all the talk of swaddling clothes and basinettes.

As "the day" approached, Sonya was serene and happy. She
was surrounded by those she loved, and treated with exceptional
kindness and attentiveness. Everything was indeed so pleasant that
a new sense of tenderness awakened within her. Tolstoy, wanting
to be with her when she went into labor, remained close at hand,
and she had great pity for his extreme anxiety about the imminent
birth. The leather couch on which Tolstoy and his sister and brothers had been born was moved into the Tolstoys' bedroom.

The "well-calculated day" came only to be followed by a week
of impatient waiting. Then early in the evening of June 27, 1863,
Sonya felt unwell and went to their room, Tolstoy following her.
He was superstitious about dates, and he considered the twenty-
eighth (he was born on August 28) lucky. "Do you think you can
wait until after midnight?" he asked. Laughing, she nodded and
told him to return to their guests. Later, when he joined her for the
night, she appeared to him to be in pain.

"Has it begun?" he asked in a frightened voice. She stood, a
candle in her hand, by the side of the bed, "a peculiarly sweet and
significant smile" on her face.

"I only felt a little unwell," she explained and, putting out the
candle, got into bed. Two hours later he was awakened by her
touch on his shoulder. "Lyova, don't be frightened, but I think we
must send for Marya Ivanovna," she said gently, almost apologeti-
cally. (Marya Ivanovna Abramovich was the local midwife whom
Dr. Shmigaro had recommended.)

Sonya had lit a candle and was sitting on the edge of the bed
"holding in her hands some knitting she had lately been doing."

As he leapt from the bed in near panic, she smiled reassuringly
and said, "Please don't be frightened. I'm not a bit afraid." She
took his hand and pressed it to her breast and then to her lips.

He dressed hastily, woke Sonya's maid, Dushka, who was
sleeping on a mat outside the bedroom door, and sent her to fetch
Lyubov Alexandrovna. Then, after going to order his horse sad-

dled, he ran back to the bedroom. Sonya was pacing up and down and "knitting, rapidly throwing the thread over the needle and giving orders." The maids were placing linens on the leather couch, preparing it as the "birth bed." Lyubov Alexandrovna brushed past him, and mother and daughter briefly and tearfully embraced. Sonya let out a sudden cry, and then moaning was helped to the couch by the three women. Tolstoy ran to the stable shouting for his horse. He set out for Dr. Shmigaro's house since Alexei Stepanovich had already gone for Marya Ivanovna. On the road he passed the midwife, who was on her way to Yasnaya Polyana in a small cart.

The doctor was asleep, but Tolstoy insisted his footman wake him; and when Shmigaro did not come down within a minute or two, he called for him to hurry. Tolstoy returned with the doctor to find Sonya in great pain. He grasped her damp hand and began to pray. He was terrified by her suffering, by the agony and strain apparent on her face. Finally Marya Ivanovna, a Polish woman of forty-five, with a broad pleasant face and large competent hands, insisted he leave the room. In the dining room, to Aunt Toinette's great irritation, Dr. Shmigaro was chain-smoking rather foul-smelling cigarettes.

Lyubov Alexandrovna, her face flushed, her hair damply falling over her forehead, rushed in for the doctor and Tolstoy started out after them. "No, get the icon from over Natalya Petrovna's bed," his mother-in-law ordered.

Tolstoy did as he was told, although it seemed a ridiculous thing for him to do at that moment. When he reached Sonya's bedside and placed the silver-gilt icon behind her pillows, she appeared not to recognize him. Her face was deep red, her eyes glazed, and she was mumbling to herself. As she began screaming, the doctor and the midwife insisted he leave; but when he turned to go Sonya called his name. He came back to her side, but again she did not seem to recognize him.

The screams came again, and then, falling back in exhaustion, Sonya turned to him and cried, "Don't go! Don't go! I am not afraid." But in the next breath she sobbed, "I shall die . . . die! . . . Go! Go!" and screamed "a scream unlike any other cry."

Tolstoy ran sobbing into the adjoining room. He no longer cared whether or not the child lived; he only wanted Sonya's suffering to end. Just when he thought Sonya's screams had reached the utmost limit of horror, there was a sharp, sudden silence. It's over, he thought and tore back into the room. He fell to his knees at Sonya's side, and she, "looking unusually beautiful and calm, gaz[ed] silently at him, trying unsuccessfully to smile."

"Alive! Alive! And a boy!" Marya Ivanovna announced in her deeply accented voice. She stood at the foot of the bed holding a gleaming wet infant, which she then slapped vigorously on the back.

Sonya turned to Lyubov Alexandrovna. "Mama, is it true?" she asked. Her mother's answer was lost in the baby's lusty cries.

The rest of the household was gathered in the dining room waiting for news. It was not yet daylight, and the room blazed with candles. Tolstoy, his face pale, his eyes red with weeping, with Aunt Toinette at his side, came in; and Aunt Toinette announced, "God has presented Sonya and Lyovochka with a son."

Upstairs Sonya was weary but happy. Downstairs her husband, mother, sister, brother, and brother-in-law, as well as the doctor, Aunt Toinette, Natalya Petrovna, and even Agatha Mikhailovna and Alexei Stepanovich, were celebrating with champagne, and she could hear their toasts and laughter.

Tolstoy wanted to call the baby Nikolai, in memory of his father, but Sonya protested that Nikolai (thinking of Tolstoy's brother, who had died only a short time before) was an unlucky name. They settled on the name Sergey, in honor of Tolstoy's brother Sergey Nikolaevich. And since June 28 was the feast day of St. Sergius and St. Herman, the miracle workers, this choice seemed especially apt. To Aunt Toinette's delight, she was named the child's godmother.

Childbirth had drained Sonya of her strength, and her recovery was slow, in large part because of her husband's theories about infant care. He was adamantly opposed to the employment of a wet nurse, a practice almost universal among women of Sonya's class. He thought it obscene and immoral for a woman not to nurse her own child, and was disgusted by the thought of his child sucking at an alien teat, growing strong from the milk of a hired nurse. To please him, Sonya persisted in her efforts to nurse little Sergey despite the almost unbearable pain in her breasts.

The midwife left after ten days. Sonya, pale and thin, was so weak she could scarcely stand. Her mother and Tanya had stayed on after the birth, and Lyubov Alexandrovna was incensed by Tolstoy's refusal to allow a wet nurse to be hired. With great reluctance he did agree to having a peasant girl (Dunyasha's sister) assist in the care of the baby, but he remained adamantly opposed to a wet nurse. Lyubov Alexandrovna fought angrily to no avail, and she sought out Aunt Toinette in desperation. "Lyovochka is always trying to be original; he wants Sonechka's life to be like a peasant woman's," she argued. "But infant care with us is not the same as it is for a peasant woman down in the village, and you cannot compare their strength anyway. He doesn't want to understand this. Besides, the feeding is going badly and soon Sonya will hardly be able to nurse little Sergey at all!"

Tolstoy turned an indifferent ear, convinced that Sonya was not as ill as her mother claimed. At no time during his wife's pregnancy had he stated his attitude toward breast feeding, and Sonya was dumbstruck by his impassioned insistence that she nurse their child. She feared that if she refused she would lose his love, and so, in continuous pain, she grew weaker and thinner.

At last Lyubov Alexandrovna, unable to bear the sight of Sonya's suffering, sent Tanya for Dr. Shmigaro. He was shocked to find open fissures on her seriously inflamed breasts. He forbade her to nurse the baby and advised Tolstoy that his wife was in a dangerously weakened condition and that if he didn't want her to become an invalid he should engage a wet nurse that very day. Furious, Tolstoy accused Shmigaro of improprieties in his examination of Sonya and fostering corruption by depriving her of the "only means which might have kept her from coquetry." He continued to insist that Sonya meet her maternal duties, but now the women in the house were united against him. Grudgingly he finally agreed to a wet nurse but went about the house despondent, as if mourning Sonya's fall from grace.

Sonya, seeing his unhappiness, was determined to try whenever possible to breast-feed her child. On the day Tolstoy went into Tula to bring back the wet nurse, Sonya wrote in her diary, "I have a great longing to rest, to enjoy the open fields, and I feel like a prisoner in jail. I am waiting anxiously for my husband's return from Tula. I love him with all my heart, with a good, steady love, though with a slight feeling of inferiority. I'm going now to sacrifice myself to the child."

Lyubov Alexandrovna returned to Moscow a month after the baby's birth, leaving Tanya to help her sister. Dr. Behrs, horrified by his wife's reports about Sonya's health, immediately wrote his daughter and son-in-law a scathing letter.

Unfortunately, my dear friends, I must inform you that you are living without any sense. You cannot even humble yourselves before circumstances which you have brought on yourselves by your thoughtless actions. Your dilemma to engage or not to engage a wet nurse is put on a par with Hamlet's "to be or not to be," and you have been acting out this tragedy for six long weeks in spite of all requests and exhortations from those who wish you well. You have acceded to them only after you had endured the utmost in physical and mental suffering, which are still going on.

I couldn't read your heartbreaking letter of July 31 through for a second time, Sonya dear. Once was enough to set my nerves on edge. You think you are a thoroughly unhappy mother because you found yourself forced to engage a wet nurse; the husband comforts his wife by promising not to enter the nursery because its atmosphere disgusts him and so forth. . . . I see that you have both gone out of your minds and that I shall have to pay you a visit in order to restore you to sanity. Can it be unknown to you, good husband, that mental suffering has a harmful and injurious effect on the organism and especially on a woman after a recent confinement? . . . Such a frame of mind, as Sonya is now in, can lead to very bad results indeed. Stop acting foolish, dear Sonya, calm yourself and don't make mountains out of molehills. Aren't you shamed to take to heart the most commonplace setbacks which occur so frequently in the course of a lifetime? Is it such a disgrace that you could not manage to breast-feed your baby, and whose fault is it? Your own and especially your husband's, who, without considering his wife's condition, forces her to do things which can only prove injurious to her. . . .

Tanya, stay at your restless sister's heels and give her constant scoldings for indulging in fancies and angering God; as for Lyov-ochka, just wallop him with the first thing that comes to your hand so he may become wiser. He is a great master of words and of writing but when it comes to deeds, it is a different matter. Let him write a

story about a husband who tortures his sick wife and wants her to
continue nursing her baby; all the women will stone him. Give him
no quarter and see that he comforts his wife to the utmost.

But Dr. Behrs's letter did not greatly alter Tolstoy's attitudes,
and he was infuriated by the sight of the wet nurse in her fine lace
headdress—a stranger with his child sucking at her breast. The
situation remained at an angry impasse. Tolstoy withdrew from
the life of the household, which now centered in the nursery, and
his paternal feelings for Sergey were slow to develop. He thought
of the child as a "strange little red being, squirming and burying
his head in the edge of his swaddling clothes." And was astonished
that he also had "a nose, crossed eyes and sucking lips." He compared the infant's face to a little old man's which became even more
wrinkled when he sneezed. The child he had wanted so much was
now an interloper, disturbing the quiet routine of the house and
bringing chaos to his life with Sonya.

With each passing day Sonya became more distraught. Her
husband was angry at her, but she saw no way of placating him.
Their difficulties were compounded by Tolstoy's belief that enjoyment of sexual relations with a nursing woman was the lowest form
of bestiality. So unpleasant was he, that she tried to avoid him.
"When he says: 'I'm going to sleep,' or 'I'm going for a bath,' I say
to myself, 'Thank God,' " she wrote in her diary, knowing as well
that he would read this confession. "When I look at the boy, my
heart breaks, God has taken from me both my husband and my
child. . . . Everything seems to be at an end. . . . I have just been
reading his diary. . . . Everything seems wrong to him."

A day later she made a fevered, irrational entry of only a few
lines. "Not written for my feeble brains . . . wasting his time . . .
wouldn't it be a good thing if you cleared out of here, Sonya
Andreyevna? It makes me unhappy to be treated like this. I am
determined never to mention it [her hatred of breast feeding] to
him again. Perhaps it will pass off."

That night, after another heated discussion, she wrote, "It is
revolting not to nurse one's own child—who says it isn't? But what
can be done against a bodily defect? I instinctively feel that he is
unjust to me. Why should he go on torturing me like this? . . . and

just as he would like to wash me off the face of the earth, because
I am suffering and am not taking proper care of the child, so I don't
want to see him because he goes on writing and doesn't suffer.
. . . What a weakness on his part not to be able to be patient until
I am better. I suffer and endure ten times as much as he."

Tolstoy read Sonya's agonized words a short time later and,
feeling a strong (but fleeting) guilt, wrote an apology directly below
them:

> Sonya, forgive me, I now realize my fault, and I know how great it
> is. There are days when one seems to be guided not by one's own
> will, but by some irresistible outside power. That's why I treated
> you so badly. . . . I always knew that I had many faults, but thought
> that I at least had a tiny spark of feeling and generosity within me.
> And yet I could be cruel and unkind—and to whom? to the one
> being who alone loves me—Sonya. I know that one doesn't forgive
> and forget such things; but I know you better now, and realize more
> fully all my meanness. Sonya, my darling, I was unkind and revolt-
> ing and—but there is a good man within me who sometimes falls
> asleep. Love him, Sonya, and don't blame him.

Only an hour or so after Tolstoy had written this plea for her
forgiveness, he walked into their bedroom and found her handing
the baby to the wet nurse. In a rage, he tore open her diary and
crossed out the apology with a large bold "X." Just below it Sonya
wrote, "Lyova wrote this as he asked my forgiveness. But soon
afterward, he lost his temper and crossed it all out. It was at the
time when I had those terrible pains in my breasts and *was unable*
to, when all I longed for was to be able to do it. I deserved those
few lines of kindness and remorse, yet in his irritation against me
he crossed them out before I had even time to read them."

Tolstoy seemed driven by irrational impulses, and he was
seized by a tormented jealousy which made him suspicious of
Sonya's every move. Later, explaining his emotions during this
period of their life, he said that "seeing how easily she abandoned
her moral obligations as a mother, I rightly, though unconsciously,
concluded that it would be equally easy for her to disregard her
duty as a wife."

When one of his former teachers at the school talked pleasantly
to Sonya, it seemed to him that the young man was regarding her

lustfully. "How dare he think about her, or dream of a romance with her!" was his outraged reaction, and he was furious that Sonya not only tolerated the young man's attentions but was quite pleased by them.

The fault, he believed, was not Sonya's but that of the society in which she had been raised, a society which held that a woman's vocation was to afford pleasure to a man. It was his opinion that, like serfs, women had been corrupted by the attitude of dependent subservience they had been forced to assume. Of course, he was right in holding that Sonya had been educated to please a man. But she had also been raised to be a sensitive, intelligent woman, bilingual, musical, well versed in all the arts and with a developed talent for literature. To Tolstoy, however, these accomplishments had little bearing on what had become a central intellectual and emotional concern for him—the morality of sexual relations. He had begun to regard marital chastity as the ideal state to which every couple must strive and to view any sexual act not directed toward procreation as immoral. Sonya sensed the development of these attitudes, which she found repellent. And so both continued to be tormented and to torment each other.

Remembering the man who had courted her, who had been so extravagant in his admiration and so won over by her pride and vivacity, Sonya was bewildered by his transformation into an authoritarian husband who criticized her at every turn and seemed bent on making her feel inadequate and unattractive.

"I have been meditating and remembering those mad nights of a year ago, when I was still so happy, joyful, and carefree," she confessed in her diary on August 17. "If ever I knew the full enjoyment of life, it was then. I loved, and I could feel and understand it all, and the whole world seemed so joyous and fresh. And, added to all this was the dark, poetic *Comte*, with his deep, serene, and infinitely pleasant look (that was the impression he made then). What a wonderful time that was to me, thrilled by the vague suggestion of his love."

"Again the moon is shining," she wrote on September 10, "and the nights are so warm and gentle, but they don't seem to belong to me. . . . I am a little sad that my youth is gone. . . . Lyova's look pursues me wherever I go. At the piano yesterday, it made me shudder. What were his thoughts just then? I had never seen such an expression in his eyes before. Was he remembering anything about the past? Jealousy?"

Only nineteen, she was an extraordinarily beautiful woman, and her delicate condition lent a new poignancy to her expressive oval face. Contrary to her own appraisal that she must look old, she appeared too young to be a wife and mother.

And on September 22: "It'll be a year tomorrow since we married. Then I looked forward to happiness, now I anticipate unhappiness. I had thought that all this about going to war was a joke, but there seems something in it."

The war Sonya was referring to was a revolutionary movement in Russian-held Poland which had erupted into a bloody uprising. The Tsar had sent in troops, and Tolstoy had impulsively spoken of donning his uniform again. The insurrection failed, and despite Sonya's fears he did not desert his family "to gallop across the battlefield and revel in the romance of war and listen to the whistling of bullets to die in a foreign land."

Yet, the distant sound of war drums echoed in Tolstoy's head. To Sonya's great relief, he shifted his attention to his writing. He had long considered composing a large-scale historical novel and had first thought of basing this work on the Decembrist revolt of 1825. Now he decided that the Napoleonic invasion of Russia would be at the center of his epic, which would span the years from 1805 to 1820. This new novel, which absorbed all his energies that autumn, was to be more about peace than about war. It was to be a family chronicle in the spirit of a Dickens novel, and he intended to charge it with intense contemporary relevance, thus rebutting those critics who had condemned him for ignoring the important issues of the day in his fiction.

Everyone in the Behrs family was involved in Tolstoy's new project. Dr. Behrs put together batches of references to source material on Napoleon's invasion. Even Lisa answered an urgent request for aid. She had read a great deal about that period of history and sent him a lengthy bibliography as well as detailed and meticulously annotated answers to questions he had posed.

Once he began writing, Sonya took on the task of making a fair copy of his nearly illegible manuscript. At first the story confused her; she could make no sense of "all those conversations . . . between Countess So-and-So and Princess So-and-So." But she worked on, spending hours at her desk in the sitting room, with Dora sleeping at her feet. And as she laboriously deciphered the badly blotted pages written in her husband's small, cramped, careless hand, she became absorbed by his epic tale.

In October the nobility of Tula gave a ball in honor of the young Tsarevich, who was visiting the city. The Tolstoys were of course invited, but Tolstoy decided Sonya should not attend. He was concerned about the frailty of her health, but more importantly he believed that it was improper for a nursing mother to attend any sort of formal social gathering. She wept bitterly, but he did not relent. Although he had decided to stay at home as well, Sonya insisted that he go. And so he took an ecstatic Tanya in his wife's place. Sonya asked the Baroness Mengden, who was in Tula, to accompany them, as it was not quite proper for Tanya to go alone with Lev Nikolaevich. She also sent Tanya into Tula for fabric to make a ball gown. Not once during all the preparations for the ball did Sonya appear downcast or jealous that Tanya was to enjoy what should rightly have been her moment of glory—her first appearance in Tula society as the Countess Tolstoy. In fact, the excitement of preparing Tanya for her first ball seemed to put life back into her eyes and give a spring to her step.

Tanya rose at eight the morning of the gala event and was in a fever of excitement all day. Her filmy white gown with its deep neckline was almost ready; Sonya was just finishing the last of the dozens of pink silk rosebuds she had embroidered on the dress. Sonya subscribed to the French fashion magazines, and she sat her sister before a mirror and, with Dunyasha's help and many pins and ribbons, copied a most flattering ball hairdo. When Tanya left the house with Lev Nikolaevich, himself splendid in a black silk dress jacket, she looked every inch a beauty, from her delicate satin dancing slippers to the pink silk rose pinned in her black hair. She ran back to hug her sister and then was gone, her cries and laughter echoing behind her.

Sonya stood in the hallway alone and listened to the *dormeuse* (which Tolstoy had ordered out for this special occasion) move slowly down Yasnaya Polyana's rutted drive. Then she went to her room and pensively imagined the excitement and splendor that awaited her sister. There would be red-liveried footmen, women in satin and ermine, brightly lit rooms filled with music and scented by a dazzling array of flowers. And of course there would be the young and handsome Tsarevich, Nikolai Alexandrovich, with his brilliant retinue of young people from St. Petersburg, the men in uniform and the women in the latest French gowns. The violins would sing, and the couples would whirl, dancing polonaises, mazurkas, and waltzes. It was impossible for Sonya not to envy Tanya, not to feel that her life was rather bleak. She had never attended a ball as festive as she knew this one would be. And never again would she be young and carefree and wear a dress with yards of cascading butterfly-bright fabric swirling about her feet while she danced.

It was time for the baby's early morning feeding when Sonya heard the heavy wheels of the *dormeuse*. Moments later Tanya—glowing, looking even lovelier than when she had left—ran breathlessly into Sonya's room, unable to contain her bubbling excitement.

"Oh, Sonya," she cried, "I fell in love the moment I entered the room! Oh, not with anyone in particular, but with everyone! Oh, if only you were not ill and could have seen how glittering and wonderful it all was!"

"Well," Sonya said petulantly, "I could not have gone even if I had been well."

"But why?"

"Surely you know Lyovochka's views. Could I dress in a ball gown with an open neck? That is entirely unthinkable. How often has he condemned married women who 'go naked'?" For a moment her mouth quivered, but then a smile flickered across her face. She sat Tanya down, and soon they were both laughing over her giddy chatter.

Now deeply involved in his novel, Tolstoy was spending less time with Sonya, leaving the management of the house and the farm more in her hands. Although his writing had become in a sense her rival, she was proud of his fame and his achievement, and longed for him to become wealthy. She did, however, keenly feel his coldness, both emotional and physical, toward her.

"I try to suppress all human feelings in myself," she wrote in her diary on November 13. "While the machine works and warms the milk and knits a blanket and walks up and down without thinking, life is still bearable. He has stopped loving me. Why was I not able to keep his love?"

As she did her wifely chores or copied her husband's manuscript, she would often glance out the wide windows of Yasnaya Polyana. And sometimes she would see Tanya running out into the fields with the peasant girls to dig potatoes. Tanya, her laughter streaming behind her like crimson ribbons, young and vibrant, dreaming rapturous dreams that might yet come true. Yasnaya Polyana was enjoying a "wife's [Indian] summer." Gossamer covered the fields like a smoky veil; and when Tanya returned, her face flushed with excitement, it clung to her hands, hair, and dress. Sonya loved her younger sister deeply and yet was envious of her youth, her fire, and her enjoyment of life which enchanted everyone—young and old—including Tolstoy. There was every reason for Sonya to be wistful over the loss of her own girlish freedom and innocence.

Tolstoy's brother Sergey Nikolaevich, whose estate, Pirogovo, was only a short distance away from Yasnaya Polyana, was now a constant visitor. His Gypsy mistress, Marya Shiskin (Masha), never accompanied him on these visits. His attention to Tanya and her receptiveness to him were regarded with alarm by everyone in the Tolstoy household except Sonya. Without doubt Sergey Nikolaevich had fallen deeply in love with the vital, lovely, still naive Tanya. Sonya stood alone in her approval of this match. Her encouragement of the lovers may have sprung from a feeling that Tanya posed a threat to her own marriage, but it seems more likely that Sonya was swept up in vicarious enjoyment of her sister's first serious romance.

Tanya's visit, however, only brought disruption. The attraction between her and Sergey Nikolaevich came to a melodramatic climax when, riding together alone at Pirogovo, they were forced by a storm to take refuge for the night in a deserted house on the estate. Though they came close to becoming lovers, they did (with great difficulty) restrain themselves.

When Tolstoy learned they had spent a night alone, he was furious at his brother's "indiscretion," and for the next few days Sergey Nikolaevich stayed away from Yasnaya Polyana. Tanya told Sonya the entire story, confessing, "I believe I'm in love with him," and confiding her most intimate feelings—as once she had done by the flickering icon candle in their bedrooms in Moscow and Pokrovskoye. But even as Tanya was talking of her great happiness, Sonya's mind turned to the difficulties facing her sister. Tanya would not be seventeen until the following month. And there was the Gypsy woman who had borne Sergey Nikolaevich three children and with whom he was still intimate. Even if Lev Nikolaevich should become an ally, Dr. Behrs was bound to be adamant in his opposition to such an alliance. And, of course, Sergey Nikolaevich had not proposed! Still, Sonya's sympathies were entirely with her beloved Tanyachka, and being a romantic, she desperately wanted these two vital people to overcome all obstacles.

Several weeks later Sergey Nikolaevich returned to Yasnaya Polyana to ask Tanya to be his wife. To the lovers' amazement, Tolstoy had relented and seemed to feel marriage between the two was not impossible. They would, of course, have to wait a year or more, because of Tanya's youth. And Dr. Behrs's approval would have to be won, and a dispensation from the Tsar would have to be obtained (it was illegal for two brothers to marry two sisters). Sergey Nikolaevich would also have to settle his "affairs." Tanya did not quite know what this meant. She was aware of his Gypsy mistress and had met their son, Grisha, but the Tolstoys had kept from her the fact that Sergey Nikolaevich still spent a great part of his life with Masha. Tanya also was unaware (as were the Tolstoys) that Sergey Nikolaevich and his mistress were expecting a fourth child.

The prospect of Tanya marrying Sergey Nikolaevich delighted Sonya, for it meant that "the little imp" would always be nearby. For the present, it was decided that Tanya would extend her stay at Yasnaya Polyana, and nothing could have pleased Sonya more.

Within a few days of his proposal, Sergey Nikolaevich left to hunt in the Kursk province. The romance between him and Tanya had been a distraction for the Tolstoys from their disagreements over breast feeding before his visit. Life at Yasnaya Polyana became much more cheerful. The wet nurse, Natalya, contracted mastitis and a decision was made, after correspondence with Dr. Behrs, to wean little Seryozha onto the bottle. Tolstoy seemed to approve of this and in the beginning even fed the child himself. He wrote to his cousin Alexandra in St. Petersburg describing himself as "a happy and tranquil husband" and saying that "Seryozha means a good, sweet smile with bright eyes—there's nothing more to him." His work was going well and in this same letter he told her, "Now, I am a writer with *all* the strength of my soul, and I write and think as I have never thought or written before." He had given up the school—though, as he wrote her, "The children come to me in the evenings and bring with them memories for me of the teacher that used to be in me and is there no longer"—and had become completely consumed by his writing.

There were no more "outsiders" at Yasnaya Polyana. Even Seryozha's nurse—now that the wet nurse was gone—had once been a serf on the estate. She was Marya Afanasyevna Arbuzova, a kind, gentle, intelligent woman of about forty-five, whose only fault appeared to be that upon occasion she took a drink. But she never became intoxicated, and with her elaborate lace headdress and the bright folded kerchief she wore around her neck, she was a colorful addition to the household.

Sonya felt suddenly liberated. Seryozha was now fed by bottle, and she no longer had to be concerned about nursing him. Also to her great joy, it was decided that she and Lev Nikolaevich would accompany Tanya to Moscow, where her sister was to stay until the spring.

9

The ice had already hardened on the Moscow River, and it was crowded with sleighs and skaters. Sonya and Tanya clasped hands as they neared the red gates of the Kremlin, which were crowned with snow and sparkled in the winter sunlight. Suddenly, and for the first time since her marriage, Sonya felt young again. The birch trees in the Zoological Gardens were laden with snow, but the day was clear and frosty. Carriage tops, silk hats, church domes, all shimmered in the sunlight. The clean-swept paths between Moscow's narrow houses were thronged with people. Sledges streamed down the ice hills, skaters whirled on the lakes. True, Moscow might not be the most sophisticated city in Russia, but it was gay at Christmastime; and somehow, perhaps because town life kept them so busy, the Tolstoys quarreled less and Lev Nikolaevich was most often in good spirits.

They stayed in Moscow only five days and the time passed far too quickly for Sonya. By December 16, they were back at Yasnaya Polyana, and she wrote a letter addressed to the entire Behrs family:

> Our trip to Moscow has left us with very good, very pleasant impressions—if only Papa had not been sick. He must go abroad without fail. When I recall the Kremlin, a large animated picture presents itself—the many beloved faces, the long table, the bright lights, and one face after another with such distinctive and charming expressions. . . . I can still hear Mama's voice when you were seeing us off in the sleigh and I can still see and hear all of you. Give a very special kiss to Tanya also. It is not the same at Yasnaya Polyana without her. It has become so quiet and empty. The aunties [Toinette and Natalya Petrovna] have no one to play bezique with, and they get bored. God willing, we shall kidnap her again this spring. I

shall write to her soon. Tell her that I love her very much as ever and
that I am her unfailing friend. Do you hear, Tanechka?

Sonya did indeed miss the lively companionship of her sister.
"I feel full of youth and am longing to do something crazy," Sonya
wrote in her diary on December 19. "Instead of going to bed, I
should like to turn somersaults. But with whom?"

And on December 24: "A feeling of old age seems to have
crept over me and everything around me is old. I try to suppress
every feeling of youth, for it seems strange and out of place. Seryozha [Sergey Nikolaevich] alone is younger in body and spirit
than the others [Tolstoy, Marya Nikolaevna, Aunt Toinette, and
Natalya Petrovna]."

At Christmas there was a lovely tree, and as was the custom
in the Tolstoy family, they had a gala celebration Christmas night.
The household servants, some twenty in all, dressed in their best,
joined in all sorts of games and danced to the flute of the cook,
Nikolai Mikhailovich. At one time Nikolai had been a flutist in Lev
Nikolaevich's grandfather's serf orchestra. In those days the musicians had played beside the linden trees in the garden, and their
benches still stood there. Nikolai, now an old man, had lost most
of his front teeth and his embouchure was so poor that the melody
came in puffs and wheezes. There were also some itinerant per-
formers—a trained bear and its master, and a Gypsy who sang and
played the guitar. The Christmas festivities ended with Tolstoy
reading scenes from a new work.

During the last few weeks he had put aside *1805* (the working
title for his new novel) to write a five-act comedy, *The Infected
Family*, inspired by Sonya's inability to breast-feed her child, a
failure that in his eyes transformed her into "one of those emancipated women" he found "obnoxious." Sonya intensely disliked the
play and wanted him to get back to work on *1805*. He was, however, intent on completing his comedy and then having it produced
in Moscow.

Sergey Nikolaevich returned to Yasnaya Polyana before New
Year's Day, with the news that Masha was about to deliver his
fourth child. He was distraught, torn between his desire to marry
Tanya and his responsibility to Masha.

Appalled that he had proposed to Tanya when he knew his

mistress was carrying his child, Sonya nonetheless did not want her husband to tell Tanya this shocking news. He ignored this wish and wrote Tanya not only about Masha's condition but also about Sergey's confused state of mind. Tanya sent back an angry, hurt letter, her first expression of hostility toward her brother-in-law.

Tolstoy replied:

You say I am your enemy. Your enemy is the twenty extra years which I've lived on earth. I know that whatever happens to you, you mustn't lose a grip on yourself. . . . You have your sorrows, but besides them you also have so many friends who love you (think of me), and you won't stop living, and you'll be ashamed to remember your lapse at this time, however it may turn out. Really, don't be angry with me. You'll be convinced that it's a bad thing to lose control of yourself, and all will be well.

And how do I see your future? You want to know and I'll tell you. Seryozha promised to come and see us in a couple of days' time and he hasn't come so far. We've heard that Masha is in labor, the thought tormented me that he once said, "I must end all this one way or another by marrying Masha or Tanya." Rationally speaking, I'm more sorry for Masha than for you, but when it occurred to me that he might make his mind up without us I was afraid. We wrote him a letter to say we had something important to tell him. Now she's in labor and he's present for the first time and I'm afraid. In my heart of hearts—I say this to you *with God as my witness*—I want it to be *yes*, but I'm afraid it will be *no*. Everything may appear to him in a different light in the face of her sufferings. . . .

For my part, I'm convinced that if he marries Masha he will very likely ruin himself and her. I told him that if he didn't marry her, he would instinctively be leaving himself *une porte du salut*. He said, "Yes, yes, yes." But now, if he gets married this *porte du salut* will be sealed off, and he will hate her. He can go on living with her like this, but if he married her he will come to grief. . . . God knows what will be best for you both, and you must pray to *Him*. Yes. I know one thing, that the more difficult a choice becomes in life for a person and the harder it is to live, the more he needs to take command of himself (. . . and not to lose control), because at such a moment a mistake can cost himself and others dear. Every step, every word at such moments, at the moment through which you are living, is more important than years of life afterwards. . . .

> Tanya darling, perhaps this seems like The Mirror of Virtue [a
> child's book of morals], but what can I do if my most intimate
> thoughts are like The Mirror of Virtue? Every word has been care-
> fully thought out and heartfelt.

Tanya angrily replied, "I can't stand these moral maxims from The
Mirror of Virtue, and I am not going to heed them!"

Masha gave birth to a girl, and still Sergey Nikolaevich wrote
nothing to Tanya. Had Tolstoy not written to her, she would have
been unaware of the situation. She sent Tolstoy's letters to her
brother Sasha, who was stationed in Poland, and he wrote back
telling her she must not consider marrying Sergey Nikolaevich.
But Tanya was strong-willed, and she refused to make any decision
until she had spoken to Sergey. Very shortly after his daughter's
birth, however, Sergey left for Algeria to stay for a time with his
sister, Marya Nikolaevna, who had also given birth to a girl, out
of wedlock in Algiers. The father was a Swede, Viscount Victor-
Hector de Kleen. Marya Nikolaevna had spent the two previous
winters with her child's father, behavior that Sonya found reprehensible. Not that she did not know that such family foibles as
divorce, Gypsy mistresses, foreign lovers, illegitimate children,
and huge gambling losses were not uncommon among the aristocracy of St. Petersburg—even in the Winter Palace itself (there was
always whispering about the Tsar's private life)—or for that matter
in her mother's ancestors. But in the circles in which she was raised
such things were considered immoral. Yet Lev Nikolaevich, whose
attitude toward his own wife had been self-righteous from the beginning, seemed to accept and condone his brother's outrageous
behavior, and his sister's loose morals.

In February, a dreary cold month of black skies and chill
winds, Tolstoy and Sonya returned to Moscow with the completed
manuscript of The Infected Family. Tolstoy was excitedly looking
forward to seeing his first dramatic work staged. Sonya remained
unenthusiastic about the play, but she was grateful for the chance
to escape the winter loneliness of Yasnaya Polyana and to see for
herself that Tanya was all right.

Alexander N. Ostrovski, a well-known dramatist, was prevailed upon by Tolstoy to come to the Behrses' and listen to him
read the play. The growling bearlike Ostrovski was incensed by

the theme and found the work turgid and lacking in humor. The next day he wrote Nikolai Nekrasov: "It was so hideous that I positively had to stop my ears at his reading."

This negative response did not deter Tolstoy from submitting *The Infected Family* to a number of theatrical companies. "What are you in such a hurry for?" Ostrovski asked ironically. "Are you afraid people will grow intelligent?" It was rejected by one and all, and the Tolstoys returned to Yasnaya Polyana in March. "Among other things," he wrote to Marya Nikolaevna in Algeria, "I've done a comedy that I wanted staged at Moscow. I had no success with it before Shrovetide, and the comedy, it seems, is poor. It was written to ridicule the emancipation of women and the so-called nihilists."

Sonya had been reassured by her visit that Tanya was bearing up well and went back to Yasnaya Polyana in a happy mood. Pleased that Tolstoy was returning to his novel, she took it upon herself not only to copy his work but also to lift all other responsibilities from his shoulders.

A new spark had ignited her tremendous energy. As she sat painstakingly copying and recopying her husband's pages (sometimes as many as fifteen times as he edited and revised), she became utterly convinced that he was a genius and that his new work would earn him a place among Russia's greatest writers. In those bleak, freezing days of early 1864, sitting close to the hearth in the parlor, working by flickering candlelight after the rest of the house was asleep, Sonya came to a clear and positive decision.

She would dedicate herself to helping to make her husband world famous. She was convinced that if she could keep him writing, he would, through the power of his literary achievement, become more renowned and wealthier than she had ever dreamed. And she, Countess Sonya Tolstoy, would be his beloved wife.

When the spring thaw came, Sonya was once again pregnant —a fact that pleased her greatly, because she was determined that with this child she would show her husband that she could indeed breast-feed.

Tolstoy was now totally reabsorbed in his work on *1805*. With each page Sonya copied, she became more confident of her husband's greatness. During the day she stood between him and the rest of the household, allowing no one to disturb him when he was writing in his small study on the ground floor. If the bailiff had a question, it was Sonya who gave the answer; she had taken over the management of the estate. If something was needed, it was Sonya who made sure they could afford it; she was in charge of all household accounts. "The little Countess" was regarded with a new, respectful eye as she went about her exhausting daily tasks, her keys at her waist, a lorgnette, which she had bought in Moscow, hanging from a ribbon about her neck.

In the evening, when the baby was asleep, the servants gone for the night, and while Tolstoy chatted with Aunt Toinette and Natalya Petrovna, she would sit down at her table in the parlor and by candlelight copy his day's work. It was a Herculean task, demanding the same almost telepathic ability to understand his thoughts that she had displayed when he had written initials in chalk on the game table at Ivitsy. The pages she was given were filled with incomplete sentences and abbreviated words. Lines were heavily scratched out and new sentences or phrases were written in balloons' in the margins, or scrawled between the lines, making such a maze of words that she often needed a magnifying glass to find her way. Yet somehow she managed to make sense out of pages Tolstoy himself had not been able to reread. She refused to put down her pen until every page—copied in her graceful, legible script—was ready for him to read the next morning. And never did she complain of fatigue or about the dreadfully marked up pages of her work which were returned to her the next evening to be copied again.

> I spend a great deal of time copying out Lyova's novel [she wrote in one of her now infrequent diary entries]. This is a very great pleasure to me. As I copy it, I live through a whole new world of ideas and impressions. Nothing has such an effect on me as his ideas and his genius. This is something quite new with me. Have I changed a great deal, or is it because the novel is so extraordinarily good? I don't know. I copy at great speed, and so am able to follow the gist of the story, and yet at the same time the copying is sufficiently slow to allow me to feel and ponder over each new idea. We often discuss the novel, and I am proud to say that he pays a great deal of attention to any remarks I make.

With immense interest she watched as personal experiences, remembered anecdotes, and people she knew were transformed into "fiction," becoming somehow more real in the process. The depressed moments, the quarrels had not stopped entirely; but with her great involvement in his work, Sonya had taken on a new and most satisfying role.

On April 16 Tanya returned, bringing their brother Sasha, who had a short leave from his post in Poland. Tolstoy met them in Tula in a three-horse *katki*, and swallows swooped over their heads as they passed between the twin towers of the gateway to Yasnaya Polyana. Never had the grounds looked so trim; the front gardens had been pruned and lushly planted and were just bursting into bloom. Sonya came onto the porch at the sound of the approaching carriage, and Tanya, disregarding Tolstoy's shouted warnings, stood up, waved and called out cheerfully and jumped to the ground before the *katki* had stopped. The two women ran toward each other and embraced while Dora sat back on her sleek, shining red haunches and barked.

That springtime, guests, like bees swarming around new flowering green, came to Yasnaya Polyana—alone, in twos, and in family groups—all of them drawn, it seemed, by Tanya's irrepressible gaiety. The days were filled with picnics and hunts; the evenings with games and entertainments. Sonya and Tolstoy rarely had a moment alone. She had moved her bed into a room near the nursery, since while she was pregnant she and Lev Nikolaevich would not be sleeping together. It was suggested that Tanya's bed be placed next to hers, but she said firmly, "It must be Lyova or no one."

Sonya appeared happier than she had ever been at Yasnaya Polyana. She did not seem to mind the extra work so many guests entailed. She was, however, more protective than ever about her husband's writing time and well-being. The Tolstoys grew closer and more reliant on each other than they had ever been. Neither of them made diary entries during this time, so there were no harsh words to read and fret over. Tolstoy did make frequent trips to Tula, Ivitsy, Pirogovo, and Nikolskoye; and his absences were disturbing to her. But even when he was gone for only a few days, they sent each other one or two letters daily. In answer to Sonya's charge that he might not be thinking about her, he wrote, "Not for a moment, especially when I'm with people. In the hunt, however, I do forget. I remember only about a particular woodcock."

Early May was the season when the flight of the woodcocks was at its peak, and the best time to hunt them was in the early evening. Sonya was repelled by hunting, but she wanted to share her husband's daily life. And so she decided to go with him, Sasha, Tanya, and two former teachers from the school on an evening hunt in the Zaeska forest. The six of them left in the three-horse carriage, with Tanya serving as coachman and Dora seated on the floor.

They stopped in a thicket of young trees; just beyond in the twilight lay the dark, heavy foliage of the Zaeska. Tanya remembered: "Dora was lying at Tolstoy's feet. Sonya stood very still. The silence was complete. Everything grew deadly hushed at the approach of the woodcocks with their characteristic cries and whistles. Dora, cocking her ears, crouching on her haunches, was all ears. The woodcocks came, flying singly and in pairs, swiftly, as if swaying in the air. There was a snap as the guns were cocked and then the report of the shots."

Hares cried in the distance, and the horses neighed, but Sonya breathed with relief when she realized that few of the shots had found their mark. Dora, bred to be a hunting dog, ran off to retrieve the dead birds. She did not return immediately, and Sonya recalled her father's advice in a letter they had received just that morning. "It is always better to have a trusty companion along with you; you might come across a wolf and he will drag off your dog, especially if the dog runs far away from you. We always used to beware of such an encounter, and at night kept the dog near us."

It was with immense happiness that Sonya caught sight of Dora's slick carmine body streaking through the underbrush toward them with the quarry safely in her mouth. Sonya wanted to return home, but the others, enjoying the beauty and silence of the encroaching night, dallied. The sun was gone. They were in utter darkness, for it was a starless night and the moon was covered by dark, impenetrable clouds.

Tanya, headstrong, but refusing to let Tolstoy take the reins, mounted the carriage box nervously. It was impossible to see the edges of the road, and she would have to drive almost blindly. A wind rose, sweeping leaves up from the ground and whirling them about. They were all silent as they crossed the dam over the Voronka, and Sonya grasped Tolstoy's hand anxiously.

The most difficult part—the forest—lay ahead. The wind picked up as they moved through the darkness. The swampy clay soil of the road was scarred with deep ruts, and they were tossed from side to side. Though they were less than a mile from home, the journey seemed endless. Just as they were about to emerge from the forest, the front wheel of the carriage ran heavily into some dead branches which had fallen across the road. The carriage lurched to one side, and Tanya was thrown from the coach box with a piercing scream. The horses headed with sudden abandon toward the stable, dragging the carriage after them. The hapless passengers shouted at the horses to stop, and then one by one all the men with their loaded guns fell off, leaving Sonya alone, clinging to a long, heavy seat cushion. Tolstoy ran after the carriage crying out, "Sonya, Sonya, stay seated. Don't jump!"

Sonya, however, could not hold on, and grasping the leather cushion, which had come loose from the seat, she went reeling out of the carriage, landing near a muddy ditch in the apple orchard.

The others came running to Sonya's rescue, fearing the worst, since she was, after all, four months pregnant. But as everyone converged upon her, she struggled to her feet. Miraculously none of them had been hurt, but it was Sonya's last hunting expedition for a long while.

At the beginning of June Sergey Nikolaevich arrived unexpectedly. Tanya was ecstatic. Although still disapproving, Dr. Behrs had given his approval to the couple. Plans were made for them to be married on the groom-to-be's estate in the Kursk province. Masha, he assured Tolstoy, would receive an ample settlement for herself and their children and would remain with her parents and the children in the Gypsy district of Tula where he had first met her.

There was great excitement in the house as the wedding date was set and letters were written to obtain dispensations from the Tsar and the Synod. Champagne was served every night (never vodka, for Sergey Nikolaevich considered it "the drink of porters"). Then it was brought to their attention that the wedding day would fall during the Feast days of St. Peter and St. Paul, a period during which the Church forbade marriage ceremonies. Although the date was set back only two weeks, somehow this delay seemed ominous.

Sergey Nikolaevich went to Pirogovo for a few days to attend, as he said, to business. Returning in a thoughtful, somewhat preoccupied mood, he answered evasively when Tanya asked why he was downcast, and he soon departed again. A few days later he wrote Tolstoy a heartbreaking letter. At dawn the day following his first departure he had driven to Masha's house in Tula. He had entered quietly, and in the wavering light of the icon lamp in her room he had seen her on her knees in prayer before the holy image. Her thick black hair hung loose to her waist; her face was pale and drawn, her eyes swollen from crying. When she had turned to the sound of his step and looked up at him despairingly, he had known that he could not desert her, that it was she he must marry, their children he must legitimize. His love for Tanya was, he confessed, a "one and only love that never comes again, is never over or forgotten." But for perhaps the first time in his life, his sense of duty overrode all other considerations.

Tanya was told of Sergey Nikolaevich's decision by a distraught Tolstoy, and following the custom of the day which allowed a spurned woman to save face, she wrote to him, refusing his offer of marriage. For days she wandered about Yasnaya Polyana in such extreme melancholy that Sonya was afraid to leave her alone. Then late one night, two weeks after her letter of refusal had been sent and accepted, Tanya swallowed a large dose of *allum*, a poisonous compound that was used as a cleanser in the kitchen. When the first waves of pain and nausea swept over her, she ran screaming from her room. The house quickly wakened and Agatha Mikhailovna was sent for.

Through the long night the old servant brewed herbal teas and fed them to Tanya, who vomited convulsively. Aunt Toinette and Natalya Petrovna spent these hours kneeling in prayer before the icons of their patron saints. Tanya still lay near death when Dr. Shmigaro arrived shortly after dawn; but he offered hope that, given proper care, she would survive. For a week Sonya watched over her delirious sister; she refused to leave her side and slept in the chair bed she had used on her first visit to Yasnaya Polyana. Tanya's fever finally broke, and although she was very weak, it was clear that the crisis had passed. She made the Tolstoys promise

not to tell Sergey Nikolaevich of her suicide attempt and they kept
their word. At the end of August Tanya was well enough to travel
back to Moscow; Tolstoy accompanied her but returned to Sonya
within a few days.

Two months later Tolstoy made one of his now rare entries in
his diary. "The relations between Sonya and me have grown finer,
stronger. We love, that is to say we are dearer to each other than to
anyone else in the world, and we look at each other with clear eyes.
We have no secrets and no cause for remorse."

And the more a part of her husband's work she became, the
deeper became Sonya's love for him. All her own ambitions were
transferred to him, though not without an occasional twinge of
jealousy. Although she thought from time to time about writing
something of her own, she did not act on these impulses. Her
husband's dazzling virtuosity with words and his almost mystical
ability to penetrate his characters' thoughts and feelings made her
self-consciously aware of the limitations of her own modest talents.
And, perhaps more importantly, she felt that Tolstoy was already
capturing the world she would have written about, that he had
absorbed all of her experiences. Scenes from her childhood and
adolescence appeared in his new novel, and each day she copied
brilliant pages alive with characters modeled after her mother, her
father, Lisa, Tanya, and herself.

As the character Natasha developed, Sonya saw Tanya reincarnated before her eyes. Everything Natasha did was exactly as
Tanya would have done it. Considering how romantic and lovely
a heroine Natasha was, it was not odd that Sonya would occasionally wonder about her husband's feelings toward her sister. In her
heart she believed that although Lev Nikolaevich loved Tanya, it
was "not in the vulgar sense of desiring to sexually possess her."
And as she transcribed Tolstoy's rapturous descriptions of his heroine, she became convinced that Natasha, though modeled on
Tanya, was more his own romantic invention than reality. Therefore Natasha wasn't Tanya but a dream—and dreams are intangible. Awake from a dream, and it soon vanishes. No, Lev
Nikolaevich would never be so foolish as to harbor lust in his
artist's heart or poet's soul for a dream.

Tanya and Tolstoy seemed to share what the French might

call *amitié amoureuse*, a "loving friendship." He always responded to her unexpected outbursts, her wild enthusiasms, her carelessness, with good-natured humor. And when Tanya was in one of her rare dark moods, he would be able with a jest to induce a smile, a rather sulky one at first which gradually broadened till in the end she was laughing with him. She was gay, beautiful, and clever, and she was utterly feminine. She could hunt and fish and ride all day and laugh and talk and dance and sing all night. And how she sang! Her voice was perhaps not big enough for opera, but her tone was so pure, her interpretation so exquisitely colored, that her soul seemed to shimmer through her pure, silvery voice.

That summer, anguished over losing Sergey, Tanya had sung as never before. On those warm evenings the family and guests would gather in the parlor, whose windows had been thrown open to catch the breeze. Lev Nikolaevich accompanied her on the piano, and her soul-searing voice would rise in song, bringing a deep feeling of life and love and tears to everyone in the room. And as Sonya watched Tolstoy "bent over the keyboard, his back tense with exertion," glancing up at Tanya's young ardent face, Sonya not only understood but shared the profound pleasure he took in Tanya's presence and performance.

And when Sonya had a daughter in October, the baby was named Tatyana for her young aunt.

This birth had been easier than Seryozha's, and Sonya found to her great relief that she was able to nurse the infant. The more Sonya had to do, the more she seemed to thrive. By the time Tolstoy emerged from their bedroom in the morning, still in his dressing gown, his beard uncombed, and came downstairs to his study to dress, Sonya had nursed little Tatyana, seen to the day's menus, issued the work orders for the household staff, and was dressed and serving breakfast tea in the parlor. When he joined her and Aunt Toinette and Natalya Petrovna, he always refused to sit. Wearing a gray-blue tunic, he would stand in the doorway; one hand was usually thrust into his leather belt, while in the other he held a full tumbler of tea in a silver glass holder. He sometimes stood there talking for a half-hour, not noticing that his tea was growing cold.

Sonya would finally hurry him into his study, which was under the parlor on the ground floor off the entrance hall. A partition of bookshelves divided the study into two sections, and a narrow door in the center of the shelves led to a small inner room containing Tolstoy's desk and an armchair. The walls were adorned with antlers that he had brought back from the Caucasus and a stuffed stag's head where he hung a towel. There were also photographs of Dickens, Schopenhauer, Fet as a young man, and of the *Sovremennik* (Contemporary) circle in 1856.

A marble bust of his beloved brother Nikolai stood in a niche. It had been modeled after his death mask, and Tolstoy considered it an excellent likeness. Sonya was always moved by the kind, sad face that looked so naked without a beard. There was something childlike about the way Nikolai had worn his hair, brushed smooth and parted on one side.

From the time that Tolstoy entered his study until three or four in the afternoon, Sonya insisted on silence in the house. The ground floor had to be cleaned before breakfast, and no one could use the front door during his working hours. When he finished, he would hand her his pages and with Dora and his gun set off to hunt or to ride, or simply to walk. He often returned late for dinner, apologizing while he drank his brandy from a silver tumbler.

Life with Tolstoy may have been very different from her romantic dreams, but Sonya was quite satisfied. Even in the growing cold of autumn when she woke in darkness before the house had been warmed by its many fires, she found herself in high spirits as she went about the sleeping household getting her work done before her husband rose. But in the first week of October, shortly . after Tatyana's birth, a new family crisis arose.

Early one morning Tolstoy went to hunt, riding a rather skittish horse. A rabbit darted out from under some foliage. Tolstoy set after it at full speed. Coming upon a narrow but rather deep gully, the horse refused to jump and, stopping short, catapulted his rider to the ground. Tolstoy, his right arm smashed and his shoulder dislocated, staggered to the main road about a half-mile away. There he met several peasants, who put him in a cart and took him to their hut. Dr. Shmigaro came and tried to set the arm eight times but with no success. Remaining in the peasant's hut for the night, Tolstoy waited in excruciating pain for the new young doctor from Tula. He arrived the next morning with chloroform and managed to at least set the severe break. Four weeks later Tolstoy was still unable to lift his arm and was beginning to fear that the accident might have left him permanently maimed.

Unable to write, Tolstoy now dictated to Sonya. He paced back and forth, supporting his injured arm with his good one. He spoke in spurts, unevenly, hurriedly, and Sonya was hard pressed to keep pace with him. Except to order her to "strike that out," he ignored her until finally after several hours he would collapse in a chair. "I've tortured you enough," he would say, ending the session. Sonya then took her quickly scribbled notes to her desk, transcribed them, and when he was rested read them back for him to edit with her help.

Against the orders of the young surgeon from Tula, Tolstoy soon went hunting again and carelessly cracked his cast. This new injury further damaged his arm, and Sonya insisted he go to Moscow for a consultation with her father's good friend, the eminent surgeon Alexander Petrovich Popov. She, of course, would have to remain at Yasnaya Polyana. He planned to take with him the entire first part of *1805*, which Sonya was rushing to finish copying. Irritated by his haste, she pointed out passages that needed polishing, but these occasional roughnesses did not disturb him. He was eager to see this new work in print.

"I am in doubt where and how to publish it," he wrote Mikhail Nikiforovich Katkov, who was the publisher and editor of the *Russian Herald*. "Of all the journals, I would most like to publish it in the Russian Herald, because it is the one journal which I take and read. The point is that I want to get as much money as possible for this work which I'm particularly fond of and which has cost me a great effort. I want to get 300 rubles a printer's sheet for publishing it in a journal (you are the first person, and probably the last, to whom I am making this offer). Otherwise, I shall publish it in separate volumes."

So with winter settling in hard on Yasnaya Polyana, Tolstoy took his leave of Sonya and, with Alexei Stepanovich, arrived in Moscow on November 20. He saw Popov and several other surgeons. Popov prescribed immediate surgery, whereas the other doctors—believing the arm now past surgical help—recommended only steam baths and massage to ease the pain.

Tolstoy held off making a decision for a week. He was terrified of being anesthetized and of surgery. While at the same time he

abhorred the thought that if he did not take the one chance offered
to him by Dr. Popov he would be deformed. Finally, almost as a
jest, he asked Tanya if she thought it would be difficult to have a
"crippled" husband.

Tanya considered the question seriously. "Frankly, to have a
husband with but one arm would be somewhat awkward and embarrassing," she replied.

"Why?" he asked.

"Not to have a man's strength, which is necessary, this would
become an affront to the husband and so eventually to the wife."

That night Tolstoy dictated a letter to Sonya: "I'd be ashamed
even to think that I might be afraid of chloroform, and the operations," he admitted. "It would be wretched to remain without the
use of my arm—not so much for myself, but honestly more for
you, especially after the conversation I had with Tanya, which
further convinced me of this." Then he added, "Katkov agreed to
all my stipulations and this has finished all the stupid haggling. But
when I emptied my briefcase . . . I became sad for the same reason
that you are angry—that I am no longer able to revise the manuscript and make it read even better."

The following day Tolstoy submitted to the operation. It was
performed in Lyubov Alexandrovna's bedroom, which had been
emptied of its furniture and thoroughly scrubbed. There were
three surgeons—Popov and two assistants—and two of the
Behrses' manservants who were to help wrench the injured arm
and break the badly set bone. Lyubov Alexandrovna, Alexei Stepanovich, and Tanya were also present in the room. Tolstoy was
seated in a large armchair, chloroform was administered, and the
procedure was begun. But Tolstoy had not been given enough
anesthesia, and as Tanya wrote:

At one moment he leaped out of the armchair, his face pale, his eyes
opened wide and looking wild, flung the bag of chloroform from him
and, delirious, cried out loudly: "My friends, we cannot live like this
. . . I think . . . I've decided . . ." He didn't finish. They sat him
down again in the armchair and added more chloroform. Now he
finally began to go under. Sitting before me was a corpse and not Lev
Nikolaevich. Suddenly his face changed terribly and he subsided.
The two servants, upon Popov's instructions, pulled on Lev Niko-

laevich's arm with all their might until the improperly set bone was broken. This was dreadful to see. . . . A fear seized me that just at this moment he might wake up. But no—while the arm was hanging lifelessly, Popov strongly and deftly pushed the bone into place. . . . Mama handed the medicines, held his head. After the bandage was placed, they started to bring Lev Nikolaevich back to consciousness. But that was almost as difficult to do as putting him to sleep. He did not come to himself for some time. When he did regain consciousness, he complained about the pain in his arm. I spent the entire evening with him. After the chloroform he had nausea and suffered from it for a long time.

The operation was a success, though for several days Tolstoy was feverish and in pain. His spirits were quickly restored with the returned use of his hand. He was able to write, though in a shaky, near-illegible script. The gaiety that had once been such an integral part of the Behrs household seemed fast to be disappearing. Dr. Behrs had been seriously ill, and he talked of nothing but his poor health and his fears for his life; Lisa kept solemnly and quietly by herself; and Tanya looked tearful a good part of the time. Tolstoy understood quite well that the world which she had once shared with Sonya "with all the poetry and folly of youth" must seem to be lost to her. The end of her affair with Sergey Nikolaevich had deeply distressed her; the news that he was planning to marry Masha soon depressed her further. For once, ice skating, new clothes, theater, and concerts did not alleviate Tanya's gloom.

All Tolstoy could think about was returning to Sonya and Yasnaya Polyana. The postman brought long daily letters from her filled with news of the children and the farm and with sound advice on his literary affairs. Within ten days of the operation he was doing research at the Chertkov and Rumyantsev libraries. Alexei Stepanovich exercised his arm two or three times a day, and he wore a sling bandage. He went for walks, read, but he was bored and wanted only that the surgeon declare that all was well. An appointment had been made with Popov for December 12, and on December 7, Tolstoy wrote, "Oh, Sonya, won't these five days hurry up and pass."

And Sonya, whose life at Yasnaya Polyana had been brightened by a brief visit from her Uncle Kostya who played the piano and filled the house with music, replied:

Music, which I have missed for so long, immediately carried me away from the atmosphere of nursery, diapers, and babies—an atmosphere that I have not been able to leave for a single minute—and brought visions of faraway places where everything is different. I cannot believe that I had silenced in myself these strings that ache and feel at the sound of music or at the sight of nature so that you could not sense them and were irritated with me. Now I can feel everything, and though it hurts me, I like it. We mothers would be better off if we never felt like this . . . I look around your study and I remember . . . how you sat at the table and wrote, how I opened the door and—afraid to disturb you—peeped inside, and how you, sensing that I was afraid, said, "Come in." That was all I wanted. I remember when you were sick how you lay on the sofa. I remember the painful nights you spent after the accident, Agatha [Mikhailovna] dozing on the floor under the dim lights, and I can never tell you how sad it makes me.

Sonya's letter made Tolstoy yearn even more to be back at Yasnaya Polyana. He became pettish and difficult. The Kremlin apartment had lost its sparkle for him. Even the Behrses' guests irritated him. When Alexander Islenyev, Sonya's grandfather from Ivitsy, whom he had always admired, came to visit, Tolstoy was deliberately cold and rude so that he would not call again. Islenyev's departure impelled Tolstoy to analyze the Behrs family in a lengthy letter to Sonya.

Alexander Mikhailovich . . . has become so loathsome to me . . . that I can't look at him impassively, and I deliberately treated him so coldly in the end that he won't call to see us. He left yesterday at 5 o'clock. All the black people in your family are nice and sympathetic. Lyubov Alexandrovna is awfully like you. The other day she was making a lampshade, just like you—once you set to work, nothing will distract you. Even your bad features are identical. I sometimes hear her confidently starting to say something she doesn't know and to make positive assertions and to exaggerate, and then I recognize you. But you are dear to me whatever you are like. I'm writing in the study, and in front of me are pictures of you at four different ages. Sonya, my darling. What a clear woman you are in everything you want to think about. For that reason I say that you are indifferent to intellectual interest, but so far from being narrow-minded, you are intelligent, very intelligent. And the same is true of all you black Behrs who are especially sympathetic to me. There are black Behrs:

Lyubov Alexandrovna, you, and Tanya; and white Behrs: all the others. The mind of the black Behrs is asleep; they can, but they don't want to; hence their self-confidence, sometimes inopportune, and their tact. But their mind is asleep because they love passionately, and because, moreover, the mother of the black Behrs, i.e., Lyubov Alexandrovna, was intellectually immature. The white Behrs show a great concern for intellectual interests, but their mind is feeble and shallow. Sasha is motley colored, half-white. Slavockha is like you, and I love him. I don't altogether like his upbringing with its entertainments and overindulgence, but he'll probably turn out a splendid fellow. Only Styopa, I'm afraid, will cause us all a lot more sorrow. He's bad in himself for some reason, and his upbringing is still worse. Yesterday, on account of an argument about a tutor in which Tanya, Petya, and Volodya took part and attacked the tutor, Lyubov Alexandrovna decided to send all of them except Petya to school. And I said: splendid, at least your conscience will be at rest. . . . I didn't say why you're a clever woman. As a good wife, you think about your husband as you do about yourself, and I remember your saying to me that all the military and historical side over which I'm taking such pains will turn out badly, but the rest—the family life, the characters, the psychology—will be good. That couldn't be more true. I remember how you said that to me, and I remember you just like that. And like Tanya, I feel like crying out: Mama, I want to go to Yasnaya, I want Sonya. I started writing to you in low spirits, but I'm finishing as quite a different person. My dear heart. Only love me as I love you, and nothing else counts for me and everything is fine. Goodbye; it's time to get on with my work.

Sonya had won her place in her husband's life and in history. For a number of years to come Tolstoy would depend upon her entirely not only for his well-being but also for his inspiration and for the physical and emotional freedom to work almost totally unencumbered. Her jealousies were buried for the time. The novel *1805* was her only competitor for her husband's devotion, and she felt she was an integral part of its development, almost as though it were a child of theirs whom, in this instance, he was mothering.

PART THREE
1865-1877

A Habit of Loving

*He often says that this is not really love, but merely a
habit, and that we couldn't do without each other now.
And yet I still love him in the same restless, passionate,
jealous, and poetic way . . .*

COUNTESS TOLSTOY

10

It was early November 1864, and Sonya sat before a freshly kindled fire in the parlor of Yasnaya Polyana. Dawn was breaking, and except for a few of the household servants everyone was still asleep. The heavy winter snows were late in coming, and the roads remained easily passable. Her husband was to arrive that day, and nothing should delay him.

Before she started her day's work, she had a few moments for quiet reflection. Seryozha and the new baby, whom they affectionately called Tanya, were her greatest happiness, and yet when she was with them she stopped feeling *young*, feeling instead simply happy and serene.

Her Uncle Kostya had sent some sketches to illustrate how the house could be renovated fairly inexpensively. There was a clever plan for a new salon and a larger study for Lev Nikolaevich which had particularly interested her. If *1805* met with critical acclaim and commercial success, she could have the work done and buy new furniture as well. The book would succeed, of course. No matter what other doubts she had about herself, she was confident that she had not misjudged her husband's work and that the first thirty-eight chapters of *1805* were brilliant. To her relief, she was well again and not pregnant. It dismayed her to consider how many months of her marriage she had spent in that condition. As she looked at her small plump hands, she wondered if she was still desirable. She had gained weight with each of the children, and the twenty-inch waist she had been so proud of had thickened. Marya Nikolaevna's two girls, who were making one of their frequent visits, went laughing and rushing from room to room, their youthful exuberance undamped by the recent death of their father. Lisa, the older girl, was fifteen, only six years younger than she, but Sonya felt that decades rather than years separated them.

It was, of course, true that only two years before she would never have worn the practical gray wool dresses she wore now. And while she might not have Lisa's dazzling freshness, her skin was still clear and white, her dark hair and eyes shone, and when she smiled her dimple gave her handsome features a charming piquancy. She remained strikingly attractive. Yes, her new maturity suited her well; her fuller bosom was more womanly and her new self-assurance becoming. But she did miss the carefreeness of her girlhood.

By noon the sky was filled with dark fast-moving clouds. A driving wind had risen, lashing boughs about and stripping them of their last dry leaves. A violent storm was brewing, and Tolstoy was still on the road from Tula to Yasnaya Polyana. Sonya peered through the window, hoping to glimpse a carriage on the drive to the house. Instead she saw Lisa and Varya, running with great difficulty against the sharp wind. Headed toward the house and safety, they clutched their hats while the wind whipped their skirts about their legs. As they reached the porch, a great bolt of lightning flashed across the sky. There was the crash of a tree falling, and Sonya ran out on the porch. Putting her arms about the girls' shoulders, she guided them inside.

Ever since Tolstoy's accident Sonya had been tormented by the fear that he might die. And now she was caught up in an unspeakable terror. For hours she walked from room to room trying to see through the heavy curtain of torrential rain, listening for the sounds of carriage wheels, and able to do nothing more than to utter what seemed to her "senseless prayers." Finally the rain stopped, but an angry wind still swept heavy clouds across the soot-gray sky. At last, late in the afternoon, Tolstoy arrived, dry, unscathed, but exhausted. The storm had tossed his carriage about and his injured arm had been painfully bruised.

"The Count has grown old," Dunyasha whispered to Sonya as he lowered himself slowly and with a deep sigh into his favorite chair in the sitting room. Alexei Stepanovich helped him off with his boots. The brass samovar was steaming, and everyone in the house gathered around Tolstoy. After he had answered all their questions about his own health and that of Dr. Behrs and Tanya, he told them that just before leaving Moscow he had read part of his novel aloud at the home of Basil Perfilyev. His audience, which included Tanya and Lisa, had been amused by the description of Anna Pavlovna's evening party and had commented that the Rostov family were all quite real to them. Tanya proclaimed that Vera was Lisa to the life, and although disconcerted by how closely Natasha resembled herself, she laughed merrily when her favorite childhood doll, Mimi, popped up in the story. Tanya also had remarked that the character Boris resembled Polivanov in both his appearance and his behavior.

When he told the group at the Perfilyevs' that the first installment would appear within the month, someone observed that he had given them a diversion for the winter—everyone would be busy trying to discover the real-life counterparts of each and every one of his characters. This remark irritated him greatly. "I would be ashamed to be published if all my work consisted of copying a portrait, trying to find things out, and memorizing things," he later stated.

He told them how Tanya had been his "scribe" in Moscow, how she had nursed and waited on him, how sad she looked when she waved goodbye to him from the porch of the Behrs house.

Before retiring that night, Sonya wrote her sister: "You can't imagine, Tanya, how once again I feel happy and content. Yet when I tell you this, I must think, And what of poor Tanya? What is to be done, darling? I would so like to give you happiness, but where can I get it for you?"

Tolstoy added in postscript, "I wanted to add something, but I have read Sonya's sleepy letter and there is nothing more to say. She has the knack of loving so warmly and simply and of saying it better than I ever could. . . . Write more frequently to us, darling. Everything concerning you is of interest to me. . . . What about your heartbreak, is it any better? Try to conceal it, Tanya. Play Chopin and sing. Keep hold of yourself, so that if either happiness or sadness comes to you, you will be able to face either bravely."

But Tanya was not bearing up well, and Lyubov Alexandrovna wrote that her emotional and physical state had declined since Tolstoy's departure. She had grown thinner and paler and was irritable, bitter, and envious. Nothing—not even the gayest holiday parties—and no one could lure her from the house. She spent every evening in her room with her personal maid, Feodora, listening drowsily by the light of the icon lamps to the former serf's tales of country life.

The holidays at Yasnaya Polyana were filled with children's games and family parties arranged by Lisa and Varya. There was a big tree in the room off the dining room, and Tolstoy had brought presents from Moscow for everyone. But once the festivities had passed, all thoughts turned to the publication of *1805*.

The first part was to appear in the late January and mid-February (1865) editions of the *Russian Herald*. Tolstoy had never been so apprehensive about a publication before. He was completing the second part of the book (which was approximately the same length as the first) and driving both himself and Sonya to get the work done before the first installment appeared. In addition to his work on the second part, Tolstoy labored during the Christmas season on an introduction to the book, giving Sonya three drafts to copy before he was satisfied. Tolstoy wanted his readers to understand that although the book was "more similar to a novel or a tale than to anything else," it was not a novel because he could not and did not know "how to confine the characters . . . within given limits . . ."

He wrote anxiously to many whose criticism he respected, asking for a "frank opinion" when the work was published. In a letter to Fet he said:

> In a few days the first half of the first part of *1805* will be out. Please write and tell me your opinion in detail. I value your opinion and that of a man I dislike all the more the older I get, Turgenev. He *will understand*.
>
> What I have published in the past I consider a mere trial of pen, a rough draft. What I am publishing now, although I like it more than my previous work, still seems weak—as an introduction is bound to be. But what's to follow will be—tremendous!!! Write and tell me what they say about it in the various places you know and particularly its effect on the masses.

And to his cousin Alexandra he wrote, "In a day or two, the first part of my novel *1805* is coming out. I should like you to love these children of mine. There are marvelous people in it. I love them very much!"

Tolstoy's arm did not mend as quickly as he had hoped, and the bone-chilling weather that set in soon after he arrived home made his recovery slow and painful. He seemed, as well, to have forgotten his social ideals, for he wrote a sharp letter to the governor of the Tula district demanding that action be taken against the peasants who were stealing his livestock and stored grain and hay. And on an overnight tour of his properties he wrote to Sonya telling her that he had stayed the night "in the hut of a dear Russian peasant," and remarking, "What swine and sluts they are!"

The proofs of *1805* arrived. When Tolstoy finished with them, they were black with corrections and could not be returned until Sonya disentangled the maze of nearly illegible lines, words, balloons, and arrows and copied his corrections onto a fresh set. She sat up until nearly dawn for several nights and, exhausted, finally placed them on Tolstoy's desk for a last look before she mailed them back to Katkov.

That afternoon Tolstoy returned them to her, covered once again with almost indecipherable corrections and the apology, "Sonya darling, excuse me; again I have spoiled your work. I will never do it again. We will send them off tomorrow."

Again she copied his changes onto a fresh set of proofs, and at last they were sent back to Moscow. Now only the agony of waiting for the first reviews remained.

The newspaper the *Invalid* published the first critique of *1805*. The anonymous author praised the war scenes, quoting some of them in their entirety and ended: "The characters created by Count Tolstoy are timeless; they deeply impress themselves on one's memory, and one will recall them not only with a year but much later."

But Turgenev wrote Fet that the first section of the book was "poor, tedious, and unsuccessful." When told of this assessment, Tolstoy was extremely upset.

Sonya's brother Sasha was on leave in late February and visited Yasnaya Polyana. Tolstoy had based some of the episodes involving young soldiers on stories Sasha had told him of his own exploits in the army. One "fictional" incident described an actual event so closely that Tolstoy had written Sasha for permission (which was granted) to include it in the book. Sasha, therefore, like all the family, was deeply interested in the response by the press and public to the book. Tolstoy rose early on the day the second installment was due to arrive by post in Tula. Still in his nightshirt, he went to Sasha's room and asked him to go into Tula to pick it up for him. The murky predawn darkness was bitterly cold and Sasha was reluctant to leave his warm, comfortable bed. "You wish to be a general of infantry?" Tolstoy shouted impatiently. "Yes? Well, I wish to be a general of literature! Go at once and bring me the paper!"

Sasha did as he was ordered.

There were a great number of favorable reviews of the two installments. But there were reproaches too, especially from the liberal intellectuals, who smarted because they had not been included in his vast social canvas. Tolstoy was also taken to task for historical inaccuracies, for using too much French, and for many other things. And Turgenev in a letter to Fet (forwarded to Tolstoy) wrote, "The second part of *1805* is weak, it's all shallow and contrived, and don't these endless, endless discussions about am I or am I not a coward bore Tolstoy? All this is battle-morbidity. Where in it are the traits of the times? Where the historic colors? The character of Denisov is dashingly drawn, it would be fine as a pattern against a background, but there is no background."

It was a rainy March, but spring finally showed its fresh green face. Ironically with its gay appearance came the sad news that Sergey Nikolaevich's new baby had died. The death of the Gypsy woman's child had a dramatic effect on life at the Tolstoys'. Sergey Nikolaevich again turned his attentions to Tanya, wavering in his resolution to marry Masha; and Tanya, with reborn hope, planned to return to Yasnaya Polyana. But while Tanya was arranging for her journey from Moscow, Tolstoy was thinking of the advantages Moscow held for him. There he would be close to his publisher and to the libraries he needed for his research. Certain the third part of the book would be complete by the fall, he began talking about spending the next winter there.

"He will probably be happier in Moscow," Sonya had written in her diary on February 25, "and I shall pretend that I also want to be there. I have never admitted to him that unconsciously, in order to rise in his estimation, one can be a hypocrite even with one's husband. I did not tell him that, for I am petty and vain, and even envious of people. But I shall be ashamed in Moscow not to have a carriage and a pair, with a footman in livery, and fine dresses and fine house, and everything in general. Lyova is extraordinary —he simply doesn't care about such things. It's a result of his wisdom and virtue."

Tolstoy, however, was more conscious of his relative poverty than she realized, and he was keenly aware of his responsibilities toward his growing family. And while he was extremely grateful for all the work Sonya had done for him, he resented his dependence on her. His frustration and irritation were heightened by the few negative reviews *1805* received; and following a well-established pattern, he vented his anger on her. Once again he was cold to her in bed.

Baffled by his rejection and wounded by his sarcastic and sometimes cruel comments, Sonya was mired in self-abasing speculation.

I can feel that he is strength and life itself [she wrote in her diary on March 6], while I, I am only a worm crawling and feeding on him. I am afraid of being weak . . . and I'm ashamed of it. The last cut I received from Lyova is still hurting me . . . what if his affection never again returns? . . . This evening everything seemed so strange. He went out, and I stayed here, and everything around me was silent. The children are fast asleep. The rooms upstairs are so fresh and clean and empty . . . I am almost frightened of the sound of my footsteps and I am even afraid to breathe. Lyova came in for a moment and everything at once became cheerful and bright. He seemed to bring in with him the smell of fresh air, and to me he seems like fresh air itself.

Two days later she wrote:

Lyova is cheerful, though he is still cold and indifferent to me. I'm afraid to say he *doesn't love me*, but the thought of it keeps torturing me, and my hesitation makes me shy in his presence. . . . I began to wonder whether he was seeing A[xinia]. This thought kept tormenting me all day long . . . I cannot help thinking of it each time Lyova is cold to me, or I am in a bad mood. But what if he were suddenly to come back and tell me . . . but no, this is frightful non-sense, I'm ashamed of it, and ought to confess this evil thought which, though only in a dim, vague manner, has come into my mind.

And the next day she made this entry: "Lyova is killing me with his indifference and lack of interest. He only expects me to be interested in all he does, as if he didn't know how much I love it all . . . Lyova is out shooting, while I have been busy copying all morning . . . I am afraid of Lyova. He has begun to notice all my bad points. I'm coming to believe that there is very little good in me."

On March 10 she was in a state of confusion. "Lyova is becoming more affectionate. He kissed me today and that hasn't happened for a long time. But it was all poisoned by the thought that he hasn't l[aid] me for such a long time. I do a great deal of copying for him, and am glad to be of use to him in some way."

On March 15 she wrote, "The sun came out for a moment and it affected me as much as a waltz affects a girl of sixteen. I am longing for the spring and the summer and country walks. I haven't had any letters from the family for a long time. I wonder how my pretty, poetic Tanya is? My relations with Lyova are good and simple, he says he has been greatly dissatisfied with himself these days. I love him terribly."

Letters finally arrived from Moscow, and Sonya gleefully reported, "I got a letter from Tanya yesterday, which came with her luggage. I am so glad to think of seeing her so soon, and it was like meeting old friends to come across some of my old girlish dresses among her things."

But the weeks before Tanya came proved to be most trying. Sonya suffered from a series of migraine headaches, and both children fell ill with chronic diarrhea. Since Sergey Nikolaevich's child had died from complications caused by this illness, Sonya was beside herself with concern. Both she and the children recovered quickly, but this crisis further strained her relations with Tolstoy. She was unable to tell him what was in her heart, but she did talk to Sergey Nikolaevich, who also confided in her and smilingly told her, "There is nothing good in the world except love and the moon, and music, and the nightingales."

On March 26, musing over a conversation with Sergey Niko-

laevich, she wrote in her diary, "Lyova likes a lovely, poetic existence; there must be so much fine poetry in him which he keeps all
to himself. That has taught me also to have a separate little life of
my own. I can hear him writing something; it must be his diary
too. I hardly ever read it nowadays, for if you know that anyone is
going to read your diary you stop being sincere in what you write.
. . . He also writes down the new ideas for his novel—it is all so
clear, and my empty-headedness always terrifies me when I am
with him."

Tolstoy's irascibility was caused in large part by the slow
progress he felt he was making on the third part of his book. On
March 2 he wrote in his diary, "I write, I revise. It is all clear, but
the amount of work ahead frightens me." On the nineteenth he
considered putting aside *1805* to begin another novel—"a psychological history of Alexander and Napoleon"—but nothing came of
this new project. And on the twenty-eighth he confessed, "The
writing is going badly."

Tanya arrived on April 17 and brought with her the old
gaiety. The lime avenues of the garden were turning softly green;
the cuckoos called and the songbirds trilled. Only the nightingale
was still silent. Spring was everywhere. The gardener, Kuzma,
planted flowers and watched over the apricot and cherry trees in
the hothouse. Sonya had the garden cleared of dead stumps and
fallen limbs, ignoring Tolstoy's grumbled question "What was the
matter with it before?" The straggly shrubs were pruned, and the
benches near the lindens were painted.

Marya Nikolaevna and her two daughters (who had been in
Pokrovskoye since the holidays) arrived. The Dmitry Dyakovs, Fet
and his wife, and Sergey Nikolaevich were frequent visitors. And
the Gorchakov princesses—two cousins of Tolstoy's who were in
their late twenties—visited with their despotic old mother.

Yasnaya Polyana was filled with laughter and animated conversation and a sense of hope. Dora had four pups and the "family"
was kept in Agatha Mikhailovna's grimy quarters, where Tanya
and Varya and Lisa came to see them. Cobwebs studded with flies
hung in every corner of the old woman's room, and red cockroaches
scurried across the walls. Milk had been spilled by the pillow where
Dora lay, and Agatha Mikhailovna had left it for the mice. An

image of St. Nicholas the Miraculous hung in the corner, its face toward the wall. Thinking it had been put up that way accidentally, Varya was about to change it when Agatha Mikhailovna cried, "Don't touch it, don't touch it, dearie. I did that on purpose. I prayed and prayed to him and nothing happened. So I turned him face about. Let him hang so for a while!"

The girls laughed along with Agatha Mikhailovna. Laughter and cheerfulness had returned to Yasnaya Polyana, and the light-hearted atmosphere was a tonic for Sonya. Her darker emotions were not completely calmed, however, and she had her first serious quarrel with Tanya—"for poking her nose too much into Lyova's life." Tanya had accompanied Tolstoy to Nikolskoye, and the two of them often went shooting, riding, and walking together. Though Sonya allowed her to ride Belogubka on these excursions, her jealousy flared occasionally, and on May 3 she wrote, "The two of them have gone together to the wood. I get the strangest ideas into my head."

Tanya's coquetry was a constant irritant to Sonya; and though the sisters did not have a confrontation, the tension between them eased when on June 9 it was finally settled that Tanya and Sergey Nikolaevich would be married in twenty days at Nikolskoye. The entire household was to go to Nikolskoye for the wedding and then stay on for the summer months. Sonya was elated as they packed to leave and she put her pettishness and jealousies behind her for a time. Dressed in her sheer summer dresses, she felt young and vigorous and showed new signs of independence. Without asking his approval, she replaced Tolstoy's hard leather pillow with a silk-covered down one. He grumbled about it the first night he used it but never mentioned it again.

During the twelve days after Tanya and Sergey Nikolaevich had become betrothed, there were constant shifts in the plans for the wedding and for their future. At first Sergey Nikolaevich had been eager for a short engagement; but the day after Tanya accepted his proposal, he backed off, saying, "Just wait a little, wait a little." It was obvious to Sonya that he was toying with her sister, and she found his behavior "revolting." But Tanya, though suffering from chest spasms and breathing difficulties as well as from her fiancé's changes of heart, remained loving and loyal to him until, on the twelfth day, he confessed to her that if they married he could not give up Masha.

Tanya broke off the engagement and fell into a terrible inertia. Her health declined, and it seemed that consumption was about to envelop her like a black widow's shawl.

Sonya was furious at Sergey Nikolaevich, who she believed had deceived Tanya and "behaved like a perfect cad." "My anger at Seryozha is boundless," she wrote in her diary after Tanya had ended the engagement, "and if ever I have a chance of revenge I shall take it . . . he talked the usual platitudes, building up plans for the future and what not—an utter cad. . . . Tanya's attitude to the whole affair was very noble. She loved him very much, while he only pretended. The Gypsy woman was dearer to him. But Masha is a good woman; I feel sorry for her."

It was decided that it would be best for Tanya if they all went to Nikolskoye as planned. This estate, which was in the Chern district of Tula province (about sixty miles from Yasnaya Polyana), had belonged to Tolstoy's great-grandmother Gorchakov and had come to him at his brother Nikolai's death. It was a poor estate, and for several years Tolstoy had labored with great financial sacrifice to keep it afloat. He now had a bailiff he trusted, a man named Orlov, who was just but exacting with the peasants, and who had made great improvements to the property. These gains, however, were threatened by a disastrous drought that had afflicted Tula province since the early spring. The first crops had failed, and Tolstoy had written Fet that he feared "the evil devil famine [was] already at work." But despite the desolation of the drought-stricken countryside, Nikolskoye seemed a perfect haven for a young girl with weak lungs and a broken heart. Although the house was small, it was well situated on a hill and looked out over a river and a forest to some distant villages. A cool breeze from the river always played through its rooms, easing the hot dry summer heat.

The Tolstoy family set off for Nikolskoye on little Seryozha's second birthday (June 28) in two carriages followed by baggage carts, the servants seated on top of crates. Tanya, the two children, and Marya Afanasyevna Arbuzova traveled in the coach, Sonya and Lev Nikolaevich in the calash. (At the last moment Aunt Toinette and Natalya Petrovna had decided to stay behind.) They paused several times during the day to rest and water the horses, and as the sun was setting they took lodgings for the night. Early the next morning they were once more on the road. The trip, partly on the highway and partly on a byroad, was arduous. And once they reached Chern, only a few miles from Nikolskoye, they encountered appalling poverty. The houses in the small villages were no more than hovels. Still, in the midst of the frightful squalor, the peasants were dressed in brightly embroidered homespun tunics, and the women had linen petticoats beneath their old-fashioned hand-woven dresses and wore ribbons in place of earrings in their ears.

The family arrived exhausted by the journey; but the beauty of Nikolskoye, set in hilly country with thick forests and deep ravines, quickly revived them. Tolstoy immediately drove to his sister's estate at Pokrovskoye, which was only a few miles away. Sergey Nikolaevich was visiting her, and he and Tolstoy had an unpleasant conversation. Their meeting ended so badly that Tolstoy later wrote to Dr. Behrs, "I saw him and I think it was for the last time. He has gone to Tula now. . . . The matter is completely closed. And however painful it is for Tanya and indeed for all of us, I cannot help but feel a stealthy joy at the bottom of my heart that by undergoing this lesser misfortune we've been spared a greater one."

They had come to a vacant, dirty house; and within three days Sonya had everything clean and the household machinery set in motion. There was food and drink for everyone, the samovar was polished to a golden sheen and sat gurgling on the table, and she had somehow found room in the already overcrowded house for their first visitors, Afanasy Afanasyevich Fet and his young wife, Marya Petrovna. Tolstoy and Fet shared not only their passionate involvement in literature but also an interest in what Tolstoy called "the poetry of agriculture." Fet, however, was a far more practical man and regarded farming almost exclusively as a business. He was a fervent admirer of Tolstoy's work; and although Tolstoy held most poets in low esteem, he considered many of Fet's poems masterly.

Sonya liked Fet, who was always exquisitely courteous to her, and she was glad to have a new person in the house who could distract Tanya. Fet's wife, though pleasant and gentle, was a shy young woman who treated her husband with reverential solicitude.

He was politely attentive to her, but rumor had it that on his part the marriage had been one of convenience. Marya Petrovna was a wealthy heiress, and Fet had been a poor and practical man.

The Dyakovs and Marya Nikolaevna and her daughters came by, as did a neighbor, Volkov, a timid fair-haired little man who took a great interest in the languishing Tanya. The days at Nikolskoye were filled with walks, rides, games and other summer amusements. The Upa flowed at the foot of the hill in front of the house, and swimming in its gentle currents was one of Sonya's favorite pastimes. Although there were no bathing huts in which to change, Sonya and Tanya swam in the river daily. One day two young peasants happened by and laughingly threatened to carry off the outer clothes the sisters had hung on nearby tree branches.

"Please go away," Sonya said firmly, only her head visible above water.

The men laughed louder.

"Lyovochka!" Sonya screamed, and as if by some miracle, Tolstoy appeared in the distance. He raced down and caught one of the men; picking up a stout stick, he beat him with it before ordering him off the estate.

In the evenings Tolstoy read aloud from his latest chapters of *1805*, appreciating Fet's praise perhaps more than anyone else's. Tanya's health had improved, but rarely did she sing or play the guitar. Silent, meek, and dejected, she seemed to be living in her memories. "Only a new love can supplant this love from her heart," Tolstoy wrote Dr. Behrs on July 7. "But how and when it will come, God alone knows."

Although the summer was sultry and the drought in the region severe, the Tolstoys enjoyed their stay at Nikolskoye. They returned home on October 12 without Tanya, who had gone to spend the winter with the Dyakovs on their estate. The Tolstoys had planned to go to Moscow before the holidays, but because Aunt Toinette was ill, their trip was postponed until after Christmas. Thoughts of the journey filled Sonya with great anticipation. They intended to visit her parents and leave the children with them before they went on to St. Petersburg. Even though she knew she would finally come face to face with Alexandra Tolstoy—a meeting she very much feared—Sonya's excitement ran high.

Tolstoy was most perceptive when he wrote Alexandra on

November 14: "She [Sonya] is prepared to love you, but feels a little perplexed about you; as she herself says, you interest her greatly, as no other woman has ever interested her, but at the same time, I'm sure, she feels in her soul . . . a feeling of slight hostility such as we always have toward people whom we don't know, and whom everyone, beginning with one's husband, praises beyond measure. She can't see with her husband's eyes, since a good wife sees everything with her husband's eyes except women."

Tanya's distressing affair and her own often difficult marriage had wrought great changes in Sonya's attitudes and emotions. She now held herself in higher regard. On October 26, 1865, she wrote in her diary, "It is cheerful to take up the diary again, probably because I love myself and the whole life within me." Tolstoy's coldness no longer drove her to tears or despair, but she could not dispel the core of hostility toward him that was hardening inside her. She wanted to stop nursing the baby and found little joy in the discovery that she was once again pregnant.

Tolstoy's nieces, Varya and Lisa, were at Yasnaya Polyana for Christmas, but the holiday celebrations were dimmed by the family's concern over Tanya. Dolly (Darya Alexandrovna) Dyakov, with whom she was staying, had become gravely ill, and the somber atmosphere of the Dyakov household had plunged Tanya deeper into melancholy. Her own health was poor; she was dangerously thin and brought up blood when she coughed.

Sonya and Tolstoy wrote, urging Tanya to come for the New Year. They waited impatiently for two days for her reply. Finally, after dinner on the thirty-first—only hours before the new year was to be rung in—Tanya's letter refusing their invitation arrived. Tolstoy wrote to his sister-in-law the next day:

> I felt like a thirteen-year-old. And I wanted you to come so terribly that for . . . two days I wasn't able to do anything or think of anything except you. And every minute I would run up to the window and trick the girls [Varya and Lisa] by saying, "They're coming! They're coming!" but it was always in vain. Then when your letter came, I felt as if some misfortune had overtaken us, or perhaps it was some misdeed on my part which poisoned and is now poisoning every pleasure. Both Sonya and I were so overcome with grief that we sat down right there (in Auntie's room) and fell asleep.

The Tolstoys finally took matters into their own hands. Lev Nikolaevich went to Cheremoshnya, the Dyakovs' home, and brought Tanya back to Yasnaya; and then, with Sonya, the two children, Marya Afanasyevna, Dunyasha, and Alexei Stepanovich, they set off for Moscow. The large party formed a sort of caravan —Sonya and Tolstoy in a sleigh, the rest of the family in a carriage, and the servants and the baggage in a wagon. The road was rutted and icy, and at every stop Tolstoy would hurry back to the carriage and anxiously ask Tanya, "Is it too rough for you? Did you cough?"

"I'm fine," she would reply, "but is Sonya bearing it well?"

"She can stand the road all right," he would assure her.

The stay in Moscow was not as happy as Sonya had anticipated. When they arrived at the Behrses' they found that Polivanov was a guest. He glowed with good health and looked larger and more manly than when the Tolstoys had last seen him; there was new strength in his grasp as the two men greeted each other. Polivanov spoke heatedly and intelligently on subjects that would not have interested him before, and he was not shy in contesting Tolstoy's opinions. Jealous without cause, Tolstoy accused Sonya of flirting with her former suitor and insisted they move from the warm, lively Behrs household to a stuffy six-room apartment on Dmitrovka Street, which they rented furnished for 150 rubles a month—"heat, samovar, water, dishes—everything included."

Sonya was deeply unsettled by her husband's response to Polivanov's small attentions. "Lyova really judged me a little too harshly in that matter. But at any rate it shows that he treasures me. . . . Still, I am terrified of every new *cut*. I have to humble myself all the time, which always means a loss in that pleasant sense of pride and dignity without which I could not live."

Once these domestic upsets were settled, Sonya began to enjoy her visit. They decided that because of her condition they would not go to St. Petersburg. This disappointment was soon forgotten in the whirl of Moscow life. Sonya attended many concerts and saw all her old friends, and for the first time she felt comfortable with some members of her husband's circle. Tolstoy took sculpting classes; in the evenings he worked at modeling— first a red horse and then a bust of her. They grew closer during these weeks and talked together freely and at length, often discussing *1805* and his continuing work on it. The third part was complete, but Tolstoy had decided not to publish any more of the work until a further six parts had been written. His original plans to write the book as a family novel with historical background had long been abandoned. Now he conceived of it as a sweeping work, the concentration on war, and the elaborate philosophy of history as the final scheme.

They remained in Moscow for more than two months and returned to Yasnaya Polyana in the early spring. The Voronka was still frozen, and high banks of snow lined the narrow road. Sonya was large with child, but she was uncommonly happy; she felt that her husband loved her deeply and compassionately and that they shared a great communion through his work.

On May 22, 1866, just as the first big thaw was warming the air, Sonya gave birth, four weeks prematurely, to a son whom they named Ilya. She put the child to her breast with great pain. The fissures which had been so agonizing when she breast-fed Seryozha had reopened. Desperately she worked to overcome the condition with ointments and salves; in the end she resigned herself to bear the pain. With two small children and an infant at the breast, she found she could not both keep the estate's books and continue to copy her husband's work. Therefore a new bailiff, Ivanov, was hired and the farm's accounts became his responsibility. The man arrived with his handsome young wife, Marya Ivanova. Extremely intelligent, she was a rather rabid nihilist, and Tolstoy began to seek her out and engage her in "long, lively talks on literature and politics." He often brought her back to the house, where he laughed with her, argued with her, and flattered her. Surrounded by demanding children, Sonya looked on, painfully aware that the eighteen-year-old Marya Ivanova had a twenty-inch waist, and that a youthful glow of promise still shone on her pretty face.

11

On the morning of April 4, 1866, while taking his daily walk in the Winter Garden, the Tsar was fired at. He was saved by the quick action of a muzhik, Osip Komissarov, who noticed the would-be assassin, a slightly unbalanced youth named Dmitry Karakozov, standing among a curious crowd hoping to catch a glimpse of the Tsar. A glint in the early sun caught Komissarov's eye, and as the assailant raised his gun the muzhik leaped at him and struck his arm aside. The shot went wide, and the Tsar's officers placed Karakozov under arrest.

For weeks churches were crowded with Russians giving fervent thanks for Alexander's deliverance; theater performances were begun by the strains of "God Save the Tsar." Construction of a chapel—paid for by public donation—was started on the ground where the Tsar had escaped death; when it was completed, the words "Touch Not Mine Anointed" were inscribed over its entrance. Komissarov was ennobled by the grateful Alexander and, acclaimed a hero, he was entertained by the nobility in the select English Club.

Throughout Russia there was "an overwhelming demonstration of traditional monarchist sentiment." However, Karakozov's attempted assassination indicated that there were individuals who were determined to overthrow the monarchy at any cost and by any means. Karakozov might well have been deranged, but he belonged to a noble family and had been expelled from Kazan University for having been a member of a secret group believed to be revolutionaries. The young man was hanged with thirty-four other young rebels, most of whom were condemned on insubstantial evidence of alleged associations with secret groups.

The nihilism that the fiery Marya Ivanova supported—the

revolt of the individual against superstitions, prejudices, habits, and customs which his or her own reason could not justify—began to spread. Heated discussions with Tolstoy centered on the confusion of nihilism with terrorism, a misapprehension Marya Ivanova deemed as egregious as terming stoicism or positivism a political movement. Marya Ivanova was also an agnostic who bitterly attacked the hypocrisy of the Church. She was repelled by the strictures of social etiquette and refused to smile or talk to anyone she was not genuinely pleased to greet. Many of her arguments with Tolstoy were usually about "art for art's sake." Marya Ivanova dismissed the value of objects of art—for art, she felt, was bought with money extorted from the starving peasantry or from underpaid workers. These theories were the beginnings of Tolstoy's own later philosophies. His bailiff's young wife had stirred something that had been dormant in his mind for many years.

It was understandable that Tolstoy should be attracted to this well-educated, good-looking young woman who had run away from an affluent family in order to free herself not only from the domestic yoke but also from the possible yoke of a husband. Paradoxically, however, she married soon after leaving her family, an act Marya Ivanova was able to rationalize by her husband's accord on most of her intellectual arguments. Jealous as she was of Marya Ivanova, Sonya was also fascinated by her. She listened intently when the young woman talked about not wanting children and about choosing to live in a small village like that of Yasnaya Polyana's peasants so that she could partake of the "people's life." These were sentiments she had never heard a woman voice before. The truth was, Sonya did entertain many of Marya Ivanova's opinions on woman's "serfdom" and her indenture to her husband. She also did not agree with the concept that a woman must bow to her husband's sexual wishes.

Some of Sonya's fretfulness at this time was caused by the pain she experienced in nursing the new baby, but a more important reason for her ill temper, her sense of being poorly used and neglected, was the fact that she and Tolstoy still slept in separate rooms. This choice had been his, not hers, and his rejection rankled. With little regard for his young wife's physical or emotional state, he had begun to turn his attention toward Marya Ivanova only six weeks after Sonya had given birth. He invited her to the house so often that she became part of the family circle, an action quite without precedent at Yasnaya Polyana. The vital presence of the youthful, slim, and beautiful Marya Ivanova made the still swollen Sonya immensely unhappy. A nursing mother suffering from tormenting fissures, she was married to a sensual man who refused on moral grounds to sleep with her while she had an infant at the breasts, and who would not share a room with her lest he be tempted to have relations with her. She was only twenty-two, but Sonya, with the responsibility of three children and a large household, felt like an aging hausfrau.

Retreating to her diary on July 19 she wrote, "Lyova is wrong to treat Marya Ivanova to such long speeches. It is nearly one o'clock, but I can't sleep. I just feel as if that nihilist woman is going to be my *bete noire.*"

And three days later:

This morning Lyova made some excuse for going to *that* house. So M[arya] I[vanova] told me, and she also said that he had talked to her below her balcony. What was the need of going there in the rain? It's quite obvious that he likes her, and the thought of it drives me insane. This jealousy will kill me. He is extremely cold to me. My breasts are very sore and it is real agony to nurse the child. I called in Marfusha [a wet nurse from the village] today and made her feed the child, so that my breasts might have a rest. My suffering always seems to make him treat me badly; he always grows cold, and that adds mental agony to my physical pain. I remain locked up in my own room, while she sits in the drawing room with the children. I simply can't bear her; it annoys me to see her beauty and vivaciousness, especially when Lyova is there.

That Tolstoy gave her good reason for her jealousy is evident in her entry for July 24:

Lyova went again to that house, and said afterwards that the "poor woman" found life very dull. Then he asked me why I hadn't invited them to dinner. If only I could forbid her to come into the house at all, I would gladly do it. My dear Lyova! Can't you see how easily you get caught! The pain in my breasts takes up much of my time and happiness. . . . Goodness only knows when my breasts will heal; everything seems to be all wrong. My heart leaps with joy when

I see Lyova dissatisfied with the farm work. Maybe he'll dismiss the factor, and then I'll get rid of this dreadful feeling of jealousy. I'd be sorry for him, but I cannot bear her.

By early August Sonya's distress had vanished. The fissures on her breasts had healed; all three children were happy and well. Tolstoy was back at work on his book, and she was again copying for him. Her heart lifted because she knew that, once intent on his work, her husband would have no time for flirtations, however innocent.

Tolstoy confessed that he was now writing "under the best possible circumstances," and Sonya was ecstatically happy to be working with him, and to have his attention absorbed only by fictional characters. The household was content as well. Tanya Behrs seemed to be in much better spirits; she had regained some of her lost weight, coughed less frequently, and often took long walks with Varya and Lisa Tolstoy. Little Seryozha was walking and talking; small rosy Tanya, now crawling, laughed constantly; and the baby, whom they fondly called Ilyusha, was over the fretfulness that had been caused by Sonya's breast-feeding problems.

A party was planned for Sonya's name day, September 17—the feast day of the Blessed Martyrs: Vera (Faith), Nadezhda (Hope), and Lyubov (Charity), and their mother, Sofya (Wisdom). A holiday mood prevailed, and all the women in the household dressed themselves elegantly in white summery dresses with bright ribbons on their shoulders and at their waists. It was a day of brilliant sunshine, and Sonya had a festive table bedecked with cheery garden flowers set on the terrace for dinner. It was rather a large gathering, as their neighbors, the Markovs; the Dyakovs; and Sonya's relatives from Ivitsy and Tula had joined in the celebration. There were giggles among the girls, whispered secrets from one guest to the other. It was obvious that a surprise was being planned, but no one would tell Sonya what it was.

After the guests had assembled on the terrace, at exactly five P.M. Tolstoy insisted that everyone be seated. Suddenly from the garden an orchestra, hidden by trees and bushes, struck up the overture from Sonya's favorite opera, *La Muette de Portici*. Sonya beamed, and her eyes filled with loving tenderness as she looked at her husband. All the tensions of the past seemed to melt away.

After dinner there was dancing on the terrace, and a group of young officers from a regiment stationed nearby arrived to join in. When the band struck up, almost everyone took the floor. Only the two old aunties and Dolly Dyakov (who was ailing) remained seated in their garden chairs, but even they kept a joyous hand-clapping rhythm to the music. Sonya danced the waltzes and the polkas and the quadrille, her step light and graceful. When Tolstoy announced that the next dance would be the intricate quick-stepping *kamarinskaya*, Sonya and all her guests deserted the floor, too timid to participate in such a fiery dance.

"Go ahead, dance!" Tolstoy called out as he signaled the orchestra to play louder and faster. He went up to one of the young officers and insisted, "Come now!"

The man stepped forward and stopped with a bow in front of Tanya, who hesitated for a moment; and then, one arm akimbo and the other raised, she stepped lightly toward her partner. Someone threw her a kerchief (to be used in the dance), which she swooped up as she glided by. The people, the terrace, the garden seemed to disappear for her, and she danced with a skill and grace that seemed inborn. No dance master could have taught her the ease, precision, and blithe innocence with which she performed the complex steps. When the dance was ended, the couple received hearty applause. The night was deliciously warm, and the guests descended the broad steps from the terrace into the garden and down the allee which Sonya had worked so hard to have cleared of weeds and underbrush and which was now exotically scented by the flowers and shrubs she had had planted. The party went on until one in the morning, when the band finally left, playing a march as they set off on foot.

Sonya waved goodbye to her guests, proud to have Tolstoy close beside her, looking strikingly elegant in his dark suit, his gray eyes burning with high spirit.

All through the hard winter of 1866–67—when Tanya Behrs became so ill that Tolstoy had to leave his wife alone with the three children and take her back to Moscow—Sonya held on to the memory of that night. While snow piled to the sills of the windows and ice sabers began their downward thrust from under the eaves of the house, she remembered with warmth the affectionate look in Tolstoy's eyes and recalled how lively and excited he had been. Deep into dark November she envisioned the Chinese lanterns which had lit the veranda and the gay young girls in their white muslin dresses. "The weather was lovely," she wistfully recalled in her diary, adding that she was "surprised that such a sedate and solemn matron as myself could dance with so much gusto."

Sonya had greatly retreated into her own world of thoughts, feelings, and desires. The reality of her life was not what she had expected. Her husband was not the man whom she had thought she was marrying; motherhood brought pain as well as pleasure; and country living was often harsh as well as being boring. But Sonya had discovered she could escape disappointment and tedium by entering into the children's fantasy world or into the world of "ideas and impressions" recorded in her husband's writing.

When the children were awake, she would spend every moment she could with them. She cut out elaborate paper dolls, made up stories, and often put the two together in staged puppet shows, designing, drawing, and painting the scenery herself. Many hours were also taken up with copying the pages of her husband's novel. She could copy now at great speed, and so it was possible to follow the gist of the story and still be able to "feel and ponder over each new idea."

When he was in Moscow, Tolstoy had arranged for the publication of the second part of *1805* and had done more research for the battle scenes that he tackled once he arrived home. Sonya shuddered as she copied, convinced more than ever of her husband's genius. It had not been difficult for her to picture the pond where Tolstoy's "fictional" soldiers bathed (it was the spot where she and Tanya had swum that summer); or the estate with a shady park which the elder Bolkonski built with the aid of an Italian architect (it was, of course, Yasnaya Polyana); and the Rostov house on Povarskaya Street (it was the Behrs apartment in the Kremlin). But the battle scenes were another matter. They were almost entirely out of Tolstoy's head; and his astonishing ability to transform his imaginings into scenes of truth and reality, his phantasms into breathing, flesh-and-blood people, was—to Sonya—the essence of her husband's genius.

More confusing to her were the mixed emotions she experienced as she copied scenes drawn so closely from her own life. She felt pride that her husband had thought enough of her own early attempt at writing (the story about Dublitski) to incorporate Natasha's character and even use the same fictional name. And yet somehow it distressed her to copy the details of Natasha's first ball (Tanya at the ball in Tula), as it had in the early scenes in the Rostov household. The character Natasha was becoming less and less an admixture of Sonya and Tanya. Natasha *was* Tanya. Tolstoy had even written to his illustrator and sent him a picture of Tanya to copy when drawing the young Natasha. There were so many things Sonya would have liked to write about Tanya and herself and their family, but Tolstoy seemed to be leaving her nothing; and then how could she dare consider writing anything serious when, first, she could never meet his literary standard, and, second, he thought women had no place in the literary world?

During Tolstoy's short stay in Moscow, a new member of the household arrived. She was Hannah Tarsey, a young Englishwoman about Sonya's age whom he had hired as a governess-nursemaid for the children. Hannah's sister was employed by Prince Lvov's family in Tula, and both women had been well trained for their careers. Their father was the chief gardener at Windsor Castle and their mother a palace maid. The children now passed from the care of Marya Afanasyevna into Hannah's charge. Gentle and soft-spoken, she had an extraordinary way with children—and a total ineptitude for any language but her own.

When Hannah first arrived (she was to remain at Yasnaya Polyana for six years), her sister came with her to help translate. When she returned to the Lvovs', it looked for a time as if lines of communication between Hannah and the Tolstoy household would never be established. Hannah found Russian impenetrable and did little better at French. However, the black-eyed vivacious two-year-old Tanya was soon imitating the way she spoke, and three-year-old Seryozha had quickly learned several nursery phrases such as "Wash your hands" and "Breakfast is ready." Sonya, with the help of a dictionary and the small amount of English Tolstoy had taught her in their first days of marriage, was able to make herself understood. Hannah never did learn Russian or French; the Tolstoys, however, did improve their English.

Hannah brought calm and order to the nursery, and everyone loved her. She never complained about the isolation of Yasnaya Polyana; she thought the countryside was beautiful and delighted in the children's company. The cold weather didn't disturb her. She bundled the children up and took them for sleigh rides. No work was too much for her, and she always found time to sew for the children. She carried herself "quite as a member of the family," dining and taking tea with them. At first Sonya was worried about how the rest of the staff would respond to Hannah's receiving what would be regarded as special privileges, but it soon became clear that from the beginning the other servants recognized that Hannah occupied a social rank quite apart from and well above their own.

With the first days of December, preparations began for the Christmas celebrations. A large and beautiful Christmas tree had already been brought up to the yard, and Sonya had written out her long Christmas list. The day she went into Tula to shop was extremely cold—about twenty degrees below freezing. The sun was low in the sky, giving little warmth during the short December day, and as Sonya, wrapped in two fur coats, got into the sledge, "the horses trembled; moving their ears, stamping on the frozen ground impatiently with their sharp horseshoes." Then "the three horses crunched off over the frosted snow." Indyushkin, the old coachman, drove out onto the highway. As they rode along, Sonya saw peasants walking beside their slow sledges and urging on "their shaggy horses who were covered with hoar-frost and loaded with oats to be sold in Tula." As the men shambled along, they clapped their leather-gloved hands together in an effort to keep warm.

Sonya (or "Maman" as the two older children now called her), returned from Tula in darkness, her fingers numb in spite of her thick leather and fur gloves and fox muff. She brought with her a large box of wooden dolls, which she described as "little skeletons." Small feet could be heard running across the drawing-room parquet floor as the children raced to greet her. After carrying the box and a huge basket of cloth and ribbon remnants into the salon, she sat the children and the women of the house down and showed them all how they would transform the thirty to forty naked dolls into toys to be given as Christmas gifts to the village children.

Early the following morning the work began, and the crude dolls were turned into mustachioed Turks, officers with sabers made of silver paper, Gypsies with bright shawls, clowns with pointed hats, and dancers with flowers in their hair. Sonya's ingenuity was marvelous, and dolls like these were a traditional gift at Yasnaya Polyana for many years. In the few remaining weeks before Christmas, Sonya, the children, and whatever servants were free gilded nuts and tied bright ribbons on cardboard cutouts and on fancy gingerbread, crimson apples, and other sweets to give with the dolls.

These small handmade gifts were not signs of an everyday camaraderie between the Tolstoy youngsters and the peasant children. On the contrary, the Tolstoys were forbidden to play with the village children and were thus encouraged to become arrogant and to develop an exaggerated sense of their own worth. Their world was divided into two parts—one composed of themselves, and "the other of everyone else."

On Christmas Eve the village priests came to hold a vespers service; and when the Tolstoy children woke the next morning, a tall luxuriant fir tree, standing where the dining-room table had been, filled the whole room with its woodsy scent. During Christmas Day the doors to the room were kept locked to the children, while the adults trimmed the tree and set out the presents. Seryozha and Tanya knew something exciting was happening behind the closed doors; and whenever they could scamper away from Hannah for a few moments, they would race to peek through the keyhole. Hannah made a rich cake with raisins and currants for breakfast and a huge plum pudding which, wrapped in a napkin, boiled on the stove all day. At dinner, rum was poured over it and it was set ablaze, to everyone's gasping delight, though the youngsters began to squirm impatiently once dessert was served. As soon as dinner was over, a group of village children dressed in sheepskin coats and caftans which smelled of tanned leather and sweat arrived as prearranged with their parents and crowded into the entrance hall while Hannah kept her charges apart and in the downstairs parlor.

The dining room had two doors—one that opened into the

entrance hall and the other into the parlor. Tolstoy sounded a bell, and both doors were opened; the Tolstoy children and the peasant children rushed in through their separate entries and stood in awe on opposite sides of the immense glittering tree, its gold ornaments shimmering from the flames of dozens of burning candles. Presents were distributed to all, and as the village children unwrapped their little wooden dolls and cakes and fruits and candy, Seryozha and Tanya stripped the colored paper from their gifts. Tanya had been given a "big doll that shut its eyes and said 'mama' and 'papa,' and a miniature kitchen with plates, forks, pots and pans, and a bear on wheels that nodded its head and growled," while Seryozha received horses with riders, toy mice, a small steam engine, "a gun that fired a cork and a tin watch on a chain."

The best gift for all the adults in the house that Christmas was word that Tanya Behrs had begun to return to her old self. A great part of her recovery was to be attributed to the presence in Moscow over the holidays of her cousin Alexander (Sasha) Kuzminsky. In love with Tanya since they were children, Kuzminsky renewed his campaign for her affection on a more mature level, escorting her (and her chaperone) to the theater, and to the homes of mutual friends. In her letters to Sonya, Tanya confided that she found their cousin most attractive, especially in his new army uniform (he was stationed in Tula). But Sergey Nikolaevich still possessed a part of her heart and always would, for that matter. Tanya asked Sonya if it were possible to love two men at the same time (as an old woman, Tanya might have laughed at her naivete, for she did indeed love these two men for the rest of her life). Sonya considered her sister's question seriously and answered that she believed a woman might be able to love two men simultaneously but morality demanded that she marry and be faithful to only one.

With January came a severe blizzard, bringing snowdrifts that made the narrow roads almost impassable. An occasional visitor (usually Kuzminsky), bundled in sheepskins and traveling in a small sleigh drawn by one robust horse, made it through to Yasnaya Polyana. As much in love with her husband as ever, Sonya usually would have found no other companionship necessary, but the bitterness of the winter had spawned ferment, anger, and violence in Tolstoy. Never before had Sonya found him so irascible. Sharp-tongued and pettish, he was also given to fierce wild rages.

One dark stormy day as she sat on the bedroom floor sorting out a basket of fabric scraps the door burst open and Tolstoy, glowering, his voice as sharp as the wind that slapped at the shutters, shouted, "Why are you sitting on the floor? Get up!"

"In a minute, as soon as I put these things away," she replied as calmly as she could.

"I say get up! Immediately!" he said loudly and then left, slamming the door behind him.

Following him to his study, Sonya asked anxiously, "What is the matter?"

"Get out! Get out!" he ordered, and then, as Sonya stared uncomprehendingly at him, he picked up a tea tray from his desk and threw it furiously at her feet. Sonya seemed mesmerized by the fragments of broken china on the floor. Tolstoy then grabbed the thermometer from the wall and threw that, missing Sonya by only a few inches. His face had gone white, his eyes hard gunmetal gray. Sonya left the room tearfully, saying over and over, "Why? What have I done?" and she stayed in her room sobbing for the rest of the afternoon. Tolstoy seemed unmoved by her shaken state and did not apologize for his actions.

These rages confounded the household, and even Tanya Behrs, who arrived early in the spring, was on occasion the innocent target of his angry outbursts. He was working so intensely on his novel that he seemed to be living through the war-torn days of 1812; he moved like a dazed stranger through the world of Yasnaya and Sonya. He was also tormented by the fear that he had lost his way. When he fell into exhausted sleep, he was certain he had been visited by the phantom of death, who mocked him and the life he had led. As he worked on his book (which he had now decided to call *War and Peace*), he had begun to "feel the crime of killing in war." Deeply depressed, he groped to find the way to spiritual perfection. He could not discuss with Sonya the crisis which was racking him. She was, after all, a woman and should not be told of his doubts and weaknesses. He corresponded with Fet, but even this good friend did not satisfy his desperate hunger for a kindred spirit.

Much of Tolstoy's ferment in January 1867 and the following
months had its roots in a casual meeting in Moscow the previous
November with Yuri Fyodorovich Samarin, a leading contributor
to the Slavophile journal *Russian Conversation*. Nine years older than
Tolstoy, he was also a renowned orator and was a new member of
the Moscow Duma and of the Moscow Provincial Zemstvo. Samarin had told Tolstoy that he considered him a "has-been"; and
rather than offending him, this remark aroused his curiosity. He
was, in fact, attracted to Samarin and excited by his "cold, supple,
and educated mind." Shortly after Christmas Samarin had an article published in *Russian Conversation*. This essay seems to have
precipitated Tolstoy's anguished soul-searching, and he thought
that the eminent and manly Samarin might be the kindred spirit
for whom he was searching.

On January 10 he composed a long emotional letter to Samarin. He apparently felt that it was too revealing to send, but he
kept it for the rest of his life. He stated in this letter:

> I have my partialities and habits, my vanities and ties of the heart,
> but up to now—I shall soon be 40—I have loved the truth above all
> else, and have never despaired of finding it, and I go on seeking it.
> Sometimes, and never more so than this year, I have managed to
> raise a corner of the curtain and look in that direction, but it's difficult
> and frightening on one's own, and it seems I'm losing my way. I'm
> seeking help and for some reason you alone always involuntarily
> come to mind. Since the beginning of autumn I've been meaning to
> see you and to write, but I've been putting it off—but now it's
> reached the stage where . . . I must write to Samarin, I must. So
> here I am writing. But what do I want to say to you? It's this. If I'm
> not mistaken, and you really are the person I imagine you to be,
> seeking an explanation for all this muddle that surrounds us, and if I
> am at least one hundredth part as interesting and necessary to you as
> you are to me, then let us be friends, let us help each other, work
> together and love each other, if that's possible.

He continued at some length, asking about Samarin's religious convictions, touching on issues raised by the recent Austro-Prussian
War, berating Samarin for trimming his thoughts, and doing obeisance to Samarin's potential greatness. He closed by saying:

Please tear up my letter or else write to me; but the way I regard
you, I don't see any conventional obstacles between us, and frankly
I feel myself at once completely open with respect to you. I don't
want to pose in any way before you, nor do I want to hide from you
the most intimate or the most shameful thing about myself, if you
should need to know it. I shall be very happy if I receive the same
sort of letter from you. . . . But if you don't wish it, simply write
and tell me that you have received my letter—then I shall simply be
rather ashamed to meet you.

Count L. Tolstoy

Tolstoy's irritability toward Sonya and his marked detachment that year from the children (he never was demonstrative and
did not believe that a man should kiss or fondle his offspring,
particularly his sons) caused her many unhappy moments. Tanya's
arrival in the first days of spring and the sight of the heavy deposits
of muddy snow gradually disappearing from the banks of the rivers
and sides of the country roads cheered her considerably. She was
kept busy taking care of the children, running the household, doing
the estate books, and above all copying and recopying Tolstoy's
manuscript. She remarked that there was "little time left over for
les beaux arts and for reading, I can hardly spare a moment and then
only if it is raining."

She was glad for any diversion, and she welcomed the sight of
the peddlers who came to Yasnaya Polyana in the spring. Most
came with pushcarts filled with humble wares, but the "Hungarians" had heavy two-horse wagons that were really small shops.
They carried fabrics, ribbons, buttons, shoes, ties, stationery,
kitchen equipment, musical instruments, and even musical scores.
Tolstoy bought a copy of Johann Strauss's "Acceleration Waltz"
from one of the Hungarians and played it for Sonya with delight.
At such times she felt again their past happiness, the joy of their
courtship. He remained quite handsome in her eyes, and she still
admired his brisk, self-assured movements. The words "tired" and
"I can't" simply did not exist for this "powerful, agile man." And
his sense of pride and nobility—the qualities that had made *le
Comte* such a romantic figure when she was a girl—remained unchanged.

Once again it was Tanya who vicariously satisfied Sonya's

impassioned imagination. Not one but *two* men wanted to marry her—young Sasha Kuzminsky and stout, good-natured Dmitry Dyakov, whose wife, Dolly, had recently died. It had, in fact, been Dolly Dyakov's wish that Tanya, whom she loved dearly, marry her husband after her death. Everyone in the Behrs and Tolstoy families *except* Sonya wanted Tanya to marry Dyakov, who was a kind, intelligent man, rich enough to pamper a young woman and yet wise enough to counsel a girl only half his age. Kuzminsky, so tall and smart-looking in his uniform, was, of course, her first love, rich in his own right, and only twenty-four. However, he was her cousin, and his family did not approve of Tanya for a number of reasons. It was considered unsuitable for the bride to be fewer than eight years younger than the groom. And there were the problems of their being cousins and of Tanya's health. But the main objection of the Kuzminskys was the shadow of Sergey Nikolaevich, in their minds an evil shadow from which Tanya had yet to escape. But defying all opposition, the young couple set July 27 as their wedding day. Lev Nikolaevich spent days riding to churches in the district looking for a priest who would be willing to bypass Church law and marry the cousins. At last one priest told him of an old man—a regimental chaplain—who would perform the ceremony for a fee of three hundred rubles, and on the designated morning Tanya and Sasha Kuzminsky set out in an elegant cabriolet.

Ironically, Sergey Nikolaevich had settled on that same day for his marriage to Marya Mikhailovna Shiskin; and not far from Tula, on a dusty, little-traveled road, an awkward encounter took place. Tanya, young and lovely in flimsy white muslin, and her handsome young groom sat behind a liveried coachman. The cabriolet slowed and swerved to the side to let Sergey Nikolaevich and his Gypsy bride, seated in their open trap, pass. Sergey Nikolaevich and Tanya were startled and visibly moved by this meeting. Each bowed slightly to the other, and the carriages continued on their way.

The Kuzminskys decided to settle in Tula until Sasha was mustered out of the army. Nothing could have pleased Sonya more; her sister's company made the difficulties of life at Yasnaya Polyana easier to bear. Tolstoy's fits of anger continued, his withdrawal into his work became even more intense, and his research trips were more frequent. On September 16, 1867 (the day before her twenty-third name day), Sonya wrote in her diary:

> In spite of myself, I keep thinking of the 17th of September a year ago. Heaven knows I want no music, no dancing, none of all that, but merely his desire to give me pleasure and to see me happy as then, if only he knew how grateful I still am, and always will be, for his kind thought last year. I firmly believed then that I was happy and strong and beautiful, and now I only feel that he doesn't love me, and that I am a weak, ugly, useless woman. He talked about the estate this morning, and we discussed things in such a friendly way, as though we were *one* again; we so seldom talk to each other nowadays.

That winter the news came that Lisa Behrs was engaged to marry the commander of a Hussar regiment, Gavril Yemelyanovich Paulenko. Of Ukrainian descent, Paulenko was a wealthy man and owned several estates in the south and in Pyazan province. His regiment was stationed at Lubny in the Ukraine, and he visited Moscow infrequently; but when he did, he spent what time he had at the Behrses'. A tall, imposing man of about forty, he was an ardent Tsarist, and his conversations were studded with phrases like "It is His Majesty's pleasure to. . . ." Dr. Behrs approved of the match enthusiastically, and the wedding was to be held on January 7, 1868.

On January 5, Kuzminsky and Tolstoy saw their wives off at the new train station in Tula. (A track had just been completed connecting the city with Moscow and would soon reach Yasenki Barracks, only a few miles from Yasnaya Polyana.) The women had wanted to wear their most stylish new dresses, but Tolstoy intervened, insisting that they must dress in the proper traveling attire for a lady, black *costume tailleur* with matching veiled hats. Swathed in black as they were, the women looked like they were in mourning and could be assured that no gentlemen would make overtures. Still, in defiance, each woman carried a French novel in her gloved hand.

To Sonya's confusion and embarrassment, Polivanov, more handsome and self-assured than ever, was a guest at the Behrses' and was to be a groomsman at the wedding. At first she wanted to return to Yasnaya Polyana, but Lyubov Alexandrovna persuaded her to stay until after the wedding.

The "three maidens" were now married; but had their "expectations of happiness" been fulfilled?

As the train sped through the familiar countryside carrying her back to Yasnaya Polyana, to her three children and her husband, Sonya tried to dispel her own feelings of discontent and disillusionment. She was, after all, the Countess Tolstoy, wife of Russia's most talked-about novelist. On the completion of *War and Peace*, she was certain they would be as rich as she had ever dreamed and her husband would have time once again to spend with her. Should she not feel the stirrings of joyous anticipation in her heart?

12

Tolstoy's handwriting went from poor to deplorable in the last sections of *War and Peace*. He still inserted "whole sentences between lines, in corners, or even right across the page." Sonya no longer sat in his room while he worked; she was, in fact, afraid to interrupt him. When written pages were truly indecipherable, she would timidly knock on his door, open it quietly and peer nervously at him, waiting for him to acknowledge her presence. Invariably he would look up from his work and ask irritably, "What is it you don't understand?" If he couldn't make out the passages, he would become even more annoyed at having to rewrite the lines. She often found grammatical errors in his work, but these she corrected silently, pointing out her emendations to him later. Sonya spent every free moment at her desk in the sitting room struggling to decipher Tolstoy's almost illegible pages. She was working when the children went to bed and when they rose in the morning; and during these years they regarded her as the working member of the family.

When Tolstoy disappeared into his study, it was Sonya's task to make sure the children were kept quiet and that no one disturbed him. No child dared go into the study, and therefore fear of and respect for Papa were feelings that developed early. Yet, though the children could see that Sonya worked even longer hours, she belonged to their world; and so it was permissible for her to be interrupted by cries of "I'll tell Maman," "Where's Maman?" and "Please, Maman." Sonya seemed to be everywhere—in the kitchen supervising the meals, in the nursery tending to the children, in her bedroom mending their clothes, in the sitting room copying. Her quick light footsteps clicked rhythmically as she went from room to room, doing everything, looking after everyone. And when her day's work was done, she often sat over Tolstoy's manuscript until three or four in the morning. By 1869, when the final chapters were being written, Sonya had copied most of *War and Peace* at least eight times.

The years from 1867 to 1869 also found her managing the household and farm matters as Tolstoy made frequent trips to Moscow and elsewhere to do research. Financially they were having a difficult time, and his travels took a good part of their income. In 1867 he wrote to her from Moscow, "I'm borrowing 1,000 rubles from Perfilyev, so I'll be rich, and I'll buy a fur hat and boots and everything you say. I know you'll be angry with me for borrowing. Don't be angry, I'm borrowing in order to be free, unconstrained, and untroubled by money matters during the early part of winter; and with this purpose in view I intend to save the money as much as possible and to keep it simply in order to know that there is money there. . . . You'll understand and will help me."

In the fall of 1868 Dr. Behrs took gravely ill. Sonya and the entire family traveled to Moscow on the new Moscow–Kursk Railway. Seryozha, only five at the time, was to carry the memory of the suffering on his grandfather's face for the rest of his life. Dr. Behrs died a few days after the arrival of the Tolstoys in Moscow, and they returned to Yasnaya Polyana directly after the funeral. Leaving her mother at such a time was painful for Sonya, however she was pregnant and not feeling well. Despite this caution she lost the child. Sonya suffered one more miscarriage in 1869, and the doctor in Tula feared she might not be able to have any more children. But late in the year she was again pregnant and was ordered to bed several months before the child was due. Her bedroom became the center of the active household. The children played around her bed. The servants were in and out to receive instructions. Aunt Toinette sat in a chair by the window doing her sewing. Tea was served and guests exchanged news and gossip at her bedside. A special writing desk was constructed and Sonya did her copying as always.

On May 13, Tanya Kuzminsky, who was living in Tula, gave birth to a daughter, Dasha (named in memory of Darya Alexandrovna Dyakov). Both mother and daughter nearly died. Sonya, eight months pregnant, was seriously disturbed. To ease her anxiety about Tanya's well-being, both mother and baby were brought to Yasnaya Polyana only two weeks after the birth. Tanya's health was soon restored, but little Dasha was a frail consumptive child. Tanya regarded the little girl's birth date (the thirteenth) as an ill omen. "It's a bad date; she won't live," she cried to Sonya.

Sonya went into labor early on June 8, and the doctor and midwife were sent for without delay. Tolstoy stood by the door of her room as her labor progressed. By afternoon he had grown restless and asked the doctor to take a walk with him, leaving the midwife in attendance. The two men returned a half-hour later to find that Sonya had given birth to a son, who was named Lev for his father. Ironically, of all the children he was the least like Tolstoy. Lyova, as the child was called, was sickly and nervous; he seldom slept and cried continually. Since Sonya had little trouble nursing him, she felt closer to him than the others and therefore found his ill health inexplicable.

By spring of 1869, with the publication of the final chapters (volumes five and six), the first edition of *War and Peace* was complete. There were extremely favorable reviews, but Tolstoy had not heard from Turgenev or some of his other earlier critics. He set about preparing for summer publication a second edition with the first four volumes textually revised. Once this final task was finished, he fell into a lethargic, dazed state. He was unable to write, no new creative ideas came to him; and although he read Schopenhauer with great excitement during the early part of the summer, by September his nerves were noticeably near the breaking point. Small things irritated him. The children's shrieks or the baby's cries sent him into a fury. He found little to like about Lyova and complained that children under two were uninteresting. On the pretext of looking at a small estate in the province of Penza for possible purchase, he left home with Alexei Stepanovich for a short respite from domestic cares. But death appeared to be at the end of the road, its image leering at him. "I must be reborn in order to be content," he wrote in his notebook, "and to be reborn is to die." He spent a night on his journey in the town of Arzamas. "It was two o'clock in the morning," he wrote Sonya. "I was terribly tired, I wanted to go to sleep and I felt perfectly well. But suddenly I was overcome by despair, fear and terror, the like of which I have never experienced before."

He awakened in the strange dark room of the small house where he was a guest, feeling that he had to escape from something terrible. Desperate, he pulled himself up from the couch and lurched into the hallway, trying to run from whatever or whoever it was pursuing him. "Who is it? What do I fear?" he asked himself, still feeling a baleful presence near him.

"Me," answered a voice he believed in his half-awake state was death. "I am here!"

He reeled backward into the room and fell heavily on the couch. He spent the night huddled in prayer, unable to quell his terror. Finally, an hour or two before dawn he dressed, awoke Alexei Stepanovich, and left while it was still dark. Yet the terrible specter of death seemed to follow close on his heels, and even when he reached the town of Saransk the next morning he was afraid to look back over his shoulder. This nightmare did not fade with time; the pursuing phantom remained with him for most of his life.

More than seven years had passed since Sonya had come to Yasnaya Polyana as a bride, and she was constantly struck by dramatic changes in both her and her husband. Lev Nikolaevich had lost a large measure of his youthful ebullience. And his growing taste for philosophical reflection was gradually supplanting his more worldly interests. He was remote and uncommunicative for maddeningly long periods. He had perhaps expected that the completion of *War and Peace* would drastically alter and improve his life. It had not. Riches had not suddenly deluged him, and the dread and turmoil within him had not faded away. Sonya could see him aging before her eyes. The curly hair and beard were flecked with white, the face was folding into narrow creases, the dark blue veins on his hands were growing more prominent. But the deep, piercing gray eyes were not clouded; the shoulders remained straight, the step sharp, the hand grasp vital.

Sonya's mirror told her that, although she was still quite beautiful, she too had aged. She was twenty-five, the mother of four; she had grown stouter, more matronly. Her nearsighted eyes were now so weak she had to use her lorgnette constantly. She had, of course, become more experienced, more poised. But there was so much for her to learn and so little time to devote to herself. The work on *War and Peace* done, she found time to read and to set

about writing children's stories. But when Lev Nikolaevich decided
he would attempt this genre himself, she put her own efforts aside
and instead began a notebook.

> Yasnaya Polyana
> February 14, 1870
>
> As I was reading Pushkin's life the other day, it occurred to me
> that I might render a service to posterity by recording not so much
> Lyova's everyday life as his mental activities, so far as I was able to
> watch them. . . .
>
> This is a good time to begin. *War and Peace* is complete, and
> nothing else very important has yet been begun. He spent all last
> summer reading and studying philosophy; he spoke very highly of
> Schopenhauer, but thought Hegel a bagful of empty phrases. He
> spent much time on painful reflection, and often said that his brain
> was aching with all the strain, that he was of no further use, that it
> was time to die, etc. Later on, however, these gloomy moods passed.
> He began to read Russian folk tales and folk epics. This gave him the
> idea of writing and compiling children's books. After reading folk
> tales and folk epics, he started reading an immense number of plays.
> He read Moliere, Shakespeare, and Pushkin's *Boris Godunov*, which
> he dislikes, and now he intends to try a comedy.

On February 18, 1870, she wrote, "Yesterday he said he had
given up thinking of a comedy and was looking for a subject for a
serious drama. He repeated several times: 'What a lot of work
ahead!'

"We have just been out skating. He tried hard to do all the
tricks on one and then on both legs, such as running backwards,
doing circles, etc. It amuses him like a little boy."

While Tolstoy was thrashing about trying to decide what direction his writing should take, Sonya spent most of her time dealing with the harshness of winter at Yasnaya Polyana. Hannah
Tarsey was a tremendous help, but she also caused controversy in
the household by taking the children against the nurse's directive
for long walks in the worst weather and bathing them in cold water.
(There was only one bathtub in the house and no plumbing. Water
had to be heated in big iron kettles and carried up in pails.)

The deep isolation of winter set in again. Tolstoy declared he
did not want to read criticism; and therefore, except for the

monthly *Revue des Deux Mondes* and a German periodical, they had neither papers nor magazines. Since the roads were almost always impassable, even their neighbor Alexander Nikolaevich Bibikov, whom Sonya thought pompous and silly, was a welcome visitor.

Bibikov, who was the leaseholder of a small piece of land adjoining the Tolstoy estate, had recently replaced Ivanov as bailiff at Yasnaya Polyana. He was a sturdy, muscular, attractive man with clear blue but rather cynical eyes and a pleasant smile which was tinged with irony. He tried unsuccessfully to look like a peasant, adopting the same sort of tunic and high boots that Tolstoy wore and allowing his reddish beard to grow untrimmed. Yet it was immediately evident that he was masquerading.

In fact Bibikov was the illegitimate son of a fairly affluent landowner who later suffered severe reverses. Despite his poverty Bibikov managed to attend Kharkov University, and within a short time had become a magistrate in his province. However, he was extremely liberal-minded and was known to be a nihilist and a supporter of several radical groups. When the attempt on Tsar Alexander's life was made in 1866, many liberals and nihilists were arrested, Bibikov among them. He served six months in prison and was then deported to Siberia. Although he had been allowed to come to work and live in Tula province, he was still under police supervision.

None of this discredited him in Sonya's eyes. It was the man's private life that offended her. Now in his forties, Bibikov had recently lost his wife (whom Sonya had found pleasant) and was unprincipled in his relations with women. His half-witted son, Nikolenka, needed constant supervision, and so Bibikov prevailed upon his mistress—a tall, striking woman, with dark hair and slanted slate-colored eyes—to move from Tula to the charming small farmhouse he had built upon his land. Her name was Anna Stepanovna Pirogova, and though she was living illicitly with Bibikov and was treated abusively by him, she had come from a good family. Sonya liked Anna Stepanovna, and disliked Bibikov, who was flagrantly unfaithful to his mistress. She could not understand why the bright, pleasant, captivating, and sensitive Anna should be in a delirium of infatuation over such a dissolute seducer—a man Sonya believed was incapable of real love.

In January 1870 Bibikov hired a beautiful young German girl

as a governess, explaining to the Tolstoys that Nikolenka was too demanding for Anna to manage alone. They did not have to guess at his actual motives, since he did nothing to hide his passion for the young woman. The Tolstoys were extremely upset by the situation in their bailiff's home, and Anna's heartbreak haunted them both.

On February 24, Sonya recorded in her notebook, "Last night he [Tolstoy] said that he had conceived the character of a married woman of high rank but who had lost her balance. He said that he would try to make this woman pitiable and blameless, and that no sooner had he imagined her clearly than he also visualized all the other male and female characters of the story."

Tolstoy had difficulty beginning this story, and so he turned his attention to his primer for peasant children and to his translations and adaptations of fables from Greek, Hebrew, Oriental, and Arabic sources. But this writing seems to have represented an unsettling compromise, and for the next two years, while he worked on these pieces, he was restless, bad-tempered, and at times irrational. Most of his complaints he confided in his frequent letters to Fet. On February 4, 1870, he told Fet, whose wife was on a journey, "You write: 'I'm alone! alone!' But I read it and think, Lucky man to be *alone*. I have a wife, three children, a fourth at the breast, two old aunts, a nanny and two maids, and the whole lot are suffering from fever, a temperature, debility, a headache or a cough. This is the state your letter found me in."

On the sixteenth he continued his catalogue of problems to Fet: "I hoped to visit you on the night of the 14th, but I wasn't able to. As I wrote you, we have all been ill—myself last of all—and I only went out yesterday for the first time. I had to stop, though, because of a pain in the eyes which is aggravated by the wind and by insomnia." And replying to Fet's request that Tolstoy read him his own work, he added, in response, "I don't want to read you anything, and I haven't anything to read because I'm not writing anything."

Nonetheless, only two days later he ventured out into sharp winds to pay Fet a short visit, traveling the considerable distance in a small sleigh drawn by only one horse. He had just received a review of *War and Peace* written by the eminent critic Nikolai Strakhov and published in the magazine *Zarya*, and he wanted to discuss it with Fet. Strakhov was an important editor as well as a scholar and critic, whom Tolstoy greatly respected. He ended his review with the words "The picture of human life is complete.

"The picture of the Russian of those days is complete.

"The picture of what we call history and the struggle of nations is complete.

"The picture of everything that people consider to be their happiness and greatness, their sorrow and their humiliation, is complete. That is what *War and Peace* is."

Praise was heaped upon Tolstoy from all quarters, and sales of the book were outstripping even the most optimistic estimates. He was hailed as "Russia's greatest living novelist." Sonya was able to pay their debts and anticipated a glorious future. But he remained disgruntled—a malcontent difficult to live with—and his gloomy mood darkened when he learned that Turgenev had written,

> I read the sixth volume of *War and Peace;* of course there are things that are first class. But without saying any more about the childish philosophy, it was unpleasant to see the reflection of the *system* even in the images Tolstoy draws. Why is it all his good women are not simply females—but fools? And why does he try to convince the reader that if a woman is intelligent and cultured she is necessarily a phrasemonger and a liar . . . and why is every single one of his decent people likewise some sort of blockhead—with a touch of madness?

Sonya feared that Lev Nikolaevich himself was suffering from "a touch of madness," for he had become unreasonable in his requests for silence and in his complaints about the illness in the household. It was not her fault that both Aunt Toinette and Natalya Petrovna were old and dying; or that the children had not weathered the unusually cold winter without colds and fevers; or that little Lyova was such a sickly child. Lyova's incessant crying angered Tolstoy, and Sonya spent much of her time with the child trying to keep him soothed and quiet. This irritated Tolstoy even more, since it kept Sonya from tending to many of his own needs.

But with the advent of spring Sonya's spirits lifted. The children were well again and able to play outside. Even little Lyova had improved and did not cry as much. The elderly ladies could not leave their room, but the windows were thrown open and the oppressive odor of burning incense and melting wax was dispersed. For a short time Lev Nikolaevich seemed in better humor. Occasionally he would play with the children, lifting them up, setting them on his powerful shoulders, and carrying them around the room; Tanya, her tiny hands clasped around his neck, squealed with delight and terror. And he was tender once again with Sonya and—as Lyova began to be weaned—even romantic.

Shrovetide found Sonya with renewed hope. Her husband was rich and famous, as she had always dreamed he would be, and work was going forward on the renovations Uncle Kostya had suggested for the house. Soon she would have a proper drawing room and Lev Nikolaevich a larger study. And the children were beautiful. Seryozha was fair-haired and handsome, with a glorious smile and an infectious laugh, and though only six he had already shown a gift for music. Sensitive, lively, good at his lessons, Seryozha was also adept enough at athletics to please both his father and his mother. Tanya resembled her mother as a child—huge black eyes, thick dark hair, a little mother who was happiest when she was helping with the other children. And how different Ilya was! "Hot-tempered and violent, quick to fight, but also tender and extremely sensitive. Sensuous—fond of eating and lying down in comfort," a "big-boned, fair, rosy, beaming" boy. "Bad at lessons, original in everything." The baby, Lyova, was still frail, but he had an entrancing beauty.

In the spring of 1870 Yasnaya Polyana seemed to have become a children's world. Tolstoy was working on his *ABC Book* and four reading books for children, and he entrusted to Sonya the job of translating stories from French and German, adapting them to the Russian language and customs. This work spurred a renewal of literary creativity in her and she wrote a short story, "Sparrows," and a children's story. She also wrote a Russian and a French grammar to use in teaching her own children. At Shrovetide she prepared the traditional pancakes, cabbage, baked potatoes with savory lentil oil, and almond milk.

It was Shrovetide [her children's story, "In the Village," began]. The village children were getting benches ready and pouring water over them for sliding down hills. Lessons at school had stopped for a

while, and it was a holiday everywhere once more. The peasant men
and women had been in town and bought flour for blinis, and butter,
and the richer ones had bought smelts and herrings as well. The
weather was wonderful. It had grown cold after the thaw, and the
sun was shining, the roads were smooth and slippery which was just
what the children needed for sliding.

Sonya wrote about the life she saw in the village of Yasnaya
Polyana. There was a great naivete and yet a great truth in all her
stories, and when she read them to her children they cried out with
delight and asked her to reread them over and over again. The
images she captured were ones they recognized—the little wooden
skeleton dolls that they had decorated, the village youngsters coming from their *izbas* (peasant houses) dragging their benches and
pulling their toboggans along on ropes, the children eating their
blinis and licking their buttery fingers. There were tears as well as
laughter for her audience; Sonya's characters had real-life problems, and she did not close her eyes to poverty and death.

"Easter was late that year. The streams were swollen with
melted snow that flowed rapidly in all directions from the hill of
Krasna Polya [Sonya's fictional name for Yasnaya Polyana]," her
next story began. "The children threw chips of wood and little
sticks into the water and ran after them with shrieks of amusement."

Easter in the "manor house," as the village children called
Yasnaya Polyana, was a festive occasion. On Easter Eve, after
hours of painting eggs, everyone went to church in a broad sledge
drawn by two horses. "The snow was half melted and mounds of
brown horse dung lay on the road. Here and there the snow was
discolored, the runners slid over the mud, and rivulets flowed from
the water-filled hollows. The horses' tails were bound up short.
[The children] shivered in the dark, sleepless night. At last the
lights of the church appeared. Empty carts were drawn up around
it, and on the porch stood the beggars and the blind."

The Tolstoys, dressed gaily for the holiday, made their way
through the crowd and entered the small church, joining Bibikov
and his son, Nikolenka, in the choir. As there were few landowners
in the area, most members of the congregation were peasants, who
sat on hard wooden benches, the men wearing "long overcoats over

clean, unbleached linen shirts, their hair combed and oiled, the women in bright-colored dresses with beads around their necks." They had come for a night-long service celebrating the resurrection of Christ. At midnight, after several hours of prayers, everyone in the church took up a lighted candle and joined in a procession.

"Christ is risen," the priest proclaimed and the prayers began again. It was nearly dawn before the horses pulled the sledge homeward, but none of the occupants seemed fatigued, for still ahead was the Easter egg roll.

"It was beginning to get light," she writes in her story explaining the peasants' Easter services, "and the tired children went back to their separate *izbas*, a sledge [the Tolstoys'] drawn by two horses went down the village street with a jingling of bells. . . . The lights began to go out everywhere, and only a few still glimmered . . . here and there, in *izbas* where the sick and newly born lay, they shone dimly through the windowpanes, which were frosted over on the outside."

It was obvious that Sonya had a natural talent for writing and that she was capable of vividly recreating life as she saw it and of translating the voices she heard to the written page. But she was too much in awe of Tolstoy and what she referred to as "a true literary endeavor" to approach her talent in any other way than as a *divertissement*.

Shortly after Easter, Tolstoy went to Moscow to see his sister, Marya, who had been ill. When he returned, he was withdrawn and moody; and Sonya busied herself with caring for the children. On June 5 she wrote in her diary, "I stopped nursing little Lyova four days ago. I felt almost sorrier for him than for any of the others. I blessed him as I took leave of him, and cried and prayed; this first complete separation from one's child is very painful indeed. I must not be pregnant again. With each child one gives away a part of one's own life and bends down afresh with the weight of so much illness, anxiety, and long years of responsibility."

She *was* pregnant again, and this pregnancy was to be the most difficult she had yet endured. Childbearing was exhausting to her. She missed Moscow with its bustle and excitement, its music and theater; and she longed for the days of "buoyant carefree gaiety" that she had shared with Tanya. She loved the children, yet being bound to the nursery bored her. And Lev Nikolaevich—with his varying and violent moods, opinions, and obsessions—often gave her more pain than pleasure. For the few short months between her pregnancies he was a passionate, demanding lover, but once he knew she was with child he would not admit her to his bed. He became a hostile, distant man who constantly complained about his own health and well-being while wanting to hear nothing of her problems or those of the children.

The winter of 1870–71 was particularly trying for Sonya, not only because of her pregnancy but also because Tolstoy imagined he was going insane; and his fear of madness and of death was so intense that she herself became terrified. "A shadow has passed between us, dividing us," Sonya recorded in her diary. Lev Niko-laevich was no longer the same man she had married. Something seemed to have broken in their lives, and she had lost her identity as a person. Now she was only mother and wife, and she was fearful of the alienation the future might hold.

For three months Tolstoy immersed himself in learning Greek. He complained of severe pains in his face and legs, and he developed a dry, stubborn cough that he was certain was a symp-tom of consumption—a sign death had sent to warn him of his mortality. He wrote to Fet, "I've stopped writing, and will never again write verbose nonsense like *War and Peace*. I'm guilty, but I swear I'll never do it again." He treated Sonya with increasing coolness as her pregnancy advanced. Both in their own ways were lonely, but Tolstoy demanded sympathy and attention from his friends and family, writing lists of complaints to Fet and his cousin Alexandra. Though he suffered only from rheumatism in one knee and from a hacking cough (apparently a result of nervousness, not ill health), he believed that he was seriously ill and that death was about to seize him. Sonya was forced to remain silent about her illness and exhaustion as she appeased and coddled her husband, tended her children, tried to cheer the two old aunties, and lent her sister Tanya the strength to cope with little Dasha's weakening condition.

By January, the eighth month of her pregnancy, Sonya had lost a great deal of weight. She suffered from frequent migraine headaches and spells of dizziness and nausea, and the smallest ex-ertion fatigued her. Yet Tolstoy appeared to be oblivious to her failing health, and it was Sonya who strove to keep *his* spirits up and to dispel his melancholy and despair.

Early in the dark freezing morning of February 12, 1871, Sonya went into labor. Her maid, Dunyasha, ran to fetch Tolstoy, who had already been awakened by Sonya's screams. The birth was several weeks early, and her condition was so run down that she had no strength to help in the delivery. Tolstoy paced frantically outside her room while Hannah, Agatha Mikhailovna, and Dunyasha encouraged her and tried to assist her. By the time Indyushkin brought Dr. Shmigaro and the midwife Marya Afanasyevna from Tula, Sonya had delivered a frail, pathetically small girl whose skin was almost as blue as her pale blue eyes. Delirious and in excruciating pain, Sonya was unable to straighten her legs. She screamed for the doctor to give her morphine and cried out to the Lord for help. She talked wildly about seeing death approach. She wanted the windows open and then thought that she was out in the garden and that the flowers on the wallpaper were real.

Dr. Shmigaro diagnosed her condition as puerperal fever and warned Tolstoy that ninety-nine cases in every hundred ended in death. Tanya had suffered this illness with Dasha's birth and had survived, but Sonya was weaker than her sister had been. She lay unconscious all day, and by nightfall her pulse was faint and erratic. Tanya was sent for and sat for hours holding her sister's limp hand. The next day she regained consciousness but was delirious. These two conditions—unconsciousness and delirium—came and went for another three days. Then miraculously she awoke clearheaded. "Is my child alive?" she whispered.

She was told that the tiny girl was breathing well and taking a wet nurse's breast. Then she realized that her head had been shaved while she had been unconscious. She sobbed, heartbroken, and refused to let Tolstoy into the room until she had put on a ruffled cap with scarlet ribbons. "I've failed you again." She sighed as he stood by the side of her bed. He assured her she had not and together they agreed to name the child Marya—after his sister.

By the time spring came, soft dark curls framed Sonya's pale face. Though she was still rather thin, she was regaining her strength. These months were hectic. She had five children, all

under the age of eight, to care for; a disgruntled husband; two
elderly ailing ladies to look after; and laborers to direct as work on
the house moved forward. At Easter her sixteen-year-old brother
Stepan (Styopa) arrived. A bright, strong blond-headed youth,
Styopa worshipped Tolstoy, treated the children condescendingly,
and was constantly quarreling with Sonya, who, he felt, did not
treat him as a man. Styopa had a hair-trigger temper, but Tolstoy
found him good company. And as her husband was complaining
more and more about his health, Sonya encouraged him to travel
with Styopa to the Samara steppes for the kumiss cure he had once
found so beneficial.

Tolstoy left early in June and stayed away for six weeks. His
first four letters to her were filled with complaints about his depression and ill health, and the wretched accommodations in Samara.

> We're living in a tent and drinking kumiss. . . . The discomforts of
> life would strike terror in your Kremlin heart, no beds, no crockery,
> no white bread, no spoons. . . . I make Styopa depressed, and I can
> see he's bored. . . . It's been cold at night, but yesterday, the 17th,
> a terrible heat wave began, and I said to Styopa today, when he was
> moaning, that unless you take care you could be driven to desperation
> by the heat, and especially by the thought that you literally can't find
> a single tree for hundreds of versts round about, and that you can
> only shelter from the sun in the tent, which is completely sun-baked
> and where we're sitting with nothing on and still sweating. The most
> painful thing for me is that because of my poor health I only feel one-
> tenth of what exists. There are no intellectual pleasures especially
> poetic ones. I look at everything as though I were dead. . . . I don't
> understand my condition. . . . The main thing is weakness, depres-
> sion, and wanting to play the woman and weep, and it's embarrass-
> ing, whether with the Bashkirs or with Styopa. . . . If I'm sometimes
> in a poetic mood, it's only a very sour and tearful one—I just want to
> cry. Perhaps the illness has reached the crisis. Write and tell me in
> detail about everyone at home.

Although the tone of his letters was warm and loving, he made
no inquiry in any of them about her own personal health or feelings. He returned home with the news that despite the "discomfort" of the area he had purchased 6,750 acres of land in Samara, in
the Buzuluk district, for 20,000 rubles. He enthusiastically de-

clared that they would all summer there, growing strong on the air and the simple food.

"The two-month kumiss cure has done him no good," Sonya wrote in her diary shortly after his return. "The disease is still in him, I can't see it, but I can feel it as I watch that strange apathy toward life and his surroundings which began to show itself last winter . . . I feel him dragging me into the sad and hopeless atmosphere which seems to surround him. He does not admit this hopelessness to himself, but my instincts never betray me. It is I who suffer most from his bad moods, and so I know."

Alexander Kuzminsky had been appointed to an important government post in Kutais in the Caucasus, and Tanya and little Dasha had left to join him. This was the first time Sonya and her sister had been separated by so great a distance. Through the years only Tanya had been able to infuse her with "so much new life," to console her so well in her sorrow, or to cheer her when she was sad. Tanya's departure left her disconsolate. Her depression did not last long, for Tolstoy decided to open his school again. In January 1872, classes began and Sonya helped teach the thirty-five peasant children (a small proportion of girls among them) who attended classes daily in the schoolhouse or, when the weather was most severe, on the ground floor of the house. Throughout the winter months the front hall smelled of the peasant children's sheepskin jackets. Uncle Kostya, who was supervising the renovations on the house, also taught; and even Seryozha, Tanya, and Ilya were given duties in the schoolroom. "Lesson time was very gay and lively," Ilya later recalled. "The children did exactly as they pleased, sat wherever they liked, ran about from place to place, and answered questions simultaneously, interrupting in their eagerness to help one another remember what had been read."

The autumn of 1871 had brought the Tolstoys a new intimacy and the winter a shared closeness. Sonya was pregnant again and even though Dr. Shmigaro warned her about the dangers of a pregnancy so soon after Marya's difficult birth, she felt fine and was happy. Tolstoy's health was better, and in addition to working on his primer he was attempting to write a novel about Peter the Great. He was not having much success with this new work and cast aside one beginning after another—in all he made some twenty starts. But at night after the children had gone to bed, he would discuss the book with Sonya.

Then, in January 1872, Anna Stepanovna Pirogova committed suicide.

There was now a railway station at the army barracks in Yasenki, only a few miles from Yasnaya Polyana. Anna Stepanovna had gone to Tula for the day, telling Bibikov she was going to visit her mother. He had just told her that he was planning to marry the young German governess, and when Anna left the house she was in a deranged state. She apparently spent an anguished day in Tula, and she returned to Yasenki that night, still carrying a small red bag which contained a few articles of clothing. She was seen walking up and down the platform in a distracted manner, and the stationmaster, who knew her, asked if she was going to board the next train. Without replying, Anna hurried to the end of the platform. A freight train was about to pull into the station, and the platform trembled. Anna cast her bag aside and then, making the sign of the cross, she drew her head down between her shoulders and threw herself forward, under the oncoming train.

The postmortem examination was held on a dark freezing January day, with Tolstoy in attendance. The once enchanting Anna lay on a table in the Yasenki Barracks, "her skull dissected, her naked body terribly mangled. The effect on his mind was terrible." He had seen men ravaged by war, disease, and famine, but viewing Anna Stepanovna's corpse after her violent suicide was by far his most disturbing encounter with death. The sight of the red bag lying by her side unnerved him. What could have driven her to such a horrifying end? Jealousy, hopelessness, of course. But there were less violent methods of killing oneself. As he stepped out of the barracks into the howling wind, he could make out the sound of a locomotive steaming into the Yasenki station. Tolstoy rode down in his sledge. The train was still there. A dwarfed peasant, gray-bearded and swathed in woolen rags, muttered to himself as he worked at the rails. Tolstoy's nightmare at Arzamas returned to him, and as the little man disappeared into the thick-falling snow a terrible chill seized him.

All through the spring of 1872 these grotesque images haunted him and apparently prevented him from making a solid start on his book on Peter the Great. In April his enthusiasm for the school waned, and much to Sonya's disapproval, he decided to abandon it, leaving the peasant children no educational facilities. He took a new interest in teaching his own children arithmetic and Greek, while Sonya taught them Russian and French. To Sonya's distress, Hannah Tarsey had taken ill with consumption that winter; and as Tanya was now living in a warmer climate, the English governess departed to join the Kuzminskys. Dora, another young red-cheeked Englishwoman, was engaged for seven-year-old Tanya and the babies; and a German tutor, Fyodor Fyodorovich Kaufmann, who had been recommended by Fet, came to supervise the boys. Kaufmann wore an ill-fitting wig, which immediately became the target of many boyish jokes. And even as old men the Tolstoy brothers would remember how he would pull their blankets off on cold mornings and shout, *"Auf, Kinder, auf!"*

Spring came early that year and by the first of April there was "terrible mud, but the weather [was] warm and clear." The children brought yellow crocus and purple violets into the house. Everything was green—"the leaves . . . coming out, and the grass high." In the evening while Sonya played with the children, Tolstoy went out shooting snipe. Occasionally the entire family, except for the two youngest, took an evening stroll in the woods and watched "a full moon . . . rising over the treetops."

It was an idyllic time for Sonya. She was seven months pregnant and feeling well. On April 21 she wrote in her diary, "The children and I went out to gather mushrooms. . . . We got a whole basketful . . . Lyova went shooting. . . . The setting sun was like a bright red ball of fire. It is a quiet evening. . . . The lime trees are opening up and all the other trees except the oaks are in leaf. This morning Lyova brought in a big bunch of flowers and branches."

On June 13, 1872, Sonya's sixth child and fourth son, Pyotr, was born. He was a bright, happy child and she had no trouble breast-feeding him. But that summer was an unsettling one for the Tolstoys. Lev Nikolaevich went to Samara to visit his recently purchased estate, and while he was gone one of their young bulls gored a herdsman to death. On Tolstoy's hurried return to Yasnaya Polyana the court investigator told him that, since a suit was pending against him, he could not leave the estate. After Tolstoy was forced to sign a document agreeing to this stricture, he raged that he was not only under investigation but also under arrest. He was convinced that the authorities in Tula were bent on sending him to jail, and he wrote his cousin, Alexandra:

> I've decided to emigrate to England forever, or until such time as the freedom and dignity of every man is assured in our country. My wife views the prospect with pleasure—she loves everything English; it will be good for the children; I'll have sufficient means (I'll collect 200,000 rubles from the sale of everything); and for myself, notwithstanding my aversion to European life, I hope that over there I'll stop being furious and will be able to spend the few years of life remaining to me peacefully, working on what I still have to write. Our plan is to settle at first near London, and then to select a beautiful and healthy spot by the sea, wherever there are good schools, and buy a house and some land. For life in England to be pleasant, we'll need to know some good aristocratic families. This is where you can help me, and this is what I'm asking of you. Please do this for me. If you don't know any such families, you can doubtless arrange something through your friends: two or three letters which would open the doors of a good English circle to us. This is essential for the children, who'll have to grow up there. I can't say anything yet about when we are going, since they can torment me as long as they like.

Four days later the litigation involving the bull and the gored herdsman was dismissed by the court, and Tolstoy hastened to write Alexandra

> about the new turn that my affair has taken quite unexpectedly, and as a result of which my plans have changed. Forgive me if I've alarmed you, but I'm not to blame: I've been tormented this month as never before in my life, and with my male egoism I wanted everyone to suffer with me, if only a little. I felt better as soon as I had told you about it and had made up my mind to leave. Today—just now—I received a letter from the president of the court—he writes that all the vile things done to me were a mistake, and that I shall be left in peace. If that is so, then I shan't go anywhere, and only ask you to forgive me if I've alarmed you.

Tolstoy had certainly made "everyone suffer with" him during this incident, most especially Sonya. The thought of leaving Russia, perhaps forever and with six small children, did not fill her with pleasure, as he had written Alexandra. On the contrary, she was greatly relieved when no charges were brought against Tolstoy as owner of the bull. So happy was she to know she would not have to uproot her family, that even her husband's restiveness did not cause her much concern. Peter the Great was abandoned for the time, and he was working on the primer, yet he appeared dissatisfied with what he was doing.

A royal scandal was much discussed that spring. Some years earlier Tsar Alexander, long unhappy with his ill and reclusive life, had taken a mistress—Princess Catherine Dolgoruky, a slim dark-eyed young woman with honey-blond hair. In May 1872 the Princess bore the Tsar an illegitimate son, who was christened George. Letters from Alexandra in St. Petersburg and friends in Moscow were filled with indignation. A romantic liaison was one thing, a public scandal another matter. The health of the Empress Maria was failing. Russian society was filled with anxiety and foreboding. Alexander Alexandrovich, the Tsarevich and leader of their aristocratic set, was violent in his condemnation of moral laxity and was a bitter enemy of his father's mistress. A side had to be taken, and society rallied instantly behind the heir apparent. Catherine was forced into a life of semi-seclusion. Her invitations were refused, she was invited nowhere, and she was excluded from all court functions.

Catherine's plight and ostracism were talked about at length at Yasnaya Polyana during that summer and fall, and it seemed to stir some creative drive in Tolstoy. The Dolgoruky affair had novelistic potential, but a suitable treatment of it eluded him. Frustrated, he threw himself back into his work on the primer. Sonya was disappointed by this failure, and in November she wrote her brother Styopa, "Our serious winter life is settling into a routine. Lyova is interested only in public education, schools, teachers' schools—that is, schools where public school teachers will be taught—and this takes up his entire time from morning until night. I look at it with amazement. I am sorry he is spending his strength on this work instead of on writing a novel."

By Christmas Tolstoy was seized by a renewed interest in Peter the Great, and he began to fill notebooks with small details about the dress and customs of the period—minutiae such as whether high collars were worn with the short kaftan or only with long coats. Once again he made many attempts to begin this book and abandoned each immediately.

"The machine is ready, the problem is to get it to start," he complained to Sonya. Finally in February of 1873 he went to Moscow to do some further research, and she was left alone at Yasnaya Polyana.

It was a particularly bitter winter, and death seemed close behind them all the time. Sergey Nikolaevich and Masha had lost a young child; and the burial—with priests, a pink coffin, "everything there ought to be"—had distressed both Tolstoy and Sonya. She was terrified by the thought of losing a child, while he was confused and revolted by the ritualism of burial.

"But then I began to think," he wrote Fet on January 3, "Well, what could my brother have done to carry the decomposing body of his child out of the house in the end? How should it have been carried out? By a coachman in a sack? And where should it be put, how should it be buried? What, generally speaking, is a fitting way to end things? Is there anything better than a requiem, incense, etc? (I, at least, can't think of anything.) And what about growing weak and dying? Should one wet oneself, s[hit], and nothing more?"

Death breathed down the drafty hallways at Yasnaya Polyana as Sonya helped carry water and medicines to the failing Aunt Toinette and her lifelong friend Natalya Petrovna. The desolation of the snowy cold, the smell of the incense and melting wax surrounding the enormous ancient blackened icons in the dying women's room, gave the house an eerie loneliness in spite of the gaiety and noise of the children. And with Tolstoy away, Sonya was overcome with gloominess. On February 13 she noted in her diary:

> I sometimes look into my own heart and ask myself what I really want. And much to my own horror, I reply: I want to have a good time, with flippant company, and new dresses, and I want to be admired and to hear people praise my beauty; and I want Lyova to hear and see it all, and I should like to take him away for a little from his strenuous labors and make him spend some time with me. . . . I

am having my hair waved today, and I enjoy the thought that nobody will be there to see me and that it's really quite unnecessary. I like my new ribbons, and I also want a new leather belt, and now that I've written it all down I want to cry.

With the aunties dying and Hannah gone and Tanya so far away, there was no woman for Sonya to confide in. She did not like the new English governess, remarking in her diary that "*elle est trop commune* and dreary."

To her everlasting relief, Tolstoy arrived home two weeks later, bringing Prince Leonid Dmitrievich Urusov with him. The two men discussed Peter the Great, but Urusov often drew Sonya out and they would talk about the things that both interested and worried her. She complained about her boredom, her fear that she was losing her youth, and Urusov listened attentively, assuring her she was even more beautiful, more womanly with each child and insisting she had great talent and should try to write some stories on her own. The Prince was a tall, commanding man with a gruff voice that revealed his roots in southern Russia. His face, with its large features and heavy brows, was quite homely, but his eyes held a great tenderness. He had a son he was close to, but he was estranged from his wife and daughters. This was difficult for Sonya to understand, because in no other man had she sensed such an empathy for women, their problems, and their aspirations. Urusov's presence gave Sonya new hope, and she was deeply sorry to see him leave on March 13 after only a week's visit.

When Tolstoy returned from seeing the Prince off at the Yasenki station, he was more withdrawn than ever. The next day he was especially irritable, although he did visit the aunties. On a window ledge was a book of Pushkin's, *Tales of Belkin*. Tolstoy thumbed through the book, but his attention kept returning to a line that had caught his eye: "The guests were gathering at the country house. . . ." He immediately went to his study and sat down at his desk. Pushing aside all his books and notes on Peter the Great, he took a fresh sheet of paper and wrote: "After the opera the guests gathered at the home of young Princess Vrasskaya." A new novel had taken shape in his mind and he wrote quickly in his cramped hand.

When he emerged from the study he said excitedly to Sonya, "I have written a sheet and a half and I believe it's good." Sonya thought he had made yet another start on Peter the Great. But after supper he told her that he had begun a modern novel of family life and that one of the main characters would be molded on poor Anna Stepanovna. He would call her Anna Karenina.

13

"It's a bad date; she won't live," Tanya had predicted at the birth of her daughter, Dasha Kuzminsky. And on May 13, 1873, her fifth birthday, the child died of anemia. In the spring of 1871, while in Kutais, Tanya had given birth to another daughter, Masha, which did not lessen the grief caused by the loss of her firstborn. Dasha's death struck terror in Sonya's heart. Pyotr (Petya) had also been born on that "bad date"—the thirteenth. But as she watched him her fears seemed foolish, for Petya was a large, strong baby with great energy. He would lift himself up in his bed and wriggle his chubby elbows "striving to go somewhere," and when she held him in her arms he would try to fly right out. Still her uneasiness made her feel especially protective toward him.

Sonya found outdoor activities for the children to keep the house silent until three o'clock. When Tolstoy emerged from his study, he and the older children often climbed into a wagon and rode out to the fields. Their father's strength amazed the youngsters. He could lift an ailing pig weighing two hundred pounds and was able to work in the fields as hard and as fast as the peasants did. When the mowing had begun, the Tolstoy children helped the village women and girls in their bright *sarafans* and red kerchiefs as they tossed and stacked the hay; and they often brought back enough of the fragrant dry grass to refill their mattresses (a task that was done once a month). Arriving home ravenously hungry, they would sit down to a hearty meal—typically kasha, lamb chops, and vegetables from the garden, with pancakes and jam for dessert. Sonya made the jam herself under the linden trees on a coal stove. Bees and wasps swarmed around the bubbling sweet-smelling liquid, and the children stood waiting for the frothy pink "scum" to form (this was skimmed off and they had it with their tea).

Yasnaya Polyana was especially beautiful in May, and when Sonya woke at dawn, there were silken wisps of clouds in the violet sky. Mounds of pale blue forget-me-nots and yellow expanses of wild garlic blanketed the meadows near the house. While hay was being made in one field, the plowing for the buckwheat had begun in another, and she could hear the hemp being pounded by the peasant women.

On the days when Tolstoy wasn't writing he would rise early with Seryozha and Ilyusha and take them to swim in the Voronka. Often using only saddle cloths and no stirrups, Seryozha rode "the little Kirghiz, Sharik," and Ilyusha the pink-eyed horse Kolpik, while their father was mounted on his huge newly acquired English thoroughbred mare, Frou-Frou. He drove the boys hard, demanding courage and endurance. Putting Frou-Frou to a brisk trot so that they would have to struggle to keep up, he would glance back and ask, "Not tired, are you?" "No!" would come the untrue reply. And when they limped afterward, he would laugh.

Yet there were shared tender moments on these rigorous outings. Tolstoy took his sons to the place in the stand of oaks where his brother Nikolai had said the mysterious "green stick" was buried, and he told them stories of his childhood at Yasnaya Polyana. And sometimes as they rode along through the dappled shade under the birches, he talked about his writing.

"Do you know, Ilyusha, I'm very pleased with myself," he confided to the red-cheeked seven-year-old. "For three days now I've been tormented by her [Anna Karenina] and couldn't get her to go into that house. I just couldn't do it, that's all. It wouldn't come out right. But today it suddenly occurred to me that every entrance hall has a mirror and every lady wears a hat. And as soon as I had thought of that, she went right where I wanted her to go and did everything she was supposed to do. Now you may think that a hat is a mere trifle, but it all worked out because of that hat."

Often in the late afternoons the children would go with Tolstoy for walks in the woods, or to hunt small game, or simply to talk with the pilgrims who walked on the highway that ran past Yasnaya Polyana. This road led from the north of Russia to the Ukraine, the Crimea, and the shores of the Black Sea. The pilgrims walked about twenty miles a day with bundles on their backs, sleeping wherever they could, seldom bathing or changing clothes. They carried stories and rumors and gossip with them, and Tolstoy and his children loved talking to them. And sometimes these wanderers' tales ended up in the pages of Tolstoy's work.

At the end of May the Tolstoys decided that the entire family would journey to Samara for the summer. For the past month he had worked intensely on *Anna Karenina*, completing what he called a "draft form." Then, in a tragic repetition of the accident of the year before, a Yasnaya Polyana bull gored a peasant. The bull had been chained in its stable; the worker who was feeding it stood imprudently in front of it, and the animal lunged forward. For three days the man lay dying, and Tolstoy, in a terrible state, made every effort to save him. The young doctor who had once set Tolstoy's arm was called in as was Dr. Shmigaro. And when the man died, Tolstoy contributed generously to his family and paid for his funeral. Although no legal action was taken against him, Tolstoy was distraught over this accident.

"This was . . . a terrible blow to me," he wrote Strakhov on May 31. "I've lived for forty-five years and I've never heard of any cases of people being done to death by bulls, and now two men have to be killed in one year. I can't get rid of the feeling of guilt and sadness."

He threw himself into helping Sonya with the preparations for the trip to Samara, and early on the morning of June 3, when the sun was just rising over the forest, they set out. They rode past ruined ramparts that stood at the edge of the forest—a reminder of the Tartar raids of centuries past. Yasnaya Polyana had been one of Tula's outposts of defense against the Tartars, and now they were going to see the land from which the invaders had come.

They were to take a train from the Yasenki station to Moscow, then another train to Nizhni Novgorod on the Volga, where they would board a steamer for Samara. Once they reached Samara, they would have to travel seventy miles over poor roads to reach their new estate. To make this part of the arduous journey easier for Sonya, Urusov had put his large *dormeuse*, which seated six, at her disposal, and it was sent ahead to meet the Tolstoys in Samara.

The Tolstoy party—the entire family (except for Aunt Toinette and Natalya Petrovna), Sonya's brother Styopa, Fyodor

Kaufmann (the tutor), Marya Arbuzova (the nurse) and her son, Sergey (the footman)—met Tanya, her daughter Masha, and Hannah Tarsey in Nizhni Novgorod. There was a tearful reunion and then a quick tour of the ancient city which was known as the great gateway to the East. Nizhni Novgorod's spectacular Yarmark Fair, the most popular fair in Russia, was held later in the summer; so the city, set upon a hill with the Urals rising behind it and the Volga at its feet, was not as crowded as it would be when visitors and merchants arrived from all over the world. Still, there was a feeling that they had suddenly entered an exotic land. The people were a strange mixture of Oriental and Occidental, and the children were enchanted by the babble of foreign tongues.

The trip down the Volga was made in a large steamship run by the Caucasus and Mercury Company. Although there was only one bathroom for the more than twenty first-class passengers, the travelers were comfortable in their roomy cabins. The children loved life aboard the ship and were allowed to roam about by the amiable captain, who, as luck had it, had served with Tolstoy at Sevastopol in the Crimean campaign. However, they were forbidden to venture below, where throngs of itinerants and peasants sat and slept on the open deck. Undaunted by the unpleasant odor that wafted up to the first-class deck, the children hung over the railings to watch their fellow passengers play their balalaikas and dance in the small spaces between their shabby piles of belongings.

The farther down the Volga they traveled, the more Oriental the land seemed to become. When the boat docked in Kazan in the early morning hours to take on provisions, Tolstoy, Seryozha, and Ilyusha left the others sleeping and got off to make a short exploration of the town. Tolstoy had once been a university student in Kazan and was so enrapt in telling the boys about his experiences there that, as they walked over the rough cobblestoned streets filled with Tartar men and women setting up their wares, they lost track of time. When they returned to the dock, the steamer "was a mere speck on the horizon." Ilyusha started to wail, and Seryozha looked terrified. Having no money with him, Tolstoy became alarmed and began shouting after the ship. The crowd which had gathered cheered when the vessel, as if in response to Tolstoy's cries, turned back. Realizing Tolstoy and the boys were not aboard, Sonya had asked the captain to return for them. When the steamer reached

the dock amid shouts of relief from the family, the chagrined Tolstoy, carrying Ilyusha, waited impatiently to reboard, while trying
to hold Seryozha back until the gangplank was completely lowered.

The *dormeuse*—a two-seated dickey attached to its rear and a
large wicker trunk on its roof—and a smaller carriage met them in
Samara. Six horses, two leading and four in a row behind them,
pulled the *dormeuse;* they were driven by a young peasant boy from
Yasnaya Polyana who rode on one of the front horses. Sonya,
Tanya, Hannah, Marya Arbuzova, and the four youngest children
(Petya, Masha, and Lyova Tolstoy, and Masha Kuzminsky)
crowded inside the large carriage, while Sergey Arbuzov and Fyodor Kaufmann sat outside on the coachman's bench. Tolstoy and
Styopa rode in the smaller chaise, with Seryozha, Tanya, and
Ilyusha trading places between the two-seated dickey and the one
remaining seat in the chaise. Even with Urusov's generous gift, it
was not a comfortable journey.

Halfway to their destination they stopped for the night in a
large hut. But the ragged beds were vermin-infested and no one
slept well. There was poverty and filth in every village through
which they passed. Men squatted idly in the dirt roads; the crops
had been bad, and there was no work. The few women they saw
were heavily veiled. Sonya was appalled by all she saw, and the
plight of the country people made her forget her own discomfort.

Disappointed by the small ramshackle wooden house Tolstoy
had brought them to for the summer, Sonya immediately set to
work making it habitable. Since it was not large enough for the
family, Tolstoy and Styopa slept in a fitted tent which they had
bought in Samara; and Seryozha, Ilyusha, Lyova, and their tutor
spent their nights in a shed which Sonya made as pleasant as she
could, though there was little to be done about the rats which ran
about squeaking in the darkness.

The Samara steppe was a great uncultivated plain with few
trees. The earth was coal black and the wild grass grew in thick
tufts. Brown buzzards as large as turkeys and huge white-beaked
eagles and hawks soared through the sky. The heat was intense,
but the air was dry and there was a breeze on even the hottest day.

The "estate" was really a rundown farm divided into twelve
fields, of which two (then overgrown with coarse wild grass) were
to be sown, the others being left for pasturage. Since there was no

wood, bricks of dried manure were used for fuel, and great pyramids of them, exuding a terrible stench, were stacked close to the house. There were no other landowners in the area, so the only people the Tolstoys saw were peasants and Bashkirs. The closest doctor was a day's journey away.

Throughout that summer, Sonya was painfully aware of the miasma of poverty and death that hung over each muzhik's dilapidated hut. She was so shocked by the famine that had seized these people after three years of crop failure that she urged Tolstoy to travel throughout the area to ascertain the extent of the disaster. He drove to all the villages within fifty miles and returned convinced that the winter would bring even greater catastrophe to the starving peasants. With Sonya's support he wrote a letter to the *Moscow News* appealing for help for the area. His eloquent plea was picked up and echoed by other major Russian newspapers, and by the end of the summer the government had launched a public appeal for funds. The Tolstoys contributed one hundred rubles and solicited the aid of Alexandra in St. Petersburg, who in turn interested the ailing Tsarina in the relief effort. As a result, almost two million rubles were raised in the Tsar's name to feed the people of the stricken area.

In spite of the famine in his land, and the problems caused by his liaison with Catherine Dolgoruky, the Tsar continued to be the leader of the aristocracy's glittering social life. Grand balls for as many as three thousand guests were held in the Nicholas Hall of the Winter Palace. These parties gave him great pleasure, even though his beloved Catherine could not join his Romanov relatives and the members of Russian upper class society in their gala festivities. He also bought a thousand-acre estate near Livadia in the subtropical Crimea, which, because of fear of public censure, Catherine could not visit. His passion for her had not cooled, but he was a man of great self-indulgence; he enjoyed all the privileges of his position and expected—and received—no opposition from his mistress.

The Tsar's extravagances, which continued unabated at a time when a large number of his people were starving, and the slights suffered by his declared mistress were endlessly discussed and condemned by the Tolstoys on the trip back to Yasnaya Polyana in August. The Tsar's liaison was of special interest to Tolstoy be-

cause he saw a parallel between it and that of his fictional lovers—
Vronsky and Anna Karenina. Once home, Tolstoy continued his
work on *Anna Karenina* while Sonya happily copied his pages.
Early that fall the portrait painter Ivan Kramskoye took a small
house three miles from Yasnaya Polyana with the hope of persuad-
ing Tolstoy to sit for him. With Sonya's encouragement (the artist
had promised to do a portrait of her as well), Tolstoy reluctantly
agreed. Kramskoye came to the house every afternoon, interrupting Tolstoy's work; but once the sittings were begun, Tolstoy
found he enjoyed the discussions the two of them had on art.

That fall Sonya became pregnant once again. Then in early November the event she had feared since little Dasha Kuzminsky's
death became a reality. Petya became violently sick with a throat
infection so severe that his high temperature caused convulsions.
"At nine o'clock on the morning of November 9, my little Petya
died of throat trouble," Sonya wrote in her diary two days later.
"He died peacefully after only two days' illness. I nursed him for
fourteen and a half months. He was born on the thirteenth of June,
1872. He was such a bright, happy child. My darling, I loved him
so much, and now everything seems so empty since they buried
him yesterday."

Not for a long time would she be able to shut out "the cruel
memory" of Petya's funeral, and of "the general indifference shown
to the little pink coffin, and her own heart-rending, lonely grief [at]
the sight of that pale little forehead with the curly locks on the
temples, and of the open, surprised little mouth visible in the coffin
at the instant before they covered it with the pink lid ornamented
with a gold lace cross."

"He loved me very much; I wonder if he was sorry to have to
leave me here?" she wrote after the funeral. Throughout the winter
she grieved over the death of her child. ("As soon as the grass
begins to grow on Petya's little grave, they will have to dig it up
for me; the thought haunts me unceasingly," she wrote in February
1874.) While she grew larger with child, her depression deepened,
caused not only by Petya's death but also by her own unhappiness
and by the agony of reliving the worst moments of her bereavement
as she copied the pages of *Anna Karenina*. Tolstoy was once again
drawing on Sonya's most private and tormented experiences to
create his fictional world.

"And what is it all for?" a character in *Anna Karenina* says after the death of her last child, a boy. "What will come of it all? I [haven't had] a moment's peace, now pregnant, now nursing, always cross and grumbling, tormenting myself and others, repulsive to my husband . . ."

A small revolution was brewing inside Sonya's head. She was pregnant and there was nothing she could do about that, but she recalled a conversation with Anna Stepanovna in which the woman had told her that she was afraid of having an illegitimate child by Bibikov and that she, in fact, intended to have no children even if they should marry. Until her talk with Anna Stepanovna, Sonya had never understood why some women had only one, two, or no children. On learning that pregnancy could be prevented, she had been intrigued and horrified. But such tampering with the natural order had seemed immoral to her then and it still did. Yet she did discuss this issue—in abstract terms—with Tolstoy, who then worked it into a scene in his novel. Little Lyova remained the child she doted on, and the thought that had she taken Anna Stepanovna's path he might never have existed was enough to dispel at least temporarily "the confusion of insane thoughts that whirled in her head."

Tolstoy's spiritual crisis intensified in the spring of 1874. During the year that he had been working on *Anna Karenina* he had encountered death within his own family circle for the first time, and he had become "less horrified by death than by life." Like Levin in *Anna Karenina,* he "felt like a person who has exchanged a thick fur coat for a muslin garment, and who, being out of the frost for the first time, becomes clearly convinced, not by arguments but with the whole of his being, that he is as good as naked and that he must inevitably perish miserably."

For both Tolstoy and Levin the problem was this: "If I don't accept the replies offered by Christianity to the questions my life presents, what solution do I accept?"

He took time away from his work to write letters to Strakhov and others seeking an answer to this question. But none of those whom he respected could help him. He reread Plato, Spinoza, Kant, Schilling, Hegel, and Schopenhauer and read Homyakov's theological writings for the first time. But he found no great illumination.

Levin says, "Without knowing what I am, and why I am here, it is impossible to live. Yet I cannot know that, and therefore I can't live." And though Levin was "a happy and healthy family man, [he] was several times so near to suicide that he hid a cord he had lest he should hang himself, and he feared to carry a gun lest he should shoot himself." But Levin did neither. He went on living. And so did Tolstoy—though his search for truth and Sonya's deep and growing opposition to the religious bent that his thought had taken created a new tension and disharmony in their family life. And yet how could Tolstoy have wished for a better wife? He had educated her in his ways, instilled her with his views, idealized her in his writing. How could he expect her to do a complete turnabout and become an advocate of pure Christianity, simplicity, and Platonic marriage—all ideals he was beginning to apply to his own life? Certainly this would be difficult for Sonya, when at the same time she shared his dreams of increasing his wealth with her, proudly bought cheap land from the starving Samara Bashkirs, and did nothing to help her from having one child after the other.

On April 22, in perhaps her easiest delivery, Sonya gave birth to a large healthy boy whom they christened Nikolai. His nickname was Nikolenka, but Sonya often called him Petya.

Once again it was summer and the hay harvest had begun. Tall campanulas rested their bell-shaped white and lilac blossoms on the windowsills. Blue cornflowers glowed bright in the sunshine. And on June 20 Aunt Toinette, beloved *Auntie*, died in a room on the ground floor where she had asked to be moved so that her own room would not hold unhappy memories. All of the children, the baby in Sonya's arms, were taken in to "say goodbye to her." The coffin stood before Aunt Toinette's blackened icons, and the room was permeated by the heavy odor of incense. Terrified, each one of the children walked timidly past the coffin and glanced swiftly and nervously at the corpse of their aged relative.

Aunt Toinette had lived at Yasnaya Polyana for fifty years, and she was loved not only by her family but also by all the peasants on the estate and in the village. When the funeral procession led by the priest left the house, her coffin was carried through the dirt streets of the village. At almost every door a peasant stepped forward and pressed money upon the priest, asking him to say a prayer for her soul. A day after the funeral Tolstoy wrote his cousin Alexandra, "I lived with her all my life; and I feel frightened without her."

Only a few days later her loyal maid of over fifty years, Axinia, died. Within a week Natalya Petrovna had become mentally unstable and her physical condition had declined sharply. After a painful family decision the old woman was placed on a stretcher bed in back of the *dormeuse* and driven to an old people's home that had been built on Turgenev's estate, Spasskoye. Tolstoy's elderly Aunt Pelagya, who had been living in a convent in Tula, soon moved to Yasnaya Polyana, taking the small room in which Aunt Toinette had died. An alert and extremely intelligent woman, she was welcomed by her lively grandnieces and grandnephews. Tanya returned from Kutais with Masha and a new baby girl, Vera, but without Hannah, who had remained in the Caucasus to marry a Georgian prince. Sonya was nursing Nikolenka, and even Tanya's return and the new baby's good nature did little to restore her to health. Petya's death and Tolstoy's spiritual and intellectual demands on her had taken a heavy toll.

Progress on *Anna Karenina* was slow during that summer and fall, and Tolstoy wrote Alexandra, "I cannot tear myself away from living creatures to bother about imaginary ones." However, serial rights were sold in December to Katkov at the *Russian Herald* for the magnificent sum of 20,000 rubles, and the first three parts appeared in February 1875.

The joy Sonya felt at this further sign of her husband's success was extinguished by the death on February 20 of ten-month-old Nikolenka. Two weeks earlier the child had fallen ill with meningitis, and his suffering had been a torture to everyone in the household, most especially Sonya, who never left his bedside.

This second death, so soon after Petya's, was a stunning blow. Death seemed to be nipping at her heels, and she did not know how to escape from her dark imaginings. Lev Nikolaevich, grumbling that he was tired of *Anna Karenina*, was himself so terrified of death that he was cold to her distress. Unable to console her in any other way, he let her into his bed again. And by the first days of May, when they set out to spend the summer in Samara, Sonya was almost three months pregnant. When they returned to Yasnaya Polyana in August, she was extremely weak. Country life now seemed unbearable to her, nothing but "dull, monotonous apathy day after day," coupled with hard work that she felt increasingly unable to do. In the evenings, when she wanted to spend an hour or two alone with her husband, Aunt Pelagya demanded his attention. He played patience with the old woman while Sonya was left with sewing, embroidery, or a book. And since she was pregnant, they did not sleep together.

"Sometimes I feel that I only live in my dreams," she wrote in her diary. "I dream of marvelous picture galleries or of wonderful flowers, or of crowds of people whom, instead of hating and avoiding, I love with all my heart." But she ended her entry characteristically concerned more for Tolstoy's future happiness than her own. "If one did not hope, life would be quite impossible; and I still hope that God will once again light that flame in Lyova's mind which has kept him alive in the past, and which he will need in the future."

They were not home from the Caucasus more than six weeks when all the children came down with whooping cough, and Sonya was soon exhausted by nursing them as well as the demanding Aunt Pelagya, who had suddenly begun to ail. One night after midnight as she was seeing to the smaller children in the nursery, Tolstoy was downstairs undressing for bed in the room which had been his study and was now his dressing room. Suddenly he screamed, "Sonya! Sonya!" Then he let out an eerie, terrified shriek. She ran into the dark hallway, the candle trembling in her hand, and descended the unlighted stairs as quickly as she could, calling out to him as she went. He answered only with a stifled wail. She found him standing in his dressing gown in the cold dark hallway.

"What happened, Lyovochka?" she asked, putting her shawl over his shoulders and leading him up the stairs to his bedroom.

"I lost my way," Tolstoy sobbed, leaning on her.

It was a long time before he was soothed. He then told her that the ghostly image that he had encountered at Arzamas had returned. As before, he had felt he was being pursued by death; he had panicked and had run into the dark hallway to go up to her room. But the thing that pursued him seemed to be everywhere he turned, and suddenly he could not recall where the stairs were.

"It's a bad omen," Sonya said, tears glittering in her eyes.

She awoke the next morning with a high fever, and she began to cough blood in violent spasms. Since the aging Shmigaro had retired from practice that year, Dr. Krertzer, the young doctor from Tula, was sent for. Certain that Sonya had caught whooping cough from the children, he dosed her with quinine. But her fever rose, and she grew delirious. Now alarmed, Tolstoy wrote Dr. Zakharin in Moscow to come immediately. Zakharin sent an assistant, a Dr. Chirkov, who diagnosed peritonitis and prescribed appropriate treatment. Sonya began to improve, but the illness had precipitated early labor and on the first of November, 1875, she gave birth prematurely to a girl, whom she insisted they immediately name Varya. The child lived but one hour.

Outside her window there were three small graves, and the three new headstones were soon covered by heavy snow. Sonya was ill through most of the winter, and she spent hours looking out at the snow-covered graves. Tolstoy seemed untouched by her suffering and wrote to Strakhov, "All this time—two weeks—I've been looking after a sick wife who gave birth to a stillborn child and has been at death's door. But it's a strange thing—I've never thought with such vigor about the problems which interest me at this time."

Sonya was unable to copy for him for most of the winter. The first time she could, she copied a part of a letter to Strakhov in which he wrote, "I feel that old age has begun for me. I call old age the inner spiritual condition in which all the outer phenomena of the world lose their meaning for me."

Had she lost her meaning to him as well? Would his love for her die like little Petya and Nikolenka and Varya? She paced her room, did her sewing and embroidery, read stories to the children, and listened through the open door as Tolstoy played the piano in the sitting room. Once they had played duets. But her arms were too weak for the piano, and she only had enough strength to help a few hours a day with the copying. He was giving little time to

Anna Karenina, which he claimed he now thought repulsive; he was absorbed by religious and spiritual issues which Sonya found confusing and repellent.

On December 22, while standing on a chair to hang an icon over her bed, Aunt Pelagya lost her balance and crashed to the floor, breaking several bones and suffering a severe concussion. She was in a fevered hysterical state and lay in great pain for twenty-four hours. As Sonya held the old woman's hand, Aunt Pelagya kept crying out, "*Je ne veux pas mourir!* [I don't want to die!]." But that night she did, and from the moment of her death an intangible wall was flung between Tolstoy and his wife, a wall that Sonya would try to tear down for the rest of their lives. Aunt Pelagya was Tolstoy's last link to his mother, the mother he had never truly known. With the deaths of Aunt Toinette and Aunt Pelagya, he finally accepted the fact that his mother was dead and that there was no one who could keep her spirit alive for him. Like Aunt Pelagya, Tolstoy did not want to die. With her loss he entered in earnest into a solitary combat with death and set out on a desperate search for the truth about eternal life. All Sonya was left with were what she called "phantoms."

PART FOUR
1877-1892

Watching the Phantoms

I have come to love the darkness. When it grows dark, I begin to feel happier, and my imagination begins to evoke the things I used to love, and I sit there, watching the phantoms. Last night I caught myself speaking aloud. I was so frightened: What if I am going mad?

COUNTESS TOLSTOY'S DIARY
OCTOBER 25, 1886

14

War. It was an utterly futile, sinful atrocity that no one at Yasnaya Polyana could condone. Inevitably, though, they knew it must come. For two years the Slavonic problem had been growing more pressing. The people in the nearby countries of Bosnia and Herzegovina had risen against the harsh rule of the Turks in 1875. They endured ruthless slaughter and were finally joined in their insurrection by Serbia and Montenegro. A movement calling for Russia's entrance into the war on the side of the Slavs was energetically promoted by Russia's Slavophile circle, led by Tolstoy's old friend Yuri Samarin. Almost every newspaper and letter received at Yasnaya Polyana contained reports on the horrors being suffered by the Slavs at the hands of the barbarous Turks. In Moscow, St. Petersburg, and Tula, benefits—balls, concerts, dinners, speeches —were held for these beleaguered people. Hundreds of Russians of all classes had enlisted in the Serbian army to help fight the Turks, though they proved of little use in encounters with their war-toughened adversaries. Finally, in a manifesto issued on April 24, 1877, Tsar Alexander II announced to his people that Russia was at war with Turkey.

Everyone at Yasnaya Polyana, including the children, took a great interest in the war. When the newspapers arrived from Tula, the household gathered to hear them read. The children quickly learned the names and patronymics of all the generals, and they knew their faces as well, for their pictures were reproduced in cheap prints, on calendars, and even on candy wrappers. Each boy had regiments of miniature toy soldiers, and they spent hours plotting the battles between the Russians and the Turks.

Sonya had a horror of war. She hated guns and never took any pleasure in the "sport" of hunting. Yet she was torn by conflicting emotions regarding Russia's current entanglement. She had been touched by the wave of patriotism which had swept the country, and as the Russian army suffered great losses, her moral repugnance gave way to anxiety about her countrymen and anger toward the Turks.

One day Tolstoy took the older boys to see the Turkish soldiers who were prisoners in the Tula barracks. The Tolstoys entered a large "yard surrounded by a stone wall, where there were a number of stalwart, good-looking young men in wide blue trousers and red fezzes." One Turkish soldier was leaning against the wall reading the Koran. As Tolstoy approached him, the soldier asked in Russian for cigarettes. Tolstoy gave some tobacco and papers along with a few coins. Then he engaged him in a conversation about religion, and "persuaded two of the biggest men to give a demonstration of Turkish wrestling."

"What charming, gentle, handsome men they are," he commented as they drove away, confusing the boys, who could not understand why their father was so friendly with "those terrible Turks" whom they had been told to regard as their enemy.

Life went on as it always had from September to May at Yasnaya Polyana. The children rose about eight. Tolstoy joined them for breakfast an hour later. He was usually grumpy in the morning, and the children tried to avoid speaking to him. He would gulp down two soft-boiled eggs and then retire to his study with a glass of tea and cigarettes which Sonya rolled for him. (She also cut his beard once a month on the appearance of the new moon.) He did not reappear until late in the afternoon, when the house came suddenly alive as he emerged from his study and the children were permitted to play unrestrained.

Dinner was always at five, but seldom did everyone arrive on time. After dinner was family time. At ten, tea was served and then the children went to bed. Within two hours Tolstoy usually followed, leaving Sonya to do her work in the silence of the sleeping household.

These quiet hours in the middle of the night constituted Sonya's private world. Candles burned on her writing table, sending wavering shadows up the walls. Darkness, except for an occasional red glow from the embers of a fire dying in a hearth, existed in the rest of the house. She worked with a shawl tied securely about her shoulders, but by three in the morning the fire had turned to ash and her hands and feet were chilled through. Her neck and shoulders stiff from bending over her work and her eyes bleary, she carefully blotted her work, closed the inkwell, and snuffed all candles but one. Carrying this taper and Tolstoy's notebook with the freshly copied pages inside it, she tiptoed to his study, left the notebook on his desk (for him to have when he began work a few hours later) and then went quietly through the dark corridors of the chilled house to her bed, setting the bedside clock to rouse her in three hours to nurse her baby (there seemed always to be a baby at her breast). It was a harsh schedule, but Sonya enjoyed being part of her husband's work and she was enthralled by the story of *Anna Karenina*.

Work on *Anna Karenina* was nearing completion, a prospect that Tolstoy, unlike Sonya, regarded with relief. This book had never brought him great satisfaction. He had written to Fet in 1875, "I am now setting to work again on my *tedious, vulgar Karenina*, with only one wish, to get it out of the way as soon as possible." The following year, after reading the proof sheets for one section, he complained to Strakhov, "*Everything* in it is *execrable* and the whole thing ought to be rewritten—all that has been published too—scratched out, thrown away, repudiated; I ought to say: 'I'm sorry, I won't do it any more,' and try to write something fresh instead of this incoherent, neither-fish-nor-fowl-sort of stuff." In 1877 he wrote Strakhov again, amazed that this installment had been well received and that readers "should like anything so ordinary and *insignificant*."

When Sonya praised a passage she had just copied, he roared, "What's so difficult in writing about an officer falling in love with a married woman? There's nothing difficult in that, and, what's more, nothing good either. It's bad and it serves no purpose!" Had it not been for Sonya and his commitment to his publisher, he would have destroyed the novel.

The declaration of war almost coincided with Tolstoy's completion of the chapter in which Anna Karenina throws herself beneath an oncoming train. He had killed his "heroine." It was not to have been the end of the book, but he was at an impasse. "I can't write anything while the war is going on," he told Sonya. "One has the same feeling when there's a fire in the town; the excitement is so great that you can't give your attention to anything else."

Entered into with great bravado, the war was proving a costly, painful disappointment to the Russians. The Turks were heroic soldiers, and their defense in the critical battle of Plevna held up the Russian advance for several months. By the time the Russian army reached Constantinople, England and Austria—fearing Russia's expansion into Turkey—were close to declaring war against Russia. Faced with this danger, the Tsar surrendered to European pressures; and after tense weeks of negotiations Russia not only gave up most of the territory it had gained during the war but also allowed Bosnia and Herzegovina to pass under Austrian control. The battles had been won, but the Russian people considered the year-long war a humiliating defeat and blamed the Tsar for this failure. The war over, Tolstoy's mind turned to philosophic-religious questions. He was concerned with "showing the absolute necessity for religion," and he recorded his speculations in a large, impressively bound notebook.

The non-religious man Sonya had married was now zealously orthodox. She accepted Russian Orthodoxy without questioning any of its tenets, and it was not an important force in her life. She taught the children to say their prayers before going to sleep, blessed them with icons, and took them to church on holidays. Try as she might, she could not become a fervent believer as Tolstoy had done. He fasted, prayed for long hours, and attended church more regularly. He asked Sonya to go with him to confession, and when she finally agreed he warned her, "The priest will ask you if you eat lenten food."

"I know."

"Well, you must not eat it or else lie to him."

Sonya chose a third alternative. She accompanied him to confession less frequently.

Finally, though, the last section of the book, Part VIII, fell into place for him, and to Sonya's delight he began to write again. "We are now really at work on *Anna Karenina*," she wrote Tanya. "That is writing without interruption. Lyovochka is in a lively, concentrated state of mind. He adds a whole chapter each day. I work hard on the copying and already, lying under this very

Above, Sonya Andreyevna Behrs, seated, at 14 years of age, and her sister Tanya Andreyevna, at 12.
Above right, Tolstoy, left, with his brother Nikolai Nikolaevich, who died in 1860. He was Lev's favorite brother.
Below, Lisa Andreyevna Behrs, Sonya's sister, around 1860.
Below right, Tanya Kuzminsky, Sonya's sister, 1864.

Sonya Andreyevna Behrs in 1860, before marriage to Tolstoy.

Tolstoy at the time of his marriage in 1862.

Opposite, Yasnaya Polyana.
Opposite bottom left, Agatha Mikhailovna and Misha Stakhovich at Yasnaya Polyana.
Opposite bottom right, Maria Afanasyevna and Nikolai Mikhailovich, nurse and cook in the Tolstoy household.
Below, the Tolstoy family with Tolstoy in rear, about 1870. From left, Sonya holding the infant Lev; her daughter Tanya; "Big Masha," daughter of Sonya's sister Tanya; the woman in black, with two of her children. Front row, Ilya and Sergey.

Above, Sonya in 1883 with her sister Tanya (left) and daughter Tanya (right).
Left, the Tolstoys, 1887.
Below, Sonya's bedroom at the house in Moscow.
Opposite top, Moscow, around 1890.
Opposite bottom, Sonya with younger children, 1890. From left, Misha, Andrey, Sasha, Vanichka.

Above, behind Tolstoy stands Misha, and in front of Tolstoy, Vanichka and Sasha. Back row: Lev, with beard; Andrey; Tanya; Sonya; Masha.
Below, Tolstoy playing tennis at Yasnaya Polyana, 1890s. In the trio at the far right stands Sonya, with Tanya (seated). Across the net at the center is Sasha.
Right, in the parlor at Yasnaya Polyana, 1890s. From left, Tolstoy (with Belka at his feet), Tanya, Masha, and Sonya. Vanichka and Sasha are perched on bedpost.

Above left, Sonya and Repin in the garden at Yasnaya Polyana, 1907.
Above right, Chertkov, around 1900.
Below, a rare photo of Taneyev (left) and Goldenweiser during a visit to
Yasnaya Polyana. Photo by Countess Tolstoy.

Above left, Sergey Nikolaevich Tolstoy, Tolstoy's brother. *Right*, Ivan Turgenev. Photo by Nadar.
Below, Anton Chekhov, left, with Tolstoy in the Crimea, 1900. Photo by Chertkov.

Opposite top, 1905: from left, Dr. Makovitsky, Sasha, Elizabeth Obolensky, Chertkov, Tolstoy, Sonya, Masha Obolensky, Tolstoy's secretary, and Varvara Feokritova.

Opposite bottom, Tolstoy with his secretary, Valentin Bulgakov, about 1909.

Right, Tolstoy in 1901. Photo by Countess Tolstoy.

Below, Varvara Feokritova, who was Sonya's secretary, and Sasha playing with Sasha's poodle on Tolstoy's 80th birthday.

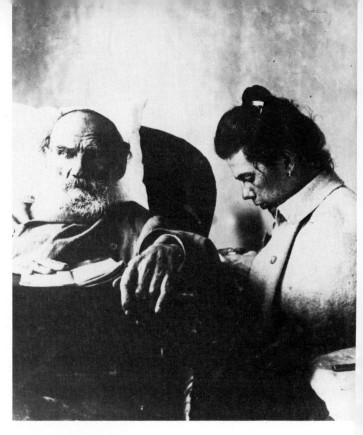

Above, Tanya at the bedside of her sick father, Gaspra, 1902.
Left, The last photograph of the Tolstoys, taken on their 48th anniversary, September 23, 1910.
Opposite top, the station at Astapovo, where Tolstoy died in November 1910.
Opposite center, funeral procession bearing Tolstoy's body for burial at Yasnaya Polyana.
Opposite bottom, Tolstoy's grave, Yasnaya Polyana.

Sonya during her widowhood.

letter, I have the fresh copies of the new chapter he wrote yesterday."

In his last section Tolstoy maintained that the Russian people should have no interest in a war between the Serbs and the Turks. Angered by this opposition to the war, Katkov, the publisher, refused to print what Tolstoy had written and instead published a note stating that the story ended with Anna's death and giving a brief summary of the fates of the other major characters.

Strakhov came to Yasnaya Polyana during June and July 1877 to help Tolstoy prepare the entire novel for publication in book form. Sonya's household that summer was extremely busy. Besides Strakhov, Tanya and her family were occupying the wing where the school had once been, a practice that was to continue each summer for years to come. The house was overrun by children of all ages and their tutors, nurses, and teachers. Two young men arrived on Saturdays and Sundays to give the boys additional lessons. And Sonya was pregnant and due to deliver in early December. Since Masha's birth (which had almost killed her), she had been reluctant to become pregnant again. Her arguments for employing some form of birth control (namely her husband's withdrawal before orgasm) shocked and repelled Tolstoy. More than once they had quarreled violently about this subject. Sonya saw that if she wanted to avoid becoming pregnant, she must forgo sexual relations with her husband. It appeared that this difficult renunciation would be far more painful for her than for Tolstoy. He, in fact, had recently described marriage as "domesticated prostitution." Sexual restraint when she was pregnant no longer seemed enough to assuage his guilt; he had begun to believe that total abstention was necessary to achieve salvation.

Sonya did not know how to respond to Tolstoy's consuming concern with morality. His quest for religious truth was "a passionate and sincere seeking," but she did not want to follow his spiritual wandering. Nor did she believe she had the right to do so with so many children reliant upon her. "How can I turn like a weathercock in every direction?" she cried.

A boy, named Andrey, after her father, was born on the morning of December 6, 1877. The child's birth seemed, as Sonya said, "to liberate L[ev] N[ikolaevich] from mental chains." He began a novel about the Decembrists. For a short time he was his old spirited self, but then he put aside the novel and returned to his philosophic-religious writings. To the older children he was now "a stern and censorious moralist." He would sit Seryozha, Ilyusha, Tanya, and Lyova down and present all his troubling theses and questions. Frightened by these fervent outpourings, the children "slunk away," and Sonya resented his disturbance of their carefree happiness. "I teach and nurse like a machine from morn to night, from night to morn," she wrote Tanya after Andrey's birth.

Then the financial reward for all the years of work suddenly swept in. *Anna Karenina* was earning huge sums in royalties, and their income for the year, based in part on her astute management of the farm, was nearly thirty thousand rubles. They were rich, and at least one of Sonya's dreams had come true.

She felt like a widow coming out of an excessively long period of mourning. She looked longingly at the dresses in her fashion magazines, the watered silks and bright satins with their low necklines set off by hand-sewn flowers. But knowing Tolstoy would never approve any of them, she sent away to St. Petersburg for a fashionable black silk travel dress to wear on a planned trip to Moscow. She refurbished some of the rooms in the house and augmented the staff. To Tolstoy's distaste, she employed two footmen and dressed them in red waistcoats and white gloves which were knitted by Agatha Mikhailovna. A French governess, Mlle. Gachet, was found for Tanya, who was almost fourteen. Knowing that Tanya would soon have to be launched into society, Sonya was trying without success to convince Tolstoy that they should have a house in Moscow. Masha had an Englishwoman, Annie, to see to her needs; the boys had Monsieur Nief, their French tutor; little Andrey had a nanny. The children also had tutors for Russian, drawing, Greek, music, and German; and these teachers came to the house for meals and lessons.

For a short time it seemed that Sonya's happiness was complete. There was the pain, of course, whenever she glanced out the window at the three small graves, but she now had six beautiful chicks in her brood. Masha was a frail child, and as Lyova had been, the new baby was troubled by croup and night restlessness. But they were all bright, loving children. Seryozha could be a bit stuffy and quarrelsome at times (he did, however, play the piano well), and Ilyusha was always in and out of mischievous trouble. But all families had their small problems. What mattered most was that Lev Nikolaevich was working on a new novel and that they were out of debt and able to afford a few luxuries.

Then as suddenly as Tolstoy had embraced orthodoxy, he turned away from it. No longer did he fast or pray. He began to criticize the rites and practices of the Church and refused to attend services. An incident at the Optina Pustyn Monastery had disillusioned him. He had made a pilgrimage there on foot with his servant Sergey Arbuzov (Alexei Stepanovich now elderly and retired), and the monks, taking Tolstoy for a poor peasant, lodged him in a filthy lice-infested cell. Sergey Arbuzov, furious that the Count had been treated so shabbily, informed the monks of his master's identity. Tolstoy was then moved to the best room, and elaborate meals were prepared for him. This obsequiousness disgusted him, and his disenchantment with the Church was immediate.

Without belief in orthodoxy, there seemed nowhere he could turn. He suffered from great guilt and a desperate need to repent. He talked about suicide and feared he would take his life. He stopped going out hunting in terror that he might turn the gun on himself. His gloom spread through the entire household, and Sonya wrote Tanya, "His eyes are fixed in a strange gaze, he scarcely talks, he has quite left this world and is absolutely incapable of thinking about everyday matters."

The children were baffled. Their world seemed to be divided into two camps; Tolstoy was in one and Sonya and "everyone else in the other." As Ilya later wrote, this was Tolstoy's "dark period of the burning of the idols."

Having idealized family life and lovingly depicted in three novels the background of a nobleman's life that resembled his own, he suddenly began to denounce and decry it; having prepared his sons for a classical and university education according to the methods of the day, he began to condemn current scholarship; having regularly consulted Dr. Zakharin and sent to Moscow for doctors for his wife and children, he began to denounce medicine; having always been a passionate sportsman and avid hunter of wolves, bears, and wild game, he began to call hunting "chasing dogs"; having accumulated money for fifteen years and bought land cheap from the Bashkirs of

Samara, he began to call property a crime and money corruption; and lastly, having devoted his entire life to literature, he began to repent of this activity and all but abandoned it forever.

At the age of fifty Tolstoy was a repentant sinner; but Sonya, having spent half of her thirty-five years living wholly for him, had little for which to repent. She saw him suffering, but he refused to turn to her for solace. No longer did they have mutual interests. Worse yet, he deprecated her interests and "chafed at their life together." His family found him "taciturn, morose, and irritable." When the children were gay—putting together a theatrical or playing a lively game of croquet or eating a good meal—he would sternly lecture them. "We stuff ourselves with cutlets and all kinds of pastry, and in Samara people are dying by the thousands, their bellies distended from starvation," or, "Here we sit in our well-heated rooms, and today a man was found frozen to death because no one would give him a night's lodging."

Seryozha was fifteen, Tanya fourteen, Ilyusha twelve, Lyova nine, and Masha seven; they were simply unable to regard the peasants and pilgrims with the intense empathy and respect that Tolstoy now displayed. From the time they were toddlers, he had made it clear to them that they were superior to the village children and that it was an absolute necessity to speak French and German and English to prepare for society, the gymnasium and university. Frustrated and disappointed that his children did not alter their lives to his new beliefs, Tolstoy felt that they failed to understand him. For their part, they suffered great melancholy and a sense of rejection and had a deep conviction that it was Papa who did not understand *them*.

With Sonya's urgings he did from time to time enter into the children's life. Still, from 1877, the year of little Andreyusha's birth and of Tolstoy's sudden religiosity, his relationship to the children seemed to them to be, "not that of a father but a teacher."

Tolstoy spent almost every waking hour surrounded by "great mountains" of philosophical and religious books and treatises; he read, wrote, and meditated about the spiritual problems that had become his central concern. The burdens of running the household and the farm fell entirely on Sonya. In summer, besides the Tolstoys' six children, there were the Kuzminskys, their four children, and a constant stream of guests and servants to care for. Sonya again suggested they move to Moscow, where life would be much easier. Tolstoy, who believed it was good for the children to live among peasants and pilgrims, remained opposed to this change.

"It's all very well to talk about ideas," Sonya argued, "but children can't be left ignorant and half educated; they have to be fed, clothed, and their health looked after." None of her arguments changed what was now a divided household. Perhaps if she had been able to alter her lifestyle to Tolstoy's—dismiss the staff, force the children to do the labor in the house, cut out croquet, horseback riding, ice skating, and singing in the evenings—life might have had a less schismatic quality. Yet, where was there proof that her husband would not once again cast about wildly and come up with still another philosophy and throw them all into further turmoil? And if she did subscribe to a self-imposed "poverty," she would have been left to do the work for the whole family—feed, sew their clothes, wash, bring up the children—while Tolstoy would have done nothing else but write his religious tracts. Where was the equality in that for her?

While Sonya awaited the birth of another child in late 1879, Tolstoy retreated deeper into his biblical and theological studies. His novel on the Decembrists was abandoned, to Sonya's distress. "Lev is working, so he says," she wrote to Tanya, "but, alas! he keeps writing religious tracts, reads and thinks until his head aches and all this to prove how inconsistent the Church is with the teachings of the gospels. There will hardly be a dozen people in Russia interested in that. But there is nothing to be done. I only wish that he would finish this as soon as possible and that it may pass like some sort of sickness."

"It's not the money I regret," she wrote in another letter to Tanya, "There is something lacking in my life, something that I loved, and that is Lyova's literary work, which had always given me such joy and inspired me with such reverence. You see, Tanya, I'm a true writer's wife, so greatly do I take his writing to heart."

On December 18 she wrote in her diary, "I am anxiously waiting for my confinement, which is already overdue. The thought of another child depresses me; my whole horizon seems to have narrowed down."

On the same day she made an entry in the journal she was

keeping on Tolstoy: "He is writing about religion and the disagreement between the Church and Christianity. He reads all day long.
. . . All his conversation is full of the teaching of Christ. His frame of mind is peaceful, meditative, and solemn. He has put aside the Decembrists and all his former labors, although he still says sometimes, 'If I ever write anything again, I shall write something quite different. All I have written so far has been mere exercise.' "

In the cold early hours of December 20, 1879, having spent the night copying her husband's work, Sonya gave birth to a boy. The child was helped into the world by Agatha Mikhailovna just minutes before the doctor and midwife arrived from Tula. The family now consisted of five sons and two daughters. The child was christened Mikhail (Misha) on Twelfth Night. For a short time the house abounded with gaiety. Occasionally Tolstoy would go to the iced-over Voronka to skate with the family. But such moments of relaxation were few.

There was a tall, beautiful Christmas tree and many dear friends—Sergey Nikolaevich, Strakhov, the Auerbachs, and Sonya's aunts and family from Tula. Prince Urusov was also a visitor. He was now permanently separated from his wife, who had moved to Paris, and he spent a good deal of time at Yasnaya Polyana discussing philosophy with Tolstoy. Urusov's visits were one of the few joys to which Sonya looked forward. She was able to open her heart to him to talk about the small and sensitive and beautiful things she could no longer discuss with her husband. The Prince shared many of his problems, hopes, and ideas with her; and a romantic attachment soon developed. They never became lovers, but Urusov's presence, his deep interest in everything Sonya considered important to her, made her even more dissatisfied with many aspects of her life with Tolstoy.

On January 30, when Misha was not yet six weeks old she confessed to Tanya, "How hard I find it to bear my hermit's life! Imagine, Tanya, I haven't been out of the house since September. It's like a prison, only brighter both morally and financially. But nonetheless I have the feeling of being locked up, held back, and I want to push through, break through and run away as quickly as possible."

A few days later she wrote Tanya again: "At times I should like to fly away to you, to Mama, to Moscow—anywhere away from my half-dark bedroom where bending over the flushed little face of a new boy fourteen times a day I have shrunk away and almost fallen into a faint from pain in my breasts."

Only the Kuzminskys' visit during the summer months gave much happiness to Sonya during 1880. Their departure in September sent her into a decline, and in October she wrote Tanya, "To my extreme horror, I'm surely pregnant again." With this new pregnancy, Sonya became deeply depressed. Her home life was filled with discord. Tolstoy had plunged into what he now regarded as "his work"—visiting prisons, justices of the peace, district courts, and recruiting stations in an effort to help the oppressed and impoverished. Suddenly he had a complete contempt for money and began to give away the large sums he had earned from *Anna Karenina* to poor peasants. Sonya had to take care of a large family on what he left her—five hundred rubles a year, a smaller income than they had possessed during the early years of their marriage.

Arguments ensued, and Sonya again wrote Tanya that she would like to leave Yasnaya Polyana and all her problems. "Truly, this is because we have begun to live a Christian life. Formerly, in my opinion, without this Christianity it was much better."

Tolstoy enjoyed folk stories, and at this time he was especially taken by the tale of a Hindu who had dedicated his life to seeking truth and had become a prophet. His neglected wife found him standing on the bank of a sacred river. Falling to the dirt and kissing the hem of his priestly robes, she cried, "Master, I know that you have renounced the life of the flesh and have attained a higher stage of wisdom. What do you command me to do?"

"Disappear from my path forever," he answered.

Silently the wife rose, walked into the river, and sank from sight. Water lilies and lotuses swept over the spot, as though to mark her watery grave, while the widower stood by impassively and watched.

But Sonya was not about to sacrifice herself for the salvation of her husband's eternal soul.

15

The Turkish war and his affair with Catherine Dolgoruky had made the Tsar unpopular even within the charmed circle of the court. The Tsarevich, despising and fearing his father's mistress and her children, openly criticized the Tsar's political and domestic behavior; and a good number of the nobility took up his cry. Catherine's exclusion from society was tightened, and Alexander was forced to live in semi-isolation, now more remote from his people than ever before. Bitter and disillusioned, he became increasingly dependent upon Catherine and his second family; he was determined to marry her, thus making her his empress and legitimizing their three children.

A small group of revolutionaries called the Will of the People party gathered on September 7, 1879, and condemned Alexander Romanov, as they styled the Tsar, to death. They concentrated their every effort toward his assassination, and several attempts were made on his life during a train journey from the Crimea, where he had vacationed with Catherine. Explosives had been planted in three places along his railway route. The first mine exploded too late, the royal train having departed only moments earlier; the second failed to fire; and the third destroyed a baggage train which was traveling directly ahead of the Tsar. Not disheartened by this failure, the terrorists continued to plot his death. Alexander reinforced his household guard and seldom left his fortified palace. The revolutionaries, however, penetrated this stronghold. On the evening of February 17, 1880, as the Tsar and his cousin the Prince of Bulgaria were about to enter the imperial dining room, it was shaken by a violent explosion. The Tsar and the Prince were unharmed, but in the chamber beneath the dining room forty palace guards lay dead or dying.

"God has saved me again," the Tsar tearfully cried.

God appeared to be his only ally. The fate of the man who
had been hailed twenty years before as the great Tsar Liberator
seemed to be of no concern to serfs whom he had freed. And among
the middle and upper classes there was little interest in this latest
attempt on his life. The German ambassador Schweinitz was being
honored that evening at a large reception given by the French
ambassador at his St. Petersburg residence. When news of the
explosion at the palace was received, the guests, many of them
prominent Russian aristocrats, were unperturbed; no chill fell over
the evening's gaiety. Schweinitz left the dinner in disgust and later
remarked that "one is tempted to regard as moribund a social body
which fails to react to such a shock."

The Tsarina was now mortally ill and confined to her bed.
Alexander imprudently moved Catherine and their children into
the palace and gave the youngsters the room directly above the
dying Empress. On June 19, 1880, Maria Alexandrovna breathed
her last. Her funeral was marked by great imperial pomp. Unfortunately Catherine was observed as she stood in the gallery of the
palace watching the coffin being carried from the church to the
burial site. The members of court considered this "boundless ef-
frontery." They were further shocked when forty days later—the
minimum waiting period required by the Orthodox Church—
Alexander morganatically married Catherine, raising her to the
rank of Princess Yurievskaya (the family name of the Romanovs).
The Tsar now committed himself to the task of making the court
and the nobility accept Catherine as his wife, and in his mind this
personal issue seemed to be more important than the great problems faced by his people.

On March 14, 1881, a small bedraggled Italian beggar knocked
on the kitchen door of Yasnaya Polyana and asked for food. Such
requests were a common occurrence, and the beggars were always
fed and given a few coins. The Italian spoke no Russian but managed a broken French. Tolstoy liked to draw these itinerant travelers into discussion.

"Life bad, nobody give money, Emperor dead." The man
sighed as he sopped his bread in gravy.

"How is that? When? Who did it?" Tolstoy cried. But the
man knew no more, and Tolstoy's questions went unanswered
until the arrival of the evening papers from Tula.

On March 13 Alexander had decided that he could no longer remain a prisoner in the Winter Palace and that he would attend the Sunday parade at the Michael Riding Academy. Disregarding the strong warnings of his officers, he left the palace at a quarter to one in an armor-plated carriage pulled by four spendid grays from the renowned Orlov stable. Six Cossacks rode with him, and two sledges filled with police guards followed close behind. All went well at the parade grounds, and feeling in high spirits, the Tsar decided to pay a brief call on his paternal aunt, the elderly Grand Duchess, who lived in the Michael Palace adjoining the parade grounds. This stop made him late for his appointment at the Winter Palace, and the coachman was ordered to hurry.

The entourage galloped over the hard-packed snow. Suddenly the Tsar's coachman decided to take a shortcut and swung into the broad unpatrolled and unguarded Catherine Canal Quay. Except for a small boy carrying a bread basket and a lone artillery officer, it appeared deserted. But at the corner, where the carriage had turned from its police-patrolled course, a herring woman stood with her barrow. This was Sophia Perovskaya, who was one of the leaders of the revolutionaries. The woman signaled her accomplices by waving her kerchief. A dark young man carrying a package darted into the broad quay, and as the Tsar's coach thundered toward him he hurled his parcel at it. There was a violent explosion. Horses whinnied wildly as they fell in the thick, pungent smoke, and men screamed in shock and pain. When the smoke cleared, the young bread boy, two Cossacks, and three horses lay dead.

Incredibly, though the front wheels of the carriage had been torn off by the blast, Alexander had been spared. Someone shouted that the assassin had been caught. Ignoring his equerry's plea that he remain where he was, the Tsar audaciously and incautiously stepped out of the smashed, tilted vehicle to investigate the carnage. He limped slightly from a splinter that had pierced his leg. The captured terrorist stood silently at bayonet point, his hands bound behind him, only a few yards away. The Tsar made his way to the young man. "Did you throw the bomb?" he asked. "Yes" was the unwavering reply. "What is your name?" Alexander asked. "Ryserkov, artisan," the youth said. One of the Tsar's guards came up and exclaimed, "Thank God Your Majesty is safe!" and Alexander replied, "I am, thank God, but look at these poor people. They must be seen to."

At that, another young man, dressed in the bohemian style of a radical student, emerged from the side of the quay and shouted, "Rather too soon to thank God." He threw a round white object which the officers at first thought was a snowball. It exploded at Alexander's feet. Snow and smoke and blackened blood swirled about. Screams slashed through the winter cold; the remaining horses stampeded wildly. Twenty more men had been either severely or mortally injured. The Tsar's coachman, who might well have been in league with the terrorists, was dead. Catherine Canal Quay was a battlefield, the cobblestones covered with blood and littered with severed limbs and fragments of uniforms and braid. Alexander was propped up against a broken wheel. His stomach had been ripped open; one leg was shattered, the other gone.

"Quick. Take me to the palace to die," he groaned. His equerry suggested that it might be better to carry him to a nearby house where medical aid could be administered. Alexander repeated his command. The few Cossacks who could stand lifted him onto a sledge drawn by four blood-splattered horses. The blasts had been heard as far away as the palace, and thousands of people lined the streets, silently watching the carriage's progress. As the unconscious Tsar was carried up the marble steps of the palace, he left behind a trail of black blood. He was taken down the long corridor, past the gilt-framed portraits of his imperial ancestors, to his study and was placed on the couch near his desk. The court doctors crowded around him, but it was obvious that nothing could be done. He was terrifying to look at, "his right leg torn off, his left leg shattered; innumerable wounds all over his head and face. One eye was shut, the other expressionless."

Catherine, still dressed in her morning clothes, burst into the room and cried, "Sasha! Sasha!" She kissed his blood-streaked hands, sobbing, "Oh, my God, my God!" Moments later the Tsar was dead in her arms.

The ambitious, bitter Tsarevich was now Tsar Alexander III. The new Tsar had become heir apparent on the death of his older brother, Nicholas (the young Tsarevich whom Tula's nobility had honored with the ball that Tolstoy and Tanya had attended). A young man of fine character and splendid education, Nicholas had been a liberal thinker and had shown promise of becoming a fine statesman. He had been groomed for the responsibilities of ruling, while the less-gifted Alexander had passed his early years in the army.

Envious and contentious by nature, Alexander was determined to reign with autocratic firmness. Immediately upon his accession he tore up his father's last (and unfortunately unsigned) manifesto which would have moved Russia toward a representative government. His next action was to notify his ministers that under his rule the severe measures of his grandfather, Nicholas I, would be reinstated. As his chief adviser he chose his former tutor, Konstantin Pobedonostsev, the brilliant procurator of the Holy Synod, who was one of the most reactionary public figures in Russia at that time.

The revolutionaries responsible for the assassination of Alexander II were arrested within days of his death. Six terrorists—Sophia Perovskaya, her lover, the two youths who had thrown the bombs, a brilliant young scientist, and a second woman, Hessia Helfmann—were quickly tried for the crime and condemned to hang. (Because she was pregnant, Helfmann escaped the gallows, but she died in prison the following year.) With the loss of these six leaders, the Will of the People party was left in confusion.

When the death sentence was handed down, it had not been anticipated that all five terrorists would be condemned and hanged only two weeks later. Images of the execution he had seen in Paris greatly disturbed Tolstoy. He was convinced that if the Tsar allowed the hangings to take place, he would be as guilty as the terrorists. One afternoon, he lay down on the leather sofa in his study, fell asleep, and had a horrifying nightmare. He dreamt that he—and not those condemned—was being executed; and then suddenly it seemed that he was the executioner. Awakening in terror, he immediately wrote to the Tsar begging him to act with Christian forgiveness and pardon the assassins.

The Tsar's advisers had warned him that pleas would be made for the lives of the five terrorists. Alexander had sternly replied, "Rest assured no one will dare to come to me with such a request and I promise you that [should it occur] all *six* of them *will hang*," making it clear that anyone rash enough to urge leniency would hang with the condemned.

Sonya was terrified of the repercussions should Tolstoy's letter reach the Emperor, and she implored him not to send it. Tolstoy however, could not be deterred. Although he was proved right in his belief that he was too well known for Alexander to martyr, his letter did not move the Tsar to spare the lives of the assassins.

On the bright cold morning of April 3 Perovskaya and her four male confederates were hanged in the crowd-thronged Parade Ground of the Semionovsky Regiment. Each went to the gallows wearing a placard with the word "tsaricide" printed on it. The hangman was a criminal who had been released from prison just that morning. Tolstoy refused to allow the newspapers carrying the story of the executions into the house.

On the issue of capital punishment Sonya was in agreement with Tolstoy, but in other areas she could only try to grasp the basis of her husband's philosophy. She wrote in her journal at this time:

Little by little L[ev] N[ikolaevich] realized to his horror the great disparity between the Church and Christianity . . . The Church created ritual, with which people are told to save themselves, and has put a check on Christianity; the doctrine of the kingdom of God on earth has been obscured by the fact that the people have been made to believe in complete salvation through such things as baptism, communion, and fasting.

This is L.N.'s central idea at present. He has begun to study the Gospel and to translate and interpret it. This work has now been going on for two years, and he must be about halfway through it by now. He has become, as he says, "happy in the soul." He has seen what he calls *the light*. His whole view of life has been illuminated by it. As for his relation to people, he now says that he used to have a small circle of *his own intimate* people, but that now all the millions of mankind have become his brother. Before he had *his own* wealth and estates, but now if a poor man asks for anything it must be given to him.

He sits down to his work every day surrounded with books, and works on till dinnertime. He is in much poorer health, and suffers from headaches. He has grown thin during the past winter and his hair is turning gray.

It seems to me that he is not as happy as I should like him to be, but he has become gentle, thoughtful, and tense. His cheerful, happy moods of the past, which we all loved so much, hardly ever come to him now. This must be due to overwork and excessive strain. It was all so different in the days when he was writing his chapters on the ball and hunting in *War and Peace;* he was so joyful and excited then, as though he himself were taking part in those entertainments. The calm serenity of his own soul is obvious, but thoughts of the suffering and the poverty of men—the prisoners in jail, all the hatred, oppression, and injustice in the world—all have a fearful effect on his impressionable soul and actually seem to be wearing him away.

On the surface Sonya's life at Yasnaya Polyana was the same as it had always been. When Tolstoy put a pile of manuscript pages on her table, she would still hurry to the little sitting room and would work at her copying into the early hours of the morning. She remained the keeper of his sanctum, allowing no disturbance when he was in his study. She still nursed Misha and knew she would suckle the baby she was now carrying. And she spent her free moments making clothes for her large brood as well as the gray-blue flannel tunics which, to her annoyance, Tolstoy insisted on wearing. She had suppressed her own desire to write, because Tolstoy believed that women had no place in the literary world; she had accepted his edict that woman's place was in the home with her children; she had nursed her babies as he decreed; and although reluctantly, she had subjected herself at his whim to non-stop motherhood. But his dramatic conversion had triggered a change in her. While he was contemplating a life of self-imposed poverty, she was determined that her children would not be raised as peasants. She had resolved that she would move her family to Moscow to insure that the children were educated to take their rightful place in society. And she had decided that she must get her husband to sign over to her the rights on his past works so that she could be financially independent and able to meet her own needs and those of her offspring.

It was, therefore, a new Sonya who greeted Tolstoy when he returned from a pilgrimage early that summer. Steel was in her eyes, the melodious voice was controlled. She did not ask, beg, or cajole; she stated flatly that they had to move to Moscow for the winter so that the older children could be placed in proper schools. Disconcerted by her new strength, Tolstoy reluctantly agreed. The family, however, would continue to summer at Yasnaya Polyana.

That is, Sonya and the children would stay there. Tolstoy himself was almost always away.

His absence was a welcome relief to the young people at Yasnaya Polyana. With Tolstoy gone, the children felt free to quarrel, laugh, and run through and around the house. The Kuzminskys and their four children were living in one wing of the house, and there was a great horde of children: eight small ones between the two families. The older children had friends and callers. The black-eyed, slim, graceful Tanya had grown into an attractive young woman. Name days, birthdays, and special occasions were celebrated almost daily. Without Tolstoy's restrictions, great feasts were prepared by the cooks. Fanciful desserts were baked; cakes in the shape of houses with waffle windows were served with a rich cream sauce.

Though Tolstoy had refused to sign over any of his copyrights to Sonya, she did take over the financial burden of the household in its entirety; this meant dealing with Tolstoy's royalties and outside investments, and paying the taxes and household accounts as well as managing the estate. The mill at Nikolskoye was sold, as was a section of Yasnaya Polyana's forest land. The money Sonya raised from the sales allowed her family to live in relative luxury. "Housemen polished a battalion of dirty shoes, they waited on table, cleaned the house; the chambermaids starched collars, ironed clothes; the coachmen curried the horses, busily harnessed or unharnessed them to the calèches, troikas, droshkies, tarantases, and saddled them for riding." It was to this comfortable well-to-do household that Tolstoy returned in his drab, dust-stained clothes and plaited bark sandals.

On August 21, 1881, Turgenev visited Yasnaya Polyana. There was a great excitement in the house and Tolstoy was jubilant. The two men had reconciled their differences three summers before when Tolstoy had written Turgenev a tardy apology for a violent quarrel between them that had taken place at Fet's years before—an argument precipitated by Tolstoy. Turgenev not only forgave Tolstoy but also came to Yasnaya Polyana a short time later for two days, returning again in less than a month. Three years had passed since Turgenev's visit, and Tolstoy ran down the stairs to receive his guest. The children followed at their father's heels and watched shyly as a calèche drawn by two horses stopped before the main entrance of the estate. The stately Turgenev stepped out of the carriage and walked past the stone pillars. As Tolstoy quickly advanced toward him, the older man removed his hat, revealing a thick shock of white hair. The two embraced warmly.

"Well, and how is the woodcock shooting?" Turgenev asked.

"Oh, good enough!" Tolstoy replied. "But I hope it will be still better this evening, as the weather is damp and mild."

That evening the family dined early, and then the men, joined by a friend from Tula and the delighted Seryozha, Ilyusha, and Lyova, left in a *linejka* (a long, open carriage) to hunt. As they rode, Turgenev and Tolstoy chatted amiably, but when they touched on political and religious issues the conversation became heated. Their differences were set aside during the hunt, only to be taken up again as they sat eating at the dining table, and the two men argued until past midnight.

The next day, August 22, was Sonya's thirty-seventh birthday. A festive party was arranged, many friends from Tula invited, and a band engaged. Tolstoy, angry with Turgenev, refused to take part in the festivities. But the children, greatly enjoying the occasion, all joined to dance a quadrille. Their merriment infected Turgenev. He got up and danced with Tanya's daughter Masha, and then, taking off his waistcoat, he began to fling his legs about, saying, "That's how they dance the can-can in Paris."

For the first birthday in many years Sonya's head was filled with exciting plans. A few weeks before she had gone to Moscow and rented an apartment for the family on Devezhny Lane. She was elated about the move to Moscow and happy to have the lively Turgenev as a guest. She looked radiant, much younger than her thirty-seven years. Ironically it was her sister Tanya, the eternal coquette, who was beginning to appear matronly. Given a dress made by a French couturier and a flattering new hat to frame her dark hair and piquant heart-shaped face, Sonya could have been the living replica of Anna Karenina when she was carrying Vronsky's child.

Turgenev, who had an eye for beautiful women, was enchanted by Sonya and searched out Tolstoy to tell him, "How well you did, my dear fellow, to choose such a wife!"

Tolstoy was irritated and wrote tersely in his diary that night, "Turgenev, can-can; it is sad."

Sonya's gaiety and the liveliness in his household did briefly win Tolstoy over upon his return from his arduous journeys. Someone decided that a postbox should be placed next to the grandfather clock on the landing at the top of the stairs. The box was to hold verses, articles, and stories, written by one and all and deposited during the week. On Sunday, when the entire family was assembled around the table in the salon, the box was then opened and one of the adults (Tolstoy when he was present) would read the contents aloud. Nothing was signed but it was usually easy to guess who had written each piece.

Who but Tolstoy would have written, "Why are Ustyusha, Masha, Alyona, Pyotr, etc. [the servants] obliged to cook, bake, sweep, empty slops, wait at table, while the masters eat, gorge themselves, quarrel, produce waste matter, and eat again?"

"At what age should a man or woman marry?" was asked one week. The next Sunday a reply appeared on the same paper in Tolstoy's handwriting. "At an age when they are no longer apt to fall in love with someone else." The next Sunday the paper appeared again. This time with the words "Have you gone mad?" added in Sonya's precise script.

Even in Tolstoy's lighter moods his underlying concerns were evident. His attitude toward the life led by upper-class matrons was clearly expressed in a riddle he posed: "Why is a sanitary barrel like a society lady?" The answer was "Both are taken out at night."

The pleasant life at Yasnaya Polyana that summer was disturbed by a current of fear. Throughout Russia the Tsar's repressive policies had begun to make themselves felt. Restrictions had been harshly tightened. Extraordinary license was granted local authorities to use martial law in dealing with peasant "outbreaks," strikes, student demonstrations, or any indication of abnormal activities. Alexander II's lenient policy toward the Jews had been rescinded, and pogroms swept through the southern provinces. The Tsar blandly stated that since the Jews had crucified Christ, their plight was "preordained by the Gospels." "In my heart," he told his ministers, "I am very happy when they beat the Jews."

Jews were forbidden to take up residence or buy land in rural areas unless they converted to the Russian Orthodox faith.

Sonya was certainly not deaf to the wails of the peasants or the cries of the Jews. But her husband's mellowed austerity gave her great hope during those last weeks of the summer of 1881. Packing up her household, she stood in the midst of straw and crates and mountains of books, and she suddenly felt free and young again, as she had been those long-ago summers when the Behrses had moved from Moscow to Pokrovskoye.

Most of the servants and the household effects were sent ahead by carriage, and on a crisp early fall day the Tolstoys boarded the train for Moscow. The first-class car Sonya rode in was occupied almost entirely by her own family. Yet when the express train gathered speed as it ran through thinning birch woods and flew past small roofless stations, it seemed to her that her real life would not begin until she reached Moscow. She was returning to her spiritual home. Of course, it would be a curious homecoming, with her father dead, her mother no longer living in the same apartment in the Kremlin, the "three maidens" married, and her youngest brother, Vyacheslav (born the year before she was married), now twenty years old. The life she had known as a young girl was gone; yet, she had great faith that in Moscow she and Tolstoy could build together on completely new foundations.

But Sonya's high hopes were quickly dashed. The apartment on Devezhny Lane proved to be unsuitable. The walls were thin, and the children's chatter echoed through every room. Tolstoy was irascible and unable to work in the study that she had arranged for him. Two weeks after they arrived in Moscow she wrote Tanya:

> I am in despair, and the strain of keeping everyone from making noise is considerable. Finally Lyova burst out that if I loved him and was concerned with his mental condition I would never have chosen these rooms where he never had a moment's peace, where the price of a single chair would have made a peasant's happiness—allowed him to buy a horse or a cow, that it drives him to tears, and so on and so forth. But there is no going back. Of course, he drove me to hysterics and I am walking about as in a vacuum; everything is a muddle in my head and I feel ill, as though suffering from shock. You can imagine how easy it all is, and only a fortnight before the baby is due and so much to do.

Sonya had to placate every member of the family. Seryozha, irritated because he was not permitted to play the piano, had adopted a distant attitude to the rest of the family. He harbored vague radical notions and was passionate in his new belief that science afforded the only true knowledge and enlightenment. Tolstoy was in direct opposition to this theory and often argued angrily with his son. Ilyusha and Lyova had looked forward to entering a state gymnasium; but when Tolstoy was asked to give a guarantee of their "political stability," he refused to do so, vehemently declaring, "I can't give such a guarantee even concerning myself; how could I do so for my sons?" The boys were therefore, to their great disappointment, enrolled in a private school which asked for no such guarantees but did not have the programs or facilities of a state gymnasium. Tanya, who had a talent for art, was sent to the Moscow School of Painting and Sculpture. But she was bored by her classes, and the smaller children sorely missed the freedom of the outdoors.

Her husband's unhappiness in the city was Sonya's greatest disappointment. She read in his diary: "A month has passed. The most agonizing of my life. The move to Moscow. Everything is being organized. When will they ever begin to live? All this is not for the sake of living, but to do as others. Poor people. It's no life."

But the city was a heady intoxicant for Sonya. The winter season in Moscow was not as brilliant, of course, as that in St. Petersburg. But the Winter Palace blazed with lights, and bustling crowds filled the streets. Elegant shops like Muir and Merilee were thronged with aristocratic customers. As hostesses presided over their samovars in salons throughout the city, talk centered on the great actress Sarah Bernhardt, whose tour, advertised on a scale never before known to Russia, was about to begin. Tickets for all her performances had been sold out within hours. Speculators had snapped up a good number of them which they later sold at wildly inflated prices. Sonya was in a fever to go. Tolstoy would not hear of it. He cited her advanced pregnancy and also adamantly refused to be a party to the unsavory aura of speculation that now enveloped the Moscow theater. When a friend was having tea in the salon on Devezhny Lane, Tolstoy belligerently asked, "Are you going to see Sarah Bernhardt?"

"Of course!" the man replied.

Tolstoy struck the table hard with his fist and angrily condemned his guest's frivolity. Then he smiled and said, "But do you know, I am awfully sorry that I'm not going!"

Tolstoy refused to enter the whirl of upper-class social life. He preferred to spend his free hours walking the streets of Moscow searching out the most poverty-stricken areas. "Stinks, stones, luxury, poverty, corruption," he wrote on October 5 in his diary. "The wicked have gathered together, robbed the people, collected soldiers and judges to guard their orgies—and they feast. There is nothing left for the common people to do but prey on their passions, to get back some of that which has been stolen from them."

Horrified by the squalor, filth, and stench of the city's poorest inhabitants, he would return distraught and sobbing to "the thick-carpeted luxury of the apartment." As the children sat down to a hearty meal, he would scream, "One *can't* live like this! It's impossible!" Then moments later, when he had settled into his study to write, he would loudly complain that he could not live in a house with paper-thin walls. Sonya thought he was becoming deranged and feared he would drive her to madness as well. She was, in fact, close to a nervous collapse, but was saved when the next months brought some surcease from her difficulties. Tolstoy decided he needed a quiet place in which to work, and he rented two rooms for six rubles a month in the building next door. Vasily Syutayev, a serious-minded man from St. Petersburg whom he had met in Samara that summer, came to Moscow to stay with them. Syutayev was poor and of simple dignity. Thoughtful and quiet, he had unshakable convictions—he preached love and brotherhood among all people and nations and complete communism of possessions—that were in almost total accord with those of Tolstoy.

With Syutayev's arrival, Tolstoy became less dejected. In the mornings he read and wrote; then he would cross the river to the Sparrow Hills and chop wood with the peasants. In the evenings he and Syutayev would talk. His new friend, Tolstoy claimed, had brought him true religious exultation, a faith in God and in the teachings of Christ. Several years before, Syutayev had abandoned his work as a tombstone maker because he had come to regard the spirit of competition in business as immoral; he had retired to the country, working as a herdsman, sharing all his salary with fellow workers and using no whip to drive his horse. He began preaching publicly and soon drew a large following. Tolstoy was charmed by him; and within a short time Syutayev was speaking about his anti-state, anti-church doctrines in drawing rooms all over Moscow, his gentle manner and soft voice winning him many supporters. The police soon came to the house to question both Tolstoy and Syutayev. A form of harassment—frequent police visits—followed.

On October 31, 1881, Sonya gave birth to another son, Alexei, affectionately called Alyosha. The birth was not an easy one, and Sonya was determined that this would be her last child. Tolstoy showed no interest in the baby, who was a sickly child suffering coughing spasms during the night. Once Sonya had recovered from the birth, Tolstoy made a new demand on her strength and emotional well-being. He had seen the very worst of Moscow, and now he insisted that his wife and children go into the slums and charity hospitals with him. They were appalled by the sights they saw, and Sonya wrote in her diary, "I often wonder why Lyova is always making me out to be guilty. No doubt because he wants to see me suffer at the sight of poverty and illness and misfortune and actually *look* for it . . . and he is expecting the same from the children. . . . Is there any need for a healthy human being constantly made to keep going to hospitals to look at the suffering and agony of the sick and listen to their groans? If you come across a sick man in your own life, take pity on him and help him. But why go *searching* for him?"

At the end of January Tolstoy, accompanied by Syutayev, returned to Yasnaya Polyana, leaving Sonya in charge of the house in Moscow. A series of letters flew between them.

"My little one [Alyosha] is still unwell and I am tender and pitying," Sonya wrote in reply to his first dutiful letter telling her of his safe arrival and of how much he had learned from Syutayev. "You and Syutayev may not especially love your *own* children," she sarcastically continued, "but we simple mortals are neither able nor wish to distort our feelings or to justify our lack of love for a *person* by professing some love or other for the *whole* world."

There was a suggestion of hysteria in the letters she wrote during the first weeks Tolstoy was away. She was torn between love and hate, censure and self-castigation. "I'm vile, sick, my life is hateful; I cry all day, and if there were poison at hand, it seems as though I would do away with myself," she wrote in an early letter. "How I wish to wound you, but if you knew how I weep every day, when after a day of torment for the *life of the flesh* as you call it, I remain alone at night with my own thoughts and grief." And in her next letter she confessed she did not look forward to his return when "you will again begin to suffer, be bored, be alive although entirely silent, while censuring my life in Moscow. God, how this wearies me and torments my soul!"

Syutayev left Yasnaya Polyana in late February, and Tolstoy, alone in the house, felt repentant, reflective and mellow. He wrote to Sonya suggesting that the Kuzminskys leave Kutais and move to Yasnaya Polyana and ended the letter warmly: "Goodbye, darling, kisses to you and the children." Then on March 1 he wrote, "I was in the worst apathetic, depressed state; but I do not regret it nor am I complaining. Like a man who has been frozen and regains consciousness and feels pain, so I in all probability am morally *regaining consciousness*—experiencing all sorts of unnecessary impressions—and am returning to the control of my own self."

Sonya replied immediately:

When I think of you (which is practically all day), my heart aches, because the impression you make nowadays is that you are unhappy. I am sorry for you and at the same time bewildered: Why is this so? For what purpose? All around you everything is all right and happy.

Please do try to be happy and gay, ask anything of me to that end, anything of course in my power and to the hurt of none but me. There is only one thing that I want now: that is your peace of mind and happiness. Goodbye, my dear one; if I had not come to the end of the sheet I would have written a lot more. I kiss you.

He answered soulfully: "I lay out solitaires, I read and I think. I'd like very much to write the article I began. But even if I do not do it this week I shall not be upset. . . . Just now Agatha Mikhailovna has been entertaining me with stories about you, and about what sort of a person I would have been if I had married the Arsenyev girl. 'And now *you've gone and left her, with her eight children—do as you see fit, but there you sit at home and smooth your beard.*' "

He returned to Moscow feeling great guilt for having deserted Sonya so soon after a difficult childbirth and with a sickly baby to nurse. For a time a brighter mood prevailed. Sonya's small salon was crowded with visitors, many of them new admirers of her husband, and she glowed as she poured tea from the samovar for her guests. Tolstoy would stride into the room looking radiant and greeting everyone with great courtesy. To please Sonya, he wore a jacket over his peasant smock; if the room grew warm, however, he would remove it to her only partially concealed annoyance. Sonya was enjoying her role as the aristocratic mistress of a crowded Moscow salon. She was pleased with herself—with her handsome, remarkably youthful face and still-dark hair, with her new dresses, the most elegant she had worn since her marriage, and her fashionable new bonnets.

Despite these happy moments, deep tensions persisted between husband and wife. Sonya still hoped that Tolstoy's religious quest would eventually end, although this did not seem likely. And he was disappointed in his expectation that Sonya would come to share his convictions. Since youth, she had been of an independent nature. She had lost a number of battles—most importantly about birth control and about Tolstoy's lack of interest in domestic affairs —and some skirmishes about their social life. But she was used to fighting for her own identity. The Tolstoys were therefore at an impasse.

Fearful that Tolstoy would act on his often-mentioned plan of transferring his copyrights (and therefore his royalties) to the "people," Sonya set out to protect her own interests and those of her family. Such a step would be irrevocable, and she was determined to save Tolstoy from his folly. She knew that he had come to believe that the concept of private property was immoral and that all goods, including literary works, should belong to the "people." But who specifically these "people" were was unclear to her. Someone had to print the writings, someone had to sell them, and "people" had to buy them. Money would pass through *someone's* hands, money to which she believed Tolstoy's family had a rightful claim. Her plan was to have Tolstoy assign to her the rights on the works published before 1881, which would of course include *War and Peace* and *Anna Karenina*. Anything that appeared after that date he would be free to dispose of as he wished and without her signature. It was a bold proposal, and Tolstoy would hear nothing of it. But

Sonya was not easily turned away; during the next months she continued to press him on this matter, standing firm in the face of his enraged and adamant refusals.

Tolstoy's return from Yasnaya Polyana coincided with the long-expected arrival of his cousin Alexandra Tolstoy from St. Petersburg. Sonya had made elaborate preparations for the visit of this woman whom she had never met but whose elegance and charm had so often been praised by her husband. To Tolstoy's great annoyance, every inch of their apartment had to be cleaned. The pungent smells of wax and polish filled every room. Nothing was where he remembered it being as Sonya and her Uncle Kostya rearranged the furniture. On the evening of Alexandra's arrival great baskets of hothouse flowers decorated the reception room. The children walked about stiffly in their best clothes. Sonya wore a new and most impractical white moiré dress embroidered in purple silk which she had purchased at the chic fashion house of Madame Josephine Brusi. The dress was, by Tolstoy's standards, acceptably high-necked and long-sleeved, but he thought its bustle and purple velvet train were ludicrous. It seemed to him that his entire household had gone mad. Still, Tolstoy had great fondness and respect for his cousin; he too looked forward to her coming and had put on a jacket without too much grumbling.

Countess Alexandra Andreyevna Tolstoy, who never married, had for almost her entire adult life occupied a high place at the court, and her position had remained secure under three tsars. Her last royal patron, the Grand Duchess Marie, was the only daughter of Tsar Alexander II. Now married to the Duke of Edinburgh, the second son of England's Queen Victoria, the Grand Duchess Marie was not often in Russia. Yet Alexandra still retained her grand apartments at the Marya Palace and was one of the most powerful women in court. When Tolstoy first met her in St. Petersburg twenty-five years earlier, she had been a startlingly beautiful woman of thirty-nine, two years older than his wife was now. He had fallen under her spell and had written in his diary that had she been ten years younger he would have proposed marriage to her. Through the years they had become the most steadfast of friends, their relationship cemented by their intense correspondence and by her frequent championing of his cause at court. Alexandra was, perhaps, the woman whose opinion he valued most, and he had remained enamored of her charm, intelligence, womanliness, and discretion. She had romantic feelings toward him, as well, but these she held privately to herself (confessing them only in her diaries).

But Sonya's glamorous guest from St. Petersburg was much more than a woman of charm and great social grace. She was a brilliant woman endowed with a forceful and charismatic personality, and she was quite the equal of her cousin, the famous Count Tolstoy. Of late, letters between Tolstoy and Alexandra had made it clear that in some areas they disagreed sharply. She was a thoroughly orthodox woman and she could not countenance her cousin's denial of Christ as divinity, his return to a primitive Christianity but stripped of its miracles or mysteries, or his rejection of the Church and its rites and traditions. But before her arrival she had agreed, as indeed so had he, that they would not discuss these sensitive issues. She was to visit Moscow for ten days to meet his wife and his eight children and to embrace him after far too many years of separation.

The Countess, a woman of sixty-four, commanded every room she entered, and Sonya was happy that she had allowed the "frivolous" side of her nature to prevail in her new dress and the extravagant floral bouquets throughout the house. Alexandra was, without appearing autocratic, the most regal woman she had ever encountered. Her penetrating gray eyes, so like Tolstoy's, were widely set in an intelligent, delicate face, and her smile was one of serene good will. Her traveling costume was of purple velvet with a high-necked bodice trimmed with mauve satin, purple ribbons, and fine lace—and there, indeed, was a bustle and train! And it did not escape Sonya's attention that when her husband's cousin removed her lavender corded silk hat from her thick, beautifully dressed gray hair, the label read, "Worth, Paris."

Tolstoy, suspecting that Alexandra wanted to win him back to the Church, engaged her in what soon became open warfare, taking her to task for what he considered her mistaken views on Christianity.

"I have nothing to reply," she answered coldly, "but I will only say that while you were speaking, I saw someone standing behind your chair."

Turning swiftly (perhaps expecting to see the ghost of Arzamas), he shouted, "Who is it?"

"Lucifer, himself, the incarnation of pride," she answered.

"Of course," he rejoined. "I'm proud to be the only one who has put his hand on the truth."

After another such discussion the next day he asked her with great irritation, "Dear Babouchka! So when will you decide to grow up?"

"Never! Never!" she furiously replied. "In age and appearance, I have been grown for a long time, but it's only on the outside. In matters of my soul, you know yourself, when you tamper with my sensitivity, I hurl myself through the air like a rocket, while you—"

"I remain quite calm," he finished, "as every man certain of his convictions."

"Hardly!" She laughed. "You are a lion who has already devoured two or three lambs!"

And the next morning, seeing the huge pile of letters that had arrived from his new followers, she scoffed, "What frightful nourishment for your conceit, my friend."

Alexandra debated with him during her entire stay. Any jealousy Sonya had once felt toward her was dispelled. She had a new friend, a champion who told Tolstoy he was ridiculous, who criticized his austerity, his social indifference, his imperiousness toward Sonya, and his opposition to Tanya's entering society. Though her nickname was "Granny," she was hardly the stereotype the name implied. The small children, in fact, set her on edge. "This house looks like a page out of Dostoevsky," she complained, "where everybody is short and hurrying to get somewhere."

16

The new Tsar's friends were few. He had little charm and he disliked and distrusted the members of his court. Though his voice was high-pitched and surprisingly feminine, he was a huge man, six feet four inches tall, and had awesome strength, being able to bend an iron poker in half or twist a silver fork into a knot. Opinionated, boorish, egomaniacal, and suspicious, he was, as Queen Victoria commented, "a sovereign not to be looked at as a gentleman." He hated the English and disliked the Germans. He was as despotic with his family as he was with his subjects, but ironically he dressed like a poor peasant and ate simply.

Determined to protect himself and his family from terrorist attacks, he moved the Tsarina, Marie Feodorovna (formerly Princess Dagmar of Denmark), and his household to the 900-room Gatchina Palace, twenty-five miles from St. Petersburg. Gatchina had stood empty since Tsar Paul I had been murdered there in his bed more than eighty years earlier. A great wall surrounded the palace, and at every twenty-five yards stood sentries who were changed on the hour. No one was allowed to enter or leave the palace without a special pass which was changed each week.

Surrounded by battalions of soldiers, Alexander III lived spartanly, much as his grandfather had. He was up at seven each morning, washed with cold water, dressed in peasant clothes, and made his own coffee in a glass percolator. Though he had an army of servants, he preferred to be self-sufficient.

The Tsarina, whose sister was married to the Prince of Wales (later Edward VII), had been betrothed to the Tsarevich Nicholas, and after his death she had married his brother, Alexander. Though not beautiful, she was a lithe, gay woman with soft, brown eyes. Fond of clothes and balls and dancing, she was adored by the members of the court, who admired her intelligent, witty conversation, were amused by her love of gossip, and sympathized with the difficult life her husband imposed upon her. Alexander, who loved her obsessively, did agree to spend three weeks in St. Petersburg every winter, allowing her a sortie into the glittering life she so much enjoyed. Perhaps in their attitude toward women, as in their desire for a simple life, Tolstoy and Alexander III—men of otherwise utterly disparate philosophies—were very much alike. In fact, their position on women's "proper" role seemed to be shared by virtually all their male contemporaries of whatever ideological bias or class. Women were expected to slavishly, selflessly, and willingly cater to their men. And the greater the man, the greater the demand for the woman's total dedication.

Alexander and his old tutor Konstantin Pobedonostsev had catapulted Russia into one of its most reactionary periods. Basic rights—among them freedom of the press and of public assembly—were abrogated. Spies and agents provocateurs flourished. The government relied on the force of the Cossacks and the police to carry out its policies. And those who rejected Orthodoxy or who called for a constitution were considered dangerous and frequently treated as malefactors.

Given this climate, Tolstoy's outspoken appeals to men's consciences and his denouncement of physical force, of the authority of the Church, and of the divine-right theory of kingship should have placed not only him but also his entire family in jeopardy. Yet, though discussion of political and religious problems was forbidden, Tolstoy continued to speak out and write with impunity. The government was wary of moving against him, because he had become well known in most of the major capitals of the world and because he was looked on by his numerous Russian admirers as a Christ-like figure who would lead them to a better life. Alexander III feared his growing power, but he was equally afraid of the violent protests of Tolstoy's supporters should he be made a martyr for his beliefs. Therefore, Tolstoy remained safe and his followers continued to multiply, for his was one of the few free voices in Russia at the time.

Sonya was disturbed by the power that Tolstoy now wielded, and it seemed to her that he had begun to think of himself as a messiah. He used his powerful blue-veined hands in a new way, making a fist in midair and smashing it down on a table like a guillotine, moving his fingers "as though they were perpetually modeling something out of the air." His gaze had become even more intense, his eyes probing and assessing everyone he encountered. To Sonya's alarm, Tolstoy was becoming the center of a cult which was founded on ideas she could not accept. Although she believed in his good intentions and his sense of honor, she was violently opposed to his belief that salvation could be achieved only through abnegation. She could not be one of his "anointed disciples," but during the summer of 1882, with her family gathered about her at Yasnaya Polyana, she was happy in his company. Although he had alienated many old friends by his strong views and scathing criticism, during these months he seemed more relaxed than he had been in years. No longer the man he had once been—so full of gaiety and quick to laugh—he had begun to admit his failings as a husband (his feelings of blameworthiness perhaps heightened by the outspoken criticisms of Tanya Kuzminsky and Agatha Mikhailovna), and he regarded Sonya with unaccustomed solicitude and sympathy. He was away most of the summer—in Moscow and on a short trip to Samara with Seryozha—but when he was home he was quite cheerful, and he had taken a rest from his writing.

Alexander III was crowned that summer, but Sonya was as indifferent to his coronation as she had been thrilled by that of his father. At Yasnaya Polyana she and Tanya Kuzminsky were planning young Tanya's debut, which would take place during the coming winter, and were enjoying the camaraderie they had shared as girls. Their unhappiness—Sonya's disappointment in her move to Moscow and Tanya's loathing of Kutais—were lightened by laughter.

Again this summer the postbox had been installed. One of the entries drew a marvelous word portrait of the two sisters. Though unsigned, it was almost certainly written by Tolstoy. A rather acerbic portrait of Tanya, it seemed to reveal Tolstoy's new, less-romantic assessment of his sister-in-law.

Aunt Sonya and Aunt Tanya
and Generally Speaking

What Aunt Sonya Likes and What Aunt Tanya Likes

Aunt Sonya likes making underclothes, doing *broderie anglaise* and various kinds of fine needlework. Aunt Tanya likes making dresses and knitting. Aunt Sonya likes flowers, and in early spring is seized with a passion for gardening. Her face takes on a preoccupied look, she digs in the flower beds, consults the gardener, and astonishes Aunt Tanya by using the Latin names of all the flowers. And Aunt Tanya thinks, "She really knows everything!" Aunt Tanya says she can't stand flowers, that it's not worth bothering with such rubbish but secretly delights in them.

Aunt Sonya wears a gray bathing costume, goes sedately down the bathhouse steps gasping with cold, then decorously dips into the water and swims off with smooth even strokes. Aunt Tanya puts on a tattered oilcloth cap tied under the chin with pink chintz ribbons, and with a desperate plunge sinks to the bottom where she momentarily lies flat on her back.

Aunt Sonya is afraid when the children jump into the water. Aunt Tanya shames them when they are afraid to jump in.

Aunt Sonya puts on her spectacles, collects the children, and walks resolutely [into the woods] saying, "Mind you keep close to me, my little dears," and likes to walk slowly about the forest gathering birch mushrooms, not even spurning the *agaricus torminosus*, and says, "Children, be sure to pick the brown-cap boletes, your *papa* is very fond of them pickled, and by spring what we have will all be eaten." When Aunt Tanya goes for a walk, she's always afraid that someone will interfere with her or tag along after her, and if the children do attach themselves to her, she sternly says, "Run along, but keep out of my sight, and if you get lost don't bawl!" She dashes all about the woods and hollows, likes to gather aspen mushrooms, and always carries gingerbread in her pocket.

When things are difficult, Aunt Sonya always thinks, "Who needs me most? To whom can I be the most useful?" Aunt Tanya always thinks, "Who will be most useful to me today? Whom can I send on an errand?"

Aunt Sonya washes in cold water. Aunt Tanya is afraid of cold water.

Aunt Sonya likes reading philosophy, holding serious conversations, and astounding Aunt Tanya with big words—and fully succeeds in this aim. Aunt Tanya likes to read novels and talk about love.

Aunt Sonya can't stand pouring tea. And neither can Aunt Tanya.

Aunt Sonya doesn't like hangers-on and God's fools. Aunt Tanya loves them.

When playing croquet, Aunt Sonya always finds some useful activity for the idle moments, such as sprinkling sand on the stony places or mending the mallets, and says that she is too active to sit and do nothing. Aunt Tanya follows the game with furious concentration, hating her opponent and oblivious to everything else.

Aunt Sonya is nearsighted and sees neither cobwebs in the corners nor dust on the furniture. Aunt Tanya sees all such things and has them removed.

Aunt Sonya adores children. Aunt Tanya is far from adoring them.

When the children hurt themselves, Aunt Sonya caresses them and says, "Never mind, my pet, my darling, just wait, we'll bump that old floor—there, take that, and that!" And both Aunt Sonya and the child strike the floor violently. But Aunt Tanya rubs the hurt place furiously when they bump themselves and says, "What a nuisance—who needs this! And where are those nurses, devil take them! The least you can do is to get me some water, instead of standing there with your mouths open!"

When the children are sick, Aunt Sonya consults medical books with a gloomy air and administers opium. Aunt Tanya scolds them when they're sick and gives them castor oil.

Aunt Sonya likes dressing up from time to time and surprising everyone by appearing at Sunday dinner in something outlandish. Aunt Tanya also likes dressing up, but in something that makes her look younger.

Aunt Sonya sometimes likes doing her hair à la injured innocence, and then assumes the air of a woman oppressed by man and fate, and looks so meek and innocent with her braid hanging down her back and her hair combed smooth in front that you think, "Good heavens, who could have hurt her, who is that scoundrel, and how could she have borne it?" And your eyes fill with tears at the mere thought. Aunt Tanya likes to wear her hair high on her head, revealing the nape of her neck, with little locks falling over her forehead; she imagines that this makes her eyes look bigger and keeps blinking them.

Aunt Tanya never lets you forget a quarrel. Aunt Sonya likes to start talking at once after a quarrel as if nothing had happened.

Aunt Sonya never eats anything for breakfast, and if she does boil herself a couple of eggs now and then, she surrenders them to anyone who wants them. When Aunt Tanya gets up, she says to herself, "What would my lady fancy?" Aunt Sonya eats quickly, taking little bites with her head bent low over her plate, like a hen pecking. Aunt Tanya stuffs her mouth full, and if anyone looks at her while she is eating, she tries to look as if she is only eating because she is obliged to, and not at all because she enjoys it.

Aunt Sonya likes to sit at the piano playing and singing to the children in a singsong voice. "Hop, hop, hop! Hey, faster, gallop!" And the children frolic about. Aunt Tanya can't bear mixing children and music, but though she tries to hide it, she has no objection to her own children dancing when Aunt Sonya plays.

When Aunt Sonya makes clothes for her children she allows for fifteen years' growth. Aunt Tanya leaves no margin for growth, and the clothes have to be remade after the first washing.

Aunt Sonya does not mind prolonged visits. Aunt Tanya can't stand them.

Aunt Sonya is constantly worrying about someone, especially if he has gone away. Aunt Tanya, once she has said goodbye to anyone, tries to forget him and never worries.

When Aunt Sonya is enjoying any pleasure or festivity, she instantly mingles a feeling of melancholy with her enjoyment. Aunt Tanya gives herself wholly to the pleasure of the moment.

Aunt Sonya is very delicate where someone else's property is concerned, and so when Aunt Tanya has a mushroom pie says, "You're sure I'm not robbing you, Tanechka?" (In such instances she always says "you" instead of "thee.") And with these words takes only the crust. Aunt Tanya pleads desperately with her to take the middle, but in vain: no action is taken on her appeal.

When Aunt Tanya isn't given fresh bread for breakfast, she asks Aunt Sonya, "Haven't you got any fresh bread today?" and without waiting for an answer picks up the bread and smells it, smells the butter, pushes both to one side and cries, "The bread is always sour, the butter always smells of the cow!" and then proceeds to eat other people's bread and butter.

Who has the smaller foot, Aunt Tanya or Aunt Sonya, has yet to be decided.

Many old friends came to Yasnaya Polyana that summer, and to Sonya's delight Prince Urusov was a frequent visitor. She brightened in his presence, was coquettish, and laughed girlishly. But although Sonya did not conceal her attraction for Urusov, Tolstoy showed no jealousy or disgust over her "improper" behavior. His uncharacteristic equanimity may have had its source in his warm regard for Urusov. This affection was returned; being with the Tolstoy family was a great balm for Urusov. He amused everyone and endeared himself to Agatha Mikhailovna by talking to the dogs and claiming they understood him. He organized croquet matches and spent hours with the children. Like Kostya Islavin, who was also a frequent guest that summer, he was a bit of an eccentric. He often observed that all great people were born in August—Napoleon, Goethe, Tolstoy, himself, and Sonya. He maintained that he was clairvoyant, stating that he had accurately predicted the day of Alexander II's assassination and claiming that he knew when Tolstoy would die, although he never revealed the date.

Sergey Nikolaevich came often, always without his wife. No mention was made of the past, nor was attention called to the attraction that was still so obvious between Tanya and him. The household remarked the looks that passed between them, but neither of the former lovers ever stepped over the boundaries of propriety.

The domestic harmony that had reigned at Yasnaya Polyana that summer was abruptly broken a few days after Sonya's thirty-eighth birthday when Ilya took sick with what was first diagnosed as typhus. Small, frequent doses of quinine were prescribed by the doctor. Although Sonya went without sleep for twenty-four hours, Tolstoy did not allow his son's illness to interrupt his schedule. Hostility festered within Sonya as she ministered to Ilya, who lay in the sitting room shivering with fever. Finally at about one in the morning, exhausted and enraged by her husband's neglect of his son and of her, she rushed into their bedroom, where she found Tolstoy half asleep. She accused him of being indifferent and cold toward her and the children and of being a hypocrite who spent his time and his emotion on sick peasant children simply because they were poor but who would not even wipe the brow of his own son. Furious, Tolstoy shouted that his most sincere wish was to leave her and the children and go away and continue his work in peace. Throwing the bed clothes off, he jumped out of bed; still shouting abusively at her, he slammed out of the room and stormed down to his dressing room, where he locked himself in for the rest of the night. For several hours Sonya roamed through the silent house in near hysteria. She would spend some minutes at Ilya's bedside and then go to stand at the door of her husband's retreat; unable to gather the courage to knock, she would return to her son. At four A.M. she sat down and wrote in her diary:

August 26, 1882

Twenty years ago, when I was a happy young woman, I started writing this book, the story of my love for Lyova. It deals with almost nothing else. And now, after twenty years, I am sitting up in the middle of the night weeping over its loss. For the first time in my life Lyova has run away from me and has spent the night in his study. We quarreled over mere trifles; I blamed him for not taking a sufficient interest in the children, for not helping me to nurse Ilya, who is ill. . . . It's a question of his increasing coldness toward me and the children. He cried out aloud today that his most passionate desire was to get away from his family. To my last breath shall I remember this candid exclamation, which seemed to tear out my heart. I am begging God to let me die, for I cannot live without his love; I realized this the moment his love vanished. I can't tell him now how much I love him—it is the same love which I have given him all these twenty years. It humiliates *me* and annoys *him*. He is full of Christianity and the idea of self-perfection. . . . I am careful to give [Ilya] his quinine at the right intervals, which are short ones —so that I must be careful not to miss them. I shan't lie down on the bed which my husband has abandoned. God help me! I want to kill myself—my thoughts are all confused. The clock is striking four. If he doesn't come back I shall know that he loves another woman.

An hour later she was still awake and added, "He hasn't come back. . . . My duty? I've always known what my duty was. But what is my duty now?"

When Tolstoy finally approached her at dawn, remorseful and tender, a truce was made.

"We both wept, and I saw with joy that the old love, the loss of which I had bemoaned during all that dreadful night, was still alive in him," she later wrote. "I shall never forget that lovely bright morning, with the silver dew sparkling on every leaf, when, after a sleepless night, I walked through the woods toward the bathing cabin. I have seldom seen Nature in such triumphant beauty. I stayed for a long time in the ice-cold water, hoping to catch a chill and die. But I did not catch a chill, and instead went home and nursed my happy, smiling little Alyosha."

Feeling remorse for the unhappiness he had caused Sonya, Tolstoy went to Moscow early in September to look for a house that would suit both him and his family. He quickly found a small estate on Dolgo-Khamovnicheski Street, a pretty, wooded, but not fashionable area, and bought it for 27,000 rubles. The main house was a two-storied wooden structure standing in the center of a large courtyard. A high fence surrounded the entire property. There were a number of smaller buildings within the enclosure—a porter's lodge, carriage house, cowshed, stables, and kitchens. Behind the house was a tree-filled park whose paths were lined with flowering shrubs.

Although there were several factories, a mill, a distillery, and a brewery nearby, the house had a rather rural air, and Tolstoy wrote to Sonya, "What a lovely garden. You sit by a window looking out into the garden, and you feel lighthearted and calm. You go into the street; you feel depressed and agitated." He liked the city no more than in the past, but now he wanted to be close to the publisher of his new works. Deciding that the house was not large enough, he had construction begun on an annex which he planned to use as a study. The three older boys were with him in Moscow preparing to return to school, while Sonya remained at Yasnaya Polyana with the rest of the family until the building and repairs were done.

Sonya returned to Moscow on October 8. Tolstoy met the train with two carriages and was extremely animated on the drive to their new home, which was in the southwest outskirts of the city not far from the Moskva River and therefore quite a lengthy ride from the station. Dinner was waiting for them when they arrived, the samovar was filled with hot tea, and an extravagant bowl of fruit sat on the table. But Sonya, tired by a week's packing and a tedious journey, found nothing to her liking. She was disappointed with the house's location and shabbiness, irritated by the odors from the factories, and dismayed by the lack of indoor plumbing and by the fact that the well was even farther from the house than it was at Yasnaya Polyana. And with characteristic inattention to details, Tolstoy had bought a house that had no rooms for the servants. She solved this last problem temporarily by crowding the three older boys into one room, Tanya and Masha into another, and turning the back parlor into a nursery for the three youngest children and their nanny.

Soon after her arrival, Sonya cheered the house up by repainting the dingy brown walls of the reception rooms a deep rose and the outside shutters bright green. The porter's lodge and carriage house were frugally refurbished for the servants. While Sonya was occupied with putting her household in order, Tolstoy had found another passion—the Hebrew language, which he studied with the same intensity he had earlier shown in learning Greek.

For all its problems, the new house was a marvelous place for the children. In the spring and summer the garden with its overgrown thickets and maze of paths was perfect for hide-and-seek; there were green hillocks to climb, trees laden with fruit, and a summer house lined with a frieze of galloping horses. As winter approached, the youngsters took to their skating rink, which was made by pouring hundreds of barrels of water onto a space in the courtyard. To Sonya's relief, Tolstoy seemed to like the house and enjoyed taking long walks through the grounds with Belka, his newly acquired Eskimo dog, at his heels.

Sonya soon had the house painted and furnished, and she then turned her attention to launching Tanya into society. The young woman was not as attractive as her handsome, engaging mother, but she was vivacious, graceful, amusing, and pretty enough with her glistening dark eyes and her pert uptilted nose. To Tolstoy's irritation, both women enjoyed a great success in the Moscow salons that winter. Offended by what he regarded as barren, frivolous existence, he fled to the sensible country refuge at Yasnaya Polyana.

"You are probably getting ready to go to a ball," he wrote Sonya. "How I pity you and Tanya!"

But Sonya was happy in a way she had not been for years.

"It was a wonderful ball last night," she wrote her sister. "Tanya wore a shell-pink dress with plush roses. My velvet dress was lilac with pansies of every possible shade of yellow. Tomorrow we go to another ball, for which Tanya has a wonderful dress— tulle—'Illusion,' pale greenish with pinkish lily of the valley. Next night another ball at the Obolenskys'. They are all simply running me and Tanya off our feet!"

Tolstoy did not approve of her "empty, sumptuous deceitful Moscow life," but his constant reproaches did not deter Sonya.

"Of course it's impossible to dispute your theory that it would be fine if people could be perfect; and of course you are right to remind them of this and to point out the path of perfection," she wrote him. "Yet I can't refrain from saying that it is hard to give up all the *toys* of life. Perhaps I grasp these toys more eagerly than others. I do so love the way they glitter, tinkle, delight."

The battle continued when Tolstoy returned to Moscow. "Aren't you ashamed to live like this?" he asked as Sonya and Tanya were leaving the house for a gala affair that he refused to attend with them. "A *bal costumé* at the Governor General's! Dressing up and exposing your bare arms and shoulders! With your furs and in your fine, warm rooms perhaps it doesn't matter; but our old coachman has to wait for you till four in the morning in twenty degrees of frost! Pity might at least be felt for him!"

Although he criticized Sonya's life in Moscow, he did not forbid her pursuit of social prestige. However, whenever he was addressed by his title or as "Your Excellency," he would sternly say, "I am called simply Lev Nikolaevich." And while Sonya flitted from tea to ball in dazzling velvets and furs, he went to the slums to walk among the poor, returning home with his eyes glittering and his head aching.

Masha had a new French governess, Mme. Anna Seuron, a widow with a son to support. Glancing out the window at eight o'clock one freezing morning, the conventional and narrow-minded Mme. Seuron was appalled to see *le Comte* (which she insisted on calling him to his great annoyance) harnessed to a hand sledge to which a tub was attached. He dragged it from the yard, filled the tub with water from the well, and then, as the servants watched with awe, slowly pulled it to the kitchen. This and other domestic chores—stoking his stove, lighting the samovar, doing his room, and cleaning his boots—became part of his daily routine. He went about in shabby clothes, visiting peasants and society friends alike in a sheepskin coat and cap and greased high boots. He refused to wear gloves, and as he walked about he kept his hands tucked into his sleeves or pockets.

Tolstoy's followers continued to increase, and they flocked to the house on Dolgo-Khamovnicheski Street as well as to Yasnaya

Polyana. He was in Anna Seuron's words a "new-baked prophet, who sits in his reception room like a Delphic oracle . . . his legs crossed under him *à la turque*, or with only one leg tucked under him *à la Tolstoy* and hears the plaints of humanity. He listens to them all: those who do not know what to do with their gold; those whose wives are too much or too little for them; those who stung by conscience confess to him; to each he says a few words."

In Moscow he had two rooms of his own (an open archway between them) which were usually crowded with visitors who smoked so much that on entering it was almost impossible to distinguish their faces in the haze. Sometimes as many as thirty persons were gathered in the low-ceilinged nine-by-fifteen-foot rooms. Everybody talked at once, but Tolstoy always spoke the final word. After their discussions he would lead the group into the dining room, where Sonya served them tea.

Tolstoy retreated often that year to Yasnaya Polyana, where people from all classes of society journeyed like pilgrims to a holy place. Yet in the village of Yasnaya Polyana he was not well beloved. He had done almost nothing there to improve the peasants' achingly difficult and impoverished lives. Their houses still had thatched roofs, which made them firetraps, and dirt floors, which gave no protection against the cold. The peasants could not afford heat or warm clothing, and the few rubles Tolstoy gave to those who came to him made no real difference in their lives. Preaching self-help, he began to make his own boots (rather poorly), clean up his quarters, empty his slop bowls. But the people of the village had been following Tolstoy's newfound philosophy of self-help since they were old enough to walk.

The winter of 1883 was a most severe one for the Yasnaya Polyana peasants. The previous spring the entire village of sixty thatched-roofed, wattle-fenced wooden hovels had gone up in flames. Tolstoy was at Yasnaya Polyana at the time and worked shoulder to shoulder with the peasants to try to check the raging blaze. But their efforts were hampered by a lack of water; the village had only two wells, and water had to be drawn up by hand in wooden buckets. After the devastation he gave the destitute peasants one hundred quarts of seed oats so that they could regain their "independence" and "confidence in their own strength." No effort was made to improve the water supply of the burnt-out village or its fire brigade; nor were the new houses (meagerly subsidized by insurance) built of less flammable materials. But the fire in Yasnaya Polyana did seem to precipitate one action on Tolstoy's part. Within three months—to rid himself of the weight of material cares—he had signed over to Sonya full power of attorney to conduct all matters concerning his property; he then went off to Samara and left her with the problems of a village struggling to rebuild itself out of ashes.

Tolstoy, his beard untrimmed, wearing a tunic and handmade boots, was beginning to look like the pilgrims who stopped at Yasnaya Polyana as they wandered from monastery to monastery. Once he had walked to the high road to meet them; now they came to his house to seek alms, sympathy, a meal, a night's lodging. Tolstoy received everyone who came through his gates, and he dealt out money and food to each mendicant. In the beginning he gave each pilgrim at least three and sometimes as many as six rubles. After a few months, his generosity decreased considerably and he became more selective. His servant, Sergey Arbuzov, complained that there was no end to the pilgrims who invaded Yasnaya Polyana and that they told "all sorts of lies to get more money," ploys that were invariably successful. Although Tolstoy was scornful of Sonya's profitable management of the estate, his philanthropy could not have continued for long without her hard work and business acumen.

Not for an instant did Sonya believe that the ills of humankind could be cured by her husband's example. While believing that he was a great writer, she was not at all convinced that he was a great man, much less a prophet. A great man should be without hypocrisy. But while Tolstoy avoided soiling his hands by touching money and refused to contaminate himself by earning it, he demanded great sums for his personal charities. Was that the philosophy of a great man—to allow the money he needed to be raised by someone whose financial skill he condemned as a source of corruption? And would a great man be so bountiful and loving to strangers and so cold to his own family? Would he declare that sexual activity (unless directed toward procreation) was filthy and

demeaning? Would a great man describe women in degrading
terms, and would lust be evident in his demeanor toward both
large-breasted peasant girls and lithe aristocratic ladies?

Sonya began to reread his diary to look for explanations, but
she found only more contradictions. His youthful actions appeared
to reveal deficiencies in his moral sense. He had gambled compul-
sively, losing the main house of Yasnaya Polyana and a considerable fortune as well. Did he now, even though no former creditor
had pressed, try to repay any of his unsettled debts? He had contracted a venereal disease which had on occasion recurred. Had he
ever admitted to being infected or protected any of the women with
whom he was intimate? He had fathered a bastard child. Had he
shown any interest in the boy? He preached the equality of all
men, while relegating women to a subservient position. No, there
was little evidence to convince Sonya that her husband was a great
man or a prophet, and she mourned the man—the writer of genius
and the passionate lover—he seemed determined to bury.

Poor mendicants were not the only seekers who made their
way to Yasnaya Polyana and the house in Moscow. "Those oppressed by riches and ennui came in carriages, on horseback, and
on foot, seeking a balm for their boredom." After speaking to Tolstoy, wealthy young men who had already skimmed the cream
from life "discarded money and lands and went into the desert to
work with peasants and live on locusts"; well-to-do women whose
girlhood illusions had lost their bloom came to Yasnaya Polyana
and, wearing galoshes and white satin dressing jackets, worked at
manuring the fields. Students in search of a spiritual leader sat at
Tolstoy's feet or stood with him under the huge maple in Yasnaya
Polyana's garden where he greeted the stream of poor peasants who
waited patiently for alms or advice and where Sonya spent hours
distributing medicines and cloth and the money her husband refused to carry.

Tolstoy plowed and worked with the Yasnaya Polyana peasants, but when he was in bad humor, a not infrequent circumstance, the sixteenth-century serf owner awoke in him and he
would speak to them in an angry and demeaning manner. But these
incidents did not counteract the growing mystical regard in which
he was held by the poor throughout Russia. Most of these peasants
could not read his writings, and they did not know the political,

economic, and religious theories his group of followers, who called themselves Tolstoyans, espoused. His growing fame as the prophet of a new social order, which was making him a national figure of great importance and the Tsar's rival, was based mainly on his wearing peasant dress, dispensing rubles, and working in the fields with his former serfs. To the millions of inarticulate, uneducated, and impoverished Russian peasants who bore the yoke of a ruthless autocracy and a soulless bureaucracy, he appeared to be the one nobleman who stood with them against their former masters.

Sonya was not the only one to bemoan Tolstoy's abandonment of his literary career for a religious crusade. On June 28, 1883, from Bougival, near Paris, Turgenev wrote him in a penciled scrawl:

> Kind and Dear Lev Nikolaevich— For long I have not written to you because to tell the truth, I have been and am, on my deathbed. I cannot recover: That is out of the question. I am writing to you especially to say how glad I have been to be your contemporary, and to express my last and sincere request. My friend, return to literary activity! That gift came to you from whence comes all the rest. Ah, how happy I should be if I could think my request would have an effect on you! I am played out—the doctors do not even know what to call my malady, *Néuralgique stomacale goutteuse.* I can neither walk, nor eat, nor sleep. It is wearisome even to repeat it all! My friend— great writer of our Russian land—listen to my request! Let me know you have received this scrap of paper, and allow me yet once more cordially to embrace you, your wife, and all yours. . . . I can write no more. . . . I am tired.

Two months later, on Sonya's birthday, August 22, Turgenev died. She was, perhaps, even more desolated by his death than was Tolstoy. She had lost a strong ally, a man who she had hoped would bring Lev Nikolaevich back to his true vocation.

In the autumn of 1883 a new friend entered Tolstoy's life: the thirty-year-old Vladimir Grigorevich Chertkov, whom Sonya would come to regard as the devil incarnate. Like Socrates's devoted disciple Alcibiades, the young, strikingly attractive Chertkov was rich and aristocratic—the only son of a regal, domineering mother, who had been a close friend of the Empress Maria Alexandrovna [the Tsar's mother], and a military father who had served as an adjutant general under Alexander II. He was tall and slim and wore his clothes in a graceful, almost foppish fashion. His deep-set black eyes—so dark that there seemed to be no distinction between iris and pupil—had a rather cynical cast. His nose was aquiline; his expression suggested that he was an intense and willful man, and in fact these traits had shaped his life. At an early age he had resigned his commission in the Horse Guards and had set out on a licentious life. As Tolstoy had once done, he gave himself over to drinking, gambling, and dissipation. Several years later, under the threat of disinheritance, Chertkov took a sharp turn toward more useful activities. However, he had no clear idea of what he wanted to do, and he floundered about accomplishing little and wasting his financial resources. Within a relatively short time he worked, to little effect, in local government and also founded an unsuccessful trade school, an underequipped clinic, and a financially insecure credit and savings company. He then threw himself (and a good part of the income from his estates) into charitable works inspired by what he had read and heard about Tolstoy's philosophy. He was now determined to assist the master himself.

In the beginning Sonya was disarmed by Chertkov, who aroused a certain pity in her. He spoke in a curiously high and drawling voice, a mannerism that he obviously hoped would disguise his slight stutter but that instead drew attention to it. Wearing knickerbockers and a Norfolk jacket, he cut a ludicrous figure as he walked with the peasant-garbed Tolstoy in Yasnaya Polyana's fields; and his inept attempts to help with the harvesting made him an object of fun. Sonya's amused compassion turned into a more reserved caution, however, when he began to display a frightening moodiness; he was gloomy and irritable one moment, fiercely animated and restless the next. Tolstoy did not share his wife's growing coolness toward Chertkov. He was delighted by his new disciple and confidant, and within six months of their first meeting, he wrote in his diary, "He and I are amazingly as one." His intimacy with Chertkov appeared to ease the painful feeling of solitariness which had dogged Tolstoy during the years since his brother Nikolai's death. In his eyes Chertkov may have been the brother who should have lived, the son who was old and experienced enough to understand him, the companion in purpose and thought that Sonya was no longer. Tolstoy may have seen himself in his young protégé; they shared many of the same traits—contempt of public opinion, an audacious independence and fearlessness in their dealings with those in authority, and a readiness to suffer for their convictions. And Chertkov had broken with St. Petersburg society as he had done, thus relinquishing the privileges of an aristocratic and pampered life which were his by birth. Tolstoy valued this renunciation highly.

By early 1884 Chertkov had gained a firm hold on Tolstoy's affections and an important place in his daily life. The family had returned to Moscow, but Tolstoy spent a good part of the winter at Yasnaya Polyana with Chertkov.

There was much unpleasantness between husband and wife whenever he returned to the city. Now nearly forty, Sonya was once again pregnant and was beside herself with anger, self-pity, and resentment. She had not wanted another child and she hated every sign of the child's growth within her. She dreaded the chilly and remote air that Tolstoy adopted toward her while she was pregnant. She had once written in her diary,

> I have nothing in me but this humiliating love and a bad temper; and these two things have been the cause of all my misfortunes, for my temper has always intefered with my love. I want nothing but his love and sympathy, and he won't give it to me; and all my pride is trampled in the mud; I am nothing but a miserable crushed worm, whom no one wants, whom no one loves, a useless creature with morning sickness, and a big belly . . . a bad temper, a battered sense of dignity, and a love which nobody wants and which nearly drives me insane.

Now, seventeen years later, Sonya was once again racked by this same anguish, and she appeared to be teetering on the brink of madness. She wept constantly and in an effort to conceal her appearance demanded that the house be kept in near darkness. The children suddenly seemed to be a crushing burden, and she cried to her husband that she would not be able to endure the ordeal of yet another birth or the addition of another child to her overwhelming responsibilities.

Absorbed by his own spiritual quest, Tolstoy had little sympathy for her distress. He had been criticized in the press for preaching self-denial while living in luxury, and he began to speak of leaving her and the children to take up an ascetic life. Sonya was devastated by this suggestion, and the estrangement between them deepened. Tolstoy went about the house in thick gloom, sat alone in his study late into the night, and left the house for long periods of time. One night when he returned after one of these absences Sonya confronted him. "Lyovochka," she pleaded, "I don't want to bear a child, I don't want to! You want to leave us, go away!" Tolstoy furiously accused her of harboring sinful thoughts. The next morning Sonya went to Tula to see the midwife and to have an abortion.

"No, Countess," the woman told her with fear in her dark eyes. "If it was someone else, I would do it with pleasure; but as for doing it for you, if you plaster me with gold, I'm not going to do it!"

Sonya would not give up easily. She returned to Tula several times to beg for help, but the midwife stood firm. She took hot baths which scalded her but had no other effect. Then she climbed on top of the chest of drawers in her room and jumped, just as the children's nanny entered.

"What are you doing, Sonya Andreyevna!" the horrified woman rasped in a coarse voice. "How can you? You know you may lose your life that way!"

"I don't want to bear the child, Niania," Sonya wept. "The Count doesn't love me any more. He wants to leave us to go away!" Once again Sonya climbed atop the chest and jumped, but to no avail.

"She is seriously mentally ill, and the cause is this pregnancy," Tolstoy wrote in his diary after a heated discussion about her efforts to abort. "It is a sin and a *shame*."

It seems likely that Tolstoy himself was distressed by Sonya's pregnancy. Only the year before he had written a young journalist, "If I knew nothing of Christ's teaching apart from these five rules I would be just as much a Christian as I am now: (1) Do not be angry. (2) Do not fornicate. (3) Do not swear. (4) Do not judge. (5) Do not make war. This is what the essence of Christ's teaching is for me."

The child his wife carried showed him to be a sinner. He had broken his own "second commandment," a transgression which filled him with shame. Their arguments grew more violent, and he returned to Yasnaya Polyana. He was alone there, since Chertkov had agreed to accompany his mother on a trip to England. A series of emotional letters passed between the two men.

"His mother, as is natural, hates me," Tolstoy wrote in his diary. This observation was true. Mrs. Chertkov feared Tolstoy's influence over her son, just as Sonya feared Chertkov's influence over her husband. "Will you always *intentionally* close your eyes to people to whom you do not wish to see anything except what is good? Truly this is blindness!" Sonya wrote to Tolstoy about Chertkov.

With Tolstoy at Yasnaya Polyana, Sonya's life in Moscow arranged itself quite pleasantly. Seryozha was a student at the university, Ilya and Lyova were enrolled in private schools, and the younger children had their lessons at home. As Sonya's pregnancy advanced, she could no longer accompany her daughter to evening parties and dances, so Tanya went out less often. Sonya, however, made the most of their seclusion. She held "drawing evenings" under the guidance of Pryanishnikov, an artist known for his society portraits; "literary evenings" which Fet and other well-known writers attended; and "musical evenings" at which eminent musicians performed. Sonya was hostess of a salon like that of Alexandra Tolstoy, which she had always envied. There were many new acquaintances—professors, nobles, provincial governors, artists, writers, and musicians—none of whom met Tolstoy's approval.

In May, Sonya and her family and the Kuzminskys joined Tolstoy at Yasnaya Polyana. Due to deliver within a few weeks, Sonya was faced with a larger household and a smaller staff. Tolstoy had dismissed a number of servants, reasoning that it was morally wrong for so many to wait upon so few. Relations between husband and wife were immediately strained. When Tolstoy attacked Sonya's life in Moscow, she retaliated with sharp criticism of the new Tolstoyans. Tolstoy grew morose and threatened to leave with one of the peasant women and start a new life. Sonya assumed that he had again become attracted to Axinia, whom she had seen quite frequently in the village. (Timofei, Tolstoy's son by Axinia, was now a strong broad-shouldered young man. Although he was industrious and clever, he had never been taught to read or write and was working as a woodsman at Yasnaya Polyana, a de-motion of sorts from his former easier work in the stables.)

On the night of June 18 the entire household, including the Kuzminskys and Anna Seuron and her son, were seated about the tea table when someone mentioned that the horses on the estate seemed in poor condition since Tolstoy had decreased the stable staff. Sonya remarked that he had done much the same thing in Samara, where he had bought some well-bred horses and then let them die from neglect and overwork.

Furious at this accusation, Tolstoy rose from the table, saying sharply that the horses meant nothing to her and that her only interest was the money that had been spent for them. Sonya countered with an angry denouncement of his many charities. There was, she claimed, "no undertaking, no definite work, no man or group of men" which he especially wished to support or assist. He did not have a thought-out plan; everything he did, all that he gave, was based on a social philosophy that constantly changed. And if he was allowed to have his head, he would soon squander what money they had. Then what would become of his children and his unborn child? Would they all end up living on charity?

Tolstoy bolted from the room exclaiming that he was leaving for America. Moments after he had run from the house, Sonya's labor pains began. Ignoring her sister's pleas to lie down until the midwife arrived, Sonya sat in the garden waiting for Tolstoy to return. Finally, as her pains grew worse, she was forced to go to her room. At five o'clock in the morning she heard him enter the house, and, her dark hair flowing loosely about her pale face, she stumbled awkwardly down the stairs. Tolstoy stood looking an-grily at her, his gray eyes critical, piercing. "Lyova," she said, "I am feeling very ill, the child will soon be born. Why are you angry? Forgive me if I am to blame for anything; for all I know I may not survive the day."

He moved away coldly, and terror filled Sonya's heart. "I have never loved anyone but you," she cried.

He turned round and stared silently at her. He had changed much since the early days. He was now close to sixty; his hair was gray and his skin sallow. Yet he still moved with electricity and looked at her in a way that made a current flash between them. His grip was strong, his step solid. Nothing, no amount of humiliation and coldness, seemed to diminish her love and desire for him.

A pain seized her, and with the midwife's help she returned to her room, where a large healthy daughter with a shock of black hair was born an hour later, without her father's attendance. The last three children had been boys, and everyone in the house was delighted with the new baby girl. Named Alexandra for Tolstoy's cousin, she was affectionately called Sasha.

The remainder of the summer was a nightmare for Sonya. She refused to nurse Sasha and hired a stout peasant woman from a nearby village to nurse the new child along with her own.

Tolstoy wrote Chertkov on June 24, "My wife has given birth to a little girl. But my joy has been poisoned by the fact that my wife, despite my clearly stated opinion that to hire a wet nurse away from her child to feed a stranger is a most inhuman, unreasonable, and un-Christian act, nevertheless and without any reason took a wet nurse from her living child. All this happens somehow without our understanding, as if in a dream. I wrestle with myself, but it's hard. I am sorry for my wife."

Sonya, having been asked by Tolstoy to copy this letter, wrote in her diary, "He turned to Christianity. The martyrdom was mine, not his."

Letters arrived almost daily from Chertkov. Early in July he wrote from England, "Even while thinking of you, I notice a nasty little devil in my relation to you. A rascally feeling of smugness often takes the place of my sincere friendship when I realize that I am in close, intimate relations with such a 'remarkable' man as you. I feel this is quite like that vain satisfaction I formerly experienced when the Emperor or even some Grand Duke favored me with special attention in the presence of others."

Tolstoy replied, "In your letters there is little simple love for me, as for a human being who loves you."

Chertkov answered, "I love you, although I love separate personalities very little . . . with the exception of children, and in particular little boys, whom I especially love. But I positively love you, although I'm a little afraid."

In another letter Chertkov wrote, "I have now arranged things so that I shall again sleep in the same room with Peter [a young servant]. I do not know why, but when I sleep in the same room with someone, I sleep much better and more quieter in this manner."

Tolstoy then urged him to marry. Chertkov answered that he was not in love with anyone and that, in any case, no woman he chose would please his mother. Tolstoy countered this by warning him of the dangerous temptations of the flesh which buffeted a single man. To which Chertkov answered, "I do not want to marry merely for physical reasons."

The two men had become so close that Tolstoy wrote to him about his intimate life with Sonya:

> On one occasion this year I lay in bed beside my wife. She was not asleep nor was I, and I suffered grievously from a consciousness of my own isolation in the family because of my beliefs, and because all of them in my eyes, seeing the truth, turn away from it. . . . With tears in my eyes I began to pray to God to open the heart of my wife. She fell asleep. I heard her quiet breathing, and suddenly it came into my head: I suffer because my wife does not share my convictions. When I speak with her under the influence of vexation about her repulsing me, I often speak coldly, even in a hostile manner; never have I entreated her with tears to believe in the truth or told her all simply, lovingly, softly; yet here she lies beside me and I say nothing to her, but what ought to be said to her I say to God.

The Chertkov-Tolstoy exchange of letters contained more than discussions of domestic life. They also dealt with doctrinal matters. Chertkov believed strongly in Tolstoy as a prophet, but his letters revealed an extraordinary ego. "I am firmly convinced that what is the truth for me, is the truth for all people," he stated dogmatically.

On the night of July 7, less than three weeks after Sonya had given birth, Tolstoy, restless and angry from a quarrel they had just had, insisted upon his "husbandly right." Sonya refused him. He rose furiously from the bed and went downstairs and wrote in his diary, "The companion of my nights? She provokes me, she makes it into a game." Returning to their bed, he persisted in his advances and she finally yielded. She began to hemorrhage almost immediately, and the midwife had to be sent for early the next morning. After tending to Sonya, the woman angrily rebuked Tolstoy for his brutality and schoolboy haste and forbade him to have intimate relations with his wife for a month, during which time Sonya was ordered not to walk or go out driving or to get upset.

Alarmed at her condition, Tolstoy was filled with concern and guilt. This tenderness was, however, characteristically short-lived. On July 18 he wrote in his diary, "Cohabitation with a woman alien in spirit, i.e., with her, is terribly disgusting." That night he packed his things, awoke her to tell her he was leaving, and then finally, after she had reasoned with him, agreed to stay. In the morning he wrote, "I do not understand how to save myself from suffering or her from the destruction toward which she flies with haste."

He became so disturbed by her presence that he proposed she return with the children to Moscow. The train journey was difficult, and when she arrived she sent for a doctor. Tolstoy, irritated at this, wrote her not to "pay too much attention to what the Moscow doctors say, as they can only ruin our lives." After the doctor had seen her for a second time, Sonya wrote her husband that he had ordered a prolonged abstention from sexual relations.

Tolstoy answered remorsefully: "Yesterday I received the letter you sent after seeing the doctor, and it has grieved and pained me, and above all disgusted me with myself. All this is nobody's fault but my own, brutal, selfish beast that I am! And I set myself up to judge others and ape righteousness! I cannot tell you how upset I am. Yesterday I saw myself in a dream, full of contempt for myself."

By the next post Sonya replied: "You are absolutely not to blame; we are both at fault; perhaps it is the result of some mechanical thing that went wrong when the baby was born. Yesterday I was in great pain, something was flowing inside me as though an abscess had burst, but today there's not a drop and the pain is much less."

Once Sonya regained her health, her most pressing problem was money. She made as much as she could from the farm and from the few other properties her husband had not yet sold. Tolstoy had a substantial income from royalties, but he gave away this and more. With two homes and nine children, Sonya knew that something had to be done to increase their income or one day her

family would be out on the street. Once again she became convinced that the key to the family's financial security lay in Tolstoy's
novels. A new idea took hold of her: Why couldn't she publish and
sell her husband's works in Russia? Dostoevsky's widow had succeeded at printing her husband's work, and Sonya believed in her
own business abilities. Russia's two great novelists had never met,
but Sonya sought out Anna Grigoryevna Dostoevsky to find out
how she had gone about beginning her publishing company. The
two women became instant friends, and with good reason, for they
had much in common. They were close in age, Anna Grigoryevna
being two years younger than Sonya. Dostoevsky's first wife had
died, and he was forty-three when he married his secretary, Anna
Grigoryevna, who was then eighteen. For the fourteen years that
they had lived together before his death she had devoted herself
entirely to guarding his study door, copying his work, raising the
children, handling the finances of the family, and enduring much
hardship on his behalf. Although she did not share her husband's
ideas, she worked so that he might be able to write. Since his death
in 1881, she had devoted herself to seeing that his works were
properly published.

　　After several consultations with Anna Grigoryevna, Sonya
decided to go forward with her project. But first, of course, she
would have to obtain her husband's permission. Tolstoy was horrified by her plan and repelled by her hardheaded business sense,
which he regarded as rapacity. More importantly, any show of
independence and initiative by any woman, and most especially by
his wife, seemed to him to be unnatural and immoral. The problems which existed between them he attributed to her refusal to
accept his beliefs as her own and to live her life as he chose to live
his. But she had too much strength of character to pose as a staunch
supporter of her husband's ideas. Sonya tried to tell him her own
strong feelings and to get him to recognize the inequality, the hypocrisy of expecting her to cast off her own opinions and beliefs
and to take on his simply because he was her husband. On December 9, 1884, she had written to him:

> You and I have been following different paths since childhood. You
> love the country, the people, the peasant children, you love the prim-
> itive life you abandoned when you married me. I am a city dweller,

and no matter how I try to reason with myself and force myself to love the country and the common people, I shall never be able to devote myself to them body and soul. I do not understand and never shall understand the peasants. What I love is nature and nature alone, and with nature I could joyfully spend the rest of my days. Your descriptions of the little muzhiks, the life of the people, etc. Your tales and your conversation—it is all exactly the same as in the days of your school at Yasnaya Polyana. But it is too bad that you care so little for your own children. If they belonged to some peasant woman it would be a different story!

To start her enterprise Sonya borrowed ten thousand rubles from her mother, and fifteen thousand rubles from Strakhov. Her extraordinary energy and purposefulness were well suited to the business of publication, and work on the edition went ahead rapidly. Her new occupation seems to have buoyed her confidence in herself, and in February 1885 she wrote to Tolstoy in an authoritative fashion: "I'm distressed that such intellectual powers should be wasted on chopping wood, tending samovars, and stitching boots—all that is fine as a rest or change of occupation, but not as a special employment. Well, enough of that! Had I not written it, I should have remained vexed, but now it is past, and the thing amuses me, and I have grown calm, repeating the old proverb: 'Let the child amuse itself as it likes, so long as it doesn't cry.' " Other letters in this frank manner followed, frequently expressing her distress that he was giving away more money than she was able to make.

This new Sonya caught Tolstoy off guard, and instead of lashing back at her he replied, "Do not be angry, darling, that I cannot attribute any importance to these money matters. That life should not appear trivial, one must take a wider and deeper view." He ended telling her that "how much our income shrinks cannot occupy me. If one attributes importance to that, it hides what is really important."

"In all relations I am sometimes inexpressibly sad without you," she replied, "but I have accepted the idea of *fulfilling* my duty in my relation to you as a writer, as a man requiring first of all his freedom, and therefore, I demand nothing of you."

Sonya did not speak idly; she was determined to do justice to Tolstoy the writer. Thus, despite her distaste for his recent spiritual works, she decided that they must be included in her edition. To this end, she went to St. Petersburg in February 1885 to obtain permission to publish *A Confession, What I Believe,* and *What Then Must We Do?*—three religious works which he had written after his conversion and which had been suppressed by the censor.

On the night train for St. Petersburg with a much excited Tanya, Sonya lay awake in the comfortable berth of the first-class car listening to the rumble of the train as it swept through the darkness. By dawn she was dressed and peering out through the ice-rimmed window at the snow-covered marshes and the leafless trees that looked in the dim light like row upon row of gallows. The northern landscape of St. Petersburg was desolate and disappointing. Then in the distance there was a spray of lights against the dark sky. Suddenly there were bridges everywhere she looked.

"Hurry, Tanya, hurry," she called out as her daughter scrambled into her clothes.

The whistle sounded; the train slowed and finally jolted to a stop in Nikolaevsky Station. Great clouds of steam swirled up from the dusky platform. Sonya moved briskly, grasping Tanya firmly as she walked along the platform. They had almost reached the exit when Sonya's cousin Anatoly Shostak—whom she had once asked to leave Yasnaya Polyana because he was too ardent in his courtship of her sister Tanya—came running up to them. They were to stay in St. Petersburg with his mother, Ekaterina Shostak, who was Sonya's first cousin. Ironically Anatoly was now married to Alexander Kuzminsky's half-sister, so Tanya, the girl who had been his first love, was now his sister-in-law.

As Sonya and her daughter, led by Anatoly, left the station for their carriage, icy winds whirled around them. Winter nights in the northern city were long, and though it was morning they rode through near darkness. The Venice of the North was not at all as Sonya had imagined it would be. But by the time she reached her cousin's house, she had been touched by the city's charms. Cold gray daylight washed over the sky, lights flickered on, and sleigh bells rang through the moaning winds. Sonya was entranced by St. Petersburg's Italianate atmosphere. Huge baroque palaces, painted red and green and blue and yellow, rose up along the banks of the frozen Neva. The smaller buildings which lined the broad boulevards resembled those in Canaletto's paintings of Venice; all were gaily painted and ornately decorated. It was a city built on water, spanning nineteen islands, tied together by graceful bridges, intertwined by twisting canals. By noon St. Petersburg blazed with light. In the great palaces along the Neva, tall ornamented windows, balconies, and columned doorways were brilliantly lighted.

Sonya missed little during her stay in the capital. She paid a visit to the House of Fabergé, reveling in its opulence. Ladies, she learned, slept until noon, received their hairdressers at home, and wore diamonds at luncheon. The members of the haut monde spoke only French and attended the theater or the Imperial Ballet almost every night, after which, bundled in lavish furs, they rode in bright red sleighs to restaurant clubs for supper and dancing. Sonya moved easily in this world and spent her evenings at parties or at musical performances which were followed by midnight suppers. Servants passed glasses of champagne on silver salvers; tables were covered with exotic delicacies. Lev Nikolaevich would have been disgusted by it all, but Sonya was like a child given her first glimpse of a shining Christmas tree glimmering with brightly burning candles.

The high point of Sonya's visit was her meeting with the Empress Maria Feodorovna. The Empress, who was a friend of the elderly and frail Madame Shostak, paid an unexpected call while Sonya and her cousin were sitting together. Although Maria Feodorovna was not a handsome woman—her hair and eyes pale brown, her body somewhat too angular, her gray wool dress rather dowdy—she had an amazing presence. Only a few inches taller than Sonya, she appeared, because of her stately carriage, to tower above her; and her gestures—slow, graceful, sure—were regal.

"Have you been here long?" the Empress asked Sonya, speaking French with a strong Danish accent.

"No, madame, only since yesterday," Sonya replied after a deep curtsy.

"How is your husband's health?" Maria Feodorovna inquired with some archness.

Sonya became slightly agitated, because she knew Tolstoy was greatly out of favor in court circles. Nonetheless she answered with equanimity, "Your Majesty is kind; he is well."

"I hope that he is writing something."

"No, madame, not at the moment, but I believe that he intends to write something for the schools in the nature of *What Men Live By*."

Madame Shostak broke in: "Countess Alexandra Tolstoy says that he will never again write any novels."

The Empress looked at Sonya with surprise. "Surely you do not desire this; it astonishes me."

Eager to avoid this issue, Sonya quickly posed an indirect question. "I hope that Your Majesty's children have read my husband's books."

Smiling, the Empress replied, "Oh, I surely believe so." The conversation then turned to less sensitive topics.

Despite the influence both Alexandra Tolstoy and Madame Shostak had at court, permission to publish Tolstoy's suppressed works was not granted. But all the same, the trip to St. Petersburg, though it lasted less than a fortnight, was memorable for Sonya; and she returned to Moscow at the beginning of March refreshed and vital.

She had an empty shed adjoining the house converted into a publishing office. Tolstoy refused to take any part in this project, so Sonya attended to the proofs herself—working on them till late at night as she had once done with her copying—while handling all the business of being a publisher during the day.

Sonya and the children joined Tolstoy at Yasnaya Polyana for the summer. As always, the house was filled with relatives and guests, but Sonya's work on the new edition continued. Proofs were sent back and forth from Moscow, and when she returned to the city in the fall she placed advertisements in the newspapers to attract subscribers. Tolstoy's fury grew through the months, and on December 16, 1885, he wrote Chertkov a long, self-indulgent tirade. In this letter, which was never sent, he complained, "During the last few days, the subscription and sale of my books has begun, on terms that are very advantageous for us and very hard on the booksellers. I go out and see a buyer looking at me, the humbug, the man who writes against property and, through my wife's business, extorts every cent he can out of the people who read him. Oh, if only someone could trumpet the ignominy of it all in the newspapers, loud and clear and devastating!"

Two nights after Tolstoy had written this letter, Sonya was

sitting at her writing table when he entered the room and gravely announced, "I've come to say that I wish to divorce you; I cannot live this way; I'm going to Paris or America."

Sonya was stunned. "What has happened?"

"Nothing," he replied, "but if the cart is loaded more and more, the horse stands and does not pull it."

He began to pace and shout at her, denouncing her for not making herself over in his image, for not seeing to it that his children accepted his philosophy. Sonya sat immobile, staring at him, unable to speak. He screamed obscenities at her, reproaching her for her materialism and her sensualism and accusing her of wantonness.

"Where you are, the air is poisoned," he hissed, bending close to her.

Slowly, proudly, Sonya stood and walked past him into the hallway, where she found four of the older children standing with shocked, frightened faces.

"Have my trunk brought around so that I can pack," she told Ilya. "I'll visit the Kuzminskys for a few days." She was trembling.

"I'll go with you," Tanya cried.

Tolstoy then stepped out into the hallway. "Don't leave," he commanded. Then his voice quavering, he begged, "Remain." His body twitched and he began sobbing. After a time and with her family's persuasion, Sonya agreed to stay. When Tolstoy finally became calm several hours later, he made no apology and showed no repentance. For the next few days he walked about the house in a dour and withdrawn mood. Finally, he decided to go to the country with Tanya to visit some family friends. Before he left, he wrote Sonya an unusually long letter; its almost illegible script, careless syntax, and omitted words show it was written by a man under great emotional stress. Throughout the letter he repeatedly insisted on her hearing out all his complaints, promising each time that he would soon speak about her. ("The subject at the moment is *me*—I'll speak about you later. . . . Put aside all thoughts of yourself for the time being. Later on I'll talk about you, about your feelings and your situation.") But he never carried through this promise, breaking off abruptly after stating only his grievances.

There can be no agreement and no loving life between us until you come to what I have come to. . . . I said until *you* come to me; I didn't say until I come to you, because that is impossible for me. It is impossible because the things you live by are the very things I have only just escaped from, as from a horrible and monstrous thing which nearly brought me to suicide. . . . But you can try to come to something you haven't yet known . . . a life devoted to God and to other people and not to one's own pleasure. . . . You publish my works so assiduously, you went to so much trouble in St. Petersburg, and you hotly defended my articles which were banned. But what was written in those articles?

After discussing his attempts to overcome despair, he flatly states, "Whichever way I turn I can't help suffering living the life we live!"

Several pages follow, chastising her for her opposition to his philosophy: "I renounced my property, began to give what people asked of me, renounced ambition for myself and the children know that what you were arranging for them . . . was the temptation of the love of fame, and of exalting oneself above others, a millstone we were putting about their necks."

"What are we to do about it?" he finally asks her. "It's strange to answer, because the answer is the simplest one; we must . . . find out where the obstacle comes from, and having found out, destroy it, or having recognized it to be insurmountable, bow down to it. . . . You attribute what has happened to everything except this one thing, that you are the unwitting, unintentional cause of my sufferings."

And he ends on an ominous note: "A struggle to the death is going on between us. Either God's works, or not God's works. And since God is within you . . ."

He ended there, in mid-thought and mid-sentence, and left the unsigned letter in an envelope atop her desk.

Had he given Sonya a chance to reply to this diatribe, she might well have countered with her own complaints. Since the age of eighteen she had devoted her life to caring for him and his home, to ensuring his financial security, to bearing twelve children, nine of whom were still alive. She had followed his dictates on family life, childbearing, nursing, and education. Now he demanded that she abandon the life he had once insisted upon and become com-

pletely obedient to his own interpretation of God's commandments. Tolstoy might reiterate forever that "a real wife has the
ability to absorb and assimilate ideas until she sees everything
through her husband's eyes." But Sonya had been married to half
a dozen Lev Nikolaeviches during their twenty-three years together. Which one of these men was she to "absorb and assimilate"?
Was she to live her life in blind and insincere mimicry?

She said none of these things, and when his first letter came
from the country telling her he was calmer, she replied, "I would
give anything to know how you are. But I am afraid to touch these
painful wounds which are not only unhealed but, it seems to me,
have started to bleed again. . . . I am happy to think that away
from me your shattered nerves have been calmed. Maybe you will
even be able to do some work."

This soft approach apparently made Tolstoy see how he had
hurt her. "I do not tell you this to pacify you, but truly I see how
badly I have wronged you. The moment I understood this and
expelled from my soul all sorts of imaginary grievances and resur-
rected my love for you . . . I felt well again!"

Tolstoy returned to Moscow in a mellower mood. Prince Urusov was now living in that city, and the two men became closer
than they had been.

To Sonya's chagrin, for she had considered Urusov more her
friend than Tolstoy's, they went off together on a trip to the Crimea. Tolstoy's grief and Sonya's disbelief were strong when Urusov died on this journey. Sonya had lost the one person whom she
sincerely believed was a kindred spirit.

Her sense of loss was intensified by her growing awareness of
Chertkov's competitive attitude toward her. He had returned to
Russia earlier that year, and his friendship with Tolstoy had grown
even more intimate. He had become determined to support the
growing cult of Tolstoyism through his own publication of Tolstoy's works, and his proprietary attitude toward her husband's
writings stunned Sonya. He wanted certain works for his own
publishing venture, a literary magazine to be called *Intermediary*,
and he was ruthless in his designs to obtain them and in his disregard for her position. A bitter lifelong battle had been joined.

17

Sonya's vibrant spirit was evident in her rapid, intense manner of speaking and her animated smile, which swept twenty years from her face. At forty-one, after bearing twelve children, she remained a handsome woman—her figure elegant, her hair dark and her skin smooth except for laugh lines about her dark eyes.

The unsureness she had once felt in gatherings of literary and social lions had disappeared. Her successful publishing enterprise had brought her great self-assurance, and friendships with women like Alexandra Tolstoy and Anna Dostoevsky had given her confidence in her ability to attract lively and interesting acquaintances. And as she worked on the proofs of Tolstoy's works, she came to recognize how much her own literary gifts had contributed to these writings. This new sense of her talent was heightened when magazine and newspaper editors asked her to write literary critiques, and authors sought her advice. Although she did not yet feel she should accept either of these responsibilities, her energy was prodigious. Never was she idle and seldom did she sleep more than five hours a night. She kept her own account books, wrote all her own letters, proofread every word she published, and dealt with the business of purchasing, selling, and distributing her books. Most of the menial tasks, both in her business and her household, fell to her small staff; but every decision that was made was hers.

Despite the additional work she had taken on, Sonya remained dedicated to the welfare of her husband and children. She might have fought against her pregnancies, but once the child was born she was a fiercely devoted mother. The future of each one of her brood constantly worried her. Seryozha, now twenty-two, was a gifted musician and wanted to become a composer, but Sonya feared he lacked the discipline to achieve this goal. Though artistically talented, the twenty-one-year-old Tanya, whom her mother regarded as a close friend and ally, longed only to marry and have children. Sonya was moved by the girl's preparations for motherhood—she struggled to overcome her habit of sleeping on her stomach, because she thought this position would be awkward during pregnancy, and she insisted on washing her breasts with freezing water and drying them with rough flannel to prepare for suckling. Yet, pretty and bright as she was, Tanya had attracted no serious suitor.

Ilya, nineteen, was Sonya's gravest concern. The most clever and sensitive of her children, Ilya spent his evenings drinking and playing cards and, as a consequence, was doing poorly at school. Lyova, sixteen, who bore the most striking resemblance to her, had become very much involved in his father's philosophy and was showing a skill for writing. There was a strong bond between Lyova and Masha, fourteen, who was the frailest, most easily led of the children. Masha had an ardent interest in the Tolstoyan philosophy, which Sonya felt had its roots in Lyova's influence rather than in a true desire to follow her father's path. A homely young girl, she maintained a watchful, rather wary attitude toward her mother.

These five children formed one group and the younger ones another. Andreyusha, the eldest of the four "little ones," was eight, Misha, six, Alyosha, four, and Sasha not yet two. Of the little ones, Alyosha was the most appealing, a child of sharply varying moods—meditative and withdrawn at times, charming and gay at others—but with little of the handsomeness of the other Tolstoy boys. Half Andreyusha's age, he was still the chief "protector," the leader among the four youngsters. Like Sonya, he was both willful and gracious. As in all families, the children fought among themselves, but he stood apart from such petty interchanges.

On January 16, 1886, Alyosha insisted on going for a walk with Ilya. It was a cold blustery morning with a strong north wind; but though he was small and slight, he was a healthy child and there was no reason to keep him at home. Well bundled up, he went off, hands in pockets and running to keep up with his brother. Less than an hour later Ilya brought him home coughing and complaining about sharp pains in his throat. A doctor examined him and, finding nothing more than a slight inflammation, gave him some mild medication. Two hours later Alyosha lay delirious on his small bed, running a dangerously high fever. The doctor returned and recognized his blunder. Abscesses, which had developed on the child's tonsils, had erupted, and the poisonous fluid was now traveling through his frail body.

For thirty-six hours Sonya stayed by Alyosha, snatching moments of sleep in a chair near his bed. Suddenly the fevered child wakened. "Maman?" he called out weakly.

"I'm here, Alyosha." Sonya rushed to assure him.

"Papa?" he asked.

It was the boy's dying request, and she sensed it. Anna Seuron stood in the doorway. "Hurry, get the Count," Sonya ordered.

Tolstoy was in his study when Anna Seuron burst in without knocking. "Alyosha—he's calling for you," she gasped.

Tolstoy ran through the house to the nursery; he paused at the door to collect himself and then walked calmly to the bed. Sonya stood facing him across their sick child. After looking up at his father, Alyosha raised his dreamy gray eyes toward the ceiling and murmured, "I see . . . I see . . ." A smile flickered on his face.

"What do you see?" Sonya asked gently, but no reply came. The smile faded and the child was dead.

Sonya was inconsolable, her guilt a monstrous and pervading thing. She was torn by the conviction that God had punished her for trying to abort Sasha; she had sinned and little Alyosha was dead because of it.

Tolstoy's stoicism and detachment in the face of his wife's grief intensified Sonya's terrible suffering. But her belief that she was responsible for their irreparable loss made her accept his indifference in a meek and even loving manner.

On the very day of Alyosha's death Tolstoy, with great equanimity, wrote Chertkov, "I know only that the death of a child, which formerly seemed incomprehensible and cruel to me, now appears sensible and good. The death has united us all more lovingly and closely than before." Five days later Sonya was still in a state of nervous collapse, and he replied to a distant cousin's note of sympathy: "My wife has been much afflicted by this death and I, too, am sorry that the little boy I loved is no longer here, but despair is only for those who shut their eyes to the commandments by which we are ruled."

Tolstoy had long since repudiated religious ceremonies, and in the hours after Alyosha died it appeared that he would not be buried with the usual funeral rites. Unable to sway her husband, Sonya turned to her mother to intercede. The aging, infirm Lyubov Alexandrovna succeeded where her daughter had failed, and the child was interred in the churchyard at Nikolskoye, his small grave beside that of the grandfather he had never known. A simple ceremony was performed by a priest. Tolstoy, however, refused to pay the priest for his services, and Seryozha had to step in and give him the customary offering of a few rubles.

Tormented by guilt and grief, Sonya threw herself into her publishing work with renewed intensity. The tragedy had not brought husband and wife closer together, as Tolstoy had written Chertkov; they were instead slipping further and further apart.

Influenced by this growing estrangement, the older children had split into two factions. Like Masha, Tanya embraced Tolstoy's philosophy and became somewhat distant toward her mother. Each day Sonya saw the girls making themselves more and more necessary to their father. They had begun by doing simple errands and chores for him and had moved on to more difficult tasks. Now they copied his manuscripts and tended to the needs of the poorer Tolstoyans (most of whom were peasants and workingmen) who came to the house "in greasy, smelly sheepskin coats, and muddy felt or leather boots." Lyova had once been his father's most enthusiastic supporter within the family, but now he joined Seryozha and Ilya in criticizing the "dark people," as Tanya Kuzminsky had named Tolstoy's poorer followers. The servants also found the "dark people" repellent. Reeking of tar and grease, they muddied the parquet floors, ate like a pack of greedy animals, and never had a spare kopeck to leave as a tip. The household staff much preferred the Countess's friends, who were clean, well mannered, and well fed; who drove up in carriages, sometimes attended by footmen; and who often gave generous gratuities.

When the family was in Moscow, Sonya was at home to her friends on Saturday afternoons. The footman, in dress coat and white gloves, led a procession of fashionable Moscow ladies up the stairs to the drawing room, where she rose with a great rustle of silk to meet them. Conversation was gay and bantering; the ladies' perfumes mingled with the strong aroma of tea from the steaming samovar. In the evening young people, friends of the older children, arrived. Tolstoy no longer came to greet these guests; instead he remained in his study to receive his "dark" visitors. These roughly dressed and often foul-smelling men and women had to pass through the drawing room to reach the master's lair. Furtive, embarrassed looks were exchanged by Sonya's elegant acquaintances as the footman ushered the Tolstoyans to a small door opening onto a dark corridor that led to Tolstoy's study.

Whichever house—city or country—Tolstoy occupied rapidly took on the frantic air of a revival meeting. Among his more prominent and dedicated disciples were Chertkov; the painter Nikolai N. Gay (loved and called "Grandfather" by the children but distrusted by Sonya, who found him "false and affected"); Pavel Ivanovich Biryukov, who was a close friend of Chertkov's; and the artist Ilya E. Repin. Pictures of Tolstoy and articles about him appeared in almost every issue of every newspaper and journal. He continued to have difficulties with the censor, and a number of his essays were suppressed. But, published clandestinely by sympathetic printers, these articles had a wide circulation despite the official ban.

Every day four or more petitioners arrived to see Tolstoy. That spring Tanya observed in her diary that most of them came "to beg for money or advice, or simply to have a talk and then say they had seen Lev Nikolaevich." She went on: "As for letters, there's no end to them—also mainly begging letters or requests for counsel. He also got drunkards, long-haired nihilists, priests, and rich businessmen—who would ask what to do with their money. On one occasion an officer came, and while he told his story sobbed so that we in the other room were all scared to death. Papa is nice to everybody who really needs his help or advice, but he never answers letters: two secretaries could not cope with them." In fact, Biryukov soon began to take on this task.

Not long after Alyosha's funeral the household became a bedlam of religious fervor. "Grandfather" Gay came to paint pictures on New Testament themes and to renew his faith with "holy Lev Nikolaevich." Chertkov arrived with Biryukov and a new disciple

called Anna Konstantinovna Dieterichs. Sonya had to find room
for them all in her crowded house (her Uncle Kostya, who had
suffered severe financial reverses, was also staying with the Tolstoys).

Sonya did not take to Anna Konstantinovna any more warmly
than she had to Chertkov. These two oddly matched but equally
abrasive people planned to wed. The prospective bridegroom told
Tanya that he had at last found a woman who shared his convictions, who he thought would help him in his work, and who had
agreed to bear his children even though he was not in love with
her. Tanya, a dreamy young woman, wrote skeptically in her
diary, "I hope it turns out well, but it seems risky."

Anna Konstantinovna was a thin but pretty young woman
with dark curly hair and great black eyes. A nervous little creature,
she looked "as though she would break any moment under the
weight of life, as though her frail body could not sustain the burden." Her passionate advocacy of Tolstoy's philosophy surpassed
even that of Chertkov, and she stood before the "master" with awe
and trembling. Toward Sonya, however, the girl was far less def-
erential, and within a few days of her arrival she upbraided her for
not adhering to Tolstoyan principles.

There was a condescending tone in Anna Konstantinovna's
voice which infuriated Sonya, and she heatedly retorted, "Well, I'll
tell you frankly that you are mistaken, as are many other youths
and these shaggy nihilists who come to him from everywhere. He's
not what you imagine, and I tell you plainly he is not that which
he tries to be. What if he does stitch boots and split wood? He was
and has remained a count, and all this simplicity is only affectation
. . . a kind of amusement; he always loved originality. Even in his
youth he played various tricks in order to shock people and make
them speak about him."

The two women had begun a difficult acquaintance that would
not grow easier.

Sonya mourned "the death of Tolstoy's great art" with the
same passion that she felt over the death of a child. She languished
in her grief and bewailed her loss: "He is an artist, and suddenly he
becomes a shoemaker! It is plain insanity!" Believing that his religious writings had no literary value, she called them "rubbish" and

declared, "I have refused to copy [these works]. Who wants them? Who will read them?"

Sonya was not alone in her sorrow at Tolstoy's abandonment of his fictive genius. Articles were constantly published decrying the course he had chosen, and members of the intelligentsia engaged in endless discussions over tea or kvass of Tolstoy's folly. The composer Tchaikovsky wrote in his diary:

> Why has this man become addicted to *teaching*, to a *mania for preaching for the enlightenment* of our obscured or limited minds? Formerly, from his description of the most simple and everyday scene, an unforgettable impression was created. Between the lines one read a kind of highest love toward mankind, a highest *pity* toward its helplessness, limitations, and insignificance. One would weep, not knowing why . . . but from his present writings there blows a cold wind; one senses a *fear* . . . The former Tolstoy was a demigod—the present one a *priest*. But priests are essentially *teachers, by a role they have taken upon themselves, and by virtue of a vocation.*

Tchaikovsky's opinion was more or less that held by most Russian artists and aristocrats. It was thought that Tolstoy was close to madness. He seemed to many almost a caricature—an aging man whose dread of death and hell had driven him to a desperate and joyless conviction that Christ, the ultimate physician, would "heal" his mortality.

Except for a few short stories, Tolstoy had written no fiction for almost nine years. Just as it seemed he would never again produce a major work in this genre, he began *The Death of Ivan Ilych*, a short psychological novel about an ordinary man who has lived an ordinary life, and whose sins are no greater than those of most men. At forty-five he hears a knock on the door—death has come for him. For three days Ivan Ilych, the dying man, fights desperately for his soul. Finally he sees clearly what *is* right, and having found this answer, "There was no fear because there was no death. In place of death there was light."

Tolstoy completed the novella on March 25, 1886, and one week later he decided to walk from Moscow to Yasnaya Polyana (a distance of 130 miles). Sonya could not dissuade him from embarking on what she considered a perilous journey. Accompanied by three young men, Mikhail Strakhovich, Nikolai Gay (the son of the artist), and S. Pisarenko, he set off with a large linen knapsack heavy with food, a second pair of shoes, a change of clothing, and a notebook with a pencil attached. Within twenty-four hours Strakhovich and Pisarenko decided to turn back; Tolstoy and Gay, however, pressed on, sleeping in hovels and eating and talking with pilgrims they encountered. They arrived at the gates of Yasnaya Polyana on the fifth evening in high spirits, tanned by sun and wind. Sonya, the family, Anna Seuron, and the Kuzminskys joined Tolstoy on the eleventh of May.

After an unusually harsh winter, the spring crops were poor, and many of the villagers of Yasnaya Polyana were hungry and ill. Masha, now a tall but rather frail girl, devoted herself to helping the unfortunate peasants. She had a talent for nursing and went from door to door visiting the sick, a practice Sonya could not help but admire. Her daughter's adoption of peasant dress and manners she found less praiseworthy. Masha insisted upon doing her own laundry, and Sonya would come upon her "barefoot with her sleeves turned up above her elbows . . . bent down over the landing of [the] pond [as she] rinsed the clothes with a broad swinging motion, then heaped a piece, flattened it with one blow of the bat, and then with another powerful blow, pressed out the water." In these blows, which echoed over the pond, Sonya felt her daughter's defiance, and she flinched at the sound.

Early in June, Ilya arrived, his spring term at the university completed. Desperately in love with Sofya Nikolaevna Filosofova, a young woman he had recently met, he considered himself engaged and was dreaming of getting married. "The general atmosphere in the house was one of falling in love. Ilya, Sonya [Kuzminsky], Masha, Alcide [Anna Seuron's son]—all of them . . . I love nobody," Tanya wrote in her diary.

During that summer a passion for physical labor seized everyone at Yasnaya Polyana. Sasha Kuzminsky, who was now a middle-aged, somewhat stuffy government official, "mowed so vigorously that his hands were covered with blisters." And even Sonya, wearing a gay sarafan, went out to the fields and took up a rake. It was a scorching summer, and the hay had to be brought in quickly. "The grass in the fields had been burned by the sun and was dry and stiff as wire," Ilya recalled. "It was only very early in the morning when the dew was on it that it yielded easily to the scythe." And so the occupants of Yasnaya Polyana got up at dawn to complete the task they had set themselves. When the sun was high, they tedded the hay, gathering it into haycocks. When the evening dew fell, they set out again with their scythes and worked until nightfall.

Tanya wrote in her diary: "I rise at seven, carry my dinner with me (sometimes it is brought out) and do not come home until eight in the evening. Our peasants, both men and women, are fine folk, so jolly; the site is wonderfully beautiful—starting from [the peasant] Mitrofan's cottage, then down the river right to the clearing. We have already made fifty [hay]cocks. . . . Yesterday we were carting, and I simply could not pitch, that is terribly hard work and I was afraid of straining myself."

Her hours in the fields left Sonya with a painful sunburn and several pulled ligaments. Suffering great discomfort, she was bedridden for most of the next weeks. She had been caught up in the family's enthusiasm, but she now thought their summer's occupation was as mad as her husband's efforts to make the peasants sign a pledge to give up alcohol and tobacco (he himself still smoked and drank). Her illness and her grief over Alyosha's death made her even more short-tempered with Chertkov, and the hostility between them intensified. Chertkov was gaining a fast-growing hold over her husband, and Tolstoy now leaned heavily on him, demanding his opinion about his literary endeavors and relying on his help in propagating the Tolstoyan philosophy. Recognizing Chertkov's considerable organizational ability, Sonya saw that he was moving toward becoming Tolstoy's "secretary" and the self-appointed business manager for Tolstoyism. The two men exchanged diaries as Tolstoy and Sonya had in the early years of their marriage. Intimate confessions crowded the pages of their voluminous correspondence, and Chertkov claimed that Tolstoy was closer to him than any other being save Christ. In one letter to Tolstoy, Chertkov complained that Sonya "is less well disposed toward me . . . when I'm away . . . than when I am in her presence. I fear that this arises from the fact that when she hears of my activities concerning the publication of your works, she ascribes motives to me that I do not at all have."

Chertkov published Tolstoy's writings in cheap editions which sold for only a few kopecks, making them available to the more affluent and educated peasants, whereas Sonya's editions were too expensive for them. Ostensibly a non-profit venture, Chertkov's publications had a wide circulation, and Sonya was convinced that he was appropriating Tolstoy's royalties. She accused him of treating Tolstoy's writings as though they were his own to profit from and dispose of as he saw fit. Tolstoy tried to make peace between them, but neither would bend and they became fiercely competitive. Sonya published *The Death of Ivan Ilych* that summer (it met with immediate success) and was preparing a thirteenth edition of Tolstoy's complete works, which Chertkov himself wished to publish cheaply.

Determined that her edition would appear first, Sonya worked doggedly, but she had no sooner become well enough to resume her household and publishing tasks than Tolstoy fell while carting hay for a poor widow and badly gashed his foot. He continued to work in the fields, walking through the low tangled brush and dry dirt in his open sandals. The wound became infected, and when erysipelas developed, he was ordered by the Tula doctor to remain in bed. As his fever rose, his condition grew worse. Conscious that his life was in danger, he overcame his distrust of medical science and sent Sonya to Moscow to seek a physician. She returned within a few days with a Dr. Chirkov, who inserted a drainage tube into the ulcer. Although she carefully followed Chirkov's strict instructions about Tolstoy's care, on September 4 his fever rose again, and intense pain made him groan through the night. The doctor from Tula was summoned and diagnosed a fresh erysipelas, warning that if it spread up the leg Tolstoy could die. Days of severe suffering followed, and at times Tolstoy shrieked so horribly that only Sonya could bear to stay with him. More than once the doctor from Tula was sent for in the middle of the night. By the beginning of October, after nine weeks of illness, Tolstoy finally began to improve. Told he must refrain from walking for another four weeks, he began to dictate a new play to Sonya. When he was allowed to move to a sofa, he demanded a writing board, pen, and paper and continued work on the drama, which was titled *The Power of Darkness*.

> For all its pain [Sonya wrote in her diary on October 25], these two months of Lev Nikolaevich's illness were, strangely enough, the last time of real happiness I have had. I nursed him day and night. It was such a happy, natural thing—the only thing I can do really well —to make a *personal* sacrifice for the man one loves. The harder it was, the happier it made me. Now he wanders about, and is nearly well. He has shown me clearly that he doesn't need me any longer, and now I am cast aside as of no further use, although I am, nevertheless, expected to do impossible things, like renouncing my property, giving up my convictions, and the education and welfare of my children—things others who firmly believe in this form of righteousness are incapable of doing. . . .
>
> I shall probably have to go to Moscow again, still keep the family together, and have to handle all the publishing side, and to get all the money, which Lev Nikolaevich, with an injured air of indifference, is the first to ask for, and which he then distributes among his favorites and his poor, who aren't poor at all, but are merely more insolent than the others and better at begging from him.

Sonya's attempts to limit the amount of money that was given away were fiercely resented by Tolstoy and by Tanya and Masha. Their scorn drove her into frequent spells of depression, darker and more frightening than ever before. The hours in the middle of the night when she was the only one awake in the dark house were the worst for her, and she feared she was going mad.

On November 11 Lyubov Alexandrovna died in Yalta, where she had gone for the winter with the hope that a warmer climate would restore her health. A decision was made not to bring her body back to Moscow, and she was buried in Yalta by two of her sons—Sasha and Stepan (Styopa). Sonya and her other children did not attend the burial. Ten days after her mother's death Sonya returned with her family from Yasnaya Polyana to Moscow. She greatly missed Lyubov Alexandrovna, and the depression she had experienced at Yasnaya Polyana intensified. "I sometimes have some beautiful moments devoted to the contemplation of death," she wrote in her diary several months later. In contrast to Tolstoy's anguished speculations about death is her serene statement: "I

clearly realize the duality of the physical and the spiritual consciousness, and the certain immortality of both."

Sonya was not able to regard her domestic life with this same
composure. She was "grieved at Ilya's shady and evil way of living.
Idleness, vodka, much lying, bad company, and above all, this
complete absence of any spiritual life." Tanya and Lyova had "developed a deplorable passion for *vint* [a game resembling auction
bridge]." Sonya seemed to have "lost all *educative* influence over the
young ones." She had thought she would find some peace when
they returned to Moscow and Tolstoy settled back to work. But
the same arguments about money and Chertkov persisted.

> Last week [she wrote on March 9, 1887] he [Tolstoy] again took
> up his vegetarianism, and it is already having an effect on his frame
> of mind. Today he purposely started talking about the evils of wealth
> and money in front of me, and alluded to my desire to keep things
> for the children. I said nothing at first but finally lost my temper and
> said, "I sell the twelve-volume edition for eight rubles, while you
> used to charge ten rubles for *War and Peace* alone." He grew angry
> but said nothing. His so-called *friends*, the new Christians, try terri-
> bly hard to put L. N. against me—and are not always unsuccessful.
> I read over Chertkov's letter in which he spoke of the happy spiritual
> communion between himself and his wife [Chertkov and Anna had
> married during the winter] and expressed his sympathy and regret
> that such a worthy man as L. N. should be ignorant of such happi-
> ness, and be deprived of such a *communion*—an obvious allusion to
> me. I read it over, and it hurt me. That blunt, sly, untruthful man,
> having succeeded in getting round L. N. with his flattery, is now
> trying (I suppose that's Christian) to destroy the bond which has so
> closely kept us together for nearly twenty-five years! . . . This rela-
> tion with Chertkov must be put to an end. It is all false and evil and
> we must get away from it.

As Chertkov bedeviled Sonya, Tolstoy was again plagued by
official opposition to his writing. Pobedonostsev denounced *The
Power of Darkness* as "a negation of ideals . . . a debasing of moral
feelings . . . and an offense against taste." The Tsar, who had earlier declared the play to be "a marvelous thing," judiciously
changed his position, writing to his minister that "one ought to put
an end to this mischief of L. Tolstoy. He is a downright nihilist

and atheist. It would not be bad now to forbid the sale of his drama *The Power of Darkness*, for he has already succeeded in selling enough of his nastiness and in spreading it among the people." But, although public performances of the work were banned, no action was taken to prevent its publication and sale. Appearing as an inexpensive pamphlet in 1887, *The Power of Darkness* was widely read. This grim play was based on a crime that had come to light in Tula several years before. At the wedding of his stepdaughter, a peasant had confessed to the assembled guests that he had murdered a child he had had by the bride and had also attempted to kill his own six-year-old daughter. Tolstoy's drama presented horrific episodes involving poison, adultery, and infanticide; and he himself cried whenever he read the scene in which the peasant kills his child, crushing it with a board until its "bones crunched."

In this play Tolstoy strikes a characteristic theme—sexual passion is a malignant force which drives men into foul baseness and precipitates unspeakable violence. He was unshakable in his conviction that the vilest elements of human nature found their expression in sexuality, and he was determined that his sons should accept this truth. He warned them that sexual activity was an evil to be avoided. And when the twenty-one-year-old Ilya, who planned to be married soon, told him he was still a virgin, Tolstoy wept tears of joy. "A sound, healthy woman," he warned Lev, "is a wild beast." To all three of his older sons he declared that "the most intelligent woman is less intelligent than the most stupid man." Yet he himself had always been and still was surrounded and supported by women; he turned for assistance not to his sons but to Sonya and his two older daughters.

As the cold, bleak winter wore on, Tolstoy suffered from chronic indigestion, which was most likely caused by his irregular eating habits. One day he would eat rich foods and fatty meat; on the next day he would follow a spartan vegetarian diet; and on the following day he would eat almost nothing but would smoke heavily and consume great quantities of rum and water. When a sharp pain developed in his side, Tolstoy consulted a physician who diagnosed his complaint as catarrhal jaundice. After telling him to wear warm clothing and an unbleached flannel waistband, the doctor ordered Tolstoy to smoke less, to eat frequent small meals, and to drink warm mineral water at frequent intervals during the day. As always when Sonya was nursing him, she was happier and he became more considerate.

As soon as he was well enough to travel, Tolstoy left for Yasnaya Polyana, where Sonya and the family joined him a few weeks later in early May. The forest was half in leaf, the wood violets were prematurely in bloom, and Sonya's garden was a mass of lively color. Tolstoy took great pleasure in flowers. He liked to see a bright bowl of them on the table; he often thrust a blossom behind his belt or carried one in his hand. "You should see," wrote Anna Seuron, "with what enjoyment he lifts them from time to time to his big nose and how he then looks around mildly, as if thanking the creator for giving us flowers."

During the summer of 1887 Tolstoy was absorbed in composing a lengthy didactic essay. It was first called "On Life and Death," but the final title was "On Life"—"for there is no death, the human soul is immortal." After copying and editing this work, Sonya translated it into French, which greatly pleased him.

It was one of the happiest summers Sonya had spent at Yasnaya Polyana since Tolstoy had turned to religion ten years before. And it was happy in spite of all the work that fell to her. Although the house had never been so filled with guests, she had only the cook, Nikolai, one housemaid, and the coachman as servants. The nurse, her sister Tanya's maid, and Anna Seuron, however, helped with the children. As always the Kuzminskys (who now had five children) were occupying a wing. There was also a parade of strangers and friends: the well-known writer Nikolai S. Leskov; the brilliant jurist A. F. Koni; Tomas G. Masaryk, a young doctor of philosophy (who would one day be president of Czechoslovakia); Vasily N. Andreyev-Burlak, a celebrated Russian actor, who read from Dostoevsky in the evenings; and a young violinist, Yuri Liassota, who had been engaged to help Seryozha with his music. Tolstoy's old friend Nikolai Strakhov arrived for a lengthy visit. The artist Ilya Repin came to paint Tolstoy. Crowds of sick and needy peasants appeared daily at the house, and Sonya used a book of home remedies to treat them. "It is mental agony," she wrote, "when you don't know what kind of disease it is and how it can really be helped. That is why I sometimes feel like giving it all up, but when I go out and see their touching faith, and imploring eyes, I begin to feel sorry, and although it grieves me to think that I am doing the wrong thing, I hand out the medicine and then try to forget all about the poor devils."

When the Kuzminskys were at Yasnaya Polyana, Sergey Nikolaevich seldom visited, but his daughter Vera, of whom the Tolstoys were extremely fond, stayed with them. Sergey Nikolaevich was beset by great financial problems, and Sonya was selling a small piece of land to raise some money for him. Of the Tolstoys' children, only Ilya was not with them that summer, having—to his father's anger and his mother's astonishment—joined the army.

Though in constant correspondence with Tolstoy, Chertkov and Anna (who was pregnant) were away; and Isaac B. Feinermann, another ardent follower, was also absent. Without these three disciples it seemed to Sonya that her husband was once more "the same happy joyful father of the family." His interest in music was rekindled, and in the evenings he played Mozart, Weber, and Haydn. Accompanied by Liassota on the violin, Seryozha, an accomplished pianist, played Beethoven's "Kreutzer Sonata." "What a powerful work, expressing every possible emotion!" Sonya noted. Tanya Kuzminsky sang with the same purity and passion as she had in her youth. The great affection between Tolstoy and his sister-in-law had cooled. She still had a deep reverence for his genius, but she did not agree with his new beliefs and was not afraid to express her frank opinions. Tolstoy's sarcasm, which had replaced his former lively humor, was parried by Tanya's sharp, mocking comments.

"There are roses and resedas standing on my table and we are going to have such a fine dinner," Sonya wrote on July 3. "The previous night Seryozha had been playing a waltz and Lyova came up to me, saying: 'Let us do a round.' This we did, to the great delight of all the young people." She was gay and relaxed; Tolstoy was loving. As the days grew warmer, she went bathing and experimented with a camera she had bought in Moscow, taking pictures of Tolstoy and the children. The disciples were not much in evidence during the early summer, and this idyllic time confirmed Sonya's belief that the discord between Tolstoy and her was caused by these invidious outsiders. Then in mid-July the disciples once again invaded her household, and the warm familial atmosphere turned sour.

"What disagreeable characters all these disciples of Lev Nikolaevich are!" she wrote on July 19. "Not a single sane person among them! Most of the women are hysterical. Marya Alexandrovna Schmidt has just left. In the old days she would have been a nun; now she is an enthusiastic worshipper of Lev Nikolaevich's ideas! . . . Every time she meets him or says goodbye she weeps hysterically."

P. D. Golokhvastov, a poet and writer who was extremely orthodox and a Slavophile, and an argumentative, unpleasant man, came with his wife and a pupil of theirs for a long visit. A. S. Butkevich, a former revolutionary, arrived, followed by Biryukov (one of the few disciples Sonya liked). "The Abameleks were here too," Sonya complained, "and brought the Helbigs, mother and daughter, with them; her maiden name is Princess Shakhovskoy, and she is married to a German professor; she and her daughter also came to see that Russian celebrity—Tolstoy." She found it tedious to play the charming hostess to people she did not like. "[Life here] is very noisy and tiring," she wrote. "I long for some of the intimacy of the family circle, and a more orderly existence, as regards both work and recreation."

There was one person she was delighted to see—Countess Alexandra Andreyevna Tolstoy, who arrived at Yasnaya Polyana on July 25 for a ten-day visit. The aging aristocrat did not like the state of the household and instantly aligned herself with Sonya, sparring sharply with Tolstoy. She favored the morning hours for discussion and was waiting for him at the breakfast table. Their conversations always began calmly enough. He would read her passages from his favorite poets. These works were usually religious, and when the name of Christ inevitably appeared, his voice would tremble and his eyes fill with tears. Alexandra was indignant at this show of feeling. Was not such emotion hypocritical when he did not accept the divinity of the Savior? A rather sharp discussion would follow, with each careful not to offend the other, yet refusing to relinquish a single conviction.

After breakfast—perhaps to make a peace offering, or perhaps simply to keep his beloved but stern critic occupied—he would give her all the mail he had received the previous day and would then disappear into his study. He was now receiving letters from all over the world and had large groups of followers in many countries, including France and the United States. When he emerged in the afternoon, she would return the stack to him, once commenting, "What fearful pap for your pride, my dear friend. I really fear that one day you will turn into a Nebuchadnezzar before his conversion."

Chertkov's pandering letters infuriated Alexandra the most. She was harsh in her judgment of the man and highly critical of the views he espoused. In fact, she was scornful of the entire Tolstoyan philosophy and pointed out that "for all his convictions about the evils of money, Tolstoy still continued to dole out kopecks to the numerous beggars who applied to him."

Appalled at Sonya's workload, Alexandra helped her by taking dictation from Tolstoy. She later recalled, "He dictated and I wrote. Entirely unexpectedly such awkward phrases began to burst forth that I involuntarily recalled the 'impassable swamp' that Turgenev once mentioned apropos of Tolstoy, and I could not resolve to circumvent the swamp or to set it down for printing in just this form." Alexandra then conscripted Sasha Kuzminsky to assist her in recopying this work. "Kuzminsky, although he agreed with me, reckoned it impossible for a simple mortal to dare correct Tolstoy." His chariness annoyed Alexandra, and she remarked to Tolstoy, "Do you know, my dear, that I am just about to correct your prose to the great scandal of your brother-in-law?" He answered mildly, "And you would be perfectly right, for I am concerned only with the idea and pay no attention to my style."

This statement was not entirely true. Sonya did edit his work, correcting grammatical errors and calling inconsistencies and unclear passages to his attention; but Tolstoy fastidiously reworked and rewrote his prose, producing a final draft which was inimitably "Tolstoyan" in style.

When Alexandra left on August 4, she felt closer to Sonya than before; she pitied her and worried about Tolstoy's unorthodox faith. The day after Alexandra's departure, Sonya's brother Stepan —whom she had not seen in nine years—arrived for an extended stay with his wife, Marya Petrovna, a former provincial actress.

The young woman was somewhat aloof, and her efforts to help with the household chores seemed to make more rather than less work for Sonya.

Stepan was shocked by the dramatic change in Tolstoy. It was not simply that Tolstoy had grown older and grayer—his whole personality seemed to have altered. His *joie de vivre*, once so enlivening to others, had now vanished, and he was consumed by an arid moralism. He denounced education as harmful and considered politeness a sign of selfishness. He had adopted the peasants' manner of speech as well as their dress, and the regard he had once felt toward the aristocracy had been replaced by sympathy for the peasants; the lower a man stood in the social scale the more Tolstoy admired him. Once rather reserved, he was now completely accessible to everyone. Stepan had known him as a man eager to build up his financial resources, but Tolstoy now thought money evil, "ignored his property, refused to have anything to do with it or to care about its fate, and ceased to make use of it except that he continued to live at Yasnaya Polyana." He had also given up hunting and abandoned sport for physical work such as plowing and hut building.

Stepan Behrs and Marya Petrovna were at Yasnaya Polyana for eight weeks, although Stepan did spend some of that time in St. Petersburg, leaving his wife with his sister and her family. Tolstoy was displeased with his former protégé, believing Behrs had not grown and developed in the years since they had last met. Neither man was ever able to regain his former love or regard for the other. Their relationship was further strained a decade later when Stepan Behrs published his *Recollections* and took Sonya's side in the conflict between husband and wife. He presented Sonya's plight succinctly:

> She [has] been the closest witness of all his spiritual sufferings, and in general of the gradual development of his thought, and in consequence she has again and again had to suffer on her husband's account. She [has] involuntarily developed a dread and abhorrence of his teaching and its consequences. Feeling how powerless she was to influence his genius or aid him in his spiritual evolution, she was driven to think only of her children, and to oppose those demands of her husband which related to them, that is, in regard to the distribution of his property and to their education. The saying "between

two fires" but feebly describe[s] her position between her husband's
demands on the one side, and the impossibility . . . of submitting to
those demands on the other.

Stepan Behrs had correctly assessed Sonya's awesome dilemma. Did she owe her first allegiance to her husband or to her
children? The household took on a split personality. The humor-
less, stern, hardworking Tolstoy, shabbily dressed, was surrounded by his "dark, dark people" and crowds of beggars. The
elegant, fastidious Sonya delighted in the gay company of her sister
and of their aristocratic guests. It was an impossible situation, one
that, after the idyllic weeks of the early summer, began to depress
Sonya.

"I am losing my moral strength," she wrote in her diary on
August 19. On the twenty-second she celebrated her forty-third
birthday. She was again pregnant and was plagued by the fear that
she would not survive the birth of another child. "I spent all day
looking through Lyova's manuscripts, and sorting them out. I want
to take them to the Rumiantsev Museum. Some of them are in a
dreadful muddle. . . . I also want to take his letters, diaries, portraits, and everything else relating to him. . . . Does my desire to
put everything in order mean that I shall soon die?"

But by September 23, the Tolstoys' silver wedding anniversary, Sonya's trepidation had left her. There was a great party,
which displeased Tolstoy; but Sonya did not let his irritation cloud
her happiness. She had come to believe that with this new pregnancy God had given her a chance to undo the evil (the attempted
abortion of Sasha) that had, she was certain, caused little Alyosha's
death. For the first time in twenty years she was pleased to be
pregnant and was certain that this child would be blessed and
would in turn bless her marital union.

The family returned to Moscow that fall, and Sonya's pregnancy proceeded uneventfully. On February 28, 1888, Ilya married Sofya Nikolaevna Filosofova, and this event (the first wedding
among her children) filled her with great happiness. But the extrav-
agance of the wedding, the religious ceremony, the fine clothes of
the guests, and the boisterous singing at the reception offended
Tolstoy's new sense of propriety. Even the happiest of occasions

served to point up the deep and bitter differences between husband and wife.

A month later, on March 31, 1888, Sonya gave birth to her thirteenth child and ninth son, Ivan, affectionately called Vanichka. She again suffered from a breast fissure, which made nursing an agony. The child was small and sickly, and she insisted she needed a wet nurse. Tolstoy was obdurate in his refusal to bend to her pleas. Three weeks after his son's birth and in the face of his wife's bitter protests, he left Moscow on foot for Yasnaya Polyana accompanied by young Nikolai Gay. "God gave the infant, and God will give it food," he wrote Sonya upon his arrival at Yasnaya Polyana. She, in turn, hastily dispatched a letter to her sister Tanya, who was now living in St. Petersburg. "Never was Lyovochka so extremely stubborn and obstinate in his lunacies as during this past year," she complained. However, she did not engage a wet nurse and endured the pain of her sore breasts.

18

Sonya and her husband were rapidly becoming spiritual and intellectual strangers. The one bond left was physical. Sex preyed constantly on the sixty-year-old Tolstoy's mind. He believed that leaving Sonya so soon after the ordeal of a childbirth was an act of Christian righteousness. By separating himself from his wife he removed any chance of seduction on Sonya's part or of "bestial behavior" on his own. He was obsessed with the idea that to follow Christ one had to refrain entirely from sexual activity. Husband and wife must sleep in separate rooms. If this did not remove temptation and a child was conceived, under no circumstances should an evil be compounded by the husband and wife having intercourse while the child was at her breast. "Let everyone try not to marry," he wrote Chertkov, whom only two years before he had advised to wed, "and, if he be married, to live with his wife as brother and sister . . . you will object that this would mean the end of the human race? . . . What a great misfortune! The antediluvian animals are gone from the earth, human animals will disappear, too. . . . I have no more pity for these two-footed beasts than for the ichthyosaurus."

In this mood of misanthropy he began a new work of fiction, *The Kreutzer Sonata.* The story was suggested by a conversation with Andreyev-Burlak in which the actor recalled meeting a stranger on a train who tearfully confided all his conjugal woes. In Tolstoy's work a man (a violinist) who has killed his wife tells a stranger who shares his train compartment how he came to commit the crime. The protagonist maintains that Christ, in saying, "Everyone that looketh on a woman to lust after her hath committed adultery with her already in his heart," was condemning carnal passion even within marriage. The theme of the story was the

302

necessity of striving for absolute purity of thought; the conclusion was that sexual passion should be eliminated from human life.

From March to May Tolstoy stayed at Yasnaya Polyana and worked on a first draft of his new work. He put it away when Sonya and the family joined him for the summer. It had become clear to Sonya that Tolstoy's religiosity would not be short-lived; her hope that his spiritual enthusiasm would pass had vanished. Since she would never capitulate to him, it appeared that they would be at an impasse for the rest of their lives. Added to this new comprehension of her position was her own changing attitude toward the strong sexual ties that had always bound them. Tolstoy now declared sexual abstinence to be an absolute good and considered all intercourse evil. Therefore, he viewed even those infrequent times that they made love as acts of depravity on both their parts. Sonya concluded that her husband no longer lay with her from love but from lust, an emotion he considered degrading. She could have been any female; she could have been a whore. Feeling debased and sexually abused, she spurned with disgust any physical overture he made.

But when Sonya did not have an outlet for her sexual passion, she tended to suffer from anxiety, depression, hysteria, and suicidal impulses. The first signs of what many of Tolstoy's future biographers would regard as madness in her became evident during the summer of 1888. She desperately needed assurance that she was still—at forty-four and after twenty-six years of marriage—a desirable woman. Yet she was now repulsed by the thought of sexual activity with her husband. Her passions were temporarily submerged in a renewed dedication to motherhood, and Vanichka became the recipient of her intense emotions. Tolstoy, free for the time from temptation, took up a daily routine of hard physical labor and turned to his older daughters, most especially Masha, for the blind devotion that his wife withheld. He wrote little, spending his time plowing, sowing, harvesting, tending his "flock," sending his disciples off to start colonies based on his philosophy.

By now Tolstoyan colonies were springing up in sparsely populated areas throughout Russia. Tolstoy had not spelled out the practical application of his philosophy, and these colonists faced what proved to be insurmountable problems in establishing communities based on Tolstoyan principles. The master condemned

landlordism, capitalism, commerce, and professional medicine; but
the colonists had to buy or rent land and equipment. And while
Tolstoy denounced civil and criminal law as an abomination, his
followers had to settle on some way of governing their colonies.
Adherence to Tolstoyan principles also led the colonists to abstain
from sexual activity, alcohol, and tobacco, to adopt a vegetarian
diet (most difficult in those areas of Russia with little produce), and
to renounce worldly goods. The colonists were therefore people
who "were led to abandon their accustomed ways of life, to uproot
themselves from the places where they were known, to break off
their family connections, and to start life anew on fresh lines, ab-
juring the things that according to [Tolstoy] made life hideous,
arid, and vile."

To ease the colonists' hardship and sacrifice, Tolstoy prescribed hard manual labor; but his followers were mostly educated
people without skill, who tilled the land and built houses as poorly
as Tolstoy made boots. Yet Tolstoy showed no concern for the
members of these colonies (which now numbered over fifty). As
one Russian writer noted: "He listened so intently to the noise in
his own ears that he hardly heard what other people were saying!"

The family was back in Moscow by November. Tolstoy found
little time to write as he went about what he called "bread-labor":
shoemaking, wood chopping, fire building, water carting, and
cleaning his room. The house on Dolgo-Khamovnicheski Street
was crowded with earnest young people who came to catch a
glimpse of or hear the word of the master. Sonya was more irritated
than ever by these intruders. Her more pressing concern, however,
was the misery and havoc that, in her opinion, Tolstoy was causing
among their own children. Masha seemed to Sonya to be the most
affected. The girl's unnaturally strong attachment to her father,
her adoption of peasant dress, and her coolness toward her mother
—toward, in fact, every member of the family except Tolstoy—
gravely disturbed Sonya. The special relationship between Masha
and her father was creating rancor between her and her sisters
Tanya and young Alexandra. (In his diary Tolstoy wrote at this
time, "I feel great tenderness toward [Masha]. Her only. She makes
up for the others, I might say.")

Although the fair-haired Masha had her father's deep-set dark gray eyes and strong cheekbones, she was a rather homely girl. Her mouth was too large, her teeth crooked, her nose rather bulbous, her forehead somewhat too high. But she was slender and graceful, and whatever she set her hands to she did well. During her adolescent years Masha—certain that her mother (with whom she had always felt awkward) preferred her brother Lyova—drew away from Sonya. And during the months they had spent in Yasnaya Polyana, the breech between them seemed unbridgeable. To her mother's anger, Masha spent her days pitching hay. She set out wearing a plain cotton dress, a kerchief on her head and a rake across her narrow bony shoulders; when she returned, her back streaked with sweat, and her hair clinging to her damp neck, she smelled like a peasant woman. Masha's attachment to the village women—she shared their secrets, advised them, helped like a midwife at the birth of their children—also repelled Sonya. But it was the young woman's closeness to her father—her assistance with his literary work in Moscow and at Yasnaya Polyana—that created the greatest rift between Sonya and Masha.

In the spring of 1889 Tolstoy resumed work on *The Kreutzer Sonata*. One of the leaders of the American Shakers visited Yasnaya Polyana and later sent Tolstoy tracts about their movement. The Shakers preached abstention from sexual intercourse, and on April 9 he wrote in his diary, "I read the writings of the Shakers. Excellent. Complete sexual restraint. How strange I should receive this just when I am concerned with the question." He wrote Chertkov the next day, "I shall not overcome this problem [lust] in a hurry, because I am a dirty, libidinous old man!" The same day he noted in his journal, "Must propose the Shaker arrangement to [Sonya]."

He threw himself into work on *The Kreutzer Sonata*. Tanya became deeply depressed as she assisted in the copying. She wrote in her diary, "I feel lost, unhappy and lonely. I do not know what will become of me or what I ought to do. I have only just decided —since the inception of *The Kreutzer Sonata*—and decided firmly, not to get married; it used to seem easy and desirable, but now it is all a tangle; my will is shaken, i.e., I cannot dream of remaining single and ought not to think about the opposite." A few weeks later she wrote, "I am quite envious to see how kind and attentive Papa is to Masha (she is not well), and have been feeling lonely and unloved; the idea even came into my head to go out and catch a cold, if only to enjoy Papa being tender to me. . . . I often think of [Papa's] dying and wonder whatever will happen to us. . . . Perhaps if one married, one would grow used to being without him? But, first, why marry while he is here? And then, secondly, if one did, there would be the terrible fear of losing contact with him."

Sonya did most of the copying, and as she worked she was both fascinated and disgusted by the story. The tension between husband and wife was heightened when she read in his diary "This morning and last night I thought much and clearly about *The Kreutzer Sonata*. Sonya copies it; it agitates her, and last night she spoke about the disillusionment of the young woman, about the feelings of the man, so strange at first because of his lack of feeling toward the children. She is unjust, and because she wishes to justify herself; but in order to understand and speak the truth, one must repent." A few days later, however, he wrote less coldly of her: "After dinner Sonya, while looking at an oncoming train, spoke of how she wished to throw herself under it. And I became very sorry for her."

This guilt which Sonya provoked in Tolstoy also seems to have roused his "evil" sexual feelings toward her. "The devil fell upon me," he despaired. This "devil" of sexual desire possessed him for twenty-four hours. "I slept badly. It was so loathsome, as after a crime," he confessed. That day he could control his passion no longer and forced himself on Sonya. "Still more powerfully possessed," he wrote, "I fell." Conscience-stricken, he asked a few days later, "What if a child should be born? How shameful, especially before the children. They will reckon when it happened, and they will read what I write [*The Kreutzer Sonata*]. It has become shameful, sad."

During a discussion with one of Tolstoy's followers shortly after this incident, Sonya remarked sharply, "It is fine for Lev Nikolaevich to write and advise others to be chaste, but what of himself?" Sonya had once again been unable to resist her husband's sexual overture and was filled with resentment toward Tolstoy on this account.

Tolstoy recorded the denouement of this domestic crisis in his diary. "Sonya came with the news that she is not pregnant. I said that it is necessary to sleep apart. I spoke with Sonya. She says she is glad (that she is not pregnant). But that she does not wish to be apart." Sonya seems to have been willing to share Tolstoy's bed even though doing so would place them in a situation where they would both have to struggle against their natural physical desires.

Early in November of 1889, less than a week after it was completed, and before it was approved by the censor, eight hundred copies of *The Kreutzer Sonata* were secretly lithographed in the editorial offices of *Intermediary* and were circulated in St. Petersburg. Within a matter of two weeks that number had multiplied astronomically as the book was copied in Moscow and the provinces. Its appearance created a sensation, and the controversy it generated catapulted the Tolstoys into chaos.

For the next year husband and wife quarreled constantly about the book, which had caused an uproar throughout Russia. The Tsar refused to sanction its official publication. Scathing letters flew back and forth between Tolstoy and his cousin Alexandra in St. Petersburg. The immediate family took sides, Lyova and Seryozha sharing Sonya's deep distaste for the book, Masha hotly defending its truth, and the others at times supporting one side and at times the other. The Tolstoys were being torn apart, and finally, on November 20, 1890, Sonya bitterly wrote:

> Lyova has broken off all relations with me. . . . I read his diaries on the quiet, and tried to see what I could bring into his life which would unite us again. But his diaries only deepened my despair: he evidently discovered that I had been reading them, for he hid them away. However, he didn't say anything to me.
>
> In the old days it gave me joy to copy out what he wrote. Now he keeps giving it to his daughters and carefully hides it from me. He makes me frantic with his way of systematically excluding me from his personal life, and it is unbearably painful. This unfriendly existence at times drives me to the depths of despair. I feel like killing myself or running away, or falling in love with someone, anything to escape from a man whom, in spite of everything, for some unknown reason, I have loved all my life, although I now see clearly that I idealized him, without realizing that there was nothing in him except sensuality.

"I am going on copying Lyova's diary," she wrote a few days later. "I don't think I have ever got over all the horror I experienced when I read Lyova's diaries before our marriage, and I doubt that the sharp sting of jealousy and my bewilderment at the thought of such filth and debauchery, has ever quite disappeared. . . . But my dreams are sinful, and I feel very restless, especially sometimes."

Sonya was copying Tolstoy's diary because she believed that everything he wrote should be preserved. No matter how repellent she found his writing (be it a novel such as *The Kreutzer Sonata* or the pages of his diaries), she was devoted to serving his literary genius. Yet she could hardly be unaffected by the entries she now copied and compared with the jottings she had read before their marriage. Even in his youth her husband had thought the devil was incarnate in any sexually attractive woman. But while he had then condemned only lust, he now damned all sexual relations. It seemed to Sonya that only one conclusion could be drawn: Tolstoy had always felt an aversion to sexual intercourse, but his deeply sensual nature had often driven him to betray his true feelings.

Her marriage had been Sonya's one security—the steel support of all her future happiness. Now that support was eroding; the concepts of marriage and family on which she had built her life were crumbling. The drama of their life together had become a tragedy. All she had believed in—indeed, all of her marriage— seemed a brutal sham. "I have been copying Lyova's diary ever since morning, and it always brings so many thoughts to my mind," she agonized in her own diary. "It occurred to me, for instance, that you can't really love someone who knows you intimately, with all your weaknesses, and to whom you can't only show one side of the medal. That's why married people drift apart in their old age—i.e., when no further illusions are left, and everything is too obvious to be hidden from either of them."

Three days later on December 14 she wrote, "I copied Lyova's diaries up to where he says, 'There is no love, there is only the physical craving for intercourse and the rational need of a life companion.' If only I had read this opinion twenty-nine years ago, I should never have married him."

Two days later she remained morbidly engrossed in his diaries:

> [His] self-adoration comes out in every one of his diaries. It is amazing how people existed for him insofar as they affected him personally. And the women! I caught myself up today on an evil

thought. I copy his diaries with the zest of a drunkard, and my drunkenness consists in working myself up into a state of jealousness over the women in his early diaries he describes. . . . I am still restless and cannot shake off those memories. Never. . . . Another thing in his diaries strikes me as curious. The fact that, simultaneously with his daily debauches, he also tried *to do a good deed* every day. And now, too, when he goes for his walks on the high road, he will show a drunken man the way, help to harness a horse, or pull a cart out of the ditch—it is still a case of looking *for good deeds*.

On December 17 she observed, "It is beginning to worry him that I have been copying his diaries. . . . He would like to destroy his old diaries and to appear before his children and the public only in his patriarchal robes. His vanity is immense!" For a time during the holidays Sonya put aside his diaries and felt "calmer and cleaner."

The diaries and the pain they caused were not the only cross Sonya bore during the Christmas season of 1890. A large group of the "dark ones" arrived at Yasnaya Polyana (where the Tolstoys were in residence), which meant that their family holiday would be shared with people Sonya could not abide. ("Miserable abortions of human society, aimless babblers, uneducated loafers," she called them.) Her work was endless. Besides the invasion of the "dark ones" there were terrible snowstorms and the younger children were ill. Ilya and his wife had had a daughter, Anna, but Sonya's joy was dimmed by worry over her son's debts. She had decided to sell the Samara estate to help him; this gave her yet another task to do, since she had to obtain all the plans and accounts of the estate in order to complete the transaction. She planned to publish a new (the thirteenth) edition of her husband's complete works, the thirteenth volume of which was to contain *The Kreutzer Sonata*. This work had been suppressed by the censor, but Sonya was determined to have the ban lifted and wrote to anyone she thought could be helpful. The decision to include the hated *Kreutzer Sonata* in this volume had not been easy. But since she had resolved to publish a complete edition of her husband's works, Sonya put her own feelings aside and had this story, which she found so distasteful, set in type.

That Christmas was also shadowed by her continuing conflict

with Masha. The summer before, perhaps to please her father (or to spite her mother), Masha had accepted a proposal of marriage from Pavel Biryukov, her father's disciple. Biryukov offered a sexless union in which they would share their lives in true "brotherhood." Sonya was appalled and employed every tactic from reason to hysteria to dissuade Masha. To Sonya's fury, Tolstoy, though not pleased, did not intervene in any way. Biryukov was one of the few Tolstoyans of whom Sonya approved, but such an "arrangement" for her daughter seemed intolerable. Mother and daughter fought constantly over the engagement. In early December Masha had told her flippantly, "Let me marry him and put an end to it. Didn't you say he was a good man?"

On December 14 Sonya noted in her diary, "I talked to Masha about Biryukov. She said that she will either marry him or, if I object, refuse to marry at all. But she added later on, 'But don't worry. All kinds of things may happen.' It struck me as though she would be only too glad to get rid of these casual ties." Sonya's diary shows the range of emotions roused by her difficult daughter. On one day Sonya is moved by maternal concern: "My Masha is very thin and depressed." But on another, jealousy and exasperation have the upper hand: "Why am I trying to keep her back? Let her marry Biryukov by all means, for I can then once again take my place beside Lyova and do his copying for him and put his papers and letters in order and gradually get him away from this hateful world of 'the dark ones.' "

On Christmas day Sonya gave a party for eighty of the village children. That evening her own children decided to have a fancy dress party. Tolstoy remained aloof, but the servants came in dressed in costumes and danced to the piano and concertina. Masha was the last to enter. "When Masha came in," Sonya recorded, "Lyova and I simply gasped. She was wearing a pair of boy's breeches which were far too tight behind and were thoroughly indecent." Within a matter of weeks, to Sonya's relief and Biryukov's great disappointment (for he would have liked nothing better than to be wed to the master's favorite daughter), the engagement was broken. Masha now turned even more to her father and ignored all the young men with whom she was in contact.

Despite her sexual problems with her husband, romance was lurking in Sonya's heart. "I am terribly afraid of becoming pregnant, for everybody will hear of this disgrace and gleefully repeat the recent Moscow joke—'*Voilà le véritable postscriptum de la Sonate de Kreutzer!*' " She withdrew into the less perilous world of romantic dreams, and memories returned of Urusov (now dead) and their platonic love—"that pure, delicate relationship which was undoubtedly more than mere friendliness, and yet left not the slightest shadow of remorse, but filled so many years of my life with happiness. But who has need of my life now? And who will give me care and affection—little Vanichka perhaps, but who else? Yet thank God for that at least."

Vanichka, that blessed little boy. More and more she turned to the child for affection, and the love he gave her helped her through this most difficult period in her marriage. To amuse him, she again began to write children's stories and make cardboard puppets. These activities were a welcome outlet for her creative energy and inspired her to try her hand at a more serious literary endeavor.

Tolstoy had included incidents and details from their family life in *The Kreutzer Sonata*, and this had offended Sonya almost more than the moral he had drawn. She was certain that the world now thought of her as the "lustful, evil" wife in the novel. As spring approached, she sat down to write a story in her defense, which would negate Tolstoy's conclusions by telling the story from the woman's point of view. She showed the finished story to Anna Dostoevsky, Seryozha and Lyova, and read it aloud when her friends gathered in the salon for tea and Tolstoy was safely in his study. Although "Whose Fault?" met with positive reactions, Sonya finally and reluctantly decided not to publish it. Once again her respect for her husband's genius and her desire to publish all his work won out. And it would have been impossible to include *The Kreutzer Sonata* in the new edition after the publication of "Whose Fault?"

When *The Kreutzer Sonata* was originally submitted to the Tsar, the Tsarina had read it first; she had been shocked by it and had prevailed on her husband to forbid publication. There seemed little chance that he would reverse his decision, but Sonya (against Tolstoy's will) decided to go to St. Petersburg and appeal the ban. On the night of March 28, 1891, Tanya and Vanichka saw her off at the Yasenki station (Tolstoy had refused to accompany her). The

next morning she was met in Moscow by young Lyova, exuber-
antly happy because two periodicals had recently published stories
of his. He had earned money and the stories had been well received; he was on his way as a writer and pleased with himself. He
took his mother to lunch, accompanied her to the bank where she
had business to transact, and then put her on the train for St.
Petersburg. She traveled in "a very cozy second class compartment" with a landowner's wife, and arriving in St. Petersburg early
the next morning, she went to stay with the Kuzminskys. The ice
on the Neva had begun to crack, and the winter season was over.
Lent, which was near its end, was rather strictly observed in the
capital—there were no soirées and no rounds of social festivities
from Ash Wednesday until Easter. The Tsar's aunt, the Grand
Duchess Olga Feodorovna, had just died, and from the window of
the Kuzminsky house Sonya and Tanya watched the funeral
procession which accompanied the coffin from the station to the
fortress of St. Peter and St. Paul. Since the royal family was in
mourning, it would be some time before Sonya was granted an
audience. But neither the royal death nor the delay it caused dulled
Sonya's pleasure at being in St. Petersburg. The two sisters had a
marvelous time shopping, visiting friends, entertaining small gatherings; and Sonya enjoyed being the Countess Tolstoy.

Not in many years had she looked so glowing. Her eyes
blazed; she was fired with energy. Always a handsome woman, she
was now dazzling. Everything about her appeared to have acceler-
ated: her speech, her quickness to laugh, her gestures, her step.
She moved in a great rustle of silk. In a carriage she would rap her
tortoiseshell lorgnette on the divider that separated driver and passengers and impatiently call out, "Faster, faster." Tanya, still attractive but now appearing to be the older of the two sisters,
studied Sonya with alarm, very much aware that Sonya was on the
edge of hysteria. Tanya could not bring herself to discuss the Tolstoys' marital relations with Sonya, though *The Kreutzer Sonata* had
led her to guess that their union was not happy. Sonya had been
the most sexually alive of the three sisters. While Tanya was satisfied with flattery, Sonya demanded much more.

It was decided that Sonya would send a letter to the Tsar
requesting an audience. Several of Alexandra Tolstoy's court

friends rallied to help. A letter was composed, but Sonya was not satisfied by it. Her youngest brother, Vyacheslav, was in St. Petersburg, and he made some alterations. Sonya then wrote a third and final draft dated March 31, 1891:

> I take the audacity to humbly beg Your Majesty to allow me to place personally before you my request on behalf of my husband, L. N. Tolstoy. Your Majesty's generous attention will allow me to explain the circumstances which might help my husband to return to his former literary work and also to show that certain allegations made against his present activities are so false and painful that they undermine the spirit and energy of the Russian writer whose health, as it is, is none too good, but who perhaps still could work to the glory of his country.
>
> Your Imperial Majesty's humble subject,
> Countess Sonya Tolstoy

Twelve days later—after Alexandra Tolstoy and her friend Countess Elena Sheremetyev (*née* Stroganov), the Tsar's cousin, had exercised the influence they had at court—Alexander granted Sonya an audience. Dressed in an elegant but conservative black silk dress and a black lace hat with a veil, she left the house at eleven-fifteen in the morning, an hour when the city was quiet. The wheels of the grand coach she had been lent for the occasion rumbled through almost deserted streets. The footman helped her out of the carriage in the palace courtyard, where she was greeted by salutes from the palace guard. When she entered the great hall, there were a few moments of confusion as a porter told her he had no record of her appointment with the Tsar. Another porter was consulted, and Sonya was soon on her way. She was led up a steep stairway covered with "a very ugly bright green carpet." Nervousness almost overcame her when she was ushered into the Tsar's antechamber by a youth in a crimson and gold uniform and a plumed three-cornered hat. When the young man disappeared, Sonya felt she might faint. She got up and paced the room; after surreptitiously loosening her stays, she sat down. The court courier returned, bidding her to follow him to the Tsar's study. As she caught her first glimpse of the Tsar, she was startled by his great girth and height. Nearly bald, his head was narrow "as if slightly compressed." There was something feminine in his posture, something high and musical in his voice that made her think of Chertkov.

The Empress was not present. Sonya and the towering Alexander were to be alone. She swept into the room, curtsied deeply, and then determinedly began her plea. Telling an outrageous lie, she informed the Tsar that Tolstoy was casting aside his philosophical writings to begin work on a novel, a fitting sequel to *War and Peace*. After some discussion of her husband's literary talents, she brought up *The Kreutzer Sonata*. Defending it warmly, she explained: "Unfortunately the story has taken a rather extreme form, but the idea underlying it is this: The ideal is always unobtainable; if this ideal is perfect chastity, it can only be pure in matrimony." This was a willful misrepresentation of Tolstoy's work, and he would have been furious had he heard it.

Sonya now made her plea that the ban be lifted from the book. The Tsar replied that he could not do so because "It is written in such a way that I'm sure even you would not give it to your children to read." He added that he was not at all pleased with the influence Tolstoy had gained over the peasants.

Sonya passionately defended Tolstoy and the Tolstoyans. The Emperor brought up Chertkov and the influence he appeared to have over Tolstoy. Sonya was taken aback but after a moment stated that her husband's friendship with Chertkov had grown less intimate since Chertkov's marriage and especially since the birth of his child, which had broken his wife's health. Then, appealing to his pride, Sonya asked if he would consent to being the first to read her husband's future literary works. He accepted with a pleased smile. Once again Sonya petitioned for the removal of the ban. Alexander stood thoughtfully for a maddeningly long time. "We might allow you to print it in the complete works, because not everyone could afford to buy the full set, and it would not be too widely disseminated," he finally agreed. Then he suggested she pay her respects to the Empress, which Sonya was delighted to do. Alexander asked after the health of Sonya's children. Sonya replied that they were all well, with the exception of Misha, who had chickenpox. "That isn't dangerous. The main thing is to avoid catching a chill," the Emperor said.

Sonya agreed and curtsied as the Emperor warmly took her

hand. The courier appeared and led her into the Empress's boudoir, which was decorated in red damask. Two huge gilt mirrors
hung between the arches which divided the boudoir from the drawing room, and there were blazing scarlet azaleas and masses of
plants everywhere. The window looked out onto a paved courtyard, where two coaches were standing and some soldiers were
marching up and down. Sonya waited for fifteen or twenty minutes
before an elderly footman ushered her into Marie Feodorovna's
reception room. The women had met briefly some years before at
Madame Shostak's. Still a slender, light-footed woman, the Empress was wearing "a black woolen dress with a very tight waist,
high neck, and narrow sleeves . . . her chestnut-brown hair was as
neatly arranged as though it were pasted on." Marie Feodorovna
stepped forward, offered her hand, and asked Sonya to be seated.
The two women spoke rather formally in French about Madame
Shostak, the Tolstoy children, and the Empress's children, who
were then at Gatchina Palace. After five minutes Marie Feodorovna
rose and the audience was over. Sonya curtsied and left the Empress's apartments and was escorted to her waiting coach.

Sonya had cleverly swayed Alexander to her side; she had won
her battle but at a price—she had had to agree to make about two
hundred textual changes in *The Kreutzer Sonata*, toning down certain sections and eliminating much of the forthright realism of the
language. The text of the story that appeared in the thirteenth
edition was therefore quite different from that which had been
clandestinely lithographed. The pirated edition of the book, of
which there were hundreds of thousands of copies, had made Tolstoy the most popular topic of discussion in Russia. There was
little talk in the salons or on the streets about anything else; and in
a way this served Alexander well, for talk of Tolstoy distracted his
subjects from the economic chaos and famine that were creeping
across the land.

Sonya arrived in Moscow on Sunday, April 14, 1891, the day
after her meeting with the Emperor. Tolstoy was at Yasnaya Polyana, and young Lyova and her old friend Dmitry Dyakov met
the train. As they lunched together at the station, Sonya excitedly
told them all the details of her palace meeting. When the train for
Yasnaya was about to depart, Sonya met a friend who asked her
and Lyova to join her family in their compartment. It was a gay,

festive journey, and Tanya and the younger children met her at the station. Sonya was thrilled to be home, proud of her achievement. Tolstoy, however, was displeased with the adventures, and particularly with her audience with the Emperor.

Life at Yasnaya Polyana was frenetic and tense. The Tolstoys had terrible battles, and after walking away from one of their arguments Sonya wrote, "I couldn't talk to him while he screamed that way any more than I could talk to a barking dog." The "dark ones" had arrived, and Tolstoy was frenziedly insisting that vegetarianism was the only humane way to exist. After going to the slaughterhouse, he terrified the children by telling them that the bulls were stripped of their hides while they were still alive. One evening he took a chicken and tied it to Tanya Kuzminsky's chair at the dinner table. Placing an ax by her plate, he told her that if she wanted to eat a chicken she would have to kill it herself.

The Tolstoys were not sharing a bed, and Sonya claimed that she was developing a disgust of "bodily intimacy" and yearned for spiritual closeness. She was, however, unable to resist her husband's occasional nocturnal or early morning "raids," and it seems likely she was disgusted, not by her own physicality but by the shame and fears sexual intercourse with Tolstoy gave rise to. Whenever they engaged in sexual activity, she knew she was not responding to her husband's love but was submitting to his lust. She had been reduced to a sexual object in his eyes, nothing more. And since she knew this, every submission filled her with guilt and self-loathing.

There were other, more immediate reasons why she avoided intercourse with her husband. She was terrified of becoming pregnant. And she was offended by Tolstoy's increasing disregard of personal cleanliness. "Last night I became so angry that I would not talk to him," she wrote in April. "He kept me awake until two in the morning. To begin with, he was downstairs washing himself for so long that I thought he was ill. For him washing is an event. He told me that his feet were so calloused with dirt that they had become sore. It quite revolted me. Then he lay down and read for a long time. I am in his way when I am not needed for his satisfaction. These days of aversion to the physical side of my husband's life are terribly depressing, but I cannot get used to it. I can never get used to the dirt, the smell."

In June, Tolstoy's sister, Marya Nikolaevna, who was now a nun, arrived. Given Marya Nikolaevna's past (the divorce, the lover, the illegitimate child), Sonya found her conversion hypocritical in the extreme. Marya Nikolaevna's visit was tense, and Sonya's nerves seemed stretched to the limit when Ilya came to her with his money problems. There were heated arguments between them about the estate and Ilya's share in it. Sonya once became so enraged that she told him to "go to hell!" To add to these problems, she was up most mornings until two or three correcting proofs of the thirteenth volume of the new edition. The entire family including the Countess Alexandra Tolstoy gathered at Yasnaya Polyana during the month of June. As always, Alexandra brought a sense of aristocracy into the house. Her authoritative bearing and her power over Tolstoy awed the Tolstoy children. During one conversation Tolstoy listened gloomily as Alexandra attacked his vegetarianism and his cold mistreatment, in her eyes, of his wife and children, who hadn't "the slightest calling for beggary and work in the fields, or for life in a peasant hut." Tolstoy sighed deeply and said, "It is hard for me." Alexandra did not allow her criticisms to be passed off so easily. "Still one word more, my dear Lev. Instead of mourning over the fantastic, the impossible, and I might even say, over the useless, have you never thought seriously over your responsibility to your children? All of them produce the effect on me of wandering between heaven and earth. What will you give them in place of beliefs that you have probably weaned them from? For they love you too much not to attempt to follow you." Tolstoy's face grew dark as Alexandra swept from the room in an autocratic manner that dismissed him completely.

Tolstoy had now decided to dispose of all his possessions, property, and personal wealth. It was impossible to sway him from this course. Every evening, therefore, the family gathered around the samovar for tea and discussed the division of Tolstoy's estate. Masha was the only participant who wanted no share whatsoever, but no agreement had yet been reached among the others. Then on July 21 Tolstoy came down before dinner and declared that he was writing a letter to several newspapers renouncing copyright on all his latest works. Sonya was shocked by this announcement. Such an action would have a devastating effect on the sales of the thirteenth edition (and she had just placed an order with the printer for

20,000 additional copies). She also realized that such a declaration would be an open avowal of his disagreement with her. Distraught, she said he was "vainglorious." He answered that she was "a greedy, stupid woman always out for money." Shouting "Leave me alone! Leave me alone!" he stalked from the house.

Sonya was seized by a suicidal impulse, and hysterically and rather ridiculously she set off through the Zahak wood to drown herself in the Voronka. It was quite dark in the forest, and as she reached a ravine a beast (her shortsighted eyes could not discern if it was a dog or a fox or a wolf) suddenly jumped at her. When she screamed, the animal ran off and Sonya turned back hurriedly, having lost her courage. When everyone in the house had gone to bed, Tolstoy returned, kissed her, and made some conciliatory remarks. Telling him to go ahead and publish his announcement, she asked him to refrain from mentioning the matter again. He answered that he could not do this until she *understood* why it must be done. She answered that she would never understand, and they were at an impasse. He approached her sexually, but she repulsed him, exclaiming that she would never again live with him as his wife.

The next day he spoke passionately of his love for her. He did not continue to press his plan for the copyrights, and for a short time they were calm, even content. "His sensuality is contagious, and yet my whole moral being protests against it," she wrote nearly a week later. "I am terribly dissatisfied with myself. Lyova woke me this morning with passionate kisses. . . . Then I picked up Bourget's *Un Coeur de femme*, and read it in bed till 11:30, which I hardly ever do. To think what unpardonable debauchery I go in for at my age! I am sad and ashamed. I feel a sinful and unhappy woman, and however much I try, I can't do anything about it. So I stayed in bed."

Bourget's book made a strong impression on Sonya. She was moved by his story of a society woman in love with two men who were both in love with her. "I can understand this double love. . . . Why, indeed should one love exclude another? And why can one not love and remain pure at the same time?"

Sonya believed that the wide circulation of the cheap illegal copies of *The Kreutzer Sonata* had sated the hunger of the curious

and that her edition in thirteen volumes would be bought in complete sets by those who respected Tolstoy as one of Russia's great
literary figures. She did not anticipate that booksellers would sell
the last volume (which contained *The Kreutzer Sonata*) separately
and at a price that students could afford, and could acquire without
fear of purchasing an illegally printed book. The huge sales of this
volume brought Sonya under attack from all sides.

Tsar Alexander's old tutor Pobedonostsev was overcome with
wrath, and in the autumn of 1891 he wrote with considerable
venom to the Tsar:

> I have decided to write Your Majesty about unpleasant matters. If I
> had known in advance that the wife of Lev Tolstoy had requested an
> audience of Your Majesty, I would have begged you not to receive
> her. What has happened is what one might have feared. Countess
> Tolstoy returned from you with the thought that her husband has in
> you a defense and justification for all those things in him over which
> the healthy-minded and religious people of Russia are indignant. You
> permitted her to print *The Kreutzer Sonata* in the complete works of
> Tolstoy. It might have been possible to foresee how they would make
> use of this permission. . . . They have placed this book on sale sep-
> arately, and already three separate editions of it have appeared. Now
> this book is in the hands of *Gymnasium* students and young girls. On
> the road from Sevastopol, I saw it on sale in the station and being
> read in the trains. The book market is full of the thirteenth volume of
> Tolstoy. . . . Tolstoy is a fanatic in the matter of his own insensate
> ideas, and unfortunately attracts and leads to madness thousands of
> giddy people. The amount of harm and ruin he has produced would
> be difficult to estimate. . . . It is impossible to conceal from oneself
> that in the last few years the intellectual stimulation under the influ-
> ence of Count Tolstoy has greatly strengthened and threatens to
> spread strange, perverted notions about faith, the Church, govern-
> ment, and society. The direction is entirely negative, alien not only
> to the Church, but to nationality. A kind of insanity that is epidemic
> has taken possession of people's minds.

Sonya had acted in good faith, but Alexander was never to
know this. He felt that Countess Tolstoy had abused his benefi-
cence, and he expressed his chagrin to Alexandra Tolstoy. That
aristocratic and still influential lady did what she could to mollify

the Tsar, but Alexander remained outraged. Countess Tolstoy, he proclaimed, had acted in bad faith. Her plan of publishing the complete works had always been a subterfuge whose aim was to gain vast profits from the sale of *The Kreutzer Sonata*. Sonya's aspirations of further audiences at court had been smashed.

19

Sonya was always a sensual woman, but her full sexuality did not reach its peak until she was in her mid-forties. Her diary at this time is filled with musings on her sexual needs, frustrations, and fantasies. Ironically, Sonya's sexual flowering coincided with Tolstoy's total abandonment of the romantic approach. No longer did they ride through the woods together or "look at the moon with the same eye, hold hands, or share secrets." Missing such moments Sonya took pleasure from chaste reveries about Urusov, passages from erotic novels, and fantasies about a possible second *pure* love. Tanya Kuzminsky had successfully balanced two loves (Kuzminsky and Sergey Nikolaevich) without reproach or criticism from any quarter, because she had always been *physically* faithful to her husband. In Tanya's achievement lay Sonya's salvation—or so it now seemed.

Yet with all her yearnings for a pure love, Sonya responded to Tolstoy's "lust." Each remained sexually obsessed with the other. Sonya would have preferred that her romantic dream and her lustful lover were embodied in one man—her husband. "These outbursts of passion always [are] followed by long periods of coldness," she wrote in her diary on August 15, 1891, a week before her forty-seventh birthday. "I sometimes feel the need of a warm, gentle affection, and of mutual friendliness; and I feel that it is never too late, yet every time I try to establish this cordial friendly relationship I come up against his dull look of surprise, and his coldness, his terrible coldness. And his excuse for this gulf between us is always the same: 'I live a Christian life and you refuse to recognize it. . . .' I may be a pagan, but I love my children and, alas, I still love this frigid Christian so much that it breaks my heart."

Tolstoy's vacillations between the extremes of passion and in-difference enraged and confounded Sonya. At this time it is pos-sible she might have preferred his absolute celibacy to the violent shifts in attitude which so distressed her. It is difficult to surmise how she would have dealt with her own sexuality had he become unswervingly chaste, but it does seem that they both would have benefited from an end to the war between them, whatever the problems an armed truce would present. As it was, Sonya could only regard her husband as a hypocrite and herself as the abused object of his lust. His diary indicates that to Tolstoy Sonya was his private devil, seducing him, creating evil in him merely by her presence. Unlike Feinermann and some of his other disciples, he was unable to desert his family and live a celibate life. Instead he expected Sonya to remove all temptation from him. When she did not (or could not), he was angry and cold to her and miserable with himself.

In early September Sonya's niece Masha Kuzminsky was mar-ried at Yasnaya Polyana to Ivan (Vanya) Egorovich Erdeli. The next evening, after many of the guests had departed, Sonya sug-gested to Tolstoy that they stroll through the grounds of the estate. As they walked, she talked of the preparations she was making for the family's return to Moscow, and he then told her that he was not going back with her. "Very well, then; that settles it. I shall not go to Moscow either, and we will start looking out for new teachers [for the children]," Sonya instantly replied.

"No, I don't want that," he said. "You must go to Moscow and put them in school."

"But this is like a divorce," she cried, "for you will see neither me nor the five children for the whole winter."

"I don't see much of them anyway," he reasoned, "but you could come here now and then."

"Me. No, never!" she sobbed. Later that night, when she was recording this exchange in her diary, she remarked that he seemed embarrassed by her tears. Following this comment, some eighty words are crossed out, and it is probable that this section, presum-ably deleted by Sonya, recorded some harsh words between them.

Touched by her anguish, Tolstoy finally admitted, "I pity you. I can see you are suffering, and yet I do not know how to help you."

"But I can tell you," Sonya replied. "I call it immoral to tear the family in half for no proper reason; so I shall sacrifice Lyova and Andreyusha and their education and shall stay here with our daughters."

"There you are, talking of *sacrifice*, and then you'll be blaming me," he countered.

"But what can I do?" she begged. "Tell me, what can I do?"

He was silent for a while. "I can't tell you now," he said at last. "Let me think it over till tomorrow."

They parted, and Tolstoy went off to see a sick villager. Sonya, frightened and despairing, wept as she walked home through the dark wood. Terror suddenly seized her, and she ran wildly in the direction of the house. She regained her composure only when the children came out to greet her.

The next day, quite calmly, Tolstoy said, "Go to Moscow and take the children with you."

The financial demands which Ilya, and to a lesser degree their other sons, made on Sonya had concerned Tolstoy for a long time. More than a year before he decided that she should return to Moscow without him, he had written in his diary, "My sons swamp Sonya with requests for money. It will get still worse. Would it not be better if she should reject at least the income from literature? How it would leave her in peace, her sons morally healthful, me joyous, and how useful to people and pleasing to God."

Sonya's adamant refusal to sign away her family's future security was at the root of most of the Tolstoys' stormy confrontations. After their bitter quarrel in July, when Sonya's thoughts had flown to suicide, Tolstoy wrote in his diary, "She does not understand, and the children do not understand, that . . . every ruble squandered by them out of the profits of the books is my suffering and shame."

Finally in September Tolstoy again raised the issue of publicly renouncing his copyrights on all the works he had written since 1881 excepting *The Death of Ivan Ilych* (which he had previously given to Sonya). At first Sonya stood firm in her resistance to what she viewed as a rash and irreparable act and to what she considered his "madness." However, she soon weakened, believing that her agreement might bind him more closely to her. The question of the disposal of Tolstoy's land holdings and material possessions had been settled earlier, during Passion Week. Tolstoy had agreed it should be done and set his mind to it. Sergey and Ilya joined the family at Yasnaya Polyana, and the Tolstoys and their nine children gathered around the dining-room table. Tolstoy stated that although they wanted him to sign everything over to them, he would do so only with the greatest reluctance. He went on to say that he had long since rejected the idea of private property. Signing the documents they proposed would make a travesty of the convictions he had publicly espoused. It would amount to an admission that he did, in fact, subscribe to a system in which property could be owned and transferred.

Tanya wrote in her diary:

> It was so pitiable, because it was like a man who has been condemned to death hurrying to stick his head into the noose which he knows he cannot avoid. And we were the noose. It hurt me terribly to be a cause of unpleasantness to him, but I know this partition will remove such a lot of unpleasantness between Ilya and Mamma, so I consider it my duty to participate in it. I envied Masha for refusing to take her part, and I made every effort to work it all out honestly with myself, how to behave, and came to the following conclusion: first, I have no right not to take my share, because I know that they will make it over to me, but in Mamma's name, and she will give me the income from it and apart from that look after it. Secondly, I still have so many demands and so little advantage comes of me, that I should merely be a millstone around somebody's neck. My first concern must be to diminish my demands. I shall always manage to get rid of the money. I still manage so badly with what I have and so often want more money, that there could be no thought of my renouncing my share.

The children were to divide all the land Tolstoy held, except for Yasnaya Polyana (which had always passed to the youngest son and so would belong to Vanichka) and Grinevka, the estate on which Ilya was living. Sonya insisted the properties could only be distributed fairly by drawing lots, and Sasha and Vanichka were chosen to carry out this task. Although Masha refused any share, Sonya, certain the girl would someday change her mind, held property in central Russia for her as well as money. Sonya received only the 55,000 rubles she had taken into the marriage as her dowry, but of course she held the early copyrights.

On September 16, 1891, an announcement in the form of a letter to the editor was printed giving free permission to all to publish in Russia and abroad in Russian and translation, and also to perform on the stage, all of Tolstoy's works which had been written since 1881, and giving up all rights to works appearing in the future. Her agreement to this was an act Sonya instantly regretted and to which she would never become reconciled. It meant that no member of the Tolstoy family would profit from Tolstoy's future work (or from his philosophical writings of the previous decade or from *The Kreutzer Sonata*). And any edition of these works which she might publish would have to compete in the marketplace with dozens of cheaper versions. Although Sonya was never able to understand why her husband had made what she considered a disastrous, willful, and ill-conceived move, she was delighted to see a happy change in him once the affair was settled. As in the days when the older children had been young, Tolstoy joined in games with Sasha, then seven, and Vanichka, who was three.

To Sasha, Tolstoy seemed remote, and everything surrounding him was "especially important: his study with the vaulted ceiling into which big rings were screwed, the desk, the big old-fashioned armchair—so long that one could stretch out on it as if in a bed; and the peculiar smell, perhaps of leather, and perhaps of old paper which emanated from all his things." It would never have occurred to the child to touch even a pencil on his desk, or to run to him and be kissed or held. But in the weeks after the public renunciation of his copyrights, Tolstoy seemed to have regained some of his old joy in being part of a children's world. He would leave his study early to give himself time before dinner to carry Vanichka on his shoulders, or to make Sasha turn somersaults, or to drag the little ones about the house in the large clothes hamper, its top shut, and then have them try to guess where they were. Squeals of childish delight filled the house. Sonya was radiant, pleased, loving. There was even a renewal of shared laughter— something the Tolstoys had not experienced for years.

One night all but Sonya (who had gone into Tula on business) were gathered in the dining room for dinner. Tolstoy insisted, though the soup was getting cold, that they wait for "the lady of the house." When the rustle of Sonya's silk skirts and the melodic sound of her hello were heard in the entrance hall, Tolstoy whispered, "One, two, three, quick—all under the table!" In the few moments it took Sonya to walk from the entrance hall to the dining room, Tolstoy, the Kuzminskys, the English governess, the older children, and Sasha and Vanichka were beneath the table, choking back their laughter. "But where is everyone?" Sonya asked as she looked about myopically. "I cannot tell you, Excellency," the waiter answered, covering his grin with a white-gloved hand. Shouts of laughter burst from beneath the table and everyone scrambled out. Sonya, laughing so hard that she cried, said, "You were always good at inventing some foolishness, Lyovochka."

A few days later Tolstoy had the two little ones join hands and make a chain with him. He led them on tiptoe through Yasnaya Polyana's darkened rooms and a seldom-used back staircase on a quest for a ghost. "Quiet, quiet," he whispered. "He'll hear us!" The children were terrified. "Shhh-sh-sh," he hissed at them as they stealthily entered a shuttered room. "Here *he* is!" Tolstoy called out. The children shrieked madly and ran out of the room, their father ahead of them. They all collided with Sonya, who hugged the youngsters to her and scolded Tolstoy. But there was a gentleness in her manner that was a form of approval. Once again a camaraderie was beginning to grow between them. This warm affection might have altered much in their lives had it had time to mature, but the growing horror of a national famine intervened.

When word of the famine first reached Yasnaya Polyana in the summer of 1891, Tolstoy did not believe that it was either severe or widespread, and he did little to help the afflicted. A Tula official, Ivan I. Rayevsky, after being refused aid rather unpleasantly by Tolstoy, went about collecting data and statistics on his own. Tolstoy remained outwardly dispassionate. He did, however, reply to a letter from an old friend, Nikolai S. Leskov, in which a similar request for help was made. Tolstoy's letter was in essence a second refusal. "There is a famine in some places . . . and it will get worse, but . . . it can certainly not be averted by collecting and borrowing money and buying bread and giving it to those who need it, because it's all a question of distributing the bread people have . . . it's all a question of teaching them (those who have bread) to share. . . . Until this happens, there will always be famine.

There always has been, and there has never ceased to be famine of the body, famine of the mind, famine of the soul."

Tolstoy then stated that those who were trying to raise money were acting from impure motives; since they were not inspired by Christian love, but by "vanity, ambition, or fear that the people might become embittered," their efforts would "produce nothing but sin." To cure social problems, "people [must] do as many good deeds as possible. . . . And a good deed consists not in feeding the hungry with bread, but in loving both the hungry, and the well-fed." He then told Leskov that "the most effective remedy against the famine is to write something which might touch the hearts of the rich."

This letter, excerpts from which were published in a news-paper without Tolstoy's knowledge or permission, was met with a public outcry of indignation. To those working for famine relief it seemed ridiculous to suggest that starving people should not be helped until love moved the more fortunate to share with them. In order to answer his critics, Tolstoy decided to visit a famine-stricken region, and in late September he went to Pirogovo, his brother Sergey Nikolaevich's estate. He was appalled by the starving, disease-ridden peasants he saw, and reversing his stand, he declared that food had to be gotten to these unfortunate people as quickly as possible. He searched out Rayevsky, whose pleas he had earlier ignored, and proposed that free kitchens be set up in the villages. Rayevsky jumped at this idea and asked Tolstoy to help with this project by spending the winter at Begichevka, his estate in Ryazan province (which had been severely affected by the famine). Tolstoy agreed, and Masha and Tanya promised to join him in this work.

Sonya had hoped that the family would be together in Moscow during the winter months, and initially she was not enthusiastic about Tolstoy's new humanitarian mission. But, moved by stories of the peasants' suffering, she did give her consent. She took the younger children to Moscow, and on October 26, Tolstoy and his two daughters and his niece Vera Kuzminsky set out on the two-day journey to Rayevsky's estate.

The Russian government had refused to acknowledge the extent and severity of the famine, and Alexander III persisted in describing the situation as "a failure of crops," which was confined to a small number of areas. But in his statements and articles Tolstoy described the horrors he saw, and the truth about the catastrophe which had visited the Russian countryside became known throughout Russia and then throughout the world.

Under Tolstoy's supervision, in less than a month, thirty free kitchens were set up in twenty villages. No meat was served, and bread, which was not as cheap as cabbage soup, porridge, potatoes, peas, and millet broth, was doled out in small quantities. In late November Rayevsky suddenly died from influenza, leaving Tolstoy to carry on their work.

In Moscow Sonya too was concerned about the victims of the famine. She sent Tolstoy 750 rubles and gave 100 rubles to the Red Cross and 300 rubles to young Lyova when he left to join his father. The house on Dolgo-Khamovnicheski Street was lonely without the older children and Tolstoy. Their dear friend Dmitry Dyakov died after an agonizing illness. Sonya went to the funeral and returned home shattered. Her loneliness, her depression over the famine, and finally her grief at Dyakov's terrible death pushed her close to a breakdown. Then all four younger children fell ill with influenza. During the sleepless nights she spent watching over them, Sonya was haunted by thoughts of the starving mothers who could do nothing to help their dying children. She composed an appeal for contributions and took it to the *Russian Gazette*, which published it on Sunday, November 3. In this letter she tried to "touch the hearts of the rich."

> My whole family has separated and gone to help in the relief effort for the starving people. . . . Compelled to remain in Moscow with my four young children, all I can do to help is send money and supplies. But the needs are immense, and isolated individuals are powerless to satisfy them. And yet, if we think of all the people who are dying of hunger in this moment, every hour we spend in a well-heated house and every piece of bread we eat are living reproaches. We all live in the lap of luxury here, we cannot tolerate the slightest discomfort for our own children: Would we be able to endure the sight of exhausted, heartbroken mothers who must watch their children die of hunger and cold, or of old people who can find nothing to eat? Thirteen rubles will see one person through the next harvest. . . . If each of us, according to his means, could feed one, two, ten,

or a hundred people in this way, our consciences might be eased.
. . . Therefore I have decided to turn for help to all those who can
and will contribute by their gifts to the work begun by my family.

Sonya's appeal was reprinted by newspapers throughout Russia and in France, England, and the United States. By November
12 she had received 9,000 rubles in contributions. She spent 3,000
rubles on rye and corn, which she had sent to Tolstoy along with
1,273 rubles, holding the rest of the money she had received to
await his instructions. But if she thought her actions would please
him she was wrong.

On November 9, upon hearing what Sonya had done, Tolstoy
wrote to Isaac Feinermann, who was living in a Tolstoyan colony:
"There is much here that is not right. Money from Sonya Andreyevna, and money that has been collected and the relation between
the feeders and the fed—there is no end to the sin of it all, but I
cannot sit at home and write. I feel the necessity of taking part and
doing something. I know I am not doing the right thing, but I can't
do the right thing, and I can't do nothing. I dread the praise of men
and ask myself every hour, 'Am I sinning?' "

Three weeks later he wrote to Feinermann again: "I don't
know myself how I was trapped into this work of feeding the
starving. . . . It is unsuitable for me to feed those by whom I am
myself fed, but I have been dragged into it and I find myself
distributing the vomit thrown up by the rich. I feel that this is
abominable and disgusting, but I cannot stand aside; not that I do
not think I ought to, for I do think so, but that I have not the
strength to do . . . my wife wrote a letter which has caused dona-
tions to be sent, and almost without my noticing it I have become
a distributor, and am, as it were, under an obligation to the people
here."

Hurt by his reaction to her efforts, Sonya nonetheless perse-
vered. She even managed to collect royalties on *The Fruits of Enlightenment* (one of those works whose copyrights Tolstoy had
renounced). She noted in her diary, "I had a reply from the Minister of the Court. In view of the worthy purpose for which I want
the money, he has promised to let me have the royalties from *The
Fruits of Enlightenment*." Once again Tolstoy was enraged by her
efforts to raise money, but when he and their children returned to

Yasnaya Polyana for a short time in January, they were drawn together by their concern for the famine victims. Sonya decided to return with Tolstoy to Ryazan, and leaving Tanya to look after the younger children in Moscow, she traveled to the Rayevsky estate with him and Masha.

On February 16, 1892, shortly after her return to Moscow, Sonya described this trip in her diary:

On [January] 27th we traveled from Tula to Klekotka, along the dreary Syzran-Viazma line. I had a fit of nerves and asthma in the train. Lyova [Tolstoy] kept going out all the time, and was fussy, careless, and silent. The weather was dreadful—it was snowing and raining, the sky was leaden gray, and there was a terrible wind. We drove on in two sledges—Masha, old Fedot [a footman], the Rayevskys' chef, and Marie Kirillovna [a seamstress and maid] in one, and Lyova and I in the other. We were uncomfortable and it was dark and eerie. Masha was sick all the way, and I was worried in case Lyova caught cold in such weather. We reached our destination late in the evening, and Ilya . . . met us at Begichevka. Ilya was in a queer, timid mood, fearing all the time to see Ivan Ivanovich Rayevsky's ghost. The next day he left, and we stayed there with our female assistants. Lyova and I lived in one room. I took all the manuscripts and looked through them. Then I went to see the kitchens. I went into one hut, where I found about ten people, but by and by thirty-eight more came in. They were all in rags, looking sad and ill. On entering, they all made the sign of the cross and sat down in orderly rows. The woman in charge then carried the bread basket around and they would all take one piece each. Then she placed a large tureen of soup on the table. The soup had no meat in it, only a little lenten oil. The boys sat on the one side of the table and they were cheerful and friendly and ate happily. After the soup they got a potato stew, or else peas, porridge, or a dish of beetroot. Usually there were two courses for lunch and two for dinner. I went around several of these kitchens and at first rather wondered what the people really thought of them. In the second kitchen I went to, I met a young girl, so pale and ill, who gave me such a sad look that I nearly broke into tears. It must be very hard for a girl like that and for the old man who was with her, and for many others to accept this charity. "May God grant that we give and not take" is a true saying of the people. But later on I got used to the kitchens, and realized things would be even worse without them.

The most difficult task of all is to discover the very poorest. It is difficult to decide who ought to be allowed to make use of the kitchens, and how best to distribute the clothes, wood, etc. When I first made my list, there were eighty-six kitchens. Now there are fully a hundred. The other day—it was glorious and sunny—Lyova and I drove round the various villages. We asked about the flour supply at the mill; then we went to the food store to find out how the distribution was being carried on; lastly, we opened another kitchen at Kulikovko, the village that was burned down. We saw the head of the village council and told him to bring along some of the older peasants. They all came in and sat down on the benches. We inquired who were the poorest families in the village, and told them how many persons per family could make use of the kitchens. Then I took down all the names. Lyova told them to come for the provisions on Tuesday, and suggested that the headman's wife might arrange a kitchen at her house, just like the other people whose huts were burned down.

It was getting dark as we drove home; there was a red sunset on one side, and the moon had risen on the other. We drove through the steppe and along the Don, a dull and monotonous landscape, except for some country houses—both old and new—beautifully situated on the banks of the river. In the forenoons I helped the tailor to make coats for the peasants from the cloth we had received, and he finished twenty-three; the village boys were overjoyed with these coats and fur jackets. They are *warm* and *new*—something that some of them have never seen before. I stayed ten days in Begichevka. There were several snowstorms, and once all our women assistants went off and didn't come back at night—we were greatly worried. They are both very good girls. Persidskaya is a Cossack girl, red-cheeked, and energetic, who gives the people medical help, and whom they called "the Princess." The other is a thin, delicate little girl, the daughter of a priest; a little sentimental, but a good worker, too. They used to go around inspecting or opening up new kitchens, distributing clothes, and making notes about the fuel, clothes, and food that had to be given out.

In Moscow Sonya was faced with the wrath of Pobedonostsev, now minister of the interior, whose hatred of Tolstoy had been intensified by an unfortunate incident. An English journalist had managed to obtain an anti-government article on the famine by Tolstoy (which he claimed was not meant for publication) and published it in England. The views expressed in this article gave Pobedonostsev grounds for imprisoning Tolstoy or banishing him and his family. Sonya was warned by those close to the court that the axe was about to fall. She wrote letters to Pobedonostsev, to his undersecretary, and to the major newspapers vehemently denying that Tolstoy was in any sense an anarchist. Receiving no answer, she wrote Alexandra Tolstoy a desperate letter begging for help. That grande dame, unfailing in her affection and sympathy for her cousin, sent an urgent request for an audience to the Tsar. To her astonishment, Alexander replied immediately—he would call upon her that afternoon.

At last the Emperor entered [Alexandra later wrote]. I noticed that he looked tired and that he was upset about something. On his asking what I had to say to him, I replied directly: "In a day or two a report will be made to you in favor of incarcerating Russia's greatest genius in a Monastery."

The Emperor's face instantly changed and he became stern and profoundly sad.

"Tolstoy?" asked he briefly.

"You have guessed rightly, sire!" replied I.

"Then he has designs on my life?" asked the Emperor.

I was amazed, but secretly encouraged: I thought that *only that* would induce the Emperor to confirm the Minister's decision.

I recounted to the Emperor all that I had learned from the Minister about Lev's offense, and I saw to my great delight that his face gradually assumed its usual mild and extremely friendly expression. Soon he rose to leave. I only allowed myself to say one thing at parting, namely, that it was of course not on the Minister that the general indignation—both in Russia and abroad—would fall if his recommendation were acted upon.

Two days later I learnt that . . . having listened to the Minister's report of what had occurred and of the (alleged) great public excitement, the Emperor, putting aside the report, replied literally as follows:

"I request you not to touch Tolstoy. I have no intention of making a martyr of him and bringing universal indignation upon myself. If he is guilty, so much the worse for him!"

I also learnt that the Minister returned from Gatchina making a show of being, as he expressed it, a "perfectly happy man." Had his

recommendations been confirmed, much reproach would of course
have fallen on him also. He quite understood that and played the
part of a "happy man" very cleverly.

Sonya pleaded with Tolstoy to defend himself, and he finally
wrote a statement for publication in the *Government Messenger*, a
Moscow newspaper. Although he presented no apologia for his
actions in this letter, he did deny that he was a revolutionary. The
Tsar appeared satisfied by this repudiation, and the matter was
dropped.

The Tolstoys were apart for long periods during the two years
(1891–93) of the terrible famine. Always close to Tolstoy's side,
Chertkov used these separations to strengthen his own position,
and he did so in a most devious fashion. Invidiously he began a
campaign to undermine Sonya by discrediting her to her children.

Chertkov was now determined to exercise control over every
scrap of paper on which Tolstoy had written. Most importantly,
he wanted to gain possession of his notebooks. Although his motives remain obscure, he claimed to be driven by a desire to protect
Tolstoy. He constantly urged Tolstoy and his children to regard
these private papers as documents of a uniquely valuable import
which must not be sullied by commercial publication. He further
suggested that it would be an outrage for anyone (that is, Sonya) to
profit from this record of Tolstoy's spiritual journey.

The diaries, notebooks, and letters had not been among the
works whose copyrights Tolstoy had renounced, and under the
terms of his will they were to go to Tanya and Masha. Chertkov
began to bombard Tanya with letters of advice, suggesting that
these papers must remain out of her mother's hands. Tanya finally
asked Tolstoy what he wanted done with these writings after his
death. He replied that while he had no objection to their being read
by Tanya, Masha, and the other children, he did not want them to
be published. Tanya then said that she believed his will left the
decision about publication to Masha and her. "And to Chertkov,"
he added, saying that no one understood him as Chertkov did.

Tanya did not share her father's wholehearted admiration for
his disciple and remarked in her diary that "Chertkov's nerves [have
gone] all to pieces." Observing that many of the Tolstoyans were

showing signs of emotional strain, she wondered why they were so distressed: "What is happening? What is the cause and how has it come about?" Although Tanya was baffled by this malaise, it is likely that the Tolstoyans were finding adherence to the master's principles an almost intolerable burden. Achieving the ideal of marital chastity was especially difficult for many. Chertkov, however, seemed to experience little hardship in observing the stricture against marital intercourse. Since the birth of their child Anna Chertkov had been a semi-invalid, yet Chertkov never recorded any feelings of sexual frustration in his correspondence, perhaps because his obsessive love of Tolstoy overwhelmed all other emotions. This intense devotion had begun to nettle Tanya. "I have had a letter from Chertkov," she noted in her diary, "in which he writes that I ought to renounce two things—property, which has passed to me by Papa's error [the diaries and notebooks], and fine clothes. Apart from that, he advises me to spend some days or weeks drawing closer to Mamma, and the moment I reach the 'maximum of mutual softening tenderly, cautiously, yet firmly and without ambiguity to tell her all you think, before God, of her persistent antagonism to God in your father.' . . . I do not agree with him . . . and what he wrote . . . made disagreeable reading."

Six months earlier Sonya had written in her diary, "I have just learned from Chertkov that he and Colonel Trepov in St. Petersburg hold many of Lev Nikolaevich's Mms between them. I must tell the children. . . . Chertkov *would* take away all Lev Nikolaevich's Mms, and take them to Christ Church, in England."

It is unclear how these manuscripts came into Chertkov's hands. (Since there is no evidence that Tolstoy gave them to him, he may have stolen them.) In any event, once they were his, he had them placed under police lock by Dmitry Feodorovich Trepov, who was a friend of the Chertkov family. This act was a further indication of his determination to wrest control of Tolstoy's works from Sonya and the family. He repeatedly asserted that the master's writings, through which the Tolstoyan gospel would be brought to the masses, could be properly published only by a true disciple.

But was Chertkov, in fact, the ardent and faithful follower he claimed to be? While he did practice vegetarianism and lived in a fairly simple manner, he never gave away his own inherited wealth.

He kept a good home with servants and seemed to be in no financial need throughout his life. And while he maintained that he did not profit from the publication of Tolstoy's works, it has never been satisfactorily established how the money derived from this venture was dispensed. Sonya, her censure of Chertkov's actions silenced by her husband, had little doubt that this money fell into Chertkov's hands. "The evil spirits have seized upon the man I love," she wrote in her diary on November 5, 1893. "If only I can maintain the strength of my prayer! If not all is lost, may God shield us from any influence but his own!"

PART FIVE
1893-1910

That Endless Dream

*Is there anything interesting in Lev Nikolaevich's life?
Or in Taneyev's? One does not love them for their external life, but for that dream, that endless dream which
flows from their work.*

COUNTESS TOLSTOY

20

In September 1894, while he was at the imperial hunting lodge at Spala in Poland, Tsar Alexander III became seriously ill. A specialist from Vienna, a Professor Leyden, was summoned and diagnosed his ailment as nephritis. Alexander was hurried to his summer palace at Livadia in the Crimea with the hope that the mild climate would prove beneficial. The Empress and the Tsarevich Nicholas were by his side on the imperial yacht *Polar Star* when it dropped anchor in Yalta. Within only a few weeks the Tsar's great frame had become shrunken and emaciated. His skin was livid and his cheeks hollow. The crowd which gathered to greet him was shocked. Their Emperor, that huge man of extraordinary strength and vigor, was dying.

For several days the Tsar did little more than sit in a wheelchair gazing at the sea. Then he grew weaker and was confined to his bed. The Tsarevich's future bride, the beautiful Princess Alexandra of Hesse (Queen Victoria's granddaughter) arrived from Darmstadt in response to a telegram from her fiancé. To extend a proper greeting to the future Tsarina, Alexander insisted on being helped into his full-dress uniform, and with great effort he sat erect in an armchair in his bedroom. Princess Alexandra knelt before the dying Emperor, and, blessing her, he sealed the betrothal between her and his son.

Ten agonized days later (November 1, 1894), at the age of forty-nine Alexander died, and his twenty-six-year-old son became His Imperial Majesty, Tsar Nicholas II. The young man sobbed at the thought of his new responsibilities. "What is going to happen to me?" he cried. "I am not prepared to be a Tsar. I never wanted to become one. I know nothing of the business of ruling. I have no idea of even how to talk to the ministers." The new Tsar spoke the truth; his father had failed to educate him for his future role, and only in the past year had he been permitted to attend meetings of the Council of State.

Nicholas was a young man with no firm views. Easily swayed, he was a dangerous ruler. The new Tsarina's second cousin Kaiser Wilhelm II commented that "he is not treacherous but he is weak. And weakness fulfills the functions of treachery." And the revolutionary Leon Trotsky later remarked, "This 'charmer,' without will, without aim, without imagination, was more awful than all the tyrants of ancient and modern history."

With the famine ended, Russia was enjoying an industrial boom. A great network of railways linking all major cities had just been completed, and the Trans-Siberian line was under construction. Russia had become one of the world's leading producers of oil and metals, and it was manufacturing its own locomotives and agricultural machinery. In spite of these advances, Russia's peasants were growing even poorer, and many discontented members of the working and middle classes were calling loudly for a free press and a parliamentary government.

Tolstoy had spoken out strongly against Alexander III and had been greatly harassed by his ministers, and he did not pretend to any great grief at his passing. Writing to his friend Nikolai Grot, he said that he felt no more than he would "for any man suffering and dying with a soul so grievously burdened." Pity, he closed, did not oblige him to change his opinion about "the deplorable deeds of his reign." The Tsar's death passed unrecorded in Sonya's diary and correspondence. She was absorbed by domestic difficulties: her problems with Chertkov continued; young Lyova, who had become emotionally ill, was about to undergo "electrical treatment"; and her husband was once again cold and distant.

Tolstoy was now a great celebrity, recognized everywhere he went. He could not walk down a street in Moscow without people pulling at his jacket, and crowds often gathered at the gates of his house. Wearied by this adulation, he remained for longer and longer intervals at Yasnaya Polyana, usually accompanied by Masha, who had taken on the task of copying his writings. Father and daughter began to grow away from the family. They were

becoming outsiders, and for Sasha one incident would always epit-
omize their alienation.

Children's costume parties were in vogue among the Moscow
aristocracy, and before one of these Sonya had Theodore, a fashionable hairdresser, come to the house to dress Sasha's hair. Using
much pomade and powder and many pins, he arranged the child's
hair in an elaborate gray coiffure. Sasha was afraid that if he saw
her costume, Tolstoy would refuse to let her go, and she ran from
the house into the closed coach to avoid him. Once at the ball, she
forgot her father and enjoyed herself immensely. While dancing a
quadrille with a young partner, she passed near a large window in
the ballroom. A rap on the pane made her turn, and, glancing
through the misted glass, she saw two figures. Tolstoy in his round
peasant's cap and sheepskin jacket and Masha, her head covered
with a kerchief, stood peering in from the cold darkness. Sasha
wavered, wanting to join them yet reluctant to leave the dance.
Her partner was bewildered, and she saw that it would be rude
and unkind to leave him standing on the floor. She turned back to
the window to explain why she had to stay, but her father and
sister were gone.

Although most of the children were with her in Moscow,
Sonya was lonely without Tolstoy, and she turned to Vanichka,
her youngest child, for companionship. This six-year-old boy was
adored by everyone, even by Sasha, whose place as the youngest
he had usurped. Vanichka was one of those rare children who
seemed blessed and could bless in return. Tolstoy had a deep love
for him and believed that of all his children, Vanichka would be
the one to carry on his work.

Sasha later wrote:

When Vanichka approached Father, and raising his little face without
a trace of embarrassment, talked to him like a grown person, I saw
what great tenderness passed through Father's glance. He [Vanichka]
smiled, but there was suffering in the smile. Dear little Vanichka.
He was more just and wise than the grown people. With some deep
intuition he sensed the truth and reached out for it as a plant reaches
toward the sun. How many times, not knowing that he did it, he
taught older ones around him! When someone acted meanly, Va-

nichka suffered so intensely that, out of love for him, one hastened to correct the mistake. He felt that he was better loved by the family than I was, and that hurt him also. Every small injustice to me upset him. Someone would give him candy and forget about me, but he instantly remembered, "And Sasha?"

With golden ringlets surrounding his delicate face and large blue eyes, Vanichka was the most beautiful of the Tolstoy clan. His laughter had a musical ring to it; his step was exceptionally light.

Sasha later described his delight at a party:

Although he was so young, Vanichka could dance beautifully, especially the mazurka. He flew around the ballroom scarcely touching the floor—a slight, graceful little figure. He stamped the rhythm with his heels as he stood in his place, he skillfully clicked his feet together off the ground, he dropped to his knee and promenaded his lady, always taller than himself, in a circle around him. His pale face flushed, his eyes shone, his long golden curls danced about his shoulders. But in the carriage driving home, sometimes after midnight, Vanichka suddenly became quite small; his little face grew pale and drawn, and he curled up on his mother's lap and went to sleep.

The bond between Sonya and her youngest child seemed to grow stronger each day. Vanichka had an uncanny sensitivity to his mother's moods and thoughts; even when they were apart, he seemed to be aware of and share her pain and her happiness. They were seldom separated, however, for Sonya found it increasingly difficult to be away from him. Vanichka gave Sonya the affection she so desperately needed, and she clung obsessively to the small boy. Her devotion, which had taken on a monomaniacal quality, made her almost blind to the needs of her other young children. With Tolstoy away for much of the time, these children had, in effect, neither a father nor a mother. In this atmosphere of neglectful indifference, Misha and Andreyusha became shy and awkward. But it was Sasha who was most deeply wounded. Her old nurse, Nianni, had often told her that Sonya had tried to abort her, and Sasha was certain that her mother hated her. She tried in vain to attract her attention and felt superfluous whenever the three of them—Sonya, Vanichka, and Sasha—were together. Sonya, absorbed by Vanichka, was unaware of the pain and damage she caused her young daughter.

It is hard to surmise what Sonya thought Vanichka's future would be or what place she would have in it. She had begun to seem markedly eccentric and at times appeared to suffer from delusions. She would sit for hours painting with the little boy; after working over his childish efforts, she would claim that the finished picture was his. They spent long snowy afternoons talking at Sonya's desk. Sonya would record the little tales he told her; after rewriting and editing this material, she would announce that Vanichka had written a remarkable story. She even published one of these works as "Vanya's Story."

Most children would have been spoiled by such lavish attention and fulsome praise. But Vanichka had a special quality that withstood Sonya's fierce love. This slight, delicate, cheerful little boy was so good-natured that he could not bear it if somebody cried or was depressed, angry, ill, deformed, or needy. In late 1894 Vanichka insisted that Sonya ask no rich children to the Tolstoys' annual Christmas party. And so only poor youngsters were invited, and all of them were given gifts. Vanichka himself received the wagon he had longed for, but before the day was over he had given it to his special friend, Igor, a five-year-old hunchback who was the son of one of the Tolstoys' servants. Giving away his belongings was a compulsion with the child. He would often wrap up an especially valued possession, enclosing a card (usually with the message "A keepsake from Vanya"), and give it to a member of the family or to a servant.

Sonya believed that Vanichka was "an angel sent to comfort [her]," and she often told him that he was divinely blessed. These convictions made it especially hard for her to bear his ill health. He was a sickly child, inclined to fevers, anemia, and chest ailments. He seldom complained, but Sonya always seemed to be at his bedside when he awoke with a fever in the middle of the night. His illnesses provoked hysterical terror in her, and she became tormented by the fear that she would lose him. Highly emotional since childhood, Sonya now seemed in danger of being swamped by her darker, more irrational feelings. She suffered migraine headaches and fits of depression which her doctors attributed to the onset of menopause. This sign of aging horrified Sonya, for she

believed that it would signal the absolute end of her physical relationship with her husband. Vanichka's devotion no longer totally
satisfied her. By February 1895 she realized that her separations
from Tolstoy and her involvement in Vanichka had allowed her
husband to drift away from her and to grow closer to his "dark
ones."

The winter of 1895 was to Sonya what 1881 had been to
Tolstoy—a time of extreme crisis. She felt that she was moving
toward madness and believed that Tolstoy's coldness had precipitated her emotional illness. She would become well, she thought,
if she could reaffirm her position as Tolstoy's wife and closest
confidante. But she sensed that it was too late to renew their intimacy, and thoughts of suicide plagued her.

"Surely there are some happy old couples," she wrote in
her diary on February 21, 1895, "who for thirty-three years have
lived an amorous life, as we have done, and who continue to be
devoted to each other. How different here! I have these constant fits of tenderness and stupid sentimentality. The day I was
ill and he brought me two lovely apples, I planted the pips to
commemorate his unusual kindness to me. Will I ever see the
pips sprout?"

In this entry she also recounted her attempts to kill herself,
which were prompted by a violent disagreement with her husband
about the publication of Tolstoy's new story "Master and Man."
While Sonya was copying it some weeks earlier, he had mentioned
that he might give it to Lyubov Gurevich, a Jewess who published
the magazine *Northern Messenger*. Since Tolstoy refused to retain
the copyright, he would receive nothing for the story. Gurevich,
however, would make a handsome profit, and her publication of
this work would most likely reduce the sales of Sonya's planned
supplement to the Complete Works, which would include this
story. When a friend remarked to Sonya that "the Gurevich woman
had fascinated the Count apparently, as she . . . got two articles
out of him in one year," her irritation was intensified by jealousy.
She decided that she and Gurevich should be allowed to publish
"Master and Man" simultaneously. But when she suggested this
plan to Tolstoy, he grew furious and ran upstairs to dress, shouting
that he was leaving the house forever.

The first thought that flashed through my head [Sonya wrote in her diary] was the woman. I lost all self-control, and, in case he should leave the house first, I ran out into the street and down the lane. He came running after me. He was in his drawers, waistcoat, and dressing gown, and without a shirt. He begged me to come back, but I had only one idea in my mind—to die somehow or other. I remember weeping and screaming, "Let them take me to the police station, or take me to the lunatic asylum!" Lyova dragged me back, and I kept tumbling on the snow; I had only slippers on my bare feet and a chemise below my dressing gown. I got soaked to the skin and caught a chill . . . and now I feel ill and giddy and abnormal, as though I were all choked up.

We managed to calm down in the end, and next morning I helped him with the proofs for the *Northern Messenger*. He finished them just after lunch and wanted to lie down for a rest. Then I said to him, "Well, I can copy it out now—let me take it." He was lying on the sofa, but the moment I spoke he jumped up, and angrily refused, giving me no reasons whatsoever. (I still don't know what the reasons are.) I did not lose my temper; I simply implored him to let me copy the story—the tears were choking me. I promised him not to publish the book without his express permission—I was only asking him to let me copy it. And although he did not refuse point-blank, I was overcome by his furious expression. I couldn't understand it at all. Why should he take the interests of the Gurevich woman and her magazine so much to heart and not let me publish the story simultaneously as the supplement to volume xiii? . . .

The feeling of jealousy and irritation—the thought that he had *never* in his life done *anything* for me—broke out with terrible violence. I threw the proofs on the table, and, putting on a light fur coat and hat and my galoshes, I went out of the house. Fortunately or unfortunately—I don't know—Masha noticed the desperate look on my face, and she followed me, though at first I did not notice her. I went toward the Virgin Monastery, wanting to be frozen to death in a wood or on the Sparrow Hills. I seemed to like the idea of perishing of cold like Vassili Andreich in the very story that was going to be the cause of my death ["Master and Man"]. I regretted nothing. I had staked all my life on one card—my love for my husband—and now the game was lost, and it was no good living any longer. I did not feel sorry for the children; after all, it is *we* who love *them*, and not *they* who love *us;* so they can live without me. Masha, as it turned out later, did not let me out of her sight for a second, and it was she who

took me back home. My despair did not subside for two more days.
I again wanted to go away; I called for a cab in the street and drove
off to the Kursk station. I don't know how the children guessed that
I had gone there, but Seryozha and Masha caught me at the station
and took me home again. I felt so ashamed at being taken home like
that. I was very ill at night [February 7]. All my nerves were on edge,
and it occurred to me that any person whom Lyova's hand had
touched, was bound to perish. . . . I wanted to pray God to save all
men from Lyova's influence. Even now I feel that my love for him
will kill me—kill my soul. If I rid myself of this love, I shall be
saved; if not, it will be the end of me. He has already killed my inner
self; so that I am no longer really alive.

That night, as I was weeping bitterly, he came into my room
and, kneeling down, asked my forgiveness. If he could only always
have a spark of the love he felt for me at that moment, I might still be
happy.

Having harassed me to the last degree, he called for the doctors.
It was comic to see how each doctor prescribed his own special
treatment. The nerve specialist ordered bromide; the dietetic specialist ordered a mixture and Vichy water; while Snegirev, the gynecol-
ogist, gave me something else, making some cynical remark about
my "critical period." I didn't touch any of the medicines. I am no
better.

Having run about in the cold for three days, with hardly anything on, I naturally caught a chill . . . and all the blood has rushed
to my head and heart—and, of course, I'm ill. The girls were
frightened; Misha burst out crying, Andreyusha went to tell Ilya all
about it, Sasha and Vanya were puzzled, as children are, and Lyova
got quite worried—but I liked Seryozha best of all; he was so kind
and gentle and made no sign of reproach. Lyova, you Christian, how
easily do you condemn, and how little love and pity there is in you!
—And the whole *business* was simply the result of my boundless love
for him. He always keeps looking for my *spitefulness;* if only he would
realize that I have plenty of different motives, but not *that* one; and
how can I help my restless and passionate character?

[And she ended] Both the *Northern Messenger* and I have been
given the story. But at what a price! I am busy correcting the proofs,
and, with joy in my heart, am realizing the greatness of the literary
work. At times my eyes are filled with tears of happiness.

Vanichka had been ill with a fever throughout the winter. The
doctor had regularly visited the house, and the child was treated

with quinine but did not improve. He was frailer than ever, and Sonya was haunted by the fear that he was going to die. For the entire month of January she had been able to think of little else. She sat by the child's bed day and night reading to him and talking with him. Then his fever suddenly broke, and he seemed well once more. He went walking with the other children and resumed his dancing lessons. Sonya still watched him anxiously, however, afraid that his recovery would be short-lived. On February 6, the day before she attempted to kill herself, Vanichka had frightened her by deciding to give away all his personal possessions. He attached small labels to each "gift": "To Masha from Vanya," "To our chef, Simion Nikolaevich from Vanya," and the like. Then he took the pictures from the wall in his room and hung them in his brother Misha's room. Unnerved, Sonya tried to interest him in a book she was reading. The small boy pensively stared out of the window and asked, "Mummy, is Alyosha an angel now?"

"Yes," Sonya replied. "Children who die before they are seven are said to become angels."

"It might be better for me if I die before I am seven. It'll soon be my birthday [March 31], but I may be an angel yet. But if I don't die, dear Mummy, will you let me fast, so that I may have no sins?"

On February 21 Vanichka was taken to the clinic for a routine examination. The doctors found him so greatly improved that they agreed that he could eat and do whatever he wanted. He had a large lunch, went for a walk with Sasha, ate a good dinner, and asked Masha to read him a chapter of Dickens's *Great Expectations* before he went to sleep. When Sonya came in to kiss him good night, he said, "It was terribly sad, Mummy. Fancy, Estella didn't marry Pip after all!" Suddenly, there were tears in his eyes and he moaned. "Oh, Mummy, it's back again. The fever."

Checking his temperature, Sonya found it was elevated. His eyes were sore, and she thought he might have caught the measles. Losing control of herself, she began to cry. Vanichka had recovered only to get ill again.

"Don't, Mummy, don't," the child soothed his mother. "It's the will of God." He wanted her to say the Lord's Prayer. As she did, he stopped her at the words "Thy will be done" and asked her to explain the meaning of this phrase.

When his brother Misha came in to see him a few moments later, Vanichka whispered to him, "I know I'm going to die this time."

By morning his temperature had risen to 104 degrees. He was delirious through the day, and the doctor diagnosed his illness as scarlet fever. The family tried to force Sonya to go to bed that evening, but when the fevered child awoke at three A.M. she was at his side. "Forgive me, Mummy, for having kept you awake," he said softly.

"I have been sleeping, darling," Sonya assured him. "We are taking it in turns."

"Is it Tanya's turn next?"

"No, it's Masha's."

"Won't you call Masha, and go to bed?" He pressed his dry lips against Sonya's.

"Is anything hurting you?" she asked.

"No, nothing," he replied. "Are you just sad?"

"Yes, I am just sad," she answered.

A few minutes later the child slipped into unconsciousness, and just before eleven that evening he died.

"My dear Vanichka died at 11 o'clock at night," Sonya wrote in her diary on February 23, 1895. "And, my God! to think that I am still alive!" It was the last entry she was to make for two years.

Tolstoy was as distraught as Sonya. He led her out of the nursery and into Tanya's room; there he sat with her on the sofa, holding her in his arms and stroking her head as it lay on his breast. Masha and Marya Nikolaevna prayed over the dead child, while Nianni lay sobbing across the foot of the small bed. Tanya, distracted and agitated, wandered in and out of the nursery in a purposeless manner. After Masha had dressed Vanichka in a white jacket and combed his hair, the Tolstoys returned to their son's bed. Sonya placed a small icon on the dead child's chest, and Tanya lit a wax candle and put it near his head. As the light flickered over his still face, Sonya began shrieking and had to be taken from the room. The doctor was called and she was given a sedative.

> Dead stillness reigned in the house [Sasha later recalled]. Everyone spoke in whispers and walked on tiptoes. From time to time, wild insane cries pierced the silence. Mother, out of her mind with despair, was convulsed with hysterics.

They did not allow me to go into the nursery, but in the night when the house was quiet I crept in, shivering in my nightgown. The powerful, sweetish fragrance of flowers mixed with that of wax and incense struck me. Upon a table in the middle of the room stood a small coffin. Candles were burning. I stood on my toes and looked in. It was Vanichka, but the expression was not his. It was important and alien. I reached over and kissed his forehead. An icy cold pierced me. I shrieked and ran headlong from the room.

Three days later a funeral mass was said, and the coffin was closed. At noon Tolstoy, all of Vanichka's brothers, and Pavel Ivanovich Biryukov carried the coffin from the house and placed it on a large sledge. Sonya sat at one end, with Tolstoy at the other facing her. The funeral procession moved slowly through the freezing winter day to the Nikolskoye cemetery, where Vanichka would be buried beside Alyosha. Ilya stood in front of Sonya to protect her from the sight of the open grave, and Tolstoy put his arm around her. While the coffin was being lowered into the earth, she fainted. As she regained consciousness, the laughter of village children playing close by was the first sound she heard.

They returned to the house, where for the first time Tolstoy broke down and wept. "And I always thought that, of all my sons, Vanichka alone would carry on my good work on earth. Well, it cannot be helped." In his diary he wrote, "We have buried Vanichka. A fearful loss! No, not fearful, but a great spiritual experience. I thank thee, Father."

Sonya walked about the house half crazed. She would awaken and jump out of bed and cry out that she was being pursued "by a hallucination of *smell* (sweet flowers and incense and melting wax)." At times she thought she heard Vanichka's voice; on one occasion she was sure she had heard him saying, "Kiss me hard, Mummy, and put your head beside mine, and breathe on my chest, so that I can fall asleep feeling your warm breath."

Stooped and with a look of great sadness in his eyes, Tolstoy wandered through the desolate house. Family and friends—Anna Dostoevsky, Mikhail Stakhovich, the now elderly Baroness Mengden, and the enfeebled Uncle Kostya—gathered around Sonya, but no one was able to bring her out of her deep depression. On March 27, 1895, Tolstoy wrote in his diary, "Sonya is suffering as much as ever, and is unable to raise to a religious level. The reason is that she has confused all her spiritual powers with the animal love for her child."

"Sometimes," Sasha recalled, "she became a little quieter, gathered Vanichka's playthings, handled them over and over again, had his pictures rephotographed; then again she wept and shouted that she was going to kill herself. 'Why, why is God so unjust to me? Why? Why did he take Vanichka from me?' she cried. And once she sobbed out, beside herself, 'Why—why Vanichka? Why not Sasha?' "

Overhearing this anguished question, Sasha ran to her room sobbing, "Lord, O Lord, why did Vanichka die? Why not I?"

If Sonya could have turned to her youngest daughter, she might have found a kindred spirit. Like her mother, Sasha bore a great love for the dead Vanichka and she was also haunted by the odors she associated with the boy's death. (She later wrote, "I thought of Vanichka often but for a long time was unable to picture him alive. I saw him as he lay in his coffin, and the fragrance of hyacinths and incense pursued me relentlessly.") But Sonya could not embrace the little girl, and that terrible, thoughtless cry— "Why Vanichka? Why not Sasha?"—would always stand between them.

21

After Vanichka's death, Sonya sought comfort in religion. Swathed in mourning, she went to church every day with the hope that confession and communion would bring her peace. She made daily visits to the cemetery in Nikolskoye where Vanichka and his brother Alyosha were buried. She wept constantly, trembling with muffled, choked sobs. Her grief enveloped the entire household, and the children and the servants were too timid to approach her. Tolstoy alone did not fear for her health. He believed that her great grief would work a spiritual transformation in her, and he wrote to his cousin Alexandra, "We never before felt so near to each other as now, and never before, neither in Sonya nor in myself, have I felt such a need for love and such a revulsion for every element of disunion and evil. I never loved Sonya as I do now. [Vanichka] was one of these children God sends into this world too early, a world not yet ready to receive them, like swallows that come too soon and are frozen. And now he has been taken from her, and despite her motherhood, nothing seems left to her in this world. In spite of herself, she has to ascend into another and spiritual world where she never lived before."

He watched over Sonya tenderly, eager to detect the slightest sign of a spiritual awakening. Sharing each "symptom" joyously with Chertkov, he confided that the beauty of her soul, which grief had revealed, dazzled him. But Sonya was not experiencing a "spiritual ecstasy" which would finally unite her and her husband, and Tanya Kuzminsky, who came to help Sonya through her grief, saw the futility of Tolstoy's hopes. When, by April, Sonya's mental condition had not improved, it was decided that the two sisters would take a short holiday in Kiev. Tolstoy agreed to this journey. He had come to recognize that his first assessment of Sonya's grief had been incorrect; he now believed that her melancholy was rooted in self-indulgence and would not lead to an obeisance to God.

Kiev was famous for its churches and monasteries, but it was music not religion that helped lift Sonya from her deep depression. The composer-pianist Sergey Ivanovich Taneyev was performing in Kiev during the sisters' visit. Taneyev's reputation was great, and as the director of the Moscow Conservatory he had been a helpful adviser to Seryozha in his studies. Sonya had met him in Moscow; but as Tolstoy disapproved of concerts, she had not seen him perform.

Taneyev, a bachelor of forty, had been a child prodigy, discovered at the age of ten by Nikolai Rubinstein, one of Russia's greatest pianists. Admitted at that tender age to the Moscow Conservatory, he had studied harmony with Tchaikovsky and piano with Rubinstein. At nineteen, he had made a spectacularly successful Moscow debut. Tchaikovsky was then a director of the Conservatory and chief professor of harmony, and Taneyev became his protégé and close friend. When Tchaikovsky retired from the Conservatory in 1878, he named Taneyev to succeed him, and on Rubinstein's death in 1881, he took over Rubinstein's pianoforte classes as well. In the front rank of Russian virtuosi, Taneyev was considered a master of tonal shading and the greatest interpreter of Tchaikovsky's piano works. His pianistic style was strongly romantic, and he had a great female following. Short and stout, he was not a good-looking man; his chunky body seemed about to burst from his clothes. There were no special charms in his thinning red hair, his small red-brown eyes, the reddened fleshy tip of his rather feminine nose, his flushed face which glistened as if oiled, or his sparse auburn beard. Yet at the piano his ruddy glow seemed a natural and most attractive expression of the passion of his performance.

Sonya and Tanya attended one of his concerts shortly after their arrival in Kiev. His performance greatly moved Sonya, and release from her terrible grief had come as Beethoven's "Appassionata" sonata swept over her. Later, as the sisters were about to step into their carriage, they saw Taneyev leaving the hall with Pelagya Vasilievna (an elderly woman who had been his childhood nurse and who still lived with him). He was immediately surrounded by

a crowd of screaming young women. These excited admirers
pressed close to him, grabbing at him; one bent down to kiss his
galoshes, another snatched the handkerchief with which he was
wiping his face, and ripped it to pieces to share with the crowd.
Taneyev tried unsuccessfully to break loose. Finally his stooped
companion shouted, "Sergey Ivanovich is tired! Leave him be."

Sonya murmured to Tanya and their footman that they must
help Taneyev, and she walked toward him. The footman instantly
ran before her. "Make way for Her Excellency, Countess Tolstoy,"
he called out sharply. Taneyev's admirers fell back, reacting perhaps to the Tolstoy name or perhaps to Sonya herself, so stately
and moving in her costume of deep mourning. Taneyev's own
carriage had been delayed, and Sonya offered to share hers with
him and the pettish Vasilievna. As she and Tanya and the celebrated musician drove through the late-night streets of Kiev,
Sonya's dark eyes shone with tears, and there was about her that
"spiritual ecstasy" that Tolstoy had hoped so fervently she would
experience. Believing that she had been reborn through Taneyev's
art, she saw him frequently in Kiev. Tanya always accompanied
them and saw no impropriety in their friendship. Not only was
Tanya sure that her sister was above reproach, but she was also
convinced that Taneyev's slightly feminine character precluded his
having any unseemly feelings for Sonya. The maestro often played
for the sisters, and at times Sonya sat beside him while he showed
her how to play a particular piece. Sonya now decided that she
would return to her study of the piano, which she had forsaken
when she married Tolstoy.

For the first time in many months, Sonya forgot her grief. But
once back in Moscow—in the house that had held Vanichka's sweet
voice, his soft quick footstep—she was again overwhelmed by sorrow. In June 1895 she wrote to Tanya in St. Petersburg, "Nothing
concerns me, nothing agitates me except one living, burning feeling
of anguish, of hopeless grief without Vanichka." She felt desperately alone. Uncle Kostya was ill and senile, and Tanya was with
Masha and their father at Yasnaya Polyana. It intensified her loneliness when Tanya wrote that Tolstoy was spending every afternoon with Chertkov and his wife, who had moved to a small estate
next to Yasnaya Polyana. She called on Taneyev several times in
Moscow, and when she left for Yasnaya Polyana three weeks after

her return from Kiev, she invited him to visit. Although Tolstoy was politely distant to his wife's new friend when he arrived a week later, Taneyev felt honored to be his guest. In his diary, which he wrote in Esperanto, the musician kept a detailed account of his stay, including his conversations with Tolstoy about art.

In July, Seryozha married Marya Konstantinovna Rachinski, a union which pleased neither of his parents. Their new daughter-in-law, who was called "Manya," was a cold, sharp-tongued young woman, and Sonya feared for the future happiness of her eldest son. August found the family at Yasnaya Polyana with a new guest, the writer Anton Chekhov, whom Sonya liked on sight. The thirty-five-year-old Chekhov had a charming, but wistful smile, and a shadow of sadness often darkened his expressive gray eyes. He suffered from a nagging cough and had all the early symptoms of tuberculosis. Although Chekhov came from a poor family (iron-ically, his grandfather had been a serf who was owned by Chert-kov's father), as a young man he had decided to become a doctor. At the age of nineteen he began his medical studies in Moscow, supporting himself by writing sketches for comic papers. He received his medical degree in 1884, but by then he was committed to a career as a writer.

In 1882 Chekhov was attracted to Tolstoyism and for the next six years was greatly influenced by it. Gradually, however, he became outraged by what he regarded as Tolstoy's arrogance, and after reading *The Kreutzer Sonata*, he angrily wrote to a friend, "There is one thing for which one does not readily forgive him: the impudence with which he writes about things of which he has no knowledge and, from sheer obstinacy, refuses to acquire any. Thus the judgments he lays down on syphilis, on houses of correction, on woman's horror of the sexual act, etc., not only can be disputed, [but] also reveal an ignorant man who during his long life has not taken the trouble to read two or three works written by experts."

Some four years later, in 1894, he wrote to another friend: "The Tolstoyan philosophy affected me deeply . . . though it was not its fundamental precepts that attracted me . . . but the way in which Tolstoy expressed himself, his immense common sense and, no doubt, too, a sort of hypnosis. But now something inside me challenges it. Logic and a sense of justice tell me that there is more neighborly love in electricity and steam than there is in chastity and abstention from eating meat."

Although Chekhov had published strongly anti-Tolstoyan works—notably, "A Dismal Story" (1889) and *Ward No. 6*—he still revered Tolstoy's artistic genius. He longed to meet him and was in high spirits when he arrived at Yasnaya Polyana early on a glorious August morning in 1895. Tolstoy was on his way to the Voronka for a swim, and Chekhov joined him; "naked, up to their necks in water," the men animatedly argued their totally disparate opinions. Chekhov later remarked, "When you talk to Tolstoy, you feel entirely in his power." And Tolstoy, who deplored Chekhov's anti-religious views, was charmed by him and referred to him glowingly as "that Pushkin in prose."

Chekhov adored beautiful women, especially if they were intelligent, and so for Sonya his visit was an immense delight. He spent hours in her company discussing her publishing enterprise. She had a brief hope that he might be attracted to Tanya, who was now thirty-one (to Sonya's despair Tanya's only attachments had been to various of Tolstoy's "dark" disciples). But Chekhov's romantic thoughts were elsewhere. He did, however, take special note of both Tanya and Masha and wrote to a friend, "Tolstoy's daughters are very appealing. They deify their father and believe in him fanatically. And this means that Tolstoy is really a great force since, if he were insincere and not irreproachable, the first ones to regard him skeptically would be his daughters, because daughters are like sparrows: You won't take them in with chaff."

With the end of summer Sonya's melancholy returned. Tolstoy was concerned about her health, and in a compassionate gesture he rode with her on the train to Moscow, even though he did not intend to stay in the city. Later he wrote in his diary, "She was sitting in the carriage and I became terribly sorry for her, not because she was departing, but sorry for her, for her soul. I'm sorry now and I hold my tears back with difficulty. I'm sorry because it is so hard for her, because she is so sad and alone. She has no one but me, no one else to cling to, and in the depths of her soul she is afraid that I do not love her, do not love her as I can love with all my soul, and that the reason for this is our different views of life. And she thinks that I do not love her because she did not come to me." His next lines addressed Sonya directly: "Do not think this. I love you still more, I understand all and I know that you *could not* come to me, and for that reason you have remained alone. But you are not alone: I am with you, I love you just as you are, and will love you to the very end as hard as it is possible to love."

During the summer of 1895 Tolstoy had felt great fondness for Sonya. Her grief over her dead child had not brought a new and elevated spirituality to her, but it had repressed her sexuality. During the long summer months at Yasnaya Polyana she had been content to live chastely. This exalted Tolstoy and gave him great hope for their future.

Alone in Moscow, Sonya became restless and agitated. Tolstoy now kept his diary locked away, but she found the key and read the most recent entries. Appalled by his harsh judgments of her, she wrote to him on October 12:

> Why do you always, when you mention my name in your diaries, speak so ill of me? Why do you want all future generations and our descendants to hold my name in contempt, as that of a *frivolous*, ill-tempered wife, who caused you unhappiness? Of course it adds to your glory that you were a *victim*. Yet how much this does to destroy me! If you simply scolded or even beat me for what I do that is wrong in your eyes, why, that would be immeasurably easier on me, that would pass—but this remains. . . . You promised you would strike out the bad words about me in your diaries. But you did not do it; [are you] afraid that your glory after death will be diminished unless you show me to have been your torment and yourself as a martyr, bearing a cross in the form of your wife?

Tolstoy appears to have been touched by this letter, and on October 13 he wrote in his diary:

> In looking through the diary, I found a place, there were several of them—in which I repent of the angry words I had written about her —these words were written in moments of exasperation. Now I repeat once more for the benefit of all who may chance on these diaries: I was often exasperated by her because of her hot, thoughtless temper, but as Fet used to say, every man has the wife he needs. She, so I now see, was the very wife I needed. She was an ideal wife

in the heathen sense of loyalty, devotion to family life, self-sacrifice, family affection, yet heathen as she is, she has in her the possibilities of a Christian friend. I saw that after Vanichka's death. Will it develop in her? O Father, help her.

During the next months the letters between Tolstoy and Sonya showed a renewed fondness and understanding. On October 25 he wrote to her that he felt "an entirely new love . . . such a holy, fine feeling that I ought not to speak about it, but I know you will be glad to hear it, and I know from the very fact that I express it that it will not change."

And in early November she sent him an affectionate, reassuring letter:

The little clouds which, as it seems to you, still darken at times our good relations—are not at all terrible. They are purely external—the result of life, habits, reluctance to change, weakness—but they do not in any way derive from inner causes. Inwardly, the very basis of our relationship remains serious, firm, and harmonious . . . I am rejoiced that you are well and living happily. I feel a little envious because you are not involved from morning to night with upholsterers, printers, governesses, the noise of carriages, policemen, and the spending of money. Amid this chaos it is difficult to remain in an attitude of contemplation of God or a peaceful, prayerful mood. Anyhow I shall strive to extricate myself from this earthly crust so that I shall not be altogether mired in the mud. But it is difficult!

Sonya's life in Moscow was fraught with problems that fall. Her long period of mourning had created chaos in her business affairs, and she had to work doubly hard to assure that her family would be well provided for in the coming year. Her temper was shorter than usual, and she was intense, unapproachable, frantic. She discarded her mourning clothes for brighter attire and put decorators to work making the nursery into a proper bedroom for Sasha, who was now a young girl of eleven.

In December Taneyev returned to Moscow from a tour and took a small charming house on Mertvy Lane. He and Sonya renewed their friendship, and she became absorbed by music. She attended concerts and devoted herself to studying the piano under Taneyev's tutelage. Marya Nikolaevna's daughter Lisa, who was now forty-three, was staying with Sonya in Moscow for the winter. She had been married to Prince Leonid Dmitrievich Obolensky, a brother of Tolstoy's old friend from Pokrovskoye, but he had died in 1888. Left an impoverished widow, Lisa now "managed" by extended visits to relatives and friends. As young women, she and her older sister Varya spent many summers at Yasnaya Polyana with the Tolstoys, but even then there was little affection between her and Sonya, who was only six years her senior. Lisa had been a favorite of Tolstoy's and was extremely jealous of Sonya, who created further animosity by her fondness for Varya.

"Aunt Sonya has undergone a great change which is displeasing to everyone," Lisa wrote to her daughter in St. Petersburg. "She has become restless, never stays at home; she has begun to dress up a lot . . . she has begun to go to the theater, to concerts, and in general she makes the impression of a person who is living with terrible speed and not losing a minute."

Sonya's new "giddiness" was difficult for her daughters—from the mature Tanya to the young Sasha—to understand. They feared she was driven by a "dread of old age and a desire not to appear an old woman." Aware that her behavior was at times eccentric, Sonya perceptively remarked to Lisa, "I have a somewhat disjointed restless life, like a lost soul, and yet I cannot do otherwise."

Her daughters were gentle with her, treating her condescendingly, like a child. They did not criticize her directly; in fact, there was little she did with which they could legitimately find fault. Sasha later asked, "Was there anything wrong with mother's being carried away by music, or in the fact that she preferred to spend her time with S. I. Taneyev, that nice, talented composer and pianist?" Certainly no one believed there was anything reprehensible in the conduct of Sonya and Taneyev. But her daughters did think her ardent friendship with a man who was ten years younger than she and who was engaged in a profession—music—that Tolstoy regarded as frivolous was a public declaration of her disdain for her husband's philosophy and showed a lack of loyalty to him as a man.

Elegantly dressed and animated by a renewed liveliness, Sonya took Sasha with her to the Thursday evening concerts at the glittering Hall of Nobility. They sat beside Taneyev in the sixth row, and Sasha was often asleep before the end of the first selection. At the concert's close, her mother and Taneyev chatted and the three of them usually rode home together. In the spring they went home on foot; during this brisk hour-long walk, her mother and Taneyev talked vivaciously while the sleepy-eyed Sasha tagged along behind.

Taneyev was now a frequent visitor to Dolgo-Khamovnicheski Street, even when Tolstoy was in Moscow. An intelligent and witty conversationalist, he enjoyed playing the piano for friends, and music filled the house. Sonya became more and more cordial toward him, and she was relaxed and informal in his company. Tolstoy and the children, however, began to resent Taneyev, regarding him as an intrusive presence in their family circle.

Every morning the Tolstoys' "sleigh, a fur-trimmed robe ready for use, a dark gray mare, Lira, in the harness," stood at the door of the house. As he waited for the Countess, the coachman, the stout, red-faced Emelyanych, huge in his padded coat, sat holding "the taut reins [which vibrated] slightly in his hands." Sonya, wrapped in fashionable furs and wearing a saucy sealskin hat, would sweep from the house ready for her marketing chores. She would drive out to Hunters Row and return with "numberless hampers filled with delectably smelling bags and boxes all tied with gay ribbons from Trembles' [the finest bakery in Moscow]." After the children had had their supper, the dining-room table was covered with a white cloth and laid with "various preserves, cakes, fruits, candies, sandwiches with anchovies, hard-boiled eggs, soft caviar, and a slim-waisted samovar fuming and sputtering on a silver tray." At about nine o'clock Taneyev would arrive, his shiny red face beaming with good humor. Hurried off to bed by her mother, Sasha would be disgruntled—"All that food can't be just for him!"—and her angry tears often made sleep impossible.

Sometimes when Sasha accompanied Sonya on a shopping tour, her mother would "give a light knock on the broad padded back of Emelyanych with her tortoiseshell lorgnette and say, 'You will turn into Mertvy Lane.'" She would then announce to her daughter, "We must see how Sergey Ivanovich's old nurse is getting along."

By some happy chance Sonya and her daughter always found Taneyev at home. He was usually playing the piano or drinking tea in his tiny dining room, but on seeing Sonya he would jump up clumsily and become frantically busy—helping them off with their wraps, seating them, and proposing refreshments. In the end the shuffling Pelagya Vasilievna would calm him and serve tea. As spring brought warmer weather, Sasha went with Sonya and Taneyev on carriage rides through the countryside. On these light-hearted excursions the stylishly dressed Sonya acted in a manner which Tolstoy most certainly would have censured as "frivolous."

The dichotomy of Sonya's life with and without Tolstoy created great tension for her. She began to suffer from severe migraine headaches, and she sought psychiatric care from Dr. Snegiryov (who had also treated young Lyova), who claimed that menopause was aggravating an underlying nervous disorder of long duration. Rest and drugs which were thought to have a soothing effect on the nerves were prescribed, but nothing seemed to help. Tolstoy's way of life was more intolerable to her than ever, and she was happy only when she was caught up in music or in the Moscow life of teas, visits, dinners, and balls.

"What can I tell you, dear, of my inner life?" she wrote to Tolstoy in March 1896. "I know nothing about it and dare not own up to it because there is no good in the vanity amid which I continue in order to drown out everything that torments me in life and all that still hurts. While I was praying and fasting during Lent I was better off: but now I am either seeking distractions and sensations or I am overwhelmed with a wave of depression and nervousness and then I rush out anywhere—away from my home, away from myself."

Tolstoy replied, "I should like to tell you that your desire to lose yourself—very natural as it may be—is not sound; that if you do lose yourself you only postpone the solution of your problems, it will still remain the same and it is just as necessary to solve it, if not in this world then in the next, that is, after our physical death."

Sonya disregarded Tolstoy's solemn advice. Moscow was alive with celebrations for the Tsar's impending coronation, and she was determined to enjoy every moment.

22

Tradition decreed that after a twelve-month period of mourning the coronation of a Russian tsar be held in Moscow, the ancient capital of the Grand Duchy of Russia, rather than in the more westernized St. Petersburg. Tradition also dictated that the entrance of the uncrowned Tsar into Moscow should be made on the day before the coronation. Nicholas and Alexandra therefore waited outside the city in the Petrovsky Palace and spent the days before the ceremony in fasting and in prayer.

After Alexander III's death, the Tolstoys, like most members of the Russian intelligentsia, had hoped that the new Tsar would introduce some badly needed reforms. In the manifesto he had issued on his accession, however, Nicholas had reaffirmed the reactionary policies of his ancestors. The document outraged Tolstoy, and he described it as "exceptionally indecent." Sonya too thought the Tsar's statement contemptible, but unlike her husband she did not refuse to attend his coronation.

All of Moscow was in a jubilant mood. Houses had been freshly painted and whitewashed; doors were decorated with evergreen branches; and white, red, and blue Russian flags flew from almost every window. Peasants had journeyed from all corners of the huge empire in open wagons. Siberians, Caucasians, and Turks arrived by train, the crowded cars a mass of scarlet tunics, rich furs, and tall red fezzes. Drunken soldiers and cheering peasants filled the city's streets. A three-day holiday had been declared, fines and taxes had been temporarily lifted, and prisoners with minor sentences had been granted pardons. For Sonya there were memories of standing in Kremlin Square, imagining the coronation of Alexander II in Uspensky Cathedral. Now, however, she was the Countess Tolstoy, an adult member of the nobility; she would sit inside the church and see the Tsar place the crown on his head.

Baroness Mengden's house faced the main avenue leading to the Kremlin, and Sonya stood on her balcony to watch Nicholas's entrance into Moscow. It was a brilliant May afternoon, and as the Imperial Guard Cavalry entered the city, their golden helmets and saber sheaths reflected the dazzling sun. Then came the Cossacks of the Guard in their red and purple coats, their sabers curving down to touch their shiny black boots. The gilded carriages of the nobility rolled past, and then on foot came the court orchestra and the officials of the court, all in gold-embroidered red uniforms. Finally Nicholas appeared on a huge white stallion. He wore a severe dark blue army tunic, buttoned to his chin, and "his hand [was] raised to his visor in a fixed salute."

Next in the regal cavalcade was the elaborately gilded carriage which had been made for Catherine the Great. Topped by a glittering replica of the imperial crown, it was drawn by eight massive white horses, and inside, waving to the thousands of spectators who lined the streets, was the Dowager Empress Marie. Then followed the equally splendid carriage of the uncrowned Empress, Alexandra Feodorovna. Her white satin gown was elaborately jeweled and embroidered, and a blazing diamond necklace encircled her long, slender throat.

Sonya awoke the next morning, May 26, 1896, to the sound of trumpets and the cries of heralds proclaiming that this was the day the Tsar would be crowned. She remembered her childhood inside the Kremlin, and she knew that royal servants had been working through the night to lay the crimson velvet carpet on the Red Staircase to the Uspensky Cathedral. Sasha, Misha, and the governess were to attend the coronation with her and there was a great deal of excitement in the household as they dressed. (Andreyusha, to everyone's horror, had joined the army and was serving in Tver, and the rest of the Tolstoys were at Yasnaya Polyana.)

The Uspensky Cathedral was brilliantly lit for the ceremony; the gilded murals which covered its walls and ceiling blazed in the light from thousands of flaming candles. Sonya and her family took their seats and, like the rest of the distinguished gathering, waited in excited anticipation. As the imperial couple entered the cathedral, a choir garbed in silver and bright blue sang a triumphant processional. Nicholas wore the vivid blue-green uniform of the Preobojensky Guard with a scarlet sash across his chest. Beside him was Alexandra; she wore a single strand of rare pink pearls and a shimmering silver-white gown with a wide crimson ribbon across its bodice. Followed by their many attendants and train bearers, the royal couple walked slowly toward their coronation thrones: for Nicholas, the 250-year-old diamond throne of Tsar Alexis, which was encrusted with rubies, sapphires, emeralds, pearls, and 870 diamonds; and for Alexandra, the ingeniously carved Byzantium ivory throne.

That evening Sonya was one of the seven thousand guests at the coronation banquet. A huge ballroom had been set aside for the peasants who were present by hereditary right (one of their ancestors had saved the life of a Tsar). They were dressed simply and were the only guests of whom Tolstoy would have approved. He certainly would have condemned the many noblewomen who had chosen gowns with deep necklines which bared their shoulders and emphasized their breasts. By contrast, Sonya's elegant new mauve silk gown seemed rather modestly cut. And unlike most of the women present, she wore no spectacular jewels—only pearls at her throat, and in her ears the small diamonds which had been her mother's. Nonetheless she was a strikingly handsome woman, and her wide-eyed gaze gave her a piquant charm (in truth, she was too vain to use her lorgnette; myopia, not flirtatiousness, gave her eyes their lively intensity).

Leaving early but exhilarated, she rode home through a night turned into day by the brilliance of the illuminations celebrating the coronation. Electric lights shone from the Kremlin for the first time; earlier that evening the Empress Alexandra had lit up the vast old fortress by pressing a button concealed in a bouquet of roses. But by morning the excitement and glamour of the week's festivities turned abruptly into horror.

Traditionally the people of Moscow celebrated on the day following a Tsar's coronation. So a massive open-air feast at which Nicholas and Alexandra were to be present had been planned for May 27. It was to be held in Khodanka Meadow, a troop training grounds. Although this was a rather grim park with a network of shallow trenches, no other area could have accommodated the hundreds of thousands of expected celebrants, a good number of whom arrived before dawn to be the first to sample the free beer and souvenirs that had been promised by the authorities. As wagons laden with beer barrels began to arrive, a rumor passed through the crowd (then estimated at 500,000) that there would not be enough beer for all. Suddenly a large boisterous group rushed toward the wagons, pushing aside the single squadron of Cossacks which had been assigned to keep order. Panic set in. Horses, soldiers, men, women, and children fell or were pushed into the ditches which crisscrossed the meadow. People were thrown to the ground, trampled, and left to suffocate or die of their wounds. Within an hour thousands lay dead on Khodanka Meadow, and thousands more lay moaning from their injuries.

Both peasantry and the nobility saw this horrifying event as an ill omen, "a sign of future tragedy in the reign." The Tsar himself seemed determined to court disaster. Just hours after more than three thousand of his subjects had been killed, he foolishly decided to attend a ball given by the French ambassador, the Marquis de Montebello. He acted on the advice of his ministers, who were fearful that his absence would deeply offend the French, who were among the Russians' strongest allies. Great preparations had been made for this gala party. Priceless tapestries and silver serving pieces from Paris and Versailles had been lent by the French government, and 100,000 roses had been sent from the south of France. But as the first guests arrived, it was clear that the gathering would be a somber one. Her eyes swollen from crying, Alexandra opened the ball by dancing a quadrille with Nicholas. The imperial couple left soon after, and with their departure this awkward reception drew to a close.

The Tsar had the victims of the tragic stampede buried in separate coffins at his own expense (a common grave in such a disaster would have been customary), and he gave each victim's family a thousand rubles. But while these acts were soon forgotten, his people never forgave him for "dancing at a time of mourning."

Despite the national tragedy, there had been reason for private rejoicing in the Tolstoy family. On May 15, eleven days before the coronation, young Lyova was married to Dora Westerlund, the daughter of a Swedish physician. She was only seventeen and spoke no Russian, but Tanya and Misha, who went to Sweden for the ceremony, were charmed by the vibrantly lovely young woman. Sonya had not gone with them, because Dr. Snegiryov had warned her that the long journey might prove extremely hazardous for her. (The reason for Tolstoy's absence remains unexplained.) Sonya was pleased with the marriage and held Dr. Westerlund, the bride's father, in high regard. When Dr. Snegiryov had no longer been able to help Lyova, he had suggested that the young man go to Sweden and place himself under Westerlund's care. After following this advice, Lyova had experienced a remarkable improvement in his emotional health. No doubt the vivacious young Dora had played a great part in his recovery; Sonya recognized this and was most grateful to her new daughter-in-law.

The happiness of Lyova's marriage was small compensation, however, for the sadness caused by Sergey's marital trials. (Family speculation, based on hints in Sergey's letters, gave sexual incompatibility as the reason for his problems.) Soon after his wedding Seryozha had taken his bride abroad for six months, returning in February 1896 to Moscow, where he embarked on his musical career. Sonya knew that this was an extremely difficult time for Seryozha and his wife, but Manya was hostile to any friendly gesture by members of the Tolstoy family. Seryozha remained somewhat aloof in his small house in Nikolskoye-Vyoziniskoye, pouring out his heart in his music and receiving professional counsel from Taneyev.

Taneyev now conducted many musical evenings at the Conservatory which were attended by most members of the Tolstoy family. He even included Tanya and her close friend Mikhail S. Sukhotin, an older man who was married and the father of six children. Sonya refused to believe that her oldest daughter could be in love with or even attracted to Sukhotin, who, rumor had it, had never been faithful to his wife. Tanya would not discuss Sukhotin with her mother, and although their friendship disturbed Sonya, she said nothing about it to Tolstoy.

Another problem involving romance upset the settled summer routine of the Tolstoys. Tanya Kuzminsky's oldest son, Misha, had grown into a bit of a rake and had recently been involved in several escapades with peasant girls. He gave detailed accounts of these adventures to his cousin Misha Tolstoy, who was several years his junior. Sonya believed her son was being corrupted, and her criticism of Misha Kuzminsky precipitated the first serious argument between her and her sister. And so, in the summer of 1896, the Kuzminskys did not occupy the wing of Yasnaya Polyana which for many years had been their summer home. Sonya offered these rooms to Taneyev and the aged Pelagya Vasilievna. After insisting on paying a token rental (125 rubles for a planned stay of four months), Taneyev moved to Yasnaya Polyana while Sonya attended the Tsar's coronation; and he was well entrenched when she joined him and Tolstoy there a few days later.

As he grew older, Tolstoy's attitude to music changed. The works of the great classical composers, which he had once enjoyed, now irritated him; he had come to believe that only folk music expressed the highest values of musical art. "All folk music," he told Seryozha, "can be understood by all people throughout the world. A Persian peasant will understand the songs of a Russian peasant and vice versa. But the pretentious insincerities of the great —like Richard Strauss for instance—even the great won't be able to understand." He liked only fragments of Bach, Haydn, Mozart, and Chopin. He disliked Wagner intensely and despised opera ("I cannot bear to see a fat yelling gentleman in tights," he complained to Seryozha). About Beethoven's Sonata in C sharp, he remarked, "It is like a conversation between man and wife—a toy sonata." The composer who was most out of favor with Tolstoy during Taneyev's stay at Yasnaya Polyana was Tchaikovsky. He often left the room when a piece of Tchaikovsky's was being played, and he told Tanya that his works were "nonsensical."

On May 27, 1896, Tolstoy wrote in his diary, "Taneyev annoys me with his air of moral self-satisfaction, his artistic obtuseness (deep-seated, not just superficial), and his position as cock-of-the-walk in the house." He kept his annoyance in check, however, and on the whole he was a cordial though somewhat formal host. He played chess with Taneyev (the musician was an inferior player), talked with him, and with reluctance listened to him play. This last could hardly be avoided, for Taneyev played nearly every evening in the salon. The pieces he favored—Mozart's Rondo in A flat, Beethoven's sonatas including the "Appassionata," and works by Schubert, Schumann, Chopin, Mendelssohn, Liszt, Arensky, Wagner, and of course Tchaikovsky—did not please Tolstoy.

Yasnaya Polyana seemed to be permeated by Taneyev's

music. As Tolstoy walked through the sunny rooms, whose windows had been thrown open to the summer breezes, the incessant sound of the piano drove him to fury. The musician had brought his own instrument, and he practiced in his apartments from eight A.M. to noon every day. After a walk and a swim, he joined the family for dinner at two. Yusha Pomerantsev, Taneyev's young protégé, had come with him to Yasnaya Polyana, and each afternoon they worked at the piano until tea was served on the terrace at five. After tea Taneyev often joined in the young people's games, and though rather clumsy, he played tennis and cycled. On inclement days he played chess with Tolstoy while one of the children read aloud (usually from a book chosen by his host). Taneyev did not discuss Tolstoy's religious philosophy with him; he did not mingle with any of the "dark people" and was almost rude in his avoidance of Chertkov.

With Tanayev's presence at Yasnaya Polyana a dramatic change had taken place in Sonya. Her depression had passed; she was bright and cheerful and looked younger and more attractive than she had in years. She seldom quarreled with her husband, and there were few bitter complaints about his inattentiveness or about the constant presence of his disciples. This change should have pleased Tolstoy, but of course it did not. Never had he encouraged her to search out her own artistic or intellectual pleasures. What he had demanded and expected was her total acceptance of his own beliefs. He was humiliated that her grief over Vanichka's death had not ended in her spiritual union with him but had been dispelled by music and a foolish flirtation. Yet he did not demand that Taneyev leave his house, perhaps believing this act would be an admission of his jealousy.

Undisturbed by Tolstoy's disapproval and motivated perhaps by his obsessive closeness to Chertkov, Sonya did not conceal her admiration for Taneyev. They had long tête-à-têtes about music and poetry in the salon, on the terrace, and in the garden; and these conversations were punctuated by sighs, laughter, and exclamations of delighted agreement. He introduced her to a favorite poem of his by Feodor Ivanovich Tyutchev and she memorized it, reciting a particular verse over and over to Sasha: "Oh how in our declining days/We love more tenderly and sadly." Sasha hated the poem and the look of ecstasy that lit her mother's face as she softly repeated it. "A repulsive poem," Tolstoy barked, "praises driveling old age love!" For Sonya, however, the idea that romantic love could still enter her life was a great consolation. Although Taneyev may have been unaware of the strength of the passion he had roused in Sonya, he did nothing to discourage her admiration.

In early July she spent two weeks in Moscow to see to some publishing business and returned to Yasnaya Polyana with several new dresses and a coiffure by Theodore which was topped with a bright coquettish bow. The sharp-tongued Lisa Obolensky wrote to her daughter Masha in September:

> Aunt Sonya arrived on the last day of my stay at Yasnaya Polyana. She looked young, gay, was well-dressed and beautiful. For the first time I did not find her very agreeable. Her strange attitude toward Taneyev (I call it strange because I do not know how to define these feelings on the part of a fifty-two-year-old woman) reached such a point that finally Lev Nikolaevich could not stand it and began to make a scene of jealousy, outrage, offense and indignation. Whereupon she started in the direction of Kozlovka station, with the idea of throwing herself in front of the train. She was gone all night in the garden, and in general raised a dreadful fuss and quite exhausted everyone. Tanya went to the Olsufievs, Masha became quite ill from the constant nervous tension. I can see that one cannot respect such a mother. This has not just happened, it was during the summer . . . after the departure of that "sack with sounds" as I call him. All this slid off her like water off a duck's back; she was as gay and chipper as ever, has taken season tickets for all the concerts and is impervious to everything!

"Morning. Did not sleep all night. Heart bothering me . . . unable to overcome pride and indignation," Tolstoy noted in his diary on July 26, 1896. Four days later he wrote, "I console myself with the thought that I ought to pity her, that she is suffering, and that I am infinitely to blame. We talked of the Gospels. Taneyev tried to prove to me, *in jest*, that Christ was in favor of castration. I lost my temper. I am ashamed of myself."

Taneyev must have recognized the awkwardness of his position at Yasnaya Polyana, for in August, four weeks before he had originally intended to leave, he returned to Moscow with Pelagya Vasilievna, his pupil, and his piano.

Taneyev was not the only guest at Yasnaya Polyana that summer. The young pianist Alexander Goldenweiser came, as well as many others; and several new disciples had become members of the household. One, Leonila Annenkova, a short, plump, smiling woman with a soft southern accent, had arrived a few summers before and had never left. Seldom speaking, she sat knitting, listening to Tolstoy's every word. Sonya liked this warm, retiring woman and confided in her. Leonila Annenkova returned this affection, and they corresponded after Sonya returned to Moscow. In one letter Leonila Annenkova mildly rebuked her about her friendship with Taneyev, and Sonya replied:

> As to my attitude toward the man who has disrupted my married life, against his will and without his knowledge, I can only say that I try not to think about him any more. It is hard for me to sever my friendly relations with him and to offend such a fine person and good and gentle man; but I am obstinately compelled to do so. He left Yasnaya Polyana a month ago, and I shall undoubtedly see him [in Moscow] in a few days. I do not know what I shall feel when I see him again. Joy, perhaps, or perhaps nothing at all. Sometimes my heart rebels and I refuse to abandon this artistic, musical happiness he gave me; I do not want to live without this relationship, so simple and tender, which has given me so many shining hours in the past two years. But when I think of my husband's sufferings and his insane jealousy, I feel deeply bitter and ashamed and I don't want to go on living. It is better for me to die than to hear such offensive accusations made against me, who have always taken care to behave so that neither my husband nor my children should have any cause to blush for me. And it is ludicrous now to have suspicions of any kind about a woman at my time of life—over fifty-two years old. Anyway, that's not what I mean to say: There are no *suspicions*, nor can there be; there is only his demanding, tyrannical nature and his possessive love of himself and his family, and I must try to submit to it.

But Sonya did not submit; on the contrary, she continued to attend concerts and saw Taneyev as often as he would allow. Taneyev had aspirations of becoming as renowned a composer as he was a performer, and for many years he had been working on an operatic trilogy, *Oresteia*. The first, *Agamemnon*, had been presented the previous year in St. Petersburg (to unenthusiastic notices); the second, *Choephoroi*, was to premiere in the capital in February. Sonya, after a terrible argument with Tolstoy, promised that she would not go to either the rehearsals or the first performance of Taneyev's new work.

The fact that she had even considered attending cut Tolstoy deeply; he wrote in his diary of Sonya's "degrading madness" and in anguish complained that in Moscow "there are nothing but pastimes of all kinds and guzzling and senile flirtation or still worse. It is abominable. I'm writing this down so that people may at least know after my death. . . . She is sick." He continued on in this vein, ending the entry with a reaffirmation of his devotion to God and a list of his own good deeds and sacrifices. Tearing the page from the book, he sent it to Chertkov (with whom he was closer than ever) with a note asking him to destroy it immediately after reading it. (Chertkov followed the letter if not the spirit of this request; he photographed the page before destroying it and added the copy to his massive collection of Tolstoy's private papers.)

In late January Sonya wrote to Tolstoy, who was at Yasnaya Polyana, that despite her promise, she had decided to go to St. Petersburg to see Taneyev's new opera. Tolstoy answered immediately: "It is dreadfully painful and humiliatingly embarrassing that a complete stranger [Taneyev], a person of no use, of no kind of interest, should be directing our lives, poisoning the last years of our life; it is humiliating and agonizing, that we must be governed by when he goes where, by what rehearsals, by when he plays. It is horribly horribly disgusting and shameful."

Taneyev—who was one of Russia's finest musicians, who was the director of the Moscow Conservatory, and who at this time was selflessly helping Tolstoy's oldest son get a solid start in his musical career—was certainly not "a person of no use." Tolstoy's disparaging phrase suggests that perhaps he, and not Sonya, was in the grip of a "degrading madness." She, after all, was guilty of little more than harboring romantic illusions and indulging in rather giddy behavior. The letters that passed between Taneyev and Sonya were no more than polite social notes, and though she was acting the coquette, her sexual faithfulness to her husband was never in doubt.

Chertkov had been forced to leave Russia in February of 1897 and his absence left Tolstoy in a highly irascible state. The tension between the Tolstoys increased throughout the spring, perhaps exacerbated further by the tangled romantic affairs of their children. Tanya had now confessed her love for the married Mikhail Sukhotin. "I have ruined my life—soiled it and ruined it irrevocably," Tanya wrote in her diary on March 7, 1897. "My present attachment stands across my life and, in addition to cutting me off from the possibility of marriage, it leaves a stain which nothing can wash away. How to get rid of my love I don't know. I am strongly attached, I have grown used to him, I have come to love his soul, I am grieved by its corruption and I rejoice at every sign that the divine essence in him is not wholly stifled. . . . I am ashamed before his wife, before his children, even though he says that I take nothing away from them, and although I know that his wife ceased loving him long ago."

The marriage of the Tolstoys' oldest son had been troubled for some time, and in January 1897 Seryozha's wife, Manya, left him and returned to her father's home. Eight months later she gave birth to their son, Sergey. It was rumored that she had fallen in love with another man, and there was much speculation about the child's paternity. Seryozha himself seemed baffled by the abrupt end of his marriage.

Several of the other Tolstoy children were also proving troublesome. Misha had failed his university examinations; Andreyusha was living a "non-Christian" life in the army; Ilya was as incapable as ever of making ends meet and, despite the financial settlement already made on him, was in dire need of assistance; and Sasha had become an overly emotional and moody young girl. The most worrisome of all the children, however, was Masha.

Lisa Obolensky's son, Nikolai (Kolasha), had come to live with the Tolstoys on Dolgo-Khamovnicheski Street during the winter of 1896–97. In his final year at the university, the handsome Kolasha was arrogant and lazy. He rose late, seldom attended classes, and spent his days lying about the house reading novels, smoking cigarettes, and flirting rather irresponsibly with Masha. It was a shock to everyone when Masha fell in love with this dandified cousin who rolled his r's elegantly in the French manner. He rep-

resented everything that Masha had once righteously declared she
abhorred, and she knew that there were few suitors who would be
less acceptable to her father. Still, she was in love with him and
had accepted his proposal of marriage without consulting Sonya or
Tolstoy.

Kolasha, in the manner of his arrogant ancestors, refused to
work for wages and insisted that Masha ask for the property and
money she had previously so adamantly refused. Life promised to
be difficult for Masha, because her share of the estate would never
support Kolasha's extravagances. But Masha would not be dis-
suaded, and she married her cousin in Tula on June 3, 1897. Her
mother and her sisters attended the bleak ceremony, which was
held in the registry and performed by a clerk. (The priest had
refused to marry them because of their kinship.) Tolstoy was despondent over Masha's defection, but his great love for her prevailed (although he did not attend the wedding). He endured his
disappointment in loving and indulgent silence while turning his
wrath upon Sonya. Three weeks before Masha's wedding he
drafted a parting letter to his wife:

> Your intimacy with [Taneyev] disgusts me and I cannot tolerate
> it calmly. If I go on living with you on these terms, I shall only be
> shortening and poisoning my own life. For a year now I have not
> been living at all. You know this. I have told it to you in exasperation
> and with prayers. Lately I have tried silence. I have tried everything,
> and nothing is of any use; the intimacy goes on and I can see that it
> may well go on like this to the end. I cannot stand it any longer. It is
> obvious that you cannot give it up: only one thing remains—to part,
> I have firmly made up my mind to this. But must consider the best
> way of doing it. I think the very best thing would be for me to go
> abroad. We shall think out what would be for the best. One thing is
> certain—we cannot go on like this.

He then wrote another draft in which he proposed some solu-
tions to their problems. The first and best, he noted, was for her to
break all relations with Taneyev; the second was for him to go
abroad; and the third was for her to go abroad with him. Then,
perhaps deciding he needed more time to think, he hid the two
letters in the upholstery of a chair (they were not found for over a

decade) and went off to Pirogovo to stay with his brother Sergey Nikolaevich. Sonya arrived from Moscow the next day, and a few days later Tolstoy returned to Yasnaya Polyana. On the day of Masha's wedding Taneyev arrived. Sonya had not told her husband that Taneyev would be a guest, and he was furious. On June 4 she wrote in her diary, "This morning, I had an unpleasant talk about Taneyev with Lev Nikolaevich. The same unbearable jealousy! Tears choked me. I flung some bitter words at my husband, who is suffering—and regretted it for the rest of the day."

Taneyev, aware that he was not welcome, prepared to leave the next day. Sonya was distraught. She waited all morning on the veranda hoping to have coffee with him before he left, and then in a state of nervous agitation she walked through the garden to the small hill that Vanichka had loved. She often spoke to the dead child in the places he had frequented, and she now asked him if there was any evil in her feeling for Taneyev. She later wrote, "Vanichka seemed to turn me away from him—he must have felt sorry for his father, but I know he is not blaming me; for it is he who has sent me Taneyev, and he will not take him away from me."

Taneyev had departed while she was wandering distractedly about the house and gardens. After dinner she spent three hours copying *What Is Art?*—the essay on which Tolstoy was then working. "Above all," she ended her diary entry for June 5, "I am missing Taneyev."

Depression plagued her throughout June. She pruned the rose bushes, corrected proofs, copied Tolstoy's manuscripts, and spent hours on photography, not only taking pictures but also developing and printing them. But in the midst of these desperate efforts to raise her spirits, melancholy would suddenly overwhelm her. As she worked on the proofs of *The Kreutzer Sonata* for a new edition, her anger toward Tolstoy grew, and she wrote that "everywhere his hero keeps saying: *We* went in for hoggish pleasures, *we* felt surfeited, *we*, always *we*. A woman's emotions are quite different, it is wrong to generalize about any emotions, even about sexual emotions, they are so different in a man to a pure woman."

Taneyev had completed *Eumenides*, the final opera in his trilogy, and had given Sonya the original score. She sent it to Moscow to be bound, thereby causing another quarrel with Tolstoy. On June 13 she wrote, "The music has come back from the Moscow binder, and the bindings were all wrong, and—what is worse—they have thrown away the cover with the dedication in Taneyev's handwriting. I nearly wept. My annoyance displeased Lev Niko-laevich, and I tried to contain myself—but I have a quick temper which I find hard to control."

On June 15 Sonya's sister Lisa and her thirteen-year-old daughter, Vetochka, arrived. Lisa had divorced her first husband fifteen years before and had married a cousin, Alexander Alexan-drovich Behrs, who joined his family the next day. The years seemed to have lessened the sisters' animosity and Sonya was happy to see Lisa, who was now a handsome woman of fifty-four. Lisa's nature had changed little, however; after a day together, the two women were arguing, and Sonya regretted confiding some of her views on marriage and religion to her sister. Her depression deepened, and she had a series of unsettling dreams, the first one recorded in her diary on June 17, 1897:

> I dreamed that I was lying in a strange bed in a strange room. Ta-neyev comes in and, seeing me, goes straight up to the table: There are little bundles of paper there, like bills or notes all torn up. He puts on his glasses and writes something very rapidly on the bits of paper. I am frightened he will see me, and keep lying very still. But, having finished writing, he takes off his spectacles, puts all the papers in a heap, and goes out. I jump out of the bed and, picking up one of the papers, try to read it. It is a detailed description of his state of mind: all his struggles and desires. I read it quickly, but suddenly there is a knock, and I wake up. So I didn't manage to read it all; I was very sorry, and wanted to fall asleep again and read the rest; but, of course, I couldn't.

Sonya was finding the problems of the two men in her life a cumbersome burden. For many years Tolstoy had suffered from minor but painful stomach disorders, and it was Sonya who had to provide nourishing, varied vegetarian meals for him. Physicians had prescribed all the conventional remedies—"soda, powdered charcoal, magnesia, various mineral waters"—but none had eased his discomfort. Convinced that food was the cause of his ailments and therefore could be the cure, he had recently become even more particular about his diet. Every evening the cook, the robust, red-cheeked Semyon Nikolaevich (whom Sonya had brought with her from Moscow), reported to her, and they discussed the next day's menu at length. Tolstoy suspected Sonya of surreptitiously introducing forbidden foods into his meals, and in fact if he was not well, she would ask Semyon Nikolaevich to add meat broth to his mushroom soup. During the difficult month of June 1897 the chore of composing the daily menu with Semyon Nikolaevich came to represent all the oppressive elements of her life, and on June 21 she wrote:

> And now I've got to write the menu again: *soupe printanière*—oh, how I hate it! *Every* day for thirty-five years it's been *soupe printanière!* I don't want to hear any more of *soupe printanière;* I want to hear the most difficult fugue or symphony; I want to hear the most complicated harmonies every single day, so that my soul can struggle in its endeavor to understand what the composer is trying to express in his difficult musical language, and what he felt in his innermost heart while composing his work. . . . I would give so much if . . . I could listen to the cultural music which gave me so much joy last summer, that, indeed, was a *holiday* of life.

On Sunday, July 5, Taneyev arrived for an eight-day visit. Although Tolstoy maintained an air of rather chilly politeness toward his guest, he was "irritable, jealous, and most disagreeable" to Sonya. Taneyev, sensing Tolstoy's dislike, played the piano on only two evenings; on one occasion he chose pieces he thought Tolstoy would find acceptable, and on the other he played only for Sonya. She described this last evening: "Lev Nikolaevich had gone out. . . . I asked Taneyev to play me Mozart's Sonata. We were alone in the room, and I felt serene and happy. He played two sonatas and most charmingly. Then he played the lovely *andante* from his own symphony, which I had heard in Moscow and which I love. . . . No one in the world can play like him. So noble and honest is his playing, with such a sense of measure and restraint, sometimes he seems to be carried away, forgetting everything—and those moments are the most wonderful."

During Taneyev's visit he and Sonya took long walks, swam together, picnicked in the Zaeska wood, and visited the nearby coal mines. Sonya took a number of photographs on these outings, and

Taneyev appeared in almost every picture. Then he was gone. For a week Sonya frenetically worked to develop and print all her pictures; she redoubled her efforts to master the piano, but when she tried to play some of Taneyev's music, she found it too difficult. The house was in a state of "near-doom" again. Sasha was "wild, and rough and obstinate," and Tanya wept constantly over her affair with Sukhotin. Sonya and her oldest daughter had grown extraordinarily close this summer. ("I am being attracted to you more and more," Tanya had cried, "and in the end I will go back to the primitive stage and start sucking your breasts.")

The pressures on Sonya were proving too much, and her dreams returned. "I was dreaming of Vanichka last night; he was lying down, looking so thin and miserable, and stretching his arms toward me. Today I dreamed of Taneyev, also lying down, and smiling and stretching his arms toward me too."

But Sonya was occupied with more than sexual fantasies. She was beginning to lose any sense of achievement in copying an article over for her husband "for the tenth time." She was bored and fearful she would "run dry," and desperately in search of some "*independent* work." Sonya was now fighting for her own identity, her survival as an independent woman and a liaison with Taneyev was the first branch she reached out to grasp.

23

On September 1, 1897, Sonya wrote in her diary, "I shall go to Moscow, where I shall hire a piano and play; and I hope Taneyev will come and play to me. The very thought of it gives me a new lease of life." Taneyev did, indeed, come and play for her, and she attended his concerts and had him to tea. When he celebrated her name day with her and a large group of her Moscow friends, he played his symphony, dedicating it to her.

Sonya was now in open rebellion. She no longer seemed to care what Tolstoy thought about her "virginal liaison" or what Moscow society whispered about this friendship. She was happy when she was with Taneyev, and they spent many evenings together talking about art and music, Tolstoy's novels (which Taneyev greatly admired) and philosophy, and exchanging gossipy chitchat. He played the piano and encouraged her in her musical studies. As fond as she was of Taneyev, however, Sonya was not blind to his failings. "A gifted man puts all his understanding and all the subtlety of his soul into his work, while his attitude to real life is dull and indifferent," she wrote after an afternoon with him. "It is the same with my husband, who is infinitely more gifted than Taneyev. What a wonderful understanding of human psychology there is in his books, and what an extraordinary indifference and lack of understanding in his home life."

Sonya continued to see Taneyev throughout the winter and into the spring of 1898. She seemed to be greatly excited by the intimacy she enjoyed with two men of genius. No longer was she reticent about opposing either her husband or Taneyev when others were present. Indeed, she took mischievous pleasure in being outspoken. Russia was a male-dominated society; women had few rights, and wives who voiced opinions about their husbands' busi-

ness activities were considered vulgar. Sonya's publishing enterprise was still regarded as a "crude" and "shocking" venture, and
her forthrightness infuriated many members of the intelligentsia (a
class that was almost exclusively male). When Vladimir Nemirovich-Danchenko, a renowned dramatist and a director with the
Moscow Art Theater, visited Tolstoy at Yasnaya Polyana, Sonya
sat doing some needlework while the two men played chess, and as
they conversed she added her comments. When Tolstoy mentioned
that he was giving an article to an editor of whom Sonya did not
approve, she said sharply, "What? I don't understand it at all. That
monkey-face, that hypocrite! And you are going to give her an
article."

Nemirovich-Danchenko was dumfounded, and in his memoirs
he raged, "How dare a woman even though she happens to be the
wife, the most intimate companion, of this great man, how dare
she maintain toward him this vulgar commanding tone?" Outspoken, independent thinking women like Sonya were almost univer-
sally scorned; and they were presented as ridiculous comic
monsters by many contemporary playwrights and novelists. Tolstoy was considered the greatest mind in Russia, and the stormy
marriage of the Tolstoys was discussed in every salon and drawing
room. Sonya was blamed for everything Tolstoy "suffered"—the
conflict between the spartan philosophy he espoused and the bour-
geois home life she insisted upon maintaining; his children's "defections" and unsuitable marriages (Misha, without any prospects, had
just married his childhood sweetheart); and his jealous pain over
her "improper" friendship.

The knowledge that her behavior was considered scandalous
did not deter Sonya from pursuing her business interests or from
seeing Taneyev. Always a voracious reader, Sonya read more during her friendship with Taneyev than ever before; she made her
way through works of musical theory and philosophy, and she
read, almost always in their original languages, the vital new writers in Russia, France, Germany, England, and the United States.
Biographies of great composers and writers held a special interest
for her, and she noted in her diary, "I read Beethoven's life. . . .
He was one of those geniuses whose world center was his own
creative power, while all the rest of the world was merely an acces-

sory to it. Beethoven gave me an insight into Lev Nikolaevich's egoism and indifference to everything around him. The world to him is merely the environment of his genius, and he takes from it only what can serve his work. He discards the rest. . . . Yet the world worships such men."

Perhaps stimulated by the biographies she read, Sonya thought of writing a life of Tolstoy, a project she had first considered some years before. Once again she wanted to explore her own literary creativity: "I must do some *independent* work-—or else I shall go dry." But, as in the past, this energy was soon spent in dealing with her complex family, business, and social life.

In July 1898 Sonya planned to visit her friends the Maslovs at their country estate, Selishche. When Tolstoy learned that Taneyev had also been invited, he raged and fumed and threatened to leave home for Finland. Sonya ignored his histrionics and found Taneyev's playing at Selishche "pure delight." She then went to Kiev, meeting her sister Tanya there, and the two women journeyed together to Yasnaya Polyana. Late one night soon after their arrival Tolstoy and Sonya had a violent argument. The next day he wrote "A Dialogue," an account of this quarrel which appears to have been intended for Tanya Kuzminsky but which was never given to her. Earlier in the day he, Tanya, and Sonya had held lengthy and angry discussions about Sonya's friendship with Taneyev, nonetheless he opens "A Dialogue" by claiming that he had gone to bed in a "good and pleasant frame of mind." He then states that as they lay in bed together, Sonya accused him of talking too much to Tanya about Taneyev and herself. He begged her not to continue this discussion, but she persisted.

> She: I cannot stop speaking of [your dislike of Taneyev] for it is difficult for me to live in constant fear and trembling. If [Taneyev] should happen to come here, [the arguments] will start over again. He did not say anything, but he may come.
>
> I: Just as I was hoping to get some peace, you begin to prepare me again for a disagreeable happening.
>
> She: What am I to do? It may happen. He told Tanya. I didn't ask him. Perhaps he will come.
>
> I: It is of no importance whether he comes or doesn't come. . . . what is important, as I told you two years ago, is the attitude

you take to your feeling for him. If you had acknowledged this feeling to be a bad one, then you would not have even troubled to mention whether he was coming or not.

She: Well, what am I to do now?

I: Repent of your feeling in your soul.

She: I don't know how to repent and don't understand what it means.

I: It means that you have to judge for yourself whether your feeling for this man is right or wrong.

She: I haven't any feeling, either right or wrong.

I: That is not true.

She: It is such an unimportant, insignificant feeling . . . so unimportant that it cannot be bad. And I am sure there is nothing bad in it.

I: No, the exceptional feeling of an old married woman for a strange man is a wrong feeling.

She: It is not a feeling for him as a man but as a human being.

I: But this human being is a man.

She: For me he is not a man. It is not an exceptional feeling. There is only this—that after all my grief I found consolation in his music, but I have no particular feeling for the man. . . . Let us leave it that way. I did wrong to go, and it hurt you. But now it is all over with. I will do everything possible in order not to hurt your feelings.

I: You cannot do so, because the whole point is that whatever you do—go to him or not, receive him or not—the whole point lies in the attitude you take to this feeling of yours. . . . until you make up your mind whether it is a good or bad feeling and acknowledge it to be wrong, you will not be able to avoid hurting me. If you acknowledge, as you are doing, that this is a good feeling, you will never be strong enough not to wish to gratify it, that is, to see each other. And if you wish it, then you will certainly do everything you can to see him. And if you avoid seeing him, you will only be sad and always yearning to see him. So it follows that everything turns on your decision as to whether it is a good feeling or a bad one.

She: I have done nothing wrong. What I did wrong was to give you pain, and I am sincerely sorry for it.

I: That is just what is bad about it; you repent of your actions but not the feeling that guided those actions.

She: I know that I have never loved anyone, nor do I love anyone more than I love you.

Tolstoy returned to his demand that she recognize that she, an older married woman, was guilty of loving a younger man. "The same thing over and over again!" Sonya shouted. "It is simply torture! All I want is that *he* should come once a month and sit awhile and play for me, as any good acquaintance might."

Tolstoy answered, "Yes, and by those words you are proving that you have a particular feeling for this man. There is, after all, no other person whose monthly visits could give you joy. If this one visit a month would be pleasant, how much pleasanter would be a weekly or a daily visit? You have confessed to your particular feeling and unless you settle the question of whether it is good or bad, nothing can be altered."

Tolstoy followed with recriminations and examples of how she pursued Taneyev, accusing her of being "one of those ladies who never miss a concert [of Taneyev's] at the Conservatory."

Sonya became hysterical; in Tolstoy's words, she was "sobbing, laughing, and whispering meaningless and, alas, feigned protests, such as 'My head is ready to split,' and then . . . crying out, '. . . cut a vein in my neck! Oh, this is the one!' "

Tolstoy embraced his distraught wife—

I held her. I know that always helps. I kissed her brows. She could not get her breath for a long time. Then she began to yawn and sigh, and at last fell asleep and is still sleeping. I do not know how this madness can end. I cannot see any way out. It is evident that she values this feeling as much as her life and does not want to acknowledge it as wrong. And without acknowledging it as wrong, she cannot get rid of it and will continue to do the things the feeling demands, things that are tormenting and shameless for the children to witness, if not for me.

The next day Sonya noted the quarrel in her diary: "At night the same talk of jealousy began again; and again there were shouting, abuse, and reproaches. My nerves could not stand it, something that kept the balance in my brain gave way and I lost my self-command. I had a terrible attack of the nerves. I trembled all over, sobbed, raved, and kept starting up in fright. I do not remember what happened to me, but it ended in a kind of numbness."

This dispute set the tone for their summer. Just a few days after their quarrel Sergey Pavlovich Diaghileff arrived at Yasnaya Polyana. The brilliant twenty-six-year old was the editor of the *Annual of the Imperial Theater* and of *The World of Art*. He had begun a literary controversy in *The World of Art* by questioning the aesthetics of Tolstoy, and he had come to Yasnaya Polyana to argue with Tolstoy his violently opposing views. Diaghileff was a dandy, with elegant and somewhat effeminate manners and an imperious attitude. He had the habit of snapping the fingers of one hand as he gestured for what he wanted with the other. Women held no appeal to him, but social leaders and men with power did.

He turned up in time for tea, kissed Tolstoy's hands, said a few amusing things, and then began his debate. Tolstoy intensely disliked Diaghileff, whom he considered little more than a dilettante and the personification of everything of which he found Taneyev guilty. By dinnertime, Diaghileff, realizing he was unwelcome, departed and never again returned. To everyone at Yasnaya Polyana's shocked surprise, less than a week later, Taneyev, who was by now extremely powerful in court and music circles, nominated Diaghileff for a position in the Ministry of the Court. Although the Tsar disliked Diaghileff almost as intensely as did Tolstoy, he bowed to Taneyev's judgment, a decision that greatly offended Tolstoy.

Never had Tolstoy felt so alone. Sonya's dedication to him and to his work had been undermined by her liaison with Taneyev. His older daughters, once so devoted, were now involved in the cares of their own lives. Shortly after recovering from typhus, Masha had a difficult pregnancy that had ended in a stillbirth after seven months, and she had not regained her strength. Tanya was completely absorbed by Sukhotin, whose wife had recently died; and it seemed certain that after a respectable period of mourning they would marry. But perhaps the most difficult "loss" in Tolstoy's life was that of Chertkov, who, along with Biryukov, had been exiled. (They had been banished because of their work on behalf of the Dukhobors, a peasant sect which adhered to principles similar to those of Tolstoyism and which had been harshly persecuted. Tolstoy had also supported the Dukhobors, but he had escaped official censure.) Chertkov had left Russia in February

1897 for England and was not to return to his native land for a full decade.

Sonya had been quite sympathetic to Chertkov's plight; her animosity toward him did not temper her deep-seated opposition to any form of censorship and persecution. Through the years of his exile Chertkov remained in constant correspondence with Tolstoy; and as he was always the first to publish Tolstoy's work (not including the earlier work published by Sonya) he controlled everything, including all translations. He and Tolstoy continued to support the beleaguered Dukhobors; and when they were given permission to emigrate, Chertkov allocated funds from Tolstoy's foreign translations to help them settle in Canada.

More and more Tolstoy was surrounded by followers and sycophants. Many who visited him wrote articles or memoirs about their meetings with him. Every word he spoke seems to have been preserved. Only a small number of those who came actually believed in his philosophy; most were drawn by his genius and his fame. There was a certain cachet in having been to Yasnaya Polyana as the great man's "guest." (The truth was that Tolstoy still turned no one away from his gates, and only a few of the people who came had actually been invited.) But the adulation of these "strangers" did not compensate for the loss of the slavish devotion of his wife, daughters, and chief disciple.

Much disturbed, Sonya watched as bitterness and jealousy gnawed at Tolstoy. Proud and lonely, he had become an aging lion, still roaring but losing his hold over his females. He was jealous not only of Taneyev but also of Masha's handsome but ineffectual young husband, so arrogant and possessive when he appeared at her side. The older Sukhotin he could not tolerate at all. Tolstoy had never made confidants of his sons, and the only female in the household from whom he might exact dedication was Sasha, who at fourteen was awkward, unattractive, and desperate for attention. His dependence upon his two older daughters had made him overlook her, but now for the first time in the young girl's life he turned to her.

Though perhaps not intentionally, he began a campaign to enlist Sasha as the loyal lifelong daughter-disciple he had believed Masha would be. Men and marriage had caused his other daughters to draw away from him. Determined that Sasha would not be caught in the same snare, he constantly reminded her that she was too unattractive to marry and that marriage almost always had a pernicious influence on one's life. At the same time he inculcated her with the belief that her greatest satisfaction would lie in doing the Lord's work, her greatest glory in serving her fellow man. Sasha did not question the sincerity of Tolstoy's altruistic statements; feeling gawky and unwanted, she knew only that her father, that great man whom all the world idolized, needed her.

Sonya was aware of her husband's efforts to make Sasha into an unquestioning disciple, and she knew that such a deep attachment to her father would rob Sasha of a normal life as a wife and mother. But she did nothing at this time to intervene; when she finally tried to help Sasha, it was much too late. She had been transformed by her blind devotion to her father. Sonya's guilt over Sasha's fate would trouble her for the rest of her life.

Continuing to pursue her friendship with Taneyev, late in the summer of 1898 Sonya once again went to Selishche to be near him. In the fall she spent more time in Moscow than she had in previous years. She therefore saw little of Tolstoy, who remained at Yasnaya Polyana immersed in the writing of a new novel—his first in nine years. Although at first she wrote to him less frequently than in the past, family difficulties—Misha's financial problems and Andreyusha's broken engagement to a Georgian woman who in despair shot herself—resulted in a series of letters seeking Tolstoy's counsel. Their correspondence grew warmer, and she confessed she was still suffering from the hallucination that had plagued her since Vanichka's death—"the smell of a corpse" and "sweet, too sweet flowers." Her husband's replies were sympathetic, and she joined him at Yasnaya Polyana.

Tolstoy's sudden return to fiction—a novel, *Resurrection*, which he had begun and abandoned years before—had been caused by Chertkov's need to raise money to resettle the Dukhobors in Canada. Working through letters, Chertkov had already sold serial rights to the partially written novel to the Russian weekly *The Field*. In principle, Tolstoy remained absolutely opposed to demanding payment for his work, but in this instance (as in many others) he was able to alter his beliefs to the occasion.

When Sonya arrived at Yasnaya Polyana, the house was in a furor of activity. Everybody was involved in the work of copying

Tolstoy's manuscript, rushing to prepare it for publication as soon as possible. Sonya left after a few days, happy that Tolstoy was once again working on a novel (although the book itself did not please her). *Resurrection* was based on a true story which had been told to Tolstoy ten years before. A prostitute had been tried and unjustly convicted of participation in a murder. One of the jurors was a man who had seduced the woman in her youth; he did not immediately recognize her, but then, with a sense of shock and remorse, he saw in her the pure young girl whose downfall he had caused. In Tolstoy's novel, the juror, Nekhlyudov, attempts to redeem himself by "resurrecting" the pure young maiden through marriage and a new position in life. Not surprisingly, Tolstoy again based his fictional world in autobiographical incidents. Like his protagonist, in his youth Tolstoy had seduced a young servant girl in his father's house, and the relationship between the novel's two main characters was drawn from this and his affair with Axinia. Sonya found the book hollow and false. Still she was happy that he had abandoned his philosophical writings, and when Tolstoy returned to Moscow that winter she was enthusiastic in her assistance. The house was turned into an editing office, and the dining-room table was covered with heaps of manuscript pages and proofs. "Whomever I might love," Sonya wrote in her diary, "there is no one else in the world I would even compare with my husband. He has held too great a place in my whole life and in my heart."

The activity in the household during the writing of *Resurrection* did not staunch the flow of people who came, both to Moscow and Yasnaya Polyana, to catch a glimpse of or to meet and talk with Tolstoy. Even he became annoyed by these curiosity seekers. Sonya was pleased by the distinguished artists, writers, and sculptors who came to visit; but through all the years she had not been able to overcome her distaste for the strange "dark ones" who sought out her husband—these frequently dirty and ill-smelling people who, as Ernest Simmons writes, "rang his bell hoping to enter the portals of truth [and yearning] for nothing more than to be admitted to his sanctuary, where each sat patiently, like Moses, hearing the voice of God on Mt. Sinai."

On November 15, 1899, Tanya married the balding, rather stout Sukhotin. Although she was thirty-five, her family had still hoped she would make a brilliant match, and there was much sadness over her choice of a widower who had six children and who was nearer her father's age than her own. Tolstoy, who surprised everyone by attending the wedding, wept throughout the ceremony; Sonya, though unhappy, remained calm. During the past year she had found that Sukhotin was a pleasant man, cheerful and witty, who worshipped Tanya. Although she did not approve of Tanya's new husband, she sensed that, unlike the ailing, miserable Masha, Tanya would be happy in her marriage.

In December 1899 Tolstoy completed *Resurrection;* the Dukhobors were all safely in Canada, and life should have returned to some semblance of normalcy. But what was normalcy in Sonya's marriage now? A home crowded from daybreak to dark with strangers? She was desperately lonely without her daughter Tanya, and she was sharing her life with a husband whose philosophy she could not accept. (After the birth of a grandchild he wrote in his diary, "I cannot rejoice at the birth of a child into the wealthy class; it is the proliferation of parasites.")

Tolstoy continued to be preoccupied with sexual morality, and on January 16, 1900, he wrote in his diary, "The best thing one can do with the sexual drive is (1) to destroy it utterly in oneself; *next best* [in English in the original] (2) is to live with one woman who has a chaste nature and shares your faith, and bring up children with her and help her as she helps you; *next worse* [in English] (3) is to go to a brothel when you are tormented by desire; (4) to have brief relations with different women, remaining with none; (5) to have intercourse with a young girl and abandon her; (6) worse yet, to have intercourse with another man's wife; (7) worst of all, to live with a faithless and immoral woman." The page also had the notation on it, "This page must be torn out." It was not, however, and the appalling revelation remains: Tolstoy believed that if he seduced and deserted a young girl, committed adultery, or lived a debauched life, he would be less guilty of immoral behavior than if he lived with a woman who might have *thoughts* of another man. Judging his marriage by his own criteria, Tolstoy must have concluded that he was mired in depravity. Certainly his attitude toward sexuality made his relationship with Sonya extremely difficult, and now, except for Sasha, they were alone. With *Resurrection* completed they were again driven apart by the absolute differences in their drives, needs, and beliefs. Once again Sonya took refuge in music, constantly playing works Tolstoy found nonsensical. And once again she sought out Taneyev.

Taneyev was by no means the only contemporary Russian composer for whom Tolstoy had little use. On January 9, 1900, Sergey Rachmaninov, the composer-pianist who had been one of Taneyev's most gifted students, visited Tolstoy in Moscow. A young man of twenty-seven, he was caught in an agonizing spiritual crisis, and he had come, like a pilgrim to a shrine, to see Tolstoy. His friend, the singer Feodor Chaliapin, was with him, and Sonya greeted the men warmly, leading them into the salon, where Misha, Andreyusha and Seryozha joined them for tea. But it wasn't until the meal was over that a reluctant Tolstoy, accompanied by the pianist Goldenweiser, appeared in the doorway.

Chaliapin later wrote that Tolstoy spoke in "a slightly bleating voice, and that a certain letter—no doubt because several of his teeth were missing—issued with a lisping sound."

Rachmaninov, overwhelmed by being in Tolstoy's presence, whispered to his friend, "If I'm asked to play, I don't know what I shall do. My fingers are numb." But when Tolstoy did indeed ask him to play one of his own compositions, Rachmaninov performed with directness, fire, and strength. He had been strongly influenced by Tchaikovsky, however; and Tolstoy, not pleased by his music, abruptly asked him, "Tell me, has that type of music any interest whatever?" The dispirited Rachmaninov mumbled nervously that he believed and hoped it did.

Unsettled by Tolstoy's coldness, Chaliapin was reluctant to sing. He had little formal training but had a magnificent natural voice. Only twenty-seven, this robust basso profundo had been a favorite among his countrymen for four years. His voice had tremendous range and power, but his scant musical education restricted him to Russian operas and the portrayal of national types.

As he sang, Tolstoy faced him, his hands thrust through the belt in his blouse, his face somber. Chaliapin first sang a new song by Rachmaninov, "Le Destin," which was a variation on a leitmotif from Beethoven's Fifth Symphony. Rachmaninov accompanied him. At the end of the piece Tolstoy sat glowering while Sonya applauded enthusiastically. She urged him to sing again, asking him to do "Le Vieux Caporal," which she had heard him perform in concert. (This song had been written by Dargomyzhski, a Tula composer, and in theme and mood was close to a folk melody.) There was a burst of applause after the song, and Tolstoy brushed tears from his eyes. Sonya went to Chaliapin and, grasping his hand, said, "I'm sure it pleased him very much."

The publication of *Resurrection* in November 1899 had created tremendous controversy and shocked and angered the ecclesiastical world. Although the many changes and deletions demanded by the censor had been made, the novel still held Church ritual up to ridicule; and one of the more despicable characters was easily recognizable as Pobedonostsev, the procurator of the Holy Synod. This powerful official bitterly struck back at Tolstoy, urging Nicholas II to excommunicate him; but the Tsar, like his imperial predecessors, was fearful of public reaction to such a step. No action might have been taken, but Chertkov, who was still in England, published two articles in which Tolstoy had violently attacked Church ritual and then had them smuggled into Russia. Pobedonostsev and the other members of the Synod, in a frenzy of rage, demanded that the Tsar move against Tolstoy. All Russia waited to see what would happen. Nicholas was trapped. His people knew that a war was being waged between him and Tolstoy, and they would regard the victor as the most powerful man in Russia.

On Sunday February 24, 1901, an edict was published in the Synod's journal, the *Church Gazette*, which formally excommunicated Tolstoy. Within hours the streets of Moscow swarmed with thousands of outraged citizens. Sonya and Tolstoy walked with a friend, A. N. Dunayev, to Lybyanskaya Square. Several thousand students had gathered there, and Tolstoy was set upon, torn from Sonya's side, and carried through the crowd on the shoulders of a tall young man, while a thunderous cheer arose: "Hurray for Lev Nikolaevich! Hail to the great! Hurray!" Mounted police finally parted the crowd and helped Tolstoy to extricate himself from the demonstrators.

Sonya, deeply disturbed by the excommunication, quickly sent an indignant letter to Pobedonostsev, posting a copy of it to three of the Holy Synod's metropolitans. Emphasizing her own unshakable faith in the Church, she warmly defended her husband and ended by pointing out that "Many outside the Church lead a more truly Christian life than certain high ecclesiastics wearing diamond miters and stars." Sonya's letter and a reply from the Holy Synod reaffirming its decree of excommunication were published in the *Church Gazette*.

Within a month Sonya reported in her diary, "No manuscript of Lev Nikolaevich ever had such swift and wide dissemination as this letter. It has been translated into all the foreign languages. This rejoiced me, but I did not become proud, thank God! I wrote it at once, swiftly, ardently. God commanded me to do this and not my will."

Tolstoy was more perplexed than pleased by Sonya's courageous act and wrote Masha: "Your mother's letter has had a very good effect on her. It is impossible to foresee anything. With us men, thought influences action, but with women especially feminine women, actions influence thought."

A serious decline in Tolstoy's health brought husband and wife closer together. Toward the end of June 1901 he suffered a severe attack of malaria and came close to dying. Sonya nursed him attentively. At one point, he wept as she applied a compress. "Thanks, Sonya. Don't think I'm not grateful and don't love you," he whispered. They embraced emotionally, and later she wrote in her diary, "Now my Lyovochka sleeps. He's still alive, I can see and hear him and care for him, and later? My God, how unbearable my grief would be, how terrible my life without him." On September 5, when he was well enough to travel, Sonya set out with Tolstoy for Gaspra, where a wealthy friend had generously placed an estate at their disposal. Sasha, Masha and her husband, and Paul A. Boulanger, Tolstoy's good friend and disciple, accompanied them.

They traveled from Yasnaya Polyana to the Tula station in a carriage drawn by a team through a sea of mud; there they took a private car—luxuriously furnished and containing individual sleeping compartments—to Sevastopol. People thronged the platforms at Kursk as the train made a brief stop, and at Kharkov the car was engulfed by a crowd of some three thousand. Well-wishers pressed in on all sides of Tolstoy's car, peering through the windows and crying out, "Tolstoy! Tolstoy!" He ordered all the blinds to be closed, and Sonya, speaking from a small platform at the rear of the train, told them Tolstoy was ill. When the train pulled out of the station, the crowds roared for him to appear at the window. He did. "Hurrah! Get well! . . . God protect you!" they shouted as they ran beside his car until they could no longer keep up with it.

A similar ovation greeted the Tolstoys in Sevastopol, where they disembarked to spend the night. The following morning they left in two carriages for Gaspra, and late that night they arrived at the mansion where they were to be guests. The warm air and the view from the upper veranda across the open sea softened Tolstoy's first disagreeable impression of the house with all its evidence of wealth, luxury, and gaudiness. Sonya set to work making it comfortable for her husband, little realizing that they would remain there for close to a year.

Maxim Gorky frequently visited Tolstoy at Gaspra. "He is like a God," Gorky observed, "not a Sabaoth or Olympian, but the kind of Russian god who 'sits on a maple throne under a golden lime tree,' not very majestic, but perhaps more cunning than all the other gods."

Tolstoy discussed religion at length with Gorky. Tolstoy talked "of literature little, as though literature was something alien to him," but "of women he [talked] readily and much, like a French novelist, but always with the coarseness of a Russian peasant." Gorky remarked that "woman, in my opinion, he regards with implacable hostility and loves to punish her."

During one theological debate, Tolstoy asked the younger writer, "Why don't you believe in God?"

"I have no faith, Lev Nikolaevich," Gorky replied.

"It is not true. By nature you are a believer, and you cannot get on without God. You will realize that someday."

Tolstoy's spiritual force did affect Gorky; he later recalled that during one of his visits "I, who do not believe in God, looked at him for some reason very cautiously and a little timidly, I looked and thought, 'The man is godlike.' "

But Sonya did not regard Tolstoy as a god. She loved him (and this was her great tragedy) as a man. Though she thoroughly enjoyed Tolstoy's reflected glory, she was not able to ignore his faults. Her devotion to him during his long illness at Gaspra was indefatigable. She was the closest to him and bore the brunt of his impatience and bad humor. She was torn by love and tenderness for him on one hand and by regret for what her devotion had cost her on the other. "I have lived with him for forty years. For everyone else he is a celebrity, for me he is all my being," she wrote in her diary in January 1902. Three weeks later, when Tolstoy had once again become gravely ill, she wrote, "Various advertisements of concerts, about the playing of certain compositions of S. I. [Taneyev] have agitated my very soul, and just as a famished person desires food, I suddenly and passionately want music and the music of Taneyev, which with its depths acts so powerfully on me."

As soon as her husband showed signs of recovering, Sonya made a short visit to Moscow and Yasnaya Polyana. Leaving in early April, she spent one day in the country and then went to the city, where she arranged a musical evening and Taneyev played "the slight things of Arenski, Schumann's sonata, and his own charming symphony." When she returned to Gaspra, she found Tolstoy gravely ill again, this time with typhoid fever. Miraculously he recovered almost immediately upon her return and within two weeks was writing and seeing guests. By June 25 he was well enough to leave Gaspra. Once home at Yasnaya Polyana, he began work on what was to be the last extensive artistic effort in his lifetime, *Hadji Murad*, which he did not finish until 1904 and which was published posthumously in 1911.

Sonya was pleased to see her husband at work on a novel, but she was going through great personal torment and confusion. "I *must* live, take care of my husband and children; I must not betray and show my madness, and I must not see that man with whom I am morbidly in love," she wrote in her diary that year. A few days later she gloried in her chaste love for her husband: "Tonight when I had covered him up and bade him good night, he tenderly stroked my cheek as though I were a child, and I rejoiced at his paternal love." Another night she entered his bedroom and at his request massaged his stomach, which was giving him great discomfort. "His thin, ancient limbs look pitiful," she observed.

Sonya was wrestling with her own spiritual problems. While correcting the proofs for a new edition of *Anna Karenina*, she wrote that she

followed step by step the state of her soul, and I understood myself and felt terrible. But people do not deprive themselves of life in order to *avenge themselves* on someone; no, they commit suicide because they *no longer have the strength to love.* At first a struggle, then prayer, then submissiveness, then despair, and at last, helplessness and death; and then I suddenly imagined Lev Nikolaevich weeping an old man's tears and saying that no one saw what had taken place in me and that no one had helped me. But what help is there? Let S. I. [Taneyev] come or invite him, and help me establish the friendly calm relations of old age with him. So that the faults of my feeling should not weigh on me and should be *forgiven* me.

Spiritual matters were not all that was occupying Sonya's thoughts. On January 8, 1904, she wrote in her diary, "Three students from St. Petersburg Institute of Mines arrived with a message [from Vladimir G. Korolenko, a well-known revolutionary author]. I talked a great deal with them; they are intelligent people, but as with all our youths nowadays, they do not know where to apply their strength."

The Tolstoys lived in relative ease and freedom, Tolstoy's fame saving him from the increasingly repressive policies of Nicholas's government. The Tsar and his ministers were determined to stem the rising tide of revolutionary sentiment; in Russia itself many groups and individuals (among them the young lawyer Alexander Feodorovich Kerensky) were working for the complete reformation of Russian society, and abroad bands of exiled revolutionaries (notably Lenin's London-based Bolsheviks) were calling for the overthrow of the Tsarist regime. Perhaps hoping to unite his subjects in a patriotic cause, in February 1904 Nicholas entered into a war with Japan for control of Korea.

The Russian people rallied behind Nicholas, and in March 1904 Sonya wrote in her diary, "In the quiet of our village this war is exciting and interesting to everyone. The general exaltation of spirit and sympathy with the Tsar is remarkable." But as the war progressed, revolutionary disturbances became more frequent and more serious. The anti-Semitic minister of the interior, Vyacheslav Plehve, was assassinated by terrorists, and there were peasant uprisings, mass army defections, and student riots. All this anti-government activity culminated on January 22, 1905, a bitter cold day on which 120,000 St. Petersburg workers, led by a youthful priest, Father Georgi Gapon, marched peacefully toward the Winter Palace. They intended to hand Nicholas a petition asking for basic reforms. Singing hymns and carrying crosses, icons, religious banners, flags, and portraits of the Tsar, the throngs moved toward the center of the city; but they found the bridges and boulevards blocked by the infantry, Cossacks, and hussars. As Father Gapon led his peaceful marchers onward, the soldiers suddenly opened fire, shooting directly into the advancing crowds. With cries of horror, men, women, and small children fell bloodied to the hard-packed ice and snow. Hundreds died; hundreds more were severely injured.

Gapon, in hiding after a narrow escape from the Cossacks, issued a public statement: "Nicholas Romanov, formerly Tsar and at present soul-murderer of the Russian empire. The innocent blood of workers, their wives, and children is forever between you and the Russian people. . . . May all the blood which must be spilled fall upon you, you Hangman!" Gapon had become a revolutionary, and the day of the slaughter became known as "Bloody Sunday."

On August 12, 1904, the youthful Nicholas had written in his diary of one happy event during this dark time. "A great never-to-be-forgotten day when the mercy of God, has visited us so clearly. Alix gave birth to a son at one o'clock. The child has been called Alexis." Cannons roared, church bells rang out, and the royal family were in a state of high jubilation over the birth of an heir. Six weeks later, however, the child began to hemorrhage, and he lay close to death until the bleeding was finally staunched. The doctors confirmed the royal couple's most dread fear—the tiny Tsarevich was a hemophiliac. His illness, which was hidden from all but the intimate family, would be an important factor in the downfall of the Romanov dynasty.

The only one of Sonya's sons to see service in the Russo-Japanese War was Andreyusha. In January 1899 Andrey had married Countess Olga Dieterichs, Chertkov's sister-in-law, but they had not been happy together. When the war broke out, he was in love with a married woman, and to his father's disgust and his mother's consternation, he decided to extricate himself from his difficulties by enlisting in the army. Leaving his wife and children, he set off for the eastern front; Sonya, young Lyova, and Misha accompanied him to Tambov, where he was to join a cavalry regiment as an aide-de-camp.

Pride rose in Sonya when she saw him in uniform: "The orderlies rode out on horseback, and my Andrey in the lead in a light sand-colored shirt, a cap of the same, and on his charming mare. It all made an imprint on my memory. The mare's legs bound round with some white material. Andreyusha's wonderful seat on horseback, and the words of an old woman. 'Your son sits a horse like a picture, it's as though he were at home in his own study.' "

But before he saw action, Andrey suffered a nervous collapse and was discharged. Refusing to return to his wife and children, he set up a bachelor household, with Timofei, his bastard half-brother, serving as his coachman.*

On March 21, 1904, the seemingly indomitable Alexandra Tolstoy died. She was eighty-six years old. Just a few months before her death Tolstoy had once more sought her help, asking her to obtain some research material. On December 29, 1903, she wrote him her last letter in their long and brilliant correspondence: "Dear Lev, whom I have loved so long, your tender, friendly letter was all the more gratifying to me because I felt in it that very, very sincere note which always rang out between us during the days of our youth. I was also pleased by your encouraging words in which we agree in thinking that even deep into old age it's possible to be of use to others."

Sonya was deeply grieved by Alexandra's death. That proud woman had been a good friend to her, perhaps the one woman she admired above all others. Tolstoy did not grieve; the closer he drew to death himself, the more urgently he asserted that after death an immortal something, a manifestation of God, lived on.

Then on August 23, 1904, Sergey Nikolaevich died after a long and excruciatingly painful battle with cancer of the tongue. "Seryozha is dead," Tolstoy wrote in his diary three days later. "Quietly, without consciousness, without any pronounced con-

---

* This difficult son continued to bring grief to the Tolstoys, and after the war they were horrified when he became a member of the Black Hundred, a right-wing anti-Semitic group which engaged in terrorist activities against members of minority and oppressed classes. From 1900 there is no mention or record of Timofei, who would have been forty-three at the time.

sciousness that he was dying. That is the mystery." With each year
the Tolstoys' intimate circle was growing smaller, but this did not
cause them to turn to each other. Sonya continued to see Taneyev;
Tolstoy's animosity toward the musician had cooled, and he had
grown less disturbed by their friendship. In the early autumn of
1904, however, Taneyev became distant and began to shut her out
of his life. In November they attended a concert in Moscow, and
during the intermission she pressed him about his inattentiveness;
much irritated, Taneyev left her to listen to the rest of the performance by herself. That night she wrote him a letter imploring and
then demanding that he explain his action. (This letter, never
found, was probably destroyed by Taneyev.) In his reply Taneyev
refused to justify himself or to continue their argument.

November 15, 1904

Esteemed Sonya Andreyevna,
     Kindly excuse me for failing to call on you today. The reason
for this is that I have not yet replied to your letter sent to me after
Nikish's concert, and have not given you the explanations which you
so insistently demanded. As I have not yet expressed my opinion on
the questions raised by you, I do not consider it proper or right to be
your guest. This had not occurred to me at the concert last night, but
on my return home it became quite clear to me. To justify my delay
I can say that as soon as I received your letter I began to put down
explanations in writing, but having heard from you that you do not
wish the letter to be addressed either to your address in Moscow or
to Yasnaya Polyana, I then refrained from continuing. At present I
definitely cannot resume my letter for lack of time. I beg you once
more to accept my apologies and my assurances of profound respect,
and my readiness to be of service to you.

S. Taneyev

     Two days later, apparently after receiving another letter from
Sonya, Taneyev answered:

Esteemed Sonya Andreyevna,
     If it had been only a matter of explaining why I left the hall
during the interval and why, during the next part, I gave up my seat
to somebody else, it would be easy for me to reply by, say, pointing
out that everybody present at a concert can enjoy the unrestrained

right of giving up his seat as well as leaving a hall in the interval. However, the questions raised by you in your letter involved such a number of facts, relationships, and misunderstandings to make me incompetent to act as you wish and give you simple explanations, verbal or in writing. I feel it would be a real task which would require time to weigh and to think over every expression and every word. At present, however, for various reasons—including material ones—I cannot interrupt the work I am engaged upon for several days. Therefore, I again beg you to excuse me and to accept the assurance of profound respect from your sincerely devoted,

S. Taneyev

Sonya was a handsome woman with a dazzling smile, a girlishly smooth complexion, and an imperious bearing. But her dark hair was turning silver, and she had grown rather plump; she was sixty and was terrified of old age. Like Anna Stepanovna and her fictional counterpart, Anna Karenina, Sonya was desperately afraid that the man to whom she was so attached no longer found her interesting and had deserted her for a younger woman. In truth, Taneyev preferred the company of young men like his brilliant pupil Alexander Scriabin and Sonya's son Seryozha. Perhaps fearing that she was trying to press him into a physical affair, Taneyev had little choice but to break off friendship with Sonya.

After their quarrel, Sonya saw very little of Taneyev, and she felt this loss keenly. Giving up the study of the piano, she devoted herself to photography and painting. Her room, which had once been scented by expensive powders and perfumes, was now permeated by the acrid odor of paint pots and photographic chemicals. Brief descents into deep depression and flights of "madness" began to occur more frequently, and she turned to the only "child" left in the family—the twenty-year-old Sasha, who was an awkward, mannish young woman. But Sasha was obsessively devoted to her father and had little pity or compassion for her mother.

The Russo-Japanese War ended a year after it had begun. Although the Russians had technically won the war, little was gained, and the price paid for this "victory" was high. The horror of Bloody Sunday was not forgotten, and the intense civil strife of 1905 ultimately culminated in the Russian Revolution. In October 1905 a widespread strike closed down the railroad, mail, and telegraph systems throughout Russia. There was fighting in the streets of Moscow, and provisional governments were established in many small towns. The strike was settled on October 17 when the Tsar issued a manifesto granting amnesty, guaranteeing personal liberty, and establishing an elected assembly. But the Tsar's promises were soon seen to be empty, and the jubilation which had greeted the proclamation soured into rebellious outrage. The revolutionaries took to the streets. In Moscow and St. Petersburg students spent their last kopecks for revolvers, and for many months there was chaos and terror all through Russia.

Tolstoy, the aged prophet, could not speak to this new world. After Bloody Sunday, his disciples had begun falling away; his power over the Russian people was on the wane. Non-resistance in the face of the Cossacks' bayonets and bullets was not feasible, and Tolstoyans quickly entered the ranks of radical revolutionists. The exiled Biryukov wrote to him stating that the people no longer wanted Tolstoy's religious writings and urging that he return to his great artistic work to remind the people "that it is Tolstoy who speaks to them." But Tolstoy, doggedly refusing to modify his philosophy, continued to write his polemical articles.

Strikes and insurrection broke out in Moscow in December 1905, and the repercussions were felt even in isolated Yasnaya Polyana. Neighboring houses were burned down by peasants, and several landowners were murdered. Strikes immobilized nearby Tula. Sonya was terrified, but Tolstoy, though grieved by the acts of violence, calmly and politely greeted the correspondents from all over the world who had rushed to Yasnaya Polyana to seek his comments on the events.

In the beginning of 1906 Sonya invited Taneyev to Yasnaya Polyana for the first time in nine years. It was an indifferent visit, marked by a rather distant politeness on both sides. Two weeks later, while Sonya was in Moscow, she went to Taneyev's home to give him an album containing the photographs she had taken of him years before. "We were both restrained and unnatural," she wrote after this meeting. Their friendship was finally at an end.

On Sonya's return to Yasnaya Polyana she learned that Chertkov had been allowed to make a brief trip to Russia to visit his aged mother. He arrived at Yasnaya Polyana on August 24 in an extraordinarily gregarious and gay mood. Making a special effort to charm

Sonya, he saved his most amusing anecdotes for her. Her deep distrust of him remained unchanged, however, and even Sasha was disturbed by his mercurial nature. "If anyone disagreed with him, deep furrows would appear on his forehead," Sasha later recalled. "His large gray eyes would flash and his whole face assume a baleful expression. He could not tolerate opposition. His social manner and humor, his stubbornness and despotic ways, the boldness and the narrowness of his views, the impatience of a sectarian —all combined to make him strange and difficult."

Chertkov's visit brought a new strain between Sonya and Tolstoy, one that might have caused a permanent estrangement. But in September Sonya became seriously ill, experiencing severe pain in her lower abdomen. Dr. Snegiryov came from Moscow to examine her and discovered a large uterine tumor. An immediate operation was required, but Sonya was so weak that she could not be moved to a hospital. Deciding to perform the surgery in her bedroom, Snegiryov sent for his equipment and his assistants.

The more severe Sonya's pain and the closer she felt to death, the quieter, the gentler she became. She made every effort to save her family from hearing her groan or cry out. When Tolstoy came to her bedside, she feebly took his hand, kissed it, and softly said, "Lyovochka, forgive me, forgive me."

"Sashenka darling, thank you," Sonya whispered when her daughter did anything for her, and Sasha was moved by a sudden deep love for her mother. "I was ready to exert myself to the utmost to help her, to save her," Sasha later wrote. "I looked into her beautiful eyes, so helpless and full of suffering and all the corroding antipathy, even hatred, I had sometimes felt seemed like a faraway nightmare."

Just before the surgery, Sonya asked to see the priest, and Tolstoy not only agreed to her request but went to fetch him as well. While the operation was being performed, Tolstoy was unable to bear the wait and walked out into the woods. Hours later, when the procedure was over and there was hope that Sonya would survive, Ilya and Sasha went in search of their father. When they found him, he asked them to let him remain alone where he was for a time. He later wrote in his diary, "Sonya has just been operated on. They say it was successful. But it was grave. This morning she was in a good spiritual state. How [near] death can bring conciliation!"

Sasha sensed that her father had not wanted the physicians "to obstruct the natural course of her illness, to obstruct the will of God." She felt her father believed that in dying Sonya would have found her redemption and her resurrection.

A few weeks later Masha and her husband came home to Yasnaya Polyana to spend the winter with the recuperating Sonya. The last years had been extraordinarily hard for Masha; her marriage was disappointing, and her health had been broken by several pregnancies which had ended in stillbirths. November was damp, cold, and windy; and at the end of the month Masha fell ill with pneumonia. For eight days she lay near death in the vaulted room in which her mother had slept in 1862, during her first visit to Yasnaya Polyana. She grew weaker with each day but never lost consciousness. Tolstoy sat vigil by her side, and an hour before she died she opened her eyes wide, saw her father, and laid his hand on her breast. He leaned close and raised her "thin, transparent hand to his lips. 'I am dying,' she whispered almost inaudibly." Sonya stood by the window; Tanya, who had rushed to join her troubled family, was beside her; Masha's husband, Kulasha, sat on the edge of her bed; and Sasha stood in the doorway. Silently they all waited with Masha until death came at one A.M. Tolstoy then left the room before the others.

"Masha is dead," he wrote in his diary. "Strange, I feel neither any horror, nor fear, nor any consciousness that something out of the ordinary has occurred, not even any pity or pain. . . . I watched her all the while she was dying: it was so amazingly calm. For me she was a being in a state of revelation, preceding my own revelation."

Masha was carried through the village as Aunt Toinette had been, and every peasant in Yasnaya Polyana came forward to say a prayer for her. She was buried beside little Nikolenka and Petya and the hour-old Varya. At the graveside Sonya leaned heavily against Tolstoy, seeking his support, but he stiffly moved away to stand alone. Tanya gave her mother her arm, and as the family left the cemetery Sasha quickly stepped to her father's side. Silently, without hesitation, he put his arm through hers and they left the graveyard together.

24

On his return to Russia in June 1908, Chertkov bought a farm close to Yasnaya Polyana and began construction of a house to accommodate his growing staff and entourage. Tolstoyism was now a vast international business, and Chertkov, who saw himself as "heir apparent," had his own court to assist him in this enterprise. He paid his workers high wages, which were drawn from the profits of Tolstoy's writings; dedicated, selfless Tolstoyans had become a disappearing breed.

Sonya knew that she represented the only threat to Chertkov's eventual accession to the "throne," and this knowledge filled her with great foreboding. It seemed clear that Chertkov was bent on winning control over the master's writings, personal papers, translations, letters, and diaries upon Tolstoy's death. His retinue grew quickly and soon included over thirty people—from farm workers and domestics, to typists and secretaries—"who were always mysteriously busy with copying Tolstoy's manuscripts and working on the seemingly endless 'Vault' of his thoughts." All of these people ate together at a long table, helping themselves directly from the vessels in which the food had been prepared. Tolstoyan brotherhood seemed to stop at that point, however, for according to Sasha, "Chertkov sat at the head of the table, flanked by his semi-invalid wife and F. A. Strakhov, a devoted follower and director under Chertkov of the compilation of the Vault. The middle section of the table was occupied by the skilled assistants, and the lower end by the common laborers." This division of the table into three distinct classes was emphasized by the higher quality and greater variety of foods served at the head of the table. On her first visit to the Chertkovs, Sasha was shocked to hear members of the entourage refer to these three groups as "first, second, and third class."

She also overheard an exchange between two of Chertkov's stable boys. After the first remarked, "Look, look, Alyosha is trying to squeeze into the first class," the second answered, "Well, he likes rice cakes and jam and stewed fruit! I guess he's tired of boiled potatoes and sunflower oil!"

Chertkov's proximity to Yasnaya Polyana was not all Sonya had to tolerate. He seldom left her alone with her husband during the day or evening. If he was not on hand himself, one of his secretaries or a trusted Tolstoyan was. He read every word Tolstoy wrote, sometimes demanding changes, to which Tolstoy almost always agreed. He followed him around with a notebook and took down any comment or conversation he deemed significant. Once or twice a week Chertkov brought in an English photographer to record Tolstoy's encounters with noted visitors and to capture him in various attitudes and settings (walking by the Voronka, on horseback, in the fields, and so on). These photographs were added to the large collection which was already in the Vault.

Since Tolstoy's excommunication in 1901, Sonya had spent most of each year at Yasnaya Polyana. She was writing again and was working on a memoir entitled *My Life* and on a series of children's stories for her beloved grandchildren. She had her own secretary—Varvara M. (Varya) Feokritova, a spirited, bright young woman who typed Sonya's work and helped with the account books. Tolstoy also had a secretary, Nikolai N. Gusev, a Tolstoyan and a close associate of Chertkov. At night Tolstoy locked himself in his room to shut out Sonya and temptation; and Gusev, who slept in a small office near to his bedroom, was expected to help him remain chaste. If Tolstoy was restless during the night, his secretary had to rise and sit with him.

Of all the members of the Tolstoy family, Sasha was the closest to her father, but she was intensely jealous of Gusev's privileged position. "Sometimes I had my dreams," she later recalled. "My father and I would have a tiny house in the village. Father would work in the mornings while I would do the housework, clean, wash, cook; we would have a vegetable garden, one cow, several chickens. In the evenings I would copy [his] manuscripts. But what then would become of Mother? . . . She would settle down next door, with physicians, menservants, maids."

At twenty-four, Sasha should have been thinking about young

men and marriage. Instead she turned to her father. They took long walks in the woods and played with her irrepressible black poodle. Tolstoy confided in Sasha, and she still did much copying for him. He repeatedly told her that it was fortunate she was unattractive to men, that her homeliness had saved her from a terrible fate, and Sasha believed him. He dwelt at gloomy length on the problems in her sisters' marriages and on the difficulties that they had experienced during pregnancy and childbirth. "To marry ever in my life? I thought with a shudder," Sasha said many years later. "Never, not for anything in the world."

Sonya saw what was happening and was tormented by jealousy, anger, and horror. Sasha was taking her place, but although this was hard to accept, she had faced the same problem with Masha. She was far more disturbed at seeing her daughter defeminized by Tolstoy's egotistic possessiveness. Sasha might not have been a beauty, but she did have a happy disposition, merry eyes, a quick mind, great energy, and intense loyalty. The young woman was certain to make an exemplary wife and mother if only Tolstoy would loosen his hold on her. Sonya worried greatly about what would happen to her daughter when Tolstoy died. Since Sasha did not embrace the orthodox faith, she certainly would not become a nun like her Aunt Marya Nikolaevna. Sonya foresaw little happiness for this awkward daughter who mimicked her father's loping gait, adopted a masculine stance, and disdained all things feminine. She argued bitterly with Tolstoy over Sasha, but he dismissed her demand that he depend less on Sasha as a further sign of her irrational jealousy and "degrading madness."

Sasha overheard many of these quarrels. Her resentment of Sonya, so painfully mixed with flashes of compassion for her mother, created great chaos in the young woman. For most of her life she would blame her mother for causing her father pain and for trying to come between Tolstoy and her. Only as an elderly woman did she begin to understand the truth; in a great surge of guilt, she tried to suppress the autobiographical books she had written early in her life. These works, with their derogatory portrayals of Sonya, were used as reference material for innumerable biographies of Tolstoy, and Sasha came to regret deeply the damage she had done to her mother. Looking back, she believed that most of her writings about Sonya were written in a spirit of hostility rather than of fair-mindedness.

On July 2, 1908, Tolstoy began a "secret diary." Years before, he had given Chertkov a reluctant promise that he could have access to his diaries, and Chertkov had been in the habit of making copies of these journals. But now, with his disciple a daily visitor, Tolstoy found that this practice inhibited his candor. Still he was loath to go back on his word to Chertkov. To extricate himself from a trying situation, Tolstoy started a second diary and hid it in his bedroom. For sixteen days he maintained this private journal. In August, however, he became seriously ill, and fearful that he might die, he sent Chertkov the secret diary, telling him to destroy it after copying whatever material he thought worth preserving.

The diary covered a period during which Tolstoy was suffering from a "bad feeling," the phrase he used for sexual desire. He would be eighty on August 28 and his health was poor, yet he continued to experience the lustful urges that he so detested. On July 9 in his secret diary (according to Chertkov's transcription) he wrote:

All are writing my biography, and in my whole biography there will be nothing about my connection with the 7th Commandment (Thou shalt not kill). Nor will there be all the terrible filth of masturbation and worse, from my 13th and 14th year to the 15th, 16th (I do not remember when I began my debauchery in the brothels). And so up to my union with the peasant girl Axinia—she is alive. Then marriage, in which once more, though I never betrayed my wife, there was lust in my relations with her—nasty and criminal lust. There will be none of this and all the more important, since at least of all the vices this is the one of which I am the most conscious, the vice which more than all others compels recovery.

He confided in Sasha that he had a secret diary, but he neither showed it to her nor told her that he had sent it to Chertkov. Sonya, although she knew nothing of this clandestine journal, was alarmed by Chertkov's almost daily visits to Tolstoy's study. Each time he emerged, he carried away folders stuffed with personal papers and manuscripts. Afraid that her husband was growing senile, she believed that he might not be able to comprehend or resist his disciple's machinations. Sonya was certain that on Tolstoy's death Chertkov intended to publish and profit from whatever writings were then in his possession. Included in the papers Chertkov had taken were some highly salable works of fiction (such as *Hadji Murad*) which Tolstoy had written during the past twenty years but had refused to publish. Confirming her worst fears, Chertkov and Gusev ardently supported Tolstoy's long-standing wish that all his writings pass into the public domain. This meant that they felt (and Tolstoy agreed) that Sonya should surrender the rights she held to the works he had written before 1881 and should renounce any rights in the works that were unpublished at his death.

Violent quarrels on this subject were frequent and bitter throughout the autumn and winter of 1908. Chertkov was often present, taking down everything in his notebook (which he later published). One argument which he recorded occurred on December 4, 1908:

Sonya Andreyevna, turning to Lev Nikolaevich, irately asserts that the property rights of all his written, unpublished works belong to the family. Lev Nikolaevich objects. She runs to her room and fetches a pocket diary written in her hand and reads her own record to the effect that Lev Nikolaevich had given as public property only those writings which had appeared in print during his lifetime (and after 1881). Lev Nikolaevich begins to object. She shouts him down. Finally in a resolute, authoritative tone, he obliges her to hear him. (She had just said that she was not concerned about herself, but that her children would assert their own claims.) Lev Nikolaevich: "You imagine that our children are like rogues who want me to do something opposed to that which is most dear to me." Sonya Andreyevna: "Well, as for being rogues, I do not know, but . . ." Lev Nikolaevich (firmly): "No, let me finish speaking. According to you it appears that the children will play the dirtiest trick possible on me. And a dirtier trick it is impossible to play. You know the principles for which I've renounced these rights—the principles of my faith, and what do you wish, that these principles should be turned into hypocrisy? I gave you my fortune, I gave you my early writings, and now it seems that I ought to give my own life—that for which I live. Yet I daily receive abusive letters, accusing me of hypocrisy. And now that you desire that in very fact I should become a hypocrite and a scoundrel. It is astonishing how you torment yourself without any need." And he left the room, firmly closing the door behind him.

Yasnaya Polyana became a divided and embattled household. Ilya, Misha, Lev, and Andreyusha stood staunchly behind their mother. Sasha was militant in her support of her father and was a strong ally of Chertkov, the Tolstoyan secretaries, and Tolstoy's physician, Dr. Makovitsky, who now lived at Yasnaya Polyana. Tanya and Seryozha attempted to maintain a position of neutrality, always trying to reconcile their parents' differences.

In March 1909 Chertkov was forced by the government to leave Tula province because of "subversive activities." Sonya was greatly relieved to be rid of her adversary, but Tolstoy languished in loneliness. "I miss Chertkov," he wrote in his diary on April 15. Worried by his listlessness, she suggested that they visit their daughter Tanya and her husband at Kochety in Orel province. But as she set off with Tolstoy, Dr. Makovitsky, Gusev, and the cook, old Semyon Nikolaevich, she did not know that Chertkov had taken a small house in Suvorovo, almost within walking distance of Kochety. A few days after their arrival Sonya left her husband with the Sukhotins and returned to Yasnaya Polyana. Soon learning that Chertkov was nearby, Tolstoy mounted a horse and rode alone to meet his friend. "Radiant meeting," he commented in his diary and then wrote Sonya that he was extending his stay at Kochety. A month later he arrived back at Yasnaya Polyana in much improved spirits. Chertkov's company always seemed to act as a tonic for him. Tolstoy believed that a good and faithful wife should give her husband unquestioning respect and devotion, but he found these qualities in Chertkov, not in Sonya. His disciple recognized his wisdom in all matters, bowed to his word, never opposed him. The truth seems to be that Chertkov possessed a great talent for getting what he wanted through charm, flattery, cleverness, and duplicity.

During their happy rides and walks and warm talks in the Orel, Chertkov had subtly urged Tolstoy to draw up a secret will which would protect his works from Sonya's "moneymaking schemes." Chertkov bemoaned the compromise that had granted her the copyrights on Tolstoy's early and most widely read works.

Suggesting that Tolstoy's agreement with Sonya had not been
legal, he implied that a new will would ensure that the master's
wishes would be carried out after his death. If Tolstoy named an
executor who shared his beliefs, he would be certain that all of his
writings would move into the public domain. Chertkov did not
suggest he be chosen executor and Sonya be cut out, but the impli-
cation was slyly, cleverly made, and Tolstoy was most receptive.

During the summer of 1909 Sonya was driven to near madness
by her sense that Chertkov had initiated an evil scheme to supplant
and impoverish her. She appealed desperately to Tolstoy to help
her protect her rights, to give her a power of attorney to prosecute
anyone who published his early work without permission. He was
resolute in his refusal. Sonya grew increasingly hysterical and
paranoiac. She tried talking to Sasha, aware that her daughter was
keeping something from her. Sasha, indeed, was secretly planning
to go with her father to visit Chertkov, who was now living near
Moscow at Kryokshino, and discuss a new will. She was coolly
evasive with her mother. Sonya threatened to kill herself, wept,
shouted, and ran from the house, but these acts only caused more
quarrels, more hostility. Tolstoy, who was also profoundly disturbed, roamed through the house with a gun threatening to shoot
himself.

In July Tolstoy was invited to participate in the Eighteenth
International Congress of Peace in Stockholm. Such honors had
always been ignored in the past, but he saw this particular one as
an opportunity to deliver an address accusing the "Peace" Congress
of dishonesty and demanding the abolition of all armies, and he set
to work on a speech. Sonya was enraged at what Tolstoy planned
to do and raised numerous objections to his attending—his age, the
sea voyage, an epidemic of cholera in St. Petersburg, a city through
which he would have to travel. When he listened to none of those
arguments, she grew distraught. On July 26 Tolstoy wrote in his
diary, "After dinner I discussed the journey to Sweden, and it
provoked terrible hysterical exasperation. She wanted to poison
herself with morphine; I snatched it out of her hand and threw it
under the stairs. I struggled with myself. But when I lay down and
quietly thought it all over, I decided to give up the trip. I went and
told her. She was a sorry sight and I pitied her."

The next day Sonya suddenly decided to travel to Stockholm

herself and read his address to the Congress. Although he did not take this plan seriously, Tolstoy commented that as a woman and his wife she would at least be received in a more genteel manner then he would be. Sonya seemed preoccupied and vague. "For this one occasion one must be well dressed," she said, insisting that her secretary leave that night for Moscow to buy her some proper clothes. On the following day, however, the Congress announced that its meeting would be postponed for a year because of a general strike in Sweden.

Sonya's obsession with the trip to Sweden quickly passed, but her mental condition continued to deteriorate. Age had dimmed her beauty, and Chertkov was undermining her position; she felt entirely exposed, unprotected, alone. Everyone around her—her husband, Sasha, Makovitsky, Gusev, even her secretary, who was now doing work for Chertkov and had been won over by him—was set in a conspiracy against her. Those who could have helped —her older daughter, her five sons, her sister Tanya—were never there when she needed them. At times she dressed with infinite care, coiffed her hair becomingly, and smiled indulgently as she made her way past the hated "dark ones," her back straight and her chin raised. She was often, however, seized by terror and hysteria. Strands of gray hair fluttered about her face, and her dark eyes were red and swollen from weeping. During these times she would take no interest in her clothing, and her hand would tremble as she raised it to her throat—a frequent gesture, for emotional stress gave her a choking sensation. Sonya's mental illness was certainly exacerbated by Tolstoy's refusal to confirm her rights to his works. He knew that she was not driven by greed but by pride. By denying her rights to his work, he denied her importance and denied her conviction that as his wife she held a position of special dignity and prestige.

During this difficult summer Yasnaya Polyana was overrun by the "dark people" who had always been her nemeses, and the countryside was populated with revolutionary youths. But despite her illness Sonya continued to run her house in the "grand manner." The table was always set in fine style, the waiters wore their white cotton gloves, and tea was served from a silver samovar.

On August 5, 1909, the local police came to Yasnaya Polyana and, while the members of the household looked on numbly, arrested Gusev for distributing "revolutionary books" (that is, works by Tolstoy). While Tolstoy stood with tears in his eyes, his aged sister, Marya Nikolaevna, swathed in her nun's habit, spat through the window at the police escort which took Gusev away. Sonya was trembling and pale; she did not fear for Gusev, but she was terrified that the police might next move against Tolstoy himself.

Chertkov's Machiavellian designs were now beginning to take shape. On September 3 Tolstoy, accompanied by Sasha, Dr. Makovitsky, and a family servant, set off to visit Chertkov in Kryokshino. Sonya was discouraged from coming with them, and was lied to about the purpose of the journey. Tolstoy wanted to discuss a new will with Chertkov, one that would leave Sonya with no power over his writings. Both Tolstoy and Sasha fervently believed that Sonya's publications were an exploitation of his work, while Chertkov's were the "fulfillment of a sacred duty to God and man." (Ironically, however, Sasha would later be gravely dissatisfied with Chertkov's management of Tolstoy's literary estate and would accuse him of taking the lion's share of the profits for himself.)

Tolstoy had not been in Moscow in a number of years. To his surprise the terminal was thronged with cheering people, and as Chertkov and a delegation from *Intermediary* greeted him, film photographers surrounded them and then followed with their cameras onto the street. After a short stay at his old home on Dolgo-Khamovnicheski Street, he and his party boarded a third-class railway carriage for the hour-long journey to Chertkov's estate. Tolstoy did not approve wholeheartedly of Chertkov's lifestyle; nevertheless he was in high spirits as "loyal followers who accepted his every word as law and reverenced him as a living saint among sinning mankind" surrounded him.

When Sonya saw the newspaper photographs of Tolstoy and Chertkov, she became wildly jealous. Quickly packing her cases, she took the train to join Tolstoy. She suspected that a conspiracy was afoot, and once at Kryokshino she did not allow Chertkov or Sasha a moment alone with Tolstoy. Chertkov was most unpleasant, and Sonya demanded that Tolstoy return with her to Yasnaya Polyana. When he refused, she became frenzied. Seeing no other way to calm her, Tolstoy grudgingly agreed to leave with her the following day. Her victory had exhausted her, and she spent the

rest of the afternoon in her room, thus giving Tolstoy and Chertkov an opportunity to be alone. With Chertkov's consultation, he
drafted a new will, which Sasha copied. In it he once again waived
all rights to his works, while confirming Sonya's control of the
rights to his pre-1881 writings. He also named Chertkov sole executor of his literary estate. Unable to betray Sonya completely,
Tolstoy had compromised. He and three witnesses signed the document. Chertkov kept a copy and Sasha was asked to have an
attorney in Moscow certify that it was valid.

In Moscow the Tolstoys and Sasha stayed with Seryozha (who
had recently remarried) and his wife. Crowds and photographers
followed them everywhere. The next day Sasha slipped out to see
the attorney; he read the will carefully and to her disappointment
declared that it was not valid. The rights to literary works could
not be left to a "non-specific" *everyone*. A new will would have to
be drawn up giving the names of specific heirs, and Sonya would
be deceived for a second time.

> The next morning [Sasha recalled] we left the house in a landau
> drawn by a pair of horses. Father, Mother, and I. (Chertkov would
> join us on the train and accompany us as far as Serpukhovo.) But we
> were unable to drive up to the Kursk station because thousands of
> people crammed the square, waiting for Father. The carriage was
> stopped, a sea of heads engulfed us, heads were bared. Maklakov [an
> old friend of her sister Tanya] met us and we started to walk toward
> the entrance of the station. The students made a chain but the crowd
> broke through. At the entrance we were so crushed we could not
> breathe. Even my broad shoulders were powerless to protect Father.
> Maklakov and a huge policeman came to our aid. The crowd actually
> carried us or pushed us out to the platform. Here people were hang-
> ing on the posts, scrambling over the tops of cars. . . . Father was
> white as a sheet and his lower jaw was trembling as he stood bowing
> to the cheering crowd. The train pulled out. Father lay down, in-
> tending to nap, but we soon realized he had fainted in his sleep. His
> pulse was so weak that we thought he was dying.

At Yasenki, Tolstoy was carried unconscious from the train
and was taken by automobile (a new acquisition of the Tolstoys) to
Yasnaya Polyana. He remained in an incoherent state that entire

evening. Sonya roamed back and forth through the house, up and down the stairs, sobbing and muttering and wailing. Rushing to his side, she cried, "Lyovochka, Lyovochka, where are the keys?"

"I don't understand. . . . What for?" he mumbled.

"The keys, the keys to the drawer with the manuscripts!"

"Mama," Sasha begged, "please let him be, don't make him force his memory. . . . Please!"

"But I have to have the keys," she said excitedly. "He will die and the manuscripts will be stolen."

"No one will steal them. Let him be, I implore you."

Dr. Makovitsky and Sasha got Tolstoy into bed; the doctor gave him an injection to help him sleep, and Sonya put several hot water bottles at his feet. By morning Tolstoy had recovered and once again turned his attention to the business of his will. The lawyer in Moscow was ordered to draft a new, valid will, and this document was signed, without Sonya's knowledge, on November 1, 1909. The works written after 1881 were now left to Sasha, Tanya, and Seryozha, with the proviso that they give them over for general use.

A few nights later, as her father was preparing for bed, Sasha passed his door. He called her in and said, "I wanted to say this about my testament: If any money is left over from the first edition of my works, it would be good to buy Yasnaya Polyana from Mama and your brothers and turn it over to the peasants."

Sasha promised to do this. This youngest daughter—the child Sonya had not wanted, the girl she had wished had died instead of her beloved Vanichka—would therefore come to hold Sonya's life in her palm. And this embittered daughter would not act kindly.

Sasha's implacable hostility toward her mother and the intensity with which she later besmirched Sonya's character speak of a kind of Elektra madness. Her mother had indeed inflicted many emotional wounds upon her when she was a young girl. It was her father, however, who dealt her the greatest blows by taking an injured, insecure child and using her pain to his advantage. Sasha's sacrifice of the worldly, her loss of a female life, satisfied some terrible quirky anger in him. For Tanya and Masha, the call of their sex had been in the end too strong and they had "deserted" him. But they had had a vital, dominant—albeit emotional— mother to turn to. Sonya was now ill, elderly, and often pathetically deranged; she could give Sasha little support and could not serve as a model for her daughter. But however damaged she was by her mother, Sasha was undone by Tolstoy's deeply ingrained hostility toward women. Gorky had written only a short time before, "There is nothing he likes so much as to punish them [women]. Is it the revenge of a man who has not achieved as much happiness as he is capable of, or the hostility of the spirit toward the 'humiliating impulses of the flesh?' Whatever it is, it is hostility, and very bitter."

Yasnaya Polyana was filled with dark intrigues and darker emotions, and Valentin Bulgakov, a young man who came there in January 1910 as Tolstoy's secretary, remarked that the household was "a sort of fortress, with secret meetings, parleys, and so forth." Although he was a staunch Tolstoyan and an acquaintance of Chertkov's, Sonya liked and trusted him. As everyone close to Tolstoy did, he kept a diary in which he recorded his meetings with and thoughts about the master. But while he revered Tolstoy as a prophet and teacher, Bulgakov, unlike most of the other disciples, was not blind to his personal failings. He sympathized with Sonya and was disturbed as her mental condition grew worse during the spring.

In early June, Tolstoy, accompanied by Bulgakov, Sasha, and Makovitsky, went to visit Tanya Sukhotin, and on June 19 he sent Sonya "the welcome news" that the authorities had granted Chertkov permission to return to Tula. Something snapped in Sonya when she received this letter. She ran through the house wildly, screaming, weeping inconsolably, mumbling to herself, and for three nights she paced the rooms in nervous agitation. On June 22 she dictated a telegram to Varya to send to Tolstoy. "Sonya Andreyevna intensely nervous attack, insomnia, weeping, pulse hundred, Varya." The secretary added the words "Asked me to telegraph," to tell Tolstoy that the message was from Sonya. Sasha convinced her father that Sonya was in all probability feigning illness, and Tolstoy sent a wire in which, making no mention of her illness, he told her that it was not convenient for him to return immediately.

Sonya opened the message and cried out to Varya, "Don't you see that this is Chertkov's expression, that he won't let him go.

They want to kill me, but I have some opium." She ran to a cupboard and seized a vial of opium and spirits of ammonia. Varya managed to take the poisonous drugs from Sonya and agreed to send another telegram: "Implore you to come home on the 23rd." Convinced that Sonya was indeed suicidal, she added, "I think it necessary."

Tolstoy and his small entourage arrived at Yasnaya Polyana late on the night of June 23. Sonya was too ill and weak to greet him, and he went to her room. She was pale, her hair in disarray, her eyes fearful, her manner distracted. She began to sob uncontrollably as soon as he entered the room. He sat by her bed holding her hand and for an hour and a half tried to calm her, but Sonya was overwrought and made little sense. He left and sent Sasha into her with the warning "For God's sake, be careful!" Sasha remained with her mother for only a few minutes and treated her like a badly behaved child, telling her she must get hold of herself for her father's sake.

Earlier in the evening Sonya had made an entry in her diary under the heading "Memorandum Before Death." After listing all her symptoms—"spasm in the throat, sharp pains in [the] heart, a migraine headache, an inability to stop weeping"—she went on: "Is it hysteria? a nervous stroke, or the beginning of insanity? . . . Let me confess the truth. I was wretched because of this long, unaccustomed separation from Lev Nikolaevich. He has a repulsive, senile love for Chertkov (in his youth he used to fall in love with men), and he is completely subject to his will and to his homosexual designs. [During 1908–10 she had frequently accused Chertkov of homosexuality.] I am insanely jealous of Lev Nikolaevich's intimacy with Chertkov; I feel that he has taken from me all that I have lived for during 48 years." Continuing in a less coherent fashion, she made complicated plans for poisoning herself; she described her coffin—"a rounded lid covered with rose-colored or white brocade"—and remarked, "How enormous my nose will seem as it sticks up in death." The entry closes with a hysterical "Quicker! Quicker! It will be too late. . . . I have drunk the opium. . . . He is coming."

She had not taken a poisonous dose, but her delusions and mad dreams suggest that Sonya was indeed taking opium and that she was under its fearful effects quite frequently during this period.

She even admitted to Goldenweiser that she feared that she was going out of her mind but that she could not control herself. She was obviously a seriously ill woman, but, except for Bulgakov, everyone at Yasnaya Polyana persisted in regarding her as simply an unreasonable shrew. Her sons and Tanya recognized the gravity of her illness, but they were only visitors at Yasnaya Polyana, and none of her sons had any influence with their father or Sasha.

On July 1 Chertkov made his first appearance at Yasnaya Polyana (he had been meeting Tolstoy elsewhere). Insisting that he speak to her alone, Sonya demanded that he return all of Tolstoy's diaries. Chertkov, who was no longer even polite to Sonya, accused her of planning to delete any entry that was not flattering to her or her family. "Are you afraid that I will *expose* you by means of the diaries of Lev Nikolaevich?" He sneered. "I have had it in my power for a long time, and I have sufficient influence to *smirch* you and your family, and if I did not do this, it is only out of affection for Lev Nikolaevich." Sonya became distraught, and Chertkov turned and left her, saying disdainfully, "If I had such a wife, I should long ago have shot myself or run away to America."

The battle over possession of Tolstoy's diaries went on at this intense level for two more weeks.

Bulgakov recognized Sonya's victimized position and watched as the spider's web tightened about her. "It is clear to me," he wrote in his diary, "that there are times when, as a sick and elderly woman, [Sonya] should be treated with more consideration than is shown by Chertkov and Alexandra Lvovna [Sasha]. Both . . . suffer from a sort of blindness in this regard. The former aims at the moral destruction of Tolstoy's wife in order to get control of his manuscripts. The latter is either in conspiracy with him or, with typical female antagonism toward the mother, devotes herself to the struggle as to a kind of sport." And it was not only Chertkov and Sasha with whom Sonya had to contend; her secretary, Varya, whom she considered a friend and confidante, was in league with Chertkov, reporting her every action and word to him and giving him copies of everything she wrote.

Sonya's behavior was increasingly disturbed, and there were frequent discussions among Sasha and Varya and Chertkov and Tolstoy of insanity (the artist Repin's decline into madness was much talked about). Young Lyova, who was at Yasnaya Polyana, was greatly sympathetic to his mother and angrily attacked his father for his callous attitude toward Sonya's illness. During one of their arguments Tolstoy stated, "I do not agree with the scientists' definition of mental illness, insanity. In my opinion insanity is the lack of receptivity to other people's ideas. An insane person holds with certitude only to what has taken root in his own mind. He will not understand me."

Sonya, in desperation, turned to Tolstoy and asked him to take the diaries away from Chertkov. Reminding him that the diaries contained intimate and detailed accounts of their forty-eight years of marriage, she argued with great emotion that he did not have the moral right to give them to an outsider. She insisted that Chertkov intended to publish the diaries in their entirety on Tolstoy's death, thus causing her and the children great pain. During one of these stormy scenes in July, Sonya threw herself to the floor of Tolstoy's balcony and refused to be helped up. She then ran out into the forest threatening to drown herself. Lyova went after her, begging her to return and trying to calm her. Finally he came back to the house and asked his father to go after her. Tolstoy refused, and Lyova, moved by fury, shouted at his father, demanding that he accept some responsibility for Sonya's condition. In the end Tolstoy agreed to try to bring her back; he returned an hour later with a subdued, docile Sonya leaning exhaustedly against his shoulder.

Quite unexpectedly, Sonya rose the next morning determined to pay a welcoming call on Chertkov's fashionable mother. She put on an elegant silk dress and with Bulgakov set out in a carriage. Halfway to Chertkov's estate, her mood changed and she started to weep. She begged Bulgakov to ask Chertkov to return the diaries. Over and over she repeated her request: "Tell him that if he will return them to me I shall be at peace. I shall be well disposed to him again, he can visit us as before, and we shall be of service to him, will you tell him this? Tell him for God's sake!"

Weeping and trembling, Sonya gazed imploringly at the young, vulnerable Bulgakov. Recognizing the woman's desperation and sincerity, and in this matter agreeing with her, he assured her he would talk to Chertkov. Sonya did not seem to hear him, and she repeated her plea over again. Bulgakov was filled with "feelings of deep compassion," and he spoke to her gently and promised again to do her bidding. This scene was repeated yet another time before they reached Chertkov's house, but Bulgakov never lost his patience. Then, as they turned onto the estate's drive, her trembling stopped and she managed a wistful smile. As Bulgakov helped her out of the carriage, she squeezed his hand, showing him she understood he was going to do as she had asked.

As soon as Sonya arrived, she was whisked away by two secretaries to meet Chertkov's mother, and Bulgakov joined Chertkov and his "indispensable adviser," Alexei Sergeyenko, in a small study. Chertkov and Bulgakov sat down on a "Tolstoyan cot, Sergeyenko, his face tense with curiosity, sat down in a chair opposite them."

> I began telling them about Sonya Andreyevna's request [Bulgakov wrote in his diary later that day]. Vladimir Gregorevich [Chertkov] became violently agitated.
>
> "Do you mean to say," he broke in, fixing his large, light-colored, restless eyes on me, "that you came straight out and told her where the diaries were?"
>
> And with these words, to my utter amazement, Vladimir Gregorevich made a hideous grimace and stuck out his tongue at me. I stared at him, suffering inwardly because of the preposterous position he had put me in. I did not know whether to feel humiliated for myself or to feel sorry for this man who was inflicting such humiliation on himself. . . . I braced myself and, ignoring his vagary, replied:
>
> "No, I could not tell her anything, because I do not know where the diaries are."
>
> "Oh, now that is wonderful!" exclaimed Chertkov, springing up from his seat. "Please go now," he said, opening the door to the corridor. . . .
>
> The door slammed behind me and I heard the lock click. I went into the corridor stunned by the reception shown me. . . . Later I learned that it had been decided not to return the diaries.

Told of Chertkov's refusal, Sonya grew despondent. For two days she stayed in her room and refused to eat. Tolstoy for the first time had true concern for her and decided to make concessions to calm her. In a letter, which Varya gave her, he wrote:

> (1) I will not give my current diary to anyone, but will keep it in my own possession.

(2) I will take my old diaries from Chertkov and keep them myself, probably in some bank.

(3) If you are troubled by the thought that those places in my diaries where I write under the impression of the moment concerning our disagreements and conflicts may be used by future biographers who are ill-disposed toward you, then, not to mention that such expressions of temporary feelings in both my diaries and yours cannot in any way give a true understanding of our real relations—if you fear this, I am glad of the opportunity to express in my diary, or, quite simply, even in this letter, my relationship to you and my evaluation of your life.

My attitude toward you and my estimation of you are this: just as I loved you in my youth, so I have never ceased loving you, and love you still, despite various reasons for coolness. The reasons for this coolness were, first, my withdrawing further and further from the interests of temporal life and my repugnance for them, whereas you neither would nor could relinquish them, not having in your soul those principles that led me to my convictions—which is very natural and for which I do not reproach you. That at first, and the second (forgive me if what I say is unpleasant for you, but what is now taking place between us is so important that one must not be afraid to speak out and to hear the whole truth), the second is that your disposition in recent years has become more and more irritable, despotic, and lacking in self-control. The manifestation of these traits of character could not but cool, not my feeling itself, but the expression of it. That is the second reason. The third and main reason was that fatal one for which neither of us is to blame—which is our absolutely contrary understanding of the meaning and purpose of life. Everything about our conception of life has been completely antithetical: the way of life, relations to people, even the means of living—property—which I consider an evil and you consider a necessary condition of life. I have submitted to a way of life which was difficult for me in order not to part from you, while you have taken this as a concession to your views, and the misunderstanding between us has grown greater and greater. There have been other reasons for my coolness, for which we have both been guilty, but I shall not speak of them now because they are beside the point. The point is that despite these misunderstandings, I have not ceased loving and esteeming you.

My estimation of your life is this: I, a debauched man, deeply depraved in the sexual sense and no longer in my first youth, married you, a pure, beautiful, clever eighteen-year-old girl, and, my vile, dissolute past notwithstanding, you have lived with me for almost fifty years, loving me, living a hard, industrious life, bearing children, nursing them, rearing them, caring for them and for me, and not succumbing to the temptations that might easily have enticed any other strong, healthy, beautiful woman in your position. You have lived in such a way that I have nothing to reproach you for. I do not, cannot, reproach you for failing to follow me in my unusual spiritual movement, for each man's spiritual life is a mystery between him and God, and no one can require anything different of him. And if I have made demands on you, then I was mistaken, and in this I am guilty.

So here you have a true description of my relation to you and my estimation of you. And as for what can be found in the diaries, I only know that nothing harsh, nothing that would be contrary to what I am now writing, will be found there.

So that is (3), concerning what might, but should not, trouble you about the diaries.

(4) is this: if at the present moment my relations with Chertkov are painful for you, I am prepared not to see him, although I can say that this will be harder for him than for me. But if it is what you want I will do it.

And now (5), which is that if you do not accept my conditions for a good, peaceful life, then I will retract my promise not to leave you. I will go away. I will go, but certainly not to Chertkov. I shall even set as an indispensable condition that he not come to live near me, but I shall leave without fail, because it is impossible to go on living as we are now.

Think it over calmly, dear friend, listen to your heart, be sensible of it, and you will decide everything as it should be. For my part, I will say that this is how I have decided everything, and that for me it *cannot, cannot* be otherwise. Stop torturing, not others, but yourself, my darling, for you are suffering one hundred times more than anyone else. That is all.

Lev Tolstoy

Morning, 14 July 1910

On Tolstoy's instructions, Sasha and Varya went to Chertkov's to repossess the diaries (there was a tall, heavy stack of them). Without her father's knowledge Sasha helped Chertkov, Sergeyenko, and Goldenweiser and his wife hastily copy any passages that Sasha thought her mother might destroy. Several hours later Chertkov, "standing on the porch . . . with mock solemnity, made the sign of the cross three times over [Sasha] with the packet of letters, and then handed them to her. It was not easy for him to part with them."

Sonya stood impatiently waiting on the veranda of Yasnaya Polyana as Sasha and Varya returned from their mission. She grabbed the large package with such vehemence that the diaries fell to the floor. Tanya, learning of her mother's trials, had hurried to Yasnaya Polyana, and that afternoon she and Sonya went to Tula together and deposited the controversial diaries in the state bank with instructions that they be given only to Tolstoy, or by his power of attorney to Tanya's husband, Sukhotin. Tanya was gravely concerned about her mother's mental state. Sonya did not seem to understand all that was said to her and appeared quite confused, and after a consultation with Tolstoy, it was agreed that two doctors, one the eminent psychiatrist G. I. Rossolimo, be asked to come from Moscow to examine her.

After spending several hours with Sonya, the doctors stated that she was in a state of nervous collapse and was suffering from severe depression caused by menopause. Characteristically, Tolstoy did not agree; both he and Sasha continued to believe that she was simply "torturing herself and everyone else" by acting badly. The doctors left, having done nothing to improve Sonya's condition. Less than a week later Chertkov visited Yasnaya Polyana, and on seeing him Sonya became rude and antagonistic. The family and guests gathered on the terrace for tea. "The samovar boiled cheerily on the table, the bowl of raspberries stood out like a bright red patch on the white tablecloth, but those sitting around the table looked as if they were serving a prison sentence and hardly touched their tea."

Sonya felt that "something awful and irreparable had just happened," and this conviction proved true. That morning Chertkov had dispatched three emissaries (Alexei Sergeyenko, Goldenweiser, and Anatol Radinsky, a good-looking youth to whom Chertkov was quite partial) with a new revised will for Tolstoy to sign. Sasha and Tolstoy met the three "witnesses" in the woods near the village of Grumond and there, sitting on the stump of a tree, Tolstoy signed a will that placed all his works (including those written before 1881) in the public domain. He also signed a separate document, drawn up by Chertkov, which made Sasha the nominal executrix but Chertkov the actual administrator of his literary estate.

It had been done. The act which Sonya had so dreaded had been committed. The literary rights to Tolstoy's early works which she had so violently fought to keep for herself and her family had been lost.

25

On September 23, 1910, the Tolstoys celebrated their forty-eighth wedding anniversary, and Tolstoy agreed to Sonya's request that Bulgakov photograph them together. Sasha was jealous and incensed. She did not want the world to see a picture of her mother (dressed in a white silk gown like a "vestal goddess") standing next to her father, her arm linked possessively through his. A recent incident had made her ill-will toward her mother even stronger. In one of her moments of distraction, Sonya had torn up two photographs in Tolstoy's study—one of Chertkov with Ilya, and the other of Sasha with Tolstoy—and had put portraits of herself and of Tolstoy's father in their place.

As she watched her parents being photographed together on the sunny lawn of Yasnaya Polyana, Sasha was seized by an intolerable rage. She ran into Varya's small office and, standing alone, almost howled with fury. Tolstoy entered the house and, hearing her raised voice, opened the door and asked, "Sasha, what are you shouting about?"

Sasha whipped around and, forgetting the deference she usually showed her father, raged that it was wrong of him to be photographed with her mother. It was wrong of him to promise Sonya that he would not be photographed with Chertkov again, and it was wrong "of him to sacrifice the interests of a friend and of a daughter for a brainless wife and to allow her to remove photographs from his study."

Tolstoy shook his head and said, "You're very like her!" He went to his study, and a few minutes later his gong sounded. He used this signal to call Sasha, but this time she refused to go to him. He struck the gong again, but still Sasha did not stir. Bulgakov was sent to fetch her, and she reluctantly followed him to Tolstoy's study, where her father told her he wanted to dictate a letter. Sasha stiffly took out her pad, but when she glanced up her father was sobbing, his head resting on the arm of his chair. "I don't want your shorthand!" he gasped. Beside herself, Sasha begged his forgiveness; she kissed his hands and then fell prostrate in tears at his feet. He finally forgave her, but this episode put great fear into Sasha's heart, causing more resentment toward her mother, whom she held responsible for her father's displeasure with her.

Sonya's suspicion that Tolstoy had signed a new will grew, as did her jealousy and hatred of Chertkov. Convinced that her husband was having an immoral affair with his disciple, she wrote Tolstoy a wildly incoherent letter. In it she accused him of homosexual acts and quoted a passage from his earliest diary in which he had discussed his love for men. She railed obsessively at him about this friendship. Insisting he stop writing to Chertkov, she wrote, "You are always carrying on a secret amatory correspondence." Whenever she saw him leaving the house alone, she followed him, certain that he was on his way to a rendezvous with Chertkov. Terrible dreams troubled Sonya, and one night she jumped from her bed sure that she heard Chertkov and Tolstoy making love in her room. Tolstoy was disturbed when she recounted these nightmares, but he was horrified by her demand that their marital relations be resumed. This last "indiscretion" on Sonya's part drove him to plot his escape from Yasnaya Polyana. Taking Sasha into his confidence, he told her to inform Chertkov of his plans.

On the night of October 27 Sonya was terribly restless. As she drifted in and out of sleep, dreadful images of Tolstoy and Chertkov engaged in the most base sexual acts tormented her. Thinking she heard Chertkov's high laugh, she went out into the hallway. The house was dark and silent; everyone was asleep. The fires were out, and she shivered in the damp cold. Hearing no sounds from Tolstoy's room, she realized that she had been caught up in a demonic nightmare. Suddenly a new thought struck her: the terrible dreams might be a message, perhaps from Vanichka, warning her of the evils that had taken place in the house. As she stood in her nightclothes, her thick gray hair loose about her shoulders, Sonya became convinced that there *was* a new will and that she must find it that very night. She made her way stealthily to Tolstoy's study. In the adjoining room her husband wakened.

"I heard the opening doors and footsteps," he wrote in his diary the next day. "I saw . . . a bright light in the study and heard a rustling. That was Sonya Andreyevna, searching, probably reading. . . . Again footsteps and a cautious opening of doors and she went out. . . . I tried to go to sleep again but could not. I tossed about for an hour, lighted a candle, and sat up. The door opened. Sonya Andreyevna came in and asked 'How are you?' . . . My aversion and indignation grew. I choked and counted my pulse— 97. I could lie there no longer and suddenly took the final decision to go away."

Sonya left him and fell into an exhausted sleep. There were no more footsteps or sounds in the house that night. Tolstoy rose and wrote her a letter, in which he stated:

My departure wll grieve you. I am sorry for that, but please understand and believe that I could not act otherwise. My position in the house is becoming and has become unbearable. Apart from everything else, I can no longer live in these conditions of luxury in which I have been living, and I am doing what old men of my age commonly do: leaving this worldly life in order to live out my last days in peace and solitude.

Please try to understand this and do not follow me if you learn where I am. Your coming would only make your position and mine worse and would not alter my decision. I thank you for your honorable forty-eight years of life with me, and I beg you to forgive me for anything in which I have been at fault toward you, as I with all my soul forgive you for any wrong you have done me. I advise you to reconcile yourself with the new position in which my departure places you and not to have an unkindly feeling toward me. If you want to report anything to me, give it to Sasha. She will know where I am, for she has promised me not to tell anyone.

Still in his dressing gown and slippers, Tolstoy picked up his candle and went to wake Dr. Makovitsky. "I have decided to go away," he said. "You must come with me. I am going upstairs and you must come too, only don't wake Sonya Andreyevna. We won't take much with us—only what is essential. Sasha will follow us in a few days and bring what else is necessary." After returning to his room to dress, Tolstoy woke Sasha, and they packed his things together. The only plan Tolstoy had at the time was to go to Marya Nikolaevna's monastery in the province of Kaluga. Makovitsky made no effort to dissuade his patient, an eighty-two-year-old man who had suffered several strokes, from venturing off into the unknown on a damp, cold morning. Tolstoy went out to tell the coachman to harness horses to the droshky, but he became confused in the dark. He wrote in his diary, "[I] missed the path to the wing of the house, stumbled into a thicket, pricked myself, ran into the trees, fell, lost my cap, and couldn't find it, made my way out with difficulty, and got back to the house. I found another cap and with a lantern made my way back to the stable."

The sun had just risen when Sasha and Varya saw Tolstoy and Makovitsky drive off for Yasenki. There they waited for an hour in the unheated railroad station. Finally the train arrived, and they climbed stiffly aboard. Vaporous clouds of steam and of early morning dew fogged the windows as the train slowly pulled away. Tolstoy was leaving Yasnaya Polyana for the last time; he was traveling south and on the same tracks on which Anna Stepanova had ended her life.

Sonya woke with a start at eleven that morning, and she immediately went to Tolstoy's room. Not finding him there, she was hurrying to the library when she met Sasha, Bulgakov, and Varya at the top of the stairs.

"Where is Papa?" she cried, rushing toward Sasha.

"He has gone away."

"What do you mean—gone away! . . . When?"

"Last night."

"Impossible, Sasha dear," Sonya said with quiet disbelief.

"I am telling you the truth."

Sonya grasped Sasha's shoulders tightly. Her eyes were wide with fear. "Has he gone away for good?"

"Probably."

"Alone?" she pressed.

"No, with Dushan [Makovitsky]," Sasha answered coolly.

"Darling, Sasha, dear one," Sonya pleaded, taking her daughter's large practical hands. "Tell me, where has he gone to?"

"I don't know," Sasha replied, pulling away from her mother. "He told me nothing but simply gave me this letter for you."

"My God!" Sonya whispered, frantically tearing open the envelope. She read only the first words—"My departure will grieve you"—and then shrieked, "My God, my God. What is he doing to me?" Flinging the letter from her, she dashed from the room.

A few moments later Semyon Nikolaevich rushed in shouting that the Countess had left the house and was running toward the pond. "Go after her, you have boots on!" Sasha ordered Bulgakov as she hurried to put on her galoshes.

Bulgakov tore out across the garden. Behind him were Semyon Nikolaevich, Vanya the footman, several other servants, and finally Sasha. He caught a glimpse of Sonya, but then she disappeared into the bushes. Just as Bulgakov came to the pond, Sasha, skirts rustling, streaked past him. Poised at the water's edge, Sonya glanced back, saw them, and began moving rapidly along the narrow walkway to the jetty. Suddenly slipping, she screamed and fell onto the wooden planks. She lay motionless for a moment; then crawling to the edge of the jetty, she rolled into the freezing water. The pond was deep, and in its center there was a treacherous eddy. As Sonya sank beneath the surface, Sasha and Bulgakov jumped in after her. They managed to keep her from the dangerous currents, and helped by the footman Vanya, they pulled her from the pond. Sobbing softly, Sonya was gently led back to the house, where the housekeeper took her upstairs and dressed her in dry clothes. Then, to everyone's dismay, Sonya came back down and ordered Vanya to drive to Yasenki and ask the stationmaster what Tolstoy's destination had been.

Sasha sent a telegram to her father, telling him all that had happened after his departure. She also sent telegrams to Seryozha, Ilya, Tanya, Andreyusha, and Misha (Lyova was in Sweden), asking them to come quickly to Yasnaya Polyana, and by the next morning Sonya's family was gathered around her. Sonya had learned from the stationmaster that Tolstoy had purchased tickets to Belev and guessed he was on his way to Optina Pustyn monastery to see his sister, Marya Nikolaevna.

As the family arrived, Sasha received a letter from her father:

. . . Dear friend, Sasha. It is hard, and I cannot help feeling greatly
oppressed. The chief thing is not to sin, and therein lies the difficulty. Of course I have sinned and do sin, but if only I can manage
to sin less. That is what I desire for you, too, above all and first of
all, the more so as I know that a terrible task has fallen on you and on
your strength. I have not decided on anything and do not wish to
decide anything. I am trying to do only what I cannot help doing,
and to avoid what can be avoided . . . I hope very much from the
good influence of Tanya and Sergey. The chief thing is that they
should understand and try to suggest to [Sonya] that for me—with
her spying, eavesdropping, continual reproaches, and disposing of
me as she pleased, her constant control over me and feigned hatred
of the man nearest and most necessary to me, together with an evident hatred of me disguised as love—life was not merely unpleasant
but quite unendurable. If anyone should wish to drown it is certainly
not she but I. Let her know that I desire only one thing: to be free
from her, from this falsity, pretense, and the hatred which fills her
whole being.

Of course they cannot explain that to her, but they might suggest that all her actions in regard to me not merely express no love,
but seem to be done for the express purpose of killing me—which
purpose she is achieving, for I hope that the third stroke [he had
suffered two previously] which threatens me will free both her and
me from the horrible situation in which we have been living and
which I do not wish to renew.

You see, dear, how bad I am. I am not pretending to you. I am
not asking you to come yet, but shall do so as soon as possible and
very soon.

Write and tell me how you are. I kiss you.

L.T.

Not waiting until her father summoned her, Sasha immediately left with Varya Feokritova. She met her father at the monastery on the morning of October 30, and after telling him that Sonya
had discovered where he was, she urged him to leave with her.
Tolstoy, however, was reluctant to travel, and Sasha sensed that
"Papa regrets having left home." Still she pressed on; by that afternoon, plans were being made to go to Bulgaria or, if that proved
impossible, to go to the Caucasus. Sasha's fear that Sonya might
follow them were baseless. Since he had left, she had eaten noth-

ing, and she was too weak to leave the house. Her children feared
for her life and wrote letters to their father.

From Ilya:

Dear Papa: . . . Sasha will tell you what took place when you
had gone . . . but I fear her explanation will be rather one-sided, and
I am, therefore, writing too. . . . Needless to say we do not wish to,
and cannot, blame anyone. First of all we must do everything we can
to preserve and as far as possible calm Mamma. . . . She says all the
time that there is nothing for her to live for, and her state is so pitiable
that none of us can speak to her without tears. . . . Her life is certainly in great danger. One fears both a violent death and a slow
extinction from grief and anguish. That is what I think, and what I
feel that for the sake of truth we ought to tell you. I know how
painful life was for you here . . . but then you regarded that life as
your cross. . . . I am sorry you did not endure that cross to the end.
You know you are eighty-two and Mamma sixty-seven. You have
both of you lived your lives and should die becomingly. . . . I do not
call on you to return here immediately, because I know you cannot
do it. But for the sake of Mamma's tranquility . . . write to her, give
her a possibility of strengthening her nervous system and then let it
be as God may decree!

From Andrey:

Dear Papa: Tanya, Sergey, Ilya, Mikhail, and I are gathered
here, and however much we consider the matter, we have been unable to find any way but one of protecting Mamma from suicide
. . . to put her under the constant supervision of hired persons. She
will oppose this of course with all her energy, and I am convinced
will never submit to it. The present position of us brothers is an
impossible one, for we cannot abandon our families and our work in
order to remain constantly with our mother. I know that you have
finally decided not to return, but as a conscientious duty I have to
warn you that by this final decision you are killing our mother.

From Tanya: "Dear, precious Papenka: . . . Like everyone
else you have to act as best you can and as you consider necessary.
I shall never condemn you. Of Mamma I will only say she is
pitiable and touching."

The only letter that pleased Tolstoy came from Sergey: "Dear

Papa . . . I think Mamma is nervously ill and in many respects irresponsible and that it was necessary for you to separate (perhaps you should have done so long ago), however painful it is for you both. I also think that even if anything should happen to Mamma, which I do not anticipate, you should not reproach yourself. The position was desperate, and I think you chose the right way out. Forgive me for writing so frankly."

Sonya herself sent a letter to Tolstoy pleading for a meeting or for his return. He replied on October 31 that it was "quite impossible" for him to see her and ended his letter: "Farewell, dear Sonya, may God help you! Life is not a jest, and we have no right to throw it away at our own caprice. And to measure it by length of time is also unreasonable. Perhaps those months which remain to us are more important than all the years we have yet lived, and they should be lived well. L.T."

Sonya's children were afraid to leave her alone, and they decided that she must have professional help. Seryozha went to Moscow and asked Dr. Rastayaev, a noted specialist in mental illness, to see Sonya. The doctor, a nurse, and a young medical student arrived at Yasnaya Polyana on October 31; horrified by their presence, Sonya continued her hunger strike and would do nothing they asked. But by the next day the young student had won her over. He reminded her that she would have to be strong if her husband should fall ill and need her, and she finally began eating again.

On November 1 Tolstoy wrote in his diary, "Sasha was anxious lest we should be overtaken [by Sonya], so we set off [for the Caucasus]." In order to deceive Sonya, an elaborate plan had been made to travel by a circuitous route. This decision was foolish; a man of Tolstoy's stature could not keep his movements secret. In fact, his flight from Yasnaya Polyana had become international news, and reporters were converging on the area from all over the world. Police spies were following him, and one even traveled in the railroad car that took him from the monastery. Tolstoy was immediately recognized by his fellow passengers, who then came over to speak to him.

The day was cold and windy and the sky was stormy. Because of the route they had chosen, Tolstoy and his party would have to change trains several times. Some hours were spent waiting in unheated stations, and at Astapovo, their third transfer point, Tolstoy took sick with a high fever and chills. The stationmaster offered him his lodgings, and Makovitsky and Sasha helped him to bed.

Early on the morning of November 2 Sonya received a telegram from a Russian reporter telling her Tolstoy had fallen ill with pneumonia and asking for a private interview. After attempting to dissuade her from going to Astapovo, her children saw that nothing could stop her, and they reluctantly agreed to accompany her. A train was commandeered by the authorities in Tula, and that afternoon Sonya, Ilya, Andrey, Misha, Tanya, Dr. Rastayaev, and his nurse set out for Astapovo. This difficult trip was made even more arduous by Sonya's hysterical reaction to a newspaper story that revealed that Chertkov had already arrived at Astapovo (to her deep hurt, she later learned that Tolstoy had sent for him). At Tula, Dr. Semenovski, a local doctor, joined the family. When Sonya and her party arrived in Astapovo on November 3, they were met by Seryozha and by a Dr. Nikitin (two days later a Dr. Berkenheim became yet another medical consultant of the Tolstoy family). Dr. Rastayaev returned to Moscow and wrote Seryozha an assessment of Sonya's mental condition: "Sonya Andreyevna is suffering from psychopathic nervopsychic hysteria, and may under the influence of certain conditions suffer so acutely one may speak of it as *temporary* and transient mental disorder." While he did not believe the family should be unduly concerned by her suicidal threats, he urged that she have constant medical supervision during this difficult time.

The railroad car in which Sonya had traveled was shunted onto a siding, and she and her children and medical advisers lived in it while they were at Astapovo. Before anyone left the car, a family meeting was held, and it was decided that Tolstoy should not be told of Sonya's arrival. She turned away, her shoulders shaking, but after a moment she faced her children and said in a trembling, faint voice that she would agree with them because she did not wish to cause their father's death.

Tanya had brought a little pillow she had once made for her father, and she gave it to Makovitsky to place under his head. Tolstoy was now slipping in and out of consciousness, but he recognized the pillow and asked who had brought it. When Makovitsky admitted that Tanya was in Astapovo, Tolstoy said that he wanted to see her. As soon as she entered the close, crowded sick room, he asked, "Who is with [Sonya]?"

"Andrey and Misha," she replied carefully, not lying to him yet not telling him that Sonya was at Astapovo.

"Misha, too?"

"They are all quite agreed on not letting her come to you as long as you do not wish it."

"What does she do? How does she occupy herself?"

"Perhaps you had better not talk, Papenka. You get excited."

His voice breaking, he demanded, "Tell me, tell me! What can be more important to me than that? . . . Is she well?"

Tanya again told him that her mother was well, that she was waiting to be summoned by him, and that she would not come until he asked for her. Tolstoy was silent, and Tanya left and returned to her mother. There seemed to be no end to Sonya's questions about Tolstoy's condition, about their conversation, and about the people who were with him. She became upset when Tanya said that Chertkov was indeed present, but she grew calmer as she repeated Tolstoy's words, "What can be more important to me than that." Sonya was certain in her heart that he wanted to see her, that Chertkov and Sasha were keeping him from doing so. A short time later a telegram from Tolstoy (which had been addressed to Yasnaya Polyana) was delivered to her. It read: "Because my heart is so weak a meeting would be fatal, though otherwise I am better. L.T." (This telegram somehow got in a reporter's hands and was printed.)

Beside herself with grief, Sonya walked distractedly beside the tracks, the doctors, the nurse, and her children desperately trying to protect her from the crowds that pressed about. Photographers pursued her and clambered onto bystanders' shoulders in order to get a clear view of her. The whirring sound of newsreel cameras was a constant buzzing in her ears. Reporters tugged at her arms, and to the family's horror the distraught and confused Sonya talked to them. As she became more agitated, she broke away from her "keepers" and marched to the stationmaster's hut, only to be denied entrance by Sasha. Finding her position unbearably humiliating, she begged Sasha to allow her to go into the small entryway of the hut, thus making it appear to the cameramen who were filming her that she was visiting her husband. Sasha finally permitted this, but the door to Tolstoy's sickroom and the room adjoining it were kept carefully guarded. During the next days and nights Sonya haunted the damp entryway and prowled about the outside of the little house, straining to catch a glimpse of her dying husband through the closed windows. The bulletins from the sickroom brought grave news: Tolstoy was sinking.

On the evening of November 6 Tolstoy began to move his hand slowly over his breast, plucking at the blanket—an action the peasants called "getting ready." Once or twice he made a quick movement with his hand along the sheet as if he were writing. By two o'clock in the morning he had slipped into unconsciousness. His breathing was regular, but Makovitsky knew he did not have long to live. Chertkov, his languid gray eyes staring into the half-dark, sat at the head of the bed, with Seryozha opposite him. Tanya, Sasha, Varya, Andrey, and Misha were sitting in the next room, and they glanced up anxiously every few minutes as one or another of the doctors passed through. At about three A.M. Makovitsky took Tolstoy's pulse and found that his heartbeat was rapidly becoming weaker. One of the other doctors insisted that Sonya be called, saying they had no right to keep a wife from seeing her husband before he died. Misha and Andrey went to get her. Standing in the tiny drafty entryway with great tears rolling down her pale cheeks, she looked like a lost child. She grasped her sons' arms tightly and walked past Sasha and Tanya and the doctors. Chertkov had slipped into the small kitchen when he heard Sonya coming.

Tolstoy's room was lit by the single candle that burned by his bedside. She stood in the doorway for a moment, and then, on tiptoe, as though afraid she might waken him, she crossed to his side, gently kissed his forehead, and sank to her knees beside his bed. "Forgive me! Forgive me," she cried softly. Tolstoy's breath seemed to catch, and Sonya leaned closer, certain he was aware of her presence. Fearful the dying man might regain consciousness and see her, one of the doctors said gently that it would be best for her to leave. She looked up at him with wide eyes and, finding some truth in his face, rose to her feet and, holding her skirts tightly so that they would not rustle, she slowly left the room. Refusing to return to her car, she stood with Tanya in the entryway. At five thirty-five A.M. Seryozha came to the door. Sonya walked directly to him, knowing the end was approaching, and went with him into Tolstoy's room. Chertkov had left, and Tolstoy's children stood around his bed. Misha and Andrey moved aside, and Sonya knelt by him and murmured, "I have never loved anyone but you." Tolstoy's faint breathing stopped; then there were a few more breaths, another cessation, and finally a slight rattle. Makovitsky stepped in beside Sonya and closed Tolstoy's eyes. Sonya stood up and, gently weeping, leaned over the body of her husband and rested her head on his chest. Not even Sasha intervened.

PART SIX
1910-1920

A Soul Steeped in Darkness

*I have not slept at all, these dreadful nights with my soul
steeped in darkness.*

COUNTESS TOLSTOY

26

As Sonya sat at the head of Tolstoy's bed, in the chair earlier occupied by Chertkov, she was oblivious to the solemn procession of more than a thousand people who moved slowly through the stationmaster's small house to pay their last respects to her husband. Silent and dry-eyed, she shook her head slowly from side to side and clasped and unclasped her hands. She sat all through the day, looking on in disbelief as the painter Leonid Pasternak made death drawings and the sculptor Mercurov molded a death mask. She spoke only once. When the doctors asked if she would allow Tolstoy's skull to be opened for study, she answered with a sharp, resolute "No!" She averted her eyes when a medical student injected his body with formalin. That evening her sons finally prevailed upon her to return to her railway car. Two additional cars now stood on the siding. One, decorated with fir branches, would carry Tolstoy's body; the other would be used by journalists, photographers, and newsreel cameramen. During the night the four brothers carried the coffin containing their father's body to its car. In the cold darkness a crowd of mourners holding torches lined the platform. As the train pulled slowly away from the station which would later be named for Tolstoy, they ran beside it crying out and weeping. Staring ahead, Sonya sat tense and strained, as if she were trying to resist the locomotive's forward motion. Finally Astapovo was left behind and the train began its journey through the dark, empty countryside. Inside Sonya's car the frosted windows shimmered in the flickering light of the kerosene lamps. Tanya and the nurse sat facing Sonya; her sons were across the aisle, while Sasha and Dr. Makovitsky had chosen to sit together at some distance from the family.

About ten minutes after the homeward journey had begun,

Sonya made the sign of the cross and murmured, "God, forgive me everything" (ironically these were Anna Karenina's last words). Leaning back in her seat, she spent the rest of the journey in a trancelike state.

At seven A.M. on November 8 the train drew into the small Zaeska station at Yasnaya Polyana. When Seryozha and Lyova helped Sonya from the car, she started, shocked by the immense crowd on the narrow platform. Nearly four thousand people stood in the cold gray morning: friends and acquaintances; peasants from Yasnaya Polyana and from the surrounding area and from Tula; students and disciples from as far away as Moscow. (Thousands more would have come, but the government had forbidden the railroads to run extra trains.) Banners mourning Tolstoy waved overhead, and as the coffin was lifted from the train, thousands sang the dirge "Eternal Memory."

Sonya, supported by Tanya and Sasha, walked behind the coffin and led a lengthy procession up the road to the house. Chertkov (who had not been on the train) had told Sasha that the coffin should not be brought into the house but should be left unopened at the gates for a few moments before it was interred. The Tolstoy brothers, however, insisted that their mother should make the final decision and reluctantly Sasha asked Sonya what she wanted to have done. "Many people who loved your father will want to see him once more," she said softly.

Seryozha rushed ahead with Semyon Nikolaevich to pull out the door frame of Tolstoy's old study (now the library), thus ensuring that the coffin could be brought into the room. When the procession reached the house, Sonya was taken to her room, but she soon came down and sat by her husband's body. She stayed there until late in the afternoon as mourners filed past, entering through the hall and going out into the gardens. Then only the family was left. Just before the coffin was closed, Sonya stood looking impassively at Tolstoy for several minutes. She whispered a few words, and though Seryozha could not hear her clearly, he thought she asked, "Where are you?" Her eldest son gently drew her back as the coffin was sealed. With Sonya walking behind, it was carried, again by the Tolstoy sons, to the place in the Zahak wood where the green stick was said to have been buried. A grave had already been dug. The crowd was quiet as the coffin was lowered into the ground. There were thunder clouds overhead, and a sharp wind kept forcing Sonya to turn her head aside. She did not cry but, as Seryozha remarked, "bore herself silently and with restraint." She was the first to kneel on the ice-crusted earth, but the huge gathering immediately followed her example. Only one policeman remained standing; and when the crowd shouted, "On your knees!" he too knelt down. Representatives from the Holy Synod had urged that there be a priest at Tolstoy's interment, but Sonya and her family stood firm against them. Tolstoy was buried, as he wanted to be, without a religious ceremony.

A dark, cold autumn night set in, and a storm was about to break. As the crowd dispersed, Sonya took Seryozha's arm and turned away from the gravesite, the mound of freshly dug earth now heaped with leaves. "I thank God Chertkov wasn't here," she said.

Tolstoy's death had touched off student demonstrations. Young men and women thronged to the Nevsky Prospect in St. Petersburg waving red and black flags, shouting angry attacks on the Orthodox Church in the mistaken belief that Tolstoy had been buried without ritual because of his excommunication. Police and Cossacks had to be called in to disperse the crowds with sabers and threats of gunfire. In Odessa students and police, during a disorder precipitated by Tolstoy's burial, engaged in a gun battle. Sonya knew nothing of these events. She had retreated to her room, and the newspapers were kept from her so that she would not read the sensational stories which had been written about Tolstoy's "desertion" of her and his death and burial.

For the two days following Tolstoy's burial, Sonya refused to eat and sat in the darkness, clenching and unclenching her hands and shaking her head. She mumbled incoherently from time to time, but she refused to speak to anyone. On the morning of November 12, Sasha entered and pulled back the curtains to let in the daylight. Sonya glanced up startled and began shaking uncontrollably. Thinking her mother had caught a chill, Sasha was about to wrap a blanket around Sonya's shoulders. But as she drew close, her mother bolted up from the chair in which she had been sitting and let out an unearthly scream. Then all the sobs that had not come before burst from her in a wild flood. Hours later she stopped crying, but she still refused to eat. She was unable to sleep, and she seemed to be in danger of dying of grief. Her sister Tanya came from St. Petersburg, and Sonya collapsed in her arms. She remained in a kind of delirium for nearly two weeks. Tanya stayed at her bedside, and finally Sonya began to improve. On November 25 she wrote a two-word entry in her diary: "Sleepless nights." On the twenty-seventh she wrote, "Got up." Other cryptic entries followed: "Easier when people about. Terrified of solitude. No future." (November 28); "Unendurable anguish—" (November 29); "Gloomy and terrible is the life before me—" (November 30); "unendurable despair" (December 7); "My sister left. I wept inconsolably." (December 8); "The wind has risen. Wrote to Maslova, Taneyev [who had written a letter of sympathy], Andrey, and Lev." (December 10); and "Have put away husband's things to protect them from moths. . . . It is a torture to go on living." (December 11).

Sasha was estranged from her mother because of her complicity in Tolstoy's final flight and was at odds with her sister and brothers over Tolstoy's will. Less than a week after her father's death, she moved from Yasnaya Polyana with Vavara, Sonya's former secretary, to a small neighboring estate, Telyatinki, which she had owned since the division of Tolstoy's properties. Several years earlier she had sold Chertkov half of these lands, and it was here that Chertkov had built his house. The two "conspirators" now lived two hundred yards from each other, and they never again had to plan "secret meetings" or worry about Sonya's surveillance.

Despite Sasha's defection, Sonya was not alone at Yasnaya Polyana. Her nurse had remained with her; Tanya Sukhotin and her small daughter, Tanichka ("My two darling Tanichkas"), came often; and there were almost daily visits from Tolstoy's close friends who came to pay their respects to Sonya and to visit Tolstoy's grave. But in the dark, lonely night hours Sonya was tormented by a sense of responsibility for her husband's self-torture. "Oh, these terrible sleepless nights," she wrote in her diary on December 13. "Alone with my thoughts and tormented by conscience! The utter darkness of these [long] winter nights with my soul steeped in darkness!"

Goldenweiser came to Yasnaya Polyana in early December.

He went into Tolstoy's bedroom to sit quietly for a time, and when he came out Sonya was waiting for him. "I shall never forget her face and her whole figure," he wrote. "In a trembling and broken voice she began: 'What happened to me? What overcame me? How could I have done it? . . . If you only knew what I am enduring, Alexander Borovich! These terrible nights! How could I have been so blind? You know I killed him!' "

The snows came hard and fast, and Sonya wrote, "There is much snow, all is white, quiet, and beautiful, 11 degrees of frost. But where is *he*? Where?" The harsh freezing weather did not deter the stream of visitors who, like Sonya, wanted to find Tolstoy. There were always groups of peasants who knelt three times and then placed fresh fir branches on the grave. On December 18, fifty-two girl students came from St. Petersburg, walked to the grave, and invaded the house. Correspondents from Moscow, Austria, and the Caucasus came the next day.

When Andrey and Ilya arrived, there were painful conversations about their bleak financial prospects and their fears for the future. They had received nothing on their father's death, and Sonya was no longer able to help them. Tolstoy's will had placed Sasha and Chertkov in control of all his literary rights and unpublished works, and it instructed Sasha to purchase Yasnaya Polyana from her mother and to transfer it to the peasants. But this would take a year or more to execute, and until then Sonya would receive no money from her husband's estate. She had only the meager remains of the dowry she had brought into her marriage so many years before. Tolstoy had never owned any valuable antiques or art works, nor had he ever given Sonya any expensive jewelry. His library and private papers were now in Chertkov's hands. And by the conditions of the will her publishing company no longer had any rights to Tolstoy's works—she was not even permitted to sell the books that remained on hand—and within a year or two even Yasnaya Polyana would no longer be hers.

What she had feared would happen had indeed come to pass. She was anguished by the rupture that Tolstoy's will had caused with her family. Sasha's sister and brothers had turned bitterly against her, blaming her for the inequities in their father's will.

During his visit Ilya had an angry confrontation with Sasha and Chertkov at Telyatinki, and returned furious, leaving a greatly disturbed Sonya a short time later. "My son Ilya has left," she wrote in her diary. "He has been with Sasha and Chertkov, of whom we get to know more and more that is bad. He is an evil and cunning man. I went to photograph the grave. . . . In the evening developed the photographs. . . . The beauty makes me still more dejected."

After all the years of near madness, suspicion, and bitter reproach, Sonya seemed to have found the strength to let events shape themselves as they would. Her hysteria—that virulent flame that had consumed her in the past—had been snuffed out. On December 31, 1910, she ceased keeping her diary. It was as though she did not think that the progression of days and nights without Tolstoy mattered. What was of importance was the past and anything concerning the memory of Tolstoy. She was occupied with guilt and with the desperate need to survive in order to expiate that guilt. Never leaving Yasnaya Polyana, she struggled to keep the house and its surroundings as they were when Tolstoy was alive. Despite frost and freezing winds, she seldom missed her daily visit to his grave. There she would stand with her head bowed and whisper soft, tender words as she had done when he had been on his deathbed. "I loved you to the end. I love you now," she would repeat quietly, still hoping that he might somehow hear her.

Pale and drawn, Sonya looked older, but she radiated the factitious energy of one who had passed beyond fatigue. Her eyes shone, and the powerful melody of her voice was sustained. To everyone's surprise she had not passed from near madness into insanity, nor had she retreated to a catatonic state. She went on with her daily routine and set aside certain hours for work on her autobiography. She kept her hair meticulously coiffed and her clothes in good repair, and she tended the house with the same disciplined eye for order that she had always possessed. Gone were the fearful anger and unquenchable passion that had given her a terrifying force and a distracted air which her family, her doctors, and her visitors had all thought were certain indications of madness.

Yet, perversely and most humanly, these same people now perceived a different form of dementia in her. Her composure, good temper, and imperturbability were regarded as tragic signs of a mental breakdown, of a complete retreat from unpleasant reality. No one—least of all Sasha—could understand her calm acceptance of the final settling of Tolstoy's estate.

On February 26, 1913, Sasha bought Yasnaya Polyana from her mother for 400,000 rubles. (She had raised this money by selling the rights to Tolstoy's works to a printer named Ivan D. Sytin; she received 120,000 rubles for the copyright on Tolstoy's posthumous writings and 280,000 rubles for an exclusive license to publish a complete edition of his works.) On March 26, 1913, her father's long-cherished desire was fulfilled; over two-thirds of Yasnaya Polyana's land, including its fine carefully preserved woods, was transferred to the peasants. Sonya retained 540 of the estate's 1,800 acres. The previous year Sasha had sold the Moscow house with all its furnishings to the Moscow municipal government for 125,000 rubles with the request that it be used as a Tolstoy museum and library.

Sonya took the money Sasha gave her and divided it equally among the members of her family. There were, including daughters-in-law and grandchildren, thirty-eight members of the Tolstoy clan, and each received approximately 10,000 rubles, with the grandchildren's money being placed in trust until they came of age. Sonya was fulfilling her own lifelong desire to make some provision for her children. She had given away almost all she had, but a pension which the Tsar had granted her allowed her to live a quiet but comfortable life at Yasnaya Polyana.

Although she was happy that the sale of the estate's lands had enriched her children, Sonya loathed the havoc the peasants soon caused. Within a few months they had destroyed much of the forest land by wholesale felling of trees, which were then sold. The sounds of axes and the acrimonious disputes between the peasants and their timber merchant infuriated Sonya, and she became even more determined that, while she was mistress, life would be lived as it always had been in the house at Yasnaya Polyana. Her close servants—the cook Semyon Nikolaevich; the waiter Ilya Vasilievich and his assistant; and Nianna, the old nurse—remained with her. Breakfast was served at noon; and a four-course dinner at six in the evening. The waiters wore their white cotton gloves; the house was filled with the laughter of children. Some things never change.

During the years since her father's death Sasha had been occupied by responsibilities as his legatee. Her relations with the members of the family except her mother were embittered. Since Chertkov was the co-executor of Tolstoy's literary estate, she had been forced to work closely with him, and her respectful affection for him had begun to sour. Sixty-five years later Sasha admitted that Chertkov

> depressed me with his frequently senseless stubbornness and stupid dictatorial ways. I was only twenty-six [when my father died] and had had little experience, so it was hard for me to struggle with him when I thought him wrong. . . . There was no flexibility in Chertkov. He was heavy-handed in his singleness of purpose, his complete inability to adapt to circumstances. His manner, his actions, his reason—all were focused in one direction and permitted no compromise. Chertkov had no sensitivity; there was no warmth in him. His approach to people took the form of a rigid judgment . . . to Chertkov, a society lady was a zero. . . . Chertkov would never notice the half-wit standing by the door with a foolish smile, begging for a kopeck . . . to me Chertkov was tiresome; he depressed me.

Sasha had also begun to feel irritated and disappointed by the Tolstoyans. "I felt in them a lack of sincerity, a constraint, and unnaturalness," she later said. "Once [before my father's death] my little six-year-old nephew read a notice in Chertkov's house: 'Today at eight o'clock in the evening there will be a lecture on spiritual marriage.' The child asked our cook, 'Annushka, what is spiritual marriage?' Annushka, a robust, hard-working woman who daily cooked the food of these idlers, only waved her hand. 'They haven't anything else to do, so they invent foolishness. Today spiritual marriage—tomorrow we shall have spiritual children.' "

Sasha came to believe that the Tolstoyans were "idlers," and she later confessed that they were repugnant to her: "Dirty in person, smelling of unwashed clothing; they killed all joy of life [and] preserved their gloomy Lenten faces, as if fearing to spoil their state of perfection by an unnecessary smile or a happy song." The Tolstoyans were not, however, an enduring problem; despite Chertkov's great efforts to win them over, they would not accept him as their leader, and they soon drifted away.

Sasha's life had become empty. Her work on her father's estate was finished; she was alienated from her sister and brothers; her close friendship with Chertkov had cooled; and she had grown unsympathetic to her father's disciples. She turned to what she later called "my petty interests," working with the peasants to facilitate the transfer of land to them and attempting, with the aid of an agronomist, to help them improve their farming techniques. She kept a herd of pedigreed cattle, sending milk to the hospital in Tula, and she bought some thoroughbred horses. The house in Telyatinki was filled with dogs—two black poodles and two large white powerful Eskimo dogs, descèndants of Tolstoy's Belka. Varvara Feokritova lived with her, and there appeared to be a special bond between them. Sasha visited her mother often; but these curious meetings were filled with the most superficial of exchanges. Although Sasha kept busy, life had come to seem futile. Her father, her love, her God was dead. Sonya was able to laugh with her grandchildren and find some solace in her daily visits to Tolstoy's grave, but Sasha was inconsolable. Many years later she commented, "While [my father] was with me, I had no interests of my own; all that was serious and genuine was wrapped up with him. And when he departed, there remained a yawning void, an emptiness which I did not know how to fill."

Then suddenly war broke out, shocking Sonya and the household at Yasnaya Polyana; so caught up in their grief, in their fashioning of new lives without Tolstoy, they were barely conscious of the warlike mood throughout Europe, most especially in Germany.

On July 28, 1914, World War I began with Austria's declaration of war on Serbia. The Tsar ordered a full mobilization of Russia's armed forces. On August 2 Russia entered the war, its military leaders convinced—and able to convince Nicholas—that national interest made it imperative for Russia to protect Serbia.

The declaration of war gave rise to a wave of patriotism. Suddenly the Tsar was a hero, and thousands gathered outside the Winter Palace to cheer him. For one dramatic and fleeting moment in his regime Nicholas was loved by his subjects. Even Sasha was moved by patriotic fervor. In the first few months of the war relatives (Andreyusha among them), friends, and workers departed. The army commandeered Sasha's horses, the peasants traded their plows for guns, and Yasnaya Polyana and Telyatinki were desolate. Declaring that she could not sit with "folded hands," Sasha decided to go to the front as a nurse. When she went to Yasnaya Polyana to tell Sonya her decision and to say goodbye, she found her dozing in the sitting room. As soon as her daughter told her why she had come, Sonya came alive with angry disapproval.

"Why do you go to the war?" she demanded. "There is no point in it. Your father was against war, and you want to take part in it?"

"I don't think he was against my helping the sick and wounded," Sasha countered.

Sonya was not satisfied. "Well, I gave my opinion, but I know it is useless. You always have your way."

And, of course, she was right. Sasha soon left for the front. For Sonya the war and the ruin it would bring to Russia seemed to have little meaning. She had retreated into the past, and she appeared impervious to the events that touched her life in the present. Even the death of Taneyev on June 6, 1915, elicited no strong response from her. She did not attend his funeral.

Sasha returned home in the summer of 1915 to recuperate from a serious case of malaria she had contracted while serving on the Turkish front. It was dull at Telyatinki without her horses. Varvara had moved to Moscow, and Yasnaya Polyana seemed empty, too quiet. Tanya Kuzminsky, now widowed, was living at Yasnaya Polyana with Sonya, Tanya, and young Tanichka (Sukhotin had died). Sasha was shocked to see how much her mother had aged. Sonya had greeted her daughter with happy tears; then she spoke about Tolstoy's death and fell into a reverie. Her sight was failing and she could neither read nor write; little interested her, and she spent her days dozing in an armchair. Sasha was certain that she was senile, and after only three days she left to return to the front.

The war was going badly. Russia had been driven out of Serbia by the combined forces of Germany and Bulgaria. Within Russia, Rasputin's power due to his control over the Tsarina had become enormous, and the Tsar had been known to issue military directives which were based on Rasputin's dreams. The Tsarina believed the faith healer would keep her son alive. To her Rasputin was Christ reincarnated and had to be obeyed absolutely. Discontent spread throughout Russia, and there was open talk about revolution at the front.

On the evening of November 29, 1916, Rasputin was lured to the house of Prince Yussupov (a cousin to the Tsar) and was brutally murdered by a group of patriotic noblemen who were determined to break his hold over Russia. But this killing would not placate the Russian people, and his aristocratic assassins would soon be swept aside by the Revolution.

Shocked astonishment surged throughout Russia with news of Rasputin's murder, but at Yasnaya Polyana Sonya could think only of her son Andreyusha, who had recently been killed in action. For a number of years she had been profoundly distressed by his membership in the Black Hundred, a reactionary anti-Semitic organization. Although she was grieved by his death, she was consoled by the thought that he had died as a patriot in the service of Russia.

Rasputin's murder triggered an outbreak of revolutionary activity, and by February the country was in chaos. Mobs in St. Petersburg shouted and howled for Tsarina Alexandra's death. A police regiment mutinied and killed an officer rather than fire into the crowds as he had ordered. Nicholas was urged to abdicate by his advisers. A short time later six of his own soldiers barred his way as he attempted to leave the palace. The imperial family was under arrest. After the Tsar had been forced to abdicate, a provisional government was formed. The February Revolution had toppled the Tsarist regime, but the Russian Revolution had just begun. In mid-April Lenin, the Bolshevik leader who had spent the last ten years in exile, returned to St. Petersburg and was met at the Finland Station by massive cheering crowds and a brass band. The imperial family were prisoners at Tsarskoye Selo. In July Britain offered them asylum, and Kerensky, now head of the provisional government, agreed to make such arrangements as were required; but then David Lloyd George, Britain's prime minister, suddenly withdrew the offer. Still Nicholas and Alexandra had hope. They were being treated fairly and were allowed to correspond, and they knew there was a White Russian army of loyalists who refused to accept the revolution.

During the summer there was internal fighting everywhere. The long road from Moscow to Yasnaya Polyana was lined with battered houses, tumbled walls, and charred fields. Crude red flags declaring Bolshevik allegiance flew from many rooftops. Nearly every house in the district had been robbed and burned. There were rumors that Yasnaya Polyana was going to be destroyed not by the village peasants but by peasants from another area.

Ilya Vasilievich brought Sonya news of the approach of a marauding band as she dozed in her rocking chair. He shook her gently and, after telling her, cried, "What shall we do? What shall we do?" Their situation did indeed seem hopeless. Sonya was almost blind, an old woman thought by her children to be senile. But some of her old spirit came back into her voice as she rose slowly from her chair and ordered him to tell the Yasnaya Polyana peasants to arm themselves.

"With what?" he asked, knowing that all weapons had been commandeered long before by the army.

"Pitchforks and axes if they have nothing else," Sonya replied sharply.

Ilya Vasilievich went off to dispatch this advice, and Sonya had her daughter Tanya gather together the household staff. After telling them to quickly pack everything of Tolstoy's and a few personal possessions, she turned to Tanya and said, "Telegraph Kerensky. Tell him the family of Tolstoy require an army to protect his home and papers."

Tanya thought it was an old woman's madness to expect that Kerensky would spare men to defend a family of distressed aristocrats. Still, there was the ring of authority in her mother's voice, and she dispatched the telegram. Cases of Tolstoy's books and papers were brought to the salon, and the three women—Sonya, Tanya, and Tanichka (Tanya Kuzminsky had gone to St. Petersburg to see her sons)—sat and awaited the arrival of the plundering mob. They had armed themselves with knives and hammers to fight for their lives if need be.

The servants whimpered and prayed, their fear increasing with the passing of each hour. "Stop wailing!" Sonya shouted at one point. "Kerensky will send his men."

Faint beams from the rising moon fell through the windows of the salon. They sat without candles, hoping that if the terrorists saw the house in darkness they would assume that it had already been abandoned by its owners and ransacked by the village peasants. Suddenly in the distance there were loud shouts, the sound of horses' hoofs and neighing. The three women huddled closer together. The clamor lasted for nearly an hour, and then there was an unbearable silence. Sonya insisted that no one move or light a lamp or candle, and they passed about a quarter of an hour in darkness and abject fear. Then there were the sounds of footsteps on the veranda and a knock at the door. Light wavered into the room as Semyon Nikolaevich entered. For a moment no one recognized the old cook. His once-plump cheeks were unshaven, his clothes rough, and his round stomach gone. He had left Yasnaya Polyana earlier that year to farm for himself, but he still lived in the village. Hurriedly he told the women that the Yasnaya Polyana peasants had turned the rioters away from the gates with pitchforks and axes. The mob had moved on to the next estate, so they were safe.

Kerensky, who had long been an admirer of Tolstoy, in answer to Sonya's plea did indeed send a band of a hundred men the following day to guard Yasnaya Polyana during the violent summer, so Sonya, her brood, and her home were spared further encounters. In November 1917 the fighting ceased, though the looting and burning continued. Fear permeated the atmosphere, but at least the Bolsheviks, who had taken power, were arresting and shooting people with a certain discretion; and persons who had been even peripherally involved in revolutionary activity under the old government were not in any great danger.

Arriving in Yasnaya Polyana in October, Sasha found that her house and lands at Telyatinki had been declared government property and had been laid claim to by members of the village Soviet, who had taken what they wanted—horses, cows, machinery, tools, furniture, even clothes and dishes. Her mother had assured her that she had saved some gold and would manage to take care of those at Yasnaya Polyana. Sonya's composure shocked Sasha. Dinner—usually little more than beet root—was served as always at six by Ilya Vasilievich, who wore his carefully darned white gloves. There were no guests and the house was strangely silent, but Sonya's only complaint was that she could no longer read or write.

On her return to Moscow, where she stayed with Varya, Sasha received a letter from her Aunt Tanya Kuzminsky, saying she was leaving St. Petersburg and would have a few hours in Moscow before boarding the night train for Yasnaya Polyana. Tanya was frail, and Sasha feared that the poor conditions on the

newly nationalized trains would prove to be too much for her.
Simply finding a seat on one of them was a difficult and sometimes
dangerous task. On Sasha's trip from Yasnaya Polyana "people
[had] climbed through the windows and on to the roofs of the
coaches, hung on the steps, or stood on the couplings. Police [had]
menaced them with the butts of their guns, but they kept pushing
forward. Boxes and baskets [had] burst open, women shrieked,
windowpanes [had been] broken." Her aunt weighed no more than
a slender twelve-year-old, and it would be impossible for her to
endure such mayhem.

The station was mobbed when they arrived, and the only train
departing that night for Yasnaya Polyana was the "Maxim Gorky,"
a proletarian train which had only fourth-class accommodations.
Sasha found a hefty porter and gave him the few rubles she had to
look after Tanya. She left her aunt seated in a corner of the station
on one of her boxes, the porter guarding her, and prayed she would
be safe from the crowds. She then hurried to the stationmaster.

"Comrade!" she shouted through the crowd that surrounded
him. "Tolstoy's sister is taking the next train and she's an old
woman. She was Natasha Rostova in *War and Peace*. Please give her
a seat on the train. She's going to Yasnaya Polyana."

The stationmaster ignored her as he did all the others who
were begging his help. When he jumped up and walked out onto
the platform, Sasha ran after him crying, "Comrade, please, I beg
you. The sister of Tolstoy!" He strode away without even glancing
at her. Sasha went back to her aunt, and with the porter walking
behind the slight elderly lady they made their way to the train
platform. They were stopped at the gate and forced to open their
bags. Tanya's hands trembled badly and she could not find her
keys.

"Oh, Sasha, Sasha," she cried, "They will mix up my manuscripts!" (Tanya was writing her memoirs.)

"What have you got here? Flour? Bread?" the man demanded.

"Certainly not! Nothing of the kind!" Tanya replied indignantly.

"Gold!" shouted someone. "That's what to look for. She's got
gold and diamonds."

Finally Tanya found her keys in her handbag, and, satisfied

that she only had papers and some old clothes, the official let her pass.

A solid wall of people stood at the edge of the platform; those in the rear pressed forward so that they could rush onto the train as soon as it pulled in. Knowing her aunt could not manage in this crush of people, Sasha again sat her down on a box and went to seek help a second time.

"The train rumbled in," she later wrote, "and before it stopped, the crowd surged forward and up the steps. Soldiers drove them off. There were curses, cries for help. . . . Nearly everyone succeeded in squeezing on board, and only a few were left hopelessly trying to force their way in."

Finding the head conductor, Sasha begged, "Please help me. My aunt, Tolstoy's sister, must get on the train. Please give her a seat."

"No room," the man told her. "Full!" He walked briskly up the platform, Sasha hurrying behind him. Suddenly they were beside a car with empty seats.

"Who is in this car?" she asked.

"Commissars."

"Let me in. I want to speak to them."

"Impossible!"

Sasha rapped on the windows, shouting, "Comrades! Comrades!" Finally an old man with unkempt hair came to the window and asked, "What's the matter, comrade?"

"The sister of Tolstoy, an old woman of seventy, simply must go to Yasnaya Polyana today. The crowd has nearly killed her—she is sick—please take her."

"And who are you?"

"Tolstoy's daughter."

The head disappeared and in a moment popped out again. "We'll take your old lady."

Wearing an old-fashioned cloak and a little black fur hat, Tanya sat terrified on her box, while the large porter stood in front of her like a statue.

"Auntie! Auntie! Come quickly!" Sasha screamed. Tanya and the porter ran after Sasha, trying to catch the train which had already begun to move. Once alongside the car, Sasha pushed her gasping aunt from below, while the porter—who had tossed the cases in and then jumped after them—pulled her from above.

This would be Tanya Kuzminsky's final journey to Yasnaya Polyana, and she enjoyed every moment of it. Once again she was the coquette, and being the only woman in the commissars' car, she was treated most cordially and was even fed roast chicken. When she reached Yasnaya Polyana, she told Sonya all about it, her face flushed with excitement. Finally, sighing, she ended her recital: "But they were disappointed that I was not Tolstoy's sister, but only his sister-in-law." And for a brief moment there was an echo of the young Tanya in her voice, and the quicksilver shadow of Natasha Rostova in her eyes.

Early in 1918 famine spread across Russia but at Yasnaya Polyana dinner—"boiled winter beets, no meat [and] some little, very little, pieces of black bread made of flour mixed with chaff" —was still served by the white-gloved Ilya Vasilievich. Sonya insisted that a white damask cloth cover the table, that the silver be polished, and that the best plates be used. Thanks to Kerensky, her possessions had never been taken from her. The piano at which Taneyev had played still stood in the salon, and to break the tedium of the long evenings Sonya would play and Tanya Kuzminsky would sing in a "sweet, broken voice that echoed in the old hall."

Toward the end of 1918 Yasnaya Polyana was taken over by the government to be used as a farm commune, and a Yasnaya Polyana Society was organized in Tula. Its members were those few intellectuals who still remained in the area, and its task was to organize educational facilities for the peasants who worked the lands of Yasnaya Polyana. The chairman appointed by the government was a writer who had been known and disliked by Tolstoy. Although the chairman's name was forgotten by all the survivors of the war years at Yasnaya Polyana, Sergey, Ilya, and Sasha later described him quite vividly. Sasha recalled that many years before Chekhov had said that he reminded him of a funeral hearse stood on end. Tall, dark, with long arms and fingers, and stooped as if he were too tall to stand erect, he moved into the library downstairs. Sonya distrusted him from the very beginning, and with good reason. He was continually surprising the inhabitants of Yasnaya

Polyana by his noiseless entrances; he spoke in an often inaudible voice and had a deeply conspiratorial air. Yet, however much she disliked the chairman, she was grateful for the food, clothing, soap, and other necessities he was able to wheedle out of the government for her, her family, and the 150 village peasants.

Chertkov had moved to Moscow to begin preparations for the Soviet government edition of Tolstoy's complete works, but it seemed his spirit lived on in the chairman. He set himself up as the seat of authority in Sonya's household, found fault with everything, and was rude to her and her family and servants. He refused to requisition help for the heavy tasks like washing windows and putting in the winter frames. When Sasha returned for a visit and saw her mother, sister, and aunt doing these hard jobs in the cold wind of November, she angrily returned to Moscow and immediately went to see the commissar of education. Sasha cautiously made a little speech about Yasnaya Polyana and its importance to the nation, and she concluded: "I think that the Tolstoy estate ought to be not a Soviet farm but a museum, like Goethe's home, and that I should replace the current chairman." To Sasha's amazement the commissar agreed; she then returned to Yasnaya Polyana and dismissed the chairman. Sasha was now mistress in Sonya's home.

Life at Yasnaya Polyana was somewhat easier for Sonya with her daughter as commissar, but it also meant that she had to ask Sasha for even the smallest things she needed. She did not complain, however, but simply grew more quiet and withdrawn. Nearly blind, she sat in reverie most days. The hardships she had borne trimmed her portly matron's figure to the slimness she had so prided herself upon as a young woman, but her voice had faded to a soft whisper. Though old, she was still handsome, and the shadow of her youthful beauty lingered in her fine features. Her greatest happiness was her grandchildren, and when Ilya or Misha or Lev brought their families to see her, she would suddenly come alive and walk in the garden with them and tell them the stories she had written so many years before—"The Skeleton Dolls" and "How Tax, the Dog, Was Saved."

On November 1, 1919, Sasha made plans to take the midnight train to Moscow. It was a cold moonless night, and a harsh wind whipped at the shutters and rattled the windows. Firewood was extremely scarce, and Sonya, feeling a chill, had retired early to stay warm beneath her bedcovers. Sasha packed her bag and then went upstairs to have tea in the sitting room with Tanya Kuzminsky. Wrapped in a shawl and a blanket, the old lady wore worn yellow gloves on her trembling hands as she played solitaire. She sat at a table against an inside wall, away from the wind that slipped through the cracks in the windowpanes. Tanya Kuzminsky had not aged as well as her older sister; her skin was deeply wrinkled, her shoulders hunched, her once-luxuriant hair thin. But she had not lost the gay spirit and the great femininity that were so inimitably and essentially hers.

"Auntie dearest, tell me my fortune," Sasha asked, thinking that this would help while away the time until she had to leave for the station.

After finishing her game of solitaire, Tanya gathered together and shuffled the cards and asked Sasha to cut them with her left hand and spread them out. The hunched old woman stared down at the cards which lay exposed before her. A look of apprehension passed across her heavy-lidded dark eyes, and she shivered. Then, with a quick movement, she swept the cards together, saying, "Bad, very bad."

Sasha begged her to tell her what she had seen, but her aunt adamantly refused. Sasha persisted. "All right"—Tanya sighed— "if I must. Illness and death of a close relative. You won't go away tonight."

Sasha asked to cut the deck again. Tree branches brushed against the windows and the big-bellied samovar sputtered, its top making an eerie vibrating sound. Sasha turned up the seven of spades, indicating illness. "Again, Auntie," she insisted. This time she turned up the ace of spades—*death*. Tanya paled, and she quivered as she leaned back in her chair. Then her face flushed and she cried out angrily, "Nonsense! Are you mad? Forget it!" She fidgeted nervously, pulling her shawl tighter around her. She rose gingerly from her chair and began to prepare the tea. As she lifted the china, her trembling hand made the teacups clatter in their saucers. Sasha went to see if her mother would like some tea.

A small kerosene lamp burned dimly on Sonya's desk and she

lay on her bed drawn up in a fetal position, her face turned to the wall. "What is the matter, Mamma!" Sasha cried in alarm.

Sonya murmured, "I am . . . very cold . . . please cover me."

Sasha touched her and found that Sonya was burning with fever. Turning at a sound, she saw Tanya Kuzminsky in the doorway, a lost, terrified look on her sagging, pinched face. They gave Sonya tea and wine and awakened Tanya Sukhotin. The women agreed Sonya was very ill, and Ilya Vasilievich was sent for the doctor. When he arrived, he said that there was little he could do; Sonya had an advanced case of pneumonia. For three days she suffered badly, her coughing spasms too painful to watch. But she was uncomplaining, enduring, and gentle. On the third night she insisted on speaking to her two daughters.

"Are you thinking of Father?" Tanya asked, trying to help her mother sort out her confused thoughts.

"Constantly . . . constantly. Tanya . . . it torments me that I didn't get along with him better, but . . . before I die, Tanya . . . I want to tell you . . . I never, never loved anyone but him."

She looked at her daughters with large, dark, clouded eyes. Both Sasha and Tanya were crying bitterly, but Sonya was calm. The next morning she could no longer speak, but she opened her eyes wide and nodded to tell her family that she recognized them. When her sister came to her bed and took her hand in her own frail trembling one, Sonya summoned up the strength to return her grasp. Only moments later Sonya was dead. It was November 4, 1919. She was seventy-five years old and had seen four tsars, several wars, famine, revolution, the birth of thirteen children, the death of seven. She had spent forty-eight years with a man whose name would be remembered as long as the names of any of the tsars she had met or the revolutionaries who had replaced them.

Sonya was buried beside Masha at Kotchakovo Cemetery, with only her close family and her few servants present. She had been buried in a shabby flannel dressing gown. In her enormous ironbound trunk there were many fine clothes—an old-fashioned silk petticoat, dresses—but food was scarce and those things could be traded for at least forty pounds of flour and perhaps as much as ten pounds of rye. After the funeral, the clothes from the trunk were tied up in a bundle, and throwing them into the bottom of a sleigh, Sasha and a nephew drove to the village beyond Yasnaya Polyana.

The moon was shining as they returned, and yellow lights gleamed from the peasant huts they passed. Bags full of flour and grain lay at the bottom of the sleigh along with a heavy slab of bacon. There would be enough food for the winter—Sonya was still the provider for the house of Tolstoy.

AFTERWORD

The Tolstoy Family

SERGEY (Seryozha) LVOVICH TOLSTOY (1863–1947) was the only one of the Tolstoy children who did not leave Russia after the revolution; he was also the most successful of Sonya's sons. Sergey composed *Twenty-seven Scottish Songs*, *Two Belgian Songs*, and *Hindu Songs and Dances* and set poems by Pushkin, Alexei Konstantinovich Tolstoy, Fet, and Tyutchev to music. He was also an ethnomusicologist, a teacher, and a performer. From 1917 to 1928 he gave many public concerts to good reviews. In 1928–29 he lectured on musical ethnography at the Moscow Conservatory.

His book, *Tolstoy Remembered by His Son*, was published posthumously in 1961. He prepared his mother's diaries for publication and wrote an introductory essay and notated her diary for the year 1910, *The Final Struggle* (which also includes entries from Tolstoy's diary of the last year of his life). Sergey was the consultant on the definitive edition of his father's works (Jubilee Edition) for which he edited Tolstoy's "Two Hussars." He was responsible in a large part for organizing and maintaining the Yasnaya Polyana Museum.

In 1895 Sergey married Marya Konstantinovna Rachinsky, who bore him a son, Sergey, in 1897. She died in 1900. His second wife, Countess Marya Nikolaevna Zubova, whom he wed in 1906, died in 1939. In his later years Sergey lost a leg in an accident, the sight in one eye, and his hearing. Yet he was active until his death at the age of eighty-four.

ILYA (Ilyusha) LVOVICH TOLSTOY (1866–1933) served in the civil service in various posts. Ill-suited for this career, he made a determined effort to become a self-supporting journalist. His newspaper, the *New Russia*, a cooperative project, failed. He served as a war correspondent in the Balkans for the *Russian Word*, a newspaper, but took ill and had to terminate his contract.

He had married Sofya Nikolayevna Filosofova in 1890. In 1916, after they had separated Ilya emigrated to the United States. In 1918 he returned to Russia on a mission from President Theodore Roosevelt to the chairman of the Council of Ministers. Sofya Nikolayevna divorced him at that time. Bitter, Ilya returned to the U.S. to write a syndicated column on Russia and Russian-American relations and to lecture on his father's work and philosophy. A year later he married Nadezhda Klimentyevna Katulsky.

Late in the 1920s he became the consultant on the Hollywood film versions of Tolstoy's *Anna Karenina* and *Resurrection*. He wrote stories under the pseudonym of Ilya Dubrosky. One, "One Scoundrel Less," was published and shows Ilya's considerable but wasted talent. He also wrote *Reminiscences of Tolstoy*, published in 1914, perhaps the most sensitive memoir written by any of the Tolstoy children.

He was unable to support himself during the Depression and died in poverty in a New York hospital at the age of seventy-seven. His daughter, Vera Tolstoy, who was born in 1898 and came to America in 1949, now lives in New Smyrna Beach, Florida. Her sister, Anna (1888–?), was the oldest grandchild of the Lev N. Tolstoys. Ilya's other children were Mikhail (1893–1919), Andrey (1895–1920), and Ilya (1896–?).

TATYANA (Tanya) LVOVNA TOLSTOY SUKHOTIN (1864–1950) married Mikhail Sergeyevich Sukhotin in 1899. After 1918 Tanya was the caretaker of the Yasnaya Polyana Museum. For a year she operated a school of painting in Moscow. In 1923–25 she was director of the Moscow Tolstoy Museum. She then emigrated to France and later moved to Rome, where she established a Tolstoy museum.

Tanya wrote several memoirs in Russian and French—*Friends and Guests at Yasnaya Polyana* (Moscow, 1923), *About My Father's Death* and *The Reasons for His Leaving Home* (Paris, 1928)—and two that were translated into English: *The Tolstoy Home: Diaries* (London, 1950) and *Tolstoy Remembered* (New York, 1977).

She died in Rome in 1950 at the age of eighty-six. She had three children, Dorik Mikhailovich, Sergey Mikhailovich, and Tatyana Mikhailovna. Her daughter now lives in Rome.

LEV (Lyova) LVOVICH TOLSTOY (1869–1945) wrote children's stories and *The Chopin Prelude* (intended as a rebuttal to Tolstoy's *The Kreutzer Sonata*). He also wrote numerous plays, articles, and his memoir, *The Truth About My Father* (1924). He also served on the editorial staffs of several magazines.

He left Russia in 1918 for Sweden, the homeland of Dora Westerlund, his wife. After traveling to America, Italy, and France, he returned to Sweden, where he died in 1945 at the age of seventy-six.

MIKHAIL (Misha) LVOVICH TOLSTOY (1879–1944) emigrated to France after his mother's death and lived there until 1935, when he moved to Morocco. He married Alexandra Vladimirovna Glebov. He died in 1944 at the age of 65.

One son, Dr. Sergey Mikhailovich Tolstoy, lives in Paris. Another son, Vladimir Mikhailovich Tolstoy, and his wife, Olga, live in Upper Nyack, New York. They work for the Tolstoy Foundation in the neighboring Valley Cottage. Misha's other children include Ivan, Tatyana, Alexandra, Peter, and Sophy (all except Sophy are living).

ALEXANDRA (Sasha) LVOVNA TOLSTOY (1884–1979), Sonya's youngest child, wrote three memoirs—*I Worked for the Soviet* (London, 1934), *The Tragedy of Tolstoy* (New York, 1933), and *A Life of My Father* (New York, 1953).

She emigrated to Japan before finally settling in the 1930s in the United States, where she founded the Tolstoy Foundation in Valley Cottage, New York. Alexandra never married.

APPENDIX

Following are excerpts from daily articles covering Tolstoy's departure from Yasnaya Polyana and subsequent illness and death as reported in the New York *Times* in November 1910. In each case the day's article appeared on page one. Dates given in the newspaper accounts would be thirteen days forward from the Russian calendar. A great deal of journalistic license was taken by the newsmen who wrote these articles, and they did have a tendency to fictionalize.

In addition, there are a number of spelling inconsistencies, particularly names and places, from item to item.

TOLSTOY QUITS HOME; HIS REFUGE UNKNOWN
Leaves Message for Wife Saying He Will Spend His Last Days in Solitude
DOCTOR WENT WITH HIM
No Trace of Great Russian Novelist, Now 82 Years Old, Since October 10

LONDON, Nov. 11 — A special to The London Times from Moscow says that the correspondent of the Russkoe Slovo telegraphs that Count Tolstoy has left Yasnaya Polyana for an unknown destination, saying he intends to spend his last days in seclusion.

A special also says that the St. Petersburg Novoe Vremka has received the following telegram from Tula, signed by Prince Demitry Obolensky:

"Leo Tolstoy left Yasnaya Polyana at 5 A.M. Oct. 10, accompanied by his physician, Dr. Makovetsy. Neither has been heard of since. The Countess is in despair. In a letter to his wife Tolstoy says he has decided to spend his remaining days in solitary retirement.

TOLSTOY IS FOUND; WIFE TRIED SUICIDE
In Grief Over Husband's Departure to Turn Hermit, Sought Death by Drowning
SAVED BY HER DAUGHTER
Aged Novelist, Who Had Asked Not to be Traced or Followed, Said to be on Friend's Estate

MOSCOW, Nov. 12—It is reported here that Count Tolstoy, who disappeared from his home several days ago, leaving behind him a letter acquainting his wife with his purpose of spending his last days in solitary seclusion, has been found in the Mount Sensky district of Tula Province. He is on the estate of the Abrikosoffs, well-known manufacturers.

From Tula comes the news that Countess Tolstoy, after receiving the

459

letter left by her husband, attempted to drown herself, but was saved by her daughter, Alexandra. It is said that this was Countess Tolstoy's second attempt at suicide, that on an earlier occasion she tried to die by poison.

The Tolstoy family up to to-day, had obtained no clue to the Count's whereabouts. By some it was believed that Tolstoy had betaken himself to an old monastery in the Government of Kaluga, which adjoins the Government of Tula on the west. He was last seen here when he took a train last Thursday on the Kiausani Railroad. This road runs west through the capital of Kaluga, which is about fifty miles from Tula.

That the novelist, who is over 80 years old, should desire to spend the evening of his days in solitude surprises no one acquainted with his career, but that he should deliberately desert the wife who has borne him many children gives rise, even in the light of his well-known eccentricities of character, to the suggestion of failing mentality. This is accepted by many in explanation of the sudden leave taking.

TOLSTOY IN CONVENT; A TYPIST IS WITH HIM
His Letter Said He Must Have Peace from Visitors and Moving Picture Men.
DAUGHTER FOLLOWED ALSO
Convent Has Long Sheltered His Favorite Sister—Stories of Countess's Attempted Suicide Denied

LONDON, Nov. 13—The Daily Mail's Moscow correspondent says that on the morning of Count Tolstoy's disappearance his wife was awakened at 3 o'clock by his footsteps in the adjoining room. She found the old man restless, pacing the floor. He told her he had taken some medicine, requested her to retire, and closed the door. The Countess then slept until 10 o'clock, and did not hear of her husband's disappearance until the coachman who drove him away returned.

Then she found on a table a letter addressed to her in which Tolstoy said: "Do not seek me. I feel that I must retire from the trouble of life. Perpetual guests, perpetual visits and visitors, perpetual cinematograph operators, beset me at Yasnaya Polyana, and poison my life. I want to recover from the trouble of the world. It is necessary for my soul and my body which has lived 82 years upon this earth." [This is an incorrect translation of Tolstoy's last letter to Sonya.]

He added that he should not return, if he were found, and closed with an appeal for his wife's forgiveness after their forty-eight years of happiness.

The Countess was prostrated with grief, but the tales of her attempted suicide are absolutely unfounded. Count Tolstoy and his doctor traveled in a third-class carriage to Optina Pustina, and after a rest walked six and one-half miles to the Shamardinsky Convent where Tolstoy's favorite sister Maria has been a nun for many years.

The 500 nuns in the place are all engaged in manual labor, women blacksmiths being among their number. Tolstoy's daughter, Alexandria [sic], and his woman typist, followed him to the convent.

TOLSTOY VERY ILL AT WAYSIDE STATION
Meant to Go to Caucasus, But High Fever Made Further Travel Impossible
JOURNEYED AS A PEASANT
In a Crowded, Unventilated, Third-Class Carriage—His Physician and Daughter Tending Him.

TULA, Russia, Nov. 14—Broken down by the hardships of a Winter journey, mental strain, and the rupture with his family, Count Leo Tolstoy tonight lies with a high fever in the little railroad station at Astapova, barely eighty miles from his home in Yasnaya Polyana.

Tolstoy is attended by Dr. Makovetsky, who was his only companion when he left his peasant hut a few days ago and who carried along with him medicaments for just such an emergency. Tolstoy's daughter, Alexandra, is acting as his nurse.

Telegraphic reports of his condition are far from favorable. Indeed, they are considered extremely pessimistic. The temperature of the aged writer is 104, indicating probably serious congestion, and of itself an alarming symptom in one of Tolstoy's years.

The mental anguish of the patient handicaps the efforts of the physician to reduce the fever. Even if Count Tolstoy recovers there can be no question of his continuing the journey to the Caucasus, where he hoped to end his life among the Tolstoyan colony on the shores of the Black Sea.

Tolstoy had hoped to escape notice after his hasty departure from Yasnaya Polyana and to spend a quiet week of farewell with his sister, Marie, a nun in the ancient cloister of Shamardino, in the Province of Kaluga, but he insisted upon departing immediately after he found that the retreat had been discovered. He drove in a carriage last evening from Shamardino to Kozelsh, accompanied by his daughter, Alexandra, and Dr. Makovitsy, and in order to cover his movements announced that he was going to Moscow where he has a house. Later, however, the party boarded a slow local train proceeding in the direction of the Caucasus.

Tolstoy, with his two companions, made his way to an unventilated, third-class compartment, which was already crowded with peasants. The atmosphere was stifling, and he developed such a fever that Dr. Makovitsky thought it unwise to proceed to Dankeff, the first town of any considerable

size along the route. They left the train at Astapova, which is merely a little flag station. There is no hospital there and only a few peasant huts. The Count was taken into the station but . . . [Illegible] where he remained during the night.

No attempt will be made by his family to induce Count Tolstoy to abandon his self-imposed exile. His wishes are sacred to the Countess, who, however, has sent a message to her husband imploring that she be permitted to join him and share the hardships which he is determined to experience.

TOLSTOY IS BETTER; HIS WIFE WITH HIM
The Count Is Very Weak, but the Doctors Say There Is No Immediate Danger
THERE HAD BEEN A QUARREL
Countess Protested Against Her Husband's Determination to Ask No Money for His Writings

TULA, Russia, Nov. 15—Count Leo Tolstoy is suffering from bronchitis, and owing to a high fever, is in an extremely weak condition. A message from his daughter Alexandra, who is nursing him at Astopova, giving this information, adds that the physicians say no immediate danger threatens.

Count Tolstoy suffered from a severe attack of bronchitis in the Winter of 1900, and as a result was readily susceptible to a recurrence of the disease when he exposed himself to a long journey in the cold and rain.

The home of the station master at Astopova is quite comfortable, and the patient is receiving skillful attention at the hands of Dr. Makovetsky and one other physician, in addition to the loving care of his daughter. Newspaper correspondents, who are gathering around the little flag station, however, although not aggressive in their attempts to obtain the latest details, are hampering the attendants, and Alexandra Tolstoy has issued a request that her father be left in peace.

According to the official diagnosis of the physicians, Tolstoy is suffering from a catarrhal inflamation of the lower lobe of the left lung. His heart action is good. The maximum temperature to-day was 102, falling at times to 99, which is practically normal; pulse 104, dropping to 90, respiration fair. The physicians add that expectoration and diuresis are sufficient, and that the patient has enjoyed tranquil sleep, is in good spirits, and is resting quietly.

Altogether, this is considered a very satisfactory report, particularly in view of the high temperature which was maintained yesterday, and the symptoms of mental distress which Count Tolstoy was said to have developed.

Countess Sophia Tolstoy, after the first shock caused by her husband's sudden abandonment of his home and family, displayed astonishing energy this morning, and insisted upon being taken to the Count. Accompanied by her sons and Count Vladimir Tchertkoff, who was formerly Tolstoy's representative in England, she proceeded to Astopova by special train.

The illness of the great author brought about a reconciliation between the Countess and Count Tcherkoff, whose embittered feelings in recent months caused Tolstoy much anguish. Count Tchertkoff was summoned by telegraph to Yasnaya Polyana, where he joined the Countess and her sons. Tolstoy himself in a letter had expressed a particular desire for Tchertkoff's presence.

TOLSTOY NOW SAID
TO BE PAST CRISIS
St. Petersburg Received Reports
of His Death Last Night,
Which Were Later Denied.
HE REFUSES TO GO HOME

His Wife Wanted to Remove Him to
Yasnaya Polyana—Reports as to the
Gravity of His Condition Conflict

ST. PETERSBURG, Thursday, Nov. 17—A report of the death of Count Leo Tolstoy at Astapova was received here last night by the various newspapers and agencies.

The Novoe Vremya's Moscow correspondent first telegraphed that Tolstoy was dead, but at an early hour this morning he sent a further dispatch saying that a message had been received from Astapova that Tolstoy was living, that the crisis of the disease had been passed, and that the patient's temperature late last night was 99.6.

At 4:15 this morning, the Vestnik News Agency reported that the death of Tolstoy was not confirmed.

TOLSTOY DELIRIOUS;
HOPE ALMOST GONE
Physicians Admit It Will be Next
to a Miracle if the Count
Recovers
HIS HEART IS VERY WEAK
Author Said to Desire Reconciliation
with Church—Unhappy Lot of the
Special Correspondents

ASTAPOVA, Russia, Nov. 17—Although hope has not yet been given up the attendants of Count Tolstoy recognize that his life is in the balance, and that although his strong constitution of the great Russian has carried him through other grave struggles against disease his system has become so weakened and his heart has responded so feebly to restoratives that it will be next to a miracle if he recovers from his present attack.

During the early stages of the inflammation of the lungs, from which he is suffering, it was the temperature which gave cause for anxiety, now it is the heart. The patient's temperature was not particularly high to-day, but the heart action was extremely bad.

Tolstoy alternated during part of the time between unconsciousness and delirium.

TULA, Nov. 17—Count Tolstoy's condition for many hours has been such as to give rise to frequent reports that the end had come. Such a report emanated from Moscow last night, and it was some time before its falsity could be established.

SYNOD MAY FORGIVE TOLSTOY
Likely to Withdraw Excommunication —Strange Scene at Astapova.

LONDON, Friday, Nov. 18—A telegram to The Times from St. Petersburg says that the Holy Synod on Wednesday discussed the question of rescinding the writ of excommunication against Count Tolstoy. The assembled prelates are understood to be predisposed in his favor.

A great impression had been caused by Bishop Parthenius of Tula, who recently visited Tolstoy and had a prolonged conversation with him. The Bishop, without retelling the substance of Tolstoy's words, which he regards as having the secret character of those of the confessional, has proclaimed his conviction that Tolstoy wishes to be reconciled to the Church.

The Holy Synod will, it is expected, soften the rigors of excommunication. At present no prayers can be offered for Tolstoy's recovery. It is rumored that the clergy of Kozelsk refused such a request from the parishioners.

TOLSTOY NO BETTER DOCTORS STILL HOPE
Unfavorable Turn Last Night and

Oxygen Administered for Fainting Spells
DOCTORS BAR CHURCHMEN
Holy Synod Seeks to Reconcile Novelist with Church—Czar Advocates Ecclesiastical Forgiveness

ASTAPOVA, Russia, Nov. 19—After having remained practically unchanged throughout the day, the condition of Count Leo Tolstoy took an unfavorable turn late yesterday afternoon. Oxygen was administered to the patient, who frequently lost consciousness. Great anxiety was expressed by those at the bedside of the stricken novelist, but hope has not been abandoned for his ultimate recovery.

At 12:40 o'clock this morning the patient was resting quietly.

Dr. Usoff, Professor of Internal Diseases at Moscow University, and Dr. Thechurovsky, who treated Tolstoy for bronchitis in the Crimea to 1901 have been urgently summoned to Astapova.

At 7 o'clock last night Tolstoy's temperature was 97.88, pulse 110, and respiration 36. At that hour he was quite conscious but sleepy and very weak. Still later in the evening, after a clyster temperature had been taken which registered 98.2 degrees, the general feeling of the patient was better.

TOLSTOY IS DEAD; LONG FIGHT OVER
Novelist with Family About Him Sank Into Last Rest at 6:05 This Morning.
STILL UNDER CHURCH BAN
Holy Synod Refused to Lift it Though Czar's Ministers Favored Such Action

ASTAPOVA, Sunday, Nov. 20 [Nov. 7, O. S.]—Count Tolstoy died at 6:05 this morning.

The Countess Tolstoy was admitted

to the sickroom at 5:50. Tolstoy did not recognize her.

The family assembled in an adjoining room, awaiting the final event.

Tolstoy has suffered several severe attacks of heart failure during the night. During the early morning hours they followed each other in rapid succession, but were quickly relieved. Between the first and second attack the members of the family were admitted to the bedside.

The novelist's condition after each attack was what the attending physician called "deceptively encouraging." The patient slept for a little, seeming to breathe more comfortably than usual. Drs. Thechurovsky and Usoff, nevertheless, in a statement to Tolstoy's son, Michel, held out but slight hope, and did not hesitate to predict a quick end under ordinary mortal circumstances. Tolstoy, they said, was a splendid patient in mind and body, except for his heart.

When one of the heart attacks seized him Tolstoy was alone with his eldest daughter, Tatina. He suddenly clutched her hand and drew her to him. He seemed to be choking, but was able to whisper:

"Now the end has come; that is all."

Tatina was greatly frightened and tried to free herself so she might run for the doctor, but her father would not release his grasp. She called loudly from where he sat. The physicians came and injected camphor, which had an almost immediate effect in relieving the pressure. Tolstoy soon raised his head and drew himself up to a sitting position. When he had recovered his breath he said:

"There are millions of people and many sufferers in the world. Why are you so anxious about me?"

Several important communications, including that from Antonious, the Metropolitan of St. Petersburg, had not been shown to Tolstoy. The condition of the Count had been all along considered too grave to permit his being agitated by written appeals to him to make peace with the Church.

St. Petersburg, Nov. 19—The C . . [Illegible]-net last night discussed Tolstoy and his relations with the Greek Catholic Church. According to the newspapers, all of those present, including the Procurator of the Holy Synod, were in favor of removing the ban of excommunication as necessary and timely. The Synod, however, has rejected the proposal, as there is no indication of a change in Tolstoy's attitude nor is it known that he desires to be restored to the faith.

Only two Clericals of the Holy Synod favored the proposal. The majority decided that every effort to influence the novelist to modify his position should be made. The presence at Astapova of Count Tchertkoff is believed to be a stumbling block in the way of the Count's return to the church.

PEASANTS KNEEL AT TOLSTOY'S BIER
All Comers, Even Children, Admitted to Hut Where Countess Sits Beside Her Dead.
Funeral to Be To-morrow
Church Still Holds Old Antagonist Excommunicate, but Requiems Are Sung In St. Petersburg and Moscow

Astapova, Nov. 20—In a low room, hung with pine branches, Tolstoy's body lies in the rude hut in which he died early this morning. All the peasants in the district have flocked here during the day. None was excluded from the death chamber, through which there was a constant stream of visitors, including many school children. Many of them knelt beside the bier. The silence at times was broken by orthodox chants for the repose of the soul of the dead.

Countess Tolstoy sat beside the body for hours, often kissing the face. [Incorrect] "The light of the world is out," she said repeatedly. She left the hut only to attend matins in the school chapel, expecting that a requiem would be sung. When informed that this was not permitted, she fainted.

NOTES

18 Astapovo 1910. This scene has been re-created as accurately as possible with the help of a special viewing of remarkable newsreel film shot at Astapovo in 1910 and preserved in the special film archives in Moscow, and with the viewing of a documentary film, *From Riches to Rags* (produced by Jonathan Stedall), which incorporated the Russian film with film owned by the British Broadcasting Company. Additional material was found in the following books: *Tolstoy Remembered by His Son* (Sergey Tolstoy), *Tolstoy, My Father* (Ilya Tolstoy), *Tolstoy, A Life of My Father* (Alexandra Tolstoy), and the diaries of Countess Tolstoy.

19 Tolstoy re-created the death of his brother, Count Dmitry Nikolaevich Tolstoy (1827–56), in *Anna Karenina*, Part V, Chapter 21.

20 Alexandra Andreyevna Tolstoy (1817–1918), Tolstoy's third cousin, a very close friend throughout his life and a woman he much admired.

21 Princess Alexandra Alexseyevna Obolensky (born Dyakova, 1830–90). Married Prince Andrey Vasilyevich Obolensky (1819–84), governor of Moscow from 1861–66. He founded a private girls' school in St. Petersburg in 1870.

21 Kostya's full name was Konstantin Alexandrovich Islavin (1827–1903). The evening of this visit Tolstoy wrote in his diary, "Had dinner at the Behrses with Kostya. The children served at the table. What delightful gay girls!"

21 Baron Vladimir Mikhailovich Mengden (1826–1910) became a member of the State Council.

Part One

23 Epigraph: *War and Peace* (Aylmer Maude translation). In describing the atmosphere of the Rostov family, Tolstoy re-created his impressions of the Behrs family circle, which included the three young sisters—Sonya, Lisa, and Tanya. Natasha Rostov in *War and Peace* was an admixture of Sonya and Tanya, and Lisa was the model for Vera Rostov.

Chapter 1

25 Dr. Behrs's full name was Andrey Yevstafyevich Behrs (1808–68). He was Sonya's father, son of a chemist-physician on the staff of the Moscow Palace

Control Collegiate Assessor in 1842, and state councilor in 1864. The Behrses were among those families promoted to nobility through the civil service in 1843, granted through Dr. Behrs. Permission was given in 1847 for a coat of arms—a beehive and bees. The original concept—a bear (Behrs-Bar meaning bear in German) being attacked by bees—was not approved by the government.

25 Description of Pokrovsoye: *Tolstoy as I Knew Him*, Tatyana Behrs Kuzminsky.

25 The name Lisa was an affectionate family name. As in most Russian families, the Behrs children all had nicknames, which were as follows:

    Elizaveta—Lisa (1843–1919). Married Gavril Paulenko

    Sofya—Sonya (Sonechka) (1844–1919)

    Tatyana—Tanya (Tanyachka) (1846–1950) Author of *Nikolaevna Tolstoy* (St. Petersburg, 1924). Married her cousin Alexander Kuzminsky.

    Alexander—Sasha (1845–1918).

    Stepan—Styopa (1855–1909). Author of *Recollections of Count Leo Tolstoy* (London, 1893).

    Pyotr—Petya (1849–1910). Editor of *Detskii Otdekh* (1881-82). Co-editor with Leonid D. Obolensky of a collection of stories by Turgenev and Tolstoy (1883–86).

    Vladimir—Vlodny (1853–74).

    Vyacheslav—Slavatchka (1861–1907). Killed by revolutionary workmen in St. Petersburg.

26 "on the contrary it gave": *War and Peace*, Book I, Chapter 9. The Behrs family, individually and as a family, appear repeatedly in Tolstoy's works including *Childhood*, *Family Happiness*, *War and Peace*, and *Anna Karenina*.

26 Behrs family; Lyubov Alexandrovna's ancestry: *A Life of My Father*, by Alexandra L. Tolstoy; and Tatyana Kuzminsky.

26 Tsar Alexander II (1818–81), Tsar 1855–81, successor to his father, Nicholas I. His first act as Tsar was to negotiate a peace for the Crimean Wars. His most important reform was the emancipation of the serfs (1861), from which time he was called the Tsar-Liberator. His first wife was Princess Maria of Darmstadt (1824–80) with whom he fell in love when she was only fifteen and he was on a royal tour of her country as Tsarevich. Their early years were happy and they had four sons and a daughter. Princess Maria was taken into the Orthodox Church as Marya Alexandrovna. They were estranged from 1865, when Alexander II met Princess Catherine Dolgoruky, later Princess Yurievsky, who bore him three children and became his morganatic wife in 1880 after the death of the Tsarina. Tsar Alexander II was assassinated on March 13, 1881, by revolutionaries.

26 On April 11, 1856, Tsar Alexander II told representatives of the Moscow nobility, "For the contradiction on certain unfounded reports, I think it necessary to tell you that I do not at present intend to abolish serfdom; but certainly, as you well know yourselves, the existing manner of owning serfs cannot remain unchanged. It is better to abolish serfdom from above than to await the time when it will begin to abolish itself from below. I request you, gentlemen, to consider how this may be achieved and to submit my words to the nobility for their consideration": *Alexander II and the Modernization of Russia*, Werner E. Mosse.

27   Uncle Kostya: Impressions from Sonya's diary and the autobiographies of
     Ilya, Sergey, Tatyana, and Alexandra Tolstoy.
28   "another chapter": Kuzminsky.
28   "Admiral Kornilov, making the rounds": Ibid.
28   Sevastopol story. Letter from Tolstoy to Sergey N. Tolstoy. Also Kuzmin-
     sky.
28   "And now it seems": Kuzminsky.
28   Behrs family scene, the singing of "The Eighth of September": Ibid.

CHAPTER 2

31   "Poor Sonya": Kuzminsky.
31   "Sasha" was Alexander Andreyevich Behrs, the eldest of Sonya's brothers
     but still one year younger than herself.
31   "If you only go": Childhood.
32   "Don't climb trees": Ibid.
32   "Don't be a baby": Kuzminsky.
33   "Next you will give your daughters": Ibid.
33   The full names of Marya Nikolaevna Tolstoy's (1830–1912) children were
     Elizaveta (Lisa) Valeryanova Tolstoy (1852–?), who was married in 1871 to
     Prince Leonid Dmitrievich Obolensky (1844–88); Varvara (Varya) Valery-
     anova Tolstoy (Varneka) (1850–?), who married Nikolai Mikhailovich Na-
     gurnov (1845–96); and Nikolai Valeryanovich Tolstoy (1848–?).
34   Polivanov (1842–1913) became head of a sector of the Nikolayevsky railroads
     and was later manager of the Cours Stables. He married Anna Mikhailovna
     Parmont.
34   Coronation Manifesto: Mosse.
34   A ruble equaled approximately 61 cents at that time.
35   George Leveson-Gower, 2nd Earl Granville (1815–91) was a British states-
     man who was interested in the women's movement and advocated the ad-
     mission of women to classes.
35   "intelligent and amiable": British Royal Archives.

CHAPTER 3

37   Georg Büchner (1813–37) was a German dramatist whose literary reputation
     rests on three plays and a fragment of a short story.
37   Karl Vogt (1817–95), a German naturalist, was forced from his post as
     professor at Giessen by his political activities. He was a professor, from
     1852, at Geneva. An ardent supporter of Charles Darwin (1809–82), he
     wrote a great many books on natural science.
38   Ivan Sergeyevich Turgenev (1818–83) was living abroad at the time and
     became the first Russian writer to gain a wide reputation in Europe. He
     came from a gentry family and was raised by a tyrannical mother. He
     studied at the universities of Moscow, St. Petersburg, and Berlin, and was
     an ardent liberal who strongly opposed serfdom. He wrote poetry and plays
     and the novels A Month in the Country, A Nest of Gentlefolk, On the Eve, and
     Fathers and Sons. His relations with Tolstoy were always incendiary even

when they had reconciled their differences. But he was a great friend of Gustave Flaubert (1821–80), Emile Zola (1840–1902), and Henry James (1843–1916), who gave him the title of "beautiful genius."

38 "How dare you": Kuzminsky.

38 "Sasha" Kuzminsky's full name was Alexander Mikhailovich Kuzminsky (1843–1917). He was a cousin of the Behrses' and later married Tanya.

38 "If Sonya were sixteen": Kuzminsky.

38 Plan to give land to the serfs: *Leo Tolstoy*, by Ernest J. Simmons, and Tolstoy's own *A Morning of a Landed Proprietor* (published in 1856 in *Memoirs of a Fatherland*). Also, Tolstoy recorded this incident in slightly altered form in *Anna Karenina:* "Another stumbling block was the peasants' invincible mistrust of the possibility of a landlord having any other aim than that of robbing them as much as possible. They were firmly convinced that his real aim (whatever he might say) would always be hidden in what he did not tell them": *Anna Karenina*, Part III, Chapter 29.

39 Aunt Toinette—Tatyana Alexandrovna Ergolskaya (1795–1874)—also was called "Auntie" and "Auntie Tanya." She was Tolstoy's third cousin, one of the most important influences of his childhood and youth. She was the model for Sonya in *War and Peace*. Quoted descriptions are from *War and Peace*, Part I, Chapter 5.

40 Valerya Vladimirovna Arsenev (1836–1909). The Arsenev family lived at Sudakova, three miles from Yasnaya Polyana. The father and mother had died when Valerya was a baby. The family consisted of an aunt, three daughters, a son, and a French governess. They were Tolstoy's nearest neighbors and he was an old friend of the family and had been made guardian of the son. For four months, Tolstoy carried on a courtship with Valerya, who in the beginning, he noted, was "without backbone and fire—like vermicelli—but kind. And her smile is painfully submissive." But he was for a time quite passionately in love with her and intended to marry her. His letters to her were those of jealous love. (Quote is from Tolstoy's diary.)

40 "Perhaps the whole delight": Ibid.

40 "nothing at all majestic": Tolstoy recalled this twenty-five years later in *Confessions*.

40 Vasily Petrovich Botkin (1811–69) was a publicist and literary critic. He was a partisan of the art-for-art's-sake movement.

40 Grand Duchess Marie, the daughter of Nicholas I, was Tsar Alexander II's sister and wife of Prince Maximilian of Leuchtenberg.

40 "is to a journey": Simmons.

41 Valerian Petrovich Tolstoy (1813–65) was the son of Aunt Toinette's only sister, Elizaveta Alexandrovna Ergolsky and Count Pyotr Ivanovich Tolstoy (1785–1834), a cousin of Tolstoy's father.

41 "would not be the chief sultana": Simmons.

41 "a scamp of a girl": Kuzminsky.

42 "combined with the slim beauty": description of Kitty modeled from Sonya, *Anna Karenina*.

42 Tolstoy's visits to the Behrs household: Kuzminsky.

42 "not for the sake": Tolstoy, *The Devil*. Tolstoy later wrote this book based on his affair with Axinia.

43 "simple, without pretense": Ibid.

43 So strong was Tolstoy's attraction for Axinia Bazykina that he wrote about

it not only in *The Devil*, but in *Polikushka, Idilliya (An Idyll)*, and in *Tikhon and Malanya.*

43   Years later Timofei Bazykina was to serve as coachman to Ilya Tolstoy, Tolstoy's second legitimate son.

43   Tolstoy describes the bear hunt in one of his children's stories, "The Bear Hunt."

CHAPTER 4

46   "an end has been put": *Russia: A History*, by Michael Florinsky.

46   Description of Liberation Day in St. Petersburg from the *Memoirs of a Revolutionist* by Prince Peter Kropotkin (1843–1921).

46   Liberation of the serfs: *Rural Russia Under the Old Regime*, by Gerald Tanquary Robinson.

47   The statute was actually signed by the Tsar on February 19, 1869.

47   "Nothing in my life": *Tolstoy's Letters*, Reginald F. Christian.

47   Afanasy Afanasyevich Fet (1820–92) was a Russian poet. His first collection of poetry, *Liricheskiy Panteon*, appeared in 1840; later he became a cavalry soldier. He loved "Yelena" but was too poor to marry her. Their parting and her subsequent suicide devastated him, and he never forgot her. *Stikhotvoreniva* appeared in 1850. After travels abroad and a commission in the Guards he married a rich woman, Marya Petrovna, in 1856, and befriended Tolstoy and Turgenev. He retired to a farm (1858), wrote conservative articles (1862); and his poems were re-edited and decried by the radicals. In 1881 he moved to Moscow, translated Horace and other Latin poets, Schopenhauer, and Goethe's *Faust*. He published *Vecherniye ogni* (1883) and later his memoirs in prose (3 vols.). He attempted suicide and died of heart failure. Rejected by his anti-aesthetic contemporaries, Fet's poems inspired several composers.

48   "The arbitership has involved me in quarrels": Simmons.

49   "Lessons often continue": Christian.

49   "I like the Behrs family": Kuzminsky.

49   "She will make an excellent wife": Ibid.

50   Vasya (Fedka) Morozov, one of Tolstoy's favorite students, lived to an old age and wrote a memoir of his days at the Yasnaya Polyana school and his travels with Tolstoy. According to Morozov there were no female students in the Yasnaya Polyana school.

50   Kumiss (Russian *kumys*) is an intoxicating beverage originally made by the western Mongols from mare's milk. Valued in some places as a tonic and medication, kumiss is acrid in flavor. In Tolstoy's time a kumiss cure was given to people in a run-down, exhausted state and was thought to be revitalizing. These "cures" were most often given in the Caucasus and the Urals.

50   "Nihilist" was a word first applied by Turgenev in his novel *Fathers and Sons* (1862) to a theory held by many Russian revolutionaries at that time and afterward until the downfall of the Tsarist government in 1917. Nihilism stressed the need to destroy existing economic and social institutions. Acts of terrorism to achieve this end were encouraged. But on the whole, the nihilists were moderate in comparison with the revolutionaries of 1917.

50   "pedagogical nihilist": Simmons.

50 "Jewish synagogue": Ibid.
51 "an ignoramus": Ibid.
51 "What if our Lisa": Kuzminsky. It should be noted that the attitude of Dr.
    Behrs toward his wife's "matchmaking" appears in *Anna Karenina* in Book I,
    Chapter 12, in a discussion between the Rostovs.
52 "Sonya, do you love *le Comte*": Kuzminsky.
54 The Tsar was in Moscow at the Peter Palace at the time in connection with
    some army maneuvers. Tolstoy's letter to the Tsar was dated Moscow,
    August 22, 1862, and was presented through an aide de camp, S. A. Sher-
    emetev. The chief of police justified his search of Yasnaya Polyana by
    claiming student teachers were living there without resident permits. In the
    end the letter was sent to the governor of Tula with instructions that Yas-
    naya Polyana was not to be disturbed again for the same reasons.
54 "very much like a dark": Kuzminsky.
54 "The police officials burst upon": Kuzminsky.
55 "My father's a doctor": Ibid.
55 "And what else have you been doing": Countess Tolstoy's diary (recon-
    structed later by Sonya) and Kuzminsky.
56 "I have come to tell you": Kuzminsky.
56 "How pleasant and comfortable": Ibid.

CHAPTER 5

59 Nadezhda Alexandrovna Karnovich (née Islavin) (1824–1900) was a full
    sister to Sonya's mother.
59 "There's the house": Kuzminsky.
59 "Do you remember our old house": Countess Tolstoy's diary (reconstructed
    later by Sonya).
60 Natalya Petrovna Okhotnitsky (1792–1874), a childhood friend of Tolstoy's
    Aunt Toinette, was a woman of seventy at this time.
60 "Sonya is much like you": Diary.
61 "And what shall we do about a third": Ibid.
61 "something rapturous": Ibid.
61 "What are you doing here": Ibid.
62 "Would you like to ride with me": Ibid.
62 "day was different": Ibid.
63 Sofya Alexandrovna Islenyev, Lyubov Alexandrovna Behrs's stepmother,
    was a good deal younger than her husband; and her three daughters were
    only a few years older than the Behrs sisters.
63 "*Le Comte* is coming": Ibid.
63 "But we let the wolf get away": Ibid. This wolf appears in *War and Peace*,
    Book VII, Chapters 4 and 5.
64 "How stylish you look": Diary.
65 "I must go": Ibid. This is the famous scene that Tolstoy recaptured for *Anna
    Karenina* between Kitty (Sonya) and Levin (Tolstoy). It has been recon-
    structed here from the dialogue in the scene in the novel and from notes
    recorded by Sonya in her diary and by Tanya Kuzminsky in her reminis-
    cences. Sonya records that Tolstoy did not make this his proposal and that
    only Tolstoy wrote letters with chalk upon the card table. These two vari-

ances are the only differences between the actual scene as recorded by both Sonya and Tanya, and the published version. (See *Anna Karenina*, Part IV, Chapter 14.)

66   "Tanya, Sonya is taking *le Comte*": Kuzminsky.

66   "I want to have a talk with you, Mama": Ibid.

68   "I am going with you": Diary.

68   "It's so stuffy inside the coach": Ibid.

69   "A powerful sense of infinite": Ibid.

69   "When I become Empress": Ibid.

69   "What a mad night!" Ibid.

69   "You've noticed it too": Kuzminsky.

70   "Spent the night": Tolstoy's diary.

71   "Go on": Countess Tolstoy's diary (reconstructed later by Sonya).

71   The "Il Baccio" waltz was written by Luigi Arditi (1822–1903). He also wrote *L'Arditi* and *Le Tortorelle*. His operas, *I Briganti*, *Il Corsaro*, and *La Spia*, only met with fair success. It was for the "Il Baccio" waltz that he was known.

71   Letter to Sonya: *Tolstoy's Essays and Letters*, Aylmer Maude translation.

72   "What is it": Diary.

72   "Do you want to marry *le Comte*": Ibid.

73   "with remarkable nobility": Kuzminsky.

73   "sound of very, very": *Anna Karenina*, Part IV, Chapter 15. Referred to by Sonya in her autobiography as being the re-enactment of her own scene with Tolstoy.

73   "filled his own heart": Ibid.

74   "When is it to be": Ibid., Part IV, Chapter 16.

74   "You may also congratulate": Kuzminsky.

76   "You will have me": Diary.

76   "Take those dreadful books back": Ibid.

77   "I have come to say": *Anna Karenina*, Part IV, Chapter 2.

78   "You've chosen a fine time": Kuzminsky.

79   "What if I lose his love": Diary (undated).

79   Pelagya Ilyenishva Yushkov (1798–1875), who was born Countess Tolstoya, was Tolstoy's paternal aunt.

79   In her diary Sonya wrote, "The marriage ceremony has been splendidly described in *Anna Karenina*. In his account of Levin's and Kitty's wedding, Lev Nikolaevich has not only given a vivid and brilliant picture of the ceremony, but he has also described the whole psychological process in the bridegroom's (Tolstoy's) mind. As for myself, I had lived through so much excitement during the last few days that, standing at the altar, I felt and experienced absolutely nothing. It seemed to me that something obvious, natural, and inevitable was happening—nothing more."

81   "If leaving your family": Diary, under heading *L. N. Tolstoy's Marriage*.

82   "Well, show that you are the mistress": Ibid.

PART TWO

83   Epigraph: *Anna Karenina*, Part VII, Chapter 13.

CHAPTER 6

85 Description of servants: Ilya Tolstoy and Kuzminsky.
86 Description of portraits: Ilya Tolstoy.
87 Ilya Andreyevich Tolstoy (1757–1820) was the prototype for Count Rostov in *War and Peace*.
87 "Incredible happiness": September 25, 1862.
87 "I am writing from": September 28, 1862.
88 "How are you": Kuzminsky.
90 "I love her at night": October 7, 1862.
93 "Was marriage": In 1889 Tolstoy wrote *The Kreutzer Sonata*, in which he examined closely this period of his life with Sonya.
93 "No! No!" Countess Tolstoy's diary, October 9, 1862.
94 "it seems to me": Ibid.
94 "He grows colder and colder": October 11, 1862.
94 "If I am no good to him": November 3, 1862.
94 "Masha": Marya Mikhailovna Tolstoy was born Shiskin (1832–1918). A Gypsy from Tula, she was Sergey Nikolaevich's mistress for eighteen years until he married her in 1867.
94 "Today Grisha": Grisha was the eldest child of Sergey Nikolaevich's three then-illegitimate children, and at the time his only son. When Sergey finally married his Gypsy mistress, Grisha was legitimized and his name then became Count Grigory Sergeyevich Tolstoy. In 1892 he married Baroness Elena Vladimirovna Tisenhausen.
95 Belogubka means "white lips."
96 Letter to Tanya: Kuzminsky.
97 "to see things in a pure light": Countess Tolstoy's diary, November 23, 1862.

CHAPTER 7

98   "I cannot wash": from Pushkin's poem "Recollection."
100 "was brilliant": Countess Tolstoy's diary, November 23, 1862; italics Countess Tolstoy's.
102 "becoming enslaved": Ibid.
102 "as if the chains": *The Kreutzer Sonata*.
104 Story of hat: Kuzminsky.
105 Darya Ivanovna Tyutcheva Sushkov (1806–79) was the sister of the poet Fyodor Ivanovich Tyutchev (1803–73).
106 "Mama, I'm going home": Ibid.
106 "My darling, my dear one": Kuzminsky.
106 Ivan Sergeyevich Aksakov (1823–86) and his older brother, Konstantin Sergeyevich (1817–60), were Slavophile publicists. Ivan also was one of the leaders of the Slavophile movement. Dmitry Irinarkhovich Zavalishin (1804–92), a Decembrist, wrote *The Notes of a Decembrist*.
  The Decembrists were officers and noblemen who belonged to a secret political society advocating representative democracy. On December 14, 1825, they gathered 3,000 troops in Senate Square in St. Petersburg. Tsar

Nicholas I quickly suppressed the ill-organized revolt. Some Decembrists were executed or exiled.

107   "You shall come to see us": Kuzminsky.

108   The Auerbach family were landowners in Tula and were friends of both the Behrs and the Tolstoy families. Some of the family members were also involved in the manufacture of porcelain.

108   Eugene (Yevgeny) Lyovich Markov (1835–1903) was a writer and teacher. From 1860 he was headmaster of the boys' school in Tula, where he became acquainted with Tolstoy.

108   "swinish"; "a crime": *The Kreutzer Sonata*.

109   "I heard her opening the door": Kuzminsky.

109   The porcelain doll. This "dream" of Tolstoy's was actually an enlargement of the nightmare that Sonya had in Moscow when she dreamt of Axinia's illegitimate son by Tolstoy as a doll she tore to pieces. The tale is generally referred to as the "porcelain doll story" although in *Tolstoy's Letters*, translated by Reginald F. Christian, it is referred to as the "china doll story."

112   "Your Lyova": Dr. Behrs's letter, Kuzminsky.

112   "Managers, foremen": *The Life of Tolstoy*, Maude.

113   "For certainly": Kuzminsky.

114   "What can the reason be?": April 29, 1863.

114   "He already has toenails": Kuzminsky.

114   Mikhail Antonovich Marcus (1790–1865) was a former court physician and friend of Dr. Behrs.

CHAPTER 8

115   Anatoly Lvovich Shostak was second cousin to Sonya. He married Alexander Kuzminsky's half-sister, Nadia V. Shidlovskaya (1851–1889).

116   "Do you think you can wait": Kuzminsky.

116   "Has it begun": *Anna Karenina*, Countess Tolstoy's diary, and Kuzminsky confirm that Tolstoy re-created almost moment by moment the birth of his and Sonya's first child, Sergey Lvovich Tolstoy (and his reactions to it), in the birth scene in *Anna Karenina*, Part VII, Chapter 15. The main difference is that Kitty has her child in the city, whereas Sonya's confinement was in the country.

117   "No, get the icon": Kuzminsky.

118   "Alive! Alive!": Ibid.

118   "God has presented": Ibid.

119   "Lyovochka is always trying": Ibid.

119   "only means": *The Kreutzer Sonata*.

119   The original wet nurse was a woman named Evlampia Matveeva, whose husband, Phillip Rodionov, later became the Tolstoys' coachman and then bailiff. Evlampia was replaced by Natalya Kasakova.

119   "I have a great longing to rest": July 24, 1863.

120   "Unfortunately, my dear friends": Kuzminsky.

121   "A strange little red being": Tolstoy diary.

121   "When he says": July 31, 1863.

121   "When I look at the boy": August 2, 1863.

121   "Not written for": August 3, 1863.

122   "seeing how easily": Addendum to *The Kreutzer Sonata*.

123   "How dare he think": Ibid.
125   The Tsarevich Nicholas died suddenly in 1865. His brother, Alexander,
      who had been ill-prepared for the role, then became Tsarevich and in 1881
      ascended the throne as Alexander III.
125   This ball and Tanya's attitudes, dress, and demeanor were vividly recap-
      tured by Tolstoy in *War and Peace*, Part VI, Chapter 9, Natasha's first ball.
126   "Well, I could not": Kuzminsky.
127   "I believe I'm in love with him": Kuzminsky.
128   "a happy and tranquil": Simmons.

Chapter 9

131   The new novel, *1805*, was eventually to be *War and Peace*.
132   "You say I am your enemy": January 1–3, 1864, *Letters*, Christian.
133   "I can't stand these moral": Kuzminsky.
133   *The Infected Family* (also called *The Contaminated Family* and *The Progressives*)
      was never produced and was not published in Russian until 1928.
134   "It was so hideous": *A Life of My Father*, Alexandra L. Tolstoy.
134   "What are you in such a hurry for": Ibid.
134   "Among other things": Simmons.
135   "I spend a great deal of time": November 13, 1863.
136   "It must be": Diary, April 22, 1864.
136   "Not for a moment": Christian.
137   "Dora was lying": Kuzminsky.
137   "It is always better": Ibid.
138   "Sonya, Sonya": Ibid.
138   The Synod is an ecclesiastical council attended by bishops and delegated
      clergy of a nation, province, or diocese.
138   Sergey Nikolaevich's drinking preferences: Ilya Tolstoy.
139   Sergey Nikolaevich and Masha. Ibid.
139   "one and only love": Ibid.
139   Tanya's attempted suicide: Ibid.
140   "The relations between Sonya and me": September 16, 1864.
140   "not in the vulgar sense": Ilya Tolstoy.
141   "bent over the keyboard": Ibid.
141   Description of Tolstoy's early study: Ibid.
142   The *Sovremennik* circle photograph, taken on February 15, 1856, by Levit-
      sky, shows Tolstoy in his officer's uniform surrounded by well-known writ-
      ers of the time. It was autographed by all present and still hangs on the wall
      of his study in Yasnaya Polyana.
142   Still in Tolstoy's study at Yasnaya Polyana, the marble bust of Nikolai was
      made from Nikolai's death mask by the sculptor Guillaume Geefs in 1861.
      Carved on the left shoulder is the inscription "Gme. Geefs, Statuaire du
      Roi, Bruxelles, 1861" (Guillaume Geefs, Royal Sculptor, Brussels, 1861).
142   The Tula doctor's name was Preobrazhensky.
143   Popov (1816–86), no relation to Nil A. Popov, was professor of surgery at
      the University of Moscow.
143   "I am in doubt": Christian.
143   Katkov (1818–67), noted Moscow journalist, was publisher and editor of
      Russky Vestnik (translated as the *Russian Messenger* or the *Russian Herald*) and

Moskovskiye Vedomosty (Moscow Record). Katkov did publish the first part of *1805*, later to be incorporated as the first part of *War and Peace*, in the *Russian Herald* at the agreed price of 300 rubles per printer's sheets. There were ten printer's sheets in this section of the final book. (Three hundred rubles was $183.)

144   "Frankly, to have": Kuzminsky.
144   "I'd be ashamed": Ibid.
144   The surgical assistants were named Nechayev and Haak.
144   "At one moment": Kuzminsky.
145   "Oh, Sonya": Christian.
146   "Music, which I have missed": December 9, 1864. *Tolstoy and His Wife*, Tikhon Polner.
146   "Alexander Mikhailovich": Christian.

PART THREE

149   Epigraph: Countess Tolstoy's diary, July 31, 1868.

CHAPTER 10

152   "The Count has grown old": Countess Tolstoy's diary, November 3, 1864.
152   The first reading of *1805*: Kuzminsky.
153   Many characters in *1805* (later to become the first 38 chapters of *War and Peace*) were modeled after people in Tolstoy's and Sonya's lives. Some were: 1) Count Ilya Rostov, a close copy of Tolstoy's grandfather, Count Ilya Andreyevich Tolstoy; 2) The Countess Rostov, Tolstoy's grandmother, Countess Pelagya N. Tolstoy; 3) Natasha, Tanya, and Sonya; 4) Sonya, Aunt Toinette; 5) Nikolai Rostov, Tolstoy's father, Count Nikolai Ilych Tolstoy; 6) Vera, Lisa Behrs; 7) Boris, Polivanov.
153   "I would be ashamed to be published": Letter dated May 3, 1865 (Christian), to Princess L. I. Volkonskaya (1825–90), wife of Tolstoy's second cousin, Prince A. A. Volkonsky. In spite of Tolstoy's denial, Princess Volkonskaya was the prototype for the "little princess" Liza Bolkonskaya in *War and Peace*. She was also portrayed by Tolstoy as the heroine of his story "A History of Yesterday" (1851).
153   "You can't imagine, Tanya": Kuzminsky.
154   Sonya retained all three drafts. Tolstoy later wrote a fourth draft for use in the final full publication of *War and Peace*, but the third draft was used in the first Russian edition. Most English editions do not include the introduction, though it was translated into English by George Bibian from the Russian texts printed in Volume 13 of the Jubilee Edition of Tolstoy's work (Moscow 1949).
154   "more similar": Tolstoy's third draft of the introduction.
154   "In a few days": Christian.
154   "In a day or two": Ibid.
155   "in the hut": Ibid.
155   "Sonya darling": Ibid.
155   Critique in the *Invalid*: Kuzminsky.

155   Turgenev's quote: Christian. Turgenev later changed his views dramatically when the book was published in its entirety.

156   "You wish to be a general": Simmons.

156   "The second part of *1805*": Alexandra L. Tolstoy, *A Life of My Father.* (British title: *My Life with Tolstoy*).

158   "There is nothing": Diary, March 26, 1865.

159   "What was the matter": Kuzminsky.

160   "The two of them": Ibid.

160   "Just wait a little": Ibid.

161   Sergey Nikolaevich's behavior described by Sonya in her diary, July 12, 1865.

161   "the evil devil": Christian.

162   "I saw him": Kuzminsky.

163   "Please go away": Kuzminsky.

163   "Only a new love": Ibid.

164   "She is prepared to love you": Christian.

164   "I felt like": Kuzminsky.

165   "Is it too rough": Ibid.

165   "Lyova really judged me": Diary, March 12, 1866.

166   "long, lively talks": Ibid. July 19, 1866.

CHAPTER 11

167   Osip Ivanovich Komissarov was a hatter by profession. Tolstoy wrote Fet from Yasnaya Polyana in May 1866, a month after the attempted assassination: "Osip Ivanovich Komissarov, a member of various societies, public prayers about them shooting at the Tsar; students at the Ivarskaya Chapel —it's all a lot of stuff and nonsense." (Christian)

167   Dmitry I. Karakozov, although a member of a small group of communist students, appeared to have been acting on his own. He was executed within weeks of the attempt. Tolstoy wrote Fet in May, 1866: "What do you think of 4 April? For me it was the *coup de grace*. The last shred of respect and reticence on the part of the conscience of the crowd has vanished" (Christian).

168   Marya Ivanova's viewpoints, regarded as nihilism in 1866, resembled the basic tenets of Tolstoy's future philosophy. These discussions with his bailiff's wife, therefore, influenced Tolstoy more than might be thought.

170   "under the best possible circumstances": Kuzminsky.

170   Sonya's name day: Kuzminsky.

170   *La Muette de Portici*, an opera by Daniel François Esprit Auber (1782–1871), was known in the United States as *The Dumb Girl of Portici*, and in Britain as *Masaniello*. It was produced in Paris in 1828, London and Edinburgh in 1829, and New York in 1831.

171   The *kamarinskaya* was a Russian folk dance. Glinka composed an orchestral "Fantasia" based on the dance, which was later used by Rimsky-Korsakov and Gazasinov, with the same name and rhythms.

171   "Go ahead": Kuzminsky.

172   "The weather was lovely": November 12, 1866.

172   "feel and ponder": Ibid.

173   The illustrator of twenty-one drawings that appeared in the first edition of

War and Peace was Mikhail Sergeyevich Bashilov (1821–70), Sonya's second cousin. Bashilov was an artist and sculptor who was inspector at the College of Art, Sculpture, and Architecture (1855–70) and had illustrated other books, among them *The Misfortune of Being Clever* (Griboyedov) and *Provincial Sketches* (Saltykov-Shchedrin). Tolstoy writes in a letter to Bashilov (December 8, 1866), "In The Kiss [Part I, Chapter 10], can't you model Natasha on Tanyachka Behrs? Here's a picture of her at 13" (Christian).

173 Hannah Tarsey, an Englishwoman, lived as governess with the Tolstoys from 1866 to 1872. She then was employed in the same capacity by Tanya Kuzminsky for a year.

174 "quite as a member": *A Life of My Father*, Alexandra L. Tolstoy.

174 "the horses trembled" . . . and descriptions of the wooden dolls and her shopping trip to Tula were described in detail by Sonya in her short children's story "The Little Skeleton Dolls—A Christmas Tale," published by I. N. Kuzhnerev and Co. Lithographic Press, Pimenovskaya Street, Moscow, 1910, in a private limited edition of 150 copies. This children's book, entitled *The Little Skeleton Dolls and Other Tales* (five in all), has never been published in English. Only three copies of the original survive, and I am grateful to Count Sergey Mikhailovich Tolstoy (Sonya's grandson) for allowing me the use of the book and to Ms. Pamela Davidson for translating it for me. There are also eight color illustrations in the book drawn "according to the author's plan" by A. Moravov.

175 "the other of everyone else": Ilya Tolstoy.

175 Christmastime at Yasnaya Polyana: Ibid.

176 "big doll": Sergey Tolstoy.

177 "Why are you sitting on the floor": Kuzminsky.

177 "feel the crime of killing in war": Christian.

178 Tolstoy first met Samarin (1819–96), a well-known Slavophile, in 1856 and often consulted him during the writing of *War and Peace* on matters pertaining to the history of that period, on which Samarin was an expert.

178 "I have my partialities": Christian.

179 "little time left over": Kuzminsky.

179 Peddlers at Yasnaya Polyana: Ilya Tolstoy.

181 Trip to Moscow and French novels: Kuzminsky.

CHAPTER 12

183 "whole sentences": Ilya Tolstoy.

183 "What is it": Ibid.

183 "I'll tell Maman": Ibid.

184 "I'm borrowing": Christian.

185 "It's a bad date": Kuzminsky.

185 "I must be reborn": Tolstoy's Notebooks, Maude.

185 "It was two o'clock": Christian.

187 Arthur Schopenhauer (1788–1860) was a German philosopher who expounded the philosophy of pessimism.

187 Georg W. F. Hegel (1770–1831) was a major German philosopher whose teachings Schopenhauer opposed.

187 "Yesterday": Entry dated February 5—misdated—in translation. It was February 18.

188   Anna Stepanovna Pirogova (1837–72), Bibikov's mistress, was the model for Anna Karenina. She was the daughter of well-to-do Tula landowners who had originally owned Sergey Nikolaevich Tolstoy's estate, Pirogovo. Bibikov was considered beneath her, and the liaison degrading. In January 1870, when he cast her out to marry the German governess in his home, she threw herself before an oncoming train in nearby Yasenki station. Tolstoy was asked to be at the post-mortem. It was an unforgettable experience, and the following year he began *Anna Karenina*.

189   "You write": Christian.

189   "I hoped to visit": Ibid.

189   Nikolai Nikolayevich Strakhov (1828–96) was a literary critic and philosopher who admired Tolstoy and worked devotedly for him, assisting in the proofreading of *War and Peace*, *Annà Karenina*, and the *ABC* books. He was a close associate and a biographer of Dostoevsky.

190   "I read the sixth volume": Letter from Ivan Turgenev to I. P. Boresov. March 15/27, 1870. In Maude translation of *War and Peace*.

191   "Hot-tempered and violent": Tolstoy letter to Countess Alexandra Tolstoy (Christian).

191   Tolstoy's first *ABC Book* was published in 1872 and revised as *A New ABC Book* in 1875. The first edition had an extremely small sale and received negative reviews. The revised edition did considerably better.

191   Sonya's short story "Sparrow" is lost, according to Alexandra L. Tolstoy. It was about spring at Yasnaya Polyana and the arrival with it of Tanya Kuzminsky when she was still unmarried.

191   "It was Shrovetide": Countess Sonya Tolstoy's *The Little Skeleton Dolls and Other Tales*. See note for page 174.

192   "Easter was late": Ibid.

192   "The snow was half melted": Ibid.

192   "long overcoats over": Ilya Tolstoy.

193   "Christ is risen": Ibid.

193   "It was beginning to get light": "In the Village."

194   "A shadow has passed between us": August 18, 1870.

194   "I've stopped writing": Christian.

195   Sonya's difficult birth of little Masha and her battle with puerperal fever were duly recorded and "fictionalized" by Tolstoy in *Anna Karenina* in Part IV, Chapter 2, with even the details of the wallpaper (exactly like that in Sonya's room at Yasnaya Polyana) and the shaving of Sonya's hair included.

195   "Is my child alive": Kuzminsky.

195   "I've failed you again": Ibid.

196   "We're living in a tent": Christian.

197   "The two-month kumiss cure": August 18, 1871.

197   "so much new life": Ibid.

197   Peter the Great: This project took up a great deal of Tolstoy's time from 1871 to 1873. He did prodigious research and made many attempts at beginning the book. Years later he commented that the reason he couldn't write it was that the more he found out about Peter, the more a fool he believed the Tsar to be.

198   Anna Stepanovna's small red bag appears as a major prop piece in *Anna Karenina*, Part VIII, Chapter 31.

198   "her skull dissected": Countess Tolstoy's diary.

198 Tolstoy was to use the image of the old peasant combined with his experience in Arzamas throughout the text of *Anna Karenina* as a symbol of death.

199 Dora was to stay only a short while. Her last name is unknown. Fyodor Fyodorovich Kaufmann, the German tutor, remained for several years though he was disliked by all the Tolstoy boys.

199 "*Auf, kinder, auf*": Ilya Tolstoy.

199 "terrible mud": Countess Tolstoy's diary, April 1, 1872.

200 "I've decided to emigrate": September 14, 1872, Christian.

200 "about the new turn": Ibid.

201 Princess Catherine Dolgoruky was mistress and second wife of Alexander II. She was an uncrowned tsarina. In June 1880, forty days after the death of the Tsar's first wife, the Empress Maria Alexandrovna, the Tsar made the Princess his morganatic wife (she had been his mistress fifteen years) and raised her to the rank of Princess Yurievsky (the family name of the Romanovs). It was expected that the Tsar would secure her coronation and the accession of their children, the oldest being Prince George, but on March 13, 1881, Tsar Alexander II was assassinated.

201 The ostracism of Catherine Dolgoruky was indeed used by Tolstoy in *Anna Karenina*, serving as a model for Anna Karenina's own ostracism by St. Petersburg society.

201 "Our serious winter life": November 20, 1872.

202 "The machine is ready": January 31, 1873.

202 "everything there ought to be": Tolstoy to Fet, June 3, 1873, Christian.

202 "But then I began to think": Ibid.

203 Prince Urusov (1827–85) was a war hero, mathematician, historian, writer, and a well-known chess player. He was a friend of Tolstoy's from their war days together in the Crimea. Urusov wrote *Studies of the Eastern War, A Survey of the Campaigns of 1812–13*, and *Military-Mathematical Problems and the Railways*. Tolstoy consulted him when he was writing sections of *War and Peace* dealing with the philosophy of history and war. He considered his letters to Urusov, with his correspondence to his cousin Alexandra and to Nikolai Strakhov, his most important. Urusov translated to French Tolstoy's *What I Believe*. Sonya had a strong attachment to Urusov, a platonic love that had great impact on her middle years. Urusov died in the Crimea, where he had gone with Tolstoy, leaving "his most valuable possessions"—his letters from Tolstoy—to his son.

203 The first lines of *Anna Karenina*: Countess Tolstoy's diary, Alexandra L. Tolstoy, and Sergey Tolstoy. The line quoted in the text ("After the opera . . .") was eventually to become the opening of Part II, Chapter 6, of *Anna Karenina*. It wasn't until the final version that Tolstoy used the line "Everything was at sixes and sevens in the home of the Oblonskys," which was even closer to the original Pushkin inspiration.

204 "I have written a sheet and a half": Countess Tolstoy's diary, March 19, 1873.

CHAPTER 13

205 "It's a bad date": Kuzminsky.

205 Masha Kuzminsky's name was actually Marya Alexandrovna. There would

soon be three more Kuzminsky children: Mikhail Alexandrovich (Misha), Sonya Alexandrovna, and Vera Alexandrovna.

205   "striving to go somewhere": Christian.

205   Summer life at Yasnaya Polyana. Ilya Tolstoy.

206   *Froufrou* was the title of a French comedy by Henri Meilhac (1831–97) and Ludovic Halévy (1834–1908) that enjoyed great popularity in the 1870s. Tolstoy not only gave the name to his own horse, but to Vronsky's animal in *Anna Karenina*.

206   "Not tired, are you": Ilya Tolstoy.

206   "Do you know, Ilyusha": Ibid.

207   "This was": Christian.

208   Trip down the Volga: Ilya and Sergey Tolstoy.

211   "the cruel memory": Tolstoy described Sonya's grief in *Anna Karenina*, Part VI, Chapter 16.

211   "He loved me very much": Diary, November 11, 1873.

211   "As soon as the grass": Ibid, February 17, 1874.

212   "And what is it all for": Dolly says this in Part VI, Chapter 16.

212   "the confusion": Ibid.

212   "less horrified by death": Levin, *Anna Karenina*, Part VIII.

212   "felt like a person": Ibid.

212   "If I don't accept": Ibid.

213   "Without knowing what I am": Ibid.

213   "a happy and healthy family man": Ibid.

214   "I lived with her all my life": Christian.

214   "I cannot tear myself away": Ibid.

215   "dull, monotonous apathy": Diary, October 12, 1875.

215   "Sometimes I feel that": Ibid.

215   "Sonya! Sonya": Ilya Tolstoy's room was near his father's study. These shouts awakened him and, standing hidden in his own dark hallway, he was a witness to this scene.

216   "All this time": Christian.

216   "I feel that old age had begun for me": Ibid.

217   *"Je ne veux"*: *My Life* (in Russian), Countess Tolstoy.

PART FOUR

CHAPTER 14

221   Bosnia, Herzegovina, Montenegro, and Serbia, at one time independent nations, all became constituent republics of Yugoslavia in 1946. They are located, respectively, in the northern, southern, southwestern, and eastern regions of Yugoslavia.

222   "yard surrounded by a stone wall": Ilya Tolstoy.

222   "What charming, gentle": Ibid.

223   "I am now setting to work": August 25, 1875, Maude (underscorings are Tolstoy's).

223   *"Everything* in it is *execrable"*: April 8–9, 1876, Ibid. (underscorings are Tolstoy's).

223   "should like anything": January 25–26, 1877, Ibid.

223   "What's so difficult": Ilya Tolstoy.

223   "I can't write anything while the war": Diary, September 12, 1877.

224   "showing the absolute necessity": Ibid, December 26, 1877.

224   "The priest will ask you": Ilya Tolstoy.

224   "We are now really at work": December 9, 1876, *A Life of My Father*, Alexandra L. Tolstoy. The length of an average chapter in *Anna Karenina* was approximately 1,200 words.

225   "domesticated prostitution": Maude.

225   "a passionate and sincere seeking": Ibid.

225   "How can I turn": *My Life* (in Russian), Countess Tolstoy.

225   "to liberate": December 26, 1877.

226   *The Decembrists* was never completed. Several chapters were published at a future time. Tolstoy had worked on this novel in 1863 and abandoned it for *War and Peace*. In 1879 he once again let the work on it stop, but this time he did not begin again.

226   "stern and censorious moralist": Ilya Tolstoy.

226   "I teach and nurse like a machine": *A Life of My Father*.

226   Thirty thousand rubles in 1873 was about $18,500.

227   "everyone else in the other": Ilya Tolstoy.

227   "dark period": Ibid.

227   "Having idealized": Ibid.

228   "chafed at their life together": *My Life*, Countess Tolstoy.

228   "We stuff ourselves with cutlets": Sergey Tolstoy.

228   "Here we sit": Ibid.

228   "not that of a father": Ibid.

229   "It's all very well": Ibid.

229   "Lev is working, so he says": Sonya to Tanya, October 1879, *A Life of My Father*.

229   "It's not the money I regret": Sonya to Tanya, November 1879, ibid.

230   "How hard I find it": Sonya to Tanya, January 30, 1880, ibid.

230   "At times I should like to fly away": Sonya to Tanya, February 1880, ibid.

231   "To my extreme horror": Sonya to Tanya, October 1880, ibid.

231   Five hundred rubles would have been about $300 in 1880.

231   "Truly, this is because we have begun": Sonya to Tanya, November 1880, ibid.

CHAPTER 15

232   "God has saved me again": *The Russian Dagger*, Virginia Cowles.

233   "one is tempted to regard": Ibid.

233   "Life bad, nobody give money": Ilya Tolstoy.

234   "Did you throw the bomb": Mosse.

234   "Thank God Your Majesty": Ibid.

235   "Rather too soon": Ibid.

235   "Quick. Take me to the palace": Ibid.

235   "Sasha! Sasha": Ibid.

236   The young scientist Kibalchich was a pioneer of jet propulsion. Sophia Perovskaya's father was governor-general of St. Petersburg. Zhelyabov, though the son of a house serf, had managed to be admitted to the University of Odessa (though he was later expelled). Rysakov was an artisan who attended a technical school in St. Petersburg. Helfmann was the daughter

of a poor self-educated Jewish tradesman and publisher of the *Rabochaya Gazeta* (the *Workers' Paper*). The only uneducated member of the condemned group was Mikhailov, who was a metal worker.

One of the youngest recruits to this party at the time was Lenin's (1870–1924) older brother, Alexander (1866–87), who died in an assassination attempt on Alexander III in 1887. The Lenin family name was Ulyanov.

236   "Rest assured": Maude.

237   "Little by little": January 31, 1881.

239   "Housemen": *The Tragedy of Tolstoy*, Alexandra L. Tolstoy.

240   "Well, and how is the woodcock": *The Truth About My Father*, Lev Tolstoy.

240   "That's how they dance the can-can": Maude.

240   "How well you did": Ibid.

241   The postbox. There was quite a conflict of opinion among the contributors to the postbox regarding the year it began. I have, after much consideration, decided it was first instigated in the summer of 1881, but did not become a family tradition until 1884.

241   All quotes from the postbox: Ilya Tolstoy.

241   "In my heart": *Alexander III* (in Russian), Zalonchkovsky.

242   "I am in despair": September 1881, Sergey L. Tolstoy.

243   "I can't give such a guarantee": Ibid. and Ilya Tolstoy.

243   "A month has passed": October 5, 1881, Maude.

243   "Are you going to see Sarah Bernhardt": Ibid.

244   "One *can't* live like this": Lev L. Tolstoy.

245   "I often wonder": October 26, 1886.

245   "My little one": Countess Tolstoy's letters, January 1882, Yasnaya Polyana Archives.

246   "Goodbye, darling": February 27, 1882, *A Life of My Father*, Alexandra L. Tolstoy.

246   "I was in the worst": Ibid.

246   "When I think of you": March 2, 1882, ibid.

246   "I lay out solitaires": Ibid.

249   "I have nothing to reply": Countess Alexandra A. Tolstoy's memoirs (in French and Russian).

250   "Dear Babouchka": Ibid.

250   "This house looks like": Ibid.

CHAPTER 16

253   Excerpt from the postbox: Ilya Tolstoy.

258   Dialogue included in diary entry.

259   Dolgo-Khamovnicheski Street is now called Lev Tolstoy Street.

259   "What a lovely garden": *A Life of My Father*, Alexandra L. Tolstoy.

260   "You are probably getting ready to go to a ball": Ibid.

260   "It was a wonderful ball": Ibid.

261   "Of course it's impossible to dispute": *Married to Tolstoy*, Cynthia Asquith. Tolstoy had sent Sonya this article on moral perfection and asked her opinion.

261   "Aren't you ashamed": Maude.

261   "I am called simply": Ibid.
261   Mme. Anna Seuron was a widow and the grand-niece of the German com-
      poser, Karl von Weber (1786–1826). She remained with the Tolstoys as
      governess to Masha for six years. Late in her life (1895), she published a
      German language memoir, *Graf Leo Tolstoy*, about those years, a book that is
      frequently quoted in Maude.
262   "new-baked prophet": Anna Seuron's Memoir, as translated by Maude.
263   "all sorts of lies": S. P. Arbuzov's memoirs.
264   "Those oppressed by riches": Seuron.
265   "Kind and Dear Lev Nikolaevich": The letter from Turgenev (in Maude)
      was unsigned and written with a weak hand. Turgenev died in Paris in
      1883, after a year-long illness, and was buried in Russia.
265   Chertkov (1853–1936) was Tolstoy's secretary and disciple and executor of
      his will.
266   "He and I are amazingly as one": Simmons.
267   "I have nothing in me": September 12, 1867.
268   Sonya's conversations with Tolstoy and with midwife: *The Tragedy of Tolstoy*,
      Alexandra L. Tolstoy.
268   "She is seriously mentally ill": Asquith.
268   Letter with five rules was sent to Mikhail Alexandrovich Englehardt (1861–
      1915), who at the time had been exiled to his father's estate in the Smolensk
      province for taking part in the 1881 student uprisings.
269   "His mother": July 1884, Maude.
269   "Will you always *intentionally*": April 1884, Simmons.
270   "no undertaking": Maude.
270   Argument at dinner table: Diary, June 18, 1897. On Alexandra (Sasha)
      Lvovna Tolstoy's thirteenth birthday, Countess Tolstoy reconstructed her
      feelings the night the child had been born.
271   "My wife has given birth": June 24, 1884. The correspondence between
      Tolstoy and Chertkov for the period of 1884–85 has been published in full
      (volume 85) in Russian in the Jubilee Edition. The remaining letters (1,000
      in all) have been published in succeeding editions (volumes 86 and 87).
271   "He turned to Christianity": June 18, 1897.
271   "Even while thinking of you": Simmons.
271   Correspondence between Tolstoy and Chertkov: Jubilee Edition, volume
      85, and Simmons.
272   "The companion of my nights": Diary, July 7, 1884.
273   "Cohabitation": Ibid., July 18, 1884.
273   "I do not understand": Ibid., July 19, 1884.
273   "Yesterday I received": Letter, October 26, 1884.
273   "You are absolutely": Letter, October 27, 1884.
274   "You and I": Asquith.
275   "I'm distressed": Simmons.
275   "Do not be angry": Ibid.
275   "In all relations": Ibid.
276   "Hurry, Tanya, hurry": *The Tolstoy Home*, Tatyana Sukhotkina.
277   Sonya's conversation with Empress: *My Life*, Countess Tolstoy.
279   "I've come to say": Lev L. Tolstoy.
281   "I would give": *A Life of My Father*, Alexandra L. Tolstoy.
281   "I do not tell": Maude.

CHAPTER 17

284   "Maman" and all dialogue in the passage: Anna Seuron.
284   "My wife:" Tolstoy to Mrs. Young, January 23, 1886.
285   These graves were dug up in 1932 when Nikolskoye Cemetery was demolished, and the remains were removed to Kotchakovo Cemetery.
285   "in greasy": *A Life of My Father*, Alexandra L. Tolstoy.
285   Description of Sonya's Saturdays: *The Tragedy of Tolstoy*, Alexandra L. Tolstoy.
286   Gay (1831–94) first came to see Tolstoy in 1882 in a time of spiritual crisis. He stopped painting portraits after this meeting (except for illustrations for Tolstoy's *What Men Live By* and portraits of the Tolstoy family) to devote his art entirely to portraying the life of Christ.
286   "false and affected": Diary, October 30, 1886.
286   Biryukov (1860–1931), Tolstoy's friend and biographer, was briefly engaged to Masha Tolstoy, but they never married.
286   Repin (1844–1930) made several famous portraits of Tolstoy.
286   "to beg": May 6, 1885, Tatyana Sukhotkina.
287   Anna married Chertkov in 1886.
287   "as though she": *A Life of My Father*, Alexandra L. Tolstoy.
287   "Well, I'll tell you": Simmons.
287   "the death of Tolstoy's great art": Ibid.
287   "He is an artist": Ibid.
288   "Why has this man": June 29, 1886, *The Diaries of Tchaikovsky*. The italics are Tchaikovsky's. He met Tolstoy ten years before and had spent a memorable evening sitting beside him and listening to a string quartet at the Moscow Conservatory play the great composer's Andante Cantabile.
288   "There was no fear": *The Death of Ivan Ilych*.
289   "barefoot": *The Tragedy of Tolstoy*, Alexandra L. Tolstoy.
289   "The general atmosphere": May 7, 1886, *The Tolstoy Home*, Tatyana Sukhotkina.
289   "mowed so vigorously": Ilya Tolstoy.
290   "The grass in the fields": Ibid.
290   "is less well-disposed": July 1886.
292   "I sometimes have": Diary, March 6, 1887.
293   "grieved at": Ibid.
293   "a negation of ideals": Simmons.
293   "one ought to put an end": Ibid.
294   *The Power of Darkness* was finally staged in Russia in 1895. With the aid of Émile Zola (1840–1902), it was performed in Paris on February 22, 1888, at the Théâtre Libre and was well received.
294   "A sound, healthy woman": Lev L. Tolstoy.
294   "the most intelligent": Ilya Tolstoy.
295   "for there is no death": *A Life of My Father*.
295   "It is mental agony": Diary, June 18, 1887.
296   "the same happy": June 18, 1887.
296   "What a powerful": July 3, 1887.
297   "The Abameleks": July 19, 1887.

298   "What fearful": Countess Alexandra Tolstoy's memoirs.
298   "for all his convictions": Simmons.
298   "He dictated": Countess Alexandra Tolstoy's memoirs.
298   "Do you know": Ibid.
299   "ignored his property": *Recollections of Count Leo Tolstoy*, Stepan Behrs.
299   "She [has] been": Ibid.
301   "God gave": *A Life of My Father*.
301   "Never was": Ibid.

CHAPTER 18

304   "were led to abandon": Anna Seuron.
304   "He listened": *Recollections*, Stepan Behrs.
304   "I feel": *The Tragedy of Tolstoy*, Alexandra L. Tolstoy.
305   "I read": Simmons.
305   "I shall not": Ibid.
305   "Must propose": Ibid.
305   "I feel lost": *The Tolstoy Home*, Tanya Sukhotkina.
306   "This morning": Simmons.
306   "After dinner": Ibid.
306   "The devil": Ibid.
306   "It is": Ibid.
306   "Sonya came": Maude.
307   "I am going on copying": November 23, 1890.
308   "I have been copying": December 11, 1889.
308   "[His] self-adoration": December 16, 1889. Thirty-two words are missing from this entry.
309   "It is beginning": Forty words are missing from this entry.
309   "calmer and cleaner": December 20, 1890.
309   "Miserable abortions": December 17, 1890.
310   "Let me marry": December 11, 1890.
310   "My Masha": December 24, 1890.
310   "Why am I trying": December 10, 1890.
310   "When Masha came": December 27, 1890.
310   "I am terribly": December 25, 1890.
311   "that pure, delicate": December 27, 1890.
312   "a very cozy second class compartment": Lev L. Tolstoy.
313   Letter to Alexander III recorded in Countess Tolstoy's diary, April 22, 1891.
313   "a very ugly bright green carpet": Ibid.
313   Description of Alexander: Ibid.
314   "It is written": Ibid.
314   "We might allow": Ibid.
314   "That isn't dangerous": Ibid.
315   "a black woolen dress": Ibid.
316   "I couldn't talk": Diary, June 1, 1891.
316   "bodily intimacy": Simmons.
316   "Last night": Ibid.
317   "the slightest": Alexandra A. Tolstoy's memoirs.
317   "It is hard": Ibid.

318   "vainglorious": Diary, July 21, 1891.
318   "a greedy": Ibid.
318   "His sensuality": July 27, 1891.
318   Charles Joseph Paul Bourget (1852–1935) was a French critic and novelist.
      Un Coeur de femme was concerned with erotic psychology.
319   Pobedonostsev's letter to Alexander III, July 1890: Simmons.

CHAPTER 19

322   "Very well then": Diary, September 19, 1891 (dialogue included).
322   The five children left at home were Vanichka, Sasha, Misha, Andreyusha,
      and Lyova.
323   "My sons": Tolstoy's diary, June 18, 1890.
323   "She does not understand": July 1, 1891.
324   Family meeting: *The Tolstoy Home*, Tatyana Sukhotkina.
324   The Tolstoy property was divided as follows: *Sergey* received 800 dessiatines
      of land at Nikolskoye, provided he paid 28,000 rubles to his sister Tatyana
      in one year and 55,000 rubles to his mother over a period of fifteen years.
      Tatyana received the Tolstoy estate in central Russia, Oviannikovo, and
      38,000 rubles. *Ilya* received Grinevka and 368 dessiatines of the Nikolskoye
      estate. *Lev* received the house in Moscow and 394 dessiatines in the Samara
      province, with the provision that he pay 5,000 rubles to Vanichka. *Andrey*
      and *Alexandra* received 2,011 dessiatines each in the Samara province, with
      payment of 9,000 rubles to Tatyana. *Ivan* (Vanichka) was allotted 370 des-
      siatines of Yasnaya Polyana (only a section) and the house. *Countess Tolstoy*
      was returned her dowry of 55,000 rubles and held the rest of the property at
      Yasnaya Polyana for Marya (Masha) and 55,000 rubles.
325   Sasha's observations: *The Tragedy of Tolstoy*, Alexandra L. Tolstoy.
325   Story of dinner prank: Ibid.
326   Ghost hunting: Ibid.
326   Rayevsky (1831–91) was a landowner from Tula and a family friend of the
      Tolstoys.
326   Leskov (1831–95) was a novelist and a short story writer. In his early work
      he took a strongly anti-radical stand and was considered an arch-conservative
      for the remainder of his life. His most well known work is a short story, "A
      Lady Macbeth of Mtsensk District" (1865), and a trilogy about the life of an
      imaginary town, Stargorod, which included *Cathedral Folk* (1872) and *En-
      chanted Wanderer*, which have been translated into English. Chertkov intro-
      duced Leskov to Tolstoy in 1887 and the two writers exchanged more than
      sixty letters between 1887 and 1894.
326   "There is a famine": July 4, 1891, Christian.
328   "My whole family": Simmons.
329   "There is much": November 9, 1891, Maude.
329   "I don't know myself": Ibid., December 1891.
329   "I had a reply": November 12, 1891.
332   "At last": Countess Alexandra Tolstoy's memoirs.
333   Chertkov's letters to Tanya: January 31, 1894. *The Tolstoy Home*.
333   "Chertkov's nerves": Ibid., February 5, 1894.
334   "I have had a letter": Ibid., February 9, 1894.
334   "I have just learned": August 2, 1893.

334   Trepov (1855–1906), a colonel and later a major-general, was chief of the Moscow police between 1896 and 1905, and after that governor-general of St. Petersburg.

PART FIVE

337   Epigraph: Countess Tolstoy's diary, October 21, 1897.

CHAPTER 20

339   "What is going to happen to me": *Nicholas and Alexandra*, Robert Massie.
340   "he is not": Ibid.
340   "This 'charmer' ": Ibid.
340   "for any man suffering": *Tolstoy's Love Letters*, Pavel Biryukov.
341   Costume party: *The Tragedy of Tolstoy*, Alexandra L. Tolstoy.
341   "When Vanichka approached": Ibid.
342   "Although he was so young": *A Life of My Father*, Alexandra L. Tolstoy.
343   Vanya's gift giving: *My Life*, Countess Tolstoy.
343   "an angel sent": Diary.
344   "the Gurevich woman": Ibid, February 5, 1895.
345   "The first thought": Ibid.
348   "Dead stillness": *The Tragedy of Tolstoy*.
349   "And I always": Tolstoy's diary, February 26, 1895.
349   "by a hallucination": Diary.
350   "Sometimes she became": *The Tragedy of Tolstoy*.
350   "Why—why Vanichka? Why not Sasha": Alexandra (Sasha) Tolstoy never forgave or forgot this unthinking statement of Sonya's. When I visited the Tolstoy Foundation in Valley Cottage, New York, to speak with Sonya's only surviving child in 1978, Miss Tolstoy was ninety-four, weak, and ill but in full possession of her mental powers. I was reminded three times during the day of this incident and the irreparable damage it did to Sasha as a child.

CHAPTER 21

351   "We never before": February 26, 1865, Maude.
353   "Sergey Ivanovich is tired!" *The Tragedy of Tolstoy*.
353   "Make way": Ibid.
353   "Nothing concerns me": Simmons.
354   Anton Pavlovich Chekhov (1860–1904), Russian playwright, author of *The Sea Gull* (1896), *Uncle Vanya* (1899), *The Three Sisters* (1900), and *The Cherry Orchard* (1904).
354   "There is one thing": Chekhov to Alexei Pleshcheev, February 15, 1890, *Letters of Anton Chekhov*.
354   "The Tolstoyan philosophy": Chekhov to Alexei Suvorin, March 27, 1894, ibid.
355   "When you talk to Tolstoy": Chekhov to Suvorin, October 26, 1895, ibid.
355   "Tolstoy's daughters": Ibid.

355 "She was sitting": Diary, October 23, 1895.
357 "The little clouds": *The Tragedy of Tolstoy*.
358 "Aunt Sonya has": Ibid.
358 "dread of old age": Ibid.
358 "I have a somewhat": *A Life of My Father*.
358 "Was there anything": *The Tragedy of Tolstoy*.
359 "the taut reins": Ibid.
359 "numberless hampers": Ibid.
359 "various preserves": Ibid.
359 "You will turn": Ibid.
360 "What can": Ibid.
360 "I should like": Ibid.

CHAPTER 22

361 Coronation of Nicholas: Massie.
364 "a sign of ": *Russia*, Michael T. Florinsky.
364 "dancing at a": Ibid.
366 "All folk music": *Tolstoy Remembered by His Son*, Sergey L. Tolstoy.
366 "I cannot bear": Ibid.
366 "It is like": Ibid.
366 "nonsensical": Ibid.
367 Tyutchev (1803–73), who was a diplomat for twenty-two years, wrote philosophical poems and love lyrics which were completely out of the mainstream of Russian poetry at the time. He was not fully appreciated until the later symbolists hailed him as their master. He also wrote political invectives.
368 "A repulsive poem": *The Tragedy of Tolstoy*.
368 "Aunt Sonya arrived": *A Life of My Father*.
370 "degrading madness": January 12, 1897.
370 "It is dreadfully": February 1, 1897.
372 "Your intimacy": May 18, 1897, Christian.
373 "Vanichka seemed": Diary, June 5, 1897.
373 "everywhere his hero": Ibid., June 8, 1897.
374 Alexander Alexandrovich Behrs (1844–1921) was the son of Dr. Behrs's brother and Rebella Pinkerton.
374 "soda, powdered charcoal": *The Tragedy of Tolstoy*.
375 "irritable": Diary, July 5, 1897.
375 "Lev Nikolaevich had gone": Ibid., July 13, 1897.
376 "wild": Ibid., July 17, 1897.
376 "I am being": Ibid., June 22, 1897.
376 "I was dreaming": Ibid., July 21, 1897.

CHAPTER 23

377 "A gifted man": Diary, September 19, 1897.
378 "What?": *My Life in the Russian Theatre*, Vladimir Nemirovich-Danchenko.
378 "How dare": Ibid.
378 "I read": November 7, 1897.

379   "I must do": August 17, 1897.
379   "pure delight": July 15, 1898.
379   "A Dialogue": Simmons, N. N. Gusev translation.
385   During a visit to Yasnaya Polyana in 1889, A. F. Koni, the eminent jurist, told Tolstoy this story. Tolstoy worked on it intermittently from 1889 to 1890 and then in 1895–96.
386   "I cannot rejoice": July 12, 1900, on the birth of a child to Ilya and his wife.
386   "The best thing": Simmons.
387   Visit by Rachmaninov and Chaliapin: *Man and Mask*, Feodor Chaliapin.
387   "a slightly bleating": Ibid.
387   "If I'm asked": Ibid.
388   "I'm sure it pleased him": Ibid.
388   "Hurray for": Countess Tolstoy's diary, February 24, 1901.
388   "Many outside": Letter, February 26, 1901.
389   "Your mother's": April 10, 1901.
389   "Thanks, Sonya": Simmons.
389   "Now my Lyovochka": Diary, June 26, 1901.
390   "Hurrah! Get well!": Simmons.
390   "He is like a God": *Reminiscences of Tolstoy*, Maxim Gorky (1868–1936), born Alexei Maksimovich Peshkov. Author of *Sketches and Stories* (1907), *The Lower Depths* (1902), and *Mother* (1907). He also wrote autobiographical works between 1913 and 1924 and additional plays.
390   "of literature": Ibid.
390   "Why don't you believe": Ibid.
391   "the slight things": Diary.
391   "I *must* live": Simmons.
391   "followed step by": Diary.
392   Kerensky (1881–1970) went on to lead the provisional government from July to November 1917 as prime minister shortly after the Tsar's overthrow in March 1917. Author of several accounts of this period, he was forced to flee the country after the Bolshevik Revolution in November.
393   Gapon's statement: *Nicholas and Alexandra*, Massie.
393   "A great never-to-be-forgotten": Ibid.
394   "The orderlies": Diary, August 8, 1904.
394   "Dear Lev": Christian.
395   Letter from Taneyev: Sergey L. Tolstoy.
395   Letter from Taneyev: Ibid.
396   Scriabin (1872–1915) was one of Taneyev's most gifted pupils at the Moscow Conservatory, graduating in 1892. After acquiring a considerable reputation as a pianist in Western Europe, he returned as a professor to the Moscow Conservatory (1898–1903). He then devoted the rest of his life to composition.
397   "that it is": *Leo Tolstoy: His Life and Work*, Pavel I. Biryukov.
397   "We were both": Diary, February 1906.
398   "If anyone disagreed": *The Tragedy of Tolstoy*.
398   "Lyovochka, forgive me": Ibid.
398   "I was ready": Ibid.
398   "Sonya has just": September 2, 1906.
399   "to obstruct the": *The Tragedy of Tolstoy*.
399   "thin, transparent": Ibid.
399   "Masha is dead": Ibid.

CHAPTER 24

400 "who were always": Alexandra L. Tolstoy's unpublished memoirs.
400 "Chertkov sat": Ibid.
401 "Look, look": *The Tragedy of Tolstoy.*
401 "Sometimes I": Ibid.
402 "To marry ever": Alexandra L. Tolstoy's unpublished memoirs. (An excerpt entitled "The Tolstoyans" was published in *Yale Review,* December 1977.)
402 Alexandra Tolstoy grew increasingly disturbed about one particular book —her early autobiography, *The Tragedy of Tolstoy*—because of her harsh treatment of her mother in the book. And Alexandra actually succeeded in suppressing an English reprint.
403 The reference to the "7th Commandment" relates to Tolstoy's army days, his former involvement with hunting as a sport, and Chertkov's earlier carnivorous eating habits.
404 "Sonya Andreyevna": *The Last Days of Tolstoy,* Vladimir G. Chertkov.
405 "Radiant meeting": April 28, 1909.
407 "For this one": Alexandra Tolstoy's unpublished memoirs.
408 "fulfillment of a": Ibid.
408 "loyal followers": Simmons.
409 "The next morning": *A Life of My Father.*
410 "Lyovochka, Lyovochka, where are the keys": Ibid.
410 "I wanted to": Alexandra Tolstoy's unpublished memoirs.
411 "There is nothing": *Reminiscences,* Gorky.
411 "a sort of fortress": *The Last Year of Lev Tolstoy,* Valentin Bulgakov.
411 Telegrams: Ibid.
411 "Don't you see": *The Final Struggle* (the diary of 1910).
412 "For God's sake": Bulgakov.
412 "Memorandum Before Death": June 23, 1910.
413 "Are you afraid": Ibid. and Bulgakov.
414 "I do not agree": Bulgakov.
414 "Tell him": Ibid.
415 "Tolstoyan cot": Ibid.
415 "I will not": *Final Struggle.* Letter is in notes for pp. 106–109.
417 "standing on the porch": Bulgakov.
418 "torturing herself": Ibid.
418 "The samovar": Ibid.
418 "something awful": Ibid.

CHAPTER 25

420 "vestal goddess": *The Tragedy of Tolstoy.*
421 "Sasha, what are you shouting": Bulgakov.
421 "of him to sacrifice": Ibid.
421 "You're very like": Ibid.
421 "I don't want": Ibid.
421 "You are always": August 2, 1910. *Final Struggle.*
422 "I heard": October 28, 1910.

422   "My departure will": *Final Struggle*.
422   "I have decided": Makovitsky's unpublished memoirs.
423   "[I] missed the path": October 28, 1910.
423   "Where is Papa": Bulgakov (dialogue included).
425   Tolstoy's letter to Sasha: *Final Struggle*.
425   "Papa regrets": Ibid.
426   "Sasha will tell you": Ibid.
426   "Tanya, Sergey, Ilya": Ibid.
426   "Dear precious Papenka": Ibid.
427   "I think Mamma": Ibid.
427   "Farewell, dear Sonya": Simmons.
428   The Astapovo railway station is now called Lev Tolstoy station.
428   "Sonya Andreyevna is suffering": Sergey L. Tolstoy.
429   "Who is with [Sonya]": *Final Struggle*.
429   "Andrey and Misha": Ibid. for entire exchange.
429   "What can be more important": Ibid.
430   "Forgive me": Ibid.
431   "I have never loved": Sergey L. Tolstoy.

PART SIX

433   Epigraph: Diary, December 13, 1910.

CHAPTER 26

435   Leonid Pasternak was the father of writer and poet Boris Pasternak. He illustrated *Resurrection*.
436   "God, forgive me": Reported in letter to Tanya Sukhotkina, Yasnaya Polyana Archives.
436   The Zaeska station is now called Yasnaya Polyana station.
436   "Many people": Sergey L. Tolstoy.
436   "Where are you": Ibid.
437   "bore herself silently": Ibid.
437   "On your knees": Ibid.
437   "I thank God": Ibid.
438   "My two darling Tanichkas": *Final Struggle*.
439   "I shall never": *Talks with Tolstoy*, Alexander Goldenweiser.
439   "There is much snow": December 19, 1910.
440   "I loved you": Countess Tolstoy Archives, Moscow.
442   "depressed me": Alexandra Tolstoy's unpublished memoirs.
442   "I felt in them": Ibid.
442   "Dirty in person": Ibid.
443   "my petty interests": Ibid.
443   "While [my father] was with me": Ibid.
444   "Why do you go to war": Ibid. for entire exchange.
444   Grigory Yefimovich Rasputin (1872–1916) began exercising his great influence on the court of Nicholas II after he "cured" Tsarevich Alexis's hemophilia in 1904. Thereafter, with each recurrence of her son's illness, the Tsarina grew more dependent upon this starets.

445   Prince Yussupov's four co-conspirators were Grand Duke Dmitry Pavlovich, the Tsar's cousin (the son of Nicholas II's last surviving uncle, Grand Duke Paul Pavlovich); Vladimir M. Purishkevich, conservative member of the Duma, a Dr. Lazavert, and an officer named Sukhotin.

445   David Lloyd George (1863–1945) was British prime minister (1916–22), a member of Parliament (1890–1944), and chancellor of the exchequer (1908–15).

446   "What shall we do": Alexandra Tolstoy's unpublished memoirs.

446   "With what": Ibid.

446   "Telegraph Kerensky": Ibid.

446   "Stop wailing": Ibid.

448   "people [had] climbed": *A Life of My Father.*

448   "Comrade": Ibid.

448   "Oh, Sasha": Ibid.

449   "The train rumbled": Ibid.

449   "Please help me": Ibid.

449   "Who is in this car": Ibid., as entire exchange.

450   "But they were disappointed": Ibid.

450   "boiled winter beets": Alexandra L. Tolstoy's unpublished memoirs.

450   "sweet, broken voice": *A Life of My Father.*

451   "I think that the Tolstoy": Ibid.

452   "Auntie dearest, tell me": Ibid.

452   "Bad, very bad": Ibid.

452   "All right, if I must": Ibid.

452   "Again, Auntie": Ibid.

453   "What is the matter": Ibid.

453   "Are you thinking": Ilya Tolstoy.

453   "Constantly, constantly": Ibid.

BIBLIOGRAPHY

Of all the Tolstoy biographies, I have found *Leo Tolstoy* by Ernest Simmons the most comprehensive, accurate, and insightful. But it must be used in tandem with Professor Simmons's separately published pamphlet of notes and his full bibliography, which (since it was published in 1946) is now difficult to obtain. Aylmer Maude's two-volume *Life of Tolstoy* is a standard reference. However, it was written before the publication of *The Diary of Tolstoy's Wife, The Countess Tolstoy's Later Diary, The Final Struggle,* and the reminiscences of Sergey and Alexandra. It is therefore incomplete regarding the Tolstoys' home life and various portraits of those in their circle. Henri Troyat's *Tolstoy,* though a thoroughly readable and credible account of Tolstoy's literary and religious life, must be regarded with some suspicion, especially in the area of Tolstoy's family and marital relations. When Mr. Troyat's book appeared, Alexandra Tolstoy published a lengthy pamphlet (*The Real Tolstoy*) repudiating many of Troyat's statements and correcting numerous others. Simmons's book seems to be the English biography most highly regarded by the surviving members of the Tolstoy family.

Adams, Arthur E. *Imperial Russia After 1861.* Boston, 1965.
Ascher, Abraham, and the editors of Newsweek Books. *The Kremlin.* New York, 1972.
Asquith, Cynthia. *Married to Tolstoy.* Boston, Houghton Mifflin, 1961.
Behrs, Stepan. *Recollections of Count Leo Tolstoy.* London, Heinemann, 1893.
Biryukov, Pavel I. *Leo Tolstoy: His Life and Work.* New York, Scribner's, 1911.
———. *Tolstoy's Love Letters.* Richmond (England), Hogarth, 1923.
Bulgakov, Valentin. *The Last Year of Lev Tolstoy.* New York, Dial, 1971.
Chaliapin, Feodor. *Man and Mask.* New York, Knopf, 1932.
Chekhov, Anton. *Letters of Anton Chekhov.* New York, Viking, 1973.
Cherniavsky, Michael, editor. *The Structure of Russian History.* New York, 1970.
Chertkov, Vladimir. *The Last Days of Tolstoy.* London, Heinemann, 1922.
Christian, Reginald F. *Tolstoy's Letters.* London, Athlone, 1978.
Christoff, Peter K. *An Introduction to 19th Century Russian Slavophilism.* The Hague, 1961.
Cowles, Virginia. *The Russian Dagger.* New York, Harper, 1969.

Ferguson, Alan D., and Alfred Levin, editors. *Essays in Russian History*. Hamden, Conn., 1964.

Field, Daniel. *Rebels in the Name of the Tsar*. New York, 1976.

Florinsky, Michael T. *Russia: A History*. New York, Macmillan, 1953.

Footman, David. *The Alexander Conspiracy*. London, 1944.

Frank, Joseph. *Dostoevsky: The Seeds of Revolt*. Princeton, 1976.

Goldenweiser, Alexander. *Talks with Tolstoy*. Richmond (England), Woolf, 1923.

Gorky, Maxim. *Reminiscences of Tolstoy*. New York, Heubsch, 1920.

Grabbe, Paul. *Windows on the River Neva*. New York, 1977.

Guterman, Norbert, translator. *Russian Fairy Tales*. New York, 1945.

Howes, Robert C., translator. *The Confession of Mikhail Bakunin*. Ithaca, N.Y., 1977.

Klyuchevsky, Vasili. *The Rise of the Romanovs*. New York, 1970.

Kuzminsky, Tatyana (Behrs). *Tolstoy as I Knew Him*. New York, Macmillan, 1948.

Lafitte, Sophie. *Chekhov*. New York, 1973.

Mann, Thomas. *Three Essays*. New York, 1929.

Massie, Robert. *Nicholas and Alexandra*. New York, Atheneum, 1968.

Maude, Aylmer. *Family Views of Tolstoy*. Boston, 1926.

———. *The Life of Tolstoy*. London, Oxford University Press, 1929–30.

———. *Tolstoy and His Problems*. London, 1902.

Miller, Wright. *Russians as People*. New York, 1960.

———. *Who Are the Russians?* New York, 1973.

Mochulsky, Konstantin. *Dostoevsky, His Life and Work*. Princeton, 1967.

———. *Nijinsky*. New York, 1934.

Mosse, Werner E. *Alexander II and the Modernization of Russia*. London, English Universities Press, 1958.

Nazaroff, Alexander. *The Land of the Russian People*. New York, 1944.

Oliva, L. Jay, editor. *Russia and the West from Peter to Khrushchev*. Boston, 1965.

Onassis, Jacqueline. *In the Russian Style*. New York, 1976.

Pares, Bernard. *A History of Russia*. London, 1944.

Pollen, John, translator. *Russian Songs and Lyrics*. London, 1916.

Polner, Tikhon. *Tolstoy and His Wife*. New York, 1945.

Robinson, Gerald Tanquary. *Rural Russia Under the Old Regime*. New York, Macmillan, 1932.

Rolland, Romain. *Tolstoy*. New York, 1911.

Salisbury, Harrison E. *Black Night White Snow*. New York, 1978.

Seton-Watson, Hugh. *The Decline of Imperial Russia, 1855–1914*. New York, 1952.

Simmons, Ernest J. *Leo Tolstoy*. Boston, Little, Brown, 1946.

Stadling, Jonas, and Will Reason. *In the Land of Tolstoi*. London, 1897.

Stavrou, Theofanis George, editor. *Russia Under The Last Tsar*. Minneapolis, 1969.

Sukhotkina, Tatyana (Tolstoy). *The Tolstoy Home: Diaries*. London, Haverhill, 1950.

———. *Tolstoy Remembered*. New York, McGraw-Hill, 1977.

Tchaikovsky, Peter. *The Diaries of Tchaikovsky*. New York, Norton, 1945.

Tolstoy, Countess Alexandra Andreyevna, and Lev Tolstoy. *The Letters of Tolstoy and His Cousin Alexandra, 1857–1903*. Translated by Leo Islavin. New York, Dutton, 1928.

Tolstoy, Alexandra Lvovna. *A Life of My Father*. New York, Harper, 1953.

———. *The Tragedy of Tolstoy*. New Haven, Yale University Press, 1933.

Tolstoy, Ilya Lvovich. *Reminiscences of Tolstoy*. New York, Century, 1914; reprinted under the title *Tolstoy, My Father:* Chicago, Regnery, 1971.

Tolstoy, Lev Lvovich. *The Truth About My Father*. London, J. Hurray, 1924.

Tolstoy, Lev Nikolaevich. *ABC Book*. London, Oxford University Press, 1928–37.

———. *Anna Karenina*. Translated by Louise and Aylmer Maude. New York, Norton, 1970.

———. *Childhood*. London, Oxford University Press, 1928–37.

———. *The Death of Ivan Ilych*. London, Oxford University Press, 1928–37.

———. *The Devil*. London, Oxford University Press, 1928–37.

———. *Kreutzer Sonata*. London, Oxford University Press, 1928–37.

———. *The Letters of Tolstoy and His Cousin Alexandra, 1857–1903*. New York, Dutton, 1928.

———. *The Private Diary of Leo Tolstoy, 1853–1857*. Translated by Louise and Aylmer Maude. London, Heinemann, 1927.

———. *Recollections and Essays*. Translated by Aylmer Maude. London, Oxford University Press, 1937.

———. *War and Peace*. Translated by Louise and Aylmer Maude. New York, Oxford University Press, 1965.

Tolstoy, Sergey Lvovich. *Tolstoy Remembered by His Son*. New York, Atheneum, 1961.

Tolstoy, Sonya Andreyevna. *The Autobiography of Countess Sophie Tolstoi*. Richmond (England), Woolf, 1922.

———. *The Countess Tolstoy's Later Diary, 1891–1897*. London, Gollancz, 1929.

———. *The Diary of Tolstoy's Wife, 1860–1891*, London, Gollancz, 1928.

———. *The Final Struggle, Being Countess Tolstoy's Diary for 1910*. Translated by Aylmer Maude. London, Allen and Unwin, 1936.

Tomasic, Dinko. *The Impact of Russian Culture on Soviet Communism*. Glencoe, Ill., 1953.

Troyat, Henri. *Tolstoy*. New York, Doubleday, 1967.

Trotsky, Leon. *The History of the Russian Revolution*. Volume I, The Overthrow of Tsarism. New York, 1932.

Walsh, Warren B., editor. *Readings in Russian History*. Syracuse, N.Y. 1959.

———, editor. *Readings in Russian History*. Volume II, From the Reign of Paul to Alexander III. Syracuse, N.Y., 1963.

Wilson, Colin. *Rasputin and the Fall of the Romanovs*. Secaucus, N.J., 1964.

Wilson, Edmund. *A Window on Russia*. New York, 1972.

ARCHIVAL SOURCES

The typewritten manuscript of Dr. D. P. Makovitsky's Yasnaya Polyana Notes (on Tolstoy's last year and death) can be found at the L. N. Tolstoy Museum in Moscow.

The L. N. Tolstoy Museum also contains numerous manuscripts, originals of correspondence, and many of Countess Tolstoy's letters that have not yet been published.

In the Yasnaya Polyana Archives in Tula are letters, papers, and peasants' reminiscences of the Tolstoys.

Unique film footage of the Tolstoys traveling and of the last days, death, and funeral of Tolstoy can be found in the Russian Film Archives in Moscow.

Interesting Tolstoy photographs were found at Radio Times Hulton Picture Library, BBC Publications, London; Camera Press, London; The Mansell Collection Ltd., London; and Roger-Viollet, Paris.

INDEX